美国管理会计师协会（IMA）

注册管理会计师（CMA）认证考试教材之三

战 略 管 理

（第二版）

（英汉双语）

美国管理会计师协会（IMA）主编

杜美杰　译

经济科学出版社

图书在版编目（CIP）数据

战略管理：第 2 版：英汉双语 / 美国管理会计师协会主编；杜美杰译 . —北京：经济科学出版社，2007.11

书名原文：Strategic Management

注册管理会计师（CMA）认证考试教材

ISBN 978 - 7 - 5058 - 6607 - 2

Ⅰ. 战…　Ⅱ. ①美…②杜…　Ⅲ. 企业管理 - 资格考核 - 教材 - 英、汉　Ⅳ. F270

中国版本图书馆 CIP 数据核字（2007）第 146785 号

亲爱的读者朋友：

非常高兴你决定参加注册管理会计师（CMA）资格考试并选用这套全新的中文版本教材，我相信这对你来讲是一个明智的决策。这套培训教材的编写以美国管理会计师协会所确认的管理会计知识体系和学习要点为基础，教材在编写中充分利用了一些最为有效的学习技巧，我们相信这套教材能够帮助你顺利通过 CMA 考试。

我很高兴美国管理会计师协会能提供 CMA 考试及这套教材的中文版权。CMA 资格认证只授予全球各行业、各语种中最为优秀的会计人员，它是一个全球性的资格认证。希望读者朋友们能成功通过 CMA 考试并一生好运。

保罗·A·沙曼（Paul A. Sharman），ACMA
IMA 总裁兼首席执行官
2007 年 7 月 12 日

Dear Colleague:

Congratulations on your decision to pursue the Certified Management Accountant (CMA®) certification. You have made a wise choice to pursue this goal and in choosing the new Chinese version of the CMA Learning System to prepare for the exam. The CMA Learning System was developed using IMA's management accounting body of knowledge and subject matter experts. It takes advantage of some of the most effective techniques for learning. We believe that this is a valuable tool to help CMA candidates successfully pass the exam.

I am pleased that IMA can offer a Chinese language version of the CMA exam and the appropriate study materials to help you succeed. I trust you will find that the CMA is a global designation of excellence for accountants working in industry, across all industries and languages. I wish the best of luck to you with your study prep and in your future.

Sincerely,

Paul A. Sharman, ACMA
IMA President and CEO

7/12/07

总目录

The Institute of Management Accountants'
CMA Learning System

Book 3: Strategic Management

Contents

About the CMA Learning System

This product is based on the CMA body of knowledge developed by the Institute of Certified Management Accountants (ICMA). Although the text is based on the body of knowledge tested by the CMA exam and the published Learning Outcome Statements covering the four part exams, CMA Learning System program developers do not have access to the current bank exam questions. It is critical that candidates: understand all Learning Outcome Statements published by the ICMA, learn all concepts and calculations related to those statements, and, finally, that they have a solid grasp of how to write the multiple-choice and essay exams in the CMA program.

This material is designed for learning purposes and is distributed with the understanding that the publisher and authors are not offering legal or professional services.

Acknowledgements

IMA would like to acknowledge the subject matter experts who worked on the original version of this product: Kimberly Frank Charron, Ph.D., CMA; Neal J. Hannon, CMA; Charles R. Hartle, CMA, CPA; Dennis L. Neider, CMA, CPA; and Carl V. Menconi, CMA, CPA.

In addition we would like to acknowledge the following subject matter experts who were instrumental in the 2.0 version of this product: Jill Bale Ph.D., CMA, CFA; Kent Baker, Ph.D., CMA, CFA; Kenneth Cole, CMA; Saurav Dutta, Ph.D., CMA; Karen L. Jett, CMA; Joe Lanz, CMA, CFA; Paul Miesing, Ph.D.; Lou Petro, Ph.D., CMA; Terri Rittenburg, Ph.D.; Siaw-Peng Wan; Ph.D., CMA

The CMA™ Designation

The Certified Management Accountant (CMA) designation provides corporate management and finance professionals with an objective measure of knowledge and competence in the field of management accounting. The CMA designation is recognized globally as an invaluable credential for professional accountancy advancement inside organizations and for broadening professional skills and perspectives.

The four-part CMA exam is designed to develop and measure critical-thinking and decision-making skills and to meet the following objectives:

- To establish management accounting and financial management as recognized professions by identifying the role of the professional, the underlying body of knowledge, and a course of study by which such knowledge is acquired

- To encourage higher educational standards in the management accounting and financial management fields

- To establish an objective measure of an individual's knowledge and competence in the fields of management accounting and financial management

- To encourage continued professional development

Persons earning the CMA designation benefit by being able to:

- Communicate their broad business competency and strategic financial mastery.

- Obtain contemporary professional knowledge and develop skills and abilities that are valued by successful businesses.

- Convey their commitment to an exemplary standard of excellence that is grounded on a strong ethical foundation and lifelong learning.

- Enhance their career development, salary qualifications and professional promotion opportunities.

The CMA designation is granted exclusively by the Institute of Certified Management Accountants.

Overall Expectations of Candidates

The CMA exam content covers both a depth of technical accountancy and a breadth of organizational topics that are critical for management accountants to be able to assume the 'business partner' role now expected of savvy professionals.

Completing the CMA designation requires a high level of commitment. Dedicating what often amounts to two years of your life to study and complete the four-part exams in a serious investment, one that will provide a solid foundation for your career and that will enhance your career in ways that will pay dividends for a lifetime.

Your success in completing the four-part exams will rest heavily on your ability to create a solid study plan and to execute that plan. The IMA offers many resources, tools and programs to support you during this process. We encourage you to pay the CMA Entrance Fee as soon as you begin the program in order to provide you maximum access to these resources and tools. You are also encouraged to draw on these benefits with rigor and discipline in a way that supports your unique study needs.

For more information about the CMA designation, the CMA exams, or the exam preparation resources offered through IMA visit www.imanet.org.

Introduction

Welcome to Part 3 of the Institute of Management Accountants' CMA Learning System: Strategic Management.

Part 3 examines the strategic aspects of cost management. It looks at how contemporary cost management methods and practices contribute to organizational success in competitive times, beginning with an overview of strategic planning. Fundamentals of how a firm develops strategies to distinguish itself from competitors and add value for both customers and shareholders are explained. We then look at the importance of understanding product and service markets and how to best match distinctive organizational capabilities with promising value opportunities. The next section covers risk management principles and the effective selection and management of different financial instruments to support business strategies and goals; the importance of relevant data in the decision process and the strategic role of analysis and pricing in supporting profitability are then discussed. Part 3 concludes with a strategic perspective of capital budgeting and a discussion of various techniques used to investigate capital investment projects.

The Part 3 CMA Exam

Candidates for the CMA designation are required to take separate exams for Parts 1, 2, 3, and 4. Parts 1, 2, and 3 can be taken in any order; however, Part 4 can be taken only after successful completion of Parts 1, 2, and 3.

The Part 3 CMA exam consists of 110 multiple-choice questions that test all levels of cognitive skills. Candidates have three hours to complete the computer-based exam. This Part 3 book is based upon the Content Specification Outline and the Learning Outcome Statements provided by ICMA for Part 3. That outline is reflected in the table of contents of this book. The ICMA Content Specification Outline and LOS can be obtained from the IMA Web site at www.imanet.org.

It is important when preparing for the Part 3 exam that candidates learn all of the concepts presented and also understand all of the various ways calculations can be performed. It is also important that you learn (or relearn) how to write a comprehensive multiple-choice exam. You are strongly encouraged to create a study plan that details how you will accomplish your Part 3 exam preparation and when you will write the Part 3 exam.

Online Resources

Valuable resources are available to assist candidates to pass the CMA examinations. For information regarding all the resources available please go to www.imanet.org/china/examtools.

Creating a Part 3 Study Plan

The Part 3 certification exam uses a multiple-choice format to test your understanding of Part 3 concepts, terms, and calculations. Creating a study plan is a critical ingredient to planning a path to success. Managing your plan is critical to achieving success. The following tips and tactics are included to help you in preparing and managing your Part 3 study plan.

1. Because the Part 3 exam can be written anytime throughout the year, YOU need to bring structure to your exam preparation. This means setting target dates and making them a priority.

   - Decide on the date you commit to contacting the ICMA to register for the Part 3 exam. After you register, mark the date you plan to take the exam in pen.

   - Based on the dates you commit to register and sit for the exam, decide when you will start and finish studying Part 3. We recommend that you make every effort to write the exam as close as possible to the completion of your studies. A reasonable benchmark for the number of study hours required to prepare for Part 3 is 150. The actual hours you need to invest to prepare will depend on your current level of understanding of the Part 3 content and your familiarity and confidence to write exams of this nature.

   - Review each section and topic in Part 3 and rate your familiarity/confidence with each section.

2. Create a written plan or chart to track your progress and guide your completion of each component of the self-study books, section by section. We strongly recommend that you create a plan that sees you through to completion of Part 3 within six (6) months or less.

3. Use your plan on a regular basis to assess your progress. In addition, be sure to practice the section-specific questions and exercises included in the print materials.

Strategic Planning

Section A

Section overview

Today's business environment has been described as hypercompetitive. Day in and day out, organizations face myriad internal and external challenges and changes impacting their operations and even their survival. Some challenges and changes are inevitable; some are the result of deliberate efforts; others are unforeseen.

Strategic planning helps an organization to proactively address both challenge and change—whether planned or unforeseen. Certainly a strategic plan does not guarantee an organization success. However, in the absence of a well-thought-out strategic plan, the probability of that organization becoming a marketplace victim rather than a victor dramatically increases.

Historically, strategic planning was a top-down exercise for the corporate elite. During the 1990s, it became a more democratized process, capturing the perspectives of a broad range of people. Today, an inclusive initiative is much more prevalent.

Management accountants have assumed a more prominent role through the strategic planning evolution. Cost management is no longer a passive stewardship exercise of product/service costing and financial reporting. Now a cost management system must facilitate strategic management and enable a firm to deal with critical issues impacting the enterprise's success. This section describes in simple and succinct language the core concepts in the areas of strategic and tactical planning, manufacturing paradigms, and business process performance that every management accountant—at any level—should know.

Learning Outcome Statements

The Certified Management Accountant (CMA) test is based upon a series of Learning Outcome Statements (LOS) developed by the Institute of Certified Management Accountants (ICMA). The LOS describe all the knowledge and skills that make up the CMA body of knowledge, broken down by part, section and topic. The CMA Learning System (CMALS) supports the LOS by addressing all the subjects they cover. Candidates should use the LOS to ensure that they can address the concepts in different ways or through a variety of question scenarios. Candidates should also be prepared to perform calculations referred to in the LOS in total or by providing missing components of a calculation. The LOS should not be used as proxies for exact exam questions; they should be used as a guide for studying and learning the content of the CMA Learning System and ensuring that you can accomplish the objectives set out by the LOS.

The LOS included in the CMALS books are the comprehensive set, current as of the date of publication. Candidates can access the IMA Web site at www.imanet.org and click on the Certification section to locate and download a Portable Document Format (PDF) file of the current LOS.

Learning Outcome Statements

Part 3: Strategic Management — Section A. Strategic Planning

Part 3 — Section A1. Strategic and Tactical Planning

- LOS 3.A.1.a—Discuss how strategic planning determines the path an organization chooses for attaining its long-term goals and missions.

- LOS 3.A.1.b—Identify the time frame appropriate for a strategic plan.

- LOS 3.A.1.c—Identify the external factors that should be analyzed during the strategic planning process and understand how this analysis leads to recognition of organizational opportunities, limitations, and threats.

- LOS 3.A.1.d—Identify the internal factors that should be analyzed during the strategic planning process and explain how this analysis leads to recognition of organizational strengths, weaknesses, and competitive advantages.

- LOS 3.A.1.e—Demonstrate an understanding of how the analysis of external and internal factors leads to the development of the overall organizational mission and that this mission leads to the formulation of long-term business objectives such as business diversification, the addition or deletion of product lines, or the penetration of new markets.

- LOS 3.A.1.f—Identify the role of capital budgeting and capacity planning in the strategic planning process.

- LOS 3.A.1.g—Explain why short-term objectives, tactics for achieving these objectives, and operational planning (master budget) must be congruent with the strategic plan and contribute to the achievement of long-term strategic goals.

- LOS 3.A.1.h—Explain why performance measurement and other reporting systems must be congruent with and support measurement of progress on strategic and operational measures.

- LOS 3.A.1.i—Identify the characteristics of successful strategic/tactical planning.

- LOS 3.A.1.j—Define contingency planning and discuss its importance, particularly where changes in external factors might adversely impact strategic plans.

Part 3 — Section A2. Manufacturing Paradigms

- LOS 3.A.2.a—Define a just-in-time (JIT) system and describe its central purpose.

- LOS 3.A.2.b—Identify the operational benefits of implementing a just-in-time system.

- LOS 3.A.2.c—Define the term kanban and describe how kanban is used in a just-in-time system.

- LOS 3.A.2.d—Demonstrate an understanding of work cells and how they relate to just-in-time processes.

- LOS 3.A.2.e—Define material resource planning (MRP) and identify its benefits.

- LOS 3.A.2.f—Calculate subunits needed to complete an order for a finished product using MRP.

- LOS 3.A.2.g—Demonstrate an understanding of the concept of outsourcing and identify the benefits and limitations of choosing this option.

- LOS 3.A.2.h—Demonstrate an understanding of the theory of constraints and the steps involved in theory of constraints analysis.

- LOS 3.A.2.i—Define and calculate throughput contribution and demonstrate an understanding of its relationship to the theory of constraints.

- LOS 3.A.2.j—Demonstrate an understanding of a drum-buffer-rope system as a tool for managing product flow.

- LOS 3.A.2.k—Discuss how the theory of constraints and activity-based costing are complementary analytical tools.

- LOS 3.A.2.l—Identify other contemporary productivity concepts such as automation and the use of robots, computer-aided design, computer-integrated manufacturing, and flexible manufacturing systems.

Part 3 — Section A3. Business Process Performance

- LOS 3.A.3.a—Define value chain analysis.

- LOS 3.A.3.b—Identify the steps in value chain analysis.

- LOS 3.A.3.c—Demonstrate an understanding of how value chain analysis is used to better understand a firm's competitive advantage.

- LOS 3.A.3.d—Define a value-added activity and explain how the value-added concept is related to improving performance.

- LOS 3.A.3.e—Demonstrate an understanding of process analysis and how to improve business process performance through business process reengineering.

- LOS 3.A.3.f—Analyze a sequence of tasks, activities, and processes.

- LOS 3.A.3.g—Define the Pareto principle.

- LOS 3.A.3.h—Demonstrate an understanding of benchmarking process performance.

- LOS 3.A.3.i—Identify the benefits of benchmarking in creating a competitive advantage.

- LOS 3.A.3.j—Apply activity-based management principles to recommend process performance improvements.

- LOS 3.A.3.k—Demonstrate an understanding of the relationship among continuous improvement techniques, activity-based management, and quality performance.

- LOS 3.A.3.l—Demonstrate an understanding of the concept of continuous improvement (kaizen) and how it relates to implementing ideal standards and quality improvements.

- LOS 3.A.3.m—Define best practice analysis and discuss how it can be used by an organization to improve performance.

Strategic and Tactical Planning

Topic overview

Strategy *defines how a firm competes and sets forth the general direction an organization plans to follow to achieve its goals. It represents the collective soul of an organization. Strategies are developed by matching core competencies of the enterprise with industry opportunities and/or threats.*

Strategic planning (sometimes referred to as **long-range planning***) involves a comprehensive look at an organization in relation to its industry, competitors, and environment. An organization charts its destination, assesses barriers that must be overcome to reach that destination, and identifies approaches for moving forward and dealing with the barriers. Although traditionally the responsibility of top management, all organizational members should be involved in the process. Well-thought-out strategic planning can help an organization adeptly navigate through turbulent times—both good and bad.*

Strategy and Strategic Planning

Every well-managed organization formulates both strategies and strategic plans at some level. Executives and managers typically spend considerable time thinking about strategies to achieve organizational goals; these strategies are then formally incorporated in a strategic plan.

Strategy

Strategy is a broad term. Organizations generally develop strategies at different levels. Figure 3-1 shows three levels that firms commonly develop organizational strategies for:

- Corporate (or multibusiness)

- Competitive (or business unit)

- Functional (within a business)

Figure 3-1: Levels of Strategy

Corporate	■ Looks at the whole gamut of business opportunities, including international expansion and mergers and acquisitions
	■ Defines the organization's values, expressed in financial and nonfinancial terms
	■ Centers on identifying and building or acquiring key resources and capabilities
	■ Involves decisions about which industries the organization will compete in and how the businesses will be linked
	■ Determines how organizational resources will be allocated among the firm's businesses
	■ Determines constraints on what the firm will and will not do
Competitive	■ Defines how an organization competes in a given industry—how the firm creates value in an industry
	■ Involves a vision of what customers the organization serves and how it delivers value to them
	■ Combines specific activities and processes to enable the firm to create unique value
	■ Aligns organizational activities so all efforts consistently reinforce the potential advantage of the firm's competitive positioning
Functional	■ Reinforces the organization's competitive strategy
	■ Includes plans and objectives for marketing, finance, research, technology, operations, and so on
	■ Focuses on coordination among functions
	■ Defines activities and processes to help the organization maximize its competitive position
	■ Clarifies whether and how the organization's functions fit with the competitive strategy

Corporate strategy considers the big picture, determines the appropriate mix of businesses, and identifies where (in what markets) the firm competes. Competitive and functional strategies are more tactically focused on how the organization will compete in a given industry. Although the outcomes differ for the various levels of strategy, they all must be consistent and aligned.

Naturally, strategies differ between organizations. For example, how Dell, IBM, and Toshiba compete for market share in the same business computer arena is driven by different strategies. In turn, different strategies require different tasks, skills, priorities, and control systems.

In today's competitive environment, organizational strategies must be dynamic. The strength of an organization's strategy is not determined by the firm's initial move but rather by how well it:

- Anticipates competitors' actions.

- Anticipates and/or influences changing customer demands.

- Capitalizes on advantages in a changing competitive environment (for example, regulations, technology, the economy, global opportunities and events).

- Reacts to, chooses, and executes alternative competitive strategies.

Anticipation and preparation are key to an effective strategy. Every eventuality with competitors and customers and other important factors must be met and addressed with rapid countermoves.

Strategic planning

A conceptual representation of strategic planning is shown in Figure 3-2.

Figure 3-2: Key Elements of Strategic Planning

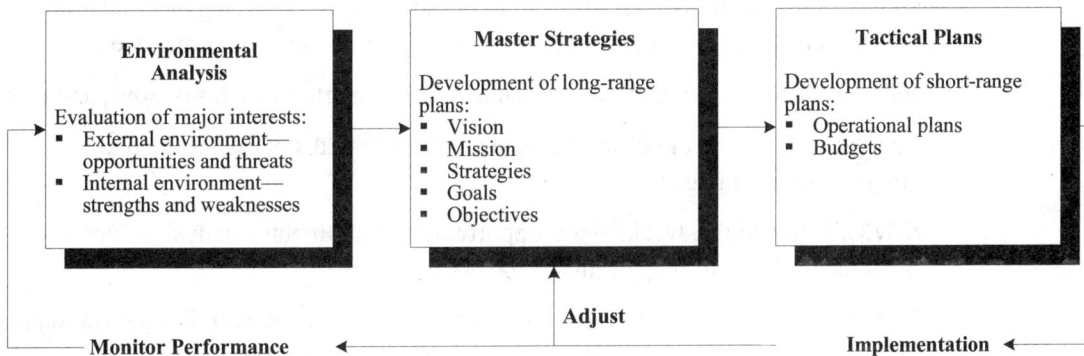

Keep in mind that the representation shown here is conceptual; it is intended to provide a general view of the strategic planning process. In practice, strategic planning terminology and approaches differ across organizations. Organizations devise their own operational models that elaborate on the specifics of their strategic planning process. The nature of the enterprise, its marketplace and stakeholders, the size, resources, and capabilities of the organization, and other factors such as the participants in the process and their power and interests ultimately dictate additional specifics that will shape the operational model.

What is the appropriate time frame for strategic planning? There is no rule regarding strategic plans being prepared at one-, three-, five-, or ten-year intervals. Organizations prepare strategic plans at different intervals depending upon the industry, the level of competition (for example, new entrants), and how fast products or services change. For example, technology-focused businesses prepare strategic plans at short time intervals to address the rapid changes and competitive pressure of their markets.

Typically, the strategic planning process is highly iterative. The core elements are interrelated; completion of one element requires a review of previous elements and entails some measure of fine-tuning. In the end, the resulting strategic plan yields insights into how an organization can position itself for sustainable competitive advantage.

The relationship between strategy and strategic planning

In practice, strategy formulation and strategic planning have much overlap. But the two processes have important conceptual differences.

On a fundamental level, strategy formulation results in new strategies and strategic planning addresses how to implement the strategies. Additional distinctions can be made:

- Strategy formulation leads to organizational goals; management creates strategies to achieve those goals.

- Strategic planning develops plans to implement strategies and achieve the goals.

- Strategic planning is typically a systematic process with a timetable and some measure of prescribed procedures.

- Ideally, strategies are continually reevaluated based on perceived opportunities and threats.

Regardless of the overlap or variances in terms and processes, strategy formulation and strategic planning will both address the following core elements at some level:

- External factors—recognition of organizational opportunities, limitations, and threats

- Internal factors—recognition of organizational strengths, weaknesses, and competitive advantages

- S.W.O.T. (strengths, weaknesses, opportunities, and threats) analysis—identification of elements that will help or hinder the organization

- Long-term vision, mission, and goals—development of the overall organizational vision and mission and the formulation of long-term business goals

- Tactics to achieve long-term goals—development of short-term plans and tactics

Subsequent content looks at each of these elements in more detail.

Analysis of External Factors Affecting Strategy

Creating strategies without first assessing the organization's business environment—what is happening and what may happen inside and outside the organization—would be a futile exercise.

The specific external factors affecting an organization's strategy are determined by its industry and broader environment. A variety of external factors typically make up an organization's business environment. Examples of key external factors shaping organizational strategy include:

- Legal and regulatory factors.

- Market forces, industry trends, and competition.

- Technological changes.

- Stakeholder groups and their social concerns.

- Globalization trends, emerging markets, and non-government organizations (for example, United Nations, World Bank, and so on).

All of these external factors need to be examined during strategic planning.

Legal and regulatory factors

Depending upon the industry, legal and regulatory factors may be interrelated. But the two factors also have some key distinctions.

Legal factors

Legal factors are rules of conduct promulgated by legal entities (for example, federal, state, county/provincial, or city laws); they are enforced by the threat of punishment. A host of legal factors can impact product/service success. Examples include:

- Patents.
- Copyrights.
- Trademarks.
- Antitrust laws.
- Trade protectionism.
- Product/service liability issues.
- Environmental liability concerns.
- Employment law and litigation.
- Compliance with the Sarbanes Oxley Act (SOX).

Regulatory factors

Regulatory factors (or regulations) are principles or rules designed to control or govern behavior. Theoretically, regulations are voluntary. But in many situations regulations can have the force of law. For example, an organization may not be able to compete in a given market if it does not comply with regulatory factors.

Agencies under legal entities as well as nongovernmental entities (for example, industry self-regulating bodies and professional societies) typically set regulations and sanctions. Unlike legal factors, which are always enforced by the threat of punishment, regulatory factors are most often enforced by some form of self-regulation, with the threat of fines and/or disenfranchisement.

General examples of regulatory factors that can affect an organization's strategy include:

- Social regulations (such as but not limited to)
  - Environmental Protection Agency (EPA) standards—restricting pollution of air, water, and land.
  - Occupational Safety and Health Administration (OSHA) standards—protecting the safety and health of American workers.
  - Federal Trade Commission (FTC) regulations—protecting consumers, requiring truthful advertising by businesses, and prohibiting collusion (for example, price fixing and allocating markets).
- Industry regulations (such as but not limited to)
  - Federal Aviation Administration (FAA) requirements—for airports, air traffic control, safety issues, and routes.
  - Federal Communications Commission (FCC) regulations—for radio and television frequencies.

> ▪ Food and Drug Administration (FDA) requirements—for safety in the food and drug industry and in medical device manufacturing.

Linkage of legal and regulatory factors to strategic planning

The influence of legal and regulatory factors on an organization's strategy can be quite pervasive. The following are just a few examples of how legal and regulatory factors can affect an organization:

- Influencing how a firm chooses to compete (for example, through antitrust laws and licensing requirements)

- Limiting global operations (for example, through trade protectionism)

- Thwarting or promoting technology innovations (for example, through tax and patent policies)

- Impacting human resource practices (for example, through equal employment opportunity/antidiscrimination laws, wage and price controls, Family and Medical Leave Act legislation, and employee safety and health regulations)

- Restricting marketing campaigns (for example, through FTC controls)

- Forcing environmental accountability (for example, through EPA controls)

- Increasing capital requirements (for example, through required technical sophistication to meet governmental control requirements)

As seen above, many legal and regulatory factors are industry-specific; others may cut across a variety of industries. Some legal and regulatory factors may even be directed at an individual company.

To no small degree, the legal and regulatory factors already noted can directly affect management accounting due to significant cost incurrence implications. For example, changes in EPA or OSHA regulations can require significant capital investments for compliance.

Consider a few additional factors that have specific implications for management accounting:

- Securities and Exchange Commission (SEC) laws and rules to protect investors and maintain the integrity of the securities markets

- The Sarbanes-Oxley Act changes regarding internal controls

- The Internal Revenue Service (IRS) code

- Congressional changes to minimum wage requirements and/or overtime compensation

- State-regulated insurance and banking commission regulations on how business is conducted and how various financial transactions are to be accounted for

Market forces, industry trends, and competition

History has shown how factors such as government deregulation, globalization, technological innovations, demanding customers, and changing demographics and social expectations can dramatically alter even stable business arenas. Thus a critical part of strategic planning is an industry analysis—a thorough assessment of the competitive arena that includes the competitors the organization must face and the structure and boundaries of the competitive arena.

As in other aspects of strategic planning, there is no one single definitive method for identifying arena boundaries or anticipating rival actions. But most industry analyses consider the following factors:

- Entry of new competitors
- Threat of substitutes
- Bargaining power of buyers
- Bargaining power of suppliers
- Rivalry among existing competitors

Michael Porter developed a model examining these five forces and their collective role in determining the strength of competition and profitability. Figure 3-3 visualizes Porter's model.

Figure 3-3: Five Forces Driving Industry Profitability

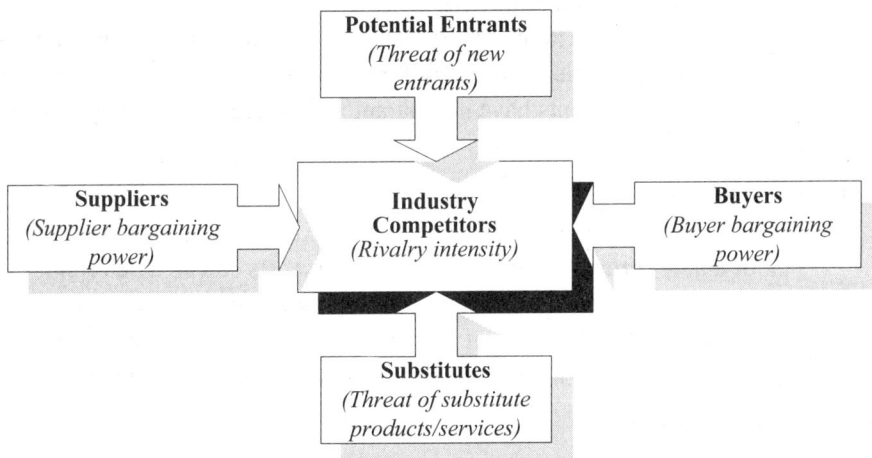

Source: Adapted from *Competitive Advantage—Creating and Sustaining Superior Performance* by Michael Porter

The discussion of Porter's five forces that follows is synthesized from two of Porter's books, *Competitive Strategy: Techniques for Analyzing Industries and Competitors* (1980) and *Competitive Advantage: Creating and Sustaining Superior Performance* (1985), and the collaborative text *Wharton on Dynamic Competitive Strategy* (Day and Reibstein 1997).

Entry of new competitors

A new player in a marketplace (an entrant) generally brings with them new capacity and resources. The profitability for an incumbent in the marketplace may be reduced if its sales prices are bid down or its product costs are increased in order to compete against this new entrant.

The threat of new competitors depends upon the magnitude of entry barriers—factors that create a disadvantage for prospective entrants and lower their profit expectations.

Examples of entry barriers include the following items.

- **Incumbent cost advantages**
  These are created when incumbents have advantages such as low labor or capital costs, preferred access to raw materials, government subsidies, favorable locations, proprietary technology and product designs, and accumulated learning experience. A start-up firm with no experience, for example, can expect higher costs than incumbents; heavy start-up losses and below- or near-cost pricing are often common in order to gain experience.

- **Economies of scale**
  Generally defined as a decline in the unit costs as the volume per period increases, economies of scale can deter an entrant. A new entrant may need to come in at a larger scale and risk encountering strong reaction from the existing players. Or a new entrant may decide to come in at a smaller scale and incur a cost disadvantage. Facilities, research, marketing, sales force coverage, and distribution are all examples of areas of economies of scale that potentially require significant entry investments.

- **Product/service differentiation**
  Differentiation refers to the brand identification and existing customer loyalties an entrant must overcome. Entrants will need to invest time and money to build a brand name. Such investments have no guarantee of success or "salvage value" should the entry fail.

- **Switching costs**
  Should a buyer consider changing from an existing supplier's product or service to that of a new entrant, the one-time switching costs can be a deterrent. Having to purchase/install new equipment or retrain employees are two common examples of switching costs. A new entrant must offer a major cost savings or potential for performance improvement to warrant a switch from an incumbent.

- **Channel crowding**
  Many distribution channels have limited capacity or exclusive relationships with manufacturers that restrict the number of product lines. Intense selling efforts are generally required to convince a distributor to take on a new product line. A new entrant may need to pay larger margins to offset the extra cost that distributors incur, or a new player may be forced to find a niche market.

- **Expected incumbent reactions**
  Depending upon how aggressively incumbents have defended their positions in the past, entry barriers may be raised or lowered. Incumbents with deep pockets and staying power who have demonstrated a willingness to take a short-term reduction in

profits to defend market share discourage entrants. Incumbents who have ignored previous entrants or have been unwilling to defend their position can encourage entrants.

Threat of substitutes

When an acceptable substitute product or service is available—one that provides the same functions and offers the same benefits—the average price that can be charged and the resulting profit margin is squeezed. The amount of product or service value is also limited. Less costly but acceptable substitutes also pose a threat.

How electronic surveillance and alarm systems have impacted security guard firms is but one example of industry threats posed by the availability of substitutes. Another example is how customers can now purchase products and services directly online in lieu of traditional distribution channels. The key in these situations is to account for similarities while looking for differentiation opportunities beyond product or service similarities. In the case of the security industry, firms offer guards and electronic surveillance systems as a value-added package, positioning the guards as skilled operators.

Bargaining power of buyers

Buyers (customers) and sellers (suppliers) of goods and services can have wide variance in their relationship. Relationships may involve tightly integrated, just-in-time manufacturing systems, or they may be at the other end of the spectrum, with mass marketing. Buyer power, in particular, is enhanced or deterred depending upon bargaining leverage and price sensitivity.

Bargaining leverage. Generally speaking, leverage is any strategic or tactical event that can be exploited to an advantage. A buyer's bargaining leverage is enhanced by the following factors:

- **Large-volume purchases made by a few key customers**
  In this situation, the seller becomes somewhat dependent on the key buyers and would encounter problems if a relationship were severed.

- **Ability for customers to easily switch**
  Customers may change suppliers if there is little product or service differentiation, low switching costs, or readily available low-cost substitutes.

- **Ability to backward-integrate**
  Current prices and/or other terms can make an alternative more attractive than continuing to buy externally. (An example of this is the purchase of an upstream supplier or the ability to bring back in house something that was previously outsourced.)

- **Customer insider knowledge**
  Bargaining leverage is gained if customers know the supplier's costs and profits or learn that the supplier needs their business to offset excess capacity or other mitigating circumstances.

Price sensitivity. Price sensitivity is an indicator of how important lower prices are to customers. Price sensitivity is heightened by the following factors:

- **Product or service impact on end product quality**
  A buyer pays more attention to price if the consequences of product or service failure are more severe than in situations where the product/service has little impact on the quality of the end product.

- **Price of the product or service relative to a customer's total costs**
  Big-ticket items tend to incur greater purchasing scrutiny; smaller incidental items often escape analysis of cost alternatives.

- **Buyer's profits**
  When customers are suffering from poor profitability, they often seek price concessions from suppliers. The pressure for concessions can become intense if survival is at stake.

Price sensitivity is further intensified if buyers perceive little difference among competing suppliers.

Bargaining power of suppliers

A supplier's ability to withstand bargaining by customers tends to mirror those conditions making buyers powerful. A supplier's bargaining power depends upon the following items:

- **Size of the supplier relative to the customer**
  A larger supplier can have a distinct advantage and leverage in dealing with a small, dispersed customer base.

- **Customer's reliance on the supplier's product or service**
  Reliance is influenced to the extent that a customer cannot buy an equivalent, the input is not storable (so the buyer cannot stockpile inventory), or switching costs are high.

- **Threat of forward integration**
  If suppliers can sell directly to end users, customers will have less leverage to get better prices.

Rivalry among existing competitors

In some environments, rivals coexist. In other environments, direct rivals constantly jockey for market share with tactics such as temporary price cuts, special promotions, advertising blitzes, aggressive new product launches, and increased customer service and extended warranties. Value often erodes as competitors match moves.

Telecommunication providers are notorious for price cutting in their efforts to secure new customers and cover fixed costs. Yet such actions often decrease profits and leave market share unchanged.

The following factors typically influence the status of competitor relations.

- **Structure of competition**
  Rivalry is generally most intense when there are a few balanced competitors or

several small players serving the same market. Antagonism may run deep between top competitors; instability often results as firms may be prone to fight and retaliate. In the case of a proliferation of smaller players, these companies may try to make moves the others will not notice. But in situations where one competitor clearly dominates, rivalry is often subdued as followers learn to coexist under the leader's umbrella.

- **Structure of costs**

  Capacity utilization is emphasized when fixed costs are high. Any excess capacity often leads to price cutting and a cycle of price matching.

- **Product or service differentiation**

  In the absence of differentiation, customers often focus on price, terms, and so on, and rivalry intensifies. Conversely, rivalry is subdued when customers develop preferences and brand loyalty due to large perceived differentiation. Product differentiation can foster buyer preferences and loyalties to particular suppliers. Naturally, organizations seek differentiation that is sustainable (for example, a feature that is difficult to imitate, remains useful, and customers are willing to pay for).

- **Customer switching costs**

  Costs that tie a buyer to one supplier provide good protection against raids by rivals. Changing a computer operating system is an example of a situation in which a customer would typically incur a general disruption of operations and expensive costs.

- **Diversity of competitors' strategies and objectives**

  It is much easier for competitors to anticipate another's intention or accurately anticipate reactions to market moves when all competitors have similar strategies, cost structures, management philosophies, and so on. When competitors come from diverse backgrounds (for example, foreign-owned, government-owned, small owner-operated firms versus large enterprises), actions and activities are much less predictable.

- **High exit barriers**

  Even when profits are depressed, exit barriers can keep players trapped. For example, firms may choose to endure the drain on profits caused by excess capacity rather than sell to other manufacturers that could threaten their other markets at a later point in time. Or management may resist an economically justified exit decision based on an emotional rationale such as loyalty to a particular business or employees.

Linkage of the five forces to strategic planning

According to Porter, the five forces in total—entry of new competitors, threat of substitutes, bargaining power of buyers, bargaining power of suppliers, and rivalry among existing competitors—determine the intensity of industry competition and profitability. In other words, the collective strength of the five competitive forces determines the ability of firms to earn rates of return on investment in excess of the cost of capital.

In industries where the strength of the five forces is favorable (for example, pharmaceuticals), profits are attractive. In industries where the strength of one or more of the forces is under fire (for example, airlines), few firms have good returns in spite of management efforts. Porter notes that industry profitability is not a function of what a product looks like or whether a service incorporates high technology or low technology, but rather it is determined by industry structure. That is why a product that looks mundane (for example, an automotive aftermarket part) may be extremely profitable, whereas a more glamorous high-tech product (for example, a cellular handset) may not be highly profitable for all the market players.

To a large extent, the five forces are moving targets. In this respect, they:

- Can vary from industry to industry.

- Can change as an industry evolves.

- Are not equally important in any one industry.

- Are vulnerable to high growth and market demand (if a surplus of competitors is attracted, leading to overcrowding).

Naturally, different firms will have unique strengths and weaknesses that influence their ability to deal with or even alter industry structure.

Understanding industry structure is a critical starting point during strategy formulation. Different forces take on prominence. The strongest force or forces assume increased importance during strategic planning and strategy formulation.

Technological changes

No industry is immune from the strategic implications of technology. Consider the following points as proof:

- Technology can result in the creation of industry substitutes (for example, wireless phones versus land lines).

- Technology can reduce the need for large-scale distribution and open a market up to new entrants (for example, Web-based e-commerce technology versus traditional distribution channels).

- Technology can accelerate new product designs and facilitate short production runs in manufacturing-based industries, leading to either intense rivalry or monopoly.

- Technology can create a shift in the balance of power between an organization and a supplier or buyer, depending on where the technology is developed and exploited.

- Technology can change industry structure and thereby either improve or degrade average profitability.

Those firms savvy in recognizing and exploiting technological changes are generally more adept at gaining and sustaining competitive advantage. To a degree, technological change is both an external factor and an internal factor. Technology impacts what products and services an organization offers, how products and services are made, how customers are serviced, and with whom the firm must compete. As such, technology must reinforce a firm's strategic intent and competitive strategy.

Characteristics of a technology assessment

Technology cuts across all of the business units and activities of an enterprise. Given the span of technology and its importance to market success, an organization needs to assess its technology capabilities on an ongoing basis.

The Portable MBA (Bruner et al. 1998) outlines a five-step process for a technology assessment:

1. Identify key technologies.

2. Analyze the potential changes in current and future technologies.

3. Analyze the competitive impact of technologies.

4. Analyze the organization's technical strengths and weaknesses.

5. Establish the organization's technology priorities.

Step 1: Identify key technologies. This initial phase in a technology assessment identifies all technologies that impact the organization. This involves current and future technologies as well as those used inside the firm or outside.

General categories that should be considered include:

- Product technology.

- Manufacturing and/or service process technology.

- Technology used by support functions (such as sales, customer service, finance and accounting).

- Information management technology.

- Technologies used by competitors.

- Technologies used by suppliers or buyers of the organization's products and services.

Consideration should be given to technologies not currently used by the enterprise, especially if they might have future implications. For example, a small business not currently using e-commerce might well explore how the technology is used in other industries and how it could impact the firm's current products and processes.

Step 2: Analyze the potential changes in current and future technologies. This next step involves evaluating short- and long-term changes in all the important technologies identified. Complex technologies may have many layers of subtechnologies. The evaluation must consider all of the subtechnologies.

- A few pointers about analyzing potential changes are:

- People with expertise in the technologies should conduct the technology evaluation.

- Evaluations should be constructively examined and challenged by others to preclude the possibility of a forecast based on unquestioned conventional wisdom.

- The effort applied to technology development varies. A technology that is critical to a competitor will most likely evolve more quickly than technologies that are necessary but not an important source of competitive advantage.

- Mature technologies do not always change slowly, especially if the need for progress or replacement of the technology exists. Mature technologies will also change rapidly when a new technology offers opportunities for new entrants.

Step 3: Analyze the competitive impact of technologies. The intent of this step is to answer the following key questions:

- What technologies or technological changes can give the organization the greatest source of competitive advantage?

- What technologies or technological changes would be the greatest threat in the hands of a competitor?

- What technologies or technological changes could significantly change the industry structure?

The competitive impact of different technologies is generally classified by base, key, or pacing characteristics.

- **Base technologies** are widely used throughout an industry. As such, they are well understood. They are considered necessary, but they do not provide competitive advantage.

- As implied by the name, **key technologies** are critical to competitive advantage. They help an organization differentiate its products or services. In some instances, they enable the firm to compete with lower costs. Patents, unpatented advances by the firm, or superior expertise in using the technology often make key technologies proprietary to an organization.

- **Pacing technologies** are those that have the potential to redefine an industry or change the whole basis of competition. Pacing technologies often replace key technologies. When firms that are not the market leader develop a pacing technology, the opportunity to change industry leadership exists. Market leaders have a dangerous tendency to overlook pacing technologies because they are often very different or they threaten to cannibalize existing products, services, and processes.

Step 4: Analyze the organization's technical strengths and weaknesses. Managers must assess the organization's strengths and weaknesses for each technology classification as well as the potential costs of developing each technology. The evaluation should compare findings with competitors' strengths and weaknesses (both current and future scenarios).

Just as in the overall organizational strengths, weaknesses, opportunities, and threats (S.W.O.T.) analysis, pride and unwillingness to acknowledge the organization's weaknesses or the strengths of a competitor can skew this assessment. To help ensure objectivity, it is best to have a team of technical specialists, who understand the technologies, and managers, who are operations and market-focused, do the assessment together.

Step 5: Establish the organization's technology priorities. Based on findings from the technology assessment process, a tentative set of priorities for the acquisition, development, and use of product, service, and process technologies can be created.

A technology assessment should also consider the pros and cons of having highly integrated technology systems—whether or not the firm currently has highly integrated systems or is contemplating them.

- **Integration benefits**
  Integration facilitates simultaneous updating of databases. Current data is available for decision making. The costs of data entry and processing are lower than for stand-alone applications.

- **Integration concerns**
  System integration typically requires huge financial investments, comprehensive designs, and careful project management and execution as well as timely training on system features and the transition process. Integration is a big commitment. It often strains an organization's resources to the point of vulnerability to competitors by inhibiting growth and flexibility for a prolonged period of time (for example, two or more years). Furthermore, failures can create customer dissatisfaction, lead to financial losses, and make the entire organization vulnerable.

Linkage of a technology assessment to strategic planning

Insights gained from the technology assessment evolve into an organizational technology strategy through a process of interaction between the firm's leaders and managers representing all the functional areas of the organization.

Characteristics of a sound technology strategy include:

- Enhancement of technology's strategic role in the organization.

- Support of the organization's corporate and competitive strategies.

- Plans for attaining short-term and long-term objectives and major projects, including goals and milestones.

- Resource allocation.

- Alignment to the organization's financial plan and budget.

- Metrics for measuring accomplishment.

A technology strategy should also be easily understood and well communicated. The commitment of key people must be secured.

The technology strategy establishes preliminary organizational priorities and commitments to innovation and technology development, always keeping the firm's strategic positioning in mind. It is in this manner that a technology assessment leads to a technology strategy and ultimately provides inputs for strategic plans.

Stakeholder groups and their social concerns

Stakeholders include people, departments, groups, organizations, or other bodies that have a "stake"—an investment or interest—in the success of or actions taken by an organization. Thus, stakeholders include:

- Executives.

- Managers and employees (including their families).

- The organization's board of directors.

- Shareholders (stockholders).

- The industry in which the organization operates.

- Customers.

- Competitors.

- Suppliers.

- Business partners.

- Consulting and advisory services.

- Creditors.

- Special interest groups—industrial, political, consumer, and so on.

- Unions.

- Regulating government bodies.

- The community in which the organization operates.

- The nation.

- The environment—plants, animals, ecosystems, natural resources.

- Educational institutions.

- The media.

- Future generations.

During strategic planning, it is important to identify the various stakeholders to understand their expectations and potential influences on the enterprise and to ensure that their needs and interests are addressed. If not on board, stakeholders can withhold resources and support and potentially undermine the legitimacy of the enterprise.

Maximizing shareholder value while being socially responsible in business

The idea of maximizing shareholder value is associated with for-profit corporations and generally refers to the market valuation of a firm. The idea of profit maximization requires consideration of marginal costs and a demand curve. Certainly, an organization must earn a profit that is at least equal to its cost of capital considering the risk. Although critical to organizational success, profit maximization and optimizing shareholder value are not the only goals for organizations.

The social responsibility approach in business implies that organizations should act as good corporate citizens and adopt socially responsible practices that will be a positive force for change and help improve the quality of people's lives. The premise behind this approach is that corporations have societal obligations that must complement—and not compete for—profit maximization. This philosophy suggests that corporate actions should balance the claims of all stakeholders and hence corporate leaders have a fiduciary responsibility to all stakeholders, not only the organization's executives and shareholders.

Organizations naturally encounter a host of challenges in attempts to be socially responsible. Consider a few common examples:

- Accounting practices—insider trading

- Advertising—accurate and truthful product/service representation

- Corporate restructuring—layoffs

- Diversity issues—race, ethnicity, gender, sexual orientation

- Employee privacy issues—drug testing, chemical dependency, AIDS

- Harassment issues—gender or age discrimination

- Environmental issues—pollution, animal rights

- International operations—conduct encountering bribery, nepotism, and other issues acceptable in other countries that challenge the organization's ethics

- Competition—predatory pricing, antitrust actions

Stakeholder analysis

Most organizations use some type of model for stakeholder analysis to assess ethical challenges and how to best be socially responsible. Stakeholder analysis provides an organization with a framework for weighing all the various claims and stakeholder concerns to reach a socially responsible decision.

A common method of stakeholder analysis uses a matrix. The main steps of this type of stakeholder analysis are listed in Figure 3-4.

Figure 3-4: Steps in a Stakeholder Analysis Framework

Step 1	Identify stakeholders; brainstorm a list of the main participants.
Step 2	Determine stakeholder needs; collect input through interviews, focus groups, surveys, and so on.
Step 3	Develop a matrix of the organization's objectives and the stakeholders' needs.
Step 4	Code the effect of the organization's objectives versus the stakeholders' needs (for example, using a plus or minus sign or question mark).
Step 5	Make a decision based on the effects recorded.

A stakeholder analysis done in this manner sets the stage for decisions to:

- Change the organization's objectives.
- Satisfy stakeholder demands.
- Mitigate potential conflict.
- Pass if compatible or acceptable.

Figure 3-5 shows an example of a stakeholder analysis. In this analysis, a produce distributor plans to build automated warehouses and install pricey high-tech gear. The matrix shown considers the stakeholders. The analysis points out that there is no one "right" way; differences in the weighting shown here can exist. The point of stakeholder analysis is to tackle such stakeholder issues and make informed and thoughtful decisions that are consistent and defensible

Figure 3-5: Stakeholder Analysis Example—Automating a Produce Warehouse

(+ or −)	Organization	Employees	Consuming Public	Suppliers	Government Inspectors
Harm and benefits	− Higher costs + Higher profits	+ More free time − Fewer hours/ potential layoffs	+ Lower prices + Quick time to market; less spoilage	− New hardware	+ Power and influence
Rights and responsibilities	+ Value + Profits for owners and shareholders	+ Competitive market position	? Possible quality concerns ? Public good	? Ability to meet demand	+ Protect the public + Regulate industry

Other methods are available for conducting a stakeholder analysis. Some organizations do a stakeholder analysis by answering a series of guiding questions such as:

- Who are the main stakeholders?
- What are the most important values of each stakeholder? (For example, What are the harm and benefits to each?)
- What rights and duties are at issue?
- What principles and rules are relevant?
- What are some relevant parallel cases?
- What should be done?

Linkage of a stakeholder analysis to strategic planning

There are many ways to manage an enterprise. The style of Xerox will differ from that of Fujitsu. Charles Schwab will approach things differently from Datek. But all firms will interact with their stakeholders.

Stakeholder analysis helps an organization frame its corporate social responsibility. It identifies the role good citizenship plays in a business. Through stakeholder analysis, a firm learns:

- How people feel about the organization and the industry it is in.

- What issues the organization should rethink/reevaluate its position on.

- What the organization should do differently to improve its position.

Shareholder value and stakeholder analysis are not mutually exclusive. Obvious decisions that balance expenses with revenues and are aligned to corporate goals are usually prudent courses for action. However, challenges can arise. For example, an organization may face a situation that violates the rights of one at the benefit for many. But most organizations also look for ways "to do the right thing" for all stakeholders while still achieving satisfactory profits for shareholders.

Globalization

Globalization describes an organization's migration to international operations. Globalization is a reflection of organizational strategy and an integrated progression of worldwide operations.

Although globalization is prevalent and a goal on which many organizations set their sights, an organization does not simply become a global entity overnight. The migration from domestic to global operations typically evolves through a series of relatively predictable stages.

- **Export**
  This is the initial stage of globalization for most organizations. Firms begin to export their products or services abroad through direct sales to customers, import/export firms, and independent agents or distributors. International sales from exports generally represent a small portion of total revenue. They are seen as an adjunct to domestic sales.

- **International division and sales subsidiaries**
  As international sales grow in importance, the organization is likely to establish a separate international division and/or sales subsidiaries. At this stage of globalization, increased communication and coordination is required between domestic and international operations.

  A sales subsidiary generally involves a branch operation in a country or countries where sales have become significantly large. Subsidiaries range from a relatively modest office to operations such as stores, service centers, or manufacturing plants, depending upon the volume and the nature of the business.

- **Multinational corporation (MNC)**
  As sales volume and the number of countries significantly increase, an organization evolves to the stage of an MNC. The MNC generally operates in several countries and views and treats each one as a relatively separate entity. It often maintains global coordination of some functions such as finance, staffing, marketing, and so on. Or the

firm may move to a regional structure with more regional headquarters and coordination.

- **Global organization**

  To a global organization, the whole world is one market. National boundaries are seamless. The organization's headquarters may be located anywhere.

  The global organization is characterized features such as but not limited to:

  - Global strategic planning.

  - Products and services designed and marketed worldwide.

  - Pursuit of technology and innovation worldwide.

  - Sharing of global technology and innovation between all operations; application to individual markets.

  - Product and service development wherever cost, quality, and cycle time are favorable and demand is sufficient.

  - Pursuit of resources (such as money, materials, parts, insurance, and people) in locations where the best quality for cost can be found.

  - Employees moving freely between countries.

- **Alliances, partnerships, joint ventures, and so on**

  This stage of globalization does not necessarily replace the MNC or global organization. But it does offer an organization a channel to capitalize upon resources (such as research and design, technology, personnel, manufacturing facilities, and so on) that would not otherwise be available.

  A couple of examples of this level of globalization are:

  - A large telecommunications firm subcontracting for technology resources in other countries, including from a major competitor.

  - Two international electronics companies pooling resources to design and develop sophisticated computer chips and distribute them in more than 120 countries.

Linkage of globalization to strategic planning

The stages of globalization are sometimes named or categorized slightly differently than those just described. And, obviously, not every organization passes through each stage in exactly the same way. Some move at an accelerated pace—due to mergers, acquisitions, and so on. Others evolve slowly in a deliberate manner and may take years to move from export to MNC and global. Some organizations overlap the stages. For example, an organization with operations in multiple countries may be at the export stage in one country and at the MNC stage in another. But regardless of the nomenclature, the number of stages, and the time frame it takes for an organization to go global, it is helpful to recognize that globalization follows a progression.

An enterprise needs to acquire additional skills and competence as it moves through the stages of globalization. Various activities and functions evolve as an organization becomes a full-fledged multinational or global organization. For example, international financial skills and tax knowledge become increasingly important along the globalization spectrum.

To compete successfully in the global arena, organizations must make considerable investments in resources and these investments should be carefully crafted during strategic planning.

Analysis of Internal Factors Affecting Strategy

To complement the assessment of external factors affecting strategy, an organization must conduct an internal capability analysis. Together these two assessments—external (looking from the outside in) and internal (looking from the inside out)—help an organization to establish its current capabilities and close the gap between those capabilities and the capabilities needed for industry success.

What to assess in internal capability analysis

In particular, an internal capability analysis helps to ensure that the organization has the resources, skills, and processes to reach its strategic and tactical goals.

- **Resources**
  An internal assessment of resources looks at the finances, facilities, equipment, and other infrastructure issues that can support or impede organizational initiatives. Assessing resources requires review of financial statements and additional analytical work and quantitative information. Supporting growth strategies requires capital investment analysis. Supporting ongoing programs involves value chain analysis and review of activity-based costing (ABC) information. (*Note: Additional information on value chain analysis is found in Topic 3 of this section, "Business Process Performance."*)

- **Skills**
  Skill assessments examine the current education levels of employees, the core knowledge and skills required, and the specific technical or organizational skills required. As organizations face competitive pressures, employees must be prepared. As warranted, a commitment to training should be made.

- **Processes**
  Cycle time and a variety of capacity issues are considered when assessing organizational processes necessary to gain competitive advantage. (*Note: Process analysis is discussed further in Topic 3 of this section, "Business Process Performance."*)

How to assess internal resources, skills, and processes

There is no one single method for analyzing internal capabilities, because every organization is unique. Examples of tools and techniques organizations may choose from include:

- Baldrige National Quality Program Criteria (for self-assessment).

- ISO 9001 quality system and ISO 14000 environmental management system requirements (for gap analysis).

- Benchmarking processes (to understand best-in-class).

- Competitive analysis (for example, analysis of the five forces to understand competitors' businesses, market share, and so on).

- Employee competency assessments (to determine current knowledge, skills, experience, and aptitude).

- Training needs analysis (to identify training needs that can support organizational initiatives).

- Internal listening posts (to gather customer data, and so on).

- Employee surveys (to determine if employees understand the organization's focus and to assess conditions and/or issues in the current work environment, compensation approaches, management, and so on).

- Audits (to verify that processes are working within established limits).

No matter how an organization chooses to assess internal factors, internal issues should not be given a lower priority than the challenges the organization faces in the external environment. Without the internal capabilities in place, an organization is hard pressed to address external business issues. An internal gap can constrain an organization's ability to fulfill strategic external initiatives.

Linkage of internal capability analysis to strategic planning

Conceptually, internal capability analysis has two phases. The first phase is establishing a snapshot of the present state and identifying gaps. The second phase involves making decisions about closing the critical gaps to desired states. Some gaps may be fairly simple and straightforward to address; others may require costly capital expenditures and time to address. The cost of developing new capabilities must be weighed against the potential payoffs.

Different capabilities support different sources of competitive advantage. An organization's future success often depends on the capabilities it develops. Capabilities that require financial investments can be risky because returns are uncertain; some investments may be irretrievable. But not investing can be just as risky due to:

- Falling behind competitors.

- Failing to sustain profits.

- Compromising existing capabilities, leading to lost opportunities.

Strategic planning stalls in many organizations because they fail to assess internal capabilities. Well-intended strategies become operational plans without an understanding of the internal requirements and capabilities to get the job done. In the end, due diligence in assessing internal capabilities and addressing them appropriately helps to position an organization for future opportunities.

S.W.O.T. (Strengths, Weaknesses, Opportunities, and Threats) Analysis

S.W.O.T. (or SWOT) is the acronym for strengths, weaknesses, opportunities, and threats. A **S.W.O.T. analysis** provides a framework to identify a variety of elements that will help or hinder an organization's progress in the environment in which it operates. S.W.O.T. analysis is sometimes called current state analysis.

An environmental analysis frames the proverbial big picture and identifies top issues an organization must deal with; a S.W.O.T. analysis takes the strategic planning process to the next level of focus. Organizations traditionally conduct a S.W.O.T. analysis to gather additional input for the strategic planning process.

Essentially, a S.W.O.T. analysis provides a means to organize the data gathered in the detailed internal and external analyses. Strengths and weakness are identified from an internal analysis of the organization; opportunities and threats are part of an external analysis of the environment in which the organization operates. (The external environment is essentially everything outside an organization that might affect it.)

Strengths

Identifying organizational strengths answers the question, what is the organization really good at? In other words, what are the skills, capabilities, and core competencies that help achieve the organization's goals and objectives and sustain its competitive position?

Organizational strengths might be any of the following:

- Strong leadership
- Financial soundness
- Organizational learning
- Research and development
- Innovative product designs
- Breakthrough technology
- Product development
- Product assembly
- Strong distribution channel
- Strong market position

One or more strengths can provide a competitive advantage and help an organization differentiate itself in the marketplace. For example, if a company is exceptional at research and development, it might focus efforts on in-house product development to build or strengthen a competitive advantage. Conversely, spreading resources too thinly across too many areas can weaken an organization's competitive position.

Weaknesses

Identifying organizational weaknesses answers the questions, what needs to improve? or what do we need that we do not currently have? More specifically, weaknesses are the skills, capabilities, and competencies that the organization lacks and that prevent the organization from achieving its goals and objectives. Weaknesses may be thought of as opportunities for improvement. Furthermore, any of the examples of strengths previously listed might be or become a weakness. In other words, an ability can become a disability.

Faced with a deficiency, an organization generally has three choices:

- Modify the goal and objective into something achievable.

- Invest the necessary capital to acquire the knowledge and/or skill required.

- Find another organization that has the expertise needed and outsource that requirement or develop an alliance.

For example, consider a small manufacturing company that does not have the funds or plant floor space for heat-treating furnaces. They would either have to outsource this "weakness" or invest capital funds if this capability was deemed critical for operations.

Opportunities and threats

Opportunities are generally described as those events, trends, and so on, that can help an organization meet goals and grow to new levels. Examples of opportunities are the chance to:

- Expand the customer base—based on growth in customer numbers due to demand, favorable demographic population shifts, and so on.

- Provide new avenues of customer access—distribution channels or bundling of services, and so on.

- Increase customer appeal of the product/service offering—new media for advertising or methods of packaging to entice customers to switch from competitors.

- Exploit a competitor's weakness—capitalize on windows of opportunity to strengthen customer acceptance of the firm's product/service.

Threats are barriers to an organization's growth. They are created mostly by events, trends, or competitor actions.

Examples of threats are situations that may:

- Reduce the size of a firm's customer base—due to economic downturns, unfavorable demographic population shifts, in-sourcing by customers, and so on.

- Make customer access more difficult or costly—due to changes in customer buying practices or doing business with smaller numbers of suppliers, and so on.

- Reduce the customer appeal of a firm's product/service—price wars or other activities that can entice the customer to choose alternatives.

- Surpass the organization's product/service offering—price cutting or new offerings that provide significant improvements (for example, technology leapfrogging).

Similar to strengths and weaknesses, opportunities and threats are dualistic—the same event or trend can be an opportunity or a threat. Organizations may address threats and opportunities in different ways. Overall, an organization should look to capitalize on opportunities and counter threats.

Example of a S.W.O.T weighted average

A weighted average can be useful in implementing S.W.O.T. analysis data.

Example:

Selecting strategies using a weighted average in conjunction with S.W.O.T. data might be done in the following manner.

ABC Company has identified the following factors that can impact market attractiveness and business strength for a product. Each item has a different proportionate weight, all summing to 1.0. The rating scale ranges from 1 (the highest) to 5 (the lowest).

Market Attractiveness	Weight	Rating (1 to 5)
Market size	0.3	4
Market profitability	0.4	5
Distribution structure	0.2	4
Government regulations	0.1	2

Business Strength	Weight	Rating (1 to 5)
Unit costs	0.4	3
Customer loyalty	0.5	2
Brand reputation	0.1	4

The calculated weighted average for market attractiveness is 4.2 and the calculated weighted average for business strength is 2.6, as shown below. Because the highly attractive market will presumably entice others to enter, planning strategies to build on the lower business strength (rather than attempting to exploit the higher market attractiveness) would be the most beneficial plan.

Market attractiveness = (0.3 x 4 + 0.4 x 5 + 0.2 x 4 + 0.1x 2 = 4.2)

Business strength = (0.4 x 3 + 0.5 x 2 + 0.1 x 4 = 2.6)

Use of a T.O.W.S. (threats, opportunities, weaknesses, and strengths) matrix

Where a S.W.O.T. analysis provides a framework to identify elements that can help or hinder an organization, a **T.O.W.S. matrix** (or **TOWS matrix**) takes the process to the next level. Using S.W.O.T. analysis data, a T.O.W.S. matrix systematically identifies relationships and helps to develop strategies by matching strengths with opportunities, using opportunities to reduce weaknesses, using strengths to overcome threats, and reducing weaknesses and avoiding threats.

The variables in T.O.W.S. matrix are not new; they are direct outcomes of the SWOT analysis. The uniqueness of the T.O.W.S. matrix is the strategy formulation based on the systematic approach. T.O.W.S. is also referred to as situational analysis.

A basic T.O.W.S. is shown in Figure 3-6.

Figure 3-6: T.O.W.S. Matrix Example

Internal factors ／ External factors	Strengths (S)	Weaknesses (W)
	A list of five to ten internal strengths goes here	A list of five to ten internal weaknesses goes here
Opportunities (O) A list of five to ten external opportunities goes here	**SO strategies** Strategies here use strengths that take advantage of opportunities	**WO strategies** Strategies here take advantage of opportunities by overcoming weaknesses
Threats (T) A list of five to ten external threats goes here	**ST strategies** Strategies here use strengths to avoid threats	**WT strategies** Strategies here minimize weaknesses and avoid threats

There are different ways of preparing a T.O.W.S. matrix and analyzing the situation. For example, an organization might begin by identifying important problems. Other approaches could be to start by identifying organizational objectives or to focus on opportunities. Another consideration is whether to start by analyzing the external environment or to begin with the organization's internal resources. There is no single best way.

A T.O.W.S. matrix provides a good framework for identifying relationships, but it can become complex as multiple factors are being identified and the combinations examined increase. Once the combinations of relationships are identified, a weighting system may be used to help formulate the strategic choices. A '+' can be used to indicate a match between the strengths of the company and external opportunities; a '0' can be used to indicate a nonexistent relationship; or, a '-' can be used to indicate a weak relationship.

But management experts caution that you cannot simply add up the number of pluses, zeroes, and minuses in interpreting the matrix. Different relationships identified in a T.O.W.S. matrix often have different potential and merit further evaluation. Similar tables can be developed to analyze the strategy boxes (SO, WO, ST, and WT).

The point in time the matrix is prepared is another consideration. As noted previously, because internal and external environments are dynamic, multiple T.O.W.S. matrices may be warranted.

In spite of these potential complexities, a T.O.W.S. matrix offers a relatively straight-forward way to identify promising strategies that use organizational strengths to take advantage of opportunities in the external environment.

Linkage of a S.W.O.T. analysis to strategic planning

The outcomes of a S.W.O.T. analysis are usually lists that an organization needs to sort through. Organizations are faced with questions such as:

- What interrelationships exist among the strengths, weaknesses, opportunities, and threats?

- Does the organization have the necessary resources and capabilities to seize the opportunities and neutralize the threats?

- How many competitors already have the same resources and competencies?

- Are there barriers to market entry?

- Could the organization gain a source of competitive advantage?

- Will acquiring a particular resource or capability create a cost disadvantage for the firm?

- Are substitutes available?

- Does the organizational structure allow the firm to take full advantage of its resources and capabilities and support potential growth/change?

The challenge in evaluating all the strengths, weaknesses, opportunities, and threats is to prioritize them and then identify appropriate actions. The basic idea is to:

- Build on strengths.

- Eliminate or deal with weaknesses.

- Exploit opportunities.

- Minimize threats.

In addressing strengths and weaknesses, the outlook can change quickly. What is true or feasible now may differ in time. For example, something that is considered a strength today can be immediately neutralized by a technological innovation, a change in a government regulation, and so on.

A S.W.O.T. analysis is an important part of strategic planning because it incorporates both internal and external assessments about an organization into one summary that is practical and useable. It helps tie up any loose ends from the environmental analysis and answers many previously unresolved organizational issues. The opportunities and limitations identified provide information for reasonable goals and action plans in the strategic planning process.

Note: The use of S.W.O.T. analysis data in the process of advantage creation is discussed in Section B, "Strategic Marketing."

Long-Term Vision, Mission, Goals, and Objectives

Organizational goals and strategies cannot be left to chance and intuition. They must be explicitly stated and clearly communicated to those in the organization responsible for their implementation. For that reason, an important step during strategic planning is to formally write out the organization's vision, mission, goals, and objectives.

Vision

An organization's **vision statement** is a guiding image of future success and achievement articulated in terms of the organization's contribution to society. It is a succinct statement of what an organization will do for future generations and how it wants to be perceived. Consider the vision statement examples shown in Figure 3-7.

Figure 3-7: Vision Statement Examples

The Boeing Company

[Our vision is] People working together as a global enterprise for aerospace leadership.

The Saturn Division of General Motors

[Our vision is] To market vehicles developed and manufactured in the U.S. that are world leaders in quality, cost, and customer satisfaction through the integration of people, technology, and business systems and to transfer knowledge, technology, and experience throughout GM.

Unfortunately, too many vision statements tend to be soulless and easily transportable between companies by simply changing the organization's name (for example, "XYZ strives to be a world-class organization committed to excellence and exceeding customer expectations."). A clear vision statement is compelling and unites everyone in the organization. It will reflect organizational values and inspire and challenge management and employees alike to action.

Mission

A **mission statement** provides the guiding compass for an organization. Similar to vision statements, mission statements are shaped by organizational values. A mission statement succinctly articulates an organization's business position. It expresses how the organization will continuously move toward its vision and provides a clear view of what the firm is trying to accomplish for its customers. A mission statement answers the question, why are we in business? In answering this question, a mission statement must be accurate, easily understood, motivating, and transferable into action.

Figure 3-8 shows two examples of corporate mission statements.

Figure 3-8: Corporate Mission Statement Examples

Southwest Airlines

The mission of Southwest Airlines is dedication to the highest quality of customer service delivered with a sense of warmth, friendliness, individual pride, and company spirit.

Courtyard by Marriot

[Our mission is] To provide economy- and quality-minded travelers with a premier, moderate-priced lodging facility that is consistently perceived as clean, comfortable, well-maintained, and attractive, staffed by friendly and attentive people.

Goals

Generally, goals may be thought of as aimed-at targets. They summarize what an organization hopes to achieve in order to fulfill its mission and achieve its vision. Goals serve as general guidelines; they tend not to be overly specific or quantifiable. A goal states the desired end result and/or the benefits of the result; it does not state the implementation plan. Organizations typically develop both strategic and tactical goals.

Strategic goals

Strategic goals are established at the highest levels of an organization. As implied by the name, strategic goals are part of the firm's strategic plan; they are long-range in nature. Examples of strategic goals are business diversification, the addition or deletion of product lines, or the penetration of new markets. Strategic goals require additional goals to be achieved at the tactical level.

Tactical goals

Tactical goals are generally established by business (also referred to as responsibility centers and strategic business units or SBUs) or functional departments at middle and lower levels of an organization. Tactical goals are short-range and usually span one year or less. "To increase product line profits by 10%" is an example of a tactical goal.

Concepts applying to strategic and tactical goals

Just as organizational strategies must be dynamic, so too must strategic and tactical goals. New things are always on the competitive horizon: new entrants, technological changes, economic upheavals, to name but a few. Goals need to be modified or changed to reflect the internal and external changes taking place as well as threats and opportunities present. At a minimum, goals should be evaluated on an annual basis.

Objectives

Objectives provide the details or actions required to support goals. Well-conceived objectives specify the quantitative measures that will be used to track progress and performance—the desired action, the timing of the action, the level of performance desired, and the function or individual responsible for the action.

Multiple objectives may support one goal. In this situation, all the objectives must be completed to realize the benefit of the goal; none of the objectives alone can ensure fulfillment of the goal. Expanding upon the previous example, "to increase product line profits by 10%," a few supporting objectives might be:

- Marketing team member A determines customer quality perceptions of product X within 30 days. Team member A prioritizes these customer perceptions and assigns a relative weight to each.

- Production team member B develops a process flow diagram of product X within 30 days, including all equipment involved.

- Accounting team member C conducts a profitability analysis of product X within 30 days, determining the profit margin percentage and the investment turnover.

Additional objectives would need to be developed. In totality, all the objectives would support the goal of increasing product line profits by 10%.

As a reminder of the specificity objectives require, the acronym **SMART** is often applied. Objectives should be **s**pecific, **m**easurable, **a**ttainable, **r**ealistic, and **t**ime-determined.

Alignment of Tactics With Long-Term Strategic Goals

As noted earlier, a strategic plan tends to have a long-range planning horizon—typically, somewhere between one and ten years, depending upon the nature of the business. By contrast, an **operational plan** focuses on the fiscal year ahead and involves more tactical issues. A strategic plan precedes an operational plan; the strategic plan provides the foundation upon which the more detailed operational plan is developed. In that sense, strategic plans are "macro" plans and operational plans are "micro" plans. An overview comparing strategic and operational plans is shown in Figure 3-9.

Figure 3-9: A Comparison of Strategic and Operational Plans

	Strategic Plan	Operational Plan
Focus	Underlies both long- and short-run planning; provides the basis for the budget.	Formulates specific goals for each business with detailed revenue and expense budgets.
Issues Examined	Identifies and analyzes issues such as: ■ New global market entrants. ■ Economic conditions. ■ Plans for diversification.	Identifies and analyzes issues such as: ■ Quarterly earnings. ■ Inventory levels. ■ Major capital expenditures. ■ Marketing plans. ■ Productions plans.
Development	Flows from top down; reflects a comprehensive analysis of external and internal factors.	Flows from bottom up; recommends specific options for the upcoming year.
Control	Reviewed annually and updated as needed to reflect high-level changes.	Reviewed and updated/modified periodically throughout the year to address changing needs (such as lagging major product sales, new pricing structures of competitors, a newly opened distribution channel, and so on).

Linkage of budgets to strategic plans

Strategic plans and operational plans lead to the formation of budgets. A budget represents a quantitative expression of proposed management actions for a set period of time. Budgets have numerous advantages. No matter what type or size an organization is, budgets can:

- Provide a blueprint for the organization to follow in an upcoming time period, identifying the resources and commitments required to meet organizational goals and objectives.

- Help to identify potential bottlenecks/problems and facilitate smoother operations across businesses.

- Serve as a communication device, indicating expected performance for all divisions and all employees for the specified time period.

- Provide a frame of reference with guidelines for operations and criteria for monitoring and control.

- Facilitate performance evaluation of divisions and employees through the comparison of expected operations with actual results.

Budgets quantify management expectations regarding income, cash flows, and financial position. An organization prepares a variety of operational budgets (production, research and design, marketing, distribution, administration, and so on). A master budget coordinates all these individual budgets into a comprehensive organization-wide budget on an annual basis.

Organizational strategies and the strategic plan provide the basis and starting point for preparing the annual master budget. Naturally, the master budget must be congruent with the strategies and strategic plan and contribute to the achievement of the organization's long-term strategic goals, mission, and vision.

How strategy flows from strategic planning through the budgeting process is shown in Figure 3-10. Strategy starts with a broad perspective. At the budget level, the focus becomes quite specific.

Figure 3-10: Flow of Organizational Strategy

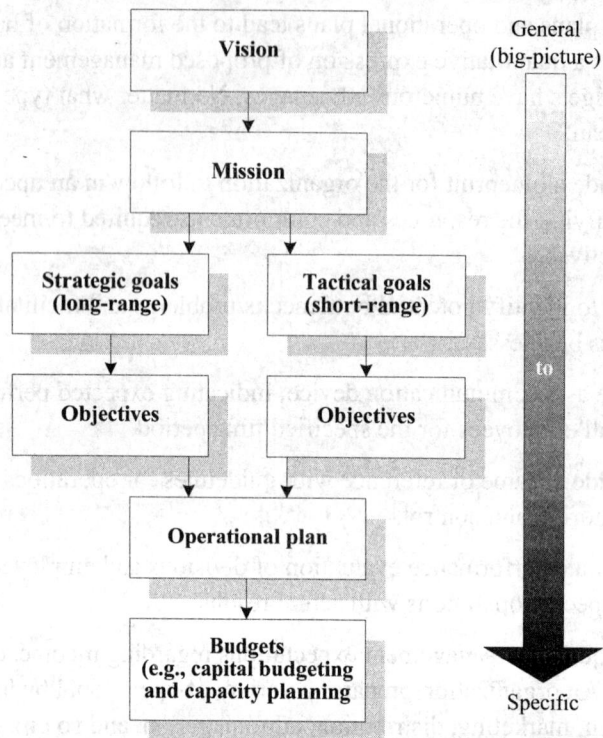

Strategic use of the balanced scorecard

The **balanced scorecard (BSC)**, developed by Robert Kaplan and David Norton during the early 1990s, was originally intended to help companies better manage intangible assets in conjunction with financial measures. Over time companies have also adapted their usage of the scorecard to help link long-term strategic planning objectives with short-term actions.

According to Kaplan and Norton, firms have introduced additional management processes to the scorecard that when used separately or collectively facilitate a successful strategic management system. Figure 3-11 summarizes this expanded use of the scorecard.

Figure 3-11: Use of the BSC as a Strategic Management System

Added BSC Process	Focus/Intent	Examples
Translating the organizational vision and strategy	Actions that senior executives take to translate the long-term drivers of organizational success into integrated objectives and measures that can be acted on at the operational levels throughout the organization.	■ To build consensus and commitment to organizational strategy, a team of executives develops a balanced scorecard that converts the corporate vision statement into a meaningful strategy that can be readily understood. ■ Terms such as "superior service" and "target customers" are further defined for the people who will have to act on the strategy.
Communicating the strategy and linking it to the organization	Actions that managers take to communicate the organizational strategy throughout the organization and link it to departmental and individual objectives.	■ Middle managers take the strategy to the next level by developing business unit scorecards and educating employees about them. ■ Internal business processes and learning and innovation objectives to support the achievement of the financial and customer goals are developed; goals are set and rewards are linked to performance measures.
Business planning	Actions that enable the organization to integrate all business initiatives and financial plans, setting priorities and allocating resources to support the long-term strategic objectives.	■ Steps are taken to link all change programs and resource allocation to long-term strategic priorities. ■ Short-term targets (milestones) are set for balanced scorecard measures. ■ Necessary investments to meet goals are identified and funded. ■ Appropriate reviews are conducted (monthly, quarterly, annually) to ensure that targets are being met.
Feedback and learning	Actions that promote strategic learning through feedback and review processes of whether the company, its departments, and individual employees are meeting/have met budgeted goals.	■ Provisions are made for continuous review of the scorecard measures as well as market conditions, customer value propositions, competitors' behavior, and internal capabilities. ■ The ongoing viability of the organizational strategy and the strategic management system is assessed/reassessed.

Kaplan and Norton note that companies have derived many benefits from this expanded BSC usage. Such an integrated and iterative strategic management system allows companies to:

- Clarify and update organizational strategy.

- More readily communicate strategy throughout the organization.

- Align business unit and individual goals to strategy.

- Link strategic objectives, long-term targets, and budgets.

- Identify and implement appropriate strategic initiatives.

- Monitor performance on an ongoing basis.

- Incorporate continuous learning into operating improvements.

Characteristics of Successful Strategic/Tactical Planning

Organizations and the industries they compete in are complex moving targets for strategists. Enterprises continually shift in response to anything that can upset the competitive balance.

The strategic planning process—no matter how large or small the organization or how formal or informal the methodology—offers several benefits in helping a firm frame its competitive strategy. It also has some limitations. Understanding both the advantages and disadvantages helps to recognize what constitutes successful strategic planning.

Benefits of strategic planning

Strategic planning provides the following benefits:

- A systematic approach to analyzing threats and opportunities and examining why some organizational strategies have better competitive and profit prospects than others

- A sound framework for developing an effective operating budget

- An organizational learning opportunity for managers to think about strategies and how to best implement them

- An exercise to align management decision making and actions with corporate strategies (for example, to gain the buy-in of managers and show how their decisions and actions support corporate programs)

- A basis for both financial and nonfinancial performance measures

- A channel of communication among all levels of management about strategies, objectives, operational plans, and so on

- Guidance for approaching new situations

Limitations of strategic planning

Strategic planning is not the end-all panacea to all organizational woes. Some of the key shortcomings of strategic planning are:

- The effort, time, and expense involved in the process.

- The fact that planning based upon predictions is not an exact science; due to a variety of factors, plans may prove to be incorrect and fail.

- The potential for resistance to change resulting from entrenched ways of doing things.

- The risk that planning can become a bureaucratic exercise devoid of fresh ideas and strategic thinking.

Contingency Planning

Well-conceived strategic plans are based on events that have a high probability of occurring. But a strategic plan should not ignore the environmental uncertainties so prevalent in today's business environment.

Contingency planning defined

Increasingly, strategic plans include a section on contingency plans to help cope with the turbulence of conditions that could lead to serious difficulty for the enterprise. Contingency plans are preparations for the "what-if" situations that might occur and are used for a specific unintended event. The purpose of contingency planning is to provide a quicker reaction time and supply much-needed guidance to managers faced with unexpected developments and possible times of crisis.

Subjects of contingency plans

Many events and conditions can occur and wreak havoc in an organization. Typical subjects for contingency plans are:

- Lower sales or profit levels.
- New entrants that can capture market share.
- Government regulations.
- Loss of a key executive or manager/succession planning for key employee replacement.
- Damage to a critical facility.
- Computer system hacking/information security issues.
- Disaster recovery.
- Sudden changes in interest rates.
- Shrinking capital availability.
- Union activity.
- Mergers, acquisitions, and takeovers.

Realistically, contingency plans cannot cover every scenario. Most organizations preparing contingency plans select no more than six critical events. The degree of criticality and the potential of probability usually influence which subjects should be addressed.

Steps in contingency planning

In most companies, contingency plans are prepared after the strategic plan is completed; the strategic planning process provides valuable data for developing the contingency plans. But contingency plans typically deal with short-range tactical strategies and not long-range strategies.

Figure 3-12 outlines basic steps for contingency planning.

Figure 3-12: Steps in Contingency Planning

Step 1	Identify potential scenarios needing contingency plans (events, "what-ifs," and so on).
Step 2	Estimate the potential impact of the subjects identified (in financial terms, competitive position, and so on).
Step 3	Develop strategies and tactical plans to deal with each possible occurrence.
Step 4	Specify trigger points or warning signals.
Step 5	Store plans off-site.
Step 6	Routinely review plans and revise as warranted (at least as often as strategic planning).

No standard format for a contingency plan exists. Ideally, a contingency plan should be succinct but include enough detail to guide actions if needed. The more critical the threat, the more detail is warranted.

A few simple examples of accounting-related contingency plans are shown in Figure 3-13.

Figure 3-13: Examples of Accounting-Related Contingency Plans

Subject	Plan
Loss of a computer system during a general ledger (GL) close	■ Identification of off-site (outsourcing) location/service for computer usage ■ Identification of company-trained associates who could work at the remote site
Loss of a chief financial officer or another key financial associate	■ Succession plan 　▪ Identification of key associates to train 　▪ Identification of back-up personnel from another division ■ Provisions/steps for an outside search
Declining major product/service sales	■ Identification of areas for analysis and/or change 　▪ Plans for the alternate use of resources 　▪ Layoff considerations

Progress Check

Directions: Read each question and respond in the space provided. Answers and page references appear on the page following the progress check questions.

1. Corporate strategy is **best** described as

   ( ) a. a detailed plan describing what a firm will do to achieve superior return on investment.

   ( ) b. a definition of organizational values, expressed in financial and nonfinancial terms.

   ( ) c. an analysis of industry attractiveness based on the five forces: buyer power, supplier power, competition, the threat of substitutes, and rivalry.

   ( ) d. the big picture of how each activity in the firm's value chain affects costs and differentiation.

2. All of the following statements characterize the five forces driving industry profitability **except**

   ( ) a. They remain constant as an industry evolves.

   ( ) b. They can vary from industry to industry.

   ( ) c. They are vulnerable to high growth and market demand.

   ( ) d. They are not equally important in any one industry.

Match the following determinants of industry profitability to the appropriate description.

3. _____ Differentiation

4. _____ Economies of scale

5. _____ Channel crowding

a. Leads to a decline in unit costs as the volume per period increases

b. Creates brand identification and existing customer loyalties an entrant must overcome

c. Results from limited capacity or exclusive relationships with manufacturers that restrict the number of product lines

6. "We believe the primary obligation of the company and its employees is to supply the public with the best modern utility service at reasonable rates." This statement exemplifies an organizational

   ( ) a. vision.

   ( ) b. mission.

   ( ) c. strategic goal.

   ( ) d. objective.

Progress check answers

1.   b (p. 3-15)

2.   a (p. 3-25)

3.   b (p. 3-22)

4.   a (p. 3-22)

5.   c (p. 3-22)

6.   a (p. 3-42)

Manufacturing Paradigms

Topic overview

By definition, a paradigm is an example or a model. In turn, a paradigm shift refers to a significant paradigm change that moves people away from one way of seeing or doing things to another.

At their inception, just-in-time systems and outsourcing represented paradigm shifts in manufacturing. The theory of constraints was also a departure from traditional manufacturing practices. These new manufacturing practices have changed the type of information needed for decision making and how data is collected. Ultimately, these practices have changed the role of the management accountant and improved the efficiency and effectiveness of information reporting.

Just-in-Time Manufacturing

All manufacturing processes required to produce a final product—from design to delivery as well as all stages of conversion from raw material onward—are involved. A **just-in-time (JIT) system** refers to a comprehensive production and inventory control methodology in which materials arrive exactly as they are needed for each stage in a production process. The goal of JIT is to create lean manufacturing by reducing or eliminating waste of resources by producing production line components as they are required rather than holding large safety stocks of inventory. Nothing is produced until it is needed.

In a JIT system, need is created by demand for a product. Theoretically, the market "pulls" a replacement product from the last position in the system. Demand triggers every step and pulls a product through production—from customer demand for a finished product at one end working all the way back to the demand for raw materials at the other end. This "demand-pull" feature of a JIT system requires high levels of quality at each point in the system and close coordination to ensure a smooth flow of goods and operations despite low inventory quantities. This often requires working more closely with fewer suppliers.

Differences between JIT and MRP systems

The demand-pull strategies of a JIT system are a stark contrast to the "push-through" **materials requirement planning (MRP) systems** traditionally used in manufacturing.

The premises underlying MRP push-though systems include:

- Demand forecasts.

- A bill of materials specifying the materials, components, and subunit tasks required to produce a final product.

- Specified quantities of materials, components, subunits, and product inventories to forecast the necessary outputs.

In MRP systems, a master production schedule indicates the quantities and timing of each part to be produced. Once the scheduled production run begins, departments push output through a system, regardless of whether that output is needed.

Example:

Using a MRP system, here's how a company might calculate subunits (parts) to produce Product P and offsets lead times.

Product P is made from:	Part A is made from:	Part B is made from:
Two parts A	One Part C	Two parts C
Three parts B	Two parts D	Two parts E.

If 100 units of Product P are required:

Part A	$2 \times$ number of Ps	$= 2 \times 100$	$= 200$
Part B	$3 \times$ number of Ps	$= 3 \times 100$	$= 300$
Part C	$1 \times$ number of As	$= 1 \times 200$	
	$+ 2 \times$ number of Bs	$+ 2 \times 300$	$= 800$
Part D	$2 \times$ number of As	$= 2 \times 200$	$= 400$
Part E	$2 \times$ number of Bs	$= 2 \times 300$	$= 600$

The lead times required are:

Product P	1 week
Part A	2 weeks
Part B	2 weeks
Part C	3 weeks
Part D	1 week
Part E	1 week

Once the date for Product P delivery is known, a schedule can be created, specifying when all the parts must be ordered and received to meet the demand for Product P.

		Week 1	Week 2	Week 3	Week 4	Week 5	Week 6	Week 7	
P	Required date							100	P lead time = 1 week
	Order placement						100		
A	Required date						200		A lead time = 2 weeks
	Order placement				200				
B	Required date						300		B lead time = 2 weeks
	Order placement				300				
C	Required date				800				C lead time = 3 weeks
	Order placement	800							
D	Required date				400				D lead time = 1 week
	Order placement			400					
E	Required date				600				E lead time = 1 week
	Order placement			600					

The MRP in this example, is based on the demand for P, the parts or subunits comprising P, and the lead times needed to obtain each part either internally of from an outside supplier.

Benefits of MRP systems

The benefits of MRP systems are:

- Less coordination required between functional areas; everyone follows the bill of materials.

- Scheduling improvements; levels load when demand is variable or relatively unpredictable.

- Predictable raw material needs; can take advantage of bulk purchasing and other price breaks.

- More efficient inventory control; schedules to use up raw materials or build finished goods.

- Additional inventory on hand to cover orders should product be damaged or lost in transit to a customer.

- Quick response to new customer demand; can supply new customers from existing inventory rather than building product after the order is received.

- Better manufacturing process control; minimizes retooling and machine setup time.

The primary downside of an MRP environment is potential inventory accumulation. Workstations may receive parts that they are not ready to process.

Components of JIT systems

The major characteristics of a JIT environment are:

- Production organized into manufacturing work cells—organization of the related manufacturing processes necessary to create a final product into clusters and then logical grouping of clusters into small groups for close proximity, improved communication, and immediate feedback.

- Multiskilled workers—cross-functional training of workers so they can perform a variety of operations and tasks on an as-needed basis to maintain smooth production flow.

- Reduced setup times—reduction of the time required to get tools, equipment, and materials ready for a production run.

- Reduced manufacturing lead times—reduction of the time from when an order is initiated to when a finished good is produced.

- Reliable suppliers—careful screening of suppliers to ensure on-time deliveries of high-quality goods for just-in-time use (sometimes within a day or less).

The use of kanban in JIT implementation

Various methods may be used to implement JIT systems; kanban is perhaps the most common. **Kanban** is a Japanese term literally meaning a visual record or a card. In JIT environments, workers use a kanban to signal the need for a specified quantity of materials or parts to move from one work cell operation or department to another in sequence. Workers respond only after receiving a kanban. When production is complete, the kanban is attached to the finished order and sent downstream to the next work cell.

A kanban is typically a card with information identifying the part, the number needed, the delivery location, and so on. However, it may also be a label, a box, a bin, a series of in-baskets, or some other visual indicator.

JIT benefits and limitations

Some of the general benefits of JIT are:

- Obvious production priorities.
- Reduced setup and manufacturing lead time.
- No overproduction occurrences.
- Improved quality control (faster feedback) and less materials waste.
- Easier inventory control (low or even zero inventory).
- Less paperwork.
- Strong supplier relationships.

JIT systems focus on controlling total manufacturing costs (versus individual costs such as raw materials or direct manufacturing labor). Typically, manufacturing costs decline and cash flow and working capital levels improve. Specific financial benefits are possible:

- Lower inventory investments

- Reduced costs for carrying and handling inventories

- Reduced risk of inventory obsolescence, damage, or "shrinkage"

- Lower investments in space (for production and inventories)

- Higher revenues resulting from a quicker response time to customers

Direct tracing of some costs that would otherwise be classified as overhead is also possible. Labor, shipping, and other costs arbitrarily allocated under another method are potentially traceable.

For all the benefits, JIT systems are not without limitations. Common ones include:

- No buffer inventory; potential for increased idle time if production needs to wait for materials.

- Reliance on suppliers to maintain adequate stock to meet unpredictable demands; highly dependent on supply chain.

- Potential stockouts at suppliers; critical parts shortages can shut down an entire line.

- Potential overtime expenses from unanticipated orders.

It should be noted that in some markets and under certain conditions, occasional stockouts are preferable to other alternatives.

Outsourcing

Outsourcing describes a company's decision to purchase a product or service from an outside supplier rather than producing it in-house. Through this option, an organization can concentrate resources on core business competencies while capitalizing on the expertise of other firms that are more efficient, effective, or knowledgeable at specialized tasks peripheral to those core business competencies. Today, many firms outsource significant parts of their information technology (IT), data processing, and human resource functions, to name a few.

The terminology "make versus buy" refers to outsourcing. Make versus buy analysis (covered in more detail in Section D of this part of the *CMA Learning System*) examines the relevant costs of keeping activities in-house versus outsourcing to external suppliers.

Some firms have extended the idea of outsourcing to **contract manufacturing**, in which another company actually manufactures a portion of the first firm's products. Contract manufacturing can provide a win-win relationship if one firm has excess capacity or expertise and another company lacks capacity or knowledge.

Benefits and limitations of outsourcing

There are many strategic reasons an organization may choose to outsource. Certainly, outsourcing offers smaller businesses resources and expertise for capabilities they may not have internally. For larger businesses, outsourcing can improve specific functions.

The following list summarizes the principal benefits of outsourcing:

- Allows management and employees to focus on core competencies and strategic revenue-generating activities

- Can improve efficiency and effectiveness by gaining outside expertise or scale

- Can provide access to current technologies at reasonable cost without the risk of obsolescence

- Can reduce expenses by gaining capabilities without incurring overhead costs (for example, staffing, benefits, space)

- May improve the quality and/or timeliness of products or services

Despite many attractive advantages, outsourcing is not the answer for all activities or functions. The following points are the key cautions associated with outsourcing:

- May cost more to go outside for specific expertise

- Can result in a loss of in-house expertise and capabilities

- Can reduce process control

- May reduce control over quality

- May lead to less flexibility (depending on the external supplier)

- May result in less-personalized service

- Creates privacy and confidentiality issues

- Can result in "giving knowledge away" and lead to competitors obtaining expertise, scale, customers, and so on

- Potential for employee morale and loyalty issues

Theory of Constraints

Benjamin Franklin is attributed with the adage "Time is money." Dr. Eliyahu Goldratt expanded the application of this time-worn statement in saying "The goal is not to save money but to make money."

In 1990, Dr. Goldratt developed the **theory of constraints (TOC)**, an overall management philosophy that has its basis in the manufacturing environment. The overriding goal of the theory of constraints is to improve speed in manufacturing processes.

The premise behind the theory of constraints is that every system has at least one constraint limiting its output in pursuit of some goal. A system is a network of connecting processes that work together to accomplish some aim. A constraint is a limiting factor—a bottleneck or barrier that slows a product's total cycle time down. Cycle time is the time it takes from beginning to end to complete a process. Constraint management refers to the process of identifying process barriers, analyzing and understanding the barriers, and removing them.

Goldratt maintains that that there is only one constraint in a system at any given time but that this bottleneck limits the output of the entire system. The remaining components of the system are known as nonconstraints (nonbottlenecks). Overall, the theory of constraints emphasizes fixing the system constraint and temporarily ignoring the nonconstraints. In this way, the theory has a profound impact on cycle time and process improvement (rather than spreading limited time, energy, and resources across an entire system, which may or may not have tangible results).

When one constraint is strengthened, however, the system does not become infinitely stronger. The constraint simply migrates to a different component of the system. (For example, some other factor becomes a bottleneck or barrier.) The system is stronger than it was but still not as strong as it could be.

Basic principles in the theory of constraints

Inventory, operational expenses, throughput contribution, and the drum-buffer-rope system are all principal concepts underlying the theory of constraints.

Inventory

Inventory refers to all the money the system invests in purchasing items it intends to resell. Typically, this refers to inventory items, but is more broadly defined to include all assets.

Operating expenses

In the TOC, operating (or operational) expenses refer the money the system spends to convert inventory into throughput. Operating expenses include expenditures such as direct and indirect labor, supplies, outside contractors, interest payments, and depreciation. Employees are responsible for turning inventory into throughput.

Throughput contribution

Throughput contribution (or throughput or throughput margin) is a TOC measure of product profitability. It is the rate at which the entire system generates money through product and/or service sales.

Throughput is represented by the following formula:

Throughput = Sales Revenue – Direct Material Costs

Throughput assumes that the material costs include all purchased components and materials handling costs. TOC analysis also assumes that labor is a fixed cost, not a direct and variable cost. Additionally, all the money that has not been generated by the organization must be deducted from sales revenue as well as other costs such as subcontracting costs, sales commissions, transportation costs, and so on.

A simple example illustrates the throughput calculation. Given the following information:

- $100 = the sales revenue for a product
- $20 = cost of parts purchased from external vendors
- $10 = sales commissions paid (10 percent of each sale)
- $5 = transportation costs

Throughput = Sales Revenue – Direct Material Costs

Throughput = ($100 – $20 – $10 – $5) = $65

Drum-buffer-rope (DBR) system

The **drum-buffer-rope (DBR) system** is a TOC method for balancing the flow of production through the constraint. The drum connotes the constraint, the rope is the sequence of processes prior to and including the constraint, and the buffer is the minimum amount of work-in-process input to keep the drum busy. The objective of the drum-buffer-rope system is to keep the process flow running smoothly through the constraint by careful timing and scheduling of the processes in the rope leading up to the constraint.

Steps in the theory of constraints

The theory of constraints includes five focusing steps designed to concentrate improvement efforts on the constraint most likely to have a positive impact on a system. Figure 3-14 summarizes the five steps.

In the theory of constraints, throughput (T), inventory (I), and operating expenses (OE) link operational and financial measures.

Figure 3-14: The Five Focusing Steps of the Theory of Constraints

Step 1	**Identify the system constraint.** In the first step, an organization identifies what part of the system constitutes the weakest link, or the constraint, and determines whether it is a physical constraint or a policy-related issue. **Example:** A management accountant works with managers and engineers to flowchart a manufacturing process for a product line. They identify the sequence and the amount of time each step requires. In doing so, the system constraint is identified (for example, subprocess taking the most time to complete—an area where work in process is idle too long).
Step 2	**Decide how to exploit the constraint.** The organization "exploits" the constraint by utilizing every bit of the constraining component without committing to potentially expensive changes and/or upgrades. **Example:** Scheduling of key machine time is changed; employees are redeployed.
Step 3	**Subordinate everything else.** With a plan in place for exploiting the constraint, an organization adjusts the rest of the system to enable the constraint to operate at maximum effectiveness and then evaluates the results to see if the constraint is still holding back system performance. If it is, the organization proceeds to Step 4. If it is not, the constraint has been eliminated and the organization skips ahead to Step 5. **Example:** Further analysis looks at actions to maximize flow through the constraint. With a focus on throughput, the accountant suggests ways to speed up (simplify) the process such as reduced setup and setup times and use of the drum-buffer-rope system. Non-value-added activities are eliminated. The idea is to keep the constraint busy without accumulating inventory or building up work in the process.
Step 4	**Elevate the constraint.** If an organization reaches Step 4, it means that Steps 2 and 3 were not sufficient in eliminating the constraint. At this point, the organization elevates the constraint by taking whatever action is needed to eliminate it. This may involve major changes to the existing system, such as reorganization, divestiture, or capital improvements. Because these typically require a substantial up-front investment, the organization should be certain that the constraint cannot be broken in Steps 1 through 3 before proceeding. **Example:** Management considers how to increase capacity of the system (should Steps 2 and 3 prove unsatisfactory in alleviating the constraint). Additional labor or more/new equipment may be necessary.
Step 5	**Go back to Step 1, but beware of inertia.** After a constraint is broken, the organization repeats the steps all over again, looking for the next thing constraining system performance. At the same time, it monitors how changes related to subsequent constraints may impact the constraints that are already broken, thus preventing solution inertia. **Example:** The organization considers a strategic response to the constraint. The goal is to improve throughput. The product or the process may be redesigned, hard-to-manufacture products may be eliminated, and so on.

As discussed in Statements on Management Accounting (SMA) No. 4HH, "Theory of Constraints (TOC) Management System Fundamentals":

- Net profit increases when T goes up or OE goes down.

- T can go up by increasing sales revenues or reducing variable costs of production.

- Measures that increase net profit increase return on investment (ROI)—as long as I remains the same.

- If I can be decreased, ROI goes up even without an increase in net profit.

- Cash flow increases when either T goes up or the time to generate T is reduced (assuming the time save is applied toward generating more T).

The theory of constraints attempts to maximize throughput while decreasing inventory, operational expenses, and other investments. Unlike traditional performance measures, which focus on direct labor efficiency and unit costs and how efficiently the company must produce a product, TOC emphasizes how efficiently an organization must manufacture products for optimum market success. The flow of product is dictated by market demand not the dictates of mass production, cheap sources of materials, machine efficiencies, or low direct labor.

Stated another way, T, I, and OE measures enable a company to understand how much money it is making and how to best leverage capabilities to improve profitability.

Theory of constraints reports

The theory of constraints focuses on eliminating constraints and improving/speeding up cycle or delivery time. Performance measures used in implementing the theory of constraints also identify critical success factors. Organizations often prepare a theory of constraints report to highlight select operating data and the throughput margin. TOC reports are valuable in identifying both profitability and critical success factors.

Figure 3-15 presents a sample TOC report.

Figure 3-15: Sample Theory of Constraints Report

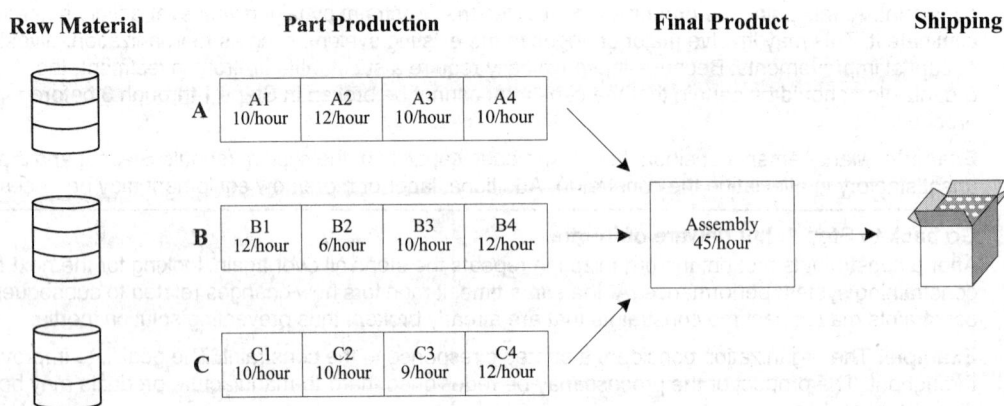

Various formats are possible for TOC reports. In looking at this sample TOC report, key points are:

- The final product is assembled from three component parts: A, B, and C.

- Each part is the result of a different series of linear operations. (For example, part A starts with the raw material and goes through operations A1, A2, A3, and A4; raw material for part B goes through B1, B2, B3, B4, and so forth.)

- The slowest operation is B2 (six per hour); the output of this constraining operation is the weakest link and determines the output of the entire system.

Having successfully identified the system constraint, steps can be taken to lessen or eliminate it. Statement on Management Accounting No. 4HH, "Theory of Constraints

(TOC) Management System Fundamentals," differentiates exploiting from elevating a constraint in the following manner:

- Exploiting the constraint changes how the organization uses the constraint without spending more money (for example, reducing internal setup times to increase utilization/optimize the activity).

- Elevating the constraint requires investing more money to increase the constrained resource's capacity (for example, buying another piece of equipment or outsourcing an activity to relieve the constraint).

Naturally, an organization should spend additional money to elevate a constraint only after exploiting it to the fullest potential.

Theory of constraints and activity-based costing

Organizations that implement the theory of constraints often use activity-based costing (ABC). ABC is an accounting technique that allocates costs to products and services, thereby allowing an enterprise to determine the actual costs associated with each product and service produced. ABC was developed to address problems associated with traditional cost management systems and their capability to accurately determine actual production and service costs and provide useful information for operating decisions.

Similar to the theory of constraints, organizations use ABC to assess product profitability.

But a few differences exist in how the two cost management methods assess profitability:

- TOC takes a short-term approach to profitability analysis (with an emphasis on materials-related costs); ABC examines long-term costing (including all product costs).

- TOC considers how to improve short-term profitability by focusing on production constraints and plausible short-term product mix adjustments.

- ABC does not consider resource constraints and process capability; it does analyze cost drivers and accurate unit costs for long-term strategic pricing and profit planning decisions. ABC is generally used as a tool for planning and control.

The short-term aspects of TOC and the long-range focus of ABC make them complementary profitability analysis methods.

Although the theory of constraints has its roots in the manufacturing environment, applications have been developed for service industries. Measures of speed and cycle time are defined appropriately for the nature of the enterprise. Additionally, specific TOC implications for management accounting have assessed the benefits of throughput accounting in business rather than traditional cost accounting.

Other Production Management Theories

Competitiveness … Productivity … Continuous improvement … Profitability … Organizations constantly strive to improve upon what they already do well and to capitalize on growth opportunities. Beyond the manufacturing paradigms previously discussed, organizations have a wide array of additional contemporary production management techniques to choose from in their quest for better, faster, and more profitable operations.

Many organizations have adopted some or all of the innovative approaches listed in Figure 3-16 in an attempt to reduce costs, increase productivity, improve quality, and increase their overall responsiveness to customers.

Figure 3-16: Contemporary Productivity Approaches

Technique	Description
Automation/robots	■ Uses reprogrammable, multifunctional robots (machines) designed to manipulate materials, parts, tools, or specialized devices through variable programmed motions ■ Applies robots to the performance of a variety of repetitive tasks

Capacity management and analysis (capacity planning)	■ Represents an important decision-making area involving strategic, tactical, and operational aspects
	■ Includes an iterative procedure that:
	  ▪ Reviews long-term demand forecasts
	  ▪ Translates forecasts into capacity requirements
	  ▪ Matches the capacity requirements to present facilities
	  ▪ Identifies mismatches between capacity requirements and projected availability
	  ▪ Devises plans to overcome mismatches and selects the best alternative

Computer-aided design (CAD)	■ Uses computers in product development, analysis, and design modification to improve the quality and performance of the product ■ Usually entails the drawing or physical layout steps of engineering design
Computer-aided manufacturing (CAM)	Applies the computer to the planning, control, and operation of a production facility
Computer-integrated manufacturing (CIM)	■ Involves a manufacturing system that completely integrates all factory and office functions within a company via a computer-based information network ■ Uses computers to control the integration and flow of information between design, engineering, manufacturing, logistics, warehousing and distribution, customers and suppliers, sales and marketing activities, and accounting ■ Facilitates hour-by-hour manufacturing management
Concurrent engineering (simultaneous engineering)	■ Integrates product or service design with input from all business units and functions throughout a product's or service's life cycle ■ Emphasizes upstream prevention versus downstream correction ■ Attempts to balance the needs of all parties in product or service design while maintaining customer requirements
Flexible manufacturing system (FMS)	Uses a computerized network of automated equipment that produces one or more groups of parts or variations of a product in a flexible manner

Progress Check

Directions: Read each question and respond in the space provided. Answers and page references appear on the page following the progress check questions.

1. What is the primary benefit of just-in-time (JIT) systems compared with traditional materials requirement planning (MRP) systems?

    ( ) a. Increased stock quantities at all levels in a system

    ( ) b. Maximization of production runs to accommodate complete product lines

    ( ) c. Replacement of a push-through manufacturing strategy with a demand-pull strategy

    ( ) d. Reduced risk of overproduction occurrences

2. A large semiconductor manufacturer plans to apply the theory of constraints (TOC) methodology to increase production capacity. How could a management accountant **best** support the initiative?

    ( ) a. Determine outsourcing costs to off-load long-term critical constraints.

    ( ) b. Design buffer management worksheets to facilitate quantitative analysis.

    ( ) c. Provide net profit, ROI, and cash flow data.

    ( ) d. Supply activity-based cost data.

Match the following terms to their appropriate description.

3. _____ Demand-pull

4. _____ Kanban

5. _____ Outsourcing

6. _____ Capacity management

    a. An iterative decision-making process intended to overcome supply and demand mismatches

    b. A decision to purchase a product or service from an external supplier rather than producing it in-house

    c. JIT system feature requiring close coordination to ensure a smooth flow of goods and operations despite low inventory quantities

    d. A visual signal indicating the need for a specified quantity of materials or parts to move from one operation or department to another in sequence

7. An organization will directly gain all of the following benefits from the TOC methodology **except**

( ) a. reduced bottlenecks.

( ) b. increased profitability.

( ) c. improved long-term planning and control.

( ) d. improved quality of products and services.

Progress check answers

1. d (p. 3-53)

2. d (p. 3-63)

3. c (p. 3-53)

4. d (p. 3-56)

5. b (p. 3-57)

6. a (p. 3-63)

7. c (p. 3-58)

Business Process Performance

Topic overview

Being competitive has organizational ramifications beyond matching or surpassing industry competitors. Customers today demand more for less. Largely due to the Internet, they generally are more informed and have unlimited sources of quality goods and services at acceptable prices. Organizations are constantly challenged to address these rising customer expectations, and analysis of business process performance is one way. A number of techniques can be used to analyze business process performance.

Value Chain Analysis

So how do organizations make intelligent choices about where to focus their energy and how to best create value in the eyes of their customers? Many organizations have found success through value chain analysis.

Value chain analysis has become an integral part of the strategic planning process. Similar to strategic planning, value chain analysis is a continuous process of gathering, evaluating, and communicating information. The basic intent of value chain analysis is to help managers envision an organization's future and implement business decisions to gain and sustain competitive advantage.

Related terms

A primer of several terms helps to understand value chain analysis.

Value

As it applies to business, the term **value** generally describes the worth, desirability, or utility of a particular asset. Value, however, is somewhat relative; it may be applied to an individual product or a service rendered, to a group of assets, or to an entire business unit. Value may also be applied as a metric such as in market value, shareholders' value, and so on.

Value activities

Value activities describe the collective activities organizations in a given industry must perform, from the processing of raw material (in a manufacturing industry) to the production and servicing of a final product. Depending on the industry, some firms may be involved in several activities whereas others may have responsibility for only a single activity. Within an organization, business units may be a further subset.

A clothing company, for example, may start with the raw textiles, design and manufacture clothing articles, and contract advertising and sales to retailers. Another clothing company may contract out manufacturing, concentrate on sales and marketing through organizational business units, and rely on retailers for distribution.

Value chain

A value chain is a system of interdependent activities, each of which is intended to add value to the final product or service. Naturally, the development of a value chain depends on the industry. Figure 3-17 shows a typical value chain for a manufacturing environment. In a service environment, the acquisition of raw materials would be absent and other activities and operations might vary and/or assume different degrees of importance.

Figure 3-17: Typical Value Chain for a Manufacturing Environment

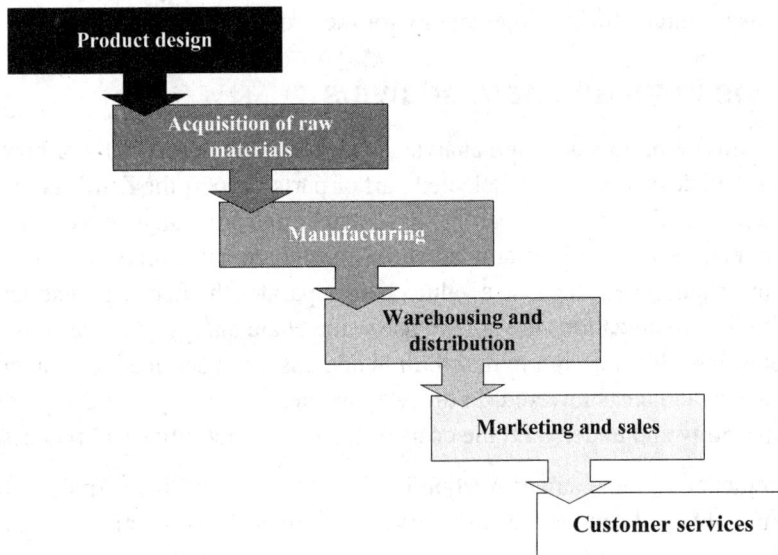

Cost driver

A **cost driver** is any factor that causes a change in the cost of an activity. Direct labor hours, machine hours, computer time, and beds occupied in a hospital are all examples. For more meaningful analysis (beyond the total costs of each value-creating activity), the causes for significant costs need to be identified. Firms examine structural cost drivers and executional cost drivers. Structural cost drivers are long-term organizational decisions that determine the economic structure driving the cost of the firm's product or service. Executional cost drivers reflect a firm's operational decisions on how to best use its resources (human and physical) to achieve organizational goals and objectives.

Supply chain

During value chain analysis, an organization examines the entire supply chain. A **supply chain** is the extended network of distributors, transporters, storage facilities, and suppliers that participate in the production, design, sale, delivery, and use of a company's product or service.

Value chain analysis, defined

Given the foundation of related terms, value chain analysis can be defined. **Value chain analysis (VCA)** is a strategic analysis tool organizations use to assess the importance of their customers' value perceptions. It consists of an integrated set of tools and processes that define current costs and performance measures and evaluate where customer value might be increased and costs reduced throughout the supply chain.

The distinct benefit of value chain analysis is that it looks at the entire value chain, not just the activities in which the organization participates. Suppliers, distributors, and others involved in a value chain have costs and profit margins impacting the final price to end users and the marketing strategy for the product or service.

Steps in value chain analysis

The purpose of a value chain analysis is to focus on the product's or service's total value chain and determine which selected part or parts support the firm's competitive advantage and strategy. Theoretically, competitive advantage and competitive strategy cannot be meaningfully examined at the organizational level as a whole or even the business unit level. Because a value chain separates the firm into distinct strategic activities, organizations are able to use value chain analysis to determine where in the operations—from design to distribution and customer service—customer value can be enhanced and costs lowered. In this way, value chain analysis helps to identify sources of profitability and understand the costs of the related activities and processes.

Statement on Management Accounting No. 4X, "Value Chain Analysis for Assessing Competitive Advantage," examines value chain analysis practices and techniques. The publication notes that value chain analysis requires a strategic framework as a starting point for organizing and analyzing internal and external information and for summarizing findings and recommendations.

There is no one standard process to conduct a value chain analysis; practices vary. The general steps in value chain analysis discussed in Statement on Management Accounting No. 4X are summarized in Figure 3-18.

Figure 3-18: A Value Chain Approach for Assessing Competitive Advantage

Step 1	**Internal cost analysis**

This step determines the sources of profitability and the relative cost of internal processes or activities. An internal cost analysis will:

- Identify the firm's value-creating processes.
- Determine the portion of the total cost of the product or service attributable to each value-creating process.
- Identify the cost drivers for each process.
- Identify the links between processes.
- Evaluate opportunities for achieving relative cost advantages.

Step 2	**Internal differentiation analysis**

During this part of the analysis, sources for creating and sustaining superior differentiation are examined. The primary focus is the customer's value perceptions of the firm's products and services. Similar to Step 1, an internal differentiation analysis first requires identifying internal value-creating processes and cost drivers. With this information, a firm can perform a differentiation analysis to:

- Identify the customers' value-creating processes.
- Evaluate differentiation strategies for enhancing customer value.
- Determine the best sustainable differentiation strategies.

Step 3	**Vertical linkage analysis**

Vertical linkage analysis is a broader application of Steps 1 and 2; it includes all upstream and downstream value-creating processes in an industry. Vertical linkage can identify which activities are the most/least critical to competitive advantage or disadvantage. It considers all links, from the source of raw materials to the disposal and/or recycling of a product. A vertical linkage analysis will:

- Identify the industry's value chain and assign costs, revenues, and assets to value-creating processes.
- Diagnose the cost drivers for each value-creating process.
- Evaluate the opportunities for sustainable competitive advantage.

The Statement on Management Accounting indicates that the three types of analysis described in Figure 3-18—internal cost analysis, internal differentiation analysis, and vertical linkage analysis—are complementary. Organizations begin by examining their internal operations and then broaden their focus to evaluate their competitive position within their industry.

Typically, a large amount of data is generated during a value chain analysis study; this data requires careful interpretation to discern the key messages of how to best create customer-perceived value.

Value-Added Concepts and Quality

Quality, like strategy and strategic planning, has many definitions and descriptions and a variety of approaches. Quality management professionals maintain that a customer ultimately defines what constitutes product or service quality. But they are also quick to note that quality is not a static perception but rather an ever-evolving perception by the customer of the value provided by a product or service. As a product or service matures (through innovation) and as alternatives (industry competition) are made available as a basis of comparison, the customer perception of quality changes. Consider any number of current consumer electronic products as examples—computers, telephones, televisions— and how customers' perceptions of quality today (due to innovations and competitive offerings) are light-years away from those of even one or two years ago. In this respect, one might say that quality is when the customer returns and the product does not.

Internal and external customers

In the quality profession, a customer is anyone who is impacted by an organization's processes, products, and services. A firm has both internal and external customers.

An **internal customer** is an employee, department, or business unit that receives an output in the form of information, a product, or a service from another employee, department, or business unit. Even the next person in a work process is an internal customer. Based on this idea, all work-related activities may be considered as a series of transactions between employees or between internal customers and internal suppliers.

An **external customer** is a person or organization who receives information, a product, or a service. Generally, external customers are thought of as being end users outside the organization.

Value chain analysis and quality performance

As organizations strive for quality performance, everyone—from the top executives to an employee on the front line—has responsibility to create or contribute to the value of the firm's processes, products, and services for the external customer or end user.

Suppliers also have a crucial role. An organization starts with external customer requirements as determined by its industry analysis and/or strategies. The firm proceeds to identify internal customer-supplier relationships and requirements and continues with external suppliers. A chain of operations produces the final product or service. The external customer is best served when every internal customer and supplier receives what they need along the chain.

Figure 3-19 illustrates the customer-supplier value chain as represented in Statement on Management Accounting No. 4R, "Managing Quality Improvements."

Figure 3-19: Customer-Supplier Value Chain

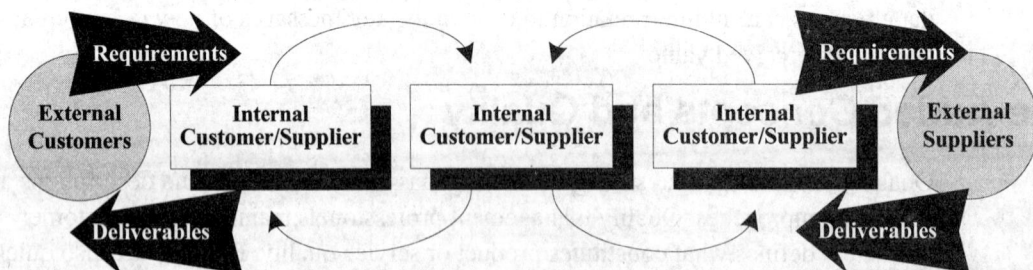

The concept of **value added** refers to activities that convert resources into products and services consistent with external customer requirements. Non-value-added activities can be eliminated with no deterioration in product or service functionality, performance, or quality in the eyes of the end user. In industries in which product and service parity is prevalent or outputs are perceived as commodities, examples of value-added activities might be some extra fabrication or customization before sale to a customer or providing more service with the sale. Activities related to materials movement or rework would most likely be non-value-added.

The goal of the customer-supplier value chain is to integrate value into every aspect of a work process. By removing non-value-added activities, work processes can be more efficient and ultimately yield a better quality product or service.

Process Analysis

To understand process analysis, it is important to first understand the concept of a process. A **process** is an activity or a group of interrelated activities that takes an input of materials and/or resources, adds value to it, and provides an output to internal or external customers. A process often spans several departmental units, such as accounting, sales, production, and shipping.

A firm should recognize and understand the array of business processes that contribute to its business profitability. One way to do this is through process analysis. **Process analysis** refers to a collection of analytic methods that can be used to examine and measure the basic elements for a process to operate. It can also identify those processes with the greatest need for improvement.

Process characteristics

The IMA self-study course "Advanced Process Analysis and Improvement" describes three characteristics that help to identify a good process fit.

- **Effectiveness:** A process is effective when it produces the desired result and meets or exceeds customers' requirements. Customers perceive an effective process as being of high quality.

- **Efficiency:** A process is efficient when it achieves results with minimal waste, expense, and/or cycle time. It has a high ratio of output to input.

- **Adaptability:** A process is adaptable when it is flexible and can react quickly to changing requirements or new competition.

A process should address all three areas. For example, a process can be the most efficient in the industry in terms of cost, but if no one wants to buy the output, it's a bad process.

"Advanced Process Analysis and Improvement" notes that the following four questions are helpful in measuring the health of a process:

- Does the process consistently produce quality products or result in good services when looked at from the customer perspective?

- Does the process get the output to the customers when and where they need it?

- Does the process produce a product that is cost-competitive?

- Can the process be changed to keep up with the changing needs of the customer?

Process reengineering/business process reengineering

An erroneous assumption in adopting quality is that process improvements can be gained only at the expense of productivity. Experience, however, has shown that quality improvements most often increase productivity. Quality improvements typically decrease waste and decrease or eliminate the need for rework. In turn, the amount of raw materials and resources needed in production processes decreases. Less input to produce output translates to productivity gains.

But process improvements and productivity gains achieved through total quality management (TQM) are generally incremental gains achieved by tweaking a system and reducing inputs. Process reengineering and business process reengineering offer deeper, more sweeping gains.

Process reengineering

Process reengineering diagrams a process in detail, evaluates and questions the process flow, and then completely redesigns the process to eliminate unnecessary steps, reduce opportunities for errors, and reduce costs. All activities that do not add value are eliminated.

Business process reengineering

Business process reengineering (BPR) is the fundamental analysis and radical redesign of business processes within and between enterprises to achieve dramatic improvements in performance (for example, cost, quality, speed, and service). Michael Hammer and James Champy brought BPR to the forefront in the early 1990s with their book *Reengineering the Corporation*. BPR promotes the idea that sometimes wiping the slate clean and radically redesigning and reorganizing an enterprise is necessary to lower costs and increase the quality of a product or service.

So how can reengineering create sweeping work-flow process changes? Hammer and Champy expand on the key aspects of BPR:

- **Fundamental**—BPR forces people to look at tacit rules and assumptions underlying the way they currently do business. Firms must answer two questions: Why do we do what we do? Why do we do it the way we do it?

- **Radical**—BPR is about reinvention, not improvement or modification. A radical redesign means disregarding existing processes and inventing new ways of doing work.

- **Dramatic**—BPR is not for the faint at heart. It should be used when the need for "heavy blasting" is required to alleviate a dire situation. If you need only a slight bump in process improvement, there is no need to reengineer.

- **Process**—BPR is about a process orientation with a heavy emphasis on the chain of activities that take input and create output of value to the customer.

The BPR model espouses that process work flow in most large corporations is based on assumptions about technology, people, and organizational goals that are no longer valid. It also maintains that information is a key enabler to achieve radical change.

Figure 3-20 lists the common tools and tactics underpinning successful BPR efforts.

Figure 3-20: Fundamentals of Business Process Reengineering

Process orientation	Organizations look at entire processes that cut across organizational boundaries, not narrowly defined tasks with predefined organizational boundaries.
Ambition	Companies aim for breakthroughs, not minor improvements.
Rule breaking	Old traditions and assumptions are deliberately abandoned.
Creative use of technology	Current/state-of-the-art technology serves as an enabler that allows organizations to do work in radically different ways.

Process reengineering and business process reengineering are strong medicine. Many well-intended reengineering efforts fail for any number of reasons. In a bit of a backlash to Hammer and Champy's initial foray, reengineering was even accused of being a cover for downsizing and layoffs. Yet the success stories show that although the boldness may have perils and may create some pain, the end gains of reengineering can be dramatic.

Linkage of quality, productivity, and process improvements

Quality, productivity, and process improvements have the following important ties:

- Productivity implies trying to improve upon what already exists.

- To improve productivity requires continuous quality improvement.

- Continuous improvement necessitates ongoing organizational learning, process improvements, and reengineering.

It is only though continuous productivity improvements that an organization can be competitive in the long term.

Application of the Pareto principle

In a quest to improve processes and productivity, organizations need to establish realistic priorities. The Pareto principle is often applied. In simplest terms, the **Pareto principle** suggests that most effects are the result of relatively few causes—that is, 80% of the effects come from 20% of the possible causes (for example, raw materials, machines, or operators). The Pareto principle was first defined by quality guru Joseph Juran in 1950 and is named after the 19th century Italian economist Vilfredo Pareto.

The percentages (80 and 20) may not always be exact, and so the expression "the vital few and the trivial many" is often associated with the Pareto principle. Juran originated the phrase. But Juran and other quality professionals later came to realize that there are no trivial problems in quality; all problems deserve attention. Juran eventually renamed "the trivial many" as "the useful many," but "the vital few and the trivial many" remains as common jargon.

In practice, the Pareto principle may be applied as a ranking system, a way of managing a project by prioritization, or a process for an orderly way of thinking about problems and their effects. Pareto charts (Pareto diagrams) are used to show frequency of occurrence or cost (money or time) as effects to an organization. In doing so, the chart visually indicates which situations are most significant.

Flowcharting

Every process requires services and products from some supplier(s). Likewise, every process produces services or products for some other process—its customer. **Flowcharting** symbolically shows the inputs from suppliers, the sequence of work activities, and the output to the customer.

One of the best ways to understand a process is to draw a picture of it. A **flowchart** is a graphical representation of the actual or ideal path followed by any service or product. It provides a visual sequence of the steps in a process, illustrates the relationship between parts, and identifies what the process does or should do.

Before a process can be improved, how it currently works must be understood. A flowchart of the current process helps to provide a complete picture of what is happening in the process from beginning to end. Attempts to change or improve a process before it is fully understood are unwise as more problems can be interjected inadvertently.

Figure 3-21 on the next page shows a simple flowchart that describes the process of getting office supplies for a meeting, incorporating commonly used flowchart symbols.

There are many other symbols that can be used to create a flowchart. For example, the simple flow chart example shown here could have been made much more detailed and additional pieces of information added.

Figure 3-21: Meeting Supplies Flowchart Example

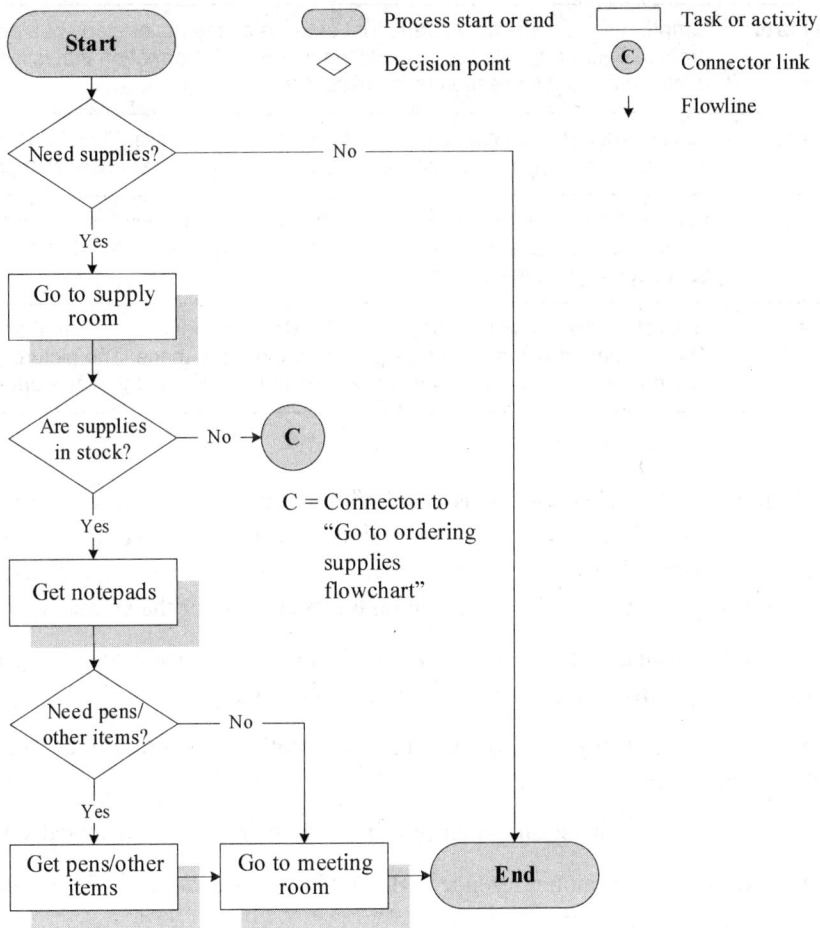

There are also several types of flowcharts. A few of the more common types of flowcharts are described in Figure 3-22.

Figure 3-22: Types of Flowcharts

Top-down flowcharts	Simple, easy-to-construct charts that emphasize the major steps of a process or project. This type of flowchart limits the amount of information that is included and is useful in highlighting essential process steps.
Detailed flowcharts	Include a lot of information about every stage in a process. The chart shows most steps in a process along with specific detail about what happens in each stage.
Deployment charts	Show the flow of a process along with the teams or employees who are responsible for the steps. They give "big picture" overviews of processes and what people are supposed to do at each step.
Work-flow diagrams	Illustrate the movement of people, materials, documents, or information in a process. The movement is sketched on a picture of the work space. The picture allows organizations to identify any inefficiencies or problems in the way work flows.

Each type of flowchart can be used to highlight different aspects of a process or task. Organizations should use the flowchart that best suits the process they intend to define. Care should be taken to accurately document the actual process and to avoid unnecessary complexity. Users must have a common understanding of the symbols.

Because flowcharts can be customized to fit a variety of needs and they can provide much useful information. A few specific benefits are:

- Provides a clear picture of how a process works by illustrating the relationship of various steps.

- Shows an organization's relationships with internal customers and suppliers.

- Provides a common reference point and a standard language for talking about an existing process or project.

- Serves as a starting point for process improvement activities.

Benchmarking

The term **benchmarking** is used to describe the continuous, systematic process of measuring products, services, and practices against the best levels of performance. Many people think of benchmarking as capturing best-in-class information, but the practice has a much wider application. Quite often, best levels are comparisons to external benchmarks of industry leaders. However, they may also be based on internal benchmarking information or measures from other organizations (outside an industry) that have similar processes.

Benchmarking process performance

Initially benchmarking was used primarily by manufacturing companies to improve products. Benchmarking practices are now commonly used in service industries as well and applied to customer service and other types of staff departments. Best levels may be financial or nonfinancial measures. Statement on Management Accounting No. 4V, "Effective Benchmarking," describes benchmarking as having seven phases:

- Selecting and prioritizing benchmarking projects
- Organizing benchmarking teams
- Documenting own work processes
- Researching and identifying best-in-class performance
- Analyzing benchmarking data and identifying enablers
- Implementing benchmarking study recommendations
- Recalibrating benchmarks.

Figure 3-23 shows a flow diagram from Statement on Management Accounting No. 4V that summarizes the activities associated with each of the seven phases.

Figure 3-23: Benchmarking Phases and Activities

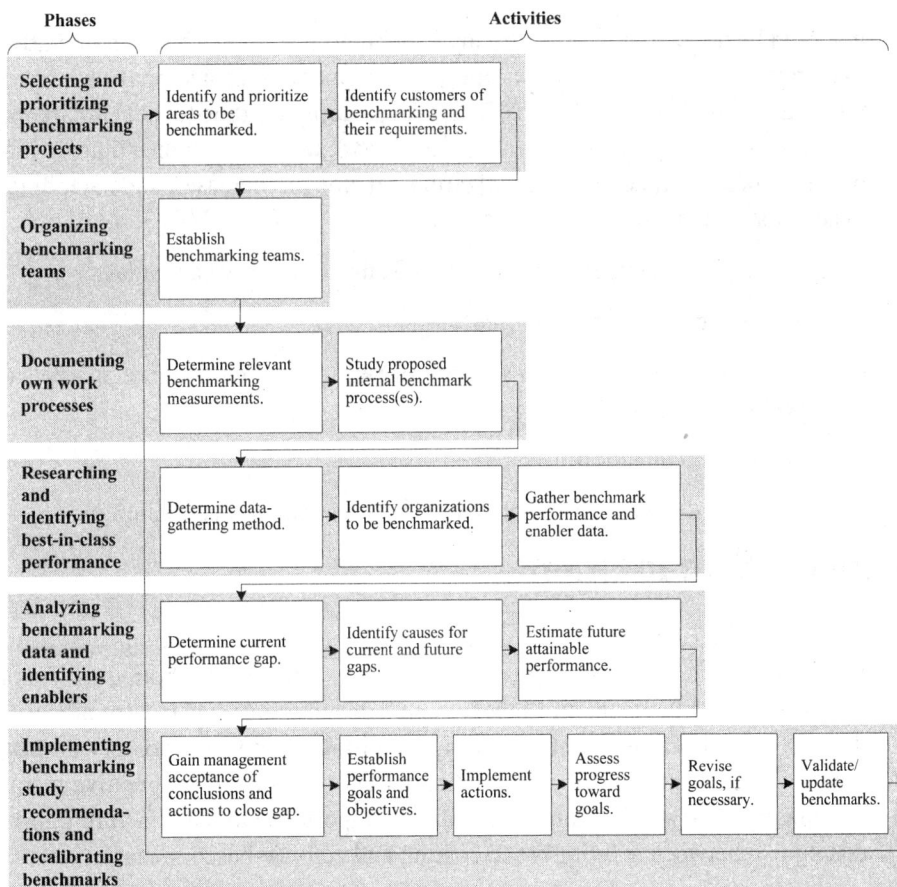

Benchmarking and creating competitive advantage

The 1990s saw a proliferation in benchmarking studies. Unfortunately, many organizations misused benchmarking. Benchmarking studies in various forms (best practice, functional, process, and competitive) were freely conducted, generally without a context. Invalid comparisons were often made (for example, comparing the growth of a highly leveraged company to one internally financed from earnings, or comparing the growth of a company in a low-cost environment to one in Silicon Valley). Given such misapplications, most of these benchmarking studies were not particularly cost-effective.

But the fact remains: Well-designed and properly applied, benchmarking can be a powerful tool in helping an organization to be competitive. Through benchmarking, a firm identifies best levels and conducts a study to help define how those levels can be adopted and lead to improved performance. As Statement on Management Accounting No. 4V notes, benchmarking provides a rational method for setting performance goals and gaining market leadership (and takes the emotion out of any arguments). Because benchmarking is based on what the best are doing, it provides an accurate assessment of what needs to change.

Strategic benchmarking

It should be noted that although many benchmarking studies have an operational focus (which is the intent of this discussion), a benchmarking project may also have a strategic focus. Strategic benchmarking is described as applying process benchmarking to the level of business strategy by incorporating benchmarking results in the strategic planning process. As such, it helps an organization develop an increased understanding and ability to address strategic business issues such as:

- Building core competencies to help sustain competitive advantage.

- Developing a new business line.

- Targeting a specific shift in strategy (for example, entering new markets or developing a new service).

- Making an acquisition.

- Creating an organization that can quickly respond to uncertainties.

Activity-Based Management

Activity-based costing, which was mentioned earlier in this section, and activity-based management are related concepts. But confusion often exists about the differentiating characteristics. Statement on Management Accounting No. 4CC, "Implementing Activity-Based Management: Avoiding the Pitfalls," cites the glossary of the Consortium for Advanced Manufacturing International (a not-for-profit, cooperative membership organization that supports areas of strategic importance to manufacturing industries) to distinguish between activity-based costing and activity-based management.

- **Activity-based costing (ABC)** is a methodology that measures the costs and performance of activities, resources, and cost objects. Specifically, resources are assigned to activities and then activities are assigned to cost objects based on their use. ABC recognizes the causal relationships of cost drivers to activities.

- **Activity-based management (ABM)** is a discipline that focuses on the management of activities as the route to improving the value received by the customer and the profit achieved by providing this value. ABM includes cost driver analysis, activity analysis, and performance measurement, drawing on ABC as its major source of data.

The bottom line is that both ABC and ABM are valuable practices for any firm striving to maintain or improve its competitive position. ABC answers the question, what do things cost? ABM takes a process view and asks, what causes costs to occur?

ABM principles and process improvements

ABM uses ABC data on process, product, and market performance and examines how to redirect and improve the use of resources to increase value for customers and other stakeholders. But where ABC is more of a static analysis of what is and is focused on controlling existing costs, ABM is forward-looking and change-oriented. ABM seeks ways to avoid unnecessary costs and put existing resources to maximum use.

Based on ABM information, organizations generally can:

- Make better decisions.

- Improve performance.

- Increase earnings on total resources deployed.

Overall, ABM supports both process reengineering and business process reengineering because it helps a firm to increase the value created by resources consumed in organizational processes and facilitates measurement of the impact of reengineering efforts.

Organizations implement ABM for a variety of reasons. Figure 3-24 summarizes general situations where a firm can benefit from ABM depending upon its stage of evolution.

Figure 3-24: General Applications for ABM

If a firm's operations are . . .	Then ABM can be useful to . . .
Growing	■ Redeploy non-value-added work. ■ Improve processes and activities.
Flat	■ Identify non-value-added costs. ■ Set priorities for improvement and effect improvement. ■ Isolate/eliminate cost drivers. ■ Determine product/service costs.
Declining	■ Cut costs. ■ Downsize. ■ Effect layoffs.
Constrained as to capacity	■ Determine product/service costs. ■ Make product/service decisions. ■ Determine activity capacity. ■ Identify bottlenecks.

ABM and quality improvements

Erroneously, ABM is sometimes thought of as a replacement for quality efforts, JIT systems, process reengineering, BPR, and benchmarking. To the contrary, ABM supports quality management and the other initiatives by providing an integrated information system that:

- Establishes accountability.

- Facilitates measuring of results.

- Enables setting of priorities.

Specific to quality, an ABM system facilitates quality implementation by:

- Identifying activity costs.

- Increasing the visibility of associated costs of quality.

- Providing quality cost measures that can be easily incorporated in cost-of-quality reports.

Because traditional accounting systems focus on functions (for example, research and design, production, sales and marketing, and so on), collecting data about the costs of quality is more problematic. With ABM, activity costs resulting from poor quality are more readily identifiable.

Continuous Improvement (Kaizen) Concepts

Kaizen is the term the Japanese use to describe continuous improvement (CI) at all levels in an organization. The premise is that as every process—beginning with the most important—is examined, worked on, and improved, the total enterprise improves. Kaizen acknowledges that innovation is valuable, but it maintains that innovations do not collectively contribute as much as continuous incremental improvements.

The kaizen process is often described as a "staircase of improvement." Moving from step to step, an organization uses a continuous process of following an improvement, maintaining an improvement, following an improvement, maintaining an improvement, and so on. Although the steps may be small, they move the organization upward toward sustained improvements.

Continuous improvements are often based on standards (organizational performance expectations and goals). Standards allow an enterprise to identify the cost to manufacture and sell a product or a service and to determine the causes of cost overruns.

Organizations can develop standards based on:

- Activity analysis.

- Historical data.

- Benchmarking.

- Market expectations.

- Strategic decisions.

Company benchmarking, for example, could be used to compare a firm's current cost structure to that of similar businesses. Once standards are determined, a series of continuous improvements could be implemented to increase efficiency and effectiveness and minimize variances.

Best Practice Analysis

A **best practice** generally refers to a process or technique that has produced outstanding results in one situation and that can be applied and/or adapted to improve effectiveness, efficiency, quality, safety, innovativeness, and/or some other performance measure in another situation. Best practice analysis refers to the collective steps in a gap analysis. A gap analysis is generally described as the difference between the current state and a desired state, or "the space between what is and what an organization hopes to be." The current state is defined by current practices; the desired state is defined by best practices.

Best practice analysis involves assessing how a firm's given performance level measures up to a best practice and then defining the logical next steps in transitioning to the desired performance level.

Typical activities are:

- Defining the gap (through a comparison to internal operational data).

- Determining the reasons for the gap.

- Examining the factors that contribute to the existence of the best practice(s).

- Developing recommendations and an approach to implement the best practice(s).

Techniques and tools for conducting a best practice analysis vary. Qualitative and quantitative tools are used. Most of the tools are common to TQM and kaizen.

It may be said that best practice analysis is the clout behind business process improvement initiatives: value chain analysis, process analysis, business process reengineering, benchmarking, total quality management, and kaizen. Through best practice analysis, performance improvements become actionable.

Progress Check

Directions: Read each question and respond in the space provided. Answers and page references appear on the page following the progress check questions.

1. Which of the following statements best characterizes value chain analysis?

   ( ) a. It emphasizes a firm's functional structure.

   ( ) b. It examines a firm's hierarchal structure.

   ( ) c. It examines distinct strategic activities.

   ( ) d. It promotes product/service differentiation.

Match the following business process concepts to the appropriate application.

2. _____ Value chain analysis

3. _____ Benchmarking

4. _____ Activity-based management

   a. Noncompetitive firms exchanging information about similar manufacturing processes

   b. An airline removing seats in a plane to give coach passengers more leg room

   c. An internal system examining past, current, and future performance

5. Which of the following statements accurately differentiates activity-based costing (ABC) and activity-based management (ABM)?

   ( ) a. ABC provides information on process, product, and market performance; ABM finds ways to improve them.

   ( ) b. ABC provides actionable information; ABM is a source of explanatory data.

   ( ) c. ABC seeks to change costs and their drivers; ABM focuses on understanding them.

   ( ) d. ABC is predominately forward-looking; ABM is primarily historical.

Progress check answers

1. c (p. 3-70)

2. b (p. 3-70)

3. a (p. 3-78)

4. c (p. 3-80)

5. a (p. 3-80)

Strategic Marketing

Section overview

Marketing is often described as a blend of science and art. From the science perspective, marketing integrates all the functions in a business. It strives to put an organization's best foot forward and reach customers through advertising, sales, and other skillful strategies. Many formal marketing tools exist and provide a framework to develop marketing strategies. On the art side, experience, intuition, and creativity also have a key role in crafting a winning marketing strategy. These collective marketing activities are why, for example, DaimlerChrysler, BMW, Ford, General Motors, and Honda all successfully sell cars—but in different ways.

To a large degree, the possibilities in marketing are limitless. But in light of prevalent survival pressures such as changing industry boundaries, new entrants, and unprecedented customer demands, one characteristic does stand out in separating the winning players from mediocrity: a market-driven strategy. No matter what type of enterprise or industry, a market-driven strategy helps to achieve success; it provides a clear, systematic approach for identifying, understanding, and meeting the customer's value perceptions. Often referred to as strategic marketing, market-driven, customer-focused marketing strategies are aligned to the organization's vision, mission, and strategic plans. When linked to the firm's corporate, competitive, and functional strategies, this customer-centric marketing approach facilitates the achievement of superior shareholder value.

Market-driven strategies are a team effort. Management accountants need to understand the basics of how a firm builds and sustains a market-driven strategy so they can provide timely information and contribute to the firm's growth and survival. This section looks at several aspects of strategic marketing: strategic role within the firm; managing marketing information; market segmentation, targeting, and positioning; managing products and services; pricing strategy; and promotional mix and distribution strategy.

Learning Outcome Statements

The Certified Management Accountant (CMA) test is based upon a series of Learning Outcome Statements (LOS) developed by the Institute of Certified Management Accountants (ICMA). The LOS describe all the knowledge and skills that make up the CMA body of knowledge, broken down by part, section and topic. The CMA Learning System (CMALS) supports the LOS by addressing all the subjects they cover. Candidates should use the LOS to ensure that they can address the concepts in different ways or through a variety of question scenarios. Candidates should also be prepared to perform calculations referred to in the LOS in total or by providing missing components of a calculation. The LOS should not be used as proxies for exact exam questions; they should be used as a guide for studying and learning the content of the CMA Learning System and ensuring that you can accomplish the objectives set out by the LOS.

The LOS included in the CMALS books are the comprehensive set, current as of the date of publication. Candidates can access the IMA Web site at www.imanet.org and click on the Certification section to locate and download a Portable Document Format (PDF) file of the current LOS.

Learning Outcome Statements

Part 3: Strategic Management — Section B. Strategic Marketing
Part 3 — Section B1. Strategic Role Within the Firm

- LOS 3.B.1.a—Identify the interrelationships between a firm's overall strategy and its marketing process.

- LOS 3.B.1.b—Demonstrate an understanding of the process of setting company marketing strategies, as well as the objectives and tactics to reach those strategic marketing goals.

- LOS 3.B.1.c—Demonstrate an understanding of strengths, weaknesses, opportunities, and threats (S.W.O.T.) analysis.

- LOS 3.B.1.d—Explain the critical importance of identifying customer needs and providing value to satisfy those customer needs.

- LOS 3.B.1.e—Define and demonstrate an understanding of business portfolio concepts.

- LOS 3.B.1.f—Demonstrate an understanding of the marketing process, including analyzing marketing opportunities, selecting target markets, developing the marketing mix, and managing the marketing effort.

- LOS 3.B.1.g—Demonstrate an understanding of the interrelationships among marketing analysis, planning, implementation, and control.

- LOS 3.B.1.h—Define strategic groups within industries and discuss why they require unique marketing strategies.

- LOS 3.B.1.i—Identify Porter's three generic strategies.

- LOS 3.B.1.j—Demonstrate an understanding of competitive changes during an industry's evolution.

- LOS 3.B.1.k—Differentiate among embryonic industries, growth industries, industry shakeout, mature industries, and declining industries.

- LOS 3.B.1.l—Demonstrate an understanding of the effect of globalization on industry structure.

- LOS 3.B.1.m—Identify internal competitive advantage and its components, including efficiency, quality, innovation, and customer satisfaction.

- LOS 3.B.1.n—Demonstrate an understanding of the value creation chain.

- LOS 3.B.1.o—Identify distinctive competencies, resources and capabilities.

- LOS 3.B.1.p—Identify reasons that marketing strategies fail and identify ways to sustain competitive advantage, including continuous improvement and benchmarking.

Part 3 — Section B2. Managing Marketing Information

- LOS 3.B.2.a—Identify marketing information needs.

- LOS 3.B.2.b—Demonstrate an understanding of the marketing information development process, including internal data collection, marketing intelligence, and marketing research.

- LOS 3.B.2.c—Define customer relationship management (CRM).

- LOS 3.B.2.d—Identify efficient methods of compiling, distributing, and using marketing information.

Part 3 — Section B3. Market Segmentation, Targeting, and Positioning

- LOS 3.B.3.a—Identify target marketing steps, including market segmentation, targeting, and positioning.

- LOS 3.B.3.b—Identify and define mass marketing, segment marketing, niche marketing, and micromarketing.

- LOS 3.B.3.c—Demonstrate an understanding of segmenting consumer markets, business markets, and international markets.

- LOS 3.B.3.d—Identify requirements for effective segmentation.

- LOS 3.B.3.e—Demonstrate an understanding of market targeting, including evaluating and selecting market segments.

- LOS 3.B.3.f—Define positioning strategy.

Part 3 — Section B4. Managing Products and Services

- LOS 3.B.4.a—Distinguish between products and services.

- LOS 3.B.4.b—Classify products and services, including consumer products, industrial products, and other marketable entities.

- LOS 3.B.4.c—Demonstrate an understanding of product attributes, branding, packaging, labeling, and product support services.

- LOS 3.B.4.d—Demonstrate an understanding of product line decisions and product mix decisions.

- LOS 3.B.4.e—Demonstrate an understanding of services marketing, including the nature and characteristics of service marketing strategies.

- LOS 3.B.4.f—Demonstrate an understanding of new product development strategies and product life-cycle strategies.

Part 3 — Section B5. Pricing Strategy

- LOS 3.B.5.a—Identify internal and external factors affecting pricing decisions.

- LOS 3.B.5.b—Demonstrate an understanding of general pricing approaches, including cost-based pricing, value-based pricing, and competition-based pricing.

- LOS 3.B.5.c—Discuss the role of the management accountant in pricing decisions.

- LOS 3.B.5.d—Demonstrate an understanding of new product pricing strategies, including market skimming pricing and market penetration pricing.

- LOS 3.B.5.e—Demonstrate an understanding of product mix pricing strategies, including product line pricing, optional product pricing, captive product pricing, by-product pricing, and product bundle pricing.

- LOS 3.B.5.f—Demonstrate an understanding of price adjustment strategies, including discount and allowance pricing, segmented pricing, psychological pricing, promotional pricing, geographical pricing, and international pricing.

- LOS 3.B.5.g—Demonstrate an understanding of how elasticity and the bargaining power of either the buyer or the seller can impact the price.

Part 3 — Section B6. Promotional Mix and Distribution Strategy

- LOS 3.B.6.a—Define marketing communication mix.

- LOS 3.B.6.b—Demonstrate an understanding of the integrated marketing communication process, including the need for integrated marketing communications.

- LOS 3.B.6.c—Identify and define the components of the overall communication mix, including advertising, sales promotion, public relations, and personal selling.

- LOS 3.B.6.d—Demonstrate an understanding of the advertising process, including setting advertising objectives, setting the advertising budget, developing advertising strategy, and advertising evaluation.

- LOS 3.B.6.e—Demonstrate an understanding of the sales promotion process, including sales promotion objectives, tools, strategy, and evaluation.

- LOS 3.B.6.f—Demonstrate an understanding of public relations and identify related tools.

- LOS 3.B.6.g—Demonstrate an understanding of the role of the personal selling process as an element of promotional mix.

- LOS 3.B.6.h—Identify the most effective component of the marketing mix (advertising, sales promotion, public relations, or personal selling) to use in a given situation.

- LOS 3.B.6.i—Define relationship marketing.

- LOS 3.B.6.j—Demonstrate an understanding of the direct marketing model, its benefits, forms of direct marketing, integrated campaign process, and ethical issues.

- LOS 3.B.6.k—Define the nature and functions of distribution channels.

- LOS 3.B.6.l—Demonstrate an understanding of distribution channel behavior and organization, including vertical, horizontal, and hybrid marketing systems and channel disintegration trends.

- LOS 3.B.6.m—Demonstrate an understanding of distribution channel design decisions, including analysis of consumer service needs, defining channel objectives and constraints, identifying and evaluating major alternatives, and global implementation.

Topic 1 — Strategic Role Within the Firm

Topic overview

A market-driven strategy attempts to address the pervasive competition in today's global business environment. Through market-driven strategies, companies assess markets and the customers comprising those markets and incorporate the information as a prominent part of their business strategy formulation.

Link Between Strategy and Marketing

Corporate strategy identifies the scope and purpose of a business; it outlines long-term objectives and capabilities and the actions and resources necessary to meet the objectives. A marketing strategy adds the customer's point of view to the mix. In addition to capturing the voice of the customer, a marketing strategy must be consistent with the overall business strategic planning priorities and must support corporate, competitive, and business unit/functional strategies.

Crafting a marketing strategy has some similarities to corporate strategy formulation:

- Analysis—developing a vision about the organization's target markets

- Strategy development—selecting and developing appropriate target market strategies and objectives

- Implementation activities—implementing and managing the marketing program strategies and meeting the value requirements of the customers in each target market

Strategic marketing takes marketing initiatives to the next level. It links an enterprise with its competitive environment and attempts to address the ever-changing conditions and the need to deliver superior customer value. It necessitates a market-driven approach to marketing strategy development that provides a basis for:

- Environmental monitoring.

- Deciding which customers to target and serve.

- Guiding product/service specifications.

- Identifying which competitors to compete against.

In strategic marketing, marketing is positioned as an organization-wide activity rather than a specialized function. Organizational performance assumes greater prominence than increasing sales.

The strategic marketing process

Across the best and the brightest business schools and the multitude of business texts, the point is made that strategic marketing process must be consistent, aligned, and supportive of the corporate strategy. The strategic planning process provides the blue-print for organizational vision, mission, strategies, goals, and objectives. The strategic marketing process supports detailed planning at a target market level.

Figure 3-25 provides a simple representation of the relationship of strategic planning and strategic marketing.

Figure 3-25 Strategic Planning and Strategic Marketing Processes

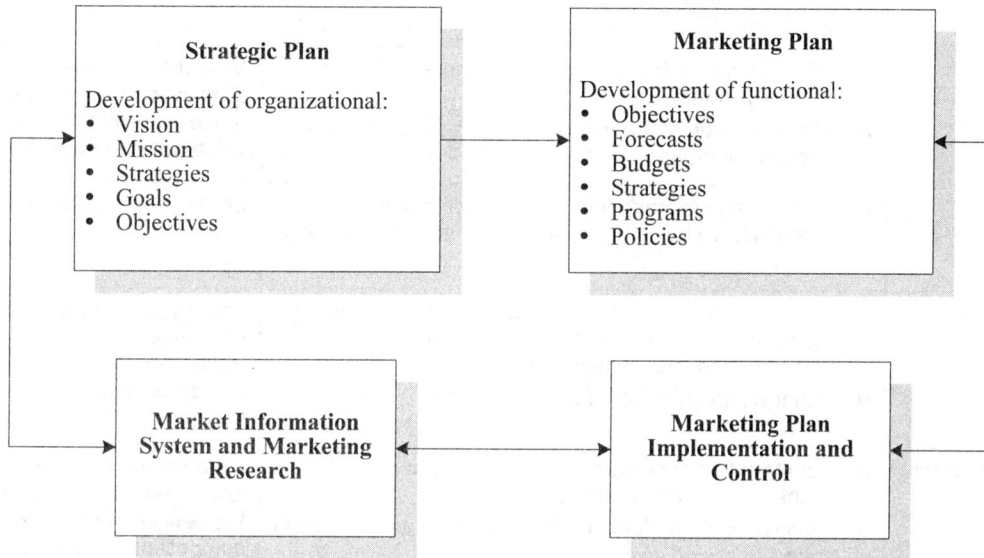

As with most models, organizations adapt steps and nomenclature in the marketing process based on circumstances. Although the end game takes precedence over the means, all marketing models account for the phases outlined in Figure 3-26. Subsequent content in this section expands on the various strategic marketing phases and activities.

Figure 3-26: Strategic Marketing Process

Phase	Actions Taken	Outcome
Analyzing marketing opportunities	■ Systematic analysis of environmental factors (e.g., cooperative, competitive, economic, social, political, and legal factors) ■ Identification of strengths, weaknesses, threats, opportunities, and counter threats ■ Definition of the customers and their preferences for products/services	Identification of profitable marketing opportunities and potential constraints on marketing activities
	■ Identification of the subgroups (segments) within the market of interest ■ Determination of the differences in needs and wants among subgroups	Market segmentation and clarification of the firm's value proposition with corresponding value requirements
	■ Use of various marketing sensing methods to understand what is happening today and what is likely to occur	Continuous learning about markets
Establishing objectives	■ Clarification of management expectations in terms of sales, market share, customer retention, profit contributions, and customer satisfaction ■ Identification of performance standards	Specification of marketing objectives (derived from/aligned to organizational objectives)
Selecting target markets	■ Identification of customer needs and what must be done to satisfy those needs ■ Estimation of the total market size and potential growth rate	Determination of how, when, and where to compete given the defined market and the competition (may be one or more segments if customer needs and wants vary)
Developing the marketing mix	■ Strategy development to satisfy the target market and achieve organizational objectives ■ Decisions about product, price, promotion, and place (distribution channels)	Product strategy, pricing strategy, promotion strategy, and distribution strategy
Managing the marketing effort	■ Putting the marketing plan into action ■ Performing marketing tasks according to the predefined schedule	Coordinated implementation of the marketing plan
	■ Measurement of the marketing plan results ■ Comparison of actual results to planned objectives ■ Decisions about any necessary adjustments	Control of the marketing plan

Customer Value and Customer Satisfaction

In today's business environment, organizational performance considered outstanding yesterday generally just meets requirements today and may be inadequate tomorrow. For a firm to successfully compete, its marketing strategy must champion customer value and customer satisfaction.

Customer value

Customer value is often described as a measure of market-perceived quality adjusted for the relative price of a product or service; value expectations and purchase decisions are based on the customers' perceptions of product or service benefits less the total costs incurred. Measures of customer satisfaction are important predictors of customers' future buying behavior, but measures of customers' perceptions of value for their dollars are often just as significant.

Value is essentially an individual thing; customers have different perceptions of value based on their:

- Ability to afford quality products and services.

- Tradeoffs or sacrifices required to afford quality.

- Perceptions of whether the products and services are worth the money paid.

Some customers may be willing to pay a high price because they will have quick delivery. Other customers may want to pay a lower price and will be willing to wait longer for the delivery.

When analyzing customer value perceptions, organizations strive to understand what causes customers to make buying decisions—why customers decide that one product or service offers better value than another. Firms typically conduct a customer value analysis to further examine the twin components of value (product and cost) and to help direct strategic marketing efforts toward enhancing customer perceptions of product worth.

A key objective in strategic marketing is getting close to customers and fostering a relationship with them so as to understand their true needs and expectations. This understanding must ultimately permeate the entire enterprise, as every part of an organization impacts customer satisfaction.

Customer satisfaction

Customer satisfaction reflects how well the customers' product use or service experience compares to their original value expectations. When customers have a very favorable experience and are extremely satisfied (compared with the expectations and value offering of competitors), superior customer value results.

Organizations typically gather both quantitative and qualitative data to assess customer satisfaction through a wide variety of measures. When both types of data are integrated, the company has comprehensive feedback, which can make future strategic marketing planning and decision-making processes easier and more effective and can increase the firm's opportunity to make better business decisions.

To achieve and sustain customer satisfaction, organizations need to:

- Determine customer satisfaction and dissatisfaction with appropriate processes, measurement methods, and data.

- Collect prompt feedback from customers on products/services and recent transactions.

- As feasible, collect and incorporate information on customer satisfaction relative to competitors and/or benchmarks.

- Keep customer satisfaction measures aligned with current business strategies.

Business Portfolio Concepts

It is more than challenging for an organization to try to satisfy all customers without falling into the trap of trying to be everything to everyone. Believe it or not, satisfaction may be irrelevant to some customers. But there are other core customers—strategic groups—who are so critical to an organization's success and survival that their satisfaction must be ensured.

Recall the Pareto principle, which was covered in the previous section, "Strategic Planning." There is always a group of core customers who are most vital to an organization's profitability. In theory, 80% of total sales volume often comes from about 20% of the total customer base. Contacts with these vital few customers are key. To a degree, an organization must focus on core customers.

So how does an organization differentiate between its customers and decide what businesses to be in? Business portfolio analysis, Michael Porter's generic competitive strategies, business life cycles, and customer profitability analysis are all important concepts that take into account organizational needs to funnel capital resources to the most viable prospects.

Business portfolio analysis

Portfolio analysis is not unique to marketing. For example, financial institutions use portfolio models to help balance risks and yields among the portfolio units (for example, stocks, products, businesses) and select an optimal portfolio.

Portfolio analysis as it pertains to marketing helps organizations put together the right portfolio mix of products and businesses to provide unrelated diversification and immunity to economic downturns. Most organizations tend to have multiple products and businesses with varying growth rates and returns. Management attempts to develop a portfolio that has multiple offerings and provides adequate cash flow and sustains long-term profits. Consider the example of PepsiCo, the parent company of Pepsi, Frito-Lay and Tropicana, which encompasses numerous product, product lines, and businesses.

Standardized portfolio models

In marketing, consulting firms have developed a wide variety of portfolio strategies. Three well-known standardized portfolio models are:

- The Boston Consulting Group's growth/share matrix.

- McKinsey & Company's multifactor analysis.

- Arthur D. Little's strategic business unit system.

Some basic similarities and differences exist across these standardized models. All three models provide product or business classification systems and include a matrix analysis.

Conceptually, the Boston Consulting Group (BCG) model and McKinsey & Company's multifactor analysis have similar actions from which to choose:

- Build—implies actions to increase market share (even at the expense of short-term earnings and cash flow)

- Hold—protects market share and competitive position

- Harvest—maximizes short-term earnings and cash flow (even at the expense of market share)

- Divest—indicates a decision to eliminate the business (either through liquidation or outright sale)

Beyond these similarities, each model then takes a slightly different approach. An overview of each model follows.

The Boston Consulting Group's growth/share matrix

The BCG business portfolio model divides business opportunities into four categories—stars, cash cows, question marks, and dogs—each requiring a different corporate strategy and marketing approach.

- **Star businesses (hold)**
  The star group of businesses holds high market share in high growth situations. An organization needs to focus its efforts (expertise, technology applications, people, and so on) in adding to customer value in these operations. Stars need to be vigilantly nurtured and sustained to maintain competitive strength in a growing market.

- **Cash cow businesses (harvest)**
  Cash cows have high market share in low growth or declining situations. They are often referred to as "gems" and are described as yesterday's stars that still provide the cash today to fund other initiatives. On a net basis, they still generate significant positive cash flows.

- **Question mark businesses (build)**
  Question marks have small market share and high growth potential. This group should always receive attention (as they may become successful stars and eventually cash cows), but they should not distract an organization from focusing on its core operations. Question marks may be large in numbers but often are small in dollar sales. An organization does not derive much profit from this group.

- **Dog businesses (divest)**
  Although some might think referring to businesses as "dogs" is in poor taste, the truth is that most organizations always have some operations that are not worth keeping. Dogs represent small market share and low growth. Bottom line, they are not profitable.

A representation of the four-quadrant BCG model is shown in Figure 3-27.

Figure 3-27: The Boston Consulting Group Chart

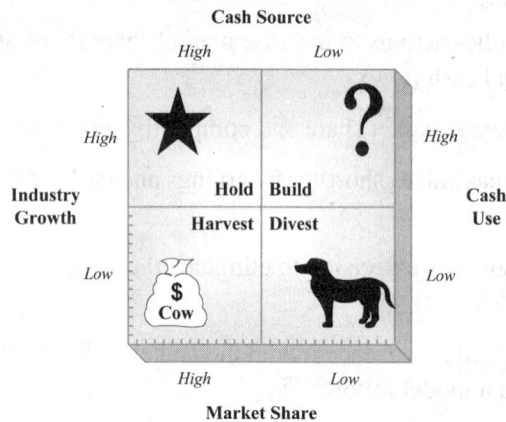

BCG studies report that high market share can be highly correlated with a higher return on investment (ROI) and lower costs due to experience. In other words, cost per unit decreases with the number of units produced over time (and cumulative experience). The BCG model supports having a stable, high market share with some operations to fund the cash needs of others.

McKinsey & Company's multifactor analysis

The McKinsey model maintains that there are two general variables governing business evaluation: industry attractiveness and business position (strength). Each variable is influenced by several industry factors. Depending upon the given industry, factors vary in importance. In total, the McKinsey model has nine quadrants, as illustrated in Figure 3-28.

Figure 3-28: McKinsey & Company's Position/Industry Attractiveness Analysis

		Low	Average	High
Business Position	**Strong**	S	I	I
	Average	H	S	I
	Weak	H	H	S

Industry Attractiveness

I = Invest and hold/grow/build or rebuild
S = Selectively invest earnings
H = Harvest/divest

Based on assessment of the quadrants, there are six generic courses of action:

- Invest and hold.

- Invest to grow.

- Invest to build/rebuild.

- Selectively invest (in promising areas).

- Harvest (milk) a cash cow.

- Divest (sell) a dog.

Arthur D. Little's strategic business unit system

The Arthur D. Little (ADL) portfolio concept revolves around strategic business units (SBUs). All business operations are classified into SBUs; the SBUs are placed in one of 24 quadrants in a matrix. The two general variables governing business evaluation are industry maturity level (ranging from embryonic to aging) and competitive position (ranging from leading to weak and nonviable).

The ADL model includes "traffic light" classifications:

- Green—indicates high market share and/or an attractive market

- Yellow—signals middle ground market characteristics

- Red—represents low market share and/or a mature market with poor prospects

Figure 3-29 shows the ADL model.

Figure 3-29: The ADL Strategic Business Unit Chart

	Embryonic	Growth	Maturity	Aging
Leading	G	G	G	G
Strong	G	G	G	Y
Favorable	G	G	Y	R
Tenable	G	Y	R	R
Weak	Y	R	R	R
Nonviable	R	R	R	R

Competitive Position (left axis)

Industry Maturity (bottom axis)

G = Green (Build) Y = Yellow (Maintain) R = Red (Liquidate)

Based on the matrix classifications, the ADL model devises generic strategies for each SBU (build, maintain, or liquidate) and then constructs appropriate tactical plans (focus, penetration, or diversification).

Variations of the three models are prevalent; other consultants have devised different approaches, and many corporations have further refined the models for specific company application. General Electric, for example, devised a model extending features of all three standardized models.

The General Electric Model

Where the BCG model assumes that market share is the sole determinant of profitability, General Electric (GE) developed a model incorporating more information and taking into account many additional factors influencing the long-term attractiveness of a market.

In the GE model, businesses are classified according to industry attractiveness and business strength (similar to McKinsey's model). Each dimension is based on a composite index of factors such as those shown in Figure 3-30.

Figure 3-30: Components of Industry Attractiveness and Business Strength in the GE Model

Industry Attractiveness		Business Strength	
• Market size	• Demand variability	**Market position**	**Competitive strengths**
• Market growth	• Market segmentation	• Domestic market share	• Leadership Quality initiatives
• Market profitability	• Distribution structure	• Global market share	• Customer loyalty
• Pricing trends	• Technology development	• Market share growth	• Technology
• Competition (intensity and rivalry)	• World scope	• Market share compared with leading competitors	• Marketing
• Market entry barriers			• Relative profits compared with leading competitors
• Opportunity to differentiate			• Relative cost position compared with leading competitors
			• Access to financial and other investment resources

Once businesses are classified by their industry attractiveness and business strengths, they are placed on a 3 × 3 matrix (similar to the McKinsey model) as shown in Figure 3-31.

Figure 3-31: General Electric's Industry Attractiveness and Business Strength Model

Business Strength

		Strong	Average	Weak
Industry Attractiveness	High	A	A	B
	Medium	A	B	C
	Low	B	C`	C

Interpretation guidelines prioritize the businesses based on where they are located in the GE matrix.

- **Priority A ("green zone")**
  High in both industry attractiveness and business strength, these businesses warrant "build share."

- **Priority B ("yellow zone")**
  Medium in both industry attractiveness and business strength, these businesses usually lead to "hold share."

- **Priority C ("red zone")**
  Low in both industry attractiveness and business strength, these businesses generally lead to "harvest or divest" actions.

Other portfolio models

Beyond the four models discussed here, there are many others. For example, there are modified risk return and stochastic (random variable) models and customized portfolio models that incorporate simulations. These more sophisticated models go beyond product or business classifications and can provide operational guidelines for resource allocation.

Over time, organizations have even adapted and applied the business portfolio concepts to customer portfolio analysis.

Benefits and limitations of portfolio management models

Overall, business portfolio management models attempt to provide the concepts and strategies necessary to create viable strategic alternatives, estimate the value of each alternative, and identify the risks inherent in each. The various models supply a framework for choosing between alternatives, for making tradeoffs between risks and opportunities, and for understanding how individual components in a portfolio will interact.

Portfolio models provide a relative snapshot. However, a general caution in using portfolio management models is that some of the grid measures are fairly subjective and, therefore, challenging to definitively assess. Business portfolio models are not meant to be used as a "cookbook" planning tool.

Generic Competitive Strategies

There are two basic requirements a firm must accomplish in order to survive and prosper in an industry. The organization must:

- Supply what customers want to buy.

- Be able to endure the competition.

Michael Porter developed three generic strategies that many firms use either singly or in combination to develop sustainable strategies to outperform industry competitors. Porter's generic competitive strategies are:

- Cost leadership (equal quality at lower costs).

- Differentiation (value above and beyond a premium price).

- Focus (zeroing in on a particular segment).

Figure 3-32 summarizes key characteristics of each strategy. The specific situation will dictate the best strategy for an organization.

Figure 3-32: Generic Competitive Strategies

Strategy	Description
Cost leadership	■ Promotes a low cost relative to those of average competitors (but not at the expense of quality, service, and other areas) ■ Requires aggressive internal economies of scale, tight cost and overhead control, vigilant pursuit of cost reductions, avoidance of marginal customer accounts, and so on ■ Results in above-average industry returns despite strong competitive forces ■ Provides high margins that can be reinvested in order to maintain cost leadership **Examples:** Wal-Mart in discount retailing, Charles Schwab in discount brokerage, Hyundai in discount automobiles
Differentiation	■ Focuses on creating a product or a service customers perceive as unique or superior and will pay a premium price for (relative to the price for competitive offerings) ■ Takes a variety of forms such as product or service design and features (e.g., durability or convenience), brand loyalty, superior customer service ■ Tends to lower price sensitivity and yield higher margins ■ Does not ignore costs; promotes cost reductions in areas that do not affect the differentiation **Examples:** Rolex in watches, Coca-Cola and Pepsi in soft drinks, Nordstrom in retailing
Focus	■ Focuses on a narrow strategic target (e.g., particular buyer group, segment of a product line, or geographic market) ■ Attempts to excel at serving the target more efficiently or effectively than competitors (who compete more broadly) ■ Achieves either cost leadership or differentiation (or both) with the target (but not necessarily within the industry) **Examples:** Porsche automobiles for high-end sports car enthusiasts, Southwest Airlines for affordable, no-frills airline travel

Industry Evolution

Industry evolution is yet another important factor in strategy formulation and business portfolio development.

Product life cycle (PLC) is a concept used to analyze the probable course of industry evolution—to anticipate shifts in the structure of an industry. It is based on the premise that an industry passes through a number of predictable stages or phases. The various stages reflect points in the rate of growth of industry sales. Competitive strategies and strategic marketing initiatives must adapt to changes in buyer diversity and preferences from stage to stage.

PLC classifications

The basic PLC classifications are embryonic, growth, shakeout, maturity, and decline.

- **Embryonic**
  "Embryonic" (also referred to as introduction, emergence, or emerging) describes a new industry or one that is re-formed as the result of a new technology, changing buyer needs, or the identification of unmet needs. The introductory phase is characterized by flat growth due to initial buyer inertia and product trials. For many years, digital photography was embryonic.

- **Growth**
  True to its name, rapid growth occurs when many buyers rush to purchase after the product has proven successful. For example, once wireless technology improved, the cell phone industry took off.

- **Shakeout**
  Shakeout occurs when the level of customer sophistication increases due to exposure to and firsthand use of a new product. Suppliers and customers concentrate around market leaders, forcing marginal players to drop out of the market. Cellular telephone manufacturers once glutted the market; many withdrew from the arena as major players emerged.

- **Maturity**
  Maturity results when market penetration is reached, causing the rapid growth to end and plateau. Microwave ovens, for example, are now a commodity kitchen appliance.

- **Decline**
  As the name implies, decline sets in as growth eventually tapers off and new product substitutes appear. Without attempts to renew the product, a dead-end course sets in. When branded pharmaceutical drugs come off patent and generic substitutes enter markets, the branded prescriptions tend to decline.

The typical PLC stages and the correlation to sales and profits are shown in Figure 3-33. Profits initially lag behind sales as expenses are often high during the introductory phase. Both sales and profits decline when a product reaches maturity (but profits typically decline before sales).

Figure 3-33: Product Life Cycle Curve

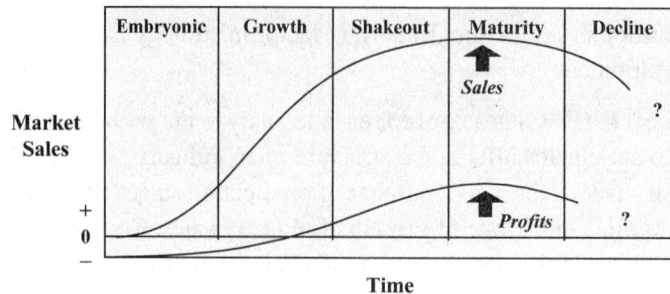

Additional PLC classifications are sometimes used. For example, "transitional" describes industries shifting from rapid growth to maturity. Products grow rapidly until market penetration is reached (for example, microwaves). The term "fragmented" characterizes an industry with a large number of relatively small firms but no dominant players (for example, lawn care). "Renewal" is sometimes used to describe an existing industry that is bouncing back from decline (often resulting from a next-generation technology or surviving competitors concentrating on cost reductions and productivity improvements to preserve market share). Basic cellular telephones entered a renewal phase when manufacturers positioned them as feature-laden mobile handsets with capabilities to transmit and receive music, games, text, images, and other forms of data.

PLC lessons learned

Over the years, the following observations have been made about the PLC stages:

- The duration of each stage varies from industry to industry.

- The demarcation points between phases are not always clear-cut.

- The S-shaped pattern can vary; sometimes industries skip a phase (for example, skip maturity and move from growth to decline).

- The nature of competition associated with each stage can vary widely across different industries.

Impact of globalization

Globalization presents additional dimensions for the PLC stages. Many different opportunities and threats are present in industries having extensive global competition (for example, telecommunications, automobiles, and consumer electronics).

International competition can impact the traditional classifications. The life cycle stages, for example, may differ depending on the country. An industry may be in rapid growth in one country while declining in other countries.

A firm's competitive and marketing strategies will also vary across countries. The benefits and limitations of a global reach and standardization must be evaluated against the potential advantages of local adaptation. A classic example is the Korean automobile manufacturer's strategies positioning Hyundai (with low prices and extended warranties) in the U.S. market against Japanese and American-made cars.

Customer Profitability Analysis

Businesses derive profits not from the manufacture of products or delivery of services but rather from the customers who buy the products and services. This simple premise is the key concept underlying customer profitability analysis.

A customer profitability analysis traces and reports customer revenues and costs; it enables a firm to determine the profitability (or unprofitability) of specific customers and provides data needed to improve profits. The two key components of a customer profitability analysis are revenue analysis and cost analysis.

Customer revenue analysis

Not all sales revenues are equal. Net proceeds from customers can vary based on factors such as:

- Sales discounts.

- Payment and delivery terms.

- Sales returns and allowances.

Different customers may generate approximately the same amount of total sales. But revenue analysis may paint an entirely different picture of net proceeds from those sales.

Consider the basic revenue analysis shown in Figure 3-34 for two different customers.

Figure 3-34: Customer Revenue Analysis

	Customer A	Customer B
Total sales	$600,000	$580,000
Less sales discounts	(30,000)	—
Net invoice	$570,000	$580,000
Less sales returns and allowances	10,000	5,000
Net sales	$560,000	$575,000
Less any cash discounts	—	8,000
Plus any finance (interest) charges	($4,000)	—
Net customer proceeds	$564,000	$567,000

Although the initial total sales from customer B are $20,000 less than those from customer A, the net proceeds from sales is $3,000 more for customer B ($567,000 minus $564,000).

Customer cost analysis

To complement the customer revenue information, customer cost analysis identifies cost activities and cost drivers associated with serving various customers. Similar to the revenue data, point-to-point comparisons can be made for individual customers or market segments. Comparisons can be made for cost classifications such as those shown in Figure 3-35.

Figure 3-35: Classifications for Customer Cost Analysis

Classification	Description	Examples
Unit-level costs	Internal resources consumed/used for each unit sold to a customer	Sales commissions, shipping costs, or restocking costs per unit
Batch-level costs	Internal resources consumed/used each time a sale occurs	Order-processing costs and invoicing costs
Service-sustaining costs	Internal resources consumed/used to service a customer regardless of the number of units or batches sold	Sales expenses, monthly statement costs, late payment collection costs
Distribution channel costs	Resources consumed/used in each distribution channel used to service customers	Operating costs for regional warehouses, distribution centers, or retail outlets
Sales-sustaining costs	Internal resources consumed/used to sustain sales and service activities that cannot be traced to an individual unit, batch, customer, or distribution channel	General company expenditures to support sales or pay salaries, fringe benefits, or bonuses

Cost drivers and their rates for each cost category can be tracked and analyzed over time for a variety of activities:

- Order taking
- Order processing
- Delivery
- Expedited order taking, processing, and delivery
- Number of customer visits
- Billing
- Sales returns and allowances
- Restocking
- Serving sales

Differences in costs to service different customers can be identified. Again, net profits can be compared.

Overall, by tracking and analyzing revenue and cost data, companies can:

- Identify activities and processes that are unprofitable for some or all of the customers.
- Measure customer profitability.
- Identify and grow their most profitable customers.

- Implement business changes to increase the profit contribution of average-performing customers and improve the profit of the worst-performing segments.

The more precise and accurate the information on the different customers, the better equipped a firm is to restructure the relationship and turn an unprofitable customer into a profitable one.

S.W.O.T. Analysis

Understanding industry competition is vital in creating realistic strategic plans and marketing strategies. Equally important is a firm's assessment of its internal competitive advantages and core competencies. An important objective of the external and internal assessments is to determine how to maximize the value of the firm's capabilities that set it apart from competitors.

Section A of this part of the CMA Learning System, "Strategic Planning," described the elements of conducting a S.W.O.T. analysis in detail—the assessment of organizational strengths, weaknesses, opportunities, and threats. The following content looks at the application of S.W.O.T. analysis data in the process of advantage creation.

Internal competitive advantage

In assessing its internal competitive advantage, a firm identifies:

- What the company is good at and what the competition is good at.
- Where the company fits in the marketplace.
- How the company's resources compare to those of the competition.

What the company is good at and what the competition is good at

S.W.O.T. data should provide a clear picture of company strengths. The 3M Company, for example, is renowned for research and development and new product introduction. Customers recognize L. L. Bean for legendary customer service. Sony is known for product quality, reliability, and durability in consumer electronics. Other distinctive capabilities resulting in competitive strengths might be advertising, distribution, etc., or internal process capabilities such as efficiency, quality, and innovation. Of course, strengths vary across companies—even within the same industry.

A competitor analysis determines what the competition's strengths are. Firms typically limit a competitor analysis to key competitors—those firms targeting the same market or market segment. An analysis of over-the-counter pain relief competitors by the manufacturer of Tylenol would include brands such as Excedrin, Anacin, Advil, Bayer, Bufferin, Aleve, and so on.

Basic information a competitor analysis should examine (for each key competitor) includes:

- Business goals, objectives, and strategies.
- Market target(s) and customer base.
- Current market share and trends.

- Capabilities (financial, technical, operating, etc.).

- Strengths, weaknesses, vulnerabilities.

- Key competitive advantages.

- Leadership and managerial capabilities.

A competitive analysis should also identify possible new competitors.

Competitive intelligence may be derived from a variety of sources such as annual reports, industry studies, trade publications, general business magazines, newspapers, reports prepared by financial analysts, government reports, and information from customers, suppliers, and salespeople. Depending on the circumstances and the level of detail warranted, a competitor analysis can become fairly sophisticated.

Armed with competitive profile data, a firm has a basis for forecasting each competitor's probable moves and their capacity to respond to industry changes.

Where the company fits in the marketplace

Key measures of a firm's market size include:

- Market share—calculated by dividing the company sales by total sales of all firms in the specified product market.

- Market potential—the maximum amount of product sales during a specified time period (to meet the needs of all buyers who are willing and able to purchase the product).

- Sales forecast—the expected product sales during a specified time period.

Market data allows a firm to evaluate market opportunities. Management can estimate the financial attractiveness of existing and new markets.

How the company's resources compare to those of the competition

Comparing the firm's resources with the competition's resources typically involves a point-by-point comparison of items such as (but not limited to):

- People (leadership, management, and staff).

- Research and design.

- Technology.

- Manufacturing.

- Sales force.

- Distribution channel.

- Cash position.

- Trade relations.

A close look at internal resources compared to the competition helps to identify core competencies.

Core competencies

Customer loyalty is often circumstantial, fragile, and fleeting. That is why an organization must strive for recognition beyond its portfolio of products and services; a firm needs to be viewed as having a portfolio of core competencies.

A **core competency** (or distinctive competency) is generally defined as fundamental knowledge, ability, or expertise in a specific subject area or skill set. Companies with specific strengths in the marketplace can be said to have a core competency in that area.

Statement on Management Accounting No. 4X, "Value Chain Analysis for Assessing Competitive Advantage," notes the following additional points about organizational core competencies:

- They are created by superior integration of technological, physical, and human resources.

- They represent distinctive skills as well as intangible intellectual assets and cultural capabilities (for example, the ability of the firm to manage change, empower teams, and promote continuous learning).

- They are the "connective tissue" that holds together seemingly diverse aspects of a business and allows managers and employees to translate insights from one business setting to another.

What distinguishes a true core competency from a "me-too" capability? There are three generally accepted characteristics:

- Enhanced customer value—A core competency makes a significant contribution to perceived customer benefits of the product or service.

- Uniqueness—A core competency reduces the threat of imitation by competitors.

- Market leverage—A core competency provides potential access to a wide variety of markets.

It has been said that the "core" part of the term indicates that a firm has a strong basis from which to develop additional products and services. Such core competency diversification is desirable because it can reduce risk and investment and promote opportunities for the transfer of learning and best practices across business units.

Value creation

As noted in earlier discussions, value is perceived by the buyer and based on the benefits and costs associated with the purchase and use of products or services. Customer satisfaction reflects how well the use experience compares with the buyer's value expectation. Superior value results from a very favorable use experience compared with competitive offerings. **Value creation** is the process of determining where and how a firm's product or service can offer superior value and then directing marketing capabilities so that a favorable competency/value match results.

Business strategies and markets are interrelated, and they are both paramount to competitive advantage. A firm must understand its current market and how that market is likely to change, or it risks being at a competitive disadvantage. **Value migration** occurs when customers shift their purchases to new or different products. The shift from traditional cameras and film to digital imaging is an example of value migration. Potential market shifts must be anticipated, and counterstrategies must be developed.

Note: Value chain analysis is covered in Section A of this part of the CMA Learning System, Topic 3, "Business Process Performance."

Why Marketing Strategies Fail

Marketing can develop great strategies, but for a variety of reason, plans can falter and sometimes fail. Consider a few key reasons why marketing strategies do not succeed.

- **Lack of organizational commitment.**
  Top management must be committed to the marketing plan. There must be a clear understanding and acceptance of how the product or service offering supports organizational goals. Cross-functional support should also be in place.

- **Improper situational analysis.**
  Weak up-front analysis can lead to erroneous product development that potentially overestimates the marketing opportunities, underestimates the competition, misinterprets trends, misses the target audience, etc. Some ill-conceived efforts may literally lead to products and services in search of markets.

- **Frequency of marketing planning.**
  If strategies are reevaluated too frequently, the organization's responses to the marketplace can become erratic. Conversely, if plans are not revised frequently enough, the organization may fail to react appropriately to environmental challenges and lose competitive position.

- **Disconnects between marketing and sales.**
  Marketing and sales are integrally linked. It is sales staff's responsibility to implement marketing strategies. If marketing fails to share the right information (for example, wrong or weak collateral support materials), sales will suffer. Also, the failure of marketing to recognize and/or implement input from salespeople regarding customer data and needs can undermine the success of a product or service offering.

- **Lack of or poor tactical planning.**
  At best, most strategic marketing plans require some fine-tuning because of changes in situational environments. For example, there may be problems with product quality or a competitor may introduce a new product. Many products and services fail due to tactical execution and control problems. Marketing executives need to continually monitor plan implementation, make necessary adjustments, and possibly redirect the plan if actual results seriously deviate from the planned results.

Even when products and services are successful, organizations should be proactive in assessing the position of the current offerings through practices such as:

- **Product or service audits**—to ascertain if the current offerings should be continued as is, improved, modified, or deleted.

- **Benchmarking**—to measure and compare current products and services against comparable ones in leading organizations and obtain information that can lead to improvements.

- **Continuous improvement**—to implement a disciplined methodology for understanding, analyzing, and continually improving products and services with the objective of meeting or exceeding customer needs and desires and sustaining competitive advantage.

Note: Benchmarking and continuous improvement are discussed in more detail in Section A of this part of the CMA Learning System, Topic 3, "Business Process Performance."

Progress Check

Directions: Read each question and respond in the space provided. Answers and page references appear on the page following the progress check questions.

1. The phase during strategic marketing that segments the market and identifies important characteristics, size estimates, and growth projections is

   ( ) a. situation analysis.

   ( ) b. strategy design.

   ( ) c. program development.

   ( ) d. strategy implementation.

2. A company is faced with the decision of investing in a strategic business unit to increase market share or divesting and deploying the capital among other businesses in the portfolio. This scenario most closely reflects which business category in the portfolio matrix concept?

   ( ) a. Star

   ( ) b. Question mark

   ( ) c. Cash cow

   ( ) d. Dog

Match the following product life cycle stages to the appropriate industry behavior.

3. _____ Embryonic

4. _____ Shakeout

5. _____ Decline

a. Competitors concentrate on productivity improvements to preserve market share.

b. Uncertainty about customer acceptance and the eventual size of the market prevails.

c. Buyers become more discriminating in their product selections.

6. A company's plan to flood the market with a new consumer electronic product priced below the cost of its major competitor's products, with the goal of recouping planned losses from the first year with larger profits in subsequent years, exemplifies which type of competitive strategy?

    ( ) a. Cost leadership

    ( ) b. Differentiation

    ( ) c. Focus

    ( ) d. Combination

7. Which of the following organizational capabilities would most likely be considered a core competency?

    ( ) a. The application of total quality management in a manufacturing operation

    ( ) b. The capability for e-commerce in customer order fulfillment

    ( ) c. The use of laptop computers by a field sales force

    ( ) d. The industry experience of a consulting firm and the tenure of its employees

Progress check answers

1. a (p. 3-90)

2. b (p. 3-95)

3. b (p. 3-101)

4. c (p. 3-101)

5. a (p. 3-101)

6. a (p. 3-100)

7. d (p. 3-107)

Topic 2 | Managing Marketing Information

Topic overview

It was not until the 1960s that the field of marketing promoted the concept of providing products and services to meet the needs and wants of customers. This was a dramatic departure from the firm-centered orientation of simply selling the customer what was produced. Today, strategic marketing champions the customer's point of view. In customer-focused organizations, all units work together in support of customer value. In cultures that place customer value as the top priority, the feeling among employees is pervasive—you serve customers or you serve people who serve customers.

Customer relationship management (CRM) is a discipline that helps organizations to become customer-driven. Relationship management starts with customers—understanding their requirements and preferences—and also encourages the development of long-term collaborative relationships with them. Information plays a key role in learning about markets and serving customers in those markets. Those firms that are most successful in customer relationship management are adept at gathering, interpreting, and using information to guide both marketing and business strategies.

An important component of customer relationship management is commitment. Commitment is the degree to which all employees have internalized the values of customer focus in every transaction—from product or service design through warranty and support. (In contrast to commitment, compliance is evident when a company or an employee merely goes through the motions.) Employees should feel that in helping customers they are helping the organization achieve its strategic goals. Knowledge gained about customers' needs and expectations should be widespread; practices and policies need to be in place so that all employees feel responsible for customer satisfaction.

Developing Marketing Information

Market-driven firms do not think that they intuitively know what customers want. Such organizations:

- Relentlessly study customers' needs and expectations.
- Seek to understand the diversity of buyer preferences.
- Stretch and look beyond traditional market boundaries.
- Include all relevant sources of knowledge and ideas.

In most industries, there is no shortage of information available. Organizations need to decide what information they need and then compare the potential benefits of the information with the costs of acquiring and analyzing the information.

Marketing Information Systems

The ability to fulfill customer needs is based on an organization's efforts to first understand customer and market needs; the ability to develop future business opportunities is based on an organization's ability to anticipate customer and market needs. This requires knowledge about long-term requirements, expectations, and preferences of the organization's target and/or potential customers and markets.

One way to better understand customer needs is to develop a rich database of product and service features that customers are now buying or requesting. Further understanding of both current and future needs can be gained from techniques such as benchmarking, advisory panels, customer interviews, focus groups, surveys, environmental scanning, employees' input, and observation.

Because information tends to be plentiful, the challenge has increasingly become knowledge management—interpreting information and building company-wide understanding. Organizations need to have a systematic way to:

- Actively listen to their customers.

- Record what they hear.

- Analyze what they hear.

- Disseminate the information internally throughout the organization.

- Act upon the information.

Without such a system, an organization runs the risk of dissatisfied customers and also leaves the door open to competition.

Many types of marketing information systems are available. Electronic systems are the norm. The specific type of information system is driven by the specific needs of the firm—factors ranging from the size of the firm and the nature of the business to the product/service mix, the type of information to be collected, etc. The marketing information requirements of a wholesale manufacturing firm supplying automotive aftermarket parts would, for example, be dramatically different from those for a retail clothing chain.

Figure 3-36 lists several common marketing information systems.

Figure 3-36: Types of Marketing Information Systems

Type	Key Characteristics
Market research studies	Customized information collected and analyzed for a specific research problem
Standardized information services	Information from outside vendors; typically purchased either on a subscription or single-purchase basis (although some services are free); the same information may be sold/available to several customers
Management information systems (MIS)	Internal computerized systems supplying information for a variety of purposes (such as order processing, invoicing, customer analysis, etc.); may include internal and external data sources
Database systems	Specialized MIS format facilitating a variety of marketing applications (for example, customer and product/service analyses, mailing lists, etc.)
Decision support systems (DSS)	Computerized systems providing decision-making assistance to managers and staff; more advanced than MIS
Customer relationship management (CRM) systems	Systems integrating all the information necessary to facilitate a seamless point of contact with the customer; can provide detailed transaction data about a customer
Market (competitor) intelligence systems	Systems designed to help monitor existing and potential competitors; may include database searches, customer surveys, interviews with suppliers and other channel members, evaluating competitive products or services, forming strategic alliances with competitors, etc.

Marketing information is typically classified in one of two broad categories:

- Information supplied on a regular basis from internal and external sources (for example, environmental scanning, S.W.O.T. analysis, salespeople, suppliers, sales cost analyses, warranty cards, customer satisfaction surveys, and market share)

- Information collected on an as-needed basis for a particular situation or problem (for example, new product concept research, brand preference studies, research on advertising effectiveness)

Marketing Research Process

Marketing research is a systematic process for obtaining information used in making marketing-related decisions. Although specific activities and nomenclature will vary, the marketing research process conceptually involves the steps outlined in Figure 3-37.

Figure 3-37: Marketing Research Process

Step	Description
Define the need.	■ Definition of the problem to be studied ■ Identification of the specific objective(s) of what is to be accomplished ■ Determination of the information necessary to solve the problem
Identify the information sources.	■ Identification of existing data to be captured from internal systems and resources ■ Identification of external information sources (e.g., government agencies, industry and trade organizations, colleges and universities, private research firms and consultants) necessary to support decision-making needs ■ Determination of whether to gather information through qualitative (e.g., observations of customer behavior) or quantitative methods (e.g., surveys)
Compile the data.	Systematic collection of qualitative and quantitative data (soft data from interviews, focus groups, etc.; hard data from reports, studies, surveys, etc.)
Analyze the data/draw inferences.	■ Statistical interpretation of hard data, identification of customer preferences and perceptions from soft data; benchmarked comparisons ■ Summary of findings and conclusions
Disseminate/ deploy the information.	■ Development of appropriate action plans based on data and prioritization ■ Deployment of customer feedback through the organization ■ Plans for ongoing monitoring; identification of ways to improve efficiency and effectiveness, reduce costs, and increase profits and market share ■ Determination of how to maintain/improve internal and external communications

Progress Check

Directions: Read each question and respond in the space provided. Answers and page references appear on the page following the progress check questions.

1. All of the following organizational activities exemplify customer relationship management (CRM) activities except

( ) a. employee compliance with call center objectives.

( ) b. increasing leverage of the Internet and a company's Web site.

( ) c. seamless coordination between sales, marketing, service, and field support.

( ) d. process technology improvements to maximize contact with distribution channel members.

Match the following marketing information systems with their appropriate description.

2. _____ Market research

3. _____ Databases

4. _____ Market intelligence

5. _____ Standardized information services

a. Monitoring of existing and potential competitors

b. Customized information collected and analyzed for a specific need

c. Specialized MIS format facilitating a variety of marketing applications

d. Data typically purchased from outside vendors

Progress check answers

1. a (p. 3-113)

2. b (p. 3-115)

3. c (p. 3-115)

4. a (p. 3-115)

5. d (p. 3-115)

Market Segmentation, Targeting, and Positioning

Topic overview

*There are two basic approaches to marketing: the mass market approach and the target market approach. Henry Ford's classic statement about the Model T, "Customers can have any color car they want as long as it is black," epitomizes the **mass marketing** approach, in which companies treat all customers the same in terms of product offerings. **Target marketing** recognizes that all customers are not alike—they have different needs and wants and those needs and wants are constantly changing. Increasingly, firms are finding that the extent to which they can meet those unique needs and wants can result in higher returns than the one-size-fits-all mass marketing approach (even though costs associated with target marketing are higher than those of mass marketing).*

The basic flow of a target marketing strategy is shown in Figure 3-38. This topic looks at each of the major components in more detail.

Figure 3-38: Target Marketing Strategy Steps

Segmentation

Develop segmentation strategies:
- Macro segments
- Micro segments
- Finer segments

Targeting

Evaluate and select market segments based on:
- Product life cycle
- Diversity of buyer preferences
- Industry structure
- Internal capabilities and resources
- Business strategies

Positioning

Identify positioning concepts for target segments for:
- The company
- Product or service mix
- Specific product or service line
- Specific brand

Market Segmentation

Market segmentation is the process whereby companies identify and analyze subgroups of buyers with similar characteristics in a given product or service market. The resulting customer segments are relatively homogenous groups of current customers or prospective buyers.

Once a firm selects the portion of the total market to be segmented, there are countless ways to segment subgroups. Firms embark on the market segmentation process through a set of interrelated activities. The overall goal is to segment customers and prospective buyers based on some common needs and characteristics. Macro and micro segmentation approaches are often used. In some situations, even finer segmentation strategies are possible. International markets have unique requirements.

Macro segmentation strategies

Macro segmentation is usually the first cut of customer or buyer data. Consider a hotel chain as an example. Vacation travelers and business travelers would represent two significant macro customer groups.

Further macro criteria could segment business travelers between extended stays and short stays or those desiring affordable accommodations versus luxury amenities. Additional segmentation criteria could include revenue generated by the business travelers. Performing a Pareto analysis of profit margin and revenue, a hotel could identify the 20% that contribute 80% of the revenue.

Another form of macro segmentation, referred to as customer-retention strategy, classifies customers by their buying behavior (for example, growing, stable, declining, or lost). Other macro approaches include segmenting competitors' customers and potential customers or segmenting the consumer market (end-user customers) versus the distribution market (business customers).

Micro segmentation strategies

A micro segmentation approach is based on a finer slice of customer variables. In his book *Competitive Advantage: Creating and Sustaining Superior Performance*, Michael Porter discusses how buyers can be classified in many ways and that all the different types of end users that a company sells to must be studied for important differences.

Variables for segmenting customers are different for buyers of consumer goods and services and buyers of commercial/industrial goods and services. For example, if selling consumer goods, a company would want to look at age, income, household size, and decision-maker characteristics. If selling industrial, commercial, or institutional products, a company would want to distinguish buyers by size, technological sophistication, and how the buyer uses the product or service.

Segmenting consumer markets

According to Porter, variables to study for important differences among buyers in the consumer market include the following:

- **Demographics**
  These variables include geographic location, age, gender, marital status, family size, social class, education, nationality, occupation, and income. For example, single business people have different needs and purchasing patterns for clothing than do families with children. In the banking industry, annual income, wealth, and educational level determine what banking services are purchased and how sensitive the customer is to the price of these services.

- **Psychographic customer characteristics**
  These variables address lifestyle issues and include consumer activities, interests, and opinions. These factors can be difficult to measure. Nevertheless, lifestyle or self-image can be important discriminators of purchasing behavior. Demographics may also be combined with this characteristic. For example, a home fitness equipment manufacturer might segment 18- to 40-year-old men and women who are active,

interested in sports, and health-conscious and who have the income to spend on sports equipment.

- **Language**

  Language defines customer segments for industries such as book publishers and the record industry and also defines segments for all end users of products and services. For example, many products come with directions written in multiple languages.

- **Decision-making unit or purchasing process**

  A household's decision-making process can be important in terms of desired quality characteristics and price sensitivities. For example, one spouse may be more interested in the price and comfort of a car whereas the other may be concerned about performance features.

- **Purchase occasion**

  Purchase occasion refers to whether a product/service is purchased as a gift or for the buyer's own use or whether the product/service is to be used routinely or as part of a special event. A buyer's use and signaling criteria are often very different depending on the occasion. For example, customers who buy pens for themselves will typically purchase practical, less expensive pens. When buying pens as gifts, customers will likely select more expensive name brands.

- **Potential buyers**

  People not currently purchasing a product or service can also represent a customer segment.

Segmenting business markets

Variables to study for important differences among buyers in the commercial/industrial market may be as basic as location, Standard Industrial Classification (SIC) code, North American Industry Classification System (NAICS) code, or number of employees. Porter notes these other variables:

- **Buyer industry**

  This variable can indicate how a product is used and the percentage of total purchases it represents. For example, a small appliance manufacturer would buy and use a plastic resin differently than an automobile manufacturer using the same resin in fabrication of a car interior.

- **Technological sophistication**

  A buyer's technological sophistication can be an important indicator of its susceptibility to differentiation and resulting price sensitivity.

- **OEM versus end user**

  Original equipment manufacturers (OEMs) that incorporate a product into their product and sell it to other firms often have differing levels of price sensitivity and sophistication than end-user firms that use the product themselves.

- **Decision-making unit or purchasing process**

  As with consumer products, specific individuals involved in purchasing decisions can have a major influence on the sophistication of the purchase decision, the desired product attributes, and price sensitivity.

- **Size**

  A company typically segments buyers on variables such as whether they are a small business or a Fortune 100 or even Fortune 500 company. According to Porter, size can be measured on three things: order size, total annual purchases, or company size.

- **Ownership**

  Ownership structure can impact a buyer's motivation. For example, private companies may value different product characteristics than public companies, or a company division may be guided by purchasing decisions made by the parent company.

- **Revenue/financial strength**

  Using this variable, a firm segments customers by revenue, such as customers with revenues of less than $1 million or in ranges such as $5 million to $10 million. According to Porter, a buyer's profitability and financial resources can determine such things as sensitivity to price, frequency of purchase, and need for credit.

Finer segmentation strategies

Several factors can work together and help a firm to identify very small segments—in some situations, even a segment of one.

Consider the following examples:

- For a host of companies, CRM system capabilities allow firms to respond to unique customer preferences in a seamless manner; firms are able to provide more attractive value in goods and services based on unique customer needs and expectations.

- In the business and home computer arena, Dell allows individual consumers and businesses to design their own computer systems, thereby satisfying specific needs and wants at prices comparable to those of mass-produced computers.

- Casio sells more than 5,000 different styles of watches because effective system design allows such variety to be created at very low costs.

When considering finer segments, an organization must assess:

- Internal capabilities to offer cost-effective, customized offerings (such as database knowledge, computer-aided design technologies, and just-in-time inventory systems).

- Customer desires/expectations for highly customized offerings.

- The advantages of closer customer relationships (such as value opportunities and potential market entry barriers).

International market segmentation

Being close to the customer remains a crucial element in any international marketing strategy. But, as one would logically expect, operating beyond the confines of a domestic marketplace orientation introduces many additional variables and challenges that must be internalized and addressed.

For the most part, international segments are all unique; although some segments may have similarities, no two will be exactly the same. It is an understatement to say that what applies in one country or region cannot be universally applied to all international operations.

International market segmentation must consider the firm's global presence. But it must also factor in local/regional tastes and how to best adapt them to variables such as:

- Area culture and values.

- Local marketing requirements.

- Level of available technology.

- Distribution structures.

- Competitors.

- The economic environment.

- The political environment.

- Trade implications, for example, tariffs and quotas.

Many firms enjoy international success through mass customization coupled with local segmentation efforts. Depending upon the location, many of the consumer and industrial characteristics investigated in domestic segmentation are still appropriate to consider. Naturally, some are irrelevant (due to local conditions).

Overall, the fundamental driving force in any international marketing effort remains the same as for a domestic effort: organizational responsiveness and value-added activities that support the changing needs and tastes of the area. Although activities should have a global coherence, they must maintain a localized sense of advantage and competition.

Requirements for effective segmentation

The fact that segmentation typically results in higher revenues is not the only impetus for segmenting markets. Organizations stand to derive numerous additional benefits such as (but certainly not limited to):

- Important insights for building and implementing strategic marketing programs.

- Clarification of the firm's own competitive position.

- Clear definition of marketing objectives and strategy.

- A sound foundation for marketing mix changes.

- Guidance for product development efforts and resource allocation.

- Strong integration of marketing with other business activities to support a firm's efforts in meeting customer needs.

These potential gains beg the question of how organizations can create effective segmentation. Figure 3-39 provides a checklist of effective market segmentation characteristics.

Figure 3-39: Effective Market Segmentation Characteristics

✓	**Leverage**	Can the segmentation plan be generalized/applied to more than one product or service?
✓	**Logical**	Do the segments reflect logical subgroups with easily distinguishable similarities and/or differences?
✓	**Research-based**	Have the segments been accurately and thoroughly analyzed?
✓	**Compatible**	Are the segment strategies aligned to corporate, competitive, and functional strategies?
✓	**Profitable**	How will the segmentation strategy support value creation? Are projected revenue-to-expense ratios for segments profitable?
✓	**Pervasive**	Will employees, suppliers, partners, and alliances support the segments? Are there any barriers that must be removed?
✓	**Win-win**	How will employees, suppliers, partners, alliances, and the segments derive mutual gains and value?

Market Targeting

During the segmentation portion of a target market strategy, a firm identifies, researches, and analyzes market segments. In other words, opportunities are identified. Through targeting, the firm picks the best market segment(s) to pursue. According to marketing guru Philip Kotler, targeting involves developing measures of segment attractiveness and then selecting a market to enter. Targeting answers the question, which segment(s) offer the most profitable opportunities for the firm? The end result of a targeting decision is how many customer groups the organization will serve.

If you were to examine the targeting strategies of market-driven companies, commonalities would surface—regardless of differences in industry, size, or other characteristics. In evaluating the profit potential of market segments and selecting which segments to target, all firms should consider the following:

- **Product life cycle**
  The stage of product maturity, the competitive industry environment, and the exposure to global competitors all influence targeting decisions. A new or emerging segment offers much different potential than one that is relatively mature or on the brink of decline. The threat or presence of international competition mandates consideration of global threats and opportunities.

- **Diversity of buyer preferences**
  Targeting should account for the value requirements of buyers in the segment. Do distinct preferences exist that a firm can appeal to through product or service specialization? Or will product variety be important to buyers?

- **Industry structure**
  Targeting should also factor in Michael Porter's five market forces. If some segment appears too good to be true, it may be a bona fide target. On the other hand, there may be some hidden downside. If a segment is truly appealing, there is a possibility that other competitors may be getting ready to target the same segment.

- **Internal capabilities and resources**
  An organization needs to be realistic and practical in targeting. In other words, can internal and external resources support the target market? There is no point in targeting a segment that is unattainable. Perhaps a competitor has a superior differential. Unless there is some potential weakness(es) the firm can exploit, the segment may be attractive but not worth going after because of a competitor's dominant position.

- **Business strategies**
  Corporate, competitive, and functional strategies should be kept in perspective. If, for example, an organization sets strategic goals of diversification and significant growth, the target markets must logically support those strategies.

Collectively, these factors influence how to best select targets.

Through targeting, a firm must ultimately decide whether to:

- **Target a single segment (single-segment concentration).**
  When a firm concentrates its marketing efforts on one particular segment, its products or services cater to the needs of that particular group. For example, Lexus targets customers looking for high-end automobiles.

- **Selectively target a few segments (market specialization or product specialization).**
  Through selective targeting, a firm decides to target different segments with distinct product or service offerings aimed at the varying groups. Commercial airlines offer first-, business-, or economy-class tickets to passengers to appeal to different groups.

- **Target all (or most) of the market segments (full or mass marketing).**
  Sometimes considered mass marketing, this approach targets the entire market (or the majority of the market) with the same offering.

Market Positioning

Once an organization selects the target market, the next step in formulating a market-driven strategy is to decide how it wants to position itself within that chosen segment. Positioning is how an organization wants to be perceived by customers in comparison to its competitors. There are different levels of positioning. Positioning may focus on:

- The entire company (for example, to be recognized for always low prices).

- A mix of products or services (for example, Ford Motor Company wants to be known for a variety of core-type vehicles as well as a selection of premier ones).

- A specific line of products or services (for example, Hewlett-Packard wants customers to choose from its complete line of laser or inkjet printers).

- A specific brand (for example, Iams® brand wants pet owners to think of its label as a premium dog and cat nutrition product).

Positioning is a pivotal part of an organization's plans to gain and sustain market share. The principal objective in positioning is to match the firm's capabilities with the customer value requirements in each target segment. The desired result is to gain an enduring position in the eyes and minds of the buyers in that target segment.

Ultimately, positioning is all about how an organization wants consumers to perceive its products and services and what strategies are necessary to reach this perceptual goal. Firms must decide if they want to position themselves close to their competitors so buyers can make direct comparisons or position themselves away from their competitors through differentiation strategies (such as low cost or distinct features and benefits).

Segmenting … Targeting … Positioning … Choosing the right market strategy can make or break an enterprise.

- Segmenting the market provides an effective way to focus marketing efforts.

- Targeting evaluates market segments and enables the firm to enter the most profitable segment(s).

- Positioning identifies how management wants buyers to perceive the firm's products or services.

Together, the three elements can dramatically affect the performance of an enterprise.

Progress Check

Directions: Read each question and respond in the space provided. Answers and page references appear on the page following the progress check questions.

1. All of the following variables are pertinent to a start-up company segmenting the consumer market except

    ( )   a.   language.

    ( )   b.   decision-making unit or purchasing process.

    ( )   c.   revenue/financial strength.

    ( )   d.   purchase occasion.

2. The plastics division of an American company is planning to market a new plastic resin internationally. Which of the following segmenting variables would be important to investigate?

    ( )   a.   Population demographics

    ( )   b.   Decision-making units

    ( )   c.   Psychographic customer characteristics

    ( )   d.   Purchase occasion

Match the market strategy to the appropriate action.

3. _____ Segmenting

4. _____ Targeting

5. _____ Positioning

a.   Provides an effective way to focus marketing efforts

b.   Identifies how management wants buyers to perceive firm's products or services

c.   Evaluates market segments and enables the firm to enter the most profitable segment(s)

Progress check answers

1. c (p. 3-120)

2. b (p. 3-121)

3. a (p. 3-126)

4. c (p. 3-126)

5. b (p. 3-126)

Managing Products and Services

Topic overview

When asked to describe the main difference between a product and a service, many people generally say a product is a "hard good" and then characterize a service as a "process." This topic looks at several aspects of managing both products and services.

Differences Between Products and Services

Consider the basic attributes listed in Figure 3-40 that are commonly used to differentiate products and services.

Figure 3-40: Product and Service Attributes

Product	Service
Tangible commodity	Intangible commodity
Durable good	Not durable
Can be inventoried	Consumed/used at delivery
Easily standardized	Delivery variations make standardization more difficult
Transaction orientation	Highly personal
Quality is more internally controlled	Quality is highly affected by customer perceptions
Low emotional investment	High emotional tie and customer sensitivity

The intangible transfer between the organization and the customer is perhaps the key distinction separating product manufacturing and service environments. Because services are intangible, they cannot be measured, tested, or verified in advance of delivery. It is not possible to inspect quality into a service or recall a defective service, as with a manufactured product.

Beyond these basic characteristics, labeling a firm as either a product or service organization can be a bit problematic. All organizations can be said to provide service to their customers—even those firms thought of as traditional hard good manufacturers. Likewise, organizations characterized as being in the service industry have tangible components. Note the following examples:

- General Motors Corporation manufactures automobiles, but they also have many pure service processes in their business portfolio that do not deliver a tangible end product to the customer. General Motors Acceptance Corporation (GMAC), a wholly owned subsidiary of General Motors, offers financing for a variety of needs (for example, automotive, home, insurance).

- Nordstrom provides a tangible product of clothing but has gained their main distinction in the industry by delivering outstanding customer service.

- Federal Express is a transportation company, but their name is typically associated with overnight delivery service and technological service innovations allowing customers easy access to information about shipments.

- The banking and financial industries are thought of as service industries, yet one can cite many tangible product offerings in both.

Further clouding a clear-cut distinction between product and service is the fact that all organizations have service departments that do not engage directly in production or other operating activities but provide some form of assistance or service vital to the overall success of the organization. Examples include human resources, internal auditing, cost accounting, purchasing, legal, day care, and an employee cafeteria.

Product Attributes

Markets exist only when there are buyers with needs who have the ability to purchase products or services and there are durable goods and services available to match those needs. People with needs and wants purchase a product or service to satisfy an organizational or household requirement. Hence the classifications of "consumer products" and "industrial products." But similar to product and service classifications, the industrial and consumer categories can overlap. Industrial businesses may be involved in the supply of components that end up in consumer products, or they may use consumer products in their processes.

In addition to the consumer and industrial classifications, other marketable entities exist. Government is perhaps the most notable of these. Both federal and state governments in the United States offer procurement bidding opportunities and contracts for a wide variety of products and services. The burgeoning global area also offers myriad supplier opportunities with governments worldwide.

Firm also try to determine why people buy specific products and brands. Both consumers and industrial buyers progress through a predictable decision-making sequence:

- Recognition—recognizing a need or a problem

- Research—collecting information about products/suppliers to satisfy the need or problem; identifying alternative products and suppliers

- Evaluation—evaluating all alternatives on the basis of important attributes

- Purchase decision—selecting a product to purchase or a supplier to contract with

Although the major decision-making stages are common to both types of buyers, the issues and activities are quite different. A consumer purchase is generally much less involved than supplier evaluation and buying criteria for industrial purchases.

The buying criteria that consumers and industrial buyers use in making purchasing decisions and whether brand was a key factor are always of interest.

Branding

Branding is typically described as a marketing strategy that creates a distinctive name and/or symbol (such as a logo, trademark, or packaging design) identifying a product or a manufacturer. The goal in branding is to differentiate a product or service from those of competitors.

The following terms and concepts are associated with branding.

- Brand is the actual term, logo, or design or a combination of these. For International Business Machines, IBM® is a brand.

- Brand name is the part of the brand that can be vocalized. IBM® is used as a brand name in product and service advertising.

- Service marks or trademarks (® or ™) are the part of the brand that is given legal protection through a first-use system, meaning that the first organization to publicly use a service mark or trademark has ownership of it.

- Brand equity refers to the value or strength of the brand and reflects the collective assets and liabilities associated with the brand (such as customer loyalty and willingness to pay a premium price, perceived quality and popularity, perceived value, awareness, market share, price, and distribution indices).

In strategic marketing, branding initiatives are intended to reflect an organization's goals and vision and articulate the firm's value proposition. A strategic brand perspective should create both customer value and shareholder value.

A strong brand offers several important advantages to buyers and sellers, as shown in Figure 3-41.

Figure 3-41: The Role of Brands

Advantages for Buyers	Advantages for Sellers
■ Helps identify/re-identify products quickly and accurately ■ Reduces purchase risk; provides an assurance of quality and consistency ■ Provides psychological rewards for purchasing brands that symbolize quality, status, and prestige	■ Facilitates repeat purchases that enhance financial performance ■ Facilitates new product introduction because of customer familiarity with the brand ■ Provides a point of focus for promotions ■ Creates a basic level of differentiation from competitors ■ Helps to build brand loyalty

Similar to positioning, there are different levels of branding. An organization may choose branding strategies for:

- A specific product (for example, Procter & Gamble's Ivory soap, Head & Shoulders shampoo, or Bounty paper towels).

- Entire product lines (for example, Palm Inc.'s line of personal digital assistants).

- A corporate name (for example, McDonald's in fast food).

- A combination strategy (for example, the General Electric name and GE logo used in combination with Whirlpool kitchen appliances).

- A private brand (for example, Safeway Stores contracting with suppliers to put the Safeway-Select label on supermarket products sold in Safeway grocery stores).

Properly leveraged, branding offers a firm significant opportunities in terms of visibility, market share, and higher sales. Investors also pay attention to the estimated value of a company's brand.

Labeling and packaging

Somewhat facetiously, it has been said that you cannot judge a book by its cover. But this is usually not the case (or the intent) in product labeling and packaging. Organizations often go to great lengths to assess their target audience, where they will be when they see a product, whether the intent is to entice the product purchase, how the product will be used, etc. Similarly, a buyer wants to know certain things by looking at the product label and package.

Typically, labeling and packaging are part of an integrated marketing communications program to promote/support brand awareness and fulfill any regulatory requirements. For many products (especially consumer ones), much consideration is given to competitive labeling and packaging and how to get the consumer to notice and select a specific product over other offerings.

General labeling considerations

Labeling serves a wide variety of purposes, as noted in Figure 3-42.

Figure 3-42: General Labeling Considerations

Purpose	Examples
Regulatory compliance	■ Compliance with current guidelines or requirements (such as food freshness dates, nutrition information, or organic qualifications) ■ Safety statements regarding product use
Recommended use	■ General how-to-use directions and intended product use ■ Age appropriateness for toys, games, etc.
Warning	■ Hazardous use/danger precautions (such as warnings about skin contact or fume inhalation) ■ Health hazards (such as the warning statement on cigarettes) ■ Precautions (such as allergy and interaction warnings on over-the-counter and prescription drugs)
General information	■ Any general information the producer wishes to promote having to do with the product or brand identity ■ Information about environmental friendliness (such as recyclable content or no animal testing) ■ Contact information for product questions/support and money-back guarantees

General packaging considerations

Packaging serves three general functions: display, convenience, and protection.

- **Display**

  Savvy marketers know that presentation is often just as important as the product. Packaging display concerns (sometimes referred to as the product "sizzle") focus primarily on those aesthetics that give a truly individual edge to any product and promote visibility and value. The options are limitless, ranging from stock-looking presentations to creative and memorable customized display presentations.

- **Convenience**

  Product suppliers need to be increasingly innovative and customer-focused with packaging that meets customer needs. Convenience considerations can range from the use of lightweight packaging materials to the easy opening and closing feature on a product or other more complicated applications.

- **Protection**

  Protective packaging generally encompasses all aspects of product packaging to prevent damage in transit, maintain the integrity/shelf life of the product during storage or use, and ensure consumer safety. Protective product packaging runs the gamut from cardboard boxes to bubble wrap, Styrofoam, and other cushioning materials, plastic laminating, shrink-wrapping, safety seals, and so forth.

Product support services

Numerous research studies have documented that customers will defect from a product because of the service attendant to it. Slow delivery, poor sales service, inaccurate invoices, unresponsive engineering modifications, and irritatingly unresponsive or slow responses to warranty or service calls are all commonly cited customer service complaints that, if ignored, escalate customer frustration. But even mundane inquiries requesting information about a product feature or how to perform a task can create customer dissatisfaction if not handled properly.

To keep customers happy and prevent customer defections, the same forethought and rigor that goes into a new product/service introduction or the production and distribution of a product should be applied to support services. Processes must be in place to facilitate the timely and satisfactory resolution of every customer contact, whether that contact is in person or via a telephone call center or an interactive voice response (IVR), electronically through a company Web site, or through any other medium.

Companies must demonstrate a commitment to building and maintaining support resources that the customer considers the appropriate medium. A software company catering to young professionals in the 25- to 50-year age bracket might provide primary customer care via the Web and give customers direct access to database files. But a small-goods manufacturer might depend solely upon affable agents for product support and not even consider alternative media.

It is widely accepted today that customer loyalty is at a premium. Providing post-sale customer support must be recognized as an integral part of the purchase of a product or a service. Effective support services must find the appropriate balance between personalized support and cost-saving technologies. Whatever the support processes chosen, they should be a natural reflection of customer needs.

Product Line and Product Mix Decisions

A firm may have a single product, a product line, or a mix of various product lines. Product line and product mix decisions deal with how a firm manages new and existing product interrelationships. In strategic marketing, companies are increasingly adopting team approaches for product line and product mix decisions.

Several organizational levels are typically involved. The specific individuals will vary depending on the organization. But it is quite common to have some combination of the following individuals participating in cross-functional teams:

- Individual product or brand managers—who act as sponsors or advocates of their products with research and development, operations, finance, sales, advertising, other departments, and SBUs

- A product group manager—who manages a group of products or brands and has group responsibilities in a business that has several products or brands

- SBU executives and/or managers—who assume principal responsibility for evaluation of the product portfolio performance and decision making about product acquisitions, research and development priorities, new product decisions, resource allocation, etc.

Today, small businesses and large corporations alike realize that merely having good or promising products is no guarantee of success. Given the myriad competitive pressures all organizations face and the ever-changing needs and wants of buyers, product success mandates a market-driven orientation and a focus on product strategies that offer superior customer value. Continuous organizational learning is at the heart of making new and existing product portfolio decisions. Ultimately, the marketing mix components must accomplish the target market objectives in a cost-effective manner.

Product Development

Innovations are critical to successfully compete in today's complex and rapidly changing business environments. But choosing the best strategy for pursuing innovation opportunities is not an easy task.

Those organizations that are successful innovators have:

- A culture that supports innovation.

- Effective processes that identify opportunities.

- Nimble processes that transform ideas into new product successes.

In other words, new products require careful planning. Market-driven companies must have processes in place to account for the activities listed in Figure 3-43. The size and type of firm, internal resources and capabilities, the need for new product growth, and external customer needs and wants all shape specific organizational strategies.

Figure 3-43: Planning for New Products

Activity	Description
Idea generation	■ Ranges from incremental improvements for existing products to new-to-the-world products ■ Often includes a variety of sources: company personnel, customers, competitors, inventors, acquisitions, and channel members ■ Generally targets within a range of current product and market involvement (for example, consistent with corporate and SBU strategies); may support more open-ended research
Screening and concept evaluation	■ Eliminates unpromising ideas as soon as possible to minimize time and money investments ■ Keeps the risk of rejecting good ideas at acceptable levels
Business analysis	■ Evaluates the commercial performance of a new product concept ■ Assesses estimated revenues, development costs, and profit projections ■ Results in a go/no-go decision
Product development and testing	■ Transforms the concept into one or more prototypes (produced by research and development rather than an established manufacturing process) ■ As feasible, gains customer feedback though trial use testing ■ Sets the stage for evaluating commercial production aspects (for example, whether the product can be manufactured in larger quantities at desired quality level and cost)
Market entry and testing	■ Involves targeting and positioning strategies (beginning at concept evaluation and proceeding through product development) ■ Includes several activities such as name selection, packaging, environmental considerations, product information, safety and service consideration ■ Gauges buyer response to new products ■ Evaluates reactions to one or more positioning strategies
Commercialization	■ Finalizes the marketing plan ■ Coordinates introduction activities with business functions ■ Implements the marketing strategy ■ Monitors and controls the product launch

New product planning applies to services as well as tangible products. Suffice it to say that products and services should not be developed in search of markets; a step-by-step planning process should be executed.

Product Life Cycle

As noted in the earlier discussion of product life cycle (PLC), an industry passes through a number of predictable stages or phases. Marketing strategies must be adjusted to correspond to changing conditions and reflect the buyer diversity and preferences of each stage.

Figure 3-44 summarizes general marketing approaches for the basic product life cycle stages.

Figure 3-44: Marketing Approaches for Product Life Cycle Stages

PLC Stage	Marketing Strategy
Embryonic	■ Inform target audience of product—build general awareness. ■ Establish the brand through brand development activities such as advertising. ■ Recover development cost.

Growth	■ Reinforce the brand though marketing efforts.
	■ Build competitive barrier to market entry by:
	    ▪ Gaining market share.
	    ▪ Reducing costs.
	    ▪ Continuing product development.

Shakeout	■ Protect and improve brand name. ■ Match the organization's distinctive capabilities to market value opportunities.
Maturity	■ Maintain loyal customers. ■ Reinvent product with product repositioning efforts to appeal to different market segments.
Decline	■ Modify and/or repackage the product. ■ Reduce costs related to administration, product development, and marketing.

Marketing Strategies for Service Firms

As noted earlier, products and services have several inherent differences. Services are distinct because they are intangible, they cannot be placed in inventory, and they are often consumed at the time of production or soon thereafter. Services also tend to be highly variable; consistency and quality cannot be engineered into delivery as with products.

Another distinguishing characteristic of services is that they are typically linked to the people who produce them. In service organizations, front-line employees not only deliver the goods, they are the goods. For example, the courtesy, efficiency, and professionalism of bank tellers, commercial airline flight crews, or hospital staff are typically what people remember about those service experiences.

Establishing a brand identity in a service industry generally requires building a bridge to the tangible aspects of the business—the people who produce the service or are somehow associated with the service. That is why airlines often showcase their employees or hospitals include physician and nursing staffs in advertising. Some companies enlist well-know personalities to pitch their services. For years, American Express built brand identity for its credit card services by having famous celebrities do commercials.

Service marketing has another important component in addition to branding and positioning through people. Service firms must also be competitor-oriented. Competitive information collected from customers via mail, telephone, and in-person research, observations of competitors, published customer and competitive data, and benchmarking should all be integrated in marketing strategies.

So for all the differences between products and services, it should be noted that success in service marketing does have a fundamental shared characteristic with product marketing: customer focus. Winners in service marketing routinely talk with customers in order to understand their real requirements and determine what they will need in the future as their requirements change. Customers become part of the strategic marketing process.

International Marketing

Conceptually, international marketing strategies are similar to domestic strategies. An organization needs to implement a systematic approach to ensure that the resulting strategies are consistent, aligned, and supportive of the corporate, competitive, and functional strategies. But the global environment is far more complex and uncertain than domestic markets; several fundamental modifications are necessary to develop successful marketing strategies.

Global market opportunity analysis

In determining which targets to pursue, a firm needs to objectively assess how company competencies and capabilities will support expansion to international markets. This foreign market assessment must evaluate home country constraints in the headquarters country (for example, political, legal, economic) as well as host country constraints in the target country (for example, economic, political, competitive, culture, distribution structure, currency, geography). Does the home country government have trade restrictions, antitrust regulations, or other legal factors that will impact an expansion to global operation? Will the political and economic climate in the host country support a new foreign market entrant?

Certainly, instant communications, global supply networks, and international finance markets can support expansion in global markets. But the market analysis must thoroughly evaluate the gamut of what-if scenarios and potential threats.

Target market adaptations

Oftentimes the marketing mix must be adapted for the international target markets. The product itself may require modifications, ranging from the brand name to features/style, packaging, service, and warranty. Pricing, promotion, and distribution could all require adaptations, too.

Companies must decide the extent to which products and strategies can be standardized across international markets (for example, standardized across multiple countries) or adapted to account for buyer differences across national and regional boundaries. Will the same product or service appeal to several different global markets? Or to what extent will country or regional preference require modifications?

It is generally problematic to try imposing a global brand on all markets. A brand's image is rarely the same throughout the world. In the United States, for example, Honda automobiles are synonymous with quality and reliability. In Japan, quality is a given, not a differential. Honda automobiles in Japanese markets mean speed, youth, and energy.

With screening information collected and target adaptations considered, a firm can then proceed to develop an international marketing strategy and move forward with implementation and control plans.

Global partnerships

Some firms competing in global markets opt to form cooperative relationships with other organizations. Joint ventures and strategic alliances can offer significant advantages in gaining market access and leveraging capabilities of individual firms. But again, benefits and limitations must be considered. An international partnership can provide mutual benefit to both parties. However, many partnerships fall apart due to an asymmetry of interests or a shift in the power balance between partners. When international partnerships derail, the emergent multinational is usually left at a distinct disadvantage.

Overall, the global arena is knowledge- and information-intensive. Entering an international market successfully usually requires much more than simple tweaking of the home marketing strategy. The lure of increased sales and low-cost labor and/or raw materials in global markets cannot preclude careful forethought and planning.

Progress Check

Directions: Read each question and respond in the space provided. Answers and page references appear on the page following the progress check questions.

1. Advertising expenditures are typically the highest during which product life cycle stage?

   ( ) a. Embryonic

   ( ) b. Shakeout

   ( ) c. Maturity

   ( ) d. Decline

2. Marketing, sales, and field support personnel at a medical device company have finalized the marketing plan and are coordinating activities for a new product launch. This product planning process is **best** described as

   ( ) a. market entry.

   ( ) b. business analysis.

   ( ) c. commercialization.

   ( ) d. screening.

Match the following product and service marketing terms to the appropriate activities.

3. _____ Branding

4. _____ Line and mix decisions

5. _____ Labeling and packaging

a. Integrated marketing communications activities to promote/support brand awareness and fulfill any regulatory requirements

b. Activities dealing with how a firm manages new and existing product interrelationships

c. Activities intended to create a distinctive name and/or symbol identifying a product or a manufacturer

Progress check answers

1. a (p. 3-135)

2. c (p. 3-134)

3. c (p. 3-131)

4. b (p. 3-134)

5. a (p. 3-132)

Pricing Strategy

Topic overview

As businesses and consumers demand more for less, global competition increases, growth slows in many markets, and myriad other industry factors create competitive pressures, setting appropriate product pricing has become an important activity for most firms. Charge too much in an attempt to capture market share or generate a quick return on investment, and the product or service may not sell; charge too little, and significant revenue and profit losses may result.

Price is also an important influence on a buyer's product value perceptions. Once implemented, a pricing strategy can be difficult to alter, especially if the change calls for a significant increase.

Suffice it to say that pricing decisions have substantial consequences. So how can companies appropriately price products? Consideration of internal and external factors and an analysis of various pricing approaches and strategies are fundamental activities.

Internal and External Factors

Several factors influence how a firm sets prices for its products. Figure 3-45 shows how these factors are generally categorized as internal or external.

Figure 3-45: Internal and External Factors Affecting Pricing

Internal Factors	External Factors
■ Materials costs	■ The industry
■ Development/manufacturing costs	■ Product maturity and stage in product life cycle
■ Overhead expenses	■ Buyers' value perception
■ Labor costs	■ Buyers' price sensitivity
■ Cycle time	■ Distribution channels
■ Time to market	■ Immediate competition
■ Estimated product or service life	■ Threat of substitutes
■ Service costs	■ Government laws and other regulatory policies
■ Product portfolio mix	■ Economic conditions
■ Bundling opportunities and/or cross-selling	■ Price that the market will bear
■ Target costs	
■ Corporate objectives and strategic fit	
■ Customer discounts for large purchases	

Pricing Approaches

Price is usually based on cost, demand, competition, or some combination of these factors. Many methods are available for setting prices. Firms typically consider the following basic approaches:

- Cost-based pricing
- Value-based pricing
- Competition-based pricing

Cost-based pricing

Cost-based pricing is described as "setting the floor" for a firm's pricing options. Such pricing reveals a product's lowest possible price levels. Two methods are associated with cost-based pricing:

- **Break-even pricing**
  Break-even pricing is used to establish a frame of reference; it is not a stand-alone method for setting price. Essentially, it determines the number of units that must be sold at a set price to cover all fixed and variable costs. The following formula is used in break-even pricing:

$$\text{Break-Even (Units)} = \frac{\text{Total Fixed Costs}}{\text{Unit Price} - \text{Unit Variable Cost}}$$

Once the break-even value is known, a firm can assess the feasibility of exceeding the break-even price and generating a profit. The price selected is typically higher than the break-even price, factoring in both demand and competition.

- **Cost-plus pricing**
  Under the **cost-plus pricing** method, a firm uses an accurate analysis of costs per unit as a basis for calculating the selling price for a product or service. A margin representing a minimally accepted return on investment (for example, 10% to 30%) is added to cost to set the price.

The formula used in markup pricing is:

$$\text{Price} = \frac{\text{Average Unit Cost}}{1 - \text{Markup Percentage*}}$$

* Where markup percentage is expressed as a decimal

Cost-plus pricing reveals the lowest reasonable price level for a product. If market conditions cannot support the price, the firm must reconsider its strategy.

The challenge of cost-based pricing is accurately accounting for all the costs that should be allocated to products or services. Firms have a tendency to overlook legitimate items (for example, research costs, customer goodwill, and overhead expenses) that should be factored into the cost calculation.

Value-based pricing

Value-based (value-added or **demand-based) pricing** estimates the value of the product or service to the buyer. The objective in setting a value-based price is to determine how much the buyer is willing to pay based on the product's or service's contribution to the buyer's needs and wants.

When using value-based pricing, a firm sets a price for its product or service based on unique characteristics that it thinks consumers value and for which they are willing to pay a premium price. Differentiation can come from a variety of factors, such as product features, service, and quality.

Value-based pricing is widely used for consumer and industrial products. Internet auctions are a recent application of the value-based pricing method.

Competition-based pricing

As the name implies, competition-based (market-based) pricing takes competitors' prices into account. Firms consider the price of other similar products or services in the marketplace and attempt to keep their price within those boundaries. Prices are set equal to or at some percentage either above or below competition prices.

The airline industry is a typical example of competition-based pricing. Market leaders usually publicize fare increases or decreases, and others in the industry adjust their prices accordingly.

New Product Pricing Strategies

Companies invest significant amounts of time, effort, and money in developing or acquiring new products. Unfortunately, there is no crystal ball to predict probable market response to the new product.

In setting a new product price, a firm must consider the:

- Cost of the product.

- Projected life span of the product.

- Estimated responses of buyers to alternative prices.

- Probable competitive reaction.

There are two basic new product pricing strategies: market skimming and market penetration.

Market skimming pricing

Market skimming pricing sets a high price for a new product with the objective of gaining maximum revenues layer by layer from the segments willing to pay the high price. The underlying logic is to convey to the buyer that because the price is high the product offers superior value.

Setting a high price for a new product can work if:

- Product features and benefits support the higher price.

- Quality and image support the higher price.

- Enough buyers want the product at that price.

- Cost of producing a small volume is not high.

- Competitors are not able to enter the market easily.

The challenge in using market skimming is that the high price may prove to be unrealistic. Buyers may disagree with the value proposition, and there may not be sufficient demand. A high price may also leave too much room for competitors to maneuver.

Market penetration pricing

Market penetration pricing is a new product pricing strategy that uses a relatively low market entry price with the objective of building volume or market position. A low price is set with the goal of attracting a large number of buyers to win a large market share.

Setting a low initial penetration price can work in the following situations:

- In new or underdeveloped markets in which customers are price-sensitive

- When product benefits are extremely high and, therefore, desirable

- When lower production and distribution costs result as sales volume increases

- When a low price will be sufficient differential to ward off the competition

The main advantage of a penetration strategy is that a supplier can build a strong presence in the market quickly and, ideally, become a market leader. The downside of using low price to undercut competition is that it usually sacrifices profitability. It may also backfire and ignite a price war.

Launching a new product and setting price appropriately requires careful analysis and astute communication. Faulty pricing can undermine the product's value proposition.

A recent McKinsey study found that 80% to 90% of poor pricing decisions are situations in which companies undercharge for products. The predicament of trying to adjust low prices up and inflate a product's value proposition is more than painful; for many companies, it becomes an impossible task.

Product Mix Pricing Strategies

When a firm has more than one product (or service), management must assess the interrelationships between those products. Careful consideration must be given to similarities and differences in the product mix and a determination made about pricing based on cost, demand, and/or competition.

Typically, not all products are equally profitable. Price structure deals with how individual items in a product mix are priced in relation to each other.

Individual products may be aimed at the same target market or at different end users. Many scenarios illustrate this point:

- Chemical products manufacturers such as Monsanto Company and Dow Chemical Company sell the same herbicide and insecticide products for agricultural crops, turf and ornamental use, and structural protection; the same products may be sold for commercial or home use.

- Large chains such as Home Depot, Sam's Club, and Costco sell many of the same products to businesses and consumers.

- Car manufacturers use essentially the same body and add luxury features for different target markets.

- Department stores and supermarkets offer store brands and premium brands.

There are many different ways to price multiple products. Key characteristics of common product mix strategies are summarized in Figure 3-46.

Figure 3-46: Product Mix Pricing Strategies

Strategy	Description
Product line pricing	■ Sets price steps between product line items ■ Establishes pricing based on the features, benefits, or some other aspects of parts of the range **Examples:** Car washes, where basic, mid-range, and deluxe packages are offered for different services and prices; different sizes of fast food menu items sold for different prices
Optional product pricing	■ Attempts to increase the amount a customer spends once they start to buy ■ Includes optional add-ons or accessories to increase the overall price of the product or service **Examples:** A tire dealer offering a lifetime replacement guarantee for a small additional charge tacked on to the new tire purchase price; home appliances with extended warranties offered at the time of purchase
Captive product pricing	Charges a premium price for products that must be used with or complement the main product **Examples:** A razor manufacturer charging a low price and then recouping its margin (and more) from the sale of refill blades that fit the razor; certain software upgrades
By-product pricing	■ Sets a price for by-products in order to make the main product's price more competitive ■ Prices low-value by-products to get rid of them **Examples:** Inedible meat-packing products sold to rendering facilities to make pet food, soap, chemicals, and fertilizers; wood waste/scraps sold to oriented strand board manufacturers for use as reconstituted building material
Product bundle pricing	Combines several products in the same package and offers them together at a reduced price **Examples:** Travel packages that bundle hotel and airfare; matching lipstick and nail color packaged together; movie videos and DVDs bundled with CD soundtracks

Price Adjustment Strategies

Pricing strategies require continuous monitoring. Changing external market conditions, actions of competitors, changes in the product life cycle, and several other factors may lead to the following price adjustment strategies:

- **Discount and allowance pricing**—price reductions to reward buyers who pay their bills early or promptly

- **Segmented (discriminatory) pricing**—adjusting prices to allow for differences in customers, products, and locations, considering the requirements of the Robinson-Patman Act and the Clayton Act covered in Part 1

- **Psychological pricing**—adjusting prices for psychological effects; trying to get the buyer to respond on an emotional perception rather than rational basis (for example, charging $799 versus $800 or even 99¢ versus $1)

- **Promotional pricing**—temporarily reducing prices to increase short-run sales or pricing to promote a product through approaches such as coupons, rebate offers, and "buy one, get one free" offers

- **Geographical pricing**—adjusting prices to account for the geographic location of the customer (for example, shipping costs based on zones)

- **International pricing**—adjusting prices based on international market conditions

Changing the price of a product or service offering is a common practice. But price adjustments can be a risky proposition, regardless of whether the change is an increase or decrease.

Price Elasticity and Other Pricing Influences

Price elasticity of demand measures the responsiveness of quantity demanded to a change in price when all other factors are held constant. It is often used to develop a sense of buyers' sensitivity to alternate prices.

Price elasticity of demand is represented by the following formula:

$$\text{Price Elasticity of Demand} = \frac{\%\text{ Change in Quantity Demanded}}{\%\text{ Change in Price}}$$

The ratio is generally negative because the quantity demanded decreases when the price increases. However, the absolute value usually is taken and price elasticity is reported as a positive number. Further, because the calculation uses proportionate changes, the result is a "unit-less" number and does not depend on the units in which the price and quantity are expressed.

A quantity demanded is said to be relatively elastic when people buy more at lower prices; a price change will cause an even larger change in quantity demanded. In some situations, however, the opposite may occur and people may buy more at higher prices; buyers equate price with quality when they are unable to evaluate the product or service and may perceive greater prestige for higher priced products. Whether people buy disproportionately more due to higher or lower price, price will be considered relatively elastic if the percentage change in the amount demanded is greater than the percentage change in price.

The quantity demanded is considered relatively inelastic when a price change will cause less of a change in quantity demanded. When the quantity demanded of a product is inelastic, a price increase results in a revenue increase, because the revenue lost by the relatively small decrease in quantity is less than the revenue gained from the higher price.

Estimating price/quantity relationships using price elasticity is highly theoretical. Firms can use methods other than price elasticity (or in addition to price elasticity) to estimate the sensitivity of customers to alternative prices. Test marketing, historical studies of price and quantity data, and consumer research on price points are all possibilities. Such approaches, in conjunction with management experience and judgment, can help to estimate the sensitivity of sales to prices.

Bargaining power of buyers or sellers

The bargaining power of either the buyer or the seller can also impact price. Consider the following examples:

- A large buyer can pressure a seller for discounted prices.

- A dominant seller, if monopolistic, can command and receive a higher price.

- A dominant seller can afford to sell at a lower price to drive out competitors.

Note: Topic 1, "Strategic and Tactical Planning," in the first section of this part of the CMA Learning System examines the bargaining power of the buyer and seller in more detail.

Public policy influences

Public policy is yet another influencing factor in product or service pricing. A wide variety of laws and regulations, ethical considerations, and product taxes can influence the pricing of goods and services.

Legal constraints

Many pricing practices undergo government scrutiny. In the United States, for example, government regulations preclude the following practices:

- Price fixing—price collusion between competitors in distribution channels

- Price discrimination—charging different customers different prices without an underlying cost basis

- Deceptive pricing—misleading a buyer with an initial high price and then subsequently reducing it to the normal price

- Partial/deceptive information disclosure—violating requirements in the form and/or availability of price information, interest rates, credit terms, and any other financial charges

Ethical considerations

Ethical considerations are more subjective in nature than legal factors, but they are nonetheless important in pricing. Many firms voluntarily develop and apply ethical guidelines in pricing decisions and practices. But deciding what is and what is not ethical is generally not clear-cut.

The high prices charged by the prescription drug industry in the United States are often the subject of government, business, and consumer concerns. Although suppliers defend high drug prices due to research and development costs, many critics question the ethics of the industry pricing and seek price controls.

Tax considerations

Public policy and pressure often comes to bear on pricing through taxes. Sales taxes, for example, may influence the prices of specific commodities. Cigarette taxes and gasoline taxes are two common examples.

Progress Check

Directions: Read each question and respond in the space provided. Answers and page references appear on the page following the progress check questions.

1. A company prices a new product significantly higher than existing products based on market research indicating that industrial customers are willing to pay more for the superior technical benefits. This pricing strategy is an example of

    ( )   a.   cost-based pricing.

    ( )   b.   cost-plus pricing.

    ( )   c.   competition-based pricing.

    ( )   d.   value-added pricing.

2. All of the following characteristics pertain to market skimming pricing **except**

    ( )   a.   Quality and image support a higher price.

    ( )   b.   Low price provides competitive differential.

    ( )   c.   The threat of new entrants in the market is low.

    ( )   d.   Strategies equate the price to superior value.

Match the following pricing strategies to the appropriate description.

3. _____ Bundle pricing

4. _____ Discount or allowance pricing

5. _____ Penetration pricing

6. _____ Psychological pricing

a.   Charging $99 rather than $100 in order to entice buyers

b.   Combining several products in the same package and offering them together at a reduced price

c.   Reducing prices to reward buyers who pay their bills early or promptly

d.   Using a relatively low market entry price with the objective of building volume or market position

Progress check answers

1. d (p. 3-143)

2. b (p. 3-143)

3. b (p. 3-145)

4. c (p. 3-146)

5. d (p. 3-144)

6. a (p. 3-146)

Topic 6
Promotional Mix and Distribution Strategy

Topic overview

The motion picture Field of Dreams popularized the expression "If you build it, they will come." But developing products or services without a promotion and distribution strategy is a high-risk proposition. Organizations must inform people about their products and services and persuade buyers, distribution channel members, and the public at large to purchase their brands.

The Marketing Communications Mix

Traditionally, marketing relied on a mix of elements focused on a product. The traditional four Ps of marketing are:

- **Product**—goods and services offered to customers; includes all product-related features such as packaging and warranties.

- **Price**—the cost of the product or service to the customer in dollars and cents.

- **Place (or distribution)**—the physical location(s) where products and services are delivered to the customer.

- **Promotion**—all advertising, personal selling, and other activities related to the selling of products and services.

Strategic marketing is driven by customer needs, and today many marketers think in terms of the four Cs of marketing:

- **Consumer** or **customer** replaces product. This recognizes the fact that organizations must be customer-focused and must study customer wants and needs. Then products and services can be designed to meet those needs.

- **Cost** replaces price. Cost analysis goes beyond calculating price in dollars and cents. It looks at the total value proposition of products and services and takes into account all of the issues that customers consider before making a purchase.

- **Convenience** replaces place. Convenience and cost/value are often interrelated, as consumers value their time. For example, being able to order a product online may make a purchase easier for prospective customers, thereby increasing sales.

- **Communication** replaces promotion. Firms use advertising, public relations, and other techniques as avenues for dialogue with the customer. The organization is listening to what customers want (through their actions and words) rather than telling customers what they need.

Every week, companies around the world spend billions of dollars promoting their products. Large and small, with big budgets or limited resources, all firms need to effectively manage their promotional expenditures and ensure that dollars spent support corporate, competitive, and functional strategies for bringing products to market.

Promotional strategy generally describes the set of interrelated communications activities—the promotional mix—firms use to communicate with customers, market targets, and other relevant audiences. Advertising, sales promotions, public relations, personal selling, and direct marketing are the tools comprising a promotional strategy. The purpose of a promotional strategy is to achieve management's desired communications objectives for each of its target audiences.

Figure 3-47 provides a basic definition of each promotional tool.

Figure 3-47: The Promotional Mix

Advertising	Any form of nonpersonal communication describing an organization, product, or idea that is paid for by a specific sponsor; attempts to influence the behavior of buyers by providing a persuasive selling message about products and/or services
Sales promotions	Various promotional activities, including use of the Internet, samples, coupons, point-of-purchase displays, trade shows, contests, and trade incentives; used to target buyers, communicate with the public, respond to special occasions, and/or creative an incentive to purchase products and/or services
Public relations	Communications about a company and its products placed in the commercial media but not paid for directly by the sponsor; encourages the relevant media (for example, a trade journal) to include company-released information in media communications
Personal selling	Verbal communication between a salesperson (or a sales team) and one or more prospective buyers with the objective of informing and persuading them to purchase products or services
Direct marketing	Various communications channels, including direct mail, catalogs, telemarketing, "infomercials," television selling, radio selling, print (magazine and newspaper) selling, electronic shopping, and kiosk shopping; enables companies to make direct contact with buyers

Each form has specific objectives, strengths, and limitations, and each promotion may vary widely in scope. Through a series of planning, implementation, and evaluation activities, a promotional strategy combines all of these elements into an integrated marketing communications (IMC) strategy that capitalizes on the advantages of each form and results in a cost-effective promotional mix.

Increasingly, integrated marketing communications are replacing traditional fragmented marketing programs. IMC strategies are generally characterized by:

▪ Comprehensive programs—Advertising, sales promotions, public relations, personal selling, and direct marketing are all considered during planning.

▪ Unified messages—All messages are supportive of a unified marketing theme.

▪ Targeted programs—All programs have the same or related target markets.

▪ Coordinated execution—All communications components are coordinated.

Relationship marketing is a pivotal part of IMC. In relationship marketing, the goal is to develop and maintain mutually satisfying arrangements between the buyer and seller.

Advertising, Sales Promotion, and Public Relations

Advertising

Organizations used paid advertising to communicate via one or more forms of media (for example, television, radio, print, Internet, direct mail, outdoor advertising).

Once the target audience is identified and described, there are four basic steps in advertising:

- Setting specific advertising objectives
- Setting the advertising budget
- Developing a creative strategy
- Evaluating the effectiveness of the strategy

Setting specific advertising objectives

Advertising objectives are set along a continuum that ranges from a general level of exposure and awareness to a specific profit contribution level.

The primary concern in setting objectives at the general level is the inability to determine the impact on purchasing behavior. It is problematic to assess how much exposure to advertising can increase the likelihood that people will buy a product.

The closer the advertising objectives are tied to the company's profit goals, the more they need to be linked to and influence the customer's purchase decision. But the specific impact can be difficult to measure due to the effect of other factors on sales and profits.

In spite of these issues, advertising has several advantages:

- Low cost per exposure
- Variety of media
- Control of exposure
- Consistent message content
- Opportunity for creative message design

Setting the advertising budget

Determining the optimal budget for advertising is challenging, because so many other factors can influence sales. Budgeting often tries to improve promotion effectiveness compared to past results.

Figure 3-48 lists the budgeting approaches firms typically use.

Figure 3-48: Advertising Budgeting Approaches

Method	Description
Objective and task	■ Sets communications objectives; determines the tasks necessary to achieve the objectives; adds up the costs ■ Popular method, but accuracy is highly dependent on the experience of the marketing team
Percentage of sales	■ Calculated as a percentage of sales ■ Often based on past expenditures
Competitive parity	■ Based on how much competitors spend ■ Difficult to account for different competitors' promotional strategies (for example, specific targets, promotional objectives, and promotional components)
"All you can afford"	■ Management sets how much can be spent on promotion ■ Driven by the reality of budget limitations prevalent in most companies

Developing a creative strategy

Creative strategy is guided by the market target and the positioning strategy. The creative theme attempts to effectively communicate the intended position to buyers.

A campaign is usually designed to do either of the following:

- Maintain the status quo and support an established brand.

- Change market conditions (for example, reposition a brand, expand the market for a brand, launch a new product).

Messages may be intended to provide specific information (such as product benefits), or they may be designed to communicate more subtle imagery and symbolism.

Evaluating the effectiveness of the strategy

Evaluation criteria should be set before the advertising strategy is implemented. Measuring the effectiveness of an advertising campaign provides a firm with feedback on which future decisions can be based.

As noted previously, the impact of advertising on sales can be difficult to pinpoint due to other factors influencing sales and profits. A regression analysis of historical data is sometimes used.

Several other methods can be used to assess the achievement of attitude, change, awareness, and exposure objectives.

A few examples include:

- Services such as Nielsen's TV ratings for the major media or Statistical Research, Inc. (SRI) for radio audience measurement, use of the yellow pages, and other media.

- Recall tests to measure consumer awareness of a specific ad.

- Test marketing.

- Consumer panels.

Sales promotion

As noted in Figure 3-47 (The Promotional Mix), many activities fit in a sales promotion program. Organizations may direct sales promotion activities to a variety of audiences:

- Industrial buyers—use of the Internet, trade shows, samples, application guides, and product information reports as well as specialty advertising items such as pens, calendars, and memo pads to maintain awareness of brands and the company name

- Consumers—use of coupons, rebates, contests, and other awards; sponsoring of events that consumers attend (for example, Visa sponsoring the Triple Crown in thoroughbred horse racing) or sponsoring of individual sports celebrities (for example, the United States Post Office sponsoring Lance Armstrong in cycling events)

- Value chain members (wholesale and retail)—use of the Internet, catalogs, and product information as well as specialty advertising items

- Salespeople—use of incentives (for example, contests, prizes, and recognition programs) and informational activities (for example, point-of-sale presentation kits) to motivate and support company sales forces

Regardless of the wide variety of possible promotional activities and target audiences, sales promotions are planned, implemented, and evaluated using tactics that are quite similar to those used in advertising. The communication task(s) to be accomplished must be defined, specific objectives must be identified, a budget needs to be set, and the relative cost-effectiveness of methods must be evaluated.

Sales promotion objectives

Overall, sales promotions are intended to build sales volume. They can be used to target various groups in the value chain and provide extra value or incentives to encourage immediate sales.

Sales promotion budgets

The same approaches used to determine advertising budgets (objective and task, percentage of sales, competitive parity, "all you can afford") apply to promotion budgets.

Sales promotion evaluation

Evaluating the effectiveness of sales promotion methods helps firms to determine those that offer the best results/cost combination. Evaluation assesses how well the promotion objective was met. For example, a trade show is evaluated by the number of contacts generated and converted to purchase. Or a firm can track its coupon redemption or rebate offers.

The primary advantage of sales promotions is that they offer a wide array of communication, incentive, and pricing capabilities. Incentives and price promotions are usually successful in triggering sales. Many types of sales promotions can be easily tracked and evaluated.

A general caution for sales promotions is that they should not be used as a substitute for advertising or personal selling; they should be used to augment other promotional initiatives. Control is also important to prevent abuse of incentives, coupons, and free offers.

Public relations

Public relations is primarily directed toward gaining public understanding and acceptance through the inclusion of company-released information in commercial media. Because a company does not purchase the coverage, the publicity is a cost-effective promotion method.

Public relations usually deals with issues rather than products or services and is used to establish and maintain goodwill with the public at large or employees. Examples of public relations include publicity about some positive community participation, a news release intended for financial analysts, or an announcement of participation and support of charitable events.

Generally speaking, people like to buy from people they know and like. Increasingly, both business customers and consumers want to know about the company behind the products. As people have growing ethical, social, and environmental concerns, they want to be reassured that the companies they are doing business with share their values and concerns. Many organizations retain public relations firms or consultants to actively pursue publicity opportunities.

But public relations can cut both ways. Although the coverage is free and cost-effective, a company cannot always control the message to the extent possible with other promotional strategies. As a result, the publicity a firm receives can be negative if the media deems the topic to be of public interest.

Personal Selling and Direct Marketing

Through personal selling, salespeople have face-to-face contact with buyers. Direct marketing reaches those same customers by mail, telephone, television, and computer.

Companies often combine these two methods. Although the promotional strategies vary in execution, they both allow an organization to communicate one on one with target audiences.

Personal selling

True to its label, personal selling is a type of personal communication that attempts to inform customers and persuade them to purchase products or services. Specific sales responsibilities range from simply taking orders to executing a consultative sale.

The target market, the specific product features, the distribution channel, the distribution policies, and the pricing strategies are all key factors shaping the salesperson's role. The role of selling must be aligned to the organization's marketing strategy.

Relationship marketing is a highly consultative personal selling approach. It usually involves a team (for example, a salesperson, a technical support representative, and a marketing manager) to assess client needs and match those needs to a product or service application. Price is relevant, but it is not the primary driver in the sale.

Through relationship marketing, team members (working individually or together) will:

- Communicate directly with the prospect or customer.

- Listen to his or her concerns.

- Answer specific questions.

- Provide additional information.

- Inform, persuade, and recommend products or services.

Across the range of personal selling roles, relationship marketing allows a firm the greatest freedom to adjust a message to satisfy customers' information needs. The consulting relationship allows companies to build customer satisfaction and increase long-term customer loyalty.

Direct marketing

The primary goal of direct marketing promotions is to obtain a purchase response from individual buyers.

Direct marketing approaches

Organizations can choose from a wide variety of direct marketing approaches, as illustrated in Figure 3-49.

Figure 3-49: Direct Marketing Approaches

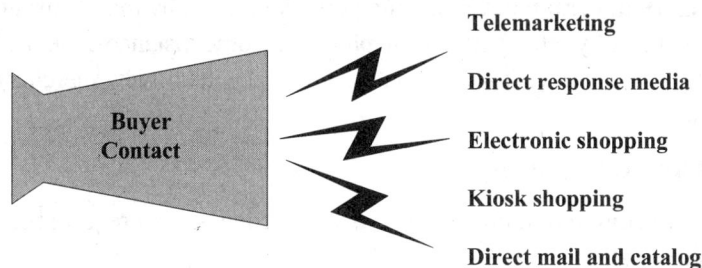

Telemarketing. Telemarketing uses the telephone to establish direct contact between the buyer and the seller. The objective is to fulfill all or some of the sales function. Low contact costs and quick access are the benefits of the method.

Direct response media. The objective of direct response media is to persuade the person hearing or reading the ad to order the product or service. Radio, magazines, and newspapers offer a broad spectrum of direct marketing advertisements. Television avenues (such as the Home Shopping Network) market a wide range of products discounted below list prices. Customers use a toll-free number to place an order. Specific products (such as music recordings, housewares, and magazines) are also sold through television commercials with toll-free numbers or mail-order addresses.

Very low exposure cost is the primary benefit of direct response media. Given the low cost, return on investment for buyers can also be substantial.

Electronic shopping. Through electronic shopping, companies can order from their suppliers via the computer and both consumers and businesses can place orders via the Internet.

Electronic methods have the following benefits:

- Facilitate routine repurchasing of standard items.

- Support a field sales force for standard ordering tasks.

- Reduce order cycles and inventory stocks.

- Cut costs.

- Monitor customer preferences.

Some sellers still resist using electronic linkages with suppliers, but the trend toward electronic ties is growing. With the growth of virtual shopping on the Internet, many more business are exploring direct marketing to computer users.

Kiosk shopping. Kiosks are akin to vending machines in concept, as they allow buyers to purchase from a small facility or stand in a retail complex (for example, shopping mall) or another public area (for example, airport). Some kiosks have Internet linkages (for example, for issuing airline or event tickets or flight insurance). Products that buyers have familiarity with from prior purchases are well-suited for kiosks. Sellers gain exposure to many people, and the buyer benefits from the convenience.

Direct mail and catalog. Contacting potential buyers by mail is usually designed to generate orders by return mail or by phone. In some instances, the method is intended to encourage buyers to visit a retail outlet or a Web site to view merchandise and make a purchase.

Direct marketing strategies

Direct marketing promotions vary widely in scope, but all require basic strategy development steps to:

- Identify market targets.

- Set objectives.

- Position the strategy.

- Formulate a communications plan.

- Implement and manage the program.

- Evaluate effectiveness against performance expectations.

Direct marketing may be the primary form of contact with the customer (such as L. L. Bean in the outdoor apparel catalog clothing market), or it may be one of several methods a firm uses in some combination (such as the women's intimate apparel retailer Victoria's Secret use of catalog, direct response media, television advertising, and electronic shopping).

Direct marketing ethical issues

The Direct Marketing Association (DMA) serves as the primary professional association for the direct marketing industry. The association promotes the general philosophy that self-regulated ethical measures are preferable to governmental mandates.

The association encourages widespread use of sound business practices related to a wide variety of direct marketing issues of concern such as (but not limited to):

- Terms of use (for example, honesty; clarity of offers and representations; disclosure; postage, shipping, and handling).

- Advance consent marketing (where the consumer gives consent to receive and pay for goods or services in the future on a continuing or periodic basis unless and until the consumer cancels the plan).

- Marketing to children (for example, parental responsibility and information from or about children).

- Special offers and claims (for example, use of the word "free," price comparisons, testimonials, and guarantees).

- Sweepstakes (for example, chances of winning, rules, prizes, and premiums).

- Fulfillment (for example, product availability and shipment).

- Collection, use, and maintenance of marketing data (for example, collection, use, and transfer of personally identifiable data, market list usage, and information security).

- Online marketing (for example, commercial solicitations online).

- Telephone marketing (for example, reasonable hours, conversation taping, and use of automated dialing equipment).

- Fund raising (for example, providing financial information regarding use of funds).

- Laws, codes, and regulations (for example, laws and regulations of the United States Postal Service, the Federal Trade Commission, the Federal Communications Commission, the Federal Reserve Board, and other applicable federal, state, and local laws governing advertising, marketing practices, and the transaction of business).

For specific information about these ethical issues in direct marketing and additional information concerning other measures, visit the DMA Web site, www.the-dma.org/guidelines/ethicalguidelines.

Distribution Channels

A **distribution channel** is a group of interrelated and interdependent institutions and agencies functioning as a network. All parties in a distribution channel cooperate and pool their efforts to distribute a product to end users. An effective and efficient distribution channel is an important factor in creating and sustaining organizational competitive advantage.

Figure 3-50 shows simple examples of distribution channels for consumer products and industrial products.

Figure 3-50: Common Distribution Channels

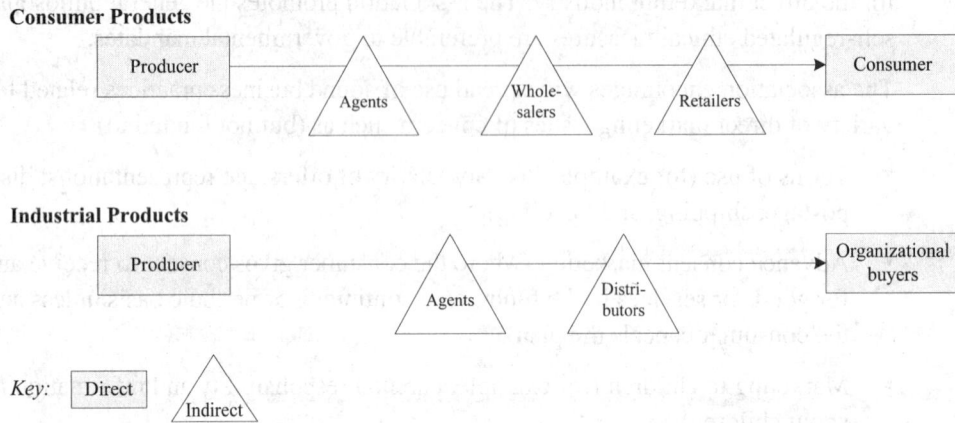

Consumer Products

Producer → Agents → Whole-salers → Retailers → Consumer

Industrial Products

Producer → Agents → Distri-butors → Organizational buyers

Key: Direct (box) / Indirect (triangle)

Value-added functions of distribution channels

Strong distribution channels perform several necessary value-added activities in moving products through the channel from producer to end user, such as those listed in Figure 3-51.

Figure 3-51: Distribution Channel Functions

Activity	Description
Marketing intermediaries	Reduce the number of transactions for producers and end users
Product inventory	Helps meet buyers' time-of-purchase and variety preferences
Transportation	Eliminates geographical/location gaps between buyers and sellers
Financing	Facilitates the monetary or currency exchange function
Processing and storage	Separates large quantities into individual orders; maintains inventory and assembles orders for shipment
Advertising and sales promotion	Communicates product availability, location, features and benefits
Pricing	Sets the basis of exchange between the buyer and the seller
Risk reduction	Provides mechanisms such as insurance, return policies, and futures trading
Personal selling	Provides sales, product information, and supporting services
Service and repairs	Provides essential customer support and service

The nature of the industry, the firm's target market and positioning strategies, the product mix, and many other factors determine which specific functions are needed to support the channel and which organizations will assume responsibility for them.

Distribution channel organization

Firms choose between different types of distribution channels.

Conventional channels

In a conventional distribution channel, independent organizations are linked vertically. Each organization fends for itself, with minimal cooperation and concern for the total performance of the channel. Communication between channel members is informal. The focus is transactional (buyer-seller transactions) rather than close collaboration throughout the channel.

Vertical marketing systems

The vertical marketing system (VMS) approach manages the channel as a coordinated or programmed system. One firm is designated as channel manager. A channel manager directs channel activities, setting operating rules and guidelines and providing management assistance and various support services to the other organizations participating in the channel. VMS channels dominate the retail sector and are increasing in popularity in the business, industrial, and service sectors.

There are four types of vertical marketing system networks. Figure 3-52 on the next page lists them and identifies key characteristics.

Typically, VMS channel performance is likely to be higher than that of conventional channels if the network is properly designed and managed. Although there are no hard and fast rules to govern operations, control is exercised in various ways. Participating firms must be amenable to making certain concessions and working toward overall VMS channel performance.

Figure 3-52: Vertical Marketing System Distribution Channels

Type	Key Characteristics
Ownership VMS	■ Channel coordinator owns the distribution channel from source of supply to end user ■ Involves a substantial capital investment by channel coordinator **Examples:** Auto manufacturers who have their own dealerships; oil companies who control their operations from "the ground to the tank"
Contractual VMS	■ May include various formal arrangements between channel participants, including franchising and voluntary chains of independent retailers ■ Contractual programs may be initiated by manufacturers, wholesalers, and retailers **Examples:** Fast food chains; hotel chains; many small retail chains
Administered VMS	Exists because one channel member has the capacity to influence other channel members due to financial position, brand strength, or some other specialized capability **Examples:** Computer operating system manufacturers; major software companies; computer chip manufacturers
Relationship VMS	■ Shares similar characteristics with administered VMS but no one member can exert control over the other channel members ■ Relationship involves close communication and sharing **Examples:** Consumer electronic chains offering wireless telephone hardware and service contracts or selling satellite television hardware and contracts

Horizontal marketing systems

In the horizontal marketing system, two or more unrelated and noncompeting companies work together to exploit a specific opportunity. The organizations join forces because independently each one lacks appropriate resources (for example, capital, know-how, or personnel) to get the job done alone or they fear the risk. The relationship may be a temporary arrangement or become a permanent relationship. In some cases, the companies may form a joint venture company or other type of strategic alliance.

An example of a horizontal arrangement is an independent car insurance company and a private credit management firm providing information about each other to their respective customers.

Hybrid marketing systems

In response to the proliferation of customer segments and distribution channel possibilities, some companies adopt a hybrid (multi-channel) approach. Hybrid or multi-channel marketing occurs when a single company uses two or more distribution channels to reach one or more customer segments.

An example of hybrid or multi-channel marketing is a producer who distributes directly to retailers who then distribute to specific consumer segment and also uses dealers who distribute to other consumer segments. The same producer may also market directly to a specific consumer segment. This is a typical approach for firms marketing via the Internet as well as through brick-and-mortar establishments.

Channel disintegration trends

The ability to sustain competitive advantage or to improve customer satisfaction and organizational effectiveness requires regular review of distribution channel operations. Often times, organizational strategic issues or cost efficiency issues mandate that channel systems be realigned and/or restructured.

Consider the following examples:

- Organizations using direct sales forces may find that indirect channels (for example, wholesalers, distributors, dealers, or retailers) may better serve part of the customer base.

- As a market matures, an organization may pursue lower-cost mass merchandisers rather than dedicated chains.

- Direct marketing programs within an existing customer base may be implemented to capitalize on the opportunity for convenience buying (shopping via mail catalogs or toll-free numbers).

- The Internet may be used to bypass traditional distributors (such as Dell Computer's virtual integration with suppliers and customers).

Many factors can lead to channel disintegration but disintermediation is perhaps the most prominent. **Disintermediation** refers to the removal of firms from the value chain. The term is generally associated with buyers using the Internet to purchase directly from a manufacturer's Web site (as was noted in the previous Dell computer example). The

Internet offers sellers the potential to eliminate previously required partners or links in the channel of distribution. The 'middleman' (the distributor and/or retailer) is often eliminated during the sale.

Disintermediation can be seen in the following additional scenarios:

- Airlines selling tickets online and bypassing travel agents and reseller Web sites such as Travelocity and Expedia.

- Entertainment companies embedding hyperlinks and promotions in their CDs and DVDs directing consumers to corporate-owned online retailers and pulling customers from retail channels.

- Auto manufacturers providing a build-to-order system allowing online shoppers to order directly from the factory or giving consumers access to new vehicle prices, an online inventory of new and used vehicles, and links to used car trade-in values and dealer Web sites, forcing dealers to disclose their costs for cars and trucks to consumers.

- Consumers shopping for clothes on-line at familiar brand name manufacturer-operated sites and bypassing traditional apparel retailers.

The benefits to buyers are convenience, fast turnaround time and, typically, lower prices. However, channel conflict tends to arise because of the exclusion of traditional intermediaries (for example, the agents and wholesalers) and the redistribution of key channel functions.

As buyers go online to purchase goods and services, many traditional retailers and suppliers may be alienated. However, a pattern of reintermediation may follow and the 'ousted' distributors or new players can come back into the picture in another role. Firms recognizing the key gaps and unmet needs between the direct relationships of a company and its customers can reenter the system as value-added intermediaries.

Channel design

The type of channel (conventional, VMS, horizontal, or hybrid) and the level of intensity (intense, selective, or exclusive) influences how many levels of organization to include in the channel and the specific kinds of intermediaries. For example, an industrial products producer might choose between independent (commissioned) manufacturing agents and a chain of distributors.

There are several factors that may influence channel design:

- Consumer needs and preferences—where the targeted end users expect to purchase products

- Product characteristics—the complexity of the product, special application requirements, and servicing needed

- Manufacturer's capabilities and resources—the collective resources and bargaining power of large producers with intermediaries (or conversely, the constraints of small producers)

- Required functions—the necessary functions to move products from the producer to the end user (such as storage, transportation, and servicing)

- Availability and skills of intermediaries—the experience, capabilities, and motivations of intermediaries

Selecting the channel strategy

Which channel to use is a key marketing decision; it affects every other marketing decision (for example, pricing, communication decisions, sales force). Factors to be taken into account in channel selection include:

- Overall organizational strategy

- Channel objectives

- End-user location and desired service levels

- Market access potential of different channels

- Product or service costs

- Economic considerations (revenue-cost impact of the channel strategy)

- Flexibility and control considerations

- Legal and ethical issues (for example, exclusive dealing and territory arrangements)

The advantages and disadvantages of major alternatives should be considered. For example, all sales being made directly to the consumer or end-user may result in unacceptable cost penalties. On the other hand, introducing intermediaries can significantly reduce the amount of control that a producer has over the relationship with the end-user. Intermediaries may help meet financial goals but at the same time result in less control over how and to whom the products are sold. Intermediaries often require some level of support (for example, training, market-research, and other capability-building programs).

Assuming multiple options can lead to profits, an organization needs to balance cost with other considerations.

International considerations

Agents, wholesalers, and retailers are present in other countries, but there are many other important differences in distribution patterns and networks. Generalizations about distribution practices across countries are not possible. Firms pursuing global expansion must:

- Study distribution patterns in the nation(s) of interest.

- Explore trends in technology (for example, satellite communications), regional cooperatives (for example, European Union), and transportation services.

- Assess the potential for global market turbulence.

- Investigate currency matters and banking institutions.

- Determine cost and capital requirements.

- Evaluate the strategic product fit.

Whether domestic or global, a primary goal of a market-driven strategy is to align the company's value chain with the ever-changing customer and competitive requirements. A distribution channel is at the heart of the value chain. Simply stated: A strong distribution channel can lead to competitive advantage.

Progress Check

Directions: Read each question and respond in the space provided. Answers and page references appear on the page following the progress check questions.

1. The four Cs of marketing are

    ( )   a.   consumer/customer, creativity, cost, communication.

    ( )   b.   consumer, competition, company, cost.

    ( )   c.   consumer/customer, cost, convenience, communication.

    ( )   d.   customer, competition, cost, channel organization.

2. A distribution channel characterized by an arm's-length buyer-seller relationship in which the purchasing department chooses the suppliers and decides when goods are needed is an example of a(n)

    ( )   a.   ownership vertical marketing system.

    ( )   b.   contractual vertical marketing system.

    ( )   c.   conventional distribution channel.

    ( )   d.   exclusive distribution channel.

3. A key characteristic of relationship marketing is

    ( )   a.   highly consultative personal selling.

    ( )   b.   persuading the prospects hearing an ad to purchase the item.

    ( )   c.   gaining public understanding and acceptance through commercial media.

    ( )   d.   consumers and businesses being able to place orders via the Internet.

4. The "all you can afford" budgeting approach in advertising is primarily influenced by

    ( )   a.   past expenditures.

    ( )   b.   how much competitors spend.

    ( )   c.   creative message design.

    ( )   d.   prevalent budget limitations.

Progress check answers

1. c (p. 3-151)

2. c (p. 3-161)

3. a (p. 3-156)

4. d (p. 3-154)

Corporate Finance

Section overview

Corporate finance is a cornerstone in advancing core business goals and achieving strategic objectives. For-profit businesses, not-for-profit institutions, and public entities all must make expenditures to cover a wide variety of costs. All investments—both short- and long-term—must support organizational core competencies. Simply stated: Corporate finances must support organizational strategies and ensure that any short-term obstacles do not disrupt long-term strategies.

Organizations may choose from several types of financial instruments. Management accountants are often called on to evaluate the appropriateness of the instruments for an organization. To do so, accountants need to understand the general uses of the different instruments and the economic risks and benefits of owning or issuing them. They must also ensure that the organization can earn a sufficient rate of return from the investments chosen to cover the costs of generating funds.

Prudent investment decisions help to ensure the financial soundness of any firm. In particular for publicly traded corporations, financial stability and value creation induce investors to purchase the firm's stocks, bonds, and securities.

This section examines key concepts in corporate finance, ranging from basic risk management principles to the effective selection and management of short- and long-term financial instruments.

Learning Outcome Statements

The Certified Management Accountant (CMA) test is based upon a series of Learning Outcome Statements (LOS) developed by the Institute of Certified Management Accountants (ICMA). The LOS describe all the knowledge and skills that make up the CMA body of knowledge, broken down by part, section and topic. The CMA Learning System (CMALS) supports the LOS by addressing all the subjects they cover. Candidates should use the LOS to ensure that they can address the concepts in different ways or through a variety of question scenarios. Candidates should also be prepared to perform calculations referred to in the LOS in total or by providing missing components of a calculation. The LOS should not be used as proxies for exact exam questions; they should be used as a guide for studying and learning the content of the CMA Learning System and ensuring that you can accomplish the objectives set out by the LOS.

The LOS included in the CMALS books are the comprehensive set, current as of the date of publication. Candidates can access the IMA Web site at www.imanet.org and click on the Certification section to locate and download a Portable Document Format (PDF) file of the current LOS.

Learning Outcome Statements

Part 3: Strategic Management — Section C. Corporate Finance

Part 3 — Section C1. Risk and Return

- LOS 3.C.1.a—Calculate rates of return.

- LOS 3.C.1.b—Identify and demonstrate an understanding of the different types of risk (systematic [market], unsystematic [company], industry, country, and so on).

- LOS 3.C.1.c—Demonstrate an understanding of the relationship between risk and return.

- LOS 3.C.1.d—Calculate expected return, standard deviation of return and coefficient of variation.

- LOS 3.C.1.e—Identify the different types of attitudes toward risk and infer how attitude might affect the management of risk.

- LOS 3.C.1.f—Define a portfolio and distinguish between individual security risk and portfolio risk.

- LOS 3.C.1.g—Define Value at Risk (VAR).

- LOS 3.C.1.h—Demonstrate an understanding of diversification.

- LOS 3.C.1.i—Differentiate between systematic and unsystematic risk.

- LOS 3.C.1.j—Demonstrate an understanding of how individual securities affect portfolio risk.

- LOS 3.C.1.k—Define beta and identify the meaning of a security's beta.

- LOS 3.C.1.l—Calculate the expected risk-adjusted returns using the capital asset pricing model (CAPM) and arbitrage pricing theory (APT).

- LOS 3.C.1.m—Define hedging and demonstrate how hedging can be used to manage financial risk.

Part 3 — Section C2. Financial Instruments

- LOS 3.C.2.a—Define and identify the characteristics of bonds, common stock, and preferred stock.

- LOS 3.C.2.b—Identify and describe the basic features of a bond, such as maturity, par value, coupon rate, provisions for redeeming, covenants, options granted to the issuer or investor, indentures, and restrictions.

- LOS 3.C.2.c—Define the different types of dividends, including cash dividends, stock dividends, and stock splits.

- LOS 3.C.2.d—Identify and discuss the factors that influence the dividend policy of a firm.

- LOS 3.C.2.e—Demonstrate an understanding of the dividend payment process for both common and preferred stock.

- LOS 3.C.2.f—Value bonds, common stock, and preferred stock using discounted cash flow methods.

- LOS 3.C.2.g—Demonstrate an understanding of the dividend discount model.

- LOS 3.C.2.h—Demonstrate an understanding of relative or comparable valuation methods, such as price-to-earnings (P/E) ratios, market-to-book ratios, and price-to-sales ratios.

- LOS 3.C.2.i—Demonstrate an understanding of duration as a measure of bond interest rate sensitivity.

- LOS 3.C.2.j—Demonstrate and understanding of how income taxes influence financing decisions.

- LOS 3.C.2.k—Define and demonstrate an understanding of derivatives, their payoff structures, and their uses.

- LOS 3.C.2.l—Distinguish between futures and forwards.

- LOS 3.C.2.m—Demonstrate an understanding of options.

- LOS 3.C.2.n—Demonstrate a basic understanding of the Black-Scholes and the binomial option-valuation models and how a change in one variable will affect the value of the option (calculation not required).

- LOS 3.C.2.o—Define and identify characteristics of other sources of long-term financing, such as leases, convertible securities, warrants, and retained earnings.

Part 3 — Section C3. Cost of Capital

- LOS 3.C.3.a—Define the cost of capital and demonstrate an understanding of its applications in capital structure decisions.

- LOS 3.C.3.b—Determine the weighted average (historical) cost of capital and the cost of its individual components.

- LOS 3.C.3.c—Calculate the marginal cost of capital and demonstrate an understanding of the significance of using the marginal cost as opposed to the historical cost.

- LOS 3.C.3.d—Demonstrate an understanding of the use of the cost of capital in capital investment decisions.

- LOS 3.C.3.e—Demonstrate an understanding of how income taxes impact capital structure and capital investment decisions.

Part 3 — Section C4. Managing Current Assets

- LOS 3.C.4.a—Define working capital and identify its components.

- LOS 3.C.4.b—Explain the benefit of short-term financial forecasts in the management of working capital.

- LOS 3.C.4.c—Identify factors influencing the levels of cash.

- LOS 3.C.4.d—Identify the three motives for holding cash.

- LOS 3.C.4.e—Demonstrate an understanding of how firms monitor cash inflows and outflows and prepare forecasts of future cash flows.

- LOS 3.C.4.f—Identify methods of speeding up cash collections.

- LOS 3.C.4.g—Calculate the net benefit of a lockbox system.

- LOS 3.C.4.h—Define concentration banking and discuss how firms utilize it.

- LOS 3.C.4.i—Demonstrate an understanding of the uses of compensating balances.

- LOS 3.C.4.j—Identify methods of slowing down disbursements.

- LOS 3.C.4.k—Define payable through draft and zero balance account.

- LOS 3.C.4.l—Demonstrate an understanding of disbursement float and overdraft systems.

- LOS 3.C.4.m—Define electronic commerce and discuss its use by firms.

- LOS 3.C.4.n—Define the different types of marketable securities, including money market instruments, T-bills, Treasury notes, Treasury bonds, repurchase agreements, federal agency securities, bankers' acceptances, commercial paper, negotiable CDs, Eurodollars, and other marketable securities.

- LOS 3.C.4.o—Demonstrate an understanding of the variables in marketable security selections, including safety, marketability, yield, maturity, and taxability.

- LOS 3.C.4.p—Demonstrate an understanding of the risk and return trade-off in the selection of marketable securities.

- LOS 3.C.4.q—List reasons for holding marketable securities.

- LOS 3.C.4.r—Identify reasons for carrying accounts receivable and the factors influencing the level of receivables.

- LOS 3.C.4.s—Demonstrate an understanding of the impact of changes in credit terms.

- LOS 3.C.4.t—Define default risk.

- LOS 3.C.4.u—Demonstrate an understanding of the factors involved in determining an optimal credit policy.

- LOS 3.C.4.v—Calculate the average collection period.

- LOS 3.C.4.w—Identify reasons for carrying inventory and the factors influencing its level.

- LOS 3.C.4.x—Identify and calculate the costs related to inventory.

- LOS 3.C.4.y—Define lead time and safety stock.

- LOS 3.C.4.z—Demonstrate an understanding of economic order quantity (EOQ) and how a change in one variable would affect the EOQ (calculation not required).

- LOS 3.C.4.aa—Define just-in-time and kanban inventory management systems.

Part 3 — Section C5. Financing Current Assets

- LOS 3.C.5.a—Demonstrate an understanding of how risk affects a firm's approach to its current asset financing policy (aggressive, conservative, and so on).

- LOS 3.C.5.b—Describe the different types of short-term credit, including trade credit, short-term bank loans, commercial paper, lines of credit, and bankers' acceptances and identify their advantages and disadvantages.

- LOS 3.C.5.c—Estimate the annual cost and effective annual interest rate of not taking a cash discount.

- LOS 3.C.5.d—Calculate the effective annual interest rate of a bank loan with a compensating balance requirement and/or a commitment fee.

- LOS 3.C.5.e—Describe the different types of secured short-term credit, including accounts receivable financing and inventory financing.

- LOS 3.C.5.f—Demonstrate an understanding of factoring accounts receivable and calculate the cost of factoring.

- LOS 3.C.5.g—Demonstrate an understanding of the maturity matching or hedging approach to financing.

Risk and Return

Topic overview

To succeed in today's economy, organizations must successfully manage a variety of business and financial risks. Poor management of risks can result in inefficiencies, business losses, and/or the demise of an enterprise.

This topic first looks at the difference between business and financial risk and then examines several aspects of financial risk and return.

Types of Risk

As conventionally used, **risk** is the probability of not receiving the expected return from an investment. Risk implies a degree of uncertainty. The greater the potential variability of returns, the riskier an investment. A one-year United States Treasury bill (T-bill) that provides a "guaranteed" rate of return on investment would be considered risk-free. The annual returns on shares of a stock or some other variable investment instrument are inherently riskier; the return may be much less than expected or, in the worst-case scenario, even less than the initial investment.

Corporate risk consists of two major types: business (operation) risk and financial risk.

Business risk

Business risk is the risk inherent with a firm's operations before the financing decision. Common examples of operational risks are any of the wide array of business decisions related to the production and marketing of products and services. Other causes of business risk include the variability of demand, sales price, and input cost; ability to adjust output prices for changes in input costs and to develop new products in a timely, cost-effective manner; foreign risk exposures; and the extent to which costs are fixed. Business risk remains the same regardless of how the firm is financed.

Included under business risk are insurable risks. As Statement on Management Accounting No. 2A, "Terminology: Management Accounting Glossary," notes, insurable risks include damage to or loss of property or other physical assets; reductions in revenue, income, or net worth resulting from tort liability; and costs incurred for occupational injury to or diseases of employees. Most organizations have a formal risk management process in place to mitigate insurable risks.

But operational and insurable risks are not typically within the direct realm of management accountants. By their nature, financial risks are.

Degree of operating leverage

Business risk is often measured by the **degree of operating leverage** (DOL). DOL is defined as the percent change in operating income given a percent change in sales. It is calculated by:

$$DOL = \frac{\text{Contribution Margin}}{\text{Operating Income}}$$

Contribution margin equals sales less variable costs. Operating income equals contribution margin less fixed costs.

Financial risk

Financial risk is the risk associated with using debt financing. Debt financing increases the variability of earnings before taxes (but after interest). Thus, along with business risk, it contributes to the uncertainty of net income and earnings per share.

Note: The different financial instruments are discussed in more detail in Topic 2 of this section, "Financial Instruments."

To no small degree, the sheer volume of choices in financial instruments and their increasing complexity affect investment risk. Additional key factors influencing the variability of investment returns are:

▪ Uncertainty about interest rates, currency exchange rates, and commodity prices.

▪ Time sensitivity of financial transactions.

Degree of financial leverage

Financial risk is often measured by the degree of financial leverage (DFL). DFL is defined as the percent change in EPS given a percent change in operating income. It is calculated by:

$$DFL = \frac{\text{Operating Income}}{\text{Operating Income} - \text{Interest Charges} - \left(\dfrac{\text{Preferred Stock Dividend}}{1 - \text{Tax Rate}} \right)}$$

Degree of total leverage

The total of business and financial risk, called the degree of total leverage (DTL), is the product of operating and financial leverage.

$$DTL = DOL \times DFL$$

or

$$DTL = \frac{\text{Contribution Margin}}{\text{Operating Income} - \text{Interest Charges} - \left(\dfrac{\text{Preferred Stock Dividend}}{1 - \text{Tax Rate}} \right)}$$

Risk Management

Given the potential ramifications of mismanaging financial risk, most companies attempt to control their exposure by implementing a risk management process. Although the formality and specifics of the process will vary across different organizations, the general steps of a risk management process are summarized in Figure 3-53 on the next page.

In addition to setting forth specific objectives and strategies with respect to risk management, organizations typically identify the roles and responsibilities of key individuals and establish a hierarchy for decision making. Consideration is also given to how performance results will be measured and reported.

Figure 3-53: Steps in the Risk Management Process

Step 1	**Determine the company's tolerance for risk.**
	This step identifies the organizational attitude toward risk. Will the company accept significant financial risks? Does the company want to take on only selective risk exposures? Must the firm eliminate all risks?
Step 2	**Evaluate the risk exposure.**
	During this step, the specific nature of the exposure must be identified. (For example, is the risk related to potential changes in interest rates or foreign exchange rates? If no, what is the primary risk factor?) The exposure must then be quantified so that a decision can be made as to whether the level of risk is acceptable to the organization.
Step 3	**Implement an appropriate risk management strategy.**
	A risk management strategy identifies what actions (if any) must be taken to manage the risk exposure. A wide variety of strategies are possible.
Step 4	**Monitor the risk exposure and the strategy.**
	Periodic monitoring assesses the status quo or any unexpected changes in the risk exposure (as a result of market volatility, and so on). This step also considers whether the risk management strategy selected is effective. Strategy adjustments may be necessary.

Risk management can help to reduce the variability of a company's future cash flows. In turn, having smooth cash flows adds value to a company. A company with smooth cash flows is generally perceived as being more stable (less risky), which can lead to a favorable borrowing position in credit markets.

Note: Content found in Topic 2 of this section, "Financial Instruments," looks at the array of investment instruments that can be used as risk management tools.

Hedging, speculation, arbitrage, and maturity matching

In general, four processes shape how companies use financial instruments in managing risk: hedging, speculation, arbitrage, and maturity matching.

Hedging

Hedging is a method of reducing exposures to adverse fluctuations in prices, interest rates, or foreign exchange rates. Companies hedge an investment by taking an offsetting position in a second investment instrument.

Common forms of hedges include futures contracts, put or call options that transfer the risk of the fluctuating prices to other parties, or the simultaneous sale and purchase of rights to goods and services for delivery at different dates. The objective of a hedging arrangement or transaction is to reduce or eliminate a company's risk.

Note: The discussion of derivatives in Topic 2 of this section, "Financial Instruments," covers futures and options in more detail.

Speculation

Speculation involves risk taking and betting on the direction of the market. Unlike hedging, which attempts to reduce risk, speculation assumes a significant risk by betting that the price of a particular investment will go up or down.

The objective in speculation is to try to predict the future in the hopes of making quick, large gains. As such, a speculation arrangement or transaction increases a company's risk.

Arbitrage

Arbitrage is the simultaneous purchase of an investment instrument in one market and the sale in another with the objective of making a profit on the price differences in the different markets.

The objective in an arbitrage arrangement or transaction is to profit from market inefficiencies. A true arbitrage should not impact a company's overall risk.

Maturity matching

Maturity is the length of time remaining before the issuer repays a security. A maturity date is the principal repayment date—the date on which the last payment is due.

Maturity matching is a management approach that involves hedging risk by matching the maturities of the company's assets and liabilities. In practice, maturity matching attempts to finance short-term projects with short-term financing and long-term projects with long-term assets. An example of maturity matching would include a company buying equipment with a project with a useful life of five years and financing the project with funds having a similar duration.

Note: Maturity matching is also discussed in Topic 5 of this section, "Financing Current Assets."

Calculating Rates of Return

Companies and investors do not typically assume risks for fun; they are seeking a return on an investment that is commensurate with its risks. A **return** (or **rate of return**) is the amount received on an investment from holding that investment for a period of time relative to the amount of the initial investment. Of course, not all returns end up as financial gains. The owner of a financial investment or asset may experience a loss over a given period of time. Returns reflect any change in market prices for the investment and are usually expressed as a percentage of the beginning market price of the investment.

At the simplest level, a return is calculated as the cash payment received (such as dividends or interest), plus the change in market price (appreciation or loss in price), divided by the beginning price of the security.

For example, the rate of return, also called the **holding period return (HPR)** for common stock over one period is:

$$R = \frac{(P_t - P_{t-1}) + D}{P_{t-1}}$$

Where:

- R = rate of return (holding period return).

- P_t = stock price at the end of the period.

- P_{t-1} = stock price at the beginning of the period.

- D_t = cash dividend at the end of the time period.

- t is the time period.

Example:

Assume that an investor buys a share of common stock for $20 exactly one year ago and the stock price rises to $22. During the period, the company pays a $2 cash dividend per share. What is the one-year holding period return for this stock?

- P_{t-1} (the previous stock price) = $20

- P_t (the current stock price) =$22

- D_t (the cash dividend) = $2

$$R = \frac{(\$22 - \$20) + \$2}{\$20} = \frac{\$4}{\$20} = 0.20 \; or \; 20\%$$

The time period (t) can be any length of time. In this case, t represents the holding period of return (HPR) for the common stock for one year. Thus, the rate of return on common stock is 20%.

Relationship Between Risk and Return

Risk is an important consideration in making financial decisions. Under rational market conditions, those investments with greater expected risk should provide a higher expected rate of return than investments with lower risk.

Numerous studies of capital market history support the idea that returns to investors are typically a reflection of the risks they take. As an example, the following generalizations can be made about United States investment instruments (based on historical performance over long periods of time—typically several decades—so average rates of returns are not distorted by fluctuations of unusually high or low returns).

- **Risk and returns from Treasury bills (T-bills)**
  United States T-bills (U.S. government securities that mature in less than one year) are very safe securities. There is no risk of default. **Default risk** is the risk that a borrower will not pay the interest and/or principal on funds borrowed when they become due. Because of the short maturity period, the prices (while subject to inflation) are relatively stable. T-bills offer the most conservative rate of return.

- **Risk and returns from bonds**
  U.S. government bonds and corporate bonds have longer maturity periods than T-bills. They also have an additional dimension: Prices fluctuate as interest rates vary. Historically, bond prices rise when interest rates fall and fall when interest rates rise. Thus, there is an inverse relation between the movement of bond prices and interest rates.

  Similar to U.S. T-bills, government bonds have no risk of default. Corporate bonds do have a default risk. Over time, bond rates of return are higher than those of T-bills. On average, corporate bonds have slightly higher returns than government bonds.

- **Risk and returns from stocks**
  Stocks provide investments signifying an ownership position (called equity) in a corporation. A stock investor also has a direct share in the risks of the enterprise.

  On average, stock returns are significantly higher than the safe rates of return from T-bills or bonds. Stock investments in small U.S. firms historically outperform the returns from large U.S. firms.

Note: Additional information on bonds, common stock, and preferred stock is found in Topic 2 of this section, "Financial Instruments."

Value at Risk (VAR)

In managing risk, organizations should not rely solely on historical data. Those managing risk should know about risks while they are being taken. As noted previously, historical performance over long periods of time average rates of return to accommodate fluctuations of unusually high or low returns. But as the name implies, "historical" provides a retrospective indication of risk. When reviewing a portfolio, historical volatility illustrates how risky the portfolio had been over the some previous period of time. It provides no indication about the current market risk of the portfolio. Value at risk gives organizations the ability to assess current risk.

Value at Risk (VAR) is the maximum loss within a given period of time and given a specified probability level (level of confidence).Unlike retrospective risk metrics that measure historical volatility, VAR is prospective. It quantifies market risk while it is being taken.

Figure 3-54 overviews key VAR concepts.

Figure 3-54: Value at Risk (VAR) Characteristics

Application	VAR can be applied to any portfolio that can reasonably be marked to market performance on a regular basis. VAR is not applicable to real estate or other illiquid assets.
Timeframe/horizon	VAR evaluates a portfolio's performance over a specific period of time such as a trading day, week, or a month.
Base currency	VAR measures risk in a currency. Any currency can be used.
VAR measurement	A resulting VAR measure summarizes a portfolio's market risk with a single number.

VAR can be calculated using any of the following methods:

- **Historical method**
  This method re-organizes actual historical returns for a time period by putting them in order from worst to best. The historical method assumes that history will repeat itself, from a risk perspective. A histogram plot correlates frequency of returns with losses. The resulting level of confidence provides a percentage that a worst-case scenario for a daily loss will not exceed. (For example, if we invest \$1000, we are 95% confident that our worst daily loss will not exceed \$40 (\$1000 × 4%).

- **Variance-covariance method**
  The variance-covariance method assumes that stock returns are normally distributed. Expected (or average) return and a standard deviation are estimated and a normal distribution curve is plotted. Reviewing the normal curve, one can see exactly where the worst percentages lie on the curve. The percentages looked at are a function of desired confidence and the standard deviation.

- **Monte Carlo simulation**
  A Monte Carlo simulation refers to any method that randomly generates trials. This method involves developing a model for future returns and running multiple hypothetical trials through the model.

Risk and return attitudes

Evaluating the trade-offs between risk and return is a major component in the maximization of shareholder wealth.

Shareholder wealth is the market value of a company's common stock. Shareholder wealth is calculated as the number of common shares outstanding times the market price per share (the price at which the firm's common stock trades for in the marketplace such as the New York Stock Exchange).

Shareholder wealth maximization (SWM) refers to the maximization of shareholders' purchasing power. In an efficient market, SWM is the maximization of the current share price. It provides a convenient framework for evaluating both the timing and the risks associated with various investment and financing strategies and relies on cash flows as a measure of returns. From a financial perspective, SWM is typically assumed to be the major goal of a firm.

Certainty equivalent (CE) is a concept that describes the amount of cash an investor would have to receive to be indifferent between the payoff and a given gamble. It answers the question, what is the smallest certain payoff an investor would accept in exchange for a risky cash flow? A certainty equivalent factor is used to convert a projected cash flow into a certain cash flow. General principles correlating the relationship of an investor's certainty equivalent and the expected monetary value are summarized in Figure 3-55.

Figure 3-55: Certainty Equivalent and Attitudes Toward Risk

When the certainty equivalent is:		Then:
Less than expected value	➔	Risk aversion (a risk adverse position) is present.
Equal to expected value	➔	Risk indifference (a risk indifferent or neutral position) is present.
Greater than expected value	➔	Risk preference (a risk seeking position) is present.

Risk aversion refers to an investor's dislike of risk and need for a higher rate of return as an inducement to take on riskier investments. Thus, high risk investments should offer an investor a higher expected return than low risk investments. In other words, the greater the risk an investment poses, the higher the expected return needed to compensate an investor for buying and holding the investment. Conversely, an investor expects to earn lower expected returns for low risk investments. Generally speaking, most investors are risk averse and seek higher returns for increasing risks.

There is no true or single measure of certainty in discussing investment returns. The concept of certainty equivalent deals with expected returns; the actual return on the investment may vary. For example, the actual return on an investment classified as less risky could very well outperform the actual return on a risky investment.

Risk typically increases with time, as there is greater uncertainty and/or variability in forecasting for distant years.

Probability distributions and risk and return

With the exception of risk-free Treasury securities, the actual rate of return is often described as a random variable subject to probability distribution. A **probability distribution** is a set of possible values that a random variable (for example, an investment) can take and the likelihood that each will occur.

Three major descriptive statistical measures in a probability distribution are:

- Expected return
- Standard deviation
- Coefficient of variation

Expected return

Expected return is the weighted average of the possible returns where the weights represent the probabilities of occurrence. It is a measure of central tendency of a probability distribution. The formula for expected return is:

$$\bar{R} = \sum_{i=1}^{n} (R_i)(P_i)$$

Where:

- $\bar{R}$ = expected return.

- R_i = return for the ith possibility.

- P_i = probability of that return occurring.

- n = total number of possibilities.

Standard deviation

Standard deviation is a statistical measure showing the variation or dispersion around the expected (most likely) return on an investment. It shows the distribution around the mean (average) and is computed as the square root of the variance. The formula for standard deviation (σ) is:

$$\sigma = \sqrt{\sum_{i=1}^{n} \left(R_i - \bar{R}\right)^2 (P_i)}$$

In the equation above, the deviations from the mean $\left(R_i - \bar{R}\right)$ are squared to eliminate the problem of minus signs. Typically, the higher the standard deviation, the greater the variability of returns and the greater the total risk.

Example:

Here's how an expected return and standard deviation of return would be computed given the following probability distributions.

Possible Return, R_i	Probability of Occurrence, P_i	Expected Return, $\bar{R}$ Calculation $(R_i)(P_i)$	Variance, σ^2 Calculation $\left(R_i - \bar{R}\right)^2 (P_i)$
-0.02	0.10	-0.002	$(-0.02 - 0.10)^2 (0.10) = 0.00144$
0.05	0.20	0.010	$(0.05 - 0.10)^2 (0.20) = 0.00050$
0.10	0.40	0.040	$(0.10 - 0.10)^2 (0.40) = 0.00000$
0.15	0.20	0.030	$(0.15 - 0.10)^2 (0.20) = 0.00050$
0.22	0.10	0.022	$(0.22 - 0.10)^2 (0.10) = 0.00144$
$\sum = 1.00$		$\sum = 0.10 = \bar{R}$	$\sum = 0.01288 = \sigma^2$

Standard deviation = $(0.01288)^5$ = 0.11349 or 11.349%

In this example:

- The distribution's variance = 0.001288

- The distribution's standard deviation = 11.349%

Coefficient of variation

Standard deviation can be misleading when comparing the risk or uncertainty of different investments if those investments are different sizes. Calculating the coefficient of variation helps to adjust for such size or scale differences.

Coefficient of variation (CV) provides a measure of relative risk. The CV is calculated by dividing the standard deviation by the mean of that distribution.

$$CV = \frac{\sigma}{\bar{\bar{R}}}$$

Example:

Investment A and Investment B with normal probability distributions have the following characteristics.

	Investment A	Investment B
Expected return, $\bar{\bar{R}}$	0.06	0.18
Standard deviation, σ	0.04	0.06

Based on a comparison of the standard deviations for both investments, the larger of the two is Investment B (0.06), seemingly making it riskier than Investment A. However, Investment A has greater variation relative to the size of the expected return. To adjust for these differences, the coefficient of variation provides a measure of risk per unit of expected return.

	Investment A	Investment B
Coefficient of variation (CV)	0.04 / 0.06 = 0.67	0.06 / 0.18 = 0.33

Using a measure of relative risk, Investment A with a CV of 0.67 is more risky than Investment B with a CV of 0.33. A higher CV indicates higher relative risk.

Risk and Return in a Portfolio Context

Investors rarely put all of their proverbial eggs in one basket and hold a single type of investment. Instead, they combine multiple investments in a portfolio.

Simply defined, a **portfolio** is a mix of two or more assets. A portfolio may include any combination of cash, bonds, stocks, mutual funds, or other investments.

Portfolio risk

Risk and return in a portfolio context differ from risk and return concepts for a single investment. Calculations used to assess the risk of a portfolio are more complicated than the standard deviation and the variance of a single investment.

Covariance and correlation are useful portfolio measures. They are both statistical measures showing the degree to which two random variables (such as two investment returns in a portfolio) move together.

Covariance

Where variance measures how a single random variable moves with itself, covariance extends the concept, measuring how one random variable moves with another random variable. Covariance shows the way two different assets in a portfolio are expected to vary together—the way returns move relative to one another—rather than independently.

For example:

- The expected returns on a stock and a put option on the stock move in opposite directions and will have a negative covariance. (*Note: Options are discussed in Topic 2: Financial Instruments.*)

- The expected returns for two stocks in the same industry would most likely move in the same direction and have a positive covariance.

- The expected return of a stock paired with a riskless Treasury security would have zero covariance because the riskless asset's returns do not move, regardless of changes in the stock's returns.

As the number of assets in a portfolio grows, the covariance between various securities that have been paired becomes more important. The more different the movement between assets, the less portfolio risk.

The basic notation for covariance between random variables, X and Y is:

$$Cov_{x,y}$$

The covariance between two asset returns using expectational data is computed as:

$$Cov_{1,2} = \sum_{i=1}^{n} \{P_i [R_{i,1} - E(R_1)][R_{i,2} - E(R_2)]\}$$

Where:

- $R_{t,1}$ = return on asset 1 in state i

- $R_{t,2}$ = return on asset 2 in state i

- P_i = probability of state I occurring

- $E(R_1)$ = expected return on asset 1

- $E(R_2)$= expected return on asset 2

For example, use the following data on returns for two assets and their associated probabilities to calculate the covariance between the two assets.

First, we must compete the expected return for each asset as follows:

$$E(R_1) = \sum_{i=1}^{n} P_i R_{i,1} = 0.25(0.06) + 0.50(0.16) + 0.25(0.26) = 0.015 + 0.080 + 0.065 = 0.160$$

$$E(R_2) = \sum_{i=1}^{n} P_i R_{i,2} = 0.25(0.25) + 0.50(0.10) + 0.25(0.05) = 0.0625 + 0.0500 + 0.0125 = 0.125$$

P_i	$R_{i,1}$	$R_{i,2}$	$(R_{i,1}) - E(R_1)$	$(R_{i,2}) - E(R_2)$	$P_i[(R_{i,1}) - E(R_1)][(R_{i,2}) - E^*(R_2)]$
0.25	0.06	0.25	-0.100	0.125	-0.00313
0.50	0.16	0.10	0.00	-0.025	0.00000
0.25	0.26	0.05	+0.100	-0.075	-0.00188

$$Cov_{1,2} = \sum_{i=1}^{n} \{P_i[R_{i,1} - E(R_1)][R_{i,2} - E(R_2)]\} = -0.00501$$

Given the negative sign of the covariance, the returns on the two assets move in opposite directions.

The covariance calculation for a portfolio depends on the variance of individual securities and the correlations between all the pairs. A matrix of weighted correlations between every possible pair must also be constructed. Depending on the number of investments in a portfolio, there are potentially a very large number of possible combinations. Also, covariance values may range from negative infinity to positive infinity and are expressed in terms of square units.

Correlation

To simply the interpretation of covariance, the covariance value is divided by the product of the random variable's standard deviations. The resulting value is the correlation coefficient (or, correlation). The formula for the correlation of expected returns for two securities (1 and 2) is:

$$Corr_{1,2} = \frac{Cov_{1,2}}{\sigma_1 \sigma_2}, \text{ which implies } Cov_{1,2} = Corr_{1,2}\sigma_1\sigma_2$$

Where:

- $\sigma 1$ and $\sigma 2$ are the standard deviations of a probability distribution of possible returns for the portfolio, security 1, and security 2, respectively.

Key characteristics to understand about the correlation of the two random variables (in this example, assets 1 and 2) are:

- Correlation measures the strength of the linear relationship between two random variables.

- Correlation has no units.

- The correlation coefficient always lies in a range from -1.0 to +1.0. This is represented as: $-1 \le Corr_{1,2} \le +1$

- A positive correlation means the securities move in the same direction. A +1.0 correlation means the random variables have perfect positive correlation. This means that a movement in one security results in an exact measurable positive movement in the other. This is represented as: Corr1,2 = +1.0

- A negative correlation implies the securities move in the opposite direction.

- A –1.0 correlation means the random variables have perfect negative correlation. This means that a movement in one security results in an exact measurable negative movement in the other. This is represented as: Corr1,2 = –1

- A 0 correlation means there is no linear relationship between the variables, indicating that prediction of R1 cannot be made on the basis of R2 using linear methods. This is represented as: Corr1,2 = 0

Risk-adverse investors would generally want to diversify holdings to include securities that have less than perfect positive correlation.

Example:

$$\sigma_p = \sqrt{w_1^2\sigma_1^2 + w_2^2\sigma_2^2 + 2w_1w_2 Corr_{1,2}\sigma_1\sigma_2}$$

Assume that w1 = 0.40 and w2 = 0.60, σ1 = 0.05 and σ2 = 0.09.

Now, assume that the correlation coefficient is +1, 0, and -1. Compute the standard deviation of the portfolio, σp, using the data above. The results will show that the standard deviation of the portfolio is largest when the correlation coefficient is +1, decline when it is 0, and declines further when it is -1.

If Corr1,2 = +1, then σp = [(0.40)2(0.05)2 + (0.60)2(0.09)2 + 2(0.40)(0.60)(1)(0.05)(0.09)]1/2

= [0.00040 + 0.00292 + 0.00216]1/2 = 0.074

If Corr1,2 = 0, then σp = [(0.40)2(0.05)2 + (0.60)2(0.09)2 + 2(0.40)(0.60)(0)(0.05)(0.09)]1/2

= [0.00040 + 0.00292 + 0.0]1/2 = 0.058

If Corr1,2 = -1, then σp = [(0.40)2(0.05)2 + (0.60)2(0.09)2 + 2(0.40)(0.60)(-1)(0.05)(0.09)]1/2

= [0.000400 + 0.00292 -0.00216]1/2 = 0.034

As the example illustrates above, the standard deviation of the portfolio decreases as the correlation coefficient goes from +1 to 0 to -1.

Portfolio return

A portfolio rate of return is the weighted average of the expected returns of all the investments comprising that portfolio. The weights represent the proportions of each item in the portfolio; the sum of the weights must be equal to 100%.

The general formula for the expected rate of return for a portfolio is:

$$\bar{R}_p = \sum_{i=1}^{n} W_i\bar{R}_i$$

Where:

- $\overline{R}_p$ = expected return of a portfolio.

- W_i = proportion or weight of the total funds invested in the security.

- $\overline{R}_i$ = expected return for security j.

- n = number of different securities in the portfolio.

A typical portfolio investment strategy is to construct an efficient portfolio (or optimal portfolio) that maximizes the rate of return for a given level of risk or minimizes risk for a given level of return.

Assume a two asset portfolio with 40% in Asset A with an expected return of 12% and 60% in Asset B with an expected return of 18%. The rate of return on this portfolio would be:

$$\overline{R}_p = 0.40(12\%) + 0.60(18\%) = 4.8\% + 10.8\% = 15.6\%$$

Diversification

Diversification refers to holding a wide range of different investments in a portfolio. The primary goal of diversification is to reduce the variability (or risk) of a portfolio.

Diversification reduces portfolio risk as long as the different investments are unlikely to all move in the same direction in perfect tandem (they are not perfectly positively correlated). For example, having ten stocks in a portfolio all from the same industry tends to result in highly correlated returns. Thus, the performance of these companies would typically move up and down in value in a similar manner. Having fewer stocks in a portfolio representing different industries is more likely to show low correlation and low portfolio return variability. That is, the probability that individual stocks in different industries move up and down in value at the same time or at the same rate is low.

Figure 3-56 provides a conceptual illustration of the offsetting variability that portfolio diversification can provide.

Figure 3-56: Diversification and Portfolio Risk

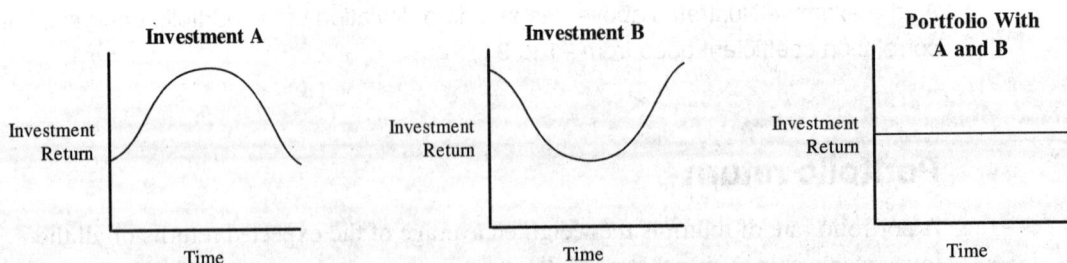

Well-conceived diversification reduces both the upside and downside potential in a portfolio and allows for more consistent performance under a wide range of economic conditions.

Systematic and unsystematic portfolio risk

Extensive market research has examined the effect of diversification on portfolio risk when randomly selected investments are combined in weighted portfolios. As shown in Figure 3-57, the level of portfolio risk reduction (standard deviation) is great at first and then tapers off as more investments are included in a portfolio.

Figure 3-57: Portfolio Risk Reduction

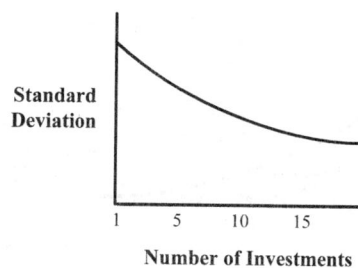

In smaller portfolios, diversification can cut variability dramatically, but the improvement is much less significant as the portfolio grows in size with numerous investment holdings (typically 15 to 20 different investments).

A portfolio's total risk, as measured by its standard deviation, consists of two specific types of risk:

- Systematic risk
- Unsystematic risk

Systematic risk

Systematic risk (also known as market risk, nondiversifiable risk, or unavoidable risk) is associated with changes in return based on the market as a whole. Systematic risk is common to an entire class of investments because of unavoidable national or global economic changes or other events that threaten the vast majority of (or all) businesses and impact large portions of the market. The value of investments usually declines across the board when investors are exposed to systematic market uncertainties. This is why, for example, stocks tend to move together in response to economy-wide or global perils.

Unsystematic risk

Unsystematic risk (also known as unique risk, diversifiable risk, or avoidable risk) is independent of economic, political, or other factors or general market movements. It is associated with a specific company or industry.

Most estimates approximate that 60% to 75% of an individual stock's total risk (standard deviation) results from unsystematic risks. For example, a new product entry in an industry could make a company's product obsolete. Labor-management issues or a strike could negatively affect a company or an entire industry.

Most variability resulting from unsystematic risk is avoidable through diversification. For this reason, unsystematic risk is sometimes called diversifiable risk. That is, holding a diversified portfolio reduces unsystematic risk because different portions of the market tend to perform differently at different times.

Figure 3-58 shows how diversification can minimize unsystematic risk but cannot eliminate systematic risk.

Figure 3-58: Systematic and Unsystematic Risk in a Portfolio

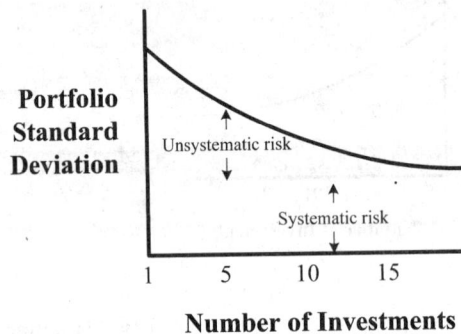

Unsystematic risk is extremely important when a portfolio has a limited number of investments. For a reasonable, well-diversified portfolio, systematic risk assumes much greater importance. That is why, for example, market changes (up or down) carry portfolios with them.

Market risk and beta

Because most investors diversify, risk is best judged in a portfolio context. An individual investment's contribution to the risk of a portfolio is a function of how that investment is most likely to be affected by a general market decline.

Beta (ß) describes an investment's sensitivity to market movements. It is a quantitative measure of the volatility of a given investment relative to the overall market.

Specifically, beta indicates the amount that investors expect an investment price to change for each additional 1% change in the market.

- United States Treasury bills have a beta of 0; the return is fixed and unaffected by market changes.
- The average beta of all stocks is 1.0.
- Stocks with a beta greater than 1.0 are unusually more sensitive to market movements; they are said to amplify overall market movements.
- Stocks with a beta less than 1.0 are unusually less sensitive to market movements. They tend to move in the same direction as the market but not as far.

Another way of describing beta measures is that a beta above 1.0 is more volatile than the overall market; a beta below 1.0 is less volatile.

Where systematic (market) risk is the primary determinant of risk in a well-diversified portfolio, the beta of an individual investment in that portfolio reflects its sensitivity to market fluctuations. In other words, the standard deviation of a well-diversified portfolio is proportional to its beta. A diversified portfolio with a beta of 1.0 has half the systematic risk of a portfolio with a beta of 2.0.

Capital Asset Pricing Model (CAPM)

The **capital asset pricing model (CAPM)** is an economic model for valuing a portfolio by relating risk and expected return. The idea behind the CAPM is that investors demand an additional expected return (also known as risk premium) when asked to accept additional risk above that found in a risk-free asset (for example, T-bills). In other words, the risk premium is the difference between the required rate of return on an investment and the risk-free rate.

The basic premise underlying the CAPM is that the risk premium varies in direct proportion to the beta in a competitive market. The expected risk premium for each investment in a portfolio should increase in proportion to its beta. This means that all investments in a portfolio should plot along a sloping line, known as the security market line.

The security market line (SML) is a graphical representation of the CAPM. The SML provides a benchmark for evaluating the relative merits of different portfolio items. The SML begins at the risk-free Treasury bills (which have a beta of 0) and slopes upward to the right. Substituting different values of beta into the CAPM equation provides different points on the SML.

The CAPM concepts of risk premium, beta, and SML are shown in Figure 3-59.

Figure 3-59: Risk Premium, Beta, and SML

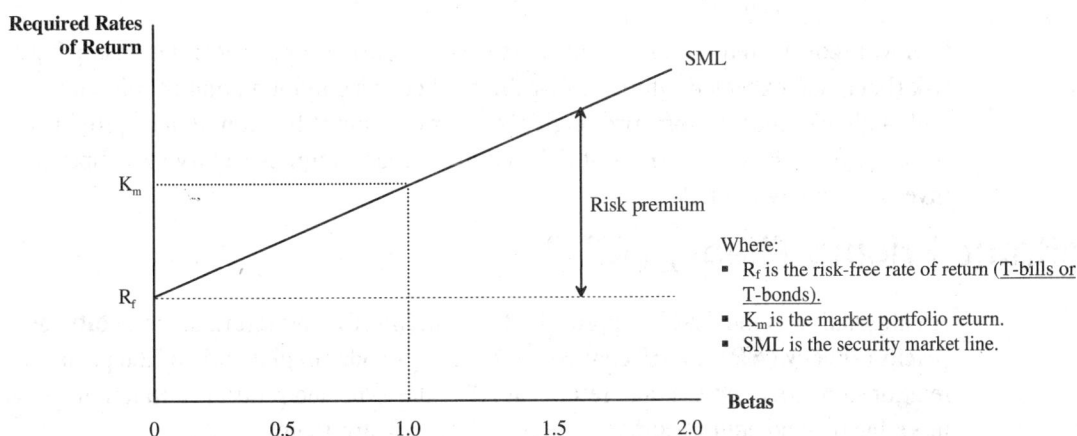

If the aim is to keep portfolio risk low, investments having low betas should be included. Conversely, if a higher return is desired, investments with high betas should be added to the portfolio.

The CAPM calculation can be used to find the required rate of return on a stock or portfolio when the return on a risk-free asset, the beta of the stock or portfolio, and the return on the market portfolio are known.

The formula for CAPM is:

$$K_e = R_f + \beta(K_m - R_f)$$

Where:

- K_e = required rate of return.
- R_f = risk-free rate (such as the return on U.S. T-bill or T-bonds).
- β = beta coefficient for the company
- K_m = return on a market portfolio.

Considerable debate exists on whether to use T-bills or T-bonds as the risk-free rate with the CAPM. Evidence shows that for capital budgeting decisions, managers tend to use T-bonds more often as a proxy for the risk-free rate than the do T-bills.

Example:

Here's how CAPM would be used find the required rate of return on a stock, assuming:

- R_f = 8% (the risk-free rate on a U.S. Treasury security)
- β = 1.50 (the beta coefficient for the company)
- K_m = 12% (the return on the market portfolio)

$$K_e = R_f + \beta(K_m - R_f)$$
$$K_e = 0.08 + 1.50(0.12 - 0.08) = 14.0\%$$

CAPM is considered a single-factor model .It establishes a positive relationship between risk (beta) and expected returns, using the market as a common point of reference. Although the model is sometimes criticized for oversimplification, it does provide one perspective of the implications of risk and the risk premium necessary to compensate investors for bearing risk.

Arbitrage Pricing Theory (APT)

An alternative to the CAPM approach of explaining risk and return is the **arbitrage pricing theory (APT)**. APT claims to provide a broader explanation of the positive relationships between risk and return. In APT, the expected return is a function of two or more factors and equilibrium is maintained through arbitrage.

APT maintains that the return on a security is sensitive to the movements of multiple factors (such as unexpected changes in interest rates, inflation, industry changes, earnings announcements) and arbitrage efficiency prevails. (Recall from the earlier discussion in this section, arbitrage means taking advantage of multiple prices for essentially the same assets or product, buying in a cheaper market and selling in a higher-priced market.

APT's consideration of multiple factors is said to give added dimension to risk and certainty.

Two-factor model

A two-factor model is represented by the following calculations.

The actual return for a security is:

$$R_j = a + b_{1j}F_1 + b_{2j}F_2 + e_j$$

Where:

- R_j is the actual rate of return for the security.

- a is the return when two factors have zero values

- F_1 and F_2 are the (uncertain) values of factors 1 and 2

- b_{1j} and b_{2j} are the reaction coefficients representing the change in the security's return to a one-unit change in a factor

- e is the error term representing specific risk or influences that are not relevant to this relationship

The expected return for the security is:

$$\bar{R}_j = \lambda_0 + b_{1j}(\lambda_1) + b_{2j}(\lambda_2)$$

Where:

- $\bar{R}_j$ is the expected rate of return for the security.

- λ_0 is the return on a risk-free security.

- (λ_1) and (λ_2) (lambda) are risk premiums for the types of risk associated with a particular factor

- b_{1j} and b_{2j} are the reaction coefficients representing the change in the security's return to a one-unit change in a factor

Example:

Here's how a two-factor analysis would be used to calculate the expected rate of return on a stock, assuming:

- λ_0 = 8% (the risk-free rate on a U.S. Treasury security)

- (λ_1) and (λ_2) are 6% and -2% respectively

- b_{1j} and b_{2j} are 1.2 and 0.8, respectively

$$\bar{R}_j = \lambda_0 + b_{1j}(\lambda_1) + b_{2j}(\lambda_2)$$
$$\bar{R}_j = 0.08 + 1.2(0.06) + 0.8(-0.02)$$
$$\bar{R}_j = 0.08 + 0.072 - 0.016 = 13.6\%$$

In this example, the first factor shows risk aversion and will require a higher rate of return; the second factor provides value and therefore lowers the expected return. The λ s represent the market prices associated with the factor risks.

Multi-factor model

The same APT calculation principles apply when considering more than two factors. The formula is extended by adding factors and their reaction coefficients. The APT results change as the sample size, from which the factors are selected, increases.

There are some specific cautions in using the APT model including:

- The potential for sampling distortions.
- The possibility of improper selection of factors
- The tendency of two factors to dominate the relationship.
- Complex computations.

Regardless of these challenges, APT provides additional insights into the way assets are priced and kept at equilibrium levels. In corporate finance, APT can be helpful in establishing the required rate of return (or, discount rate) that can then be used in capital budgeting decisions.

Note: The dividend discount model in covered in the next topic, "Financial Instruments."

Progress Check

Directions: Read each question and respond in the space provided. Answers and page references appear on the page following the progress check questions.

1. Which of the following examples exemplifies financial risk?

   ( ) a. The risk associated with a firm's common stock

   ( ) b. Credit agreements extended to new customers at low interest rates

   ( ) c. The extent to which a firm issues debt to finance real investments

   ( ) d. A lawsuit filed by an employee for an on-the-job injury

2. The standard deviation of a stock investment is best described as the

   ( ) a. variability of expected returns.

   ( ) b. sensitivity to market movements.

   ( ) c. trade-off between risk and return.

   ( ) d. variation around the mean return.

Match the following terms with their appropriate description.

3. _____ Correlation

4. _____ Security market line

5. _____ Certainty equivalent

   a. The amount of cash that would make an investor indifferent to risk at a point in time

   b. A benchmark for evaluating the relative merits of different portfolio items

   c. The degree to which two stock returns move together in a portfolio

6. A major benefit of portfolio diversification is

   ( ) a. reduced exposure to foreign exchange rates.

   ( ) b. minimization of unsystematic risk.

   ( ) c. reduction of systematic risk.

   ( ) d. a more favorable borrowing position.

Progress check answers

1. c (p. 3-171)

2. d (p. 3-180)

3. c (p. 3-183)

4. b (p. 3-189)

5. a (p. 3-178)

6. b (p. 3-186)

Financial Instruments

Topic overview

A financial instrument evidences a transaction between two parties. It has monetary value or records a monetary transaction. For one party in the transaction, the financial instrument represents an investment; for the second party, the instrument is an obligation or liability.

Risks and Returns in Investment and Financing Decisions

Firms make investment decisions on both financial (for example, stocks and bonds) and real assets (for example, plant and equipment). The investment decisions discussed below relate to financial assets. Investment decisions on real assets are discussed in Section E: Investment Decisions.

Organizations make investments in financial assets for different reasons including:

- To ensure liquidity—to cover day-to-day cash obligations in a timely manner.

- To generate interest income for cash received for which there is no immediate use.

Financing allows an organization to pursue long-term objectives through debt or equity capital. **Debt** financing implies a legal liability or obligation of an organization to repay a creditor for borrowed funds by a specified date. **Equity** financing represents selling an ownership claim in a company. Both debt and equity involve risk and return trade-offs:

- The cost of debt is represented by an interest rate; the interest paid is a tax-deductible expense.

- The value of equity is represented by a stock price or the net value of the company's assets; dividends paid on equity are not tax-deductible.

- How a company finances debt (for example, types of loan agreements) may influence operations; equity shareholders can exert control by exercising specific voting rights.

Every company should have an investment and financing strategy in place. Figure 3-60 summarizes basic aspects that investment and financing strategies should address.

Figure 3-60: Basic Investing and Financing Considerations

Investment	Financing
■ Corporate goals	■ Debt versus equity financing
■ Policies and guidelines	■ Short- versus long-term financing
■ Investment instrument selection and portfolio configuration	■ Fixed versus floating rate interest payments
■ Roles, responsibilities, and authority for investment activities	■ Secured versus unsecured debt
■ Financial controls	■ On- versus off-balance-sheet financing
■ Performance measurement	■ Tax considerations

An investment policy reflects an organization's tolerance for risk; the mix of debt and equity in borrowing determines a company's leverage and is closely linked to the firm's capital structure.

In financing, the financing mix should maximize firm value as measured by the company's stock price and should minimize the firm's weighted average cost of capital (WACC). Potential risk is reduced by matching the cash inflows of the assets being financed with the cash outflows used to finance the assets.

Income taxes' impact on financing decisions

Many financing decisions rely heavily on tax effects. Generally speaking, debt has tax advantages at the corporate level because interest payments reduce the firm's taxable income (shielding it from federal and state taxes) whereas dividends and share repurchases do not. Interest tax shields associated with this financing approach tend to support increased leverage, provided a firm balances the tax benefits of debt against the costs of financial distress.

According to trade-off theory, optimal capital structure involves a trade-off between the benefit of debt due to the interest tax shelter and the costs of debt due to financial distress and agency costs. An **agency cost** is a direct or indirect expense that the principal bears as a result of having delegated authority to an agent. An **agent** is the person authorized to act on behalf of another (the principal) to perform some duty or service. **Financial distress** refers to any general weakening in a company's financial condition caused by issuing too much debt. Bankruptcy is the extreme case of financial distress. Various economic theories challenge this trade-off theory. At issue with this shielded income proposition is whether the tax-deductibility of the interest payments associated with the borrowing affect the value of the firm.

Valuation

Valuation is the process that links risk and return to estimate the worth of an asset or a company. To understand the concept of valuation requires a baseline understanding of value and related value concepts.

The term value has different meanings, depending on whether it is applied to an asset or a company. An asset is generally thought of as a financial asset—a monetary claim on an issuer, typically a paper asset such as a bond, common stock, or preferred stock.

Related value concepts include the following.

- **Going-concern value**
  Going-concern value refers to the value of a company as an operating entity. This value depends on the ability to generate future cash flows rather than balance sheet assets.

- **Liquidation value**
  Liquidation value is the net amount of money that could be realized by selling the entity's after paying the off the liabilities (debt).

- **Liquidation value per share**
  This is the actual amount per share of common stock that stockholders would receive if the entity sells all assets, pays all liabilities (included preferred stock), and divides the remaining money among the stockholders.

- **Book value**
  Book value is the value at which an asset is carried on a balance sheet. It is the accounting value of an asset—the cost of an asset minus accumulated depreciation.

- **Book value per share of common stock**
  Book value per share of common stock refers to the ratio of stockholder equity to the average number of common shares. Book value per share may have little relation to the liquidation value per share or the market value per share

- **Market value**
  Market value is the market price at which investors buy or sell an asset at a given time. The key determinant of market value is supply and demand.

- **Intrinsic value**
  Intrinsic value is a measure of the theoretical value of an asset. Although not indicative of actual value, intrinsic value provides a basis for determining whether to buy or sell a financial asset when compared to it market value or price. Intrinsic value is also called **fundamental value**.

Generally speaking, an asset's value is influenced by:

- Cash flow of the asset over time.

- Growth rate of the cash flow.

- Riskiness of the cash flow.

Measures of cash flow are:

- The annual dividend and change in stock price per share for common stock, and preferred stock.

- The amount of interest received by the bondholder in a year plus the change in price.

Increased cash flow raises the price of an asset. If the price declines, cash flow becomes more uncertain. In financial management, basic goals are to maintain/increase cash flow and control/decrease risk. This, in turn, supports the maximization of shareholder wealth.

Risk is challenging to estimate. Future cash flows must be discounted back to present cash flows at appropriate rates to reflect risk. Thus, a key concept in valuation is: The value of an asset (the price of an asset) is the present value of all future cash flows associated with the asset.

Subsequent content in this topic examines characteristics of various debt and equity instruments. Valuation, which is a fundamental activity in financial management in estimating the intrinsic value of bonds, common stock, and preferred stock, is included. Investments are covered in Topic 4, "Managing Current Assets," and Topic 5, "Financing Current Assets." For the purposes of this discussion, Treasury bills (which mature in less than one year) are classified as short-term debt securities and covered in the later discussions of assets.

Bonds

A **bond** is a debt instrument (a loan) issued for a period of more than one year. The investor acquiring a bond earns interest by lending money while the borrower (the issuer) gets needed capital (cash).

Bonds may be bought on a short-, medium-, and long-term basis. Although these distinctions may vary slightly, the general parameters are:

- Two to five years for short-term bonds.

- Five to ten years for medium-term (intermediate) bonds.

- Ten to thirty years for long-term bonds.

Longer-term bonds normally pay returns (yields) higher than those of short-term bonds. Thus, the shape of a normal yield curve is upward sloping.

Issuers and types of bonds

There are many types of bonds, issued by several different sources. Common ones are listed in Figure 3-61.

Figure 3-61: Common Types of Bonds

Type	Description
Corporate bonds	■ Issued by large and small U.S. companies ■ Used to finance growth, expansion, and other activities
Government bonds	■ Backed by the full faith of the U.S. government ■ Used to sustain government operations and pay interest on national debt ■ Examples include U.S. Treasury bonds, Treasury notes, and savings bonds
Municipal bonds	■ Issued by various cities and states ■ Used to pay for construction projects and other activities
Agency bonds	■ Issued by various federal, state, and local government agencies ■ Examples include bonds issued by mortgage lenders (for example, Ginnie Mae, Fannie Mae, and Freddie Mac) as well as other agency bonds issued to finance operations and raise money for special projects
International bonds	Marketed simultaneously in several countries, usually by London branches of international banks and security dealers

Bond agreements

The written legal agreement among all parties involved in a bond issue is called an **indenture** (or deed of trust).

- An indenture defines the details of the bond issue, including:

- Terms and conditions of the bond issue.

- Interest rate.

- Maturity date.

- Protective covenants (restrictions placed on the issuer).

- Events of default.

- Subordination.

- Sinking fund terms (payments made by the borrower to a separate custodial account; used to repay the debt at maturity and assure creditors that adequate funds are available).

- Collateral property to be pledged (if any).

- Designation and duties of the trustee.

Covenants

Protective covenants set limits (restrictions) on certain actions the company might be taking during the term of the agreement. They are a particularly important feature in a bond indenture.

There are two types of covenants:

Negative covenants
Negative covenants limit or prohibit the borrower from certain actions. Paying too much in dividends, pledging assets to other lenders, selling major assets, merging with another firm, and acquiring more long-term debt are all examples of actions that a negative covenant may address.

Positive covenants
Positive (affirmative) covenants specify actions that the borrower promises to perform. Examples of positive covenants include maintaining certain ratios, preserving collateral in good condition, and making timely interest and principal payments. A failure to abide by positive covenants could place the bond issuer in default.

Bond administration

Bonds are administered by a qualified trustee. The trustee is a third party chosen by the bond issuer to serve as the official representative of the bondholder. Individuals or institutions may serve as trustees; banks often administer bonds.

Trustee responsibilities include:

- Authenticating the bond issue's legality.

- Ensuring that all contractual obligations are carried out; that sinking fund and interest payments are properly paid and applied.

- Initiating appropriate actions if the borrower does not meet obligations.

- Representing the bondholder in legal proceedings.

- Administering redemption.

The issuer of the bond compensates the trustee; the trustee's compensation is included in the costs of borrowing.

Bond terminology

Generally speaking, a bond is a promise to repay principal along with interest at maturity.

Bond principal

Principal (also known as par value, par, or face value) represents the dollar amount of the bond at the time it is issued. Par value is the amount the lender is repaid when the bond matures. Most bonds are sold in multiples of $1,000.

Bond interest

The interest rate stated on a bond is referred to as the **coupon rate** (or **coupon yield**). A bond's coupon rate is competitive; the rate is comparable to what other bonds being issued at that time are paying.

Three common forms of interest on bonds are:

- Fixed rate—interest paid consistently at the same rate

- Floating rate—interest varies based on economic changes

- Zero coupon rate—no ongoing interest payments (as the bond is sold at a deep discount and redeemed at full value as compound interest accrues to the par value)

Bonds are classified as fixed income securities if the coupon rate and the amount of bond payments are fixed at the time the bond is offered for sale. Traditionally, most bonds are sold at fixed rates. This is a primary reason bonds are generally considered conservative investments and less risky than stocks and other types of investments with highly variable return rates.

After the initial issue (the sale of a bond), bonds are bought and sold through brokers in the **secondary market** (a secondhand market where a security can be traded after issuance), similar to the way stocks are traded. In the secondary market, a bond's price fluctuates with interest rates. If market interest rates fall, the price will be sold above par value; market interest rates higher than the bond's coupon rate mean that the bond will be sold below par value (at a discount).

A bond's coupon rate is expressed as a percentage of the par value. Interest is usually paid semiannually or annually. For example, if a semi-annual bond has a 7% coupon, the issuer pays bondholders $35 each six months for every $1,000 par-value bond that they hold.

A zero coupon bond is an exception. As the name implies, zero coupon bonds pay no interest while the bond is maturing. Interest accrues (builds up) and is paid as a lump sum at maturity.

The term "coupon" originated because bondholders traditionally received certificates specifying the terms of the bond with attached coupons that had to be physically detached and redeemed for cash when it was time to collect interest on the bond. The vast majority of newer bonds are issued electronically (similar to stock purchases). However, many coupon certificates still exist as they have not yet reached maturity.

Bond maturity

Bonds typically have a stated maturity. This is the final date on which the bond debt becomes due for payment and the obligation is settled. **Face value** is the value of a bond at maturity.

A bond is often bought and sold during its lifetime. Some types of bonds may be paid back (called) at an earlier date. At maturity, the bondholder receives the par value of the bond. A $1,000 bond is worth $1,000 at maturity (so long as the issuer does not default in payment).

Bond ratings

A bond rating allows an investor to assess the general risks of buying a bond before making the actual purchase.

Bond issues are often rated by credit agencies based on numerous factors including:

- Current financial status of the issuer.

- Future financial prospects.

- Collateral (if any) securing the bond.

Moody's Investors Service and Standard & Poor's are two well-known credit rating services. A summary of their ratings and very general characteristics is provided in Figure 3-62.

Figure 3-62: Moody's and Standard & Poor's Bond Ratings

Moody's	Standard & Poor's	
Aaa	AAA	
Aa	AA	Generally considered high-quality bonds
A	A	
Baa	BBB	
Ba	BB	Somewhat questionable; lack some of the high-quality characteristics
B	B	
Caa	CCC	Poor quality; danger of default
Ca	CC	
C	C	Junk bonds (highly speculative bonds with a greater-than-average chance of default)
—	D	

The following are some key points to understand about bond ratings:

- Bond ratings apply to the bond issue, not the company.

- U.S. Treasury bonds are not rated because they are backed by the federal government.

- Ratings may be adjusted either up or down during the life of a bond; a downgraded rating means that future issues will need to offer higher interest rates to attract buyers.

- Bonds with Aaa and AAA ratings are sold at the lowest rates of interest.

- Because of the default risk associated with junk bonds, they are higher-yield bonds.

- Junk bonds have a greater chance of defaulting, but in some circumstances they may also be an emerging entity and provide a highly profitable return.

Bond yields

A bond's coupon rate never changes, but inflation and changes in other interest rates affect the value of a bond.

Yields and return

Current yield is the annual rate of return expressed as a percentage of the annual interest payment relative to the current price of the bond. A ten-year $1,000 bond paying 5% interest per annum earns $50 per year for ten years. If the current price of the bond is $1,250, the current yield would be 4% ($50/$1,250). The current yield is the same as the interest rate if the current price of the bond is at par.

Yield-to-maturity is the actual return on a bond from the time it is purchased to maturity, assuming that all payments received are reinvested at the same rate as the original bond's coupon rate. Yield-to maturity considers:

- Interest over the life of the bond in relation to price.

- Purchase price in relation to par value (any gains and losses based on whether the bond was purchased above or below par).

- Any coupons or interest payments reinvested.

Inflation and bond net returns

Inflation eats into the return of a bond. If a bond's return is more than the inflation rate, the bond produces a positive return. If the bond's return is less than the inflation rate, the bond produces a negative return. Consider the following examples:

- If a bond's return is 6% and inflation is 4%, the bond produces a 2% net return.

- If a bond's return is 6% and inflation is 8%, the bond produces a –2% net return.

Bond duration

Yield-to-maturity calculations assume that all payments received are reinvested at the same rate as the original bond's coupon rate. However, bonds are subject to inflation. If interest rates fall, the interest payments and principal that bond investors receive will have to be reinvested at lower rates. Thus, bond investors face reinvestment risk when interest rates fall.

Duration gives an approximate sensitivity of bond/portfolio values to changes in yield to maturity. Thus, **bond duration** considers how the price of a bond changes in response to yield changes. The best interpretation of duration is the approximate percentage price changes for a 1% change in yield to maturity. Duration is an approximation of the price yield relation because the relation follows a curve, not a straight line.

Convexity is a measure of the curvature of how the price of a bond changes as the interest rate changes. Price changes in response to rising rates are smaller than price changes in response to falling rates.

A bond price-yield curve is shown in Figure 3-63. Bond prices go up faster than they go down.

Figure 3-63: Bond Price-Yield Curve

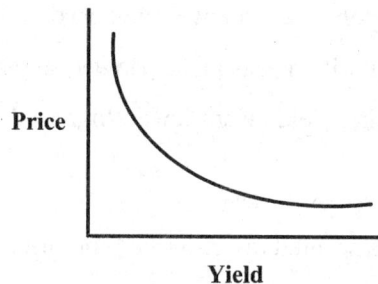

Bond duration is determined by a ratio of the percentage change in price to change in yield.

$$\text{Effective duration} = \frac{(\text{Bond price when yields fall-Bond price when yields rise})}{2 \times (\text{Initial price}) \times (\text{Change in yield in decimal form})}$$

This is often expressed as:

$$\text{Duration} = \frac{V_- - V_+}{2V_0(\Delta y)}$$

Where:

- V_- = bond value if the yield decreases by Δy.
- V_+ = bond value if the yield increases by Δy.
- V_0 = current bond price.
- Δy = change yield used to get V_- and V_+, expressed in decimal form.

Effective duration shows the average percentage price change for a 1% change in yield.

For example, consider a 10-year, semiannual-pay bond with a 9 percent coupon that is currently priced $1067.95 to yield 8%. If the yield declines by 50 basis points to 7.5%, the price of this bond will rise to $1,104.22. If the yield increases by 50 basis points to 8.5%, the price will fall to $1,033.24. Using the formula previously given, the effective duration of this bond would be:

$$Effective\ duration = \frac{\$1,104.22 - \$1,033.24}{2(\$1067.95)(0.005)} = \frac{\$70.98}{10.6795} = 6.65$$

Thus, an effective duration of 6.65 means that a 1% change in yield produces an approximate change in the price of this bond of 6.65%.

Why is bond duration important? Understanding how much a bond will move in response to changing interest rates allows investors to buy, sell, or hold bonds according to how they think they will perform. Investors can use duration to compare bonds with different issue and maturity dates, coupon rates, and yields to maturity.

Below are some relations involving bond duration. Holding other characteristics constant:

- A higher (lower) coupon means a lower (higher) duration.
- A longer (shorter) maturity means higher (lower) duration.
- A higher (lower) market yield means lower (higher) duration.

Bond security

Bonds may be issued on a secured (asset-backed) or unsecured basis.

Secured bonds

A **secured bond** is one that is backed by the collateral of a specific asset (for example, inventories, real estate, or fixed assets) or revenues created from a specific project. A secured bond provides the investor with a lien against an asset in the event of default.

Unsecured bonds

An **unsecured bond** (or **debenture**) is backed only by the good faith, integrity, and credit of the borrower and offers no specific collateral. When holding an unsecured bond, an investor has only a general claim but not against a specific asset. Because unsecured bonds have greater risk than secured bonds, they usually pay higher yields.

Bond ranking and liquidation

Bonds may be classified as equal, senior, or subordinated in relation to other debt obligations. These rankings affect priority in liquidation. If a bond issuer in default has both secured and unsecured bonds:

- Secured bondholders are paid off first; then unsecured bondholders are paid.
- Senior unsecured bondholders are paid before subordinated debenture holders.

Subordinated (or junior) debt implies a lower priority than other claims on the same asset or property. In other words, a subordinated debt is paid after other loan obligations of the issuer have been met. The more junior the debt, the greater the risk to the investor.

Bond valuation

The value of a bond is the sum of its discounted cash flows. The steps to determine the value of a bond are:

- Calculate the present value of interest payments.

- Calculate the present value of the face value.

- Add the two present values.

The traditional approach to bond valuation is to discount all cash flows by the same discount rate. The interest and the face value must be discounted at the market rate (the rate at which similar bonds are discounted).

When face value and coupon rate are known, the following formula may be used to determine the value of a bond.

$$V_b = I(PVIFA_{k,n}) + F(PVIF_{k,n})$$

Where:

- V_b = value of the bond.

- I = interest in each time period.

- PVIFA = present value interest factor annuity.

- P= principal or face value of the bond.

- PVIF = present value interest factor.

- k = discount rate.

- n = number of periods.

Example:

A company issued a 15-year annual pay bond that has 5-years before maturity. At issuance, the bond had a 10% coupon and a face value of $1,000. Now investors requires an 8% return on bonds of similar risk. Here's how to calculate the value of the bond:

- Determine the annual interest (10% x $1,000 = $100).

- Use present value annuity tables to discount the annual interest of $100 at a discount rate of 8% for five years.

- Use present value tables to discount the face value of $1,000 at a discount rate of 8% for five years.

- Add the two present values.

$$V_b = I(PVIFA_{k,n}) + F(PVIF_{k,n})$$
$$V_b = \$100(3.9927) + \$1,000(0.6806)$$
$$V_b = \$399.27 + \$680.60 = \$1,079.87$$

The value of the bond is $1,079.87. This is the price an investor would pay for the bond. In this example, the bond value is above the face value. Because the discount rate is lower that the coupon rate, the bond sells at a premium. (If the discount rate were higher than the coupon rate, the bond would sell at a discount.)

Changes in the interest rate, the coupon rate, and the term to maturity all affect bond prices. These economic forces and the passage of time affect bond value.

Other key points to understand about bond valuation include:

- When the market interest falls, the lower coupon rates mean interest paid on old bonds exceeds interest paid on new bonds. This results in **reinvestment rate risk** from the perspective of the bondholder. The reinvestment rate on coupon bonds rises and falls with market interest rates, which leads to reinvestment rate risk.

- Bond price moves inversely with market interest rate—if the interest rate rises, the bond price with a lower coupon rate declines.

- The magnitude of interest rate changes influences bond prices—the greater the moves in interest rates, the greater the swings in bond prices.

- As the maturity date approaches, the price of a bond will approach par value. This movement of bond prices toward the principal (par or face) value is called **convergence**.

Stocks

A **stock** is an equity investment instrument; it signifies an ownership position (equity) in a corporation. Stockholders (or shareholders) who buy stock (shares) in a corporation have a claim on the corporation's assets and profits based on the proportional shares of stock owned.

The level of equity ownership takes into consideration the number of shares owned and the number of shares outstanding. The term **outstanding share** refers to the number of shares of a corporation's stock held by shareholders.

Ownership is calculated by dividing the number of shares an investor owns by the total number of shares outstanding. For example, if a company has 10,000 shares of stock outstanding and an investor owns 200 of them, that investor owns 2% of the company.

Primary and secondary markets

The migration of a company from private to public ownership often occurs when a private company finds that is needs access to additional funds. The primary market and the secondary market are terms referring to where securities are created and where they are traded among investors. The initial offering of stock to investors is done in the primary market. Subsequent trading is done on the secondary market.

The primary market

As the need for expansion funds grows and exceeds money that can be raised through such sources as personal investments, trade credit, lines of credit, loans and venture capital, management goes to investment bankers who agree to underwrite a stock offering. In investments, **underwrite** is when the investment banker assumes the risk of buying a new issue of securities from the issuing corporation and reselling them to the public. By definition, the **primary market** is the market in which investors have the first opportunity to buy a newly issued security.

Underwriters help the firm prepare a prospectus. A stock prospectus is a formal written offer to sell securities to the public. It is filed with the Securities and Exchange

Commission (SEC) and made available to all investors. The prospectus includes details such as how the security is valued, the issue price per unit, usage, size and goal of the issuing company.

The primary market is basically synonymous with an initial public offering (IPO). Through the underwriting process, investment banks buy all the public shares at a set price. The corporation receives money that can be used for financing operations. After the IPO, the stock shares are traded in the secondary market but the corporation does not receive any additional income. The stock price is then determined by how much investors are willing to pay for the stock at the time of purchase.

After a firm goes public, it may continue to issue new stocks in the primary market. The only difference is that the stocks are no longer IPOs but seasoned offerings.

The secondary market

By definition, the secondary market is a market in which an investor purchases an asset from another investor rather than an issuing corporation. This is the defining characteristic of the secondary market—investors trade amongst themselves. They buy and sell previously-issued securities from other investors without the involvement of the issuing companies.

The secondary market is generally synonymous with the "stock market" and includes the New York Stock Exchange (NYSE), Nasdaq, and all major exchanges around the world.

Market value of a stock

A stock's **market value** (the last reported sale price for outstanding shares) determines the firm's market capitalization. **Market capitalization** (or **cap**) is determined by multiplying the current market price per share by the number of outstanding shares. A public corporation with 30 million shares outstanding that trade at $30 each has a market capitalization of $900 million.

Market capitalization is one of many methods used to categorize types of stocks. Figure 3-64 shows stock classifications based on market capitalization. Corporations are usually classified as large-cap, medium-cap (mid-cap), small-cap, or micro-cap, depending on their market capitalization.

Figure 3-64: Categories of Stocks Based on Capitalization

Large-cap	$15 billion and over
Mid-cap	Between $2 billion and $15 billion
Small-cap	Between $300 million and $2 billion
Micro-cap	Below $300 million

Some of the capitalization designations are arbitrary. For example, depending on the source, the separation point for micro-caps might be $250 million instead of $300 million.

A large-cap stock is the stock of a company with a market capitalization that is large relative to other companies. They frequently offer regular dividends, and the underlying company's size generally lessens the risk of company failure.

A mid-cap stock is a stock with a market capitalization that is between that of large- and small-cap stocks. Similar to large-cap stocks, mid-cap stocks also have a large volume of shares to trade but the companies are smaller and less mature than large-cap stocks. Typically, these companies offer a greater potential for growth than larger companies, but the risk is also greater.

A small-cap stock is a stock with a market capitalization that is relatively small compared to the average company. They have the potential for dramatic growth. But they also have the potential for greater volatility.

Investment returns for the different types of stocks often move in a different cycles. Micro-cap stocks are considered to be the riskiest group of all.

The following are other common stock classifications:

- Blue-chip stocks—stocks of the largest and most consistently profitable publicly traded corporations

- Growth stocks—stocks of corporations that have strong growth potential, with sales, earnings, and market share growing faster than the overall economy

- Cyclical stocks—stocks of corporations whose earnings are highly dependent on economic conditions (for example, economic upturns and slowdowns)

- Defensive stocks—conservative stocks that are relatively stable and impervious to most economic conditions

- Value stocks—stocks that appear inexpensive when compared to earnings and other performance measures

- Income stocks—stocks of typically solid performers with good track records that usually generate a steady income

- Speculative stocks—stocks that are risky investments in corporations that have yet to prove their true worth

Keep in mind that capitalization and the other classifications just mentioned are not cast in stone because companies are always changing.

Two additional stock classifications are common stock and preferred stock. Common stock and preferred stock have several distinguishing differences (as well as some similarities). Their distinct features offer corporations and investors a variety of risks and rewards.

The common and preferred stock classifications are the focus of the remaining content on stocks.

Common Stock

Common stock provides equity ownership in a corporation. That is, the owner of a common stock has an interest in the assets of the corporation and a share in the earnings. Collectively, common stockholders own the corporation. Common stock has no maturity date but shareholders may liquidate their investments by selling stock shares in the secondary market.

Equity characteristics

With common stock, there is no guarantee that an investor will make money. The equity position in a common stock means that the owner shares in the corporation's fortunes and misfortunes.

Common stock **market value per share** is the current trading price of the stock. If the stock increases in value, shareholders benefit from capital appreciation of their investment and potentially receive a dividend.

A dividend (or payout) represents a share in profits. Corporations are not required to pay dividends unless declared by the board of directors. Payments vary based on earnings and how much the board decides to pay out. Corporations usually pay cash dividends quarterly but they may also pay dividends in the form of stock.

- **Cash dividends**
  A cash dividend is paid in the form of cash, usually a check. Cash dividends are typically taxable.

- **Stock dividends**
  A stock dividend is paid as additional shares of stock (rather than cash). Stock dividends allow a corporation to conserve cash for investment purposes while still rewarding investors. When a corporation issues a stock dividend, there are typically no tax consequences until shareholders sell their shares.

- **Stock splits**
  Stock splits are similar to stock dividends in that they are a noncash dividend payout. But stock splits usually involve the issuance of more stock shares than a stock dividend.

  Corporations typically split stocks to lower the price of a stock, make the price more appealing, and stimulate trading. The rationale is that when the price of the stock is high, individual investors may be reluctant to buy shares either because the shares cost so much or because of concern that the stock price has peaked in value.

  Stocks can be split in various increments: two for one, three for one, three for two, and so on. In a two-for-one split, a stockholder with 100 shares would receive another 100 shares. If the stock is trading at $100 a share, the price drops to about $50 dollars a share. If the stock price drops to exactly $50, the total market value remains the same (200 shares at $50 dollars a share versus the original 100 shares at $100; both equal $10,000). Although the total market value initially remains the same, stockholders may profit if the price eventually goes up.

Although not a dividend, a stock may also undergo a **reverse split**. In a reverse split, the number of shares decreases and the price increases accordingly. For example, in a one-for-two reverse split, 100 shares of stock trading at $1 a share become 50 shares worth $2 dollars a share. A reverse split is often used to keep a stock at the stock market's minimum listing price or to increase the stock's general attractiveness to investors who shy away from low-priced stocks.

Stock splits and reverse splits do not result in any taxable gain or loss.

In general, dividends are considered an incentive to own common stock. Corporations offering regular dividends generally have progressed beyond the growth phase, tend not to derive much benefit from reinvesting profits, and, therefore, choose to share those profits as dividends. Thus, the stage of a company's life cycle tends to affect its dividend policy.

If corporate earnings decline, a company may decide to reduce or omit its cash dividend, which may signal a decline in the company future prospects and result in a lower stock price.

Voting rights

Ownership of common stock gives shareholders the right to vote on important company matters such as:

- Election of members of the corporate board of directors.

- Policies and changes in corporate bylaws.

- Approval of stock option plans.

- Mergers and acquisitions.

- Appointment of auditors.

Shareholders typically get one vote for each share of stock owned. Companies administer voting rights in one of two methods: traditional or cumulative.

- **Traditional voting**
  Traditional voting (also known as majority voting, majority-rule voting, or statutory voting) is a corporate voting system in which shareholders voting for the board of directors are limited to one vote per share for any single nominee. The total number of votes for each stockholder equals the number of shares owned times the number of positions open. For example, in an election in which five director candidates are running for open board positions, a shareholder owning 500 shares could cast 500 votes for each candidate, for a total of 2,500 votes.

  This traditional majority method of voting precludes minority interests from electing any of their own (minority) candidates.

- **Cumulative voting**
  A cumulative voting system allows shareholders to cast different numbers of votes for different candidates. Continuing with the five director position example, the shareholder owning 500 shares could distribute the votes equally to the five

candidates, distribute the votes among some combination of the candidates, or cast all 2,500 votes for a single candidate.

Cumulative voting attempts to give minority shareholders more voice in corporate governance by increasing their chances to elect a certain number of directors.

Some corporations issue different classes of stocks with different voting rights. In situations in which a class of shareholders is allowed extra voting rights, a small group of individuals could control the direction of the corporation while owning less than a majority of shares.

Shareholders typically cast votes by mail using a proxy statement. In addition, they may cast votes in person at the corporation's annual meeting. Some corporations allow votes to be cast by telephone or over the Internet.

A **proxy statement** is a legal document that is mailed out to all shareholders shortly before the annual meeting. The proxy statement lists the business concerns to be addressed at the annual meeting and includes a ballot for voting on company initiatives and electing the board members. Submitting a proxy ballot authorizes someone else at the meeting (usually the management team) to vote on the investor's behalf. If the management team receives proxies for over 50% of the shares voted, the team can select the entire board of directors. However, if investors do not return their proxy statements, their votes are not counted. With fewer shares being voted at the meeting, the subsequent number needed to constitute a majority is lowered.

Preemptive rights

Some common stocks offer preemptive rights. By definition, **preemptive rights** allow current shareholders to maintain their proportional ownership in the corporation should the company issue additional stock. Shareholders with preemptive rights have the right (but not the obligation) to purchase new shares before anyone else so that they can maintain their current level of equity ownership.

Liquidating value

In the event of default or liquidation, common stock shareholders have the last claim on assets of the corporation. Specifically, they have residual rights to a corporation's assets only after the claims of bondholders, other debt holders, and preferred stockholders are paid in full. But common stock shareholders also have limited liability and are not responsible for the corporation's debts; losses cannot exceed the amount of their original investment.

Common stock valuation

The return rates for a common stock can vary. As noted previously, in some years, no dividend may be paid. In other years, dividends paid may be more or less than the previous year, depending on the company's dividend policy, profitability, and availability of funds.

Valuation for a common stock requires careful projection of future growth and future dividends. Such projections are largely determined by:

- Annual dividends

- Dividend growth

- Discount rates.

There are three potential valuation scenarios. Over time, dividends may remain fixed (zero growth), grow at a constant rate, or grow at an unusual (variable) rate. Investors use valuation models to compare their results to existing prices to determine whether a stock is over-, under-, or properly valued.

Valuing common stock with zero growth (no dividend growth)

The following formula can be used for zero growth valuation.

$$V_0 = \frac{D_1}{(1 + k_s)^1} + \frac{D_2}{(1 + k_s)^2} + \frac{D_3}{(1 + k_s)^3} + ... + + \frac{D_\infty}{(1 + k_s)^\infty}$$

Where:

- V_0 = common stock price to be estimated.

- D = a constant annual dividend per share on the common stock.

- ks = the investor's required rate of return on the common stock (cost of equity).

The required rate of return is the rate depends on the risk associated with the common stock. Investors expect a high rate of return if an investment is risky. In other words, a higher payoff must be offered to entice investors to invest their money.

The formula may be further simplified:

$$V_0 = \frac{D}{k_s}$$

Example:

A company pays an annual cash dividend of $5 per share at the end of each year. Analysts expect no change in the policy. With a required rate of return of 12%, here's how to determine the value of the common stock.

$$V_0 = \frac{D}{k_s} = \frac{\$5}{0.12} = \$60.00$$

Valuing common stock with constant dividend growth

Investors may expect dividends to increase at a constant rate on an annual basis. For example, if a company recently paid a $5 dividend and dividends grow at an annual rate of 5%, the dividend next year will be:

$$\$5(1 + 0.05) = \$5(1.05)^1 = \$5.25$$

In the second year, the dividend will be:

$$5(1 + 0.05)(1 + 0.05) = \$5(1.05)^2 = \$5.51$$

This pattern would continue for future years.

The value of a common stock with a constant growth rate can also be determined by discounting future dividends at the required rate of return. This valuation method is covered under the upcoming text examining the use of the discounted dividend model.

Valuing common stock with variable dividend growth

This method estimates the stock price when dividends grow at different rate for two or more periods of time. When a common stock has varying growth rates of dividends:

- Future dividends must be projected separately.

- Projected dividends must be discounted back to present using present value interest tables.

- The present value of the terminal at the end of the growth period must be calculated.

- All present values are added together.

Example:

A company paid an annual cash dividend of $5 per share last year. Analysts expect dividends will grow at an annual rate of 20% for the next three years and then level to a normal growth rate of 5%. With a required rate of return of 12%, here's how to determine the price of the common stock today.

$$P_3 = \frac{D_3(1+g)}{k_s - g}$$

$$P_3 = \frac{\$8.64(1.05)}{0.12 - 0.05} = \frac{\$9.07}{0.07} = \$129.57$$

Where:

- D_1, D_2, D_3 = dividends in years 1,2,3, respectively.

- PVIF = present value interest factor.

- P3 = common stock price in year 3.

- ks = required rate of return on the common stock.

- g = constant (annual) dividend growth rate.

Year	Income		PVIF at 12%		Present Value of Income
1	$D_1 = \$5(1.20) = \$6.00$	×	0.8929	=	$5.36
2	$D_2 = \$6.00(1.20) = 7.20$	×	0.7972	=	5.74
3	$D_3 = \$7.20(1.20) = 8.64$	×	0.7118	=	6.15
	$P_3 = 129.57$		0.7118		92.23
			Total present value		$109.48

In this example, the price of the common stock at the end of year 3 is $129.57. When the discounted values are summed, the estimated stock price is $109.48.

Preferred Stock

Similar to common stock, **preferred stock** also provides partial ownership in a corporation. However, there are some important differences. To a degree, preferred stock is more similar to bonds than to common stock. For that reason, preferred stock is often described as a hybrid form of security having characteristics of both debt and equity.

Equity characteristics

A preferred stock generally offers a fixed dividend; the dividend amount does not fluctuate based on earnings. The term "preferred" also implies that shareholders have a right to receive their specified dividend before any dividends are paid to common stockholders.

A fixed dividend reduces investor risk, but it also limits financial rewards. Preferred stock has less volatility when markets fall. But shareholders cannot count on large price gains in rising markets. In fact, the dividend is not guaranteed. The board of directors (who votes on dividend issues) does not have to pay the fixed dividend if it so chooses.

Voting rights

Preferred stockholders do not usually have the voting rights that common stockholders have. Special voting privileges may be granted if the corporation is unable to pay the fixed dividend or the company defaults on a loan agreement or bond indenture.

Liquidating value

In the event of default or bankruptcy, preferred stockholders have a greater claim on the company's assets than common stockholders. Because preferred stock takes precedence over common stock, preferred stockholders have a greater chance of getting some of their investment back if the corporation fails than do common stock shareholders. Should asset liquidation take place, preferred stockholders are paid only after short- and long-term debt holder claims are satisfied.

Unique features

A corporation cannot deduct the dividends paid to shareholders on its tax return. This is a principal drawback to using preferred stock in corporate financing.

The following are other important characteristics of preferred stock:

- **Cumulative dividends**
  Unlike a common stock dividend, which a company is not required to pay, a preferred stock dividend is an obligation regardless of the corporation's earnings. When issuing preferred stock, a corporation often commits to offer a fixed annual dividend. However, the payment is discretionary if the company does not have

sufficient earnings to pay. In some situations, unpaid dividends for preferred stock may accumulate.

Many preferred stocks have a cumulative dividends feature that requires that all unpaid cumulative dividends on the preferred stock be paid from future earnings before common stock dividends are paid. It should be noted that if the corporation has no intention of paying out common stock dividends, there is no requirement to pay the cumulative preferred stock dividends in arrears.

- **Participating feature**

  A participating feature allows preferred stockholders to participate in increasing dividends when common stockholders' dividends reach a certain amount. The exact amount of participation varies and is determined by some predetermined formula that relates additional preferred stockholder payouts to increases in common stockholder payouts.

  Participating preferred stock gives preferred stockholders a prior claim on income and the opportunity for additional return. Unfortunately for investors, the participating feature is not as common as the cumulative feature; most preferred stock returns are limited to the fixed dividend rate.

- **Call provision**

  Preferred stock issues have a stated call price (or redemption price). A call price is specified at issuance; it is set above the original issue price and may decrease over time.

  A call provision grants the preferred stock issuer the right to buy back (or call) all or part of an issue at the call price rather than attempting to retire the issue by more expensive methods such as purchasing the stock in the open market or offering a preferred stockholder a price over market value or another security in its place.

- **Convertible feature**

  Preferred stock issues sometimes have a convertible feature (or conversion feature). Convertible preferred stock can be converted into a specified amount of common stock at the option of the holder. Corporations set a fixed ratio for the number of shares of common stock that can be exchanged for the convertible preferred stock. Once converted, the preferred stock issue is retired.

When preferred stock issues have both call provisions and conversion features, a corporation can force conversion by calling the stock if the current market value price of preferred stock is significantly higher than the call price (due to the conversion feature).

As noted previously, common stocks do not have a maturity date. Unless preferred stock has a mandatory redemption, preferred stock has no maturity date. The call provision and the convertible feature give a corporation flexibility in retiring preferred stock issues (that do not have mandatory redemption) rather than potentially having them outstanding in perpetuity.

Preferred stock valuation

If a company pays fixed a dividend at the end of each year, the valuation is determined in the following manner:

$$V_p = \frac{D}{(1 + k)^1} + \frac{D}{(1 + k)^2} + \frac{D}{(1 + k)^3} + ... + \frac{D}{(1 + k)^\infty}$$

Where:

- V_p = market value of the preferred stock.
- D = constant annual dividends per share on the common stock.
- k = discount rate.
- ∞ = infinity.

This equation can be further simplified:

$$V_p = \frac{D}{k}$$

Once the information about the dividend and discount rate is available, the value of the preferred stock is a straight-forward calculation.

Example:

A company issues preferred stock. Par value of the preferred stock is $100 and each share pays an annual cash dividend of $7 per share. The discount rate for similar preferred stock in the market is 8%. Here's how to determine the value of the preferred stock issued by the parent company.

$$V_p = \frac{D}{k}$$

$$V_p = \frac{\$7}{0.08} = \$87.50$$

Although the annual dividend rate is constant, changes in the discount rate will affect the stock price over time.

- If the market discount rate goes down, the value of the preferred stock will increase.
- If the market discount rate goes up, the value of the preferred stock will decrease.

Use of the dividend discount model

The **dividend discount model (DDM)** is a method to value common stock where the intrinsic value of the common stock is based on the discounted value (the present value) of all expected future dividends.

Dividend discount models are a type of discounted cash flow (DCF) analysis. There are several different DCF models and in turn, different DDMs, that an organization can use. There is no one best method. The method used should take into consideration:

- Measure of cash flow—the dividends and free cash flows to equity.

- Expected holding period—whether the expected period is finite (limited) or infinite.

- Pattern of expected dividends—zero growth (no growth), growth, stable (constant) growth, or supernormal growth.

Basic dividend discount model

The basic dividend discount model is represented by the following formula:

$$V_s = \sum_{t=1}^{\infty} \frac{D_t}{(1+k_s)}$$

Where:

- V_s = intrinsic value of a share of common stock.

- D_t = expected dividends per share on the common stock in period t.

- k_s = investor's required rate of return on the common stock (cost of equity).

This basic dividend discount model assumes that an investor buys a common stock and plans to hold it indefinitely. For this reason, it is sometimes referred to as an infinite period valuation model.

The constant growth dividend discount model

The constant growth dividend discount model is a valuation approach that assumes dividends per share grow at a constant rate each period that is not expected to change. The model represents a single-stage growth pattern. Substituting $D_o (1 + g)^t$ for D_t in the basic model results in the following formula.

$$V_s = \sum_{t=1}^{\infty} \frac{D_0 (1+g)^t}{(1+k_s)^t}$$

Where:

- D_o = dividends per share on the common stock in the current period

- g = constant dividend growth rate.

If k_s is greater than g, the formula can be further simplified to what is commonly known as the **Gordon constant growth model** (or **Gordon model**):

$$V_o = \frac{D_1}{k_s - g}$$

Where:

- V_0 = estimated value of common stock.

- D_1 = expected dividends per share on the common stock in year 1.

- k_s = required rate of return on the common stock.

- g = constant (annual) dividend growth rate.

Example:

A company just paid a $3 dividend per share last year. Analysts expect dividends to grow at a constant rate of 6% per year. If investors expect to receive a 12% return, what is the intrinsic value of the ABC stock?

In this example

- D_1 = $3.00 (1.06) = $3.18
- k_s = 0.12
- g = 0.06

$$V_O = \frac{D_1}{k_s - g} = \frac{\$3.18}{0.12 - 0.06} = \frac{\$3.18}{0.06} = \$53.00$$

Key points about the relationship between the required rate of return (k_s) and the growth rate (g) are summarized in Figure 3-65.

Figure 3-65: Gordon Model Key Points

If ...		Then:
The difference between k_s and g *widens*	➔	The stock value falls.
The difference between k_s and g *narrows*	➔	The stock value rises.
The difference between k_s and g *show small changes*	➔	Large changes in the stock's value can result.

Use of relative (or comparable) valuation models

Relative valuation is another valuation approach that defines "comparable" and chooses a standardized measure of value to compare companies. Value is typically some form of multiple earnings, book value of equity, or sales. Assets may be cheap based on intrinsic value but expensive based on relative valuation and how the market currently prices the assets.

Essentially the same variables considered in DCF valuation models (for example, required rate of return, expected growth rate, and so on) are used in relative valuation estimates. The major difference between the two valuation approaches is the assumptions underlying DCF valuation are explicit (clearly defined or formulated) and those applying to relative valuation models are implicit (the assumptions provide conditions that they satisfy).

Choosing comparable firms is fundamental to relative valuation. A comparable firm is one having similar business and industry characteristics to the individual firm being valued.

In relative valuation, an analyst:

- Attempts to control/minimize differences across firms (such as size).

- Computes the multiple for each comparable firm and then averages them.

- Computes the multiple for the individual firm to be valued.

- Compares the multiple for the individual firm to average.

- Evaluates any differences between the two multiples based on characteristics of the individual firm (such as growth or risk).

For example, looking at the following price-to-earnings (P/E) ratios, where:

The comparable firms' P/E = 18

The individual firm's P/E = 10

an analyst might consider the individual firm's stock as cheap (or, undervalued) because the multiple is less than average. Conversely, if the multiple were higher than average, the stock would be considered expensive (or, overvalued).

Three common relative valuation models are price-to-earning (P/E) ratios, price-to-book (P/B) ratios, and price-to-sales (P/S) ratios.

Price-to-earnings (P/E) ratios

The price-to-earnings (P/E) ratio is the most common multiple used to estimate the value of common stock. Earnings power, as measured by earnings per share (EPS), is the primary determinant of investment value. There are two versions of the P/E ratio; the difference between the two is how earnings are calculated in the denominator.

- **Trailing P/E ratios**
  Trailing P/E use earnings over the most recent 12 months. This P/E ratio is common in most popular financial press.

$$\text{Trailing P/E} = \frac{\text{Market price per share}}{\text{EPS over previous 12 months}}$$

- **Leading P/E ratios**
  Leading P/E use next year's expected earnings (either expected earnings for the next fiscal year or the next four quarters).

$$\text{Leading P/E} = \frac{\text{Market price per share}}{\text{Forecasted EPS over next 12 months}}$$

The leading P/E ratios rely on the DDM to develop a constant multiplier model for a stable firm and then explain factors in the DDM that affect a stock's P/E ratio.

Example:

A company reports $10 million in earnings in the previous fiscal year. An analyst forecasts a $1.00 EPS over the next 12 months. The company has 15 million shares outstanding at a market price of $15 per share. Given this information, here's how to determine the trailing and leading P/E ratios.

$$\text{Previous year EPS} = \frac{\$10,000,000}{15,000,000} = \$0.67$$

$$\text{Trailing P/E} = \frac{\$15.00}{\$0.67} = 22.39$$

$$\text{Leading P/E} = \frac{\$15.00}{\$1.00} = 15.0$$

Advantages of using P/E ratios include:

- They are commonly used in the investment community.

- Research shows significant relationship between P/E differences and long-run average stock returns.

Some of the disadvantages of using P/E ratios are:

- If earnings are negative, the resulting P/E ratio is useless.

- Volatility in earnings can make the interpretation of P/E ratios difficult.

- Management discretion (that is within allowable accounting practices) can distort earnings.

Price-to-book ratios

A **price-to-book (P/B) ratio** (or, **price-to-book value ratio**) shows how much the market is willing to pay for equity. Book value is a cumulative amount that is typically a positive value, even if a company reports a loss and has a negative EPS. The price-to-book ratio is represented as:

$$\text{P/B ratio} = \frac{\text{Market value of equity}}{\text{Book value of equity}} = \frac{\text{Market price per share}}{\text{Book value per share}}$$

Where:

Book value of equity   = Common shareholders' equity

                                = (Total assets – Total liabilities) – Preferred stock

Example:

Using the information in the following table, here's how the P/B ratio would be calculated for the following company.

Book Value of Equity in 200X (millions)	Sales 200X (millions)	Shares Outstanding 200X (millions)	Price 05/15/0X
$14,015	$9,450	3,400	$9.50

$$\text{Book value per share} = \frac{\text{Book value of equity}}{\text{Number of shares outstanding}}$$

$$\text{Book value per share} = \frac{\$14,015}{3,400} = \$4.12$$

$$\text{P/B ratio} = \frac{\text{Market price per share}}{\text{Book value per share}} = \frac{\$9.50}{\$4.12} = \$2.31$$

Advantages of using P/B ratios include:

- Even when EPS is negative, book value is a cumulative amount and usually positive value.

- A book value measure is more stable than EPS, so it may be more useful than a P/E ratio when EPS is high, low, or volatile.

- Book value provides an appropriate measure of net asset value for firms largely holding liquid assets (for example, finance, investment, insurance, and banking).

- P/B can be used to value a company that is expected to go out of business.

- Research shows P/B ratios help explain differences in long-run average returns.

Disadvantages of using P/B ratios are:

- P/B ratios ignore the value of nonphysical assets (for example, customer goodwill or human capital).

- P/B ratios can be misleading when there are substantial differences in the size of the assets in the firms being compared.

- The true investment made by shareholders can be obscured by different accounting conventions.

- Technological change and inflation can result in substantial differences between the book and market value of assets.

Price-to-sales ratios

A **price/sales (P/S) ratio** shows how much the market is willing to pay for a dollar of sales. The P/S ratio is an increasing function of net profit margin, the dividend payout ratio, and growth rate; it is a decreasing function of risk.

The price-to-sales ratio is represented as:

$$\text{P/S ratio} = \frac{\text{Market value of equity}}{\text{Total sales}} = \frac{\text{Market price per share}}{\text{Sales per share}}$$

Example:

Using the information in the following table, here's how the P/S ratio would be calculated for the following company.

Book Value of Equity in 200X (millions)	Sales 200X (millions)	Shares Outstanding 200X (millions)	Price 05/15/0X
$14,015	$9,450	3,400	$9.50

$$\text{Sales per share} = \frac{\text{Sales}}{\text{Number of shares outstanding}}$$

$$\text{Sales per share} = \frac{\$9,450}{3,400} = \$2.78$$

$$\text{P/S ratio} = \frac{\text{Market price per share}}{\text{Sales per share}} = \frac{\$9.50}{\$2.78} = \$3.42$$

P/S ratios have the following advantages:

- The ratio provides meaningful measure even for distressed firms.

- Sales figures tend to be more reliable than EPS and book value because they are not as easy to manipulate or distort as EPS and book value.

- P/S multiples tend to be more stable because they are not as volatile as P/E multiples.

- P/S ratios are useful for valuing a range of stocks from mature or cyclical industries to start-up companies with no record of earnings.

- Research shows significant relationships between differences in P/S ratios and differences in long-term average stock returns.

P/S ratios have the following disadvantages:

- High sales are not necessarily indicative of operating profits measured by earnings and cash flow.

- P/S ratios do not capture differences in cost structures across companies.

- Although P/S ratios are less subject to distortion than EPS and book value, revenue recognition practices can distort sales forecasts.

Derivatives

A **derivative** is a financial instrument whose characteristics and value are derived from the underlying price or value of some other, more-basic financial instrument. The underlying asset (also known as an **underlying** or **underlier**) could be a bond, an equity investment, a commodity, or currency.

A derivative involves a contract between two parties. Payment is exchanged between the two parties. The amount of the payment can be either:

- A predetermined amount triggered by a specific event (for example, the price of the underlying asset exceeding some minimum value).

- An amount resulting from the change in value of a specified quantity of the underlier; the specified quantity of the underlier is referred to as the **notional amount** (or face amount) of the contract.

Financial Accounting Standards Board (FASB) Statement 133, "Derivative Instruments and Hedging Activities," and its amendments by Statements 138, 140, 141, and 145 deal with accounting rules for derivatives. In defining a derivative, Statement 133 notes the following points:

- It includes one or more underlying assets.

- It has one or more notional amounts or payment provisions or both.

- It requires no initial net investment or it has an amount smaller than other types of contracts that would be expected to have a similar response to changes in market factors.

- The net settlement (contract payment) must be a cash payment, delivery of an asset that can be easily converted to cash, or another derivative.

Inevitably, new derivatives will be developed. In specifying these characteristics (rather than defining a derivative in terms of financial instruments considered to be derivatives), FASB's intent was to ensure that Statement 133 could be applied to new derivatives—as long as their characteristics were similar to those outlined in the statement.

Corporations do not use derivatives to raise money but buy or sell them to protect against adverse changes in market factors. For example, a corporation might use a derivative to manage the risk associated with an underlying investment and protect against fluctuations in its value.

Conceptually, there are two basic types of derivatives: options and forward contracts. Subsequent content concentrates on these derivative instruments. Other derivative instruments (for example, futures and swaps) are some combination or variation of options and forwards. Their characteristics are briefly discussed.

Derivatives are complex instruments which can be risky. The information on derivatives contained in this text is intended to provide an overview.

Much of this content summarizes information from:

- *Accounting for Derivatives and Hedging* by Mark A. Trombley.

- *AFP Learning System: Treasury.*

- Statement on Management Accounting No. 4M, "Understanding Financial Instruments."

Many other resources are also devoted to the subject of derivatives. For additional guidance on buying and selling derivatives, consulting such resources is strongly advised.

Options

An **option** (or option contract) is a contract between two parties wherein the purchaser of the contract has the right (but not the obligation) to buy or sell a given amount of an underlying asset.

Key characteristics and terminology

Some of the notable characteristics and terminology associated with option contracts follow.

- The party with the option to buy or sell is the owner of the option (also known as the buyer or holder of the option). The other party is the writer or seller of the option.

- The underlying asset may be tangible (such as shares of stock, a commodity, or currency) or intangible (such as an index value or an interest rate).

- A **call option** is a type of option contract giving the owner the right (but not the obligation) to buy the underlying asset (also called the underlier) from the writer at a fixed price during the specified time period.

- A **put option** is a type of option contract giving the owner the right (but not the obligation) to sell to the writer the underlying asset at a fixed price during the specified time period.

- **Strike price** (or **exercise price**) refers to the fixed price of the contract.

- **Exercise date** (also known as **maturity date** or **expiration date**) is the last day on which the buyer can exercise (buy or sell) the underlying asset.

- The **premium** is the initial purchase price of the option; it is usually stated on a per-unit basis. The writer (seller) of an option contract receives an up-front premium from the buyer (owner) of the contract. This premium obligates the writer to fulfill the contract (sell or buy the underlying asset) if the buyer chooses to exercise the option.

- A **European option** is a contract allowing the owner to exercise the option only at maturity.

- An **American option** is a contract allowing the owner to exercise the option at any time before maturity.

Payoff structure

Different payoffs are possible with options:

- An option is referred to as "at-the-money" if the underlying asset price equals the strike price.

- An option generally referred to as "in-the-money" requires a payment to the owner if the contract is exercised immediately.

- The option is "out-of-the-money" if there is no incentive for the holder to exercise the option.

- A call option is referred to as "out-of-the-money" if the strike price exceeds the price of the underlying asset; it is referred to as "in-the-money" if the price of the underlying asset exceeds the strike price.

- A put option is referred to as "in-the-money" if the strike price exceeds the price of the underlying asset; it is referred to as "out-of-the-money" if the price of the underlying asset exceeds the strike price.

A couple of simplified examples of call and put option payoffs follow.

Call option example. A 30-day option contract is made between a buyer and a seller for a commodity; the strike price is $50 per unit. The premium is $2 per unit. Two scenarios are possible at maturity:

- If the market price is equal to or less than the strike price of $50, the owner (buyer) would not exercise the option because buying the commodity at the current market value price would be cheaper than exercising the option. The buyer loses $2 for the option premium.

- If the market price is greater than the strike price plus the option premium ($50 + $2 = $52), the owner (buyer) would exercise the option and make a profit.

Put option example. A 60-day option contract is made between a buyer and a seller for a commodity; the strike price is $30 per unit. The premium is $1 per unit. Two scenarios are possible at maturity:

- If the market price is equal to or greater than the strike price of $30, the owner would not exercise the option. The owner can make more money by selling the commodity at the current market value price than by exercising the option. The loss is $1 for the option premium.

- If the market price is less than the strike price minus the option premium ($30 − $1 = $29), the owner makes a profit by exercising the option.

At the time an option contract is set, neither party is required to own the underlying asset. In an option involving shares of stock, for example, the writer of the option does not have to currently own the shares of stock. The writer can offer the buyer the option to buy the stock without actually owning it. However, if the owner exercises the call option, the writer must deliver the stock. If the writer does not already own the stock, the writer must buy the shares specified by the contract on the open market and deliver them to the option owner. If current market value exceeds the strike price, the option writer receives only the strike price per share as payment. The difference between the strike price and the market value must be taken as a loss.

Options have an asymmetric payoff profile. Call option owners have the opportunity for unlimited gain with limited possible losses. If the option is not exercised, it expires. No units are exchanged, and the owner's loss is limited to the premium—the price paid to· acquire the option. Call option writers may experience unlimited potential losses (unless the contract is "covered," which means that the writer already owns the underlier). On the other hand, put option owners face limited gain and limited losses and put option writers face only limited losses (but also limited gain).

Options are typically used for leverage or protection. Using an option for leverage provides the owner with equity in the underlying asset for the premium payment (which is a fraction of the actual market value). Because options provide the right to acquire the underlying asset at a fixed price for a limited time, they offer protection by guarding against price fluctuations up to the maturity date. This limits risk to forfeiture of the option premium (unless the underlier is not already owned).

A payoff diagram for a call option is shown in Figure 3-66.

Figure 3-66: Call Option Payoffs

As shown in this call option payoff diagram:

- The market value (market price) differs from the minimum value (minimum price).

- Market value exceeds minimum value in the shaded area between the curved and straight lines.

Investors are willing to pay a premium above minimum price as long as the option price continues to increase. However, as the curved market value line collapses toward the minimum value line, investors are reluctant to pay a premium for the option because any further increase in the option price will produce a minimal increase in the option value.

Price and value of options

To a degree, the price or value of an option depends on the expected future value of the underlying asset (as shown in the simple examples).

In discussing options, Statement on Management Accounting No. 4M notes that the following factors influence the theoretical value of an option:

- The current price of the underlying asset

- The time until expiration of the option

- The volatility in price of the underlying asset

- The strike price of the option

- The interest rate on risk-free income securities (usually Treasury bills) expiring at the same time as the option contract

- The present value of any expected dividends or interest for common stocks or interest-bearing securities

In practice, mathematical formulas are required to calculate the theoretical option values. Furthermore, balance sheet accounting requires that a derivative must be shown at fair value on the balance sheet as either an asset or a liability (depending on the specific contract). Accountants must be able to determine the fair value of derivatives.

Regarding option valuation, Statement 133 references Statement 107, "Disclosure About Fair Value of Financial Instruments." Statement 107 describes the following three methods for estimating the fair value of derivatives:

- Tailoring adjustments—for derivatives where a market price is available and the estimate of fair value is based on an adjustment of the quoted market price

- Pricing models—primarily for option-based derivatives where various parameters are estimated (The Black-Scholes and the binomial models are discussed next.)

- Discounted cash flows—for forward-based derivatives where future cash flow needs are estimated and the current discount rate is used to calculate the net present value of the estimated cash flows

Note: The discounted cash flow method is covered in more detail in Section E, "Investment Decisions."

The Black-Scholes and the binomial models are two models often used for option pricing.

The **Black-Scholes option model** (named after Fisher Black and Myron Scholes, who developed it) assumes that the price of heavily traded assets follow a geometric Brownian motion with constant drift and volatility. When applied to a stock option, the model incorporates the constant price variation of the stock, the time value of money, the option's strike price, and the time to the option's expiration.

Key assumptions of the Black-Scholes model include.

- The stock pays no dividends during the option's life.

- European exercise terms are used; short selling the underlying stock is possible.

- Markets are efficient; trading of the stock is continuous.

- There are no transactions costs or taxes; no commissions are charged

- The risk-free interest rate exists, remains constant, and the same for all maturity dates.

- Returns on the underlying stock are normally distributed.

The **binomial option model** produces valuations for options through an iterative mathematical computation. It traces the evolution of the option's key underlying asset using a binomial lattice (a tree). Each node, or points in time in the lattice, represents a possible price of the underlying asset, at a particular point in time between the valuation date and option expiration. This price evolution forms the basis for the option valuation.

Key features of the binomial model are that it:

- Takes a risk-neutral approach to valuation.

- Assumes that underlying asset prices can only either increase or decrease with time until the option expires.

- Removes the possibility for arbitrage.

- Assumes a perfectly efficient market.

- Shortens the duration of the option.

Both the Black-Scholes and the binomial model approaches are considerably more complex than using discounted cash flows for pricing forwards and futures. But in practice they are not overly difficult to apply with the use of computer spreadsheets and scientific calculators. In fact, the mathematical computations of the Black-Scholes model and the binomial model are frequently very close to the actual option price.

Forward contracts

A forward contract is a customized agreement between two parties to buy or sell a specific amount of an asset at a future date for a set price. Forwards are fundamentally different than options because both parties are obligated to perform according to the terms of the contract.

Key characteristics and terminology

Some of the notable characteristics and terminology associated with forwards follow.

- In a forward contract, one party purchases the contract; the other party is usually referred to as the counterparty.

- The underlying asset may be tangible (such as a commodity or currency) or intangible (such as a stock index or a debt instrument).

- The party who agrees to buy the underlying asset on a specified future date assumes a **long position** (or is said to be "long a forward contract").

- The party who agrees to sell that underlying asset on the specified date assumes a **short position** (or is said to be "short a forward contract").

- The delivery price (or contract price) is the purchase/sale price specified in the contract.

- The delivery date (or maturity date) refers to the specified future date of the contract; delivery of the contract takes place at maturity.

- The amount of the underlying asset and the delivery date are set at the time the contract is negotiated; no initial payment (premium) is made.

The counterparty in a forward contract is often a bank or a dealer or trader in foreign exchange (FX) markets (as the most common application of forwards is with FX payments). In many cases, these entities serve as "market makers" and facilitate private contracts between two parties.

Forward contracts are not traded on organized exchanges. This is a key distinction from futures contracts, which are traded on standardized exchanges.

Payoff structure

In the absence of a premium payment, the initial value of the contract to both parties is zero. The contract has no value when it is written. The forward price determines the value of the contract. A long position gains value when the underlying asset price rises and loses value when the asset price falls. Conversely, the short position gains value when the underlying asset price falls and loses value when the asset price rises.

Forwards have symmetrical payoffs; gains and losses for favorable and unfavorable positions are equal. As the value of the underlying asset changes, the value of the long and short positions in a forward contract becomes proportionally positive or negative, depending on the position held.

Forward contract example. A simple scenario illustrating use of a forward contract might be a United States importer with a 60-day invoice due in euros. Purchasing a forward contract for euros deliverable in 60 days locks in the exchange rate regardless of the fluctuation that occurs in the currency exchange rate during the 60-day period.

Futures contracts

A **futures contract** (or futures) is a forward-based contract conceptually similar to a forward contract but different in execution. The basic difference is that unlike forwards (which are often privately negotiated by an intermediary), futures are standardized contracts traded on organized exchanges.

For example, in the United States, futures are traded on:

- The New York Mercantile Exchange (for example, for metals, petroleum, and fiber).

- The Chicago Board of Trade (for example, for livestock, wood, and meat).

- The International Money Market wing of the Chicago exchange (for example, for foreign currency futures).

The exchanges dictate notional amounts and maturity dates. They also require daily settlements during the contract based on changes in the underlying asset. Gains and losses are marked against a margin account.

Futures are usually closed out before maturity. They are rarely settled by actual delivery. Final settlement is generally accomplished through a cash payment. The payoff profile from a long position and a short position in a futures contract looks exactly the same as the payoff profiles from a forward contract.

Swaps

A **swap** is a private agreement between two parties (called counterparties) to exchange (or swap) future cash payments. Similar to a forward contract, a swap agreement is usually facilitated by an intermediary. Swaps are characterized by a series of forward contracts and the exchange of payments on specified payment dates.

The most common type of swaps is an interest rate swap—where two parties (usually assisted by an intermediary) exchange future interest payments on a notational amount. The principal amount is notational because it never changes hands and it is used only to calculate the payment amounts.

In the simplest type of interest swap called a plain vanilla interest rate swap), involves trading fixed interest rate payments for floating-rate payments:

- Party A agrees to pay Party B a series of future payments that are equal to a *predetermined fixed interest rate* multiplied by the notational principal.

- Party B agrees to pay Party A a series of future payments that are equal to a *floating interest rate* multiplied by the same notational principal.

At the initiation of the swap in a single currency, Party A and Party B typically do not swap the notional principal. When payments are due, net interest is paid by the counterparty that owes it. That is, the appropriate counterparty pays the difference between the fixed-rate and variable-rate payments. At the conclusion of the swap, there is no transfer of funds because the parties did not initially swap the notional principal.

The main motivation for using interest rate swaps is to reduce exposure to adverse changes in interest rates. The parties convert a fix-rate obligation (or investment) into a floating-rate (or vice versa) that might be desirable to match the fixed or floating character of their assets and liabilities.

For example, assume the two parties, A and B, both want to borrow $10 million for 5 years. Party A has a better credit rating than Party B. Each part has been offered the following terms:

	Fixed Rate	Floating Rate
Party A	10.00%	6-month LIBOR* + 0.50%
Party B	11.00%	6-month LIBOR + 1.00%

* London Interbank Offered Rate

Also assume:

- Party A want to borrow at a floating rate

- Party B wants to borrow at a fixed rate.

- Party A has a better credit rating than Party and pays lower interest rates than in fixed and floating markets.

- Party B pays more than Party B in both markets but relatively less in the floating-rate market at a floating rate of the (LIBOR) plus 1 percentage point.

Because Party A has a comparative borrowing advantage in the fixed-rate market and Party B has a comparative borrowing advantage in the floating-rate market, the two parties enter into an interest rate swap agreement that produces a net advantage which is typically split between the two parties.

A potential risk is using swaps is either counterparty may default on the agreed-upon interest payment stream and thus potentially leave the other party liable for the original payment stream. The use of a third-party intermediary can help to mitigate such risks.

There are other forms of interest swaps as well as many other types of swaps. A couple of the more common ones are currency rate swaps, where an obligation in one currency is converted to another currency, and commodity swaps, where a floating price for a commodity is exchanged for a fixed price.

Other Long-Term Financial Instruments

In addition to the investment instruments described thus far, there are other instruments that corporations can use as sources for long-term financing. Figure 3-67 summarizes key features about leases, convertible securities, warrants, and retained earnings.

Figure 3-67: Other Long-Term Financial Instruments

Instrument	Description	Key Characteristics
Lease	Legal contract through which the owner (the lessor) of an asset grants another party (the lessee) the right to use the asset for a certain period of time in return for a specified payment	■ Binds the lessee to make payments specified in the lease contract ■ Can take various forms: 　■ Operating leases: short-term, cancelable leases where the lessor bears the risk of ownership 　■ Financial lease (also known as full payout or capital lease): usually noncancellable and fully paid out (amortized) over its term and where the lessee bears the risks. That is, the lessee bears the responsibility for maintenance, insurance, and taxes.
Convertible security	A fixed income security or a preferred stock that includes an option to exchange that security for a stated number of shares of another security	■ Typically used to convert the security into a specified number of shares of an equity security ■ Allows a corporation to raise funds at a cost of capital lower than a straight bond or common stock issue; when convertibles are exchanged, debt is removed from the balance sheet
Warrant	Long-term call option to purchase common stock directly from the corporation	■ Gives bondholders or preferred stockholders the right to purchase shares of common stock at a given price ■ Derives value from the investor's expectation that the stock price will increase beyond the strike price
Retained earnings	Net income over the life of a corporation less cash or stock dividends	■ Represents the total earnings of the corporation that have been retained in the business (not distributed to owners as cash or transferred to contributed capital because of stock dividends) ■ Ultimately represents the cheapest cost of equity capital because it allows a corporation to reinvest in itself

Progress Check

Directions: Read each question and respond in the space provided. Answers and page references appear on the page following the progress check questions.

1. Which statement accurately describes bond yields?

    (   )   a.   Higher-quality bonds typically pay lower yields than lower-grade bonds.

    (   )   b.   Short-term bonds typically pay higher yields than long-term bonds.

    (   )   c.   Fixed interest rate bonds earn more than zero coupon bonds.

    (   )   d.   Secured bonds typically pay higher yields than unsecured bonds.

2. Which type of bond is **most** attractive to buy on the secondary market when interest rates are low?

    (   )   a.   Aaa- or AAA-rated bond

    (   )   b.   Zero coupon bond

    (   )   c.   Floating rate bond

    (   )   d.   U.S. Treasury bond

Match the financial instruments with the appropriate description.

3. _____ Common stock

4. _____ Preferred stock

5. _____ Option

6. _____ Forward contract

7. _____ Warrant

8. _____ Swap

   a.   An agreement between two parties to buy or sell a specific amount of an asset at a future date for a set price

   b.   A private agreement between two parties to exchange future cash payments

   c.   Long-term call option to purchase common stock directly from the corporation

   d.   An instrument providing partial ownership in a corporation and a fixed dividend

   e.   A contract allowing the purchaser the right to buy or sell the underlying asset at a stated price on or before a specific date

   f.   An instrument providing equity interest in the assets of the corporation and a share in the earnings

9. What is a primary difference between stock splits and cash dividends?

    ( )   a. Cash dividends do not result in any taxable gain or loss; stock splits are taxable.

    ( )   b. Stock splits do not result in any taxable gain or loss; cash dividends are taxable.

    ( )   c. Cash dividends are paid quarterly; stock splits are awarded on an annual basis.

    ( )   d. Stock splits are paid quarterly; cash dividends are awarded on an annual basis.

Progress check answers

1. a (p. 3-202)

2. c (p. 3-200)

3. f (p. 3-209)

4. d (p. 3-214)

5. e (p. 3-224)

6. a (p. 3-228)

7. c (p. 3-230)

8. b (p. 3-231)

9. b (p. 3-209)

▪ Topic 3 Cost of Capital

Topic overview

As defined by Statement on Management Accounting No. 4A, "Cost of Capital," the cost of capital is a composite of the costs of various sources of funds comprising a firm's capital structure. It represents the minimum rate of return that must be earned on new investments so that shareholders' interests won't be diluted.

Cost of Capital, Defined

A corporation's management team is charged with ensuring efficiency and profitability from assets as well as minimizing the cost of the funds that the firm incurs from investments. In fulfilling this fiduciary responsibility, management makes various financing decisions that affect the firm's capital structure.

Corporations derive capital from essentially two sources: lenders and shareholders. The total capital of a firm represents a combination of debt capital and equity capital. Statement on Management Accounting (SMA) No. 4H, "Uses of the Cost of Capital," describes these capital components as follows:

▪ **Debt capital** is that portion of total capital derived from the issuance of interest-bearing instruments such as notes, bonds, or loans.

▪ **Equity capital** is that portion of total capital derived from permanent investments by shareholders, as either paid-in capital or retained earnings. A firm may issue new shares of common or preferred stock, or it may choose to retain earnings instead of distributing them as dividends.

Every activity a firm does to generate capital--either explicit or implicit--has a cost associated with it. The overall **cost of capital** represents a proportional average of the various components a firm uses for financing.

The cost of capital should be considered in capital structure decisions. Corporations can benefit from using the cost of capital to benchmark investment decisions and to more efficiently manage working capital (for example, receivables, inventories, and payables). The cost of capital can also be valuable to use in measuring and evaluating performance. For example, the actual and expected return on capital or net assets may be compared with the cost of capital associated with each.

Calculating the Cost of Capital

The cost of capital is found by determining costs for the individual types of capital and then multiplying each component cost by its proportion in the firm's total capital structure. SMA No. 4A provides the following general formula for the cost of capital:

$$k_a = p_1 k_1 + p_2 k_2 \ldots + p_n k_n$$

Where:

- n = different types of financing (each with its own cost and proportion in the capital structure).

- k = cost of an element in the capital structure.

- p = proportion that element comprises of the total capital structure.

- k_a = cost of capital (expressed as a percentage).

Cost of capital example

Consider a corporation that uses the types of financing shown in Figure 3-68:

Figure 3-68: Cost of Capital Example

Type (n)	After-Tax Cost (k)	% of Capital Structure (p)
Debt	4%	30%
Preferred stock	8%	20%
Common equity	18%	50%

$k_a = p_1 k_1 + p_2 k_2 \ldots + p_n k_n$

$= 0.30(4\%) + 0.20(8\%) + 0.50(18\%) = 1.2 + 1.6 + 9 = 11.8\%$

In calculating the cost of capital, using the current or prospective cost of the various capital components is generally more appropriate than relying on historical costs. A primary use of the cost of capital is investing new capital in such projects as new products, equipment, or facilities. Therefore, relevant costs are the marginal costs associated with incremental funds the firm plans to raise, not historical costs of capital that the firm had already raised.

Primary considerations in determining the costs of capital are:

- How to determine the cost (k) of each individual capital component.

- How to determine the respective weights (p) in the total capital structure of the firm.

Cost of Individual Capital Components

Determining the cost of each component in a firm's capital structure is the first step in calculating the cost of capital. Corporations typically use three methods of financing:

- Debt

- Preferred stock

- Common equity

Cost of debt

The cost of debt represents the required rate of return that providers of debt capital (for example, loans and bonds) require. The basic formula for the after-tax cost of debt is:

$$\text{After-Tax Cost of Debt} = k_d(1-t)$$

Where:

- k_d = the before-tax cost of debt.

- t = firm's marginal tax rate.

Considerations in determining the after-tax cost of debt are:

- What interest rate (kd) should be used?

- How should different types of debt be handled?

- What effect do income taxes have on the interest rate?

This formula does not reflect any flotation costs because most debt is privately placed.

The before-tax cost of debt is greater than the after-tax cost of debt because a firm can deduct interest payments when determining taxable income. The higher the tax rate, the lower the after-tax cost of debt.

Example:

Consider the following example where Blane Company's debt consists of 6% interest-bearing bonds, which is selling at par. The anticipated tax rate is 35%. The cost of debt would be:

$$\text{After-Tax Cost of Debt} = k_d(1-t)$$

$$= 6\%(1-0.35)$$

$$= 3.9\%$$

The current replacement cost (market value) of debt is used in calculating the cost of capital. But when one or more types of debt are involved, a weighted average of yields-to-maturity should be used to calculate the cost of debt.

The weighted average cost of debt is calculated as shown in Figure 3-69.

Figure 3-69: Weighted Average Cost of Debt Using Yields-to-Maturity

1 Debt	2 Market Value (millions)	3 % of Total	4 Yield-to- Maturity *	5 = (3 × 4) Weighted Cost
Issue A	$45	10.0%	11.2%	1.12%
Issue B	125	27.8	12.4%	3.45
Issue C	280	62.2	13.1%	8.15
Total:	$450	100.0%		12.72%

Weighted average cost of debt before taxes: 12.7%

Adjustment for income taxes (1 – .45):   .55

Weighted average cost of debt after income taxes: 6.99%

* Yield-to-maturity on a bond is the rate of discount that equates the present value of all interest and principal payments with the current price of the bond.

Cost of preferred stock

The cost associated with preferred stock is a function of the dividend paid (if any) to shareholders and flotation costs. The cost of preferred stock needs to reflect flotation costs as they can be substantial. Flotation costs include direct costs (such as underwriting fee, filing fees, legal fees, and taxes) and indirect costs (such as management time working on the new issue). Flotation costs are deducted from the selling price of the preferred stock to determine net proceeds.

The general formula for the cost of preferred stock is:

$$k_p = \frac{D_p}{P_p - F}$$

Where:

- k_p = component cost of preferred stock.
- D_p = preferred stock dividend.
- P_p = the current price per share (current or prospective cost).
- F = flotation costs as a dollar amount.

Example:

Blane company's preferred stock pays an $8 dividend per share and sells for $100 per shares. If the firm issued new shares of preferred, it would incur underwriting and other fees (flotation costs) of $2 per share. Here's how the cost of preferred stock would be calculated for the company.

$$k_p = \frac{D_p}{P_p - F} = \frac{\$8}{\$100 - \$2} = \frac{\$8}{\$98} = 8.16\%$$

In this example, the cost of the preferred stock is shown based on an annual dividend payment. If the dividend payment was quarterly, the same formula could be used and the quarterly rate multiplied by four to get the nominal annual rate.

Flotation costs may sometimes be given as a percentage of the issue. In the above example, the flotation costs were 2%. Thus, the denominator of the cost of preferred stock would be come $P_p(1-F\%)$, where F is a percent, not a dollar amount.

Because preferred stock dividends are not tax-deductible, they represent an outflow of after-tax funds. A preferred stock (par of $100) with an 11% dividend costs the firm $11 in after-tax earnings. If the firm has a 35% tax rate, it must earn $1.54 before taxes for each dividend dollar paid.

When a corporation has more than one issue of preferred stock outstanding, the weighted average rate on all preferred stock should be used.

Cost of common equity

The **cost of common equity** (or **cost of equity**) is the most difficult capital component to calculate. As noted previously, equity consists primarily of common stock issues, paid-in capital, and retained earnings. SMA No. 4A describes the cost of equity as the expected, required, or actual rate of return on the firm's common stock, which, if earned, will leave the market value of the stock unchanged. The rate is difficult to estimate because common stock has no fixed contractual payments.

Various methods ranging from simple to complex exist for estimating the cost of equity; they. Three methods of estimating the cost of internal equity follow:

- Historical rate of return.

- Dividend growth model.

- Capital asset pricing model.

Each method has distinct advantages and limitations. Firms may use more than one method to determine a reasonable estimate. The choice of the appropriate method if often a function of the information available for a given situation.

As noted earlier, companies raise equity by one of two ways:

- Internally by retaining earnings.

- Externally by selling new shares of common stock.

Mature companies tend to generate most equity internally. Flotation costs make the cost of raising new equity in the market more expensive. Additionally, if the stock is under priced, losses result from selling stock shares below the correct value Stated another way, firms generally use lower-cost retained earnings (internal equity) before issuing a new common stock (external equity) because of flotation costs and potential losses from underpricing.

Estimating the cost of internal equity using historical rate of return

As the name implies, the historical rate of return method of determining the cost of equity capital involves the historical rate stockholders have earned. It considers the rate of return earned by an investor who bought the stock in the past, held it to the present, and sold it at current market prices.

For example, consider a situation in which an issue of a common stock share purchased for $100 five years ago sells today for $110. Dividends of $8 were paid annually. Using the historical method, the average rate of return for the investor was 10% a year ($8 dividend plus $2 average annual gain/$100). The 10% is then used as the estimate of the current rate of return on the stock and the firm's cost of equity capital.

As noted in SMA No. 4A, using the historical method implies that:

- The firm's performance will not change substantially in the future.

- No significant changes in interest rates will occur.

- Investor attitude toward risk will not change.

Although this historical method is relatively easy to calculate, the limitation is that the future rarely remains the same as the past.

Estimating the cost of internal equity using the dividend growth model

The dividend growth model reflects a market value approach. As described in SMA No. 4A, the underlying logic of this model is that the market price of a stock equals the cash flow of expected future incomes, both dividends and market price appreciation, discounted to their present value. This means that when the present value of the future incomes equals the market price, the discount rate equals the cost of equity capital. An underlying assumption is that incomes will grow at a constant compound rate.

The formula for calculating dividend growth is:

$$k_s = \frac{D_1}{P_o} + g$$

Where:

- k_s = the cost of internal equity capital.

- D_1 = the dividend per share at time 1.

- P_o = the market price per share at the time 0.

- g = the expected dividend growth rate.

Example:

If Blane Company's stock is currently selling at $50 per share, the dividend at the end of the first year is expected to be $3.50 per share, and future dividends are expected to grow at 5% per year, the cost of equity capital would be:

$$k_s = \frac{\$3.50}{\$50} + 5\% = 12.00\%$$

Similar to other methods for calculating the cost of equity capital, the dividend growth rate involves an estimate. In this case, the estimate is for the value of g. The model is useful only if market expectations are for dividends to grow at that rate. Investors must believe that the past trends of earnings per share will continue. If this is the case, the trend (expressed as a percentage) may be used.

Estimating the cost of internal equity using the capital asset pricing model

The capital asset pricing model (CAPM) was previously discussed as it related to portfolio management (in Topic 1, "Risk and Return"). It is also useful in measuring the cost of equity capital for a firm.

The CAPM implies that the rate of return on any security equals the riskless rate of interest plus a premium for risk. The riskless rate is usually based on the current or anticipated rate on long-term U.S. Treasury bonds or short-term U.S. Treasury bills. The premium for risk is derived from the security's beta.

The formula for applying the CAPM to estimate the cost of equity capital is:

$$k_s = R_f + \beta(k_m - R_f)$$

Where:

- k_s = cost of internal equity capital.

- R_f = riskfree rate (for example, the rate on T-bonds or a 30-day T-bill).

- ß = stock's beta estimate (obtained from a brokerage firm, or investment advisory service, or calculated by the firm).

- k_m = estimate of the return on the market as a whole or on an average stock value.

The term ($k_m - R_f$) is called the market risk premium, which is somewhere in the area of 5% to 7%, depending on the date of the estimate and the data sources used by the analysts. Firms often add 6% to the Treasury bond rate to obtain the rate of return for the market as a whole.

Example:

If the Treasury bond rate is 8%, a firm's stock beta is 0.9, and the expected rate of return for the market is 14%, Blane Company's cost of equity capital using the CAPM would be:

$$k_s = 8\% + 0.9(14\% - 8\%)$$

$$= 8\% + 5.40\%$$

$$= 13.40\%$$

Using the CAPM involves estimates for each term in the equation. Challenges arise in deciding:

- Whether to use long- or short-term Treasury bond rates for Rf.

- Estimating the future beta investors expect.

- Estimating the expected rate of return for the market as a whole.

Estimating the cost of new equity using the dividend growth model

Determining the cost of new common stock (k_e) must consider flotation costs and possible under pricing losses. The constant growth DDM formula use to calculate the cost of existing equity (k_s) can be adjusted to account for both factors. The formula for calculating the cost of new equity is:

$$k_e = \frac{D_1}{P_o - (F + U)} + g$$

Where:

- k_e = cost of external equity capital.

- D_1 = dividend per share at time 1.

- P_o = market price per share at the time 0.

- g = expected dividend growth rate.

- F = flotation costs.

- U = under pricing losses.

Example:

Suppose Blane Company can issue stock for $50 per share, before $5 from flotation costs and under pricing losses. The dividend at the end of the first year is expected to be $6 per share, and future dividends are expected to grow at 5% per year. The estimated cost of new equity capital would be:

$$k_e = \frac{D_1}{P_o - (F + U)} + g$$

$$= \frac{\$3.50}{\$50 - \$5} + 0.05 = 13.00\%$$

Comparing the cost of new equity (13.00%) to the cost of internal equity (12%), the difference is the flotation costs and underwriting losses. These factors make the cost of new equity more costly by 1.0 percentage points.

Estimating the cost of capital, especially when the cost of equity is involved, is not exact. Decision making about inputs and the different models themselves can result in substantial differences in estimates.

Weighted Average Cost of Capital

Once the different capital components have been determined, the final goal is to calculate the relative importance of each source in the total capital structure of the firm. In other words, the individual components must be weighted to show the extent to which each one contributes to the total value of the firm's capital structure.

The **weighted average cost of capital (WACC)** is the firm's overall cost of capital and represents the risks associated with typical; or average projects.

Many companies use the following weighted average cost of capital formula:

$$WACC = \sum_{i=1}^{n} w_i k_i$$

Where:

- WACC = weighted average cost of capital.

- w_i = percentage of total permanent capital represented by each capital component.

- k_i = after-tax cost of each capital component.

- n = total number of capital components.

Because WACC includes all sources of permanent financing in a firm's capital structure, the sum of the weighted components must equal 1.0

There are three weighting schemes commonly used to calculate WACC.

- **Book value weights**
  Book value weights measure the proportion of each type of capital based on accounting (book) values shown on the firm's balance sheet.

- **Market value weights**
  Market value weights represent current proportions of each type of capital in the firm's capital structure at current market prices.

- **Target value weights**
  Target value weights represent the weights based on the firm's optimal (target) capital structure.

Book values remain stable because they do not depend on changing market values for debt and equity. They represent historical costs. However, using book values can skew WACC because book values may substantially differ from the market.

Many believe that market value weights are the most accurate way to compute WACC because market weights consider the effects of changing market conditions and the current prices of each security. Some debate exists, however, between the merits of using weights based on the actual market or the target market capital structure. Because target weights represent the best estimate of how the firm will raise money in the future, they make sense if the firm is migrating towards the target structure.

Example:

Management considers the mix as optimal and wants to maintain this target structure in raising future capital. If Blane Company raises new capital in target proportions, here's how to determine the firm's WACC.

Capital Component	Weight	After-Tax Cost	WACC
Long-term debt	0.40	3.90%	1.500%
Preferred stock	0.10	8.16	0.816
Common (internal) equity	0.50	11.80	5.900
			8.276%

* Using the average cost of the historical rate of return (10.0%), dividend growth model (12.0%), and CAPM (13.4%), the cost of common (internal) equity (retained earnings) is (11.0% + 12.0% +13.4%)/3 = 11.8%. If management thought that one method of estimating the cost of retained earnings was better than another, it could use that cost instead of determining an average based on several methods.

Thus, Blane Company's weighted average cost of capital before using external equity would be 8.276%.

$$WACC = (.30 \times 4.58\%) + (.15 \times 8.22\%) + (.55 \times 11.25\%)$$
$$= 0.0865 \text{ or } 8.65\%$$

Marginal Cost of Capital

Companies do not have unlimited sources of funds for investments. Simply stated: they cannot exceed their financial capabilities to meet financial obligations.

Market investors evaluate the financial merits of different companies, compare them, and determine reasonable limits for individual companies, beyond which investors will not make funds readily available. Should a firm attempt to extend financing beyond its market-determined limit, those funds are only available at high costs. (Recall that raising external capital has flotation costs, making the cost of new equity higher than the costs of retained earnings.)

The **marginal cost of capital (MCC)** is the last dollar of new capital that the firm raises. The **weighted marginal cost of capital (WMCC)** is the incremental cost of financing beyond the previous MCC level. The **marginal cost of capital schedule** sets a series of ranges and specifies the incremental costs a firm will incur when financing exceeds the maximum limit in each range.

MCC schedules

There are five steps to develop a MCC schedule:

1. Determine the appropriate weights of the new financing.

2. Calculate the component cost of capital associated with each amount of capital raised.

3. Calculate the range of total new financing at which the cost of the new components increases.

4. Calculate the MCC for each range of total new financing.

5. Plot a MCC schedule.

Setting MCC schedule break points

Establishing the range of total new financing at which the cost of the new components increases requires setting break points. A **break point (BP)** is defined as the total financing a firm can raise before the cost of capital increases.

The formula for calculating a MCC break point is:

$$BP_{RE} = \frac{TF_i}{w_i}$$

Where:

- BP_{RE} = break point for capital component i.

- TF_i = total amount of funds available from capital component i.

- w_i = percentage of total permanent capital represented by capital component i.

Using this formula, a break point can be determined by dividing the total amount of funds available for a particular capital component at a stated cost by its capital structure weight.

A MCC schedule may include several break points.

Example:

Blane Company's expects to have $50 million in earnings available during the next year to payout out cash dividends to common shareholders or to reinvest. The firm expects to have a 40% dividend payout ratio. Thus, the company will have $30 million [($50)(1 – 0.40)] in new retained earnings. Given the company's capital structure of 40% debt, 10%, and 50% equity, what is the breakpoint for retained earnings?

$$BP_{RE} = \frac{TF_i}{w_i}$$

$$BP_{RE} = \frac{\$30\ million}{0.50} = \$60\ million$$

Thus, Blane Company can raise $60 before having to issue external equity as the equity component of its financing mix. This $60 million will consists of $24 million in debt (0.40 × $60 million), $6 million in preferred stock (0.10 × $60 million), and $30 million in internal equity (retained earnings -- 0.50 × $60 million)). If the company has a capital budget greater than $60 million, it will need to use more expensive common stock as the equity component. Thus, the company's marginal cost of capital will increase due to the higher cost of common stock compared with retained earnings.

Calculating the MCC

Blane Company wants to calculate its marginal cost of capital after the retained earnings break point. Based on the dividend discount model, the firm's cost of retained equity is 12% but its cost of new equity is 13% when considering flotation costs and underpricing. Thus, the difference of 1 percentage point represents an estimate of the flotation and underpricing costs. Management decides to add 1 percentage point to the cost of common (internal) equity previously calculated. Thus, the estimated cost of new common stock is 12.8%, that is, 11.8% + 1.0%.

Example:

Here's how to calculate Blane Company's marginal cost of capital after the retained earnings break point of $60 million?

Capital Component	Weight	After-Tax Cost	WACC
Long-term debt	0.40	3.90%	1.500%
Preferred stock	0.10	8.16	0.816
Common (internal) equity	0.50	12.80	6.400
			8.776%

Thus, the marginal cost of capital after $60 million increases to 8.776%. The MCC schedule it plotted below.

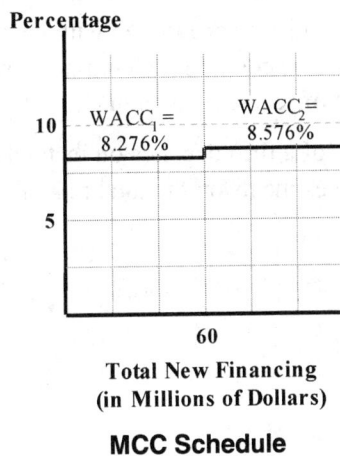

MCC Schedule

The MCC recognizes the responses of investors to increased financing requirements. The market imposes limits on different levels. Excessive levels lead to successively higher costs of capital.

Income taxes impact on capital structure and capital investment decisions

Taxes can affect a firm's capital structure in following ways:

- **Firms with large taxable income**
  Firms with large taxable income (unshielded from taxes) can possibly reduce taxes through more debt financing—which increases the total cash flows distributed to debt and equity holders.

- **Firms with volatile operating earnings**
  Firms with volatile operating earnings pose a higher business risk and lower the probability that the firm will be able to use tax deductions from borrowing during

lower income years. These firms may not want to borrow as much as other firms that have lower business risk.

Use of Cost of Capital in Investment Decisions

Corporations must decide where to invest income to gain the highest possible rate of return within the firm's risk profile. SMA No. 4A notes that firms can use the cost of capital as a discount rate of return to evaluate the present value of project cash flows or as a hurdle (threshold) rate to evaluate the internal rate of return.

Cost of capital provides a benchmark for assessing whether the risk and returns on a firm's securities are high or low. These ratings are important for the following reasons:

- High risk means a high cost of capital; low risk is indicative of a low cost of capital.

- A high cost of capital (discount rate) typically means a low valuation of the firm's securities; a low cost of capital means a high valuation for securities.

The sale of securities provides a corporation with necessary funds for investments. If the value of securities is low, the cost of financing increases. Conversely, financing costs decrease when the value of securities is high.

Ultimately, the solvency of a firm depends on its total risk. Management must consider the impact of various investments on the total risk of the firm.

Progress Check

Directions: Read each question and respond in the space provided. Answers and page references appear on the page following the progress check questions.

1. What is the cost of capital for a firm given the following information?

Type	After-Tax Cost	% of Capital Structure
Debt	8%	34%
Preferred stock	9%	26%
Common equity	10%	40%

( )   a. 8%

( )   b. 9%

( )   c. 10%

( )   d. 27%

2. Which factor makes determining the cost of debt challenging?

( )   a. Interest costs may be calculated in a variety of ways.

( )   b. Retained earnings are subject to dividend payments.

( )   c. Common stock has no fixed contractual payments.

( )   d. The firm's future performance levels are difficult to estimate.

3. An underlying premise in applying the capital asset pricing model to estimate a firm's cost of equity capital is

( )   a. Investor attitudes toward risk will not change.

( )   b. Incomes are expected to grow at a constant compound rate.

( )   c. Individual capital components must be weighted based on their contributions to the firm's capital structure.

( )   d. The return rate equals the riskless rate of return plus a premium for risk.

Match the following terms to their description.

4. _____ Cost of capital

5. _____ Cost of debt

6. _____ Cost of preferred stock

7. _____ Cost of common equity

a. The interest rate a company pays on all of its capital debt (for example, loans and bonds)

b. A function of the dividend paid (if any) to shareholders

c. The proportional average of the various components a firm uses for financing

d. The expected, required, or actual rate of return on the firm's stock which, if earned, will leave the market value of the stock unchanged

Progress check answers

1. b (p. 3-237)

2. a (p. 3-238)

3. d (p. 3-242)

4. c (p. 3-236)

5. a (p. 3-238)

6. b (p. 3-239)

7. d (p. 3-240)

Topic 4 Managing Current Assets

Topic overview

The basic components of an organization's working capital are cash, marketable securities, accounts receivable, and inventory. This topic looks at working capital and the management of each of these components.

Working Capital Terminology

Working capital (or **current capital**) generally refers to the funds a company holds in current (short-term) asset accounts. **Net working capital** refers specifically to the difference between a firm's current assets and its current liabilities. Net working capital provides a measure of immediate liquidity and indicates how much cash a firm has available to sustain and build its business. Depending on a firm's level of current liabilities, the number may be positive or negative.

Working capital management refers to decisions made about a firm's short-term assets and liabilities. Working capital management policies are generally categorized as aggressive, conservative, or moderate.

- **Aggressive working capital management**
  An **aggressive working capital management** policy focuses on high profitability potential, despite the cost of high risk and low liquidity. Aggressive asset management results in capital being minimized in current assets versus long-term investments. Aggressive financing policies include higher levels of lower cost short-term debt and less long-term capital investments. Although this lowers capital costs, it increases the risk of short-term liquidity problems.

- **Conservative working capital management**
  Conservative working capital management policy focuses on low risk, low return working capital investment and financing. A conservative policy places a greater proportion of capital in liquid assets, but at the sacrifice of some profitability. Conservative policy uses higher cost capital but postpones the principal repayment of debt, or avoids it entirely by using equity.

- **Moderate working capital management**
  A **moderate** (or **matching**) **working capital management** policy use risk and return and financing strategies that match the maturity of the assets with the maturity of the financing. The hedging approach to financing involves matching maturities of debt with specific financing needs.

As Statement on Management Accounting No. 4N, "Management of Working Capital: Cash Resources," succinctly states, effective working capital management is important for all businesses. Firms need to review the complete operations of their working capital management programs to ensure efficiencies in:

- Cash management—managing cash inflows and outflows.

- Marketable securities management—managing short-term investments and borrowing portfolios.

- Accounts receivable management—managing cash receivables and disbursements.

- Inventory management—maintaining stock of items at desired levels (for example, raw materials, work in progress, or finished products).

Working capital management consists of cash and securities management, receivables management, inventory management, and short-term credit management. Its goal is to minimize both the operating cycle and the cash cycle.

The operating cycle is the number of days of inventory on hand plus the receivables collection period.

The cash cycle is the operating cycle less the accounts payable payment cycle.

Both cycles are minimized by decreasing the number of days inventory on hand and the receivables collection period while maximizing the accounts payable payment cycle.

Subsequent content examines each of these working capital components in more detail.

Cash Management

Cash management describes the collective activities by which a corporation administers and invests its cash. The primary goal of cash management is to use cash as efficiently as possible and in a manner that is consistent with the firm's strategic objectives and risk management profile.

Finance and treasury departments are integrally involved in cash management. Working together, they must ensure that the necessary cash resources are available in a timely manner to sustain business operations, starting with the purchase of raw materials and other resources and continuing through to payment for those materials and resources, the sale of goods and services, and the collection of sales receipts.

Factors influencing cash levels

Liquidity requirements and a firm's profitability and risk policies are the primary determinants of its cash levels.

- **Liquidity requirements**
  Liquidity refers to the ability to convert assets into cash quickly without incurring loss. A firm's cash inflows (incoming cash) and cash outflows (cash expenditures) are rarely synchronized—which means that they are not for the same amount and do not occur at the same time. A business needs to monitor net working capital to cover the imbalances of cash inflows and outflows and ensure sufficient liquidity. Ultimately, an efficient cash management system can increase a firm's overall liquidity. In turn, increased liquidity can lead to increased profitability and reduced risk of insolvency.

- **Profitability and risk policies**
  Profitability typically varies inversely with liquidity. A firm must determine the

optimal levels of investment in current assets as well as the appropriate mix of short- and long-term financing necessary to support liquidity requirements. Such investments must take into account the interrelationship and trade-offs between profitability and risk. For example, offering more liberal credit terms to vendors may increase receivables. Thus, the firm may have to sell short-term securities, reduce cash balances, and/or increase short-term funding from banks to generate cash flows. On the other hand, trying to reduce idle cash in bank accounts may result in increased transaction costs. Clearly, the optimum mix of debt or equity financing can vary greatly from one company or industry to another.

The effective management of liquidity, profitability, risk, and cash requires a cash management system that must address the day-to-day management of:

- Collections—how to bring funds into the firm from customers or other payors.

- Concentration—how to concentrate funds where they can be most effectively used by moving cash from deposit banks (field banks) and other banks in the firm's collection system to a primary concentration bank.

- Disbursements—how to move funds from the concentration bank to the firm's disbursement bank(s) for payments to employees, vendors, investors, and other payees.

- Banking relations—how to manage relationships with banks and other financial service providers.

- Cash forecasting—how to forecast future cash flows and predict potential shortages or surpluses.

- Information management—how to develop and maintain appropriate information systems for collecting and analyzing financial data.

- Investing and borrowing—how to invest excess cash balances and meet short-term borrowing requirements.

- Compensation—how to cover wages and other financial benefits earned from labor.

Once again, the magnitude of these operations will vary according to the size and nature of the business enterprise. A large international corporation would, of course, have a much more complex cash management system than a small domestic company that occupies one facility.

Motives for holding cash

Corporations need sufficient financial resources (for example, cash balances in banks and securities as well as back-up lines of credit and other short-term borrowing arrangements) to maintain adequate liquidity. The reasons businesses need to manage liquidity are typically summarized as being driven by transactions, precautionary, or speculative motives.

- **Transactions motive**
  The transactions motive for holding cash addresses the unsynchronized nature of cash flows. A firm must have sufficient cash reserves or near-cash reserves to meet

financial payments arising from ordinary business operations (for example, small purchases, employee compensation, taxes, and dividends).

- **Precautionary motive**
  The precautionary motive for holding cash is to provide a buffer for unexpected cash needs. The unpredictable nature of cash inflows and outflows means that a firm must maintain sufficient levels of cash or near-cash balances to cover expenses.

- **Speculative motive**
  The speculative motive involves the use of surplus liquid reserves to take advantage of short-term investments or other temporary situations that may arise. For example, the price of a raw material may suddenly decline and offer a substantial savings if purchased with reserve funds.

Ensuring proper levels of liquidity necessitates continuous measuring, monitoring, and forecasting activities. Excess liquidity and insufficient liquidity both have disadvantages:

- Excess liquidity can translate into a loss of potential earnings because funds are not used profitably.

- Insufficient liquidity can result in a variety of negative costs such as delayed payments, additional interest from unexpected borrowing, or brokerage and administrative costs if securities must be sold. In the worst-case scenario, excessive liquidity deficits can lead to insolvency and bankruptcy.

Management of cash flows

Forecasting data and financial controls contained in a cash budget provides a starting point for cash management. But efficient cash management also involves day-to-day activities pertaining to collection, disbursement, and temporary investments.

The following types of cash flows must managed:

- **Cash inflows**—funds collected from customers; funds obtained from banks, lenders, and other financial sources; and funds received from investors and other payors

- **Concentration flows**—internal transfers among a firm's business units and between various bank accounts the firm owns to create liquid reserves

- **Cash outflows**—funds distributed from the firm's liquid reserves to employees, vendors, shareholders, and other payees of the company

The timing of these cash flows is important to maintain adequate liquidity, optimize cash resources, and manage risk. The challenge in cash flow timing is to be able to meet current and future financial obligations in a timely manner while minimizing nonearning (idle) cash balances, borrowing any necessary funds at an acceptable cost, and controlling the firm's exposure to financial risks.

A firm generally benefits from shortening the timing of cash inflows and lengthening the timing of cash outflows. Speeding up accounts receivable allows a business access to funds sooner; slowing down accounts payable provides a longer time frame for the firm to use the money it has on hand. Naturally, both must be managed carefully so as not to jeopardize vendor and customer relations and the firm's credit standing with suppliers and lenders.

Businesses can use various techniques to speed up collections and control disbursements.

Methods to speed up cash collections

A **collection system** is the set of banking arrangements and processing procedures used to process customer payments and gather incoming cash.

A firm's collection system affects the timing of cash inflows. Firms generally attempt to speed up cash collections by reducing collection float. **Collection float** is the time interval between when the payor mails a check and when the funds are available for the receiving firm to use.

Collection float has three components:

- **Mail float**—the time between when a check is mailed and when it is received by the payee or a processing site

- **Processing float**—the time between when the payee or processing site receives a check and when it is deposited at a financial institution

- **Availability float**—the time interval between when the check is deposited and when the firm's account is credited with the collected funds

Figure 3-70 provides a simple representation of collection float.

Figure 3-70: Components of Collection Float

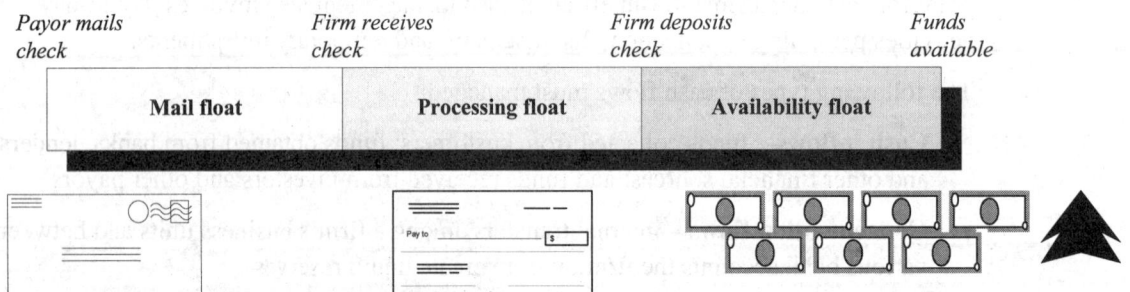

Payor mails check	Firm receives check	Firm deposits check	Funds available
Mail float	Processing float	Availability float	

In attempting to reduce collection float, important considerations include the optimal number and location of collection points, whether to use a lockbox system or an electronic payment system, and how to manage the concentration banking system.

Collection points. Depending upon the nature of the business, firms collect payments from customers over the counter, through the mail, and electronically (via home banking, telecommunications, personal computers, and the Internet). In general, the more collection points available, the shorter the collection float, especially if collection points are closer to customers or near Federal Reserve banks (for faster check clearing purposes). However, there may be higher operating costs associated with additional collection points.

Lockbox system. A **lockbox system** is an arrangement between a firm and a banking institution in which all deposits are received directly by the bank and immediately deposited into the firm's account.

The arrangement sets up the bank's post office box number for all remittances rather than the firm's address. The lockbox process is transparent to customers because the remittance envelopes and statements show the firm's name, not the bank's name. Some firms have multiple collection locations in the form of a lockbox network.

In setting up a lockbox system, a firm can request that the bank:

- Photocopy all checks received.

- Attach a photocopy of the check to the remittance.

- Include the envelope (which often notes an address change) or anything else sent with the payment.

A lockbox system ensures that deposits are handled on the day they are received which dramatically reduces processing float. Depending on the lockbox location(s), mail float and availability float can also be shortened. Once the day's receipts are deposited, the bank forwards a validated deposit slip and, if requested, the check photocopies and remittance documents to the company.

The main drawback of a lockbox system is the cost associated with the additional banking services. Lockboxes have fixed and variable costs.

- **Fixed lockbox costs**
  Fixed costs may include recurring (for example, annual or monthly) fees for renting the post office box, preparing deposits, transmitting remittance data, balance reporting, and other account maintenance activities. All fixed costs are typically bundled into a single lockbox maintenance charge.

- **Variable lockbox costs**
  Examples of variable costs include per-item deposit and processing charges, charges for transmitting remittance data, and photocopying and microfilming charges .

To decide whether to use a lockbox system, a firm needs to compare the added costs of the system with the potential income that can be gained from having accelerated funds availability.

Net Benefit From Lockbox =

Reduction in Float Opportunity Cost + Reduction in Internal Processing Costs – Lockbox Processing Costs

Float opportunity cost is a function of:

- The dollar amount of the collected items.

- The total collection time for the items.

- A firm's current investment or borrowing rate.

The lockbox system is profitable if the income is greater than the costs.

Example:

A company is considering a lockbox proposal. It has $96 million in annual sales ($8 million per month).The annual volume of checks is 12,000 and the batch of checks average size is $8,000. Internal check processing cost (assuming no lock box) is $0.20 per item. The annual opportunity costs for the company is 8%.

A lockbox processor proposes to charge $8,500 per year plus a plus a $0.45 processing cost per item.

Without A Lockbox

Batch	Dollar Amount	Collection Float Days	Total Dollars
1	$1,400,000	x 4 =	$5,600,000
2	4,400,000	x 2 =	8,800,000
3	2,200,000	x 6 =	13,200,000

Total Deposits	$8,000,000	Total Float Cost	$27,600,000
		Divided by 30 calendar days	$920,000
		Annual cost of float ($920,000 x .08)	$73,600

With A Lockbox

Batch	Dollar Amount	Collection Float Days	Total Dollars
1	$1,400,000	x 3 =	$4,200,000
2	4,400,000	x 1 =	4,400,000
3	2,200,000	x 4 =	8,800,000

Total Deposits	$8,000,000	Total Float Cost	$17,400,000
		Divided by 30 calendar days	$580,000
		Annual cost of float ($580,000 x .08)	$46,400

Annual cost of float without a lockbox	$73,600
Annual cost of float with a lockbox	($46,400)
Lockbox float savings	$27,200
Fixed lockbox costs	($8,500)
Variable lockbox costs (12,000 x $0.45)	($5,400)
Savings of internal processing costs (12,000 x $0.20)	$2,400
Net dollar benefit of a lockbox	$15,700

Based on the cost/benefit analysis that examined the trade-off between the savings from float reduction and the cost of the lockbox, the economic benefit to the company is $15,700.

Electronic payment system. An electronic payment system facilitates a payment or a transfer in an electronic format. Because electronic systems bypass mail and manual processing, they can guarantee funds availability on the payment date. In the United States, two of the primary electronic payment methods are the automated clearing house (ACH) system and Fedwire.

- The **automated clearing house (ACH)** system provides an electronic alternative to checks. Payment information is processed and settled electronically. In the United States, the Federal Reserve is the main operator of ACH. Increased reliability, efficiency, and cost-effectiveness are the primary benefits. ACH also offers the capability to transfer more information about a payment than is possible on a check.

- **Fedwire** is the Federal Reserve's funds transfer system. It provides a real-time method of immediately transferring funds between two financial institutions via their respective Federal Reserve bank accounts. Although reliable and secure, the system is relatively expensive to use.

Concentration banking system. A **concentration banking system** systematically transfers deposits received from field banks and/or lockbox banks to the firm's disbursement bank to create a centralized inventory of liquid reserves held as cash or for short-term credit or investment transactions.

Some banks require a **compensating balance**, which is a non-interest-bearing deposit maintained in the company's deposit accounts at the bank for account service charges, lines of credit, or investments. The balance requirement can be specified as a percentage of the total commitment, the unused amount of the commitment, or the outstanding borrowings.

In general, cash concentration reduces idle balances in field banks, improves control over a firm's cash inflows and outflows, and facilitates more effective investments. Naturally, there are administrative and control costs associated with a cash concentration system. Cost should be weighed against the expected value of the benefits provided.

Methods to slow down payments

A **disbursement system** is the set of banking arrangements, payment mechanisms, and processing procedures used to disburse funds to employees, vendors, suppliers, tax agencies, and other payees (for example, shareholders and/or bondholders).

A firm's disbursement system affects the timing of cash outflows and disbursement float. **Disbursement float** is the time interval between when the payor mails a check and when funds are deducted from the payor's account.

Disbursement float has three components. The first two are mail float and processing float, the same two components that are part of collection float. The third component which is different in disbursement float is called **clearing float**, which is the time interval between when the check is deposited by the payee and when the firm's account is debited.

A simple representation of disbursement float is shown in Figure 3-71.

Figure 3-71: Components of Disbursement Float

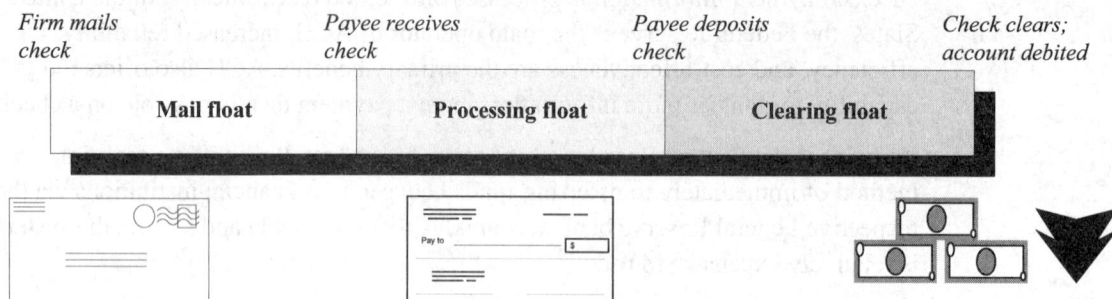

Typical costs associated with disbursement systems are time-value costs, excess balances, transaction costs, payee relations, and information and control costs. Banks and other institutions offer companies a variety of services to help control disbursement system costs. In particular, a zero balance account system is one way a firm can improve management of the disbursement process.

A **zero balance account (ZBA)** is a disbursement account against which a firm can write checks even though the balance is maintained at zero. A transfer from a master account located in the same bank covers any checks debited against the ZBA.

Firms often have several subsidiary ZBAs (for example, separate ZBAs for payroll, dividends, and other payables) under one master disbursing account. Furthermore, some ZBAs may be used for collections as well as disbursements. Funding is automatic. Credits and debits are posted daily; the bank transfers just enough funds between the master account and the ZBA to keep the balance of the ZBA at zero.

The benefits of a ZBA system include control over account balances and the elimination of idle excess balances in subsidiary accounts. Firms can more accurately invest the master account balance in securities. ZBAs can also facilitate decentralization of payables for firms with multiple locations by providing local check-writing authorization while maintaining funding control at headquarters. However, those individuals in a company with final cash management authority must accurately forecast check clearing times and ensure that the master account has sufficient reserves to cover the associated ZBAs.

Although the overall goal of a disbursement system is to make payments in a timely, accurate, and cost-effective manner, firms sometimes deliberately attempt to slow down the clearance of payments. Centralized payables and the use of payable through drafts are two methods of slowing down payments.

Centralized payables. Having centralized payables means payments are made through a single account (usually headquarters or a centralized processing center). Centralizing the payment function provides greater assurance that checks and funds will be disbursed when desired than with a decentralized payables system, where the likelihood of excess balances is greater (as well as increased transfer, reconciliation, and administrative costs).

Concentrations of excess cash can be used for loan repayments or investments. In some cases, the improved access to cash position information possible with a centralized account can allow a firm to earn a greater investment return by being able to hold the money longer. However, a centralized payables system requires careful monitoring to ensure that delayed payments do not result in the loss of cash discounts or damage relations with payees.

Payable through drafts. A payable through draft (PTD) is a payment instrument that is drawn against the payor, not the payor's bank. Unlike an ordinary check, a PTD is not payable on demand when presented at a bank. Therefore; the responsibility for paying the draft lies with the firm issuing the check.

When the issuer's bank receives the check, the bank must present it to the issuer for final acceptance. At that time, the firm deposits the funds to cover the draft. Using a PTD delays the time the firm has to have funds available and allows it to maintain smaller bank balances. The potential downside of a PTD is that banks typically impose higher service charges and suppliers may prefer checks.

Electronic commerce

From a cash management perspective, electronic commerce (or **e-commerce**) refers to the application of information and network technology to facilitate business relationships among trading partners. Many formats and communication protocols are included under the umbrella of e-commerce, including the Internet, internal intranet networks, Web-based commerce, and electronic data interchange (EDI) and the EDI subsets of electronic funds transfer (ETF) and financial EDI (FEDI).

Although the vast majority of transactions among North American companies are still paper-based, e-commerce provides an alternative. The primary benefits of e-commerce include:

- Increased productivity because it basically eliminates manual processing.
- Reduced cycle time.
- Lower error rates.
- Improved cash flow forecasting.
- Improved communication capabilities.

Hardware and software requirements and their associated costs, security issues, and the education and training of internal personnel and trading partners are the basic considerations in implementing e-commerce. Properly implemented and supported, e-commerce can facilitate stronger ties between a company and its vendors and customers.

Complex or simple, a cash management system should fulfill the following objectives (as listed in SMA No. 4N):

- Speed cash inflows.
- Slow cash outflows.
- Minimize idle cash.
- Minimize administrative costs connected with cash flows.
- Maintain good relations with customers and suppliers.

- Minimize the costs of providing back-up liquidity.

- Maximize the value of financial information provided to management.

Marketable Securities Management

Corporations need cash to meet their ongoing financial obligations. Although some amount of cash reserves is prudent, holding an excessive level involves several costs. Holding too much cash idle in bank accounts not only incurs maintenance costs but also results in a loss of potential interest income. That is why companies hold a short-term investment portfolio of interest-earning marketable securities.

Marketable securities are investments that mature in a year or less. They are generally classified as short-term investments (although balance sheet accounting differentiates securities with original maturities of three months or less as cash equivalents and those maturing in a year or less as short-term investments).

Why companies hold marketable securities

Specifically, companies invest in marketable securities for three main reasons:

- Reserve liquidity—to provide a source of near-cash (or instant cash) and cover any working capital imbalances resulting from insufficient cash inflows or unforeseen cash needs

- Controllable outflows—to earn interest on funds that are being held for predictable downstream cash outflows (such as interest payments, taxes, dividends, or insurance policies)

- Income generation—to earn interest on surplus cash for which the company has no immediate use

Variables in marketable securities selection

Before investing in a marketable security, careful consideration should be given to the choice. Safety, marketability, yield, maturity, and taxability are characteristics that firms typically evaluate.

Safety

Safety (preservation of principal) is considered the guiding principle or most basic test in selecting a security. Although a certain degree of risk is inherent in any investment, a firm must assess the specific risk associated with a security and weigh that risk against the potential for financial returns (or losses). Firms tend to look for short-term instruments that offer both safety and some level of income generation.

Marketability

The marketability of a security refers to the owner's ability to sell the security in large volumes relatively quickly without a substantial price concession. High marketability is a function of the availability of a large secondary market. A security with less active secondary markets is considered to be less liquid.

Yield

A security's yield (return) is related to its interest rate. Some securities offer variable interest, others pay a fixed rate, and some (for example, U.S. Treasury bills) pay no interest but are sold at a discount and redeemed at face value. For variable rate securities, the longer the time to maturity, the greater the potential price variation due to interest rate movements. Yield has an inverse relationship with liquidity—the more liquid a security, the lower its yield. In turn, yield has a positive relationship to risk. In general, the higher the risk, the higher the expected return.

Maturity

Maturity refers to the life of the security and represents the date on which the obligation it represents is settled. Maturity dates vary. Short-term securities are often chosen based on a maturity date on which the firm has forecasted a need for cash. Some securities may be designated for quick liquidity, while others may be earmarked for less immediate use.

Taxability

A company should evaluate the tax implications of the security. A firm's effective tax rate will determine the advantage of tax-exempt alternatives and the after-tax rate from taxable investments.

Types of marketable securities

There are two major markets for debt and equity instruments: the capital market and the money market. Stocks and long-term bonds (discussed in Topic 2, "Financial Instruments") are bought and sold in the capital market. The money market is where short-term debt securities that mature in one year or less trade.

Unlike the capital market, which has specific exchanges (for example, the New York Stock Exchange), the money market is a group of markets. Major issuers of money market securities are the U.S. government, foreign government securities dealers, commercial paper dealers, bankers' acceptance dealers, and other money market brokers specializing in short-term instruments.

Figure 3-72 on the next page provides an overview of various types of money market securities (as summarized in large part from Statements on Management Accounting No. 4M, "Understanding Financial Instruments," and No. 4N, "Management of Working Capital: Cash Resources").

Figure 3-72: Types of Marketable Securities

Instrument	Description
United States Treasury securities	<ul><li>Direct obligations of the U.S. Treasury; backed by the full faith and credit of the U.S. government.</li><li>Interest rates provide a reference point and market indicator for other securities.</li><li>Considered "safe" investments because they are free of default risk, are actively traded on a large secondary market, and are highly marketable.</li><li>Common types include:<ul><li>Treasury bills (or T-bills): do not bear interest; sold at a discount and mature to face value in 1 year or less.</li><li>Treasury notes (or T-notes): bear interest semiannually; mature within 1 to 10 years.</li><li>Treasury bonds (or T-bonds): similar to T-notes but have maturities longer than 10 years; generally not purchased for a short-term portfolio except when the bond is close to maturity.</li></ul></li></ul>
Federal agency securities (agency securities)	<ul><li>Interest-bearing securities usually offered and redeemed at face value.</li><li>Generally not backed by the full faith and credit of the U.S. government but still considered a relatively safe investment and free of default risk.</li><li>Typically smaller issues than Treasury securities; not quite as marketable but still highly liquid.</li><li>Limited tax exposure; many are exempt from state/local income taxes but not state franchise taxes.</li></ul>
Repurchase agreements (repos)	<ul><li>Purchase of a security from another party, usually a bank or security dealer who agrees to buy it back at a specified date for a fixed price.</li><li>Commonly involve U.S. Treasury securities as the underlying security to be repurchased at a rate slightly less than the U.S. Treasury securities offer.</li><li>Varying maturity, starting with overnight repurchase agreements.</li><li>Generally considered a relatively safe investment (because of the government underlier).</li><li>Often transferred to a third party to ensure that securities are available for sale if the issuer defaults.</li></ul>
Bankers' acceptances (BAs)	<ul><li>Essentially time drafts that result from commercial trade financing; frequently involve international transactions.</li><li>Involve a letter of credit "accepted" by a bank; typically implies the BA is backed by that bank.</li><li>Varying maturities and denominations.</li><li>Liquidity is provided by an active secondary market of dealers.</li></ul>
Commercial paper (CP)	<ul><li>Unsecured short-term loan issued by a corporation.</li><li>Negotiable instrument but typically held to maturity because of a weak secondary market; typically higher yield than similar securities because of its low marketability.</li><li>Maturity ranges from 1 to 270 days.</li><li>May be interest-bearing or discounted; usually discounted.</li><li>Generally rated by credit rating agencies (e.g., by Moody's or Standard & Poor's) to help investors assess risk.</li></ul>
Auction rate preferred stock	<ul><li>Equity usually purchased by other corporations that invest in short-term debt instruments.</li><li>Dividend rate is regularly reset (usually every seven weeks) to keep the price from fluctuating.</li><li>Investors usually have the opportunity to sell the stock if they do not want the adjusted rate (unless the auction process fails).</li><li>Desirable because of the 70% dividend exclusion allowance on the dividend income.</li></ul>
Negotiable certificates of deposit (CDs)	<ul><li>Interest-bearing deposits issued by banks or saving and loan institutions that can be traded in money markets; generally sold at face value in denominations of $1 million.</li><li>Most mature between 1 and 3 months; some can be for several years.</li><li>Offer fixed and variable interest rates.</li><li>Not guaranteed by the Federal Deposit Insurance Corporation (FDIC) if in excess of $100,000; therefore, issuing bank should be carefully investigated.</li><li>Highly marketable if issued by a large, established bank.</li><li>Common types include:<ul><li>Eurodollar CDs (or Euro CDs)—dollar-denominated CDs issued by foreign branches of U.S. banks and foreign banks, primarily in London.</li><li>Yankee CDs—CDs issued by U.S. branches of foreign banks.</li><li>Thrift CDs—CDs issued by savings and loan associations, savings banks, and credit unions.</li></ul></li></ul>
Eurodollar deposits	<ul><li>Typically nonnegotiable dollar-denominated time deposits held by banks outside the United States (although not necessarily in Europe); not subject to U.S. banking regulations.</li><li>May be purchased through most large U.S. banks.</li><li>Maturities range from overnight to several years; most are 6 months or less.</li></ul>
Short-term municipals	<ul><li>State and local government issues.</li><li>Two common types:<ul><li>CP instrument with float interest rate reset weekly.</li><li>Longer-term note with a 1- to 2-year maturity.</li></ul></li><li>Short-term municipal has great price stability and better marketability.</li></ul>

Accounts Receivable Management

The term **accounts receivable** refers to the money customers owe a company resulting from its decision to sell products and services on a credit basis. An item is classified as an account receivable after it is sold and an invoice is sent. An account receivable is treated as an asset on the company's balance sheet.

Why companies carry accounts receivable

Credit is often described as a sales tool. In deciding to extend credit and carry accounts receivable, companies consider the following factors:

- General economic conditions

- Target market (for example, terms necessary to attract new customers and needs of current customers)

- Industry practices (for example, credit terms competitors offer)

- Potential profit from interest income for credit terms

As with other current assets, accounts receivable have profitability and risk trade-offs. Extending credit may stimulate sales and profits. But a company incurs costs for carrying receivables and runs the risk of potential bad-debt losses. Companies must have efficient and effective policies and procedures in place for managing accounts receivable.

The general factors that influence the management of a company's receivables are:

- Defined credit policies and terms of sale.

- Provisions for the evaluation of customer creditworthiness and the determination of customer credit lines.

- Prompt billing and collection of accounts receivable.

- Accurate and up-to-date records of accounts receivable.

- Provisions for follow-up on overdue accounts and initiation of collection procedures (if necessary).

Managing credit and accounts receivable activities at a company involves the sales, accounting, and finance functions.

Credit terms

Credit terms stipulate the form and timing of payment extended to a customer for the receipt of goods and services as well as the discount terms (if any). The **credit period** is the net due date (for example, 20 days, 30 days). **Discount terms** are stated in terms of the credit period and the cash discount given for early payment. The **cash discount** is the percentage of reduction allowed for early payment. For example, terms of 25/10 net 30 mean that the total amount is due in 30 days of the invoice date but the buyer can take a 25% discount by paying within 10 days.

Common terms of credit that companies offer are described in Figure 3-73.

Figure 3-73: Types of Credit Extension

Form	Description
Open account (open book credit)	■ Seller's invoice represents the formal obligation between buyer and seller and records the sale as an account receivable. ■ Customer receives an invoice for each transaction or a monthly statement showing invoices for the period. ■ Full payment is due according to specified credit terms and any discounts; fees generally charged for late payments. ■ Includes periodic review of creditworthiness. ■ Most common type of credit.
Installment credit	■ Requires the customer to make equal monthly payments consisting of principal plus interest. ■ May involve a written contract specifying terms of the obligation, credit terms, interest rate, and so on. ■ Often used for large-value consumer purchases (for example, automobiles).
Revolving credit	■ Provides ongoing credit without requiring approval of individual transactions as long as an account is in good standing (for example, credit outstanding is below an established limit and payments are current). ■ Assesses an interest charge based on the average amount outstanding for the period if the account is past due.
Letter of credit (L/C)	■ Involves an L/C instrument where a bank guarantees the seller (not the buyer) payment for an agreed-upon purchase. ■ Buyer typically pays a fee for opening an L/C. ■ Commonly used for import/export transactions.

Extending the credit period and changing the discount terms can affect both the profitability and the risk associated with accounts receivable. Specific formulas are available to calculate the effect of changes in credit periods and cash discounts. The following content summarizes the general concepts.

- **Extending the credit period**

  A firm extends a credit period with the expectation of increased profitability from increased sales.

  Consider the following scenario: A firm changes credit terms from net 30 to net 60; the credit period is increased from one month to two months. The more liberal credit terms encourage additional sales. But the extended collection period results in additional carrying costs for the firm as customers slow down their payments.

  In extending a credit period, the firm must compare the profitability of additional sales with the opportunity costs of the additional receivables. If the increased sales profits exceed the required return on investment for the additional receivables, the change in the credit period is worthwhile.

- **Changing the discount terms**

  A firm offers a cash discount or varies an existing one in an attempt to speed up payment of receivables.

Consider the following scenario: A firm's current collection period averages 60 days with no cash discount given. The firm decides to offer the discount terms of 2/10, net 45. After one month, 70% of the firm's customers (in dollar volume) take advantage of the cash discount.

In changing the discount terms, the firm must determine if the increased speed in collections offsets the cost of offering the discount. If the opportunity costs of accelerated collections are greater than the cost of the discount, the discount is worthwhile; if the savings do not offset the cash discount, the discount is not a good idea.

Default risk

An old saying is that a receivable is only as good as the probability of it being paid. Bad debt generally refers to the slowness in the collection of receivables and the portion of receivables in default. Default occurs when a customer fails to meet the terms of an obligation. **Default risk** is the risk that a company (or an individual) will not be able to pay interest or principal on debt obligations.

To minimize default risk, firms need to set and maintain credit standards for credit extension, billing, and collection. Credit information on an applicant may be gathered from internal and external sources.

Typical sources of internal credit information are:

- A credit application completed by an applicant.

- An agreement form completed by an applicant.

- A firm's records on past dealings with the applicant (for example, payment history).

External sources of credit information include:

- Financial statements—review of audited (or unaudited) financial statements and related ratios that can be compared to industry averages.

- Trade references—contact with other companies regarding their actual payment experiences with the applicant.

- Banks and other lenders—for standardized credit information about the applicant's financial condition and available credit.

- Agencies—local and national agency reports on the credit history of most companies.

Factors contributing to optimal credit/collection policies

Credit and collection policies involve an assessment of the creditworthiness of the buyer, the credit terms extended, and the level of collection procedures required. At the very least, the gains derived from credit and collection policies should be equal to the costs associated with them.

To maximize the profitability of credit and collection polices, a firm needs to vary these policies. The optimal solution is reached based on the best possible combination of credit standards, credit terms, and collection expenditures. Typically, the following relationships have been found to exist:

- In the absence of credit standards, sales are maximized but are often offset by large bad-debt losses, collection costs, and high costs from carrying very large receivables.

- With tighter credit standards, sales revenues decline but so do the average collection period and bad-debt losses.

- Stricter credit standards increase profits up to a point, after which they decline.

Average collection period

Average collection period refers to the average time that a firm takes to collect its accounts receivable.

The following ratio is used to determine average collection period:

$$\text{Average Collection Period} = \frac{365 \text{ Days}}{\text{Accounts Receivable Turnover}}$$

The resulting ratio indicates the average number of days that the receivables are outstanding before being collected.

Consider the following example for a firm with a receivable turnover of 6.25:

$$\text{Average Collection Period} = \frac{365 \text{ Days}}{6.25}$$

$$= 58 \text{ Days}$$

To further understand the average collection period, the measure is compared with the industry average and the credit terms offered.

Comparison to the industry average provides a relative measure. If, for example, the median industry turnover ratio is 8.1 and the average industry collection period is 45 days (365 days ÷ 8.1), a 13-day difference exists.

Whether the average of 58 days is good or bad depends more on the credit terms offered than the industry average. If the terms of credit are 30 days, then an average collection period of 58 days would be cause for concern. It could be indicative of inadequate credit checks on customers, poor credit management, and/or slow collection on delinquent accounts. However, if the credit terms are 60 days, the 58-day average would be good, as most customers tend to withhold payments as long as the credit terms allow.

Changes in sales and credit terms will change average collection period, accordingly. For example, an increase in sales and a decrease in the investment in accounts receivables increases accounts receivable turnover (credit sales/accounts receivable). Thus, the average collection period decreases.

Days' sales outstanding

Days' sales outstanding (DSO) is another way to measure accounts receivable. DSO is calculated by dividing accounts receivable outstanding at the end of a specified time interval by the average daily credit sales for the period.

Example:

A company has compiled the following accounts receivable and credit information:

- Outstanding receivables at the end of month 3 = $155,000

- Credit terms = Net 60

- DSO averaging period = 3 months (90 days)

- Credit sales history

$$
\begin{aligned}
\text{Month 1} &= \text{\$40,000} \\
\text{Month 2} &= \text{\$50,000} \\
\text{Month 3} &= \text{\$65,000}
\end{aligned}
$$

$$\text{Average Daily Credit Sales} = \frac{(\$40,000 + \$50,000 + \$65,000)}{90} = \$1,722.22$$

$$\text{DSO} = \frac{\text{Outstanding Accounts Receivable}}{\text{Average Daily Credit Sales}}$$

$$\text{DSO} = \frac{\$155,000.00}{\$1,722.22} = 90 \text{ days}$$

$$\text{Average past due} = \text{DSO} - \text{Average days of credit terms}$$

$$\text{Average past due} = 90 \text{ days} - 60 \text{ days} = 30 \text{ days}$$

DSO provides a measure of a firm's overall collection efficiency. It results in a single number that can be compared to credit policy or to a historic trend. A caution in using DSO is that is can be skewed by changing trends in sales volume or by strong seasonal sales swings.

Inventory Management

To understand inventory management requires an understanding of basic inventory control terms:

- **Stock** refers to all the goods a company stores and represents a supply that is kept for future use.

- **Inventory** is a list of all the items held in stock.

- An item is a single type of product kept in stock; an item is one entry in the inventory.

- A unit is the standard size or quantity of a stock item.

Given these definitions, the concepts of inventory control and inventory management can be explained:

- Inventory control (or stock control) refers to the collective activities and procedures that ensure that the right amount of each item is held in stock.

- Inventory management refers to the process of determining and maintaining the required level of inventory that will ensure that customer orders are properly filled on time.

Why companies carry inventory

Inventory control involves balancing conflicting costs—balancing the cost of holding sufficient stock to provide a specified level of customer service with the cost of running out of stock and losing sales. The point at which those costs intersect provides answers to many inventory control issues such as what to keep in stock, when orders should be placed, how much should be ordered, and so on.

To some degree, every company holds inventory. But holding inventory is costly because of storage and handling costs, the danger of inventory obsolescence, and the costs associated with tied-up capital. When capital is tied up, businesses must forgo other profitable opportunities for investments. These disadvantages and costs for holding inventory lead to the question, why do companies carry inventory?

At a simplistic level, inventory provides a buffer between supply and demand. But there are many other reasons for holding inventory, including:

- Coverage for mismatches between supply and demand rates.

- Efficient servicing of customer demands that are larger than expected or at unexpected times.

- Coverage for delayed or insufficient supplier deliveries.

- Economies in purchasing (such as price discounts on large orders or savings on purchases when prices are low and expected to rise).

- Economies in production.

- Maintenance of consistent levels of operation.

- Coverage for emergencies.

In general, the level of inventory should be increased only if the benefits outweigh the costs of maintaining the additional inventory.

Economic order quantity

Economic order quantity (EOQ) is a classic analysis in inventory control that defines a relationship between order size, demand for an item, and the associated costs.

Determining EOQ answers two questions:

- How much should be ordered?

- How many times should orders be placed per year?

EOQ represents optimum order size—the quantity of a regularly ordered item to be purchased at a point in time that results in minimum total cost, that is, the sum of ordering and storage costs.

- **Ordering costs**

  Ordering costs include compensation paid to purchasing department employees, the cost of computer time to prepare orders, and the cost of supplies used to generate purchase orders.

  The more frequently orders are placed, the more costs incurred by the ordering process. The general relationship between ordering cost (per order) and order quantity (number of units per order) is shown in the first frame of Figure 3-74. The rationale is thus built for ordering larger quantities at one time to minimize ordering costs.

- **Storage costs**

  Storage costs (also called, carrying costs or holding costs) include storage and handling costs, obsolescence and deterioration costs, insurance, taxes, and the cost of the funds invested in inventories. Storage costs rise as the order size grows and decline when items are ordered in smaller amounts.

  The middle frame of Figure 3-72 depicts this simple relation between storage cost (per order) and order quantity (number of units per order).

EOQ can be determined when ordering and storage costs are related to demand. The last frame in Figure 3-72 illustrates EOQ.

Figure 3-74: EOQ and the Relationship between Storage Cost, Ordering Cost, and Order Quantity

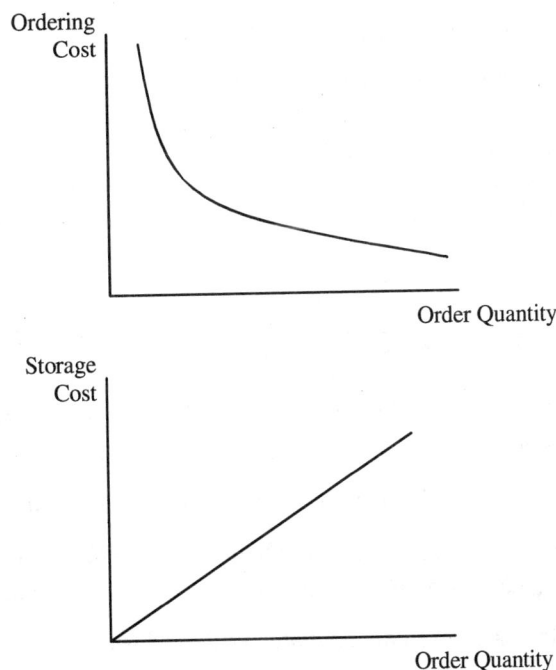

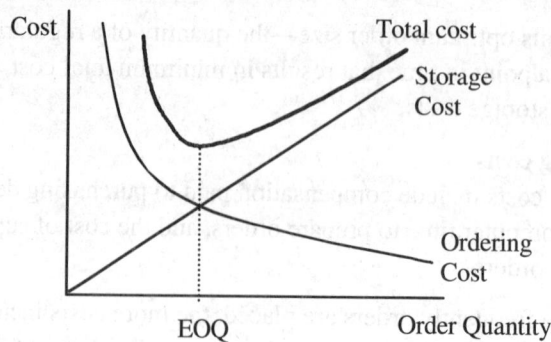

The EOQ formula is:

$$EOQ = \sqrt{\frac{2FD}{C}}$$

Where

- F = fixed order cost per order.

- D = total inventory units demanded.

- S= Storage (carrying or holding) cost per inventory unit.

If the carrying costs decrease, the EOQ increases. If total inventory units demanded or fixed order cost per order decrease, EOQ also decreases.

EOQ is based on the following assumptions:

- Lead time is constant and known.

- Demand occurs at a relatively stable and known rate.

- Operating and storage costs are known.

- Replenishment is instantaneous; there are no stockouts.

EOQ principles may also be applied to the quantities of an item to be manufactured.

For example, assume that a manufacturer of financial calculators uses 10,000 units of an item annually. Its order cost is $75 per order and storage cost of $1.50 per unit per year. The EOQ would be:

$$EOQ = \sqrt{\frac{2(10,000)(\$75)}{\$1.50}} = \sqrt{1,000,000} = 1,000 \; units$$

If the company uses 10,000 units per year and its EOQ is 1,000, the company would reorder 10 times a year (10,000/1,000).

Although widely used, EOQ analysis has the following weaknesses:

- Assumptions are sometimes unrealistic and inaccurate; situations where all relevant factors (demand, lead time, and costs) are known with complete certainty are rare.

- Calculations are based on estimated costs and forecast demands.

- In manufacturing environments, where setup costs are high, large quantities lead to excess capacity and inventory.

- Too much capacity leaves too much capital tied up in inventory.

Impact of lead time and safety stock

In practice, replenishment is not instantaneous, and when stockouts occur, they typically have myriad associated costs. In a retail or service environment, shortages can result in reduced profits from lost sales, loss of goodwill, loss of future sales, and loss of reputation. In manufacturing, disruptions in production can be considerable and costly, ranging from rescheduling issues to employee layoffs and premium prices for emergency orders and special deliveries from suppliers.

Such shortage issues can be minimized or avoided by shortening lead time and having some level of safety stock.

Lead time

Lead time is the time between placing an order and getting the units in stock and ready for use. Lead time may vary for several reasons. Effective inventory management attempts to keep lead time short by reducing the time for:

- Order preparation (the time to gather order information and prepare the order).

- Order delivery to a supplier (the time to get the order to a supplier via electronic transmissions, telecommunications, or mail).

- Order processing and fulfillment by the supplier.

- Order delivery from the supplier.

- Process delivery (getting the items into stock).

Safety stock

Safety stock (or **buffer stock**) generally refers to a quantity of stock planned and held in inventory to protect against fluctuations in supply and demand or as protection against production forecast errors and or short-term changes in backlog.

Where EOQ analysis is based on the theoretical assumption that demand and lead time are known with certainty, safety stock uses a model involving probability. Safety stock analysis attempts to address the uncertainty found in inventory systems, particularly the real-world uncertainty in demand and lead time.

Determining the level of safety stock to maintain involves balancing the probability and cost of a stockout with the cost of carrying sufficient safety stock to avoid this possibility. Specific calculations (which are beyond the scope of this text) are used. But the following general concepts apply:

- The greater the uncertainty in forecasted demand, the more safety stock a firm may wish to consider.

- The greater the uncertainty in lead time to replenish a stockout, the more safety stock a firm may want to maintain.

Safety stock analysis considers all costs associated with stockouts. But the final factor is the cost of carrying additional inventory and loss of interest income from tying up working capital. If not for these costs and loss of interest-earning investments, a firm could theoretically carry sufficient safety stock to prevent stockouts from ever occurring.

Just-in-time systems and kanban

Basic principles of just-in-time (JIT) systems and kanban are covered in Section A of this part of the *CMA Learning System*, Topic 2, "Manufacturing Paradigms." These concepts are also appropriate to mention in the context of inventory control.

The underlying objective of JIT systems is to minimize all waste in manufacturing operations by meeting production targets with the minimum amount of materials, equipment, operators, and so on. This is accomplished by completing all operations just at the time they are needed. Kanban is the simple manual method of control used in conjunction with JIT to ensure that all materials actually do arrive just as they are needed.

Some similarities exist between EOQ and JIT/kanban systems. For example, both monitor stock levels and place orders for replenishment with fixed quantities. However, a major difference is that with JIT and kanban, activity reduces stock to its reorder level and replenishments occur only after each withdrawal. The choice of EOQ versus JIT depends on a variety of factors specific to the organization.

JIT and kanban systems have been described as deceptively simple. Careful evaluation and planning are required for effective implementation. But when JIT and kanban are well-conceived and properly adopted as a means of inventory control, they can dramatically reduce stocks of raw materials and work in progress. In turn, such reductions translate to additional cost savings by:

- Reducing the manufacturing and warehousing space needed.

- Lowering property and overhead expenses.

- Reducing the investments for stock.

In the end, JIT and kanban can lead to more efficient use of working capital.

Progress Check

Directions: Read each question and respond in the space provided. Answers and page references appear on the page following the progress check questions.

1. The transactions motive for holding cash is **best** described as

    ( )   a.   using surplus liquid reserves to take advantage of short-term investments or other temporary situations.

    ( )   b.   synchronizing cash inflows and outflows so that excess cash balances can be invested in short-term instruments.

    ( )   c.   providing a buffer for unexpected cash needs that result from the unpredictable nature of cash inflows and outflows.

    ( )   d.   maintaining sufficient cash or near-cash reserves to meet financial payments arising from ordinary business operations.

2. Which of the following techniques will **not** speed up collections?

    ( )   a.   Lockbox system

    ( )   b.   ACH and Fedwire processing

    ( )   c.   Payable through draft

    ( )   d.   Cash concentration banking system

Match each type of marketable security with its characteristic.

3. _____ Federal agency securities

4. _____ Commercial paper

5. _____ Bankers' acceptances

6. _____ Negotiable certificates of deposit

7. _____ Auction rate preferred stock

a.   Interest-bearing deposits issued by banks or saving and loan institutions that can be traded in money markets

b.   Time drafts that result from commercial trade financing

c.   Relatively safe investment and free of default risk

d.   Equity usually purchased by other corporations that invest in short-term debt instruments

e.   Unsecured short-term loan issued by a corporation

8. A primary benefit that a firm expects to gain from lengthening a credit period is

    ( ) a. increased profitability resulting from increased sales.

    ( ) b. increased revenue from interest charges on past due accounts.

    ( ) c. fewer collections procedures necessary for past due accounts.

    ( ) d. improved inventory control resulting from relatively stable demand.

9. Which of the following statements accurately characterizes economic order quantity (EOQ) and safety stock principles?

    ( ) a. Both models advocate reducing stock to a predetermined reorder level.

    ( ) b. EOQ analysis assumes demand and lead time are known with certainty; safety stock uses a model involving probability.

    ( ) c. EOQ analysis and safety stock both assume demand varies but lead time is known with certainty.

    ( ) d. Both models are based on the premise that there is no true measure of certainty in inventory control.

Progress check answers

1. d (p. 3-254)

2. c (p. 3-256)

3. c (p. 3-263)

4. e (p. 3-263)

5. b (p. 3-263)

6. a (p. 3-263)

7. d (p. 3-263)

8. a (p. 3-263)

9. b (p. 3-270)

Financing Current Assets

Topic overview

Short-term financing refers to the use of debt instruments that mature in one year or less. Organizations engage in short-term financing for several reasons:

- *To ensure adequate liquidity to meet immediate cash requirements*

- *To finance current assets (such as accounts receivable and inventory)*

- *To minimize interest costs associated with borrowing*

- *To minimize insolvency risks*

- *To maximize financial flexibility by accessing a variety of short-term borrowing alternatives*

When financing current assets, it is important for a corporation to understand the financial impact of its short-term credit options. Firms can choose from several different short-term borrowing options. Market conditions and the risks involved influence the decision. The approach that yields the lowest cost is the most desirable. In particular, current liabilities are an important source of financing for many small firms.

Types of Short-Term Credit

Businesses usually meet short-term borrowing needs in one of two ways:

- By raising funds externally through financial intermediaries (for example, through banks and financial institutions or by investing in money markets)

- By issuing commercial paper

The vast majority of businesses rely on financial intermediaries to perform the lending function.

Several types of short-term credit arrangements are possible, including the use of:

- Accrued expenses.

- Trade credit.

- Unsecured short-term bank loans (lines of credit and revolving credit).

- Secured short-term loans (collateralized accounts receivable and collateralized inventory).

- Commercial paper.

- Bankers' acceptances.

A brief description of each follows.

Accrued expenses

Accrued expenses represent the amount a firm owes but has not yet paid for wages, taxes, interest, and dividends. The most common accrued expenses are wages and taxes.

Accrued expenses are considered a spontaneous source of interest-free financing. Businesses can use current funds to fulfill immediate cash needs up to the point the accrued expenses become due for payment. In that respect, accrued expenses must be used with discretion.

Trade credit

Trade credit is a source of short-term financing created when a supplier grants credit terms to customers on purchases. Trade credit is often the largest source of short-term credit for small firms.

Trade credit represents an indirect loan with the following terms:

- A seller supplies goods according to predefined credit terms.

- The credit appears as accounts receivable on the seller's books and accounts payable on the customer's books.

- The credit represents cash the customer may keep until the specified final payment date.

An open account (where a seller gives the buyer a specified time period to pay for goods or services) is the most common type of trade credit.

Note: Terms of an open account are covered in Topic 4 in this section, "Managing Current Assets," in the discussion of accounts receivable credit terms.

Unsecured short-term bank loans

An unsecured short-term bank loan is a form of bank credit that is not backed by a pledge of specific collateral or assets. Such loans are made based on the financial soundness and creditworthiness of the borrower.

Unsecured short-term bank loans are negotiated between the bank and the business. A loan agreement stipulates the terms of the loan (for example, interest to be paid, payment terms, maturity date, and so on). The borrower signs a **promissory note** as a formal obligation to repay the loan according to the specified terms.

Unsecured short-term bank loans are generally considered self-liquidating, meaning that the assets the company purchases with the loan or the current assets held by the company will generate sufficient cash flows to pay off the loan. For example, unsecured short-term bank loans are popular instruments to finance seasonal build-ups in accounts receivable or inventory.

Lines of credit and revolving credit are two types of unsecured loans that provide quick and ready sources of short-term financing for businesses.

Lines of credit

A **line of credit** (or credit line) is an agreement allowing a firm to borrow up to a specified limit during a particular time period. The borrower has access to the credit amount (which is generally substantial) but pays interest only on actual borrowing.

Borrowing against a line of credit is done through a specific short-term note. A sequence of short-term notes can be issued against the same line of credit. Maturities of the short-term notes vary; generally notes range from overnight to 90 days (although some may be longer).

Lines of credit are technically set up for a set period (usually a year), but most are renewed on an ongoing basis at maturity. Many lines of credit are kept in force for years.

Revolving credit

Revolving credit (also known as a revolver or a revolving credit agreement) allows a business to borrow, repay, and reborrow up to a specified amount. Credit terms of a revolver are similar to those of a line of credit. Although revolvers are often used for short-term borrowing, the term is often longer (ranging from two to five years).

Secured short-term loans

A secured short-term loan (or asset-based borrowing) is a form of credit based on the pledging of an asset for collateral. Accounts receivable and inventory are the most common assets used in this form of secured lending; equipment, real estate, or other tangible property is sometimes used as collateral.

Collateralized accounts receivable

In this type of arrangement, the lender spends time evaluating the borrower's business; the volume of customer purchases, the timeliness of customer payments, delinquency rates, and the number of bad-debt write-offs are all considered.

Based on this evaluation, an advance rate is determined, stated as a percentage of the accounts receivable outstanding. The percentage is then applied to the amount of pledged accounts receivable and determines the maximum amount that can be borrowed. When a loan is in force, the borrower's customers typically make payments directly to the lender, who applies them to the outstanding loan balance.

Collateralized inventory

Similar to accounts receivable financing, the amount of credit is limited by the advance rate and determined as a percentage of inventory. The advance rate also considers the risk that the borrower may not be able to sell the inventory (due to changes in market conditions, fluctuating commodity prices, or inventory obsolescence or spoilage).

In general, lenders are more willing to collateralize raw materials and finished goods than work in progress. On occasion, some lenders may calculate different advance rates for different types of inventories. Generally, the advance rate is much less for inventory than for accounts receivable.

Commercial paper

Commercial paper (CP) is an unsecured promissory note issued by a corporation. CP is sold at a discount from par value and is backed by a promise of the corporation to buy back the paper at maturity by paying par value.

The major credit rating agencies usually rate the CP of a specific issuer. CP is typically sold in denominations of $100,000. For public issues, maturities range from overnight to 270 days. Some private issues may have maturities longer than 270 days.

CP interest rates vary. The rate is market-based and is a function of the issuing company's credit rating, the size of the issue, and general market short-term interest rates.

Most CP is sold through dealers (either investment banking institutions or commercial banks). Some companies may sell their CP issues directly to investors.

In general, the use of CP for short-term financing:

- Provides a broad distribution for borrowing which results in more funds at lower rates than other methods provide.

- Allows the borrower to avoid the expense of maintaining a compensating balance with a commercial bank.

- Promotes the name of the borrower because of the broad market the borrower's name becomes more widely known.

Bankers' acceptances

A **bankers' acceptance (BA)** is a negotiable short-term instrument used primarily to finance the import and export of goods. Some issues may be used for the domestic shipment and storage of readily marketable staples.

A BA is a time draft drawn by a borrower and accepted by the bank on which it is drawn. Accepting the draft implies that the bank assumes obligation for the payment of the draft at maturity.

BAs are readily marketable and are often discounted in the money market. The borrower receives discounted proceeds as an advance and is obligated to pay the full draft amount to the accepting bank at maturity. The accepting bank pays the investor who purchased the BA.

Minimizing the Cost of Short-Term Credit

Different short-term credit options have different costs for the borrower. This section looks specifically at three types of short-term financing costs:

- Costs incurred by not taking cash discounts extended with trade credit

- The effective annual interest rate associated with unsecured short-term bank loans

- Factoring costs associated with collateralized secured short-term bank loans

Cash discounts extended with trade credit

Trade credit represents cash a firm can invest up until the specified payment date (for example, 30, 60, or 90 days). The longer the payment period, the longer the firm can use the funds.

The amount of short-term financing cost the firm saves depends on the days of credit. For example, if a firm were to use credit worth $100,000 for 30 days rather than borrowing that amount from another source at a cost of 2%, the firm would save $2,000 ($100,000 × 0.02).

Firms grant trade credit to help facilitate a sale. Discounts are offered as incentives for customers to pay early and reduce the cost of carrying receivables. The customer must weigh the discount against the option of using the trade credit and decide whether it is beneficial to take the discount and pay early. Generally, a firm saves money by taking the discount rather than extending the credit up to the original payment date.

The formula for determining the opportunity cost of giving up a discount computed at an annual rate (of 365 days) is:

$$EID = \frac{DR}{1 - DR} \times \frac{365}{N - DP}$$

Where:

- EID = effective annual rate for foregoing the trade credit discount.

- DR = discount rate.

- N = net payment period.

- DP = discount period.

Consider the following scenario:

Credit terms are 2/10 net 30. The effective annual rate of taking the cash discount is:

$$EID = \frac{0.02}{1 - 0.02} \times \frac{365}{30 - 10}$$

$$= 37.24\%$$

If the firm can borrow funds elsewhere for less than 37.24%, it should do so and take the discount for early payment of the trade credit. However, if borrowing exceeds 37.24% (or funds are not available elsewhere), the firm might want to delay payment until the net due date.

Effective annual interest rate

Banks charge interest for unsecured short-term bank loans. They generally assess a commitment fee, and they may also charge a compensating balance.

- **Interest rate**

  The interest rate charged consists of a spread added to a base rate such as prime, the British Bankers' Association (BBA) London Interbank Offered Rate (LIBOR), or the Fed rate for T-bills. In determining the interest rate, banks evaluate the customer's ability to repay the loan. The rate charged reflects the bank's assessment of the loan risk. The rate is usually variable and will be adjusted according to the changes in the base rate.

- **Commitment fee**

  In addition to interest, banks often charge a commitment fee for holding lines of credit or revolvers available for the borrower. The commitment fee is some percentage of the line or the unused portion of the line.

- **Compensating balance**

  Some banks may also require a compensating balance. The compensating balance designates the percentage of the loan the bank may require the borrower to hold on deposit without earning interest or offsetting other service charges. A compensating balance may be specified as a percentage of the total commitment, the unused portion of the commitment, or the outstanding borrowings.

A commitment fee and a compensating balance effectively reduce the amount of funds the borrower can use. In doing so, they also increase the effective annual interest rate charged for the loan. In other words, the effective annual interest rate is higher than the initial interest rate quoted by the bank.

The formula for effective annual rate of interest is:

$$EI = \left(\frac{PR + CF}{1 - CB} \right) \left(\frac{365}{M} \right)$$

Where:

- EI = effective rate of interest.

- PR = principal interest charge (%).

- CB = compensating balance (%).

- CF = commitment fee (%).

- M = loan length in days.

Consider the following scenario:

A firm negotiates a one-year loan for $1 million with an interest rate of 12%. The commitment fee is ¼ % of the total amount, and the compensating balance is 10% of the line.

$$EI = \left(\frac{0.12 + 0.0025}{1 - 0.10} \right) \left(\frac{365}{365} \right) \left(\frac{0.1225}{0.9} \right) = 13.6\%$$

The quoted rate is 12%, but the effective annual interest rate the firm will actually pay is 13.6%.

Factoring costs

Factoring is the sale or transfer of accounts receivable in a secured short-term loan to a third party (factor). A factor is a company specializing in the financing and management of receivables.

Factoring receivables is governed by a contract between the factor and the client. A factor makes credit checks on accounts and charges a percentage commission on the receivables, depending on the amount and the quality of the receivables and the overall financial soundness of the client. The factor also charges interest, which is usually variable.

A factor can liquidate collateralized assets in the event the client cannot repay the loan. To protect itself against default risk, the factor typically applies a "haircut" to the current value of the receivables. This means that the loan amount will be for substantially less than the face value of the receivables. Applying a haircut provides a buffer for the factor. Should the factor have to sell the assets at distressed prices, the factor still has a chance of covering the default loan amount.

Consider the following scenario:

The face value of accounts receivable is $200,000. The haircut is 15%, and the total charges (interest charges and commission) are $30,000.

The proceeds of the loan to the borrowing firm would be $140,000.

$170,000	Face value of accounts receivable × the haircut [$200,000 × (1 − 15%)]
$30,000	Total charges
$140,000	Loan proceeds

In some cases, factoring arrangements are transparent to the customer, who continues to make payments to the firm, which, in turn, endorses the payments to the factor. In other cases, the customer is notified of the transfer and has to make payments directly to the factor. Most arrangements are without recourse, which means that the selling company would not be liable for any receivables not collected by the factor.

Factoring arrangements can also be set up for inventories. But because inventories are the least liquid current assets, the haircut is higher and a trust receipt is required. A trust receipt allows the borrower to sell goods out of stock and remit proceeds to the factor.

Maturity Matching or Hedging Approaches to Financing

As noted in Topic 1: "Risk and Return, maturity matching is a working capital management approach that hedges risk by matching the maturities of the company's assets and liabilities. Thus, the company attempts to finance short-term projects with short-term financing and long-term projects with long-term assets.

Hedging is a method of reducing exposures to adverse fluctuations in prices, interest rates, or foreign exchange rates. Companies hedge an investment by taking an offsetting position in a second investment instrument.

The rationale to invest capital in foreign operations is generally motivated by the desire to capture a return in excess of that required. Additional contributing factors include:

- **To capitalize on gaps in international markets**
  Where domestic markets may offer only normal rates of return, international investments across different markets may present distinct opportunities to earn excess returns.

- **To lower operating costs**
  Lower labor costs and other cost efficiencies are possible through expansion into foreign markets.

- **To secure necessary raw materials**
  Companies lack sufficient raw materials and invest abroad to acquire them. Consider how mining companies and oil companies go offshore to secure necessary resources for operations.

Investments in international markets, production facilities, and raw materials are all actions that can help a firm secure a rate of return higher than through domestic activities alone.

There are some key risks associated with international opportunities including:

- **Taxation**
  Taxation becomes complex due to different tax laws and different treatments of foreign investments. The U.S. government taxes a firms with international operations differently that domestic companies. Individual countries tax the income of foreign companies doing business in their country.

- **Political risks**
  The potential for political instability in many countries ranging from mild interference in operations to expropriation warrants careful consideration.

- **Exchange rate risk exposures**
  A fundamental risk results from changes in currency exchange rates. Three specific types of exchange-rate risks are translation, transactions, and economic.

  Translation exposure is related to the accounting treatment of changes in exchange rates. There can be accounting gains or losses when assets and liabilities are translated from foreign operations into the parent company's currency.

  Transactions exposure is the gain or loss that occurs when settling a specific foreign transaction such as the purchase or sale of a foreign product or the settlement of open-credit terms.

  Economic exposure is the change in value of a company resulting from unanticipated changes in exchange rates. Economic exposure is a function of expected future cash flows.

Maturity matching and hedging are two methods a firm can use to manage exchange risk exposure. Although beyond the scope of this text, many maturity matching strategies and hedging activities exist that firms can use to offset the risk of loss from a change in foreign currency rates.

Progress Check

Directions: Read each question and respond in the space provided. Answers and page references appear on the page following the progress check questions.

Match each short-term credit arrangement with its characteristic.

1. _____ Accrued expenses

2. _____ Trade credit

3. _____ Unsecured short-term bank loans

4. _____ Secured short-term loans

5. _____ Commercial paper

6. _____ Bankers' acceptances

a. Negotiated arrangements exemplified by lines of credit and revolvers

b. Negotiable short-term instrument used primarily to finance the import and export of goods

c. Lending based on an advance rate; typically stated as a percentage of accounts receivable or inventory

d. An indirect loan between a supplier and customers for purchases

e. Spontaneous interest-free financing used to fulfill cash needs up to the point at which they become due for payment

f. An unsecured promissory note issued by a corporation and sold at a discount from par value

7. What is the effective annual interest rate on a $5 million loan with an interest rate of 8%, a commitment fee of ¼ %, and a compensating balance of 10%?

( ) a. 8%

( ) b. 8.64%

( ) c. 9.17%

( ) d. 11.11%

Progress check answers

1. e (p. 3-279)

2. d (p. 3-279)

3. a (p. 3-279)

4. c (p. 3-280)

5. f (p. 3-281)

6. b (p. 3-281)

7. c (p. 3-282)

Decision Analysis

Section overview

Decision making is a key activity in every organization. In any business, a wide variety of decisions have to be made on a daily basis. Decisions may range from small- to large-scale in scope and can be individual decisions or group decisions. Furthermore, a given decision can have short- and/or long-term consequences in regard to the resources involved in reaching the decision as well as the financial impact.

Management accountants are often called upon to provide critical data used in the decision-making process. This section reviews fundamental information that management accountants need to know about the decision-making process, the importance of relevant cost and revenue data, the use of cost/volume/profit and marginal analyses, and the application of cost-based pricing.

Learning Outcome Statements

The Certified Management Accountant (CMA) test is based upon a series of Learning Outcome Statements (LOS) developed by the Institute of Certified Management Accountants (ICMA). The LOS describe all the knowledge and skills that make up the CMA body of knowledge, broken down by part, section and topic. The CMA Learning System (CMALS) supports the LOS by addressing all the subjects they cover. Candidates should use the LOS to ensure that they can address the concepts in different ways or through a variety of question scenarios. Candidates should also be prepared to perform calculations referred to in the LOS in total or by providing missing components of a calculation. The LOS should not be used as proxies for exact exam questions; they should be used as a guide for studying and learning the content of the CMA Learning System and ensuring that you can accomplish the objectives set out by the LOS.

The LOS included in the CMALS books are the comprehensive set, current as of the date of publication. Candidates can access the IMA Web site at www.imanet.org and click on the Certification section to locate and download a Portable Document Format (PDF) file of the current LOS.

Learning Outcome Statements

Part 3: Strategic Management — Section D. Decision Analysis

Part 3 — Section D1. Decision Process

- LOS 3.D.1.a—Identify and demonstrate an understanding of the steps needed to reach a decision—in other words (i) obtain and analyze information, (ii) identify alternative courses of action, (iii) make predictions about future scenarios, (iv) choose and justify an alternative, (v) implement a decision, and (vi) evaluate performance to provide feedback.

- LOS 3.D.1.b—Demonstrate an understanding of how management should evaluate decision results.

Part 3 — Section D2. Relevant Data Concepts

- LOS 3.D.2.a—Differentiate between economic concepts of revenues and costs and accounting concepts of revenues and costs.

- LOS 3.D.2.b—Define relevant revenues (expected future revenues) and relevant costs (expected future costs).

- LOS 3.D.2.c—Recognize and identify cost behavior patterns, cost traceability, and cost relevance as it relates to various cost objects for which decisions are to be made.

- LOS 3.D.2.d—Demonstrate an understanding of various costs incurred in the value chain and the composition of such costs for decisions such as pricing, alternative operating options, contract negotiations, and outsourcing decisions.

- LOS 3.D.2.e—Differentiate between costs that are avoidable or unavoidable in a decision process setting.

- LOS 3.D.2.f—Identify relevant costs as the incremental, marginal, or differential costs among alternative courses of action and calculate the relevant costs given a numerical scenario.

- LOS 3.D.2.g—Define sunk costs and explain why they are not relevant.

- LOS 3.D.2.h—Distinguish between quantitative factors measured in numerical terms that can be

- (a) financial (for example, cost of direct labor) or (b) nonfinancial (for example, reduction in new-product development time).

- LOS 3.D.2.i—Define qualitative factors as outcomes that cannot be measured in numerical terms (for example, employee morale).

- LOS 3.D.2.j—Demonstrate an understanding of opportunity costs as the contribution to income that is forgone by not using a limited resource in its best alternative use.

- LOS 3.D.2.k—Demonstrate an understanding of the impact of income taxes on the relevant revenue and cost data employed in the decision process.

Part 3 — Section D3. Cost/Volume/Profit Analysis

- LOS 3.D.3.a—Demonstrate an understanding of how cost/volume/profit (CVP) analysis (break-even analysis) is used to examine the behavior of total revenues, total costs, and operating income as changes occur in output levels, selling prices, variable costs per unit, or fixed costs.

- LOS 3.D.3.b—Differentiate between costs that are fixed and costs that are variable with respect to levels of output.

- LOS 3.D.3.c—Demonstrate an understanding of the behavior of total revenues and total costs in relation to output within a relevant range.

- LOS 3.D.3.d—Explain why the classification of fixed vs. variable costs is affected by the time frame being considered.

- LOS 3.D.3.e—Demonstrate an understanding of how contribution margin per unit is used in CVP analysis.

- LOS 3.D.3.f—Calculate contribution margin per unit and total contribution margin.

- LOS 3.D.3.g—Calculate the break-even point in units and dollar sales to achieve targeted operating income or targeted net income.

- LOS 3.D.3.h—Demonstrate an understanding of how changes in unit sales mix affect operating income in multiple-product situations.

- LOS 3.D.3.i—Demonstrate an understanding of why there is no unique break-even point in multiple-product situations.

- LOS 3.D.3.j—Analyze and recommend a course of action using CVP analysis.

- LOS 3.D.3.k—Demonstrate an understanding of the impact of income taxes on CVP analysis.

Part 3 — Section D4. Marginal Analysis

- LOS 3.D.4.a—Demonstrate proficiency in the use of marginal analysis for decisions such as (a) introducing a new product or changing output levels of existing products, (b) accepting or rejecting special orders, (c) making or buying a product or service, (d) selling a product or performing additional processes and selling a more value-added product, and (e) adding or dropping a segment.

- LOS 3.D.4.b—Identify relevant information as the future revenues and future costs that will differ between the decisions in any type of marginal analysis.

- LOS 3.D.4.c—Explain why any cost, including any allocated costs, that does not differ between alternatives should be ignored in marginal decision analyses.

- LOS 3.D.4.d—Demonstrate an understanding of opportunity cost in marginal analysis.

- LOS 3.D.4.e—Calculate the effect of opportunity cost in a marginal analysis decision.

- LOS 3.D.4.f—Recommend a course of action using marginal analysis.

- LOS 3.D.4.g—Calculate the effect on operating income when changes in output levels occur.

- LOS 3.D.4.h—Calculate the effect on operating income of a decision to accept or reject a special order when there is idle capacity and the order has no long-run implications.

- LOS 3.D.4.i—Identify qualitative factors in make-or-buy decisions, such as product quality and dependability of suppliers.

- LOS 3.D.4.j—Calculate the effect on operating income of a decision to make or buy a product or service.

- LOS 3.D.4.k—Differentiate between avoidable and unavoidable costs in the decision to drop or add a segment.

- LOS 3.D.4.l—Demonstrate an understanding of the impact of income taxes on marginal analysis decisions.

Part 3 — Section D5. Cost-Based Pricing

- LOS 3.D.5.a—Demonstrate an understanding of cost-behavior patterns, cost traceability, cost drivers, and cost relevance in measuring the costs of products.

- LOS 3.D.5.b—Demonstrate an understanding of how the pricing of a product or service is affected by the demand for the product or service, as well as the supply availability.

- LOS 3.D.5.c—Discuss how pricing decisions in the short run can differ from pricing decisions in the long run.

- LOS 3.D.5.d—Calculate the relevant costs associated with short-run special product purchase orders.

- LOS 3.D.5.e—Discuss the importance of stable and predictable costs over an extended time period for long-run pricing decisions.

- LOS 3.D.5.f—Demonstrate an understanding of the market-based approach to the pricing decision.

- LOS 3.D.5.g—Differentiate between a cost-based approach and a market-based approach to setting prices.

- LOS 3.D.5.h—Explain why market-based pricing strategies are generally used when operating in a competitive commodities type of market.

- LOS 3.D.5.i—Define and demonstrate an understanding of target pricing and target costing.

- LOS 3.D.5.j—Identify techniques used to set prices based on understanding customers' perceptions of value, competitors' technologies, products, costs, and financial conditions.

- LOS 3.D.5.k—Identify the main steps in developing target prices and target costs.

- LOS 3.D.5.l—Define value engineering.

- LOS 3.D.5.m—Calculate the target operating income per unit and target cost per unit.

- LOS 3.D.5.n—Define and distinguish between a value-added cost and a nonvalue-added cost.

- LOS 3.D.5.o—Define the pricing technique of cost plus target rate of return.

- LOS 3.D.5.p—Define a product life cycle and life-cycle costing.

- LOS 3.D.5.q—Define peak-load pricing.

- LOS 3.D.5.r—Evaluate and recommend pricing strategies under specific market conditions or opportunities.

Topic 1 | **Decision Process**

Topic overview

At a base level, decision making is selecting between two or more alternatives. In practice, the process becomes more complex. For most business applications, decision making means having to sift through large amounts of data, only some of which may be pertinent. In determining which alternative is best, a decision maker must ultimately decide which option offers the greatest benefit for the business, generally in dollars.

Relevant Costs and Revenues

When choosing among alternative choices for a given business situation, only relevant costs and revenues should be considered. Including irrelevant cost and revenue data can cloud the issues at hand, waste time, and potentially lead to erroneous decisions.

Two criteria differentiate relevant costs and revenues from irrelevant data: (1) They have a future orientation and (2) they are different for each alternative choice.

Steps in the Decision Process

To reach a decision, the costs and benefits of one alternative must be systematically weighed against the costs and benefits of other alternatives.

Most organizational decisions are based on some type of decision model—or process—whether an individual has sole responsibility or a group of people is involved. A decision model facilitates effective decision making by providing a logical framework for discerning between relevant and irrelevant data and choosing among alternatives.

Because there are many possible decision-making approaches, discussing every type is not feasible.

Most models include a framework for quantitative and qualitative analyses and account for the steps described in Figure 3-75.

Figure 3-75: Organizational Decision-Making Steps

Step 1	**Collect information.**
	Obtaining comprehensive information at the onset helps to ensure that short-term, quick fixes are not erroneously substituted downstream as solutions.
	Example: A company must decide whether to accept a request to customize a product. Review of current costs identifies that the normal product selling price is $400 and the normal unit product cost is $200 (made up of $50 for materials, $100 for labor, and $50 for overhead).
Step 2	**Identify alternative courses of action.**
	Relevant data must be separated from irrelevant information. Courses of action may be stated in terms of short-term and long-term objectives.
	Example: The alternatives in this case are to accept or decline the opportunity. Analysis determines that the customization request will require additional materials on a per-unit basis. An annual increase in employee salaries will be in force by the time the order is fulfilled. The order would have no effect on regular sales and could be fulfilled with existing capacity.
Step 3	**Estimate future costs and revenues.**
	Based on relevant data, future relevant costs and revenues can be predicted for the different options.
	Example: The estimated unit product cost for the special order is 10% more than the current unit product costs. The additional materials are a one-time cost. The negotiated price with the client is 5% more than the normal selling price.
Step 4	**Choose and justify an alternative.**
	Evaluating the potential alternatives based on the information at hand leads to the selection of the best option.
	Example: The predicted increases in costs and the selling price for the customized units are compared. The likely effect on customer goodwill in accepting (or declining) the customization request is also considered. Management chooses to accept the order.
Step 5	**Implement a decision.**
	The optimal alternative is implemented.
	Example: The decision reached in step 4 is implemented.
Step 6	**Evaluate performance to provide feedback.**
	Evaluating the outcome of the decision option chosen provides appropriate feedback for future decisions of a similar nature. Opportunities for improvement are identified.
	Example: Labor costs are higher than predicted because additional time is required to fulfill the customization request. Management assesses that the prediction was at fault, not the implementation. Consideration is given as to how future customization requests might be better handled.

Evaluation of Decision Results

Organizational performance is largely dependent upon effective decision making. An effective decision-making process is one that addresses the six steps described in Figure 3-65: (1) systematically collecting information, (2) identifying alternative courses of action, (3) estimating future costs and revenues (4) choosing and justifying an alternative, (5) implementing the option chosen, and (6) evaluating the outcome to provide feedback.

The final step—evaluating the decision results—is critical. Performance measurement and feedback helps to ensure that the course of action taken is performing as expected.

Depending upon the nature of the decision, determinations can be made about items such as:

- Gaps between the predictions and the actual results.

- The appropriate classification—or misclassification—of relevant costs and revenues.

- How sources of unsatisfactory performance (activities and operations) can be acted upon to improve efficiency, effectiveness, and profitability.

Evaluation of decision results in this manner identifies opportunities for improvement in future decision making.

Progress Check

Directions: Read each question and respond in the space provided. Answers and page references appear on the page following the progress check questions.

1. Which two criteria differentiate relevant costs and revenues from irrelevant data?

    (   )   a.   Streamlined activities and incremental gains

    (   )   b.   Qualitative and quantitative decision outcomes

    (   )   c.   A historical basis and the given decision situation

    (   )   d.   A future orientation and different alternative choices

2. Expected financial gains from the addition of a new product have fallen short of first quarter projections. Which of the following is the most likely benefit of evaluating the decision results?

    (   )   a.   Any areas of unsatisfactory performance can be identified and corrected.

    (   )   b.   Additional opportunities for communicating a shared organizational vision can be identified.

    (   )   c.   Short-term, quick fixes can be implemented to improve productivity and revenues.

    (   )   d.   Short- and long-term objectives can be revised to be more realistic.

Progress check answers

1. d (p. 3-292)

2. a (p. 3-293)

Relevant Data Concepts

Topic overview

Several terms and concepts must be understood before decision analysis can be further explored. This topic looks at some of these important terms and concepts.

Future-Oriented Costs and Revenues

Relevant costs and revenues

By definition, a **relevant cost** is a cost yet to be incurred or a future cost. **Relevant revenues** are expected future revenues. Both relevant costs and relevant revenues are those that are different for each option available to the decision maker. Costs and revenues that have already been incurred or committed are irrelevant in decision making because there is no longer any discretion associated with them.

Avoidable and unavoidable costs

An **avoidable cost** (or escapable cost) is one that can be eliminated in whole or in part by choosing one alternative over another in the decision-making process. An avoidable cost might be eliminated by ceasing to perform an activity or by improving the efficiency of the activity. An **unavoidable cost** is an ongoing cost that remains in force regardless of any business decision or action. Avoidable costs are relevant costs whereas unavoidable costs are irrelevant.

Incremental and differential costs and revenues

An **incremental cost** (also known as outlay or out-of-pocket cost) is an additional cost incurred to obtain an extra quantity over and above existing or planned quantities of a cost object. A **differential cost** (or net relevant cost) is the difference in total costs between any two alternatives in decision making.

These two terms—incremental cost and differential cost—are often used interchangeably. Technically, an incremental cost refers to an increase in costs between alternatives whereas a **decremental cost** describes a decrease in costs. Differential costs encompass both cost increases (incremental costs) and cost decreases (decremental costs) between alternatives. All three types—incremental, decremental, and differential—are relevant costs in decision making.

Incremental revenue refers to the additional revenue that arises from pursuing an alternative course of action. **Differential revenue** is the difference in revenue between any two alternatives. The change in revenue may be in amount or timing.

An accountant views changes in costs and revenues in terms of incremental and differential. From an economic perspective, the terms **marginal cost** and **marginal revenue** are used. Marginal cost refers to the cost involved in producing one more unit of product where as marginal revenue is the revenue that can be obtained from selling one more unit of product. The basic difference between an accounting and economic perspective is that "marginal" applies to a single unit of output.

Importance of relevant data in decision making

Given that relevant costs are future costs that differ for each decision alternative, only relevant costs should logically be considered in making a decision. In other words, if a cost will be the same regardless of the alternative selected, it is irrelevant and should not be considered in the decision-making process.

Consider the following scenario to illustrate the importance of including only relevant costs in decision making. A business plans to buy a new copier and is evaluating different copier models. There is also discussion about where to put the copier. The prices for the different copiers are relevant to include in the decision-making process because those costs differ according to each copier's features and benefits. An example of an irrelevant cost is the monthly rent for the office space. The facility rent remains the same whether the business purchases the new copier, which model is selected, or where the copier is installed.

Cost behavior patterns

Cost behavior patterns refer to how fixed and variable costs react to changes in business activity levels:

- For fixed costs, the total costs remain constant within the relevant range of activity while the unit cost increases or decreases with changes in activity.

- For variable costs, the unit cost remains constant while the total cost changes with increases or decreases in activity.

Note: Topic 3 in this section, "Cost/Volume/Profit Analysis," covers cost behavior patterns in more detail.

Sunk Costs

A **sunk cost** (or past cost) is one that has already been incurred and that cannot be changed by any decision now or in the future. Sunk costs remain the same regardless of the alternatives being considered. Aside from any potential income tax effects, a sunk cost should not be included in any current decisions for increasing or decreasing present profit levels. Historical costs are sunk.

The cost of a machine previously purchased to make a product that is now obsolete is an example of a sunk cost—even if the original equipment investment was not recovered. If the decision being evaluated is whether to continue to manufacture the obsolete product, the money paid for the machine is a past cost and cannot make a difference in any future profit levels. Decision makers should ignore sunk costs.

Opportunity Costs

An **opportunity cost** is the benefit given up when one alternative is selected over another in reaching a decision. In a situation in which a business chooses to upgrade to a new computer system rather than investing in securities, the investment income foregone from the securities represents an opportunity cost.

Opportunity costs are not typically recorded in accounting. Nonetheless, they are important to consider when making business decisions. A decision alternative often has an opportunity cost associated with it. If a company chooses to buy securities instead of new computer hardware and software, the income forgone that may have resulted from increased employee productivity would be an opportunity cost.

In some situations, an opportunity cost can be quantified by determining the financial benefit of alternative options. For example, if a company decides to forego a special order because of the delay it would create in filling current orders, the potential profit from the lost order represents the opportunity cost for the decision made. But the loyalty of existing customers in this scenario, while difficult to quantify, has substantial long-term value and may tend to outweigh the potential benefits of the special order. Existing customers might cancel future orders if their current order is delayed and, thus, potentially reduce future profits.

Qualitative and Quantitative Factors

The consequences of decision alternatives are sometimes categorized as qualitative and quantitative.

Qualitative factors

Qualitative factors are decision outcomes that cannot be measured in numerical terms. Customer goodwill and employee morale are two examples.

Quantitative factors

Quantitative factors are decision outcomes that can be measured in numerical terms. Quantitative factors are further differentiated as financial and nonfinancial measures.

- **Financial measures**
  Financial measures are those easily expressed in financial terms such as the cost of direct labor or direct materials.

- **Nonfinancial measures**
  Nonfinancial measures can be expressed numerically but not in financial terms. A reduction in new product development time, a reduction in cycle time for an existing product, or a productivity improvement expressed as a percentage are all examples of nonfinancial quantitative measures.

Decision analysis generally emphasizes quantitative factors because of their financial ramifications. This does not imply that qualitative factors should be ignored. A decision should ultimately evaluate the tradeoffs between the two types.

Cost Traceability

Cost traceability refers to the ability to assign a cost to a cost object in an economically feasible way by means of a cause-and-effect relationship. Direct costs are easily traced but indirect costs are not easily and accurately traced.

Firms need to trace costs directly to cost objects and/or business segments during decision making when it is feasible to do so. For example, the rent for regional warehouses should be charged directly to regional branch operations and not included in a company-wide overhead pool.

Costs that are improperly assigned can result in cost distortion. In particular, allocating common fixed costs can make a product line or functional business unit look less profitable than it is in actuality.

Value Chain Costs

Statement on Management Accounting No. 4X, "Value Chain Analysis for Assessing Competitive Advantage," describes value chain analysis as a team effort. Management accountants need to collaborate with other functional areas of the organization that comprise the value chain—research and development, engineering (design), production (manufacturing), marketing, distribution, and service—to successfully bring a product or service to the customer and generate revenues.

Most large companies are organized as functional cost, revenue, profit, and investment centers. When considering the value chain approach, a firm needs to adopt a process perspective and a horizontal view, beginning with product inputs and culminating with outputs and customers. Costs and assets should be traced and assigned to each value-creating process identified. If cost accounting information cannot be readily aligned to processes, companies sometimes estimate the costs assignable to their value-creating processes.

Traditional management accounting focuses on internal data. Manufacturing costs are typically emphasized. Important linkages with suppliers and customers are generally ignored. In decision making, assessments of profitability may omit important costs. Consequently, management may unknowingly make decisions that result in organizational losses rather than company profits.

The value chain approach differs from traditional accounting in that it:

- Includes both internal and external data.

- Uses appropriate cost drivers for all major value-creating processes.

- Acknowledges linkages throughout the value chain.

- Accounts for upstream and downstream costs in the value chain.

"Upstream" costs and "downstream" costs are just as important in determining product profitability as manufacturing costs.

- Upstream costs are the research and development and design costs in the value chain.

- Downstream costs are the marketing, distribution, and service costs in the value chain.

On an income statement, upstream and downstream costs are usually titled, "Selling, General, and Administrative" (SG&A). In some businesses, these combined costs can comprise more than half of the firm's total costs. Consider a pharmaceutical company as an example. Research and development and marketing are a huge part of the firm's total expenditures.

When trying to determine product or service profitability for decision-making purposes, the linkages between segments in the value chain must be examined. The impact of various activities and tradeoffs between upstream and downstream costs should be considered. Additional investments in research, for example, can improve product quality and reduce service costs downstream. Innovative design decisions about product packaging can improve distribution efficiency downstream.

Management accountants are responsible for tracking the different costs incurred throughout the value chain. When costs are properly allocated informed decisions can be made about how to reduce costs in each category and improve operational effectiveness and efficiency. Examples of value-chain activities that have a role in lowering the cost structure and increasing the perceived value of products and services include: decisions to subcontract or outsource activities or to keep them in-house, pricing strategies, and decisions on the best way to structure a distribution channel.

Note: Value chain analysis is discussed in more detail in Section A of this part of the CMA Learning System, Topic 3, "Business Process Performance."

Impact of Income Taxes in the Decision Process

Tax considerations are an important part of evaluating investment proposals. In some situations, taxes rates, the methods of applying them, and the impact taxes have on relevant revenue and cost data may become the deciding factor between different proposals.

Depreciation expenses directly affect taxable income and thus influences profits. The ability to write-off depreciation in the early years results in additional funds for other investments.

Tax laws change over time. When evaluating investment proposals today, decision makers should have a thorough understanding of current tax laws and an awareness of potential future tax law changes that may affect current investments and accounting procedures.

Progress Check

Directions: Read each question and respond in the space provided. Answers and page references appear on the page following the progress check questions.

1. The difference in the amount or timing between two investment alternatives is an example of

    ( ) a. incremental revenue.

    ( ) b. differential revenue.

    ( ) c. an outlay.

    ( ) d. a net relevant cost.

2. All of the following statements accurately characterize sunk costs **except**

    ( ) a. They can be eliminated in whole or in part by eliminating an activity.

    ( ) b. They are the same regardless of the alternatives being considered.

    ( ) c. They cannot make a difference in any future profit levels.

    ( ) d. They should be ignored in decision making.

Progress check answers

1. b (p. 3-297)

2. a (p. 3-298)

Cost/Volume/Profit Analysis

Topic 3

Topic overview

Cost/volume/profit (CVP) analysis is a method for analyzing the interrelationships between total cost, volume, and profits in an organization. CVP analysis examines the interactions between the:

- *Selling prices of products and services.*

- *Sales volume (the level of activity).*

- *Per-unit variable costs.*

- *Total fixed costs.*

- *Mix of products and services sold.*

Managers can apply CVP analysis data in a wide variety of decision-making situations, such as:

- *Raising or lowering prices for existing products and services.*

- *Introducing a new product or service.*

- *Setting prices for new products and services.*

- *Expanding product and service markets.*

- *Deciding whether to replace an existing piece of equipment.*

- *Deciding whether to make or buy a product or service.*

CVP Terminology and Assumptions

CVP analysis attempts to simplify assumptions about revenue and cost behavior patterns. To explain CVP analysis further requires clarifying several terms.

- **Cost** generally refers to a resource expended to achieve a specific objective.

- A **cost driver** is any factor that affects costs. A change in a cost driver will result in a change in the total cost of a related cost object. Examples of cost drivers are the number of units manufactured or the number of packages shipped.

- A **cost object** is anything for which cost data is accumulated. Products, product lines, customers, jobs, and organizational business units are examples.

- A **fixed cost** is a cost that remains constant, in total, regardless of changes in the level of activity within a relevant range. Fixed costs have to be changed by management action.

- A **variable cost** is a cost that varies, in total, in direct proportion to changes in the level of activity within a relevant range.

- The **relevant range** is the range of activity within which the assumptions about variable and fixed costs remain valid.

- **Revenues** are inflows of assets received in exchange for products or services.

- A **revenue driver** is a factor that affects revenues (such as marketing costs, the selling prices of units, or the number of units sold).

- **Total costs** (or total expenses) are made up of variable costs (with respect to units of output) and fixed costs. Total costs are represented as follows:

  Total Costs = Variable Costs + Fixed Costs

- **Operating income** is total revenues from operations minus total costs from operations (excluding income taxes). Operating income is generally represented as follows:

  Operating Income = Total Operating Revenues – Total Operating Costs

  Companies sometimes exclude financing costs from operating income for analytical purposes.

- **Net income** is income for a period after subtracting expenses from all sources for that period. Net income is represented as:

  Net Income = Earnings before Taxes – Income Taxes

  Net income can include revenues and expenses not associated with operations.

- **Activity level** (also known as output level, measure of output, or output) refers to the number of units produced or the number of units sold. Activity level nomenclature can vary across industries. For example, instead of units, airlines use passenger miles, hospitals may use patient days or beds occupied, hotels use rooms occupied, and colleges and universities use student credit hours.

The CVP analysis explained through subsequent content specifically examines the behavior of total revenues, total costs, and operating income as changes occur in output levels, selling prices, variable costs per unit, or fixed costs. This CVP model assumes that:

- Total costs can be divided into fixed costs and variable costs with respect to levels of output.

- Total revenues and total costs have a linear (straight line) relationship to output units within a relevant range.

Fixed and variable cost behavior

Cost behavior generally refers to how a cost will react to changes in business activity levels. As the business output changes, a given cost may rise, fall, or remain constant.

A key assumption in CVP analysis is that costs can be classified as either fixed or variable with respect to activity level—the amount of goods produced or services provided by a company. Figure 3-76 summarizes how fixed and variable costs behave in total and on a per-unit basis within the relevant range. Note how fixed and variable costs behave differently if they are viewed as total costs or on a per-unit basis.

Figure 3-76: Fixed and Variable Cost Behavior within Relevant Range

Type of Cost	Behavior in Total	Behavior per Unit
Fixed	Generally not affected by changes in activity level	Increase and decrease inversely (for example, increase as activity level falls and decrease as activity level rises)
Variable	Routinely increase and decrease proportionately to changes in activity level	Remain constant

Examples of costs that are fixed irrespective of the environment in which they are incurred (for example, manufacturing, retail, or service) include insurance premiums, rental charges, property taxes, salaries, and advertising.

In manufacturing environments, examples of variable costs include direct materials and some parts of overhead such as sales commissions and shipping costs. For a retail business, examples include costs of goods sold, sales commissions, and billing costs. In a service environment such as a hospital, variable costs include the cost of prescription drugs, hospital supplies, and patient meals.

Fixed and variable classifications over time

The classifications of costs as fixed and variable can be affected by the time horizon being considered. In other words, some variable costs may be reclassified as fixed. Given an extended period of time, a fixed cost may eventually vary.

Generally, the following principles apply to fixed and variable cost classifications over time:

- The shorter the time period, the higher the percentage of total costs that can be viewed as fixed.
- The longer the time horizon, the more costs that can be viewed as variable.

Overall, whether a cost is fixed or variable is often a function of:

- Relevant range.
- Time frame.
- The given decision situation.

The example in Figure 3-77 further illustrates fixed and variable cost behavior.

Figure 3-77: Fixed and Variable Cost Behavior

	Total Cost at 10,000 Units	Cost per Unit	Total Cost at 25,000 Units	Cost per Unit	Total Cost at 50,000 Units	Cost per Unit
Direct materials	$16,000	$1.60	$40,000	$1.60	$80,000	$1.60
Direct labor	25,000	2.50	62,500	2.50	125,000	2.50
Distribution	13,000	1.30	32,500	1.30	65,000	1.30
Depreciation	50,000	5.00	50,000	2.00	80,000	1.60
Rent	25,000	2.50	25,000	1.00	40,000	0.80

The per-unit costs for materials and labor are fixed over the relevant range of capacity. Total costs for depreciation and rent are fixed whether the company produces one or 25,000 units. However, when sales increase beyond the plant's capacity of 25,000 units, the company would need to add on to its production line. Per-unit costs would increase as additional equipment and space would be required.

Total revenues and total costs

The CVP model assumes that total revenues and total costs are linear within a relevant range of activity level. Stated another way, within a limited range of output, total costs are expected to increase at an approximately linear rate. Figure 3-78 shows a simple representation of this linear relationship.

Figure 3-78: CVP Graph of Total Revenues, Total Costs, and Output Levels

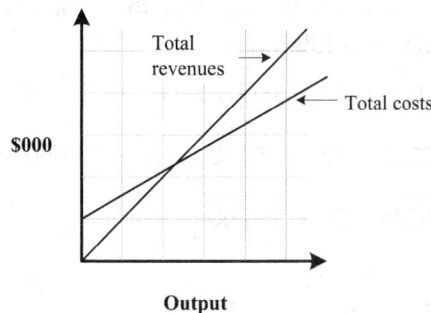

Break-Even Analysis

CVP analysis is sometimes referred to as break-even analysis. Technically, break-even analysis is only one part of CVP analysis.

A **break-even point**, also called the **operating break-even point**, is the output level at which total revenues and total costs are equal. At break-even, operating income is zero. Above the break-even point, operating income levels are profitable; below break-even, there is a loss.

Determining the break-even point is a key part of CVP analysis and assessing how various "what-if" decision alternatives will affect operating income. Break-even point may be determined using three different methods: an equation method, a contribution margin method, and a graph method. Subsequent text describes each method given the following scenario:

A company sales representative travels to a client's location to promote a new product. The unit selling price for the product is $200. The fixed costs for the product are $4,000. The variable selling costs for the product are $100, and the quantity of the product sold is 75.

Equation method

A common equation method for computing the break-even point is:

Revenues – Variable Costs – Fixed Costs = Operating Income

or

$$(USP \times Q) - (UVC \times Q) - FC = OI$$

Where:

- USP = unit selling price.

- Q = quantity sold.

- UVC = unit variable costs.

- FC = fixed costs.

- OI = operating income.

At the break-even point, operating income is zero. Setting operating income to zero and substituting the numbers in the equation, the break-even point for the example (expressed in units) is calculated as follows:

$$(USP \times Q) - (UVC \times Q) - FC = OI$$

$$(\$200 \times Q) - (\$100 \times Q) - \$4,000 = \$0$$

$$\$100 \times Q = \$4,000$$

$$Q = \frac{\$4,000}{\$100} = 40 \text{ Units}$$

In this example, selling fewer than 40 units will be a loss; selling 40 units will be break-even; selling more than 40 will make a profit.

Contribution margin method

The contribution margin method is an algebraic adaptation of the equation method. **Contribution margin** represents the amount remaining from sales revenue after variable expenses are deducted. It is found by taking revenues and subtracting all costs of the output that vary with respect to the number of output units.

The contribution margin method is based on the following equation:

$$(USP \times Q) - (UVC \times Q) - FC = OI$$

$$(USP - UVC) \times Q = FC + OI$$

$$UCM \times Q = FC + OI$$

$$Q = \frac{FC + OI}{UCM}$$

Where:

- USP = unit selling price.
- Q = quantity sold.
- UVC = unit variable costs.
- FC = fixed costs.
- OI = operating income.
- UCM = unit contribution margin (USP – UVC).

Setting operating income to zero and inserting the numbers in the contribution margin method, the break-even point (expressed in units) for the example is calculated as follows:

$$\text{Break-Even Number of Units} = \frac{\text{Fixed Costs (FC)}}{\text{Unit Contribution Margin (UCM)}}$$

$$= \frac{\$4,000}{\$100} = 40 \text{ Units}$$

A contribution income statement highlights the contribution margin by grouping line items by cost behavior patterns. A contribution margin income statement confirms the contribution margin break-even calculations.

Figure 3-79: Contribution Income Statement

Sale revenues ($200 × 40)	$8,000
Variable costs ($100 × 40)	4,000
Contribution margin	4,000
Fixed costs	4,000
Operating income	$0

Contribution margin percentage/contribution margin ratio

The contribution margin may be expressed as a percentage instead of a dollar amount per unit. Contribution margin percentage (also called, contribution margin ratio or CMR) may be calculated in two ways. Contribution margin percentage is often represented as the contribution margin per unit divided by selling price.

$$\text{Contribution Margin Percentage} = \frac{\text{Unit Contribution Margin (UCM)}}{\text{Selling Price}}$$

$$= \frac{\$100}{\$200} = 0.50 \text{ or } 50\%$$

Contribution margin percentage may also be calculated as contribution margin divided by total revenues. If 40 packages are sold:

$$\text{Contribution Margin Percentage} = \frac{\text{Contribution Margin}}{\text{Total Revenues}}$$

$$= \frac{\$4,000}{\$8,000} = 0.50 \text{ or } 50\%$$

The contribution margin percentage or CMR provides the contribution margin per dollar of revenues. In this example it indicates that 50% of each dollar (equal to $0.50) is contribution margin.

Variable cost percentage

Variable cost percentage is the complement of contribution margin percentage. In other words:

Contribution margin percentage + Variable cost percentage = 1

In the example given, contribution margin percentage = 50% so variable cost percentage = 50%. Given variable costs are $100 per unit and variable cost percentage is 50%, selling price is:

$$\$100 \div 0.50 = \$200$$

Graph method

A CVP graph (or break-even chart) shows the interrelationships among cost, volume, and profit graphically.

- The activity level (unit volume) is shown on the horizontal (X) axis.

- Dollars are shown on the vertical (Y) axis.

- Total costs and total revenues are both plotted as lines with their point of intersection being the break-even point.

Figure 3-80 shows a CVP graph of break-even analysis.

Figure 3-80: CVP Graph of Break-Even Analysis

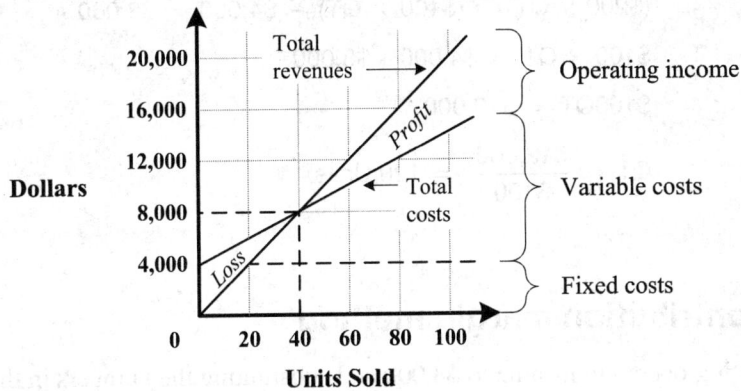

Profit Performance and Alternative Operating Levels

Break-even analysis may also be used to determine how many units must be sold to earn a target profit level—either a targeted operating income or a targeted net income. Building upon the previous scenario and setting a target operating income of $8,000, here's how the calculations in units and dollar sales would look.

Equation method

The equation used in this case is:

Revenues – Variable Costs – Fixed Costs = Target Operating Income

or

$$(USP \times QT) - (UVC \times QT) - FC = TOI$$

Where:

- USP = unit selling price.

- QT = quantity sold to earn the target operating income.

- UVC = unit variable costs.

- FC = fixed costs.

- TOI = target operating income.

Setting the target operating income to $8,000 and substituting the numbers, the number of units that must be sold is calculated as follows:

$$(USP \times QT) - (UVC \times QT) - FC = TOI$$

$$(\$200 \times QT) - (\$100 \times QT) - \$4,000 = \$8,000$$

$$\$100 \times QT = \$4,000 + \$8,000$$

$$\$100QT = \$12,000$$

$$QT = \frac{\$12,000}{\$100} = 120 \text{ Units}$$

Contribution margin method

Setting operating income to $8,000 and substituting the numbers in the contribution margin method, the numerator would consist of fixed costs plus the target operating income:

$$QT = \frac{FC + TOI}{UCM}$$

$$= \frac{\$4,000 + \$8,000}{\$100}$$

$$= \frac{\$12,000}{\$100} = 120 \text{ Units}$$

The contribution income statement would be as follows.

Figure 3-81: Contribution Income Statement

Sale revenues ($200 × 120)	$24,000
Variable costs ($100 × 120)	12,000
Contribution margin	12,000
Fixed costs	4,000
Operating income	$8,000

Calculating the break-even point in terms of revenues is also possible. Recall the previous calculation of contribution margin percentage or CMR:

$$\text{Contribution Margin Percentage} = \frac{\text{Contribution Margin}}{\text{Total Revenues}}$$

$$= \frac{\$4,000}{\$8,000} = 0.50 \text{ or } 50\%$$

In this example, 50% of each dollar (or $0.50) is contribution margin. To break even, the contribution margin must equal the fixed costs of $4,000. To earn, $4,000 of contribution margin, revenues must equal $8,000.

$$\text{Break-Even Revenues} = \frac{\text{Fixed Costs}}{\text{Contribution Margin \%}}$$

$$= \frac{\$4,000}{0.50} = \$8,000$$

Graph method

Figure 3-82 shows a profit-volume (PV) graph and how changes in output affect operating income. The level of fixed costs at zero output is $4,000. Each unit beyond the break-even point contributes to operating income.

Figure 3-82: PV Graph

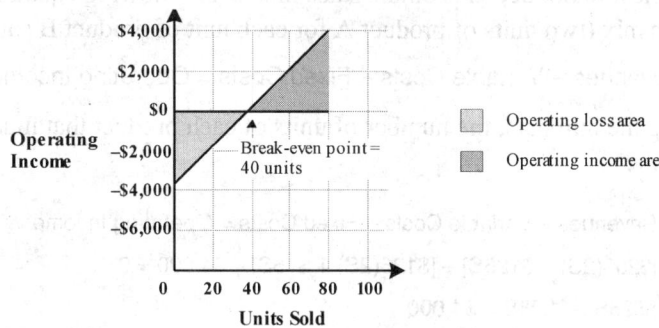

At the 60-unit level, for example, operating income would be:

$$(\$200 \times 60) - (\$100 \times 60) - \$4,000 = \$2,000$$

Analysis of Multiple Products

Sales mix (or **revenue mix**) refers to the relative proportions of products or services sold. Most companies have multiple products and/or services. Generally the different offerings are not equally profitable. Businesses typically strive for the sales mix that yields the highest profits. Profits tend to be greater if a larger proportion of the product or service mix comprises higher-margin items.

Consider the following budget projections for a company with two products (A and B).

Figure 3-83: Budget Projections

	Product A	Product B	Total
Number of units sold	100	50	150
Revenues per unit ($200 and $125)	$20,000	$6,250	$26,250
Variable costs per unit ($125 and $75)	12,500	3,750	16,250
Contribution margin per unit ($75 and $50)	7,500	2,500	10,000
Fixed costs ($4,000)			4,000
Operating income			$6,000

Because of the multiple products, there is no unique number of units for a break-even point. The number depends on the sales mix. The following equation can be used when the sales mix (two units of product A for each unit of product B sold) is constant:

Revenues – Variable Costs – Fixed Costs = Operating Income

Inserting the numbers, the number of units of each product that must be sold is calculated as follows:

Revenues – Variable Costs – Fixed Costs = Operating Income

[$200(2S) + $125S] – [$125(2S) + $75S] – $4,000 = 0

$525S – $325S = $4,000

$200S = $4,000

S = 20

2S = 40

Where:

- 2S = number of units of product A to break even.

- S i= number of units of product B to break even.

When the sales mix is 40 units of product A and 20 units of product B, the break-even point is 60. Alternate sales mixes would result in different break-even points.

Weighted average contribution method

The weighted average contribution method is another way to apply CVP analysis to a company producing multiple products. To determine the break-even point, the weighted average contribution margin per unit is computed for each of the products at the budgeted sales mix. Returning to the previous sales mix of Product A and Product B:

$$\text{Weighted Average UCM} = \frac{(\text{Product A UCM} \times \text{Number of units sold}) + (\text{Product B UCM} \times \text{Number of units sold})}{\text{Product A Number of Units Sold} + \text{Product B Number of Units Sold}}$$

$$= \frac{(\$75 \text{ per unit} \times 100 \text{ units}) + (\$50 \text{ per unit} \times 50 \text{ units})}{100 \text{ units} + 50 \text{ units}}$$

$$= \frac{\$7,500 + \$2,500}{150} = \frac{\$10,000}{150} = \$66.66 \text{ per unit}$$

Break-even point is then calculated as follows.

$$\text{Break-Even Point} = \frac{\text{Fixed Costs}}{\text{Weighted Average UCM}}$$

$$= \frac{\$4,000}{\$66.66 \text{ per unit}} = 60 \text{ units}$$

The ratio of Product A to Product B sales is 100:50 (or, 2:1), the break-even point is:

- $60/3 = 20 \times 2 = 40$ units of Product A

- $60/3 = 20$ units of Product B

At this mix, the contribution margin is \$4,000 (Product A \$75 per unit × 40 units + Product B \$50 per unit x 20 units), which is exactly equal to the company's fixed costs of \$4,000. Because the contribution margin equals fixed costs at 60 units, the company is just breaking even.

The break-even point in revenues for multiple products can also be calculated using the weighted-average contribution margin percentage.

$$\text{Weighted Average Contribution Margin \%} = \frac{\text{Total Contribution Margin}}{\text{Total Revenues}}$$

$$= \frac{\$10,000}{\$26,250} = 0.381 \text{ or } 38.1\%$$

$$\text{Total Revenues Required to Break Even} = \frac{\text{Fixed Costs}}{\text{Weighted Average Contribution Margin \%}}$$

$$= \frac{\$4,000}{0.3809523} = \$10,500.00$$

Figure 3-84 shows the breakdown of total revenues, total variable costs, and total contribution margin at the break-even point.

Figure 3-84: Budget Projections at Break-Even

	Product A	Product B	Total
Number of units sold	40	20	60
Revenues per unit ($200 and $125)	$8,000	$2,500	$10,500
Variable costs per unit ($125 and $75)	$5,000	$1,500	$6,500
Contribution margin per unit ($75 and $50)	$3,000	$1,000	$4,000
Fixed costs ($4,000)			$4,000
Operating income			$0

Using data from Figure 3-84, the $26,250 of total revenues is broken down between Product A and B as follows: 76.2% for A ($20,000/$26,250) and 23.8% for B ($6,250/$26,250). The break-even revenues of $10,500 should be split in the same ratio. This results in:

- Break-even revenues for Product A of $8,000 (76.2% × $10,500)

- Break-even revenues for Product B of $2,500 (23.8% × $10,500)

At a selling price of $200 for Product A and $125 for Product B:

- Break even for Product A = 40 units ($8,000/$200)

- Break even for Product B = 20 units ($2,500/$125)

The effects of changes in the sales mix on the operating income depend on how the original proportions of higher- and lower-margin items have changed. The following general principles usually apply:

- A shift from high-margin items to low-margin items can cause operating income to fall even though total sales may increase.

- A shift from low-margin items to high-margin items can cause operating income to rise even though total sales may decrease.

Businesses strive to maximize revenues through their sales mixes. Many factors can influence decisions as to which products to produce in what quantity and what products to emphasize. Sometimes, the best decision may not always be to produce the items having the highest contribution margin per unit. For example, a product may have a high contribution margin but the company may be able to sell insufficient units to break-even. In most cases (especially when a plant is operating at full capacity), management should focus on each product's contribution margin and select those having the highest contribution margin per unit of the constraining resource.

A **constraining resource** is a resource that restricts or limits the production or sale of products or services. In manufacturing, examples of constraining resources include contribution per machine hour or the availability of direct materials, components or skilled labor. In a retail environment, display space footage can be a constraining resource. Financial and sales factors can also be constraining resources in either environment.

A challenge arises when trying to maximize total operating income for a variety of products when each has multiple constraining resources. A company may need to stock minimum quantities of products even if these products are not very profitable. A hardware store, for example, may have to carry less-profitable items to ensure they have a wide range of products that customers need.

Income Taxes and CVP Analysis

As noted earlier, net income is often represented by operating income minus income taxes. To determine net income, the only change in the equation method for CVP analysis is to modify the target operating income to allow for taxes.

Using a tax rate of 40% and the contribution income statement shown in Figure 3-79 on page 3-323 (where the target operating income is $8,000), here is the role of taxes:

Target Net Income = Operating Income − (Operating Income × Tax Rate)

= Operating Income × (1 − Tax Rate)

$$\text{Operating Income} = \frac{\text{Target Net Income}}{1 - \text{Tax Rate}}$$

Returning to the equation method and taking income taxes into account:

$$\text{Revenues} - \text{Variable Costs} - \text{Fixed Costs} = \frac{\text{Target Net Income}}{1 - \text{Tax Rate}}$$

Substituting the numbers from the example, the equation is now:

$$\$200Q - \$120Q - \$4,000 = \frac{\$8,000}{1 - 0.40}$$

$200Q − $120Q − $4,000 = $13,333

80Q = $17,333

Q = 216.66 Units

The contribution income statement in Figure 3-85, which includes the effect of income taxes, is proof of the equation.

Figure 3-85: Income Taxes and Target Operating Income

Revenues ($200 × 216.66)	$43,332
Variable costs ($120 × 216.66)	25,999
Contribution margin	17,333
Fixed costs	4,000
Operating income	13,333
Income taxes ($13,333 × 0.40)	5,333
Net income	$8,000

Progress Check

Directions: Read each question and respond in the space provided. Answers and page references appear on the page following the progress check questions.

1. In the CVP model, total revenues and total costs

    (   )   a.   remain constant within a limited range of output.

    (   )   b.   increase and decrease inversely to changes in activity level.

    (   )   c.   increase and decrease proportionately to changes in activity level.

    (   )   d.   increase at an approximately linear rate within a relevant range of activity.

2. All of the following statements accurately describe a break-even point **except**

    (   )   a.   Operating income is zero.

    (   )   b.   Total revenues and total costs are equal.

    (   )   c.   Above break-even signifies profits; below break-even signifies loss.

    (   )   d.   Below break-even signifies profits; above break-even signifies loss.

Match the following terms with their description.

3. _____ Relevant range

4. _____ Activity level

5. _____ Cost behavior

6. _____ Contribution margin

7. _____ Sales mix

a.   How a cost will react to changes in business activity levels

b.   Activity parameters within which the assumptions about variable and fixed costs remain valid

c.   Relative proportions of products or services sold

d.   Number of units produced or sold

e.   Amount remaining from sales revenue after variable expenses are deducted

8. Given fixed costs of $8,000, variable costs of $100, and a unit contribution margin of $200, how many units must be sold to reach a target operating income of $34,000?

    (   )   a.   130

    (   )   b.   140

    (   )   c.   210

    (   )   d.   260

Progress check answers

1. d (p. 3-304)

2. d (p. 3-307)

3. b (p. 3-305)

4. d (p. 3-305)

5. a (p. 3-305)

6. e (p. 3-308)

7. c (p. 3-313)

8. c (p. 3-317)

Marginal Analysis

Topic overview

Decision making involves a choice between at least two alternatives. In some situations, there are several alternatives to consider. But other decisions may require choosing between only two alternatives, one of which may be the status quo. Regardless of the number or types of options, the costs and benefits of the various alternatives need to be evaluated during the decision process.

Marginal analysis (also known as incremental or differential analysis) is a method of analyzing decision problems that emphasizes incremental cost increases or decreases rather than total costs and benefits associated with an action (or set of alternative actions). It is often applied in the following types of situations:

- *Special orders and pricing*

- *Make or buy*

- *Sell or process further*

- *Add or drop a segment*

- *Maximize contribution per unit of the limiting factor*

The key factor in applying marginal analysis is deciding which information is relevant to the decision. As noted in Topic 2 of this section, "Relevant Data Concepts," relevant costs and relevant revenues are those that differ among options and are future-oriented. Costs and revenues that have already been incurred or committed are irrelevant in decision making. Stated another way, any costs, including allocated costs, that do not differ between alternatives should be ignored in marginal decision analyses.

This topic takes a closer look at the application of marginal analysis in organizational decision making.

Special Orders and Pricing

A special order pricing decision involves a situation in which a firm has a one-time opportunity to accept or reject a special order for a specified quantity of its product or service. Making a determination about whether to accept or decline a special order request involves an assessment of profitability (based on relevant costs and revenues and opportunity costs) as well as consideration of capacity utilization.

If there is excess capacity—more than enough to cover the order—the firm needs to identify variable costs associated with the special order that are not normally incurred. Such variable costs are relevant costs and determine the minimum acceptable (break-even) price. If the price offered for the special order is greater than the unit cost, the order is profitable and should be accepted.

If the firm is operating at or near capacity, the minimum acceptable price is the normal sale price. When there is no excess capacity, a special order should be taken only if the price offered exceeds the normal price. In the case of full capacity, a firm must also consider whether accepting the order could result in the loss of other more-profitable sales. The opportunity costs resulting from lost sales that have a higher contribution margin should be evaluated.

Special order cost analysis

Consider the following scenario:

- The unit selling price for a product is $4.

- The average variable cost per unit is $2.75.

- The average fixed cost per unit is $1.

- The total cost per unit is $3.75.

- Normal production is 500,000 units.

- Fixed costs are $500,000.

A special order for 50,000 units is offered at a selling price of $3.50 per unit.

Excess capacity

In the case of excess capacity, the correct analysis for the decision is to compare the relevant costs to the special order price. Relevant costs include the cost to produce a unit ($2.75) and the special order price offered per unit ($3.50). The fixed cost per unit ($1) remains the same whether or not the order is accepted; it is not relevant. There is a $0.75 ($3.50 − $2.75) contribution to income for each unit sold, or a total contribution of $37,500 (50,000 units × $0.75). The order is profitable and should be accepted.

A common misconception in evaluating a special order decision is to focus on the total cost per unit. If the total cost per unit is used as the comparison figure, the order would probably be rejected because the unit cost ($3.75) exceeds the special order price ($3.50).

At or near full capacity

Assuming that the firm is operating at or near full capacity, the proper decision analysis should consider the opportunity cost arising from any lost sales. For example, if the special order would result in the loss of other sales that have a higher contribution margin ($1), the opportunity cost of lost sales is $50,000 (50,000 × $1). The net contribution loss for the order is $12,500 ($50,000 − $37,500). Accepting the special order would reduce total profits by $12,500, so the order should be rejected.

In most relevant-cost analysis scenarios, fixed manufacturing costs are considered irrelevant. However, that classification could change if a firm is operating at or near full capacity. An example is when a plant near full capacity and has a relevant range that seemingly can absorb a special order. However, if additional shifts are necessary to reach full capacity and fulfill the special order, this would increase manufacturing costs and make the added fixed manufacturing costs relevant for this decision.

As the term "special order" implies, special orders are typically unexpected and infrequent. They are generally considered short-term and are accepted in those infrequent situations if they can increase total revenues. Accepting special order pricing on a regular (long-term) basis can erode normal pricing policies.

Make versus Buy

The terminology "make versus buy" refers to outsourcing. As noted in Section A of this part of the *CMA Learning System*, "Strategic Planning," outsourcing describes a company's decision to purchase a product or service from an outside supplier rather than producing it in-house. Reaching a decision about whether to make or buy generally involves a comparison of the relevant costs to make the item internally with the cost to purchase externally. In some situations, opportunity costs and qualitative factors also need to be considered.

Relevant costs represent the short-term costs to make the item in-house. They are the incremental/differential costs and usually are variable costs. Relevant costs are those that can be avoided or eliminated by buying externally.

Irrelevant costs are those unavoidable costs that will not change regardless of whether the firm makes or buys the item. They are the sunk costs or future costs that will remain in place even if the item is bought externally. Typically, these are fixed overhead costs and any depreciation costs.

If the relevant costs are less than the purchase price, the decision should be to keep production inside. If the outside purchase price is less than these avoidable costs, the logical decision is to outsource.

Make versus buy cost analysis

Consider the following scenario: A company manufactures 5,000 units of a part each year. The cost of manufacturing one unit of the part at this volume is as follows:

Figure 3-86: Manufacturing Cost

Direct materials	$2.50
Direct labor	3.50
Variable overhead	1.50
Fixed overhead	1.00
Total cost per unit	$8.50

The company can buy unlimited quantities of the part from an outside supplier at a unit cost of $7.75. Because the relevant costs are $7.50 ($8.50 – $1 for fixed overhead that will remain), the part should not be outsourced. At the 5,000-unit level, this translates to an additional $1,250 (5,000 × $0.25) in favor of continuing to make the item internally.

Consideration of opportunity costs

Opportunity costs should also be considered in reaching a make or buy decision. A common make or buy opportunity cost is whether some part of the fixed overhead could be reduced by outsourcing. Another common opportunity cost is whether some part of the space being used during internal production could be used for some other purpose.

If the space now being used to produce an item internally has no alternative use and would remain idle, the opportunity cost is zero. But if the space could be used for some other purpose, that opportunity cost should be considered when evaluating an outsourcing offer.

Returning to the example, if the company could eliminate 50% of the fixed costs per unit and also recoup $6,000 a year by leasing the space to another company, the economic benefits from outsourcing change the decision. In this situation, the $6,000 is an avoidable fixed cost and the opportunity cost per unit from renting out the space is $1.20 ($6,000 ÷ 5,000 units). The relevant cost to make is now $9.20 ($7.50 original relevant cost from before plus $0.50 of fixed cost that could be avoided if the firm outsources [that is, opportunity cost #1] plus $1.20 of lost rent [that is, opportunity cost #2]). The relevant cost to buy is $7.75. Comparing the two, the potential savings from outsourcing is now $1.45 per unit, or $7,250 in total ($1.45 × 5,000 units) in favor of buying externally.

Consideration of qualitative factors

The make or buy marginal analysis of relevant costs has a key role in the decision to outsource. But there is more to successful outsourcing than the potential profit margins. In addition to the profit alternatives in make or buy decisions, firms also need to evaluate the qualitative factors of dealing with an external supplier. Examples of such qualitative factors include the need to tap an external supplier's unique knowledge, unusually skilled labor, or its access to rare materials.

The desire to control quality has traditionally been the driving factor in the decision to make rather than buy. Increasingly, buying and selling organizations are forming quasi partnerships and alliances and collaborating on improving products and services. Buying companies now often temper the make or buy decision with the potential for mutually advantageous supplier relationships. If the buying organization can be assured that established quality and service levels will be consistent with its needs and that the supplier's practices will be continuously improved, lower prices can result. The flip side is that erratic order giving to suppliers (making parts during slack times and buying them during prosperous times) can backfire and potentially create problems in securing parts when sales demand is high but there are shortages of material and workers.

The final decision to outsource to an external supplier should not ignore the supplier's reputation for dependability and quality in:

- Ensuring on-time delivery and a smooth flow of parts and materials.

- Maintaining acceptable quality control.

The strategic aspects of retaining control over core competencies are also important. Any outsourcing of an internal capability essential to maintaining competitive position requires careful consideration.

Note: Additional information about the purpose of outsourcing and the benefits and limitations of make or buy decisions is found in Topic 2 of Section A in this part of the CMA Learning System, "Manufacturing Paradigms."

Sell or Process Further

Sell or process further concerns the decision to sell a product or service before an intermediate processing step or to add further processing and then sell the product or service for a higher price. Common examples of sell or process further include decisions to:

- Add features to a product to enhance functionality.

- Improve the flexibility or quality of a service.

- Repair defective products so they can be sold in the usual manner (rather than selling them for a discount in a defective state).

Sell or process further decisions require analysis of relevant costs. In many situations, such decisions also involve consideration of joint products or services. A key point in this type of sell or process further decision is that joint costs are irrelevant.

Joint products or **joint services** involve situations in which two or more products or services are produced from a single common input. For example, petroleum refining results in crude oil, gasoline, and natural gas. The split-off point is the point in the production process at which the joint products can be recognized as separate products. **Joint costs** describe the costs incurred up to the split-off point.

The reason joint costs are irrelevant is that they are common costs that must be incurred to get the product or service to the split-off point. Because joint costs are not directly attributable to any of the intermediate products or services or the end products or services, they are irrelevant in deciding what to do from the split-off point forward.

For sell or process further decisions, continuing to process a product or service is profitable as long as the incremental revenue received (the revenue attributable to the added processing) exceeds the incremental processing costs incurred. This rule also applies to processing beyond the split-off point in the case of joint products and services. Figure 3-87 summarizes the steps in a sell or process further decision.

Figure 3-87: Sell or Process Further Decision-Making Steps

Step 1	Determine the selling price for a product or service, or determine the selling price of each product or service in a joint production process at the split-off point.
Step 2	Determine the selling price of each product or service if it were processed further.
Step 3	Calculate the incremental revenue from processing further; subtract the step 1 amount from the step 2 amount.
Step 4	Calculate the incremental costs; subtract the cost of processing further (or the separable costs of processing each product or service beyond the split-off point) from the incremental revenue (step 3).
Step 5	Compare the incremental revenue to the incremental costs. A positive net value supports processing further, and a negative result indicates selling before processing further (or at the split-off point).

Sell or process further cost analyses

Example 1

Consider the following scenario involving a simple comparison of incremental costs and incremental revenue:

- The unit production cost for a product is $4,200.

- The unit selling price for a product is $5,000.

- The incremental processing cost per unit is $1,500.

- The new unit selling price is $5,800.

Given this information, the product should be sold as is and not processed further. The incremental revenue is $800 ($5,800 − $5,000). The incremental cost to process further ($1,500) exceeds the incremental revenue and would result in a $700 loss from further processing ($800 − $1,500 = −$700).

Example 2

Consider the following scenario involving joint products:

- A company processes raw material A into joint products B and C.

- Each 100 units of raw material A yield 60 units of product B and 40 units of product C.

- Raw material A costs $5 per unit.

- To process 100 units of raw material A into joint products B and C costs $100.

- Product C can be sold immediately for $5 per unit, or it can be processed further and sold for $15 per unit. Additional processing costs are $4 per unit.

Given this information, there is a net benefit of $6 per unit to process product C further:

- The incremental revenue for processing further is $10 ($15 − $5, which is the selling price for product C after further processing minus the selling price for product C at the split-off point).

- The incremental cost for processing further is $4.

- The net benefit of $6 is the incremental revenue minus the incremental cost ($10 – $4).

- The raw material A cost ($5) and the $100 to process raw material A into products B and C are joint costs incurred up to the split-off point; they are irrelevant costs.

Add or Drop a Segment

A decision to keep or drop a product or a service and whether to add a new one is largely determined through relevant cost analysis and the impact the decision will have on net operating income. Avoidable costs must be distinguished from unavoidable costs. Only those costs that are avoidable are relevant to consider in the decision analysis.

For example, given a product line made up of five different products, deciding to drop one of those products from the sales mix solely on the basis of a recent net operating loss is generally unwise. Instead, an attempt should be made to distinguish between traceable fixed expenses and common fixed expenses for the product. The traceable fixed expenses are potentially avoidable costs if the product is dropped. The common fixed expenses are unavoidable costs and will remain whether the product is dropped or kept.

Once avoidable costs are identified, their associated contribution margin can be determined and the decision to add, drop, or keep a segment can be made with greater assurance:

- If the avoidable fixed costs saved are less than the contribution margin amount that will be lost, the decision should be to keep the segment.

- If the avoidable fixed costs saved are greater than the contribution margin amount lost, the decision should be to eliminate the segment because overall net operating income should improve.

Add or drop a segment cost analysis

Example 1

Consider the following income statement for a product segment reporting losses:

Figure 3-88: Income Statement

Sales		$500,000
Variable expenses		200,000
Contribution margin		300,000
Fixed expenses:		
General factory overhead*	$60,000	
Salary of product manager	90,000	
Depreciation of equipment**	50,000	
Product advertising	100,000	
Rent for factory space***	70,000	
General administrative expenses*	30,000	400,000
Net loss		$(100,000)

*   Represents allocated common costs that would be redistributed to other product lines if the product is dropped

**   For equipment that has no resale value and does not wear out through use

***   For space owned by the company

Based on evaluation of this income statement, the company should keep the product.

- Allocated common costs (*) are unavoidable and would still be incurred.

- The equipment depreciation (**) is an unavoidable expense.

- The factory space (***) is owned, so it cannot be eliminated.

Figure 3-89: Cost Analysis

Lost contribution margin	($300,000)
Savings from avoided fixed costs:	
Salary of product manager	90,000
Product advertising	100,000
Net loss from dropping the line	($110,000)

The fixed costs that can be saved by dropping the product are less than the contribution margin, so the company is better off in the short run keeping the product line.

Example 2

Consider the following income statement showing segment margin for a product.

Figure 3-90: Income Statement

	Segment A	Company	Company without Segment A
Sales	$500,000	$4,000,000	$3,500,000
Variable expenses	200,000	2,000,000	1,800,000
Contribution margin	300,000	2,000,000	1,700,000
Fixed expenses:			
General factory overhead*	$60,000	$600,000	600,000
Salary of product manager	90,000	400,000	310,000
Depreciation of equipment**	50,000	300,000	300,000
Product advertising	100,000	300,000	200,000
Rent for factory space***	70,000	200,000	200,000
General administrative expenses*	30,000	100,000	100,000
Net loss	$(100,000)	$100,000	$(10,000)

* Represents allocated common costs that would be redistributed to other product lines if the product is dropped
** For equipment that has no resale value and does not wear out through use
*** For space owned by the company

As the schedule of operating data shows, in this case, the company should keep Segment A. Overall net income is greater with the segment. Avoidable fixed costs saved from discontinuing Segment A are not as much as the contribution margin amount that will be lost.

Maximize contribution per unit of the limiting factor

When the firm's ability to meet customer demand is constrained by one factor that determines capacity, the firm's goal becomes maximizing contribution margin per unit of capacity (the limiting factor). For example:

Barlow Company manufactures three products: A, B, and C. The selling price, variable costs, and contribution margin for one unit of each product follow:

	Product		
	A	B	C
Selling price	$180	$270	$240
Less variable expenses:			
Direct materials	24	72	32
Other variable expenses	102	90	148
Total variable expenses	126	162	180
Contribution margin	$54	$108	$60
Contribution margin ratio	30%	40%	25%

The same raw material is used in all three products. Barlow Company has only 5,000 pounds of raw material on hand and will not be able to obtain any more of it for several weeks due to a strike in its supplier's plant. Management is trying to decide which product(s) to concentrate on next week in filling its backlog of orders. The material costs $8 per pound. Which orders would you recommend that the company work on next week?

First, determine each product's contribution per pound of material. Next, produce the product that maximizes contribution per pound, as follows:

	A	B	C
(1) Contribution margin per unit	$54	$108	$60
(2) Direct material cost per unit	$24	$72	$32
(3) Direct material cost per pound	$8	$8	$8
(4) Pounds of material required per unit (2) ÷ (3)	3	9	4
(5) Contribution margin per pound (1) ÷ (4)	$18	$12	$15

The company should concentrate its available material on product A:

	A	B	C
Contribution margin per pound (above)	$18	$12	$15
Pounds of material available	x 5,000	x 5,000	x 5,000
Total contribution margin	$90,000	$60,000	$75,000

Although product A has the lowest contribution margin per unit and the second lowest contribution margin ratio, it is preferred over the other two products because it has the greatest amount of contribution margin per pound of material, and material is the company's constrained resource.

Income Taxes and Marginal Analysis

The decision-making process requires identifying the various types of relevant costs. A relevant cost may be variable or fixed. Typically, most variable costs are relevant because they are different for each alternative and have not been committed; the majority of fixed costs are irrelevant because they are usually the same for all options.

One erroneous assumption is classifying depreciation expenses as relevant costs. The depreciation of facilities or equipment is a portion of a committed cost. The purchase cost is allocated over the life of the asset. For this reason, depreciation expenses are sunk costs and usually irrelevant in decision analysis.

The exception to classifying depreciation expenses as irrelevant costs is when tax effects are considered. When income taxes are taken into consideration, depreciation has a positive effect because it reduces taxable income and subsequent tax expense. In this context, depreciation reduces the company's tax liability.

Progress Check

Directions: Read each question and respond in the space provided. Answers and page references appear on the page following the progress check questions.

1. For a firm that has excess capacity, a special order pricing decision should

   ( )   a.   consider the opportunity costs from potential lost sales.

   ( )   b.   compare relevant costs to the special order price.

   ( )   c.   compare the total cost per unit and the special order price.

   ( )   d.   evaluate any joint costs incurred up to the split-off point.

2. A make or buy cost analysis involves all of the following factors except

   ( )   a.   comparison of relevant internal costs with the cost to purchase externally.

   ( )   b.   consideration of opportunity costs.

   ( )   c.   evaluation of an external supplier.

   ( )   d.   comparison of incremental revenue with incremental costs.

3. What is the profit or loss of a decision to sell or process a product further given the following information?

   ▪   The unit production cost for the product is $10,000.

   ▪   The unit selling price for the product is $6,000.

   ▪   The incremental processing cost per unit is $1,000.

   ▪   The new unit selling price is $6,650.

   ( )   a.   – $350

   ( )   b.   – $650

   ( )   c.   + $350

   ( )   d.   + $650

Progress check answers

1. b (p. 3-322)

2. d (p. 3-323)

3. a (p. 3-325)

Topic 5 Cost-Based Pricing

Topic overview

To survive in today's competitive environment, a company must carefully manage both costs and prices. Long-term financial success depends on whether prices charged for products and services exceed costs and provide sufficient reserves to fund growth, finance reinvestment, and deliver a satisfactory return to investors. Management accountants have a key role in collecting, analyzing, measuring, and reporting information crucial to cost and pricing decisions.

Setting Prices

The term "pricing decision" generally refers to the collective decisions a company makes about what to charge for its products and services. There is no universally accepted method of setting prices. Yet pricing decisions can be critical in the success or failure of a business. Prices set too high tend to discourage sales; prices set too low may not cover costs.

Relevant product and service costs are an important part of pricing decisions. Earlier sections introduced the concepts of cost-behavior patterns, cost traceability, cost drivers, and cost relevance. Such contemporary cost system elements:

- Use activities and operations as intermediate cost objects to trace costs to final cost objects.

- Assign costs to final cost objects based on cost drivers.

- Provide multiple views of costs (for example, by resources consumed, activities consumed, and drivers consumed).

- Facilitate cost management of a product or a service by making the various causal relationships visible to managers.

A well-designed cost management system increases the likelihood of good pricing decisions and helps an organization to meet its strategic objectives. Other factors such as supply and demand and the time horizon for a product or service also influence decisions.

Supply and demand considerations

Traditional pricing practices in situations in which there are few competitors and demand exceeds supply are to mark up product or service costs to yield a sufficient profit. As long as demand remains strong and the competition is limited, any increases in costs can be offset with price increases.

The primary pitfall of pricing based on supply and demand in this manner is that it provides little incentive for cost management. Many companies—in various industries— have priced their products and services out of a market by perpetually increasing prices to cover costs. Furthermore, unless there are strong barriers to market entry (such as technological superiority or large capital investment requirements), such pricing creates the opportunity for competitors to enter the marketplace. As competition increases and supply exceeds demand, surviving by marking up costs to yield good profits becomes problematic.

Time horizons

Pricing decisions are often categorized as short-run or long-run.

Short-run pricing decisions have implications for a year or less. Many are for a time period of six months or less. Short-run decisions apply to one-time and short-run special product purchase orders or responses to competitive market conditions that require more immediate product line and output volume adjustments.

Long-run pricing decisions have a time horizon greater than one year. Long-run decisions generally focus on a product or service in a major market.

The time horizon—short-run or long-run—ultimately dictates which product or service costs are relevant to pricing. Some pricing decisions may have both short- and long-run implications.

Short-run costing and pricing

Consider the following scenario illustrating costing and pricing for a one-time special order. A company has decided to bid on a one-time opportunity with a quick turnaround. Excess manufacturing capacity is available, so the order will have no effect on existing sales. Current variable and fixed costs per unit are shown below for a normal production run of 100,000 units.

Figure 3-91: Fixed and Variable Costs

	Variable Cost per Unit	Fixed Cost per Unit	Variable and Fixed Costs per Unit
Manufacturing			
Direct materials	$10	—	$10
Packaging	5	—	5
Direct labor	6	—	6
Manufacturing overhead	8	$10	18
Total manufacturing costs	29	10	39
Advertising	4	12	16
Distribution	7	5	12
Total costs	$40	$27	$67

The variable manufacturing overhead ($8) represents utility costs. At the normal production run of 100,000 units, details of the total fixed manufacturing overhead costs and the fixed manufacturing overhead costs per unit are as follows:

Figure 3-92: Fixed Manufacturing Overhead Unit Costs

	Total Fixed Manufacturing Overhead Costs	Fixed Manufacturing Overhead Cost per Unit
Depreciation	$300,000	$3
Materials procurement	100,000	1
Salaries	200,000	2
Engineering	400,000	4
Total fixed manufacturing overhead costs	$1,000,000	$10

The one-time special order is for 10,000 units. If the company decides to bid on the order, the current fixed manufacturing costs ($1,000,000) will continue to be incurred. The only additional expenditures the company would incur are for materials procurement ($10,000) and engineering setups ($25,000).

The firm requesting the bid has indicated that any offer in excess of $35 per unit would be noncompetitive. The company must determine what short-term price to bid for this special offer.

Relevant costs must be analyzed. Only the additional materials procurement and engineering manufacturing costs are relevant. Advertising and distribution costs are irrelevant to the pricing decision. Existing fixed manufacturing costs are also irrelevant because they will remain whether or not the company accepts the special order. Relevant costs are summarized below:

Figure 3-93: Relevant Cost Data

Direct materials (10,000 units × $10)		$100,000
Packaging (10,000 units × $5)		50,000
Direct labor (10,000 units × $6)		60,000
Variable manufacturing overhead (10,000 units × $8)		80,000
Fixed manufacturing overhead		
Materials procurement	$10,000	
Engineering	25,000	
Total fixed manufacturing overhead costs		$35,000
Total relevant costs		$325,000

Based on this relevant cost data, per-unit relevant costs are $32.50 ($325,000 ÷ 10,000 units). This is below the $35 price deemed as competitive. Any bid above the cost per unit ($32.50) and below $35 will contribute to the company's operating income. For example, a short-term price of $34 would result in a profit of $15,000 [10,000 × ($34.00 − $32.50)].

As noted in the earlier discussion of special order pricing in Topic 4, "Marginal Analysis," making a price decision based on the total cost per unit would be misleading and would probably result in not bidding on the business. In this example, if the total cost per unit is used as the comparison figure, the order would be rejected because the company's unit cost ($67) exceeds the bid ceiling price ($35). Even if only the variable cost per unit was used in the analysis, the order would have been rejected ($40 compared to the bid ceiling of $35).

Long-run costing and pricing

Accurate cost information is essential in the decisions a company makes about what to charge for a product or service and how to best compete in the marketplace. Analysis methods make assumptions regarding costs and prices. To the extent that these constraints are stable, the analyses have a greater probability of accuracy.

Given an extended time horizon, stable and predictable costs are much preferred for pricing decisions. Stable long-run costs lead to greater price stability and reduce the need for continuous monitoring of suppliers' prices and other relevant cost data. Stable long-run costs also improve other planning decisions and foster stronger, longer-term buyer and seller relationships. Forecasting becomes easier and customer relations become stronger.

Market-Based Pricing

Companies must often compete in markets in which products and services have little differentiation. **Market-based pricing** generally prevails in such product or service parity situations.

In market-based pricing circumstances:

- Market forces strongly influence the price set for a product or service.

- Customers are reluctant to pay more than the prevailing market price.

- Companies typically charge the prevailing market rate.

Market-based pricing allows firms little latitude in setting prices above or below the market rate; a firm should do so only with discretion. Through market-based pricing, a firm:

- Considers what customers expect and want.

- Determines the intensity of competitive rivalries.

- Anticipates how customers and competitors will react to its pricing.

In market-based pricing, companies make decisions about product and service features as well as pricing decisions based on anticipated customer and competitor reactions. The general goal is to avoid setting prices that could lead to costly market destabilizing or competitive price warfare. As such, the market-based approach is a logical pricing approach in highly competitive and commodity-type markets such as airlines, oil, gas, minerals, and many farm products.

Cost-Based Pricing

The **cost-based pricing** (or **cost-plus pricing**) approach looks at the costs to develop a product or service and sets a price to recoup those costs and make a desired profit. Cost-based pricing is appropriate when some level of product or service differentiation exists and a company can exercise modest discretion in setting prices. Where market-based pricing is fairly restricted by market conditions, cost-based pricing considers market reactions as one factor in setting prices.

Under cost-based pricing, a firm:

- Determines the costs to produce and sell a product.

- Identifies a reasonable return (markup).

- Adds the markup to the cost.

- Adjusts the markup as necessary in response to market forces.

With cost-based pricing, the markup is typically expressed as a percentage of cost. A predetermined markup is applied to the cost base to determine a target selling price.

$$\text{Selling Price} = \text{Cost} + (\text{Markup \%} \times \text{Cost})$$

For example, a product costing $50 per unit with a 50% markup would have a selling price of $75.

The challenges of cost-based pricing are determining what costs to use and what the final markup should be. In the end, the desired markup is evaluated and may be modified based on the prices competitors charge for similar products and the anticipated reactions of customers to alternative prices.

Target Pricing

The traditional pricing approaches discussed thus far are all based on the idea that:

$$\text{Price} = \text{Cost} + \text{Profit Margin}$$

This equation presumes that a product or service has been developed, costs have been or can be identified, and the item is ready to be marketed once a price is set.

Target costing offers a fundamentally different way to look at the relationship of price and costs. The underlying concept of target costing is:

$$\text{Cost} = \text{Competitive Price} - \text{Profit Margin}$$

The cost for the product or service is computed by starting with the anticipated selling price and deducting the desired profit.

Key concepts and terminology

Several concepts and terms are important to understanding target costing.

Target costing

Various definitions of target costing exist. Statement on Management Accounting No. 4FF, "Implementing Target Costing," lists the following characteristics as common to most definitions:

- A competitive market environment

- A situation in which market prices drive cost (and investment) decisions

- Implementation of cost planning, cost management, and cost reduction early in product or service design and development

- Cross-functional team involvement, including management accounting

Essentially, **target costing** is a comprehensive cost management process that determines a target cost for a product or service and then develops a prototype for that product or service that can be made profitably for the identified amount. It is a proactive methodology whereby product and service costs are managed early on during the design and development processes rather than in the later stages of product development and production.

The fundamental objective of target costing is to enable businesses to manage operations profitably in a competitive market. As such, the foundation for target costing is the determination of market- and price-based costs. The cross-functional participation of research and design, engineering, production, marketing, and accounting is necessary to ensure that the proposed product or service, when sold, generates the desired profit margin. Stated another way, the cross-functional team is given the responsibility to design and develop the product or service so that it can be made for the target cost.

Target price

In target costing, the target price represents the maximum allowable price that can be charged for the product or service. It is an estimate of the amount that potential customers would be willing to pay based on their value perceptions—their needs and expectations for products and services, quality, timeliness, and price. A target price also reflects the firm's understanding of the market competition—their capabilities and probable responses. In the final outcome, a target price should result in an acceptable price to customers as well as an acceptable return to the organization.

Target cost

In defining target cost, SMA No. 4FF indicates that the term means different things to different companies. For some, target cost is the difference between the target price (set by market forces) and the target profit (set by management). Other definitions describe target cost as the difference between the allowable cost and the current cost—the amount by which costs must be reduced to achieve the allowable costs.

Allowable cost

Allowable cost is the difference between the target price and the target profit. In effect, the allowable cost represents the maximum cost that a firm can commit to a product to achieve the company's profit objective.

Target operating income per unit and target cost per unit

Other important concepts in target costing and target pricing are target operating income per unit and target cost per unit.

- Target operating income per unit is the operating income a company strives for on each unit of product or service sold.

- Target cost per unit is the estimated long-run product or service cost per unit.

Target cost per unit is determined by subtracting target operating income per unit from the target price. When a unit is produced for the target cost and sold at the target price, a company will be able to achieve its target operating income.

Consider the following scenario illustrating target operating income per unit and target cost per unit. Due to increasing market competition, a firm needs to reduce its per-unit selling price from $100 to $75. At this lower price, the firm expects to increase annual sales from 10,000 units to 12,000. Management wants to earn a 15% target operating income on sales revenues. Total current cost per unit is $80.

Total Target Sales Revenues	=	12,000 Units × $75 = $900,000
Total Target Operating Income	=	15% × $900,000 = $135,000
Target Operating Income per Unit	=	$135,000 ÷ 12,000 = $11.25
Target Cost per Unit	=	Target Price – Target operating Income per Unit
	=	$75.00 – $11.25 = $63.75

In target pricing, the market price of a product is taken as a given. The target cost per unit is usually lower than the full product or service cost per unit. This is the case in the example just presented, where the target cost per unit is $63.75 and the current (full) cost per unit is $80. But in order to make money a company must recover all of its costs. Thus, all costs—both fixed and variable—are relevant in target cost calculations. Under these circumstances, businesses are constantly challenged in target costing to improve a product or service and the associated production processes throughout the entire life cycle of the item.

Figure 3-94 on the next page summarizes basic techniques (as identified in SMA No. 4FF) that firms use to design a proposed new product or service and establish its target price and target margin.

Industry and competitive analysis used in combination with market assessment and reverse engineering data helps to facilitate setting of the target price. Financial planning and analysis facilitates the determination of the target profit margin. Internal cost analysis and cost tables facilitate the comparison of allowable and current costs and the determination of the target cost.

Figure 3-94: Target Costing Process Techniques

Technique	Description
Market assessment tools	Any of several methods to assess the market and customers' wants and needs in regard to a proposed product or service including surveys, focus groups, interviews, and customer comment cards with current, prospective, or former customers
Reverse engineering (teardown analysis)	The acquisition and disassembly of competitors' products to investigate their design, material(s), likely manufacturing processes, attributes, quality, and costs
Industry and competitive analysis	Analysis techniques used to develop an understanding of competitors and how to best position a firm and its products and services to a competitive advantage. This may include any variety of strategies (such as Michael E. Porter's strategies) for conducting comprehensive industry and competitive analysis
Financial planning and analysis	Detailed financial planning and statement analysis to examine the relationships between process, volume, and revenue. This approach also looks at cost and investments in the aggregate and for specific segment lines and individual products (or services); allows a comparison to the proposed product or service
Internal cost analysis	Determination of product and service costs and related investments for current offerings in order to estimate the costs of the proposed new product or service under existing and proposed product/service and process characteristics. This technique often involves activity-based costing (ABC) to identify costs associated with specific cost-incurring activities
Cost tables	Maintenance and use of detailed databases of cost information based on various manufacturing variables; facilitate cost projections for the proposed new product or service, assuming the use of different designs, materials, manufacturing processes, and end-user functions. This technique helps managers determine in advance the effect of alternative choices

The target costing process

Just as there is no universal definition for target costing, no definitive list of steps exists for target costing. Target costing practices in any company tend to evolve based on specific business circumstances. However, SMA No. 4FF notes that the steps shown in Figure 3-95 are common to most target costing applications.

Figure 3-95: Target Costing Steps

- Establish a target price in the context of market needs and competition.
- Establish the target profit margin.
- Determine the cost that must be achieved.
- Calculate the probable cost of current products and processes.
- Establish the target cost—the amount by which costs must be reduced.
- Establish the cross-functional team to be involved in the implementation process from the earliest design stages.
- Use tools such as concurrent engineering, value engineering, and quality function deployment in the design process.
- Implement cost reductions (for example, through kaizen and life-cycle costing) once production is under way.

Once the target cost is identified, the challenge of achieving it ensues. The emphasis on cross-functional teams promotes a high degree of interdependence between all functions in the organization. Companies will try to adapt different approaches to arrive at a product/service and process design that achieves the target cost. Most firms use some elements of concurrent engineering, value engineering, quality function deployment, and kaizen and life-cycle costing.

Concurrent engineering

Concurrent engineering is a process in which an organization designs a product or a service using input and evaluations from all business units and functions early in the process, anticipating problems and balancing the needs of all parties. The emphasis is on maintaining customer requirements and upstream prevention rather than downstream correction.

Value engineering

Value engineering is a principal technique in closing the gap between current cost and allowable cost. It is the systematic analysis of a product or service design, materials, specifications, and production processes in the context of customer requirements.

A differentiation is made between value-added costs and non-value-added costs. **Value-added costs** refer to costs that convert resources into products or services consistent with customer requirements. They are costs that customers perceive as adding value or utility to a product or service. Conversely, non-value-added costs are not critical to customer preferences. In a manufacturing environment, examples of value-added costs might be costs associated with design, assembly, tools, and machinery. Examples of non-value-added costs could be special delivery charges, rework costs, or the cost of obsolete inventory.

In practice, distinguishing between value-added and non-value-added costs can be murky. Some costs may fall in both categories given the specific circumstances. In manufacturing, testing costs or ordering costs are often difficult to differentiate between value-added and non-value-added.

The objective in value engineering is to balance overall costs and benefits and increase the ultimate value of the product. The process is best achieved using cross-functional teams, as tradeoffs between design, development, production, and cost are involved. Management accountants are often called upon to assess the potential savings resulting from the elimination of non-value-added activities and the associated costs.

For the most part, the terms "value engineering" and "value analysis" are used interchangeably. Some firms use "analysis" for the design and development stages and "engineering" for the post-development stage.

Quality function deployment

Quality function deployment (QFD) is a structured method in which customer requirements for a product or service are translated into appropriate technical requirements at each stage of development and production. The QFD process is often referred to as "listening to the voice of the customer."

Product life-cycle costing and life-cycle costing

Target costing assumes that a product or service price is stable or decreasing over time because of market conditions—due to competition on price, quality, and functionality. Companies must respond to these competitive pressures through a product's or service's life cycle.

As discussed in Section B in this part of the CMA Learning System, "Strategic Marketing," product life cycle (PLC) is a concept based on the premise that an industry (and its products and services) passes through a number of predictable stages or phases. The various stages encompass initial research and design to the point at which a product or service is eventually withdrawn from a market or support to customers is withdrawn.

Target costing is designed to reduce the overall costs of a product or service over its entire life cycle. In applying target costing principles, firms must periodically redesign products and services to simultaneously reduce price and improve value.

Life-cycle costing tracks and accumulates all actual costs associated with a product or service throughout its life cycle. Capturing all costs provides important information for a variety of planning decisions to minimize overall costs.

Kaizen costing

Content in Section A, "Strategic Planning," mentioned kaizen as the term the Japanese use to describe continuous improvement (CI) at all levels in an organization. Kaizen costing is a comprehensive and continuous approach to reducing costs once a product or service reaches the production stage. Kaizen costing (in conjunction with other CI practices such as total quality management and the theory of constraints) is used in the time between redesigns to reduce product or service costs by streamlining the supply chain and improving productivity throughout production processes.

Cost-plus target rate of return pricing

Earlier discussions of cost-based pricing described the general formula of setting a price as adding a markup percentage to the cost base. A cost-plus target rate of return is one method of determining the markup based on the target rate of return on investment.

The **target rate of return on investment** is the target operating income a firm must earn divided by its invested capital. Companies often specify a target rate of return on investment.

Consider the following scenario illustrating cost-plus target rate of return pricing:

- Full costs per unit for a product are $1,000.

- The number of units expected to be sold is 10,000.

- The pretax target rate of return is 20%.

- Invested capital (long-term or fixed assets plus current assets) is $10,000,000.

- Total target operating income is 20% × $10,000,000, or $2,000,000.

- Target operating income per unit is $2,000,000 ÷ 10,000 units, or $200.

Based on this information, the desired target operating income per unit is $200. Given the full product costs per unit of $1,000, the markup percentage that this translates to is:

$$\$200 \div \$1,000 = 20\%$$

The 20% markup represents operating income per unit as a percentage of full product cost per unit.

Peak load pricing considerations

Thus far all the pricing methods discussed have been based on costs in some manner. In some circumstances, noncost factors must be considered in setting a price. Peak load pricing is such a situation.

Peak load pricing is the practice of charging more or less for a product or service based on demand and physical capacity limits. With peak load pricing, prices differ among market segments even though there is no significant difference in the outlay costs.

Prices may go up or down with peak load pricing:

- When demand approaches capacity limits, prices go up.

- When slack or excess capacity is available, prices go down.

Peak load pricing is found in a variety of industries such as airlines, hotels, car rental, electric utilities, and telecommunications.

Progress Check

Directions: Read each question and respond in the space provided. Answers and page references appear on the page following the progress check questions.

1. What characteristics differentiate the traditional pricing approach from target pricing?

   (   )   a.   Traditional pricing is based on the premise that price equals cost plus the profit margin; target costing implies that cost equals the competitive price minus the profit margin.

   (   )   b.   Traditional pricing is based on the premise that cost equals the competitive price minus the profit margin; target costing implies that price equals cost plus the profit margin.

   (   )   c.   Traditional pricing marks up prices as a percentage of costs; target costing marks up prices in response to competitors.

   (   )   d.   Traditional pricing marks up prices in response to competitors; target costing marks up prices as a percentage of costs.

Match each pricing approach with the appropriate characteristic.

2. _____ Market-based price

3. _____ Cost-based price

4. _____ Target price

a. Generally used when some level of product or service differentiation exists and a company can exercise modest discretion in setting prices

b. Generally used in a competitive environment to enable businesses to manage operations profitably

c. Generally used in product or service parity situations and when a company has little latitude in setting prices

5. Which practice would be **most** useful in a firm's attempt to close the gap between current and allowable costs during the design process?

   (   )   a.   Reverse engineering

   (   )   b.   Product life cycle costing

   (   )   c.   Value engineering

   (   )   d.   Quality function deployment

6. What is a primary benefit of involving cross-functional teams in the target costing process?

    ( )   a.   Improved analysis of how to gain and sustain competitive advantage

    ( )   b.   More accurate input and maintenance of cost table databases

    ( )   c.   More realistic market assessment of customer wants and needs

    ( )   d.   Better assurance that the proposed product or service generates the desired profit margin

Progress check answers

1. a (p. 3-337)

2. c (p. 3-336)

3. a (p. 3-337)

4. b (p. 3-337)

5. c (p. 3-341)

6. d (p. 3-338)

Investment Decisions

Section overview

Capital is a limited organizational resource, whether it is in the form of debt or equity. Banks have limits as to the volume of credit they can extend. Even the most stable of firms can only borrow up to a certain level or issue a limited amount of shares of common stock to raise capital.

Given the fact that organizations have limited capital resources, every firm must carefully evaluate investments projects. Management accountants often have a key role in deciding whether an investment is sound and worth undertaking. Content in this section begins with an overview of the capital budgeting process and then reviews the fundamental principles that can facilitate intelligent choices between two or more investment alternatives.

Learning Outcome Statements

The Certified Management Accountant (CMA) test is based upon a series of Learning Outcome Statements (LOS) developed by the Institute of Certified Management Accountants (ICMA). The LOS describe all the knowledge and skills that make up the CMA body of knowledge, broken down by part, section and topic. The CMA Learning System (CMALS) supports the LOS by addressing all the subjects they cover. Candidates should use the LOS to ensure that they can address the concepts in different ways or through a variety of question scenarios. Candidates should also be prepared to perform calculations referred to in the LOS in total or by providing missing components of a calculation. The LOS should not be used as proxies for exact exam questions; they should be used as a guide for studying and learning the content of the CMA Learning System and ensuring that you can accomplish the objectives set out by the LOS.

The LOS included in the CMALS books are the comprehensive set, current as of the date of publication. Candidates can access the IMA Web site at www.imanet.org and click on the Certification section to locate and download a Portable Document Format (PDF) file of the current LOS.

Learning Outcome Statements

Part 3: Strategic Management — Section E. Investment Decisions

Part 3 — Section E1. Capital Budgeting Process

- LOS 3.E.1.a—Define capital budgeting.

- LOS 3.E.1.b—Demonstrate an understanding of capital budgeting applications in making decisions for project investments.

- LOS 3.E.1.c—Identify the steps or stages undertaken in developing and implementing a capital budget for a project.

- LOS 3.E.1.d—Identify and calculate the relevant cash flows of a capital investment project on both a pretax and after-tax basis.

- LOS 3.E.1.e—Demonstrate an understanding of how income taxes affect cash flows.

- LOS 3.E.1.f—Distinguish between cash flows and accounting profits and discuss the relevance to capital budgeting of the following: incremental cash flow, sunk cost, and opportunity cost.

- LOS 3.E.1.g—Explain the importance of changes in net working capital in the capital budgeting process.

- LOS 3.E.1.h—Discuss how the effects of inflation are reflected in capital budgeting analysis.

- LOS 3.E.1.i—Describe the role of the post-audit in the capital budgeting process.

Part 3 — Section E2. Discounted Cash Flow Analysis

- LOS 3.E.2.a—Demonstrate an understanding of the two main DCF methods, net present value (NPV) and internal rate of return (IRR).

- LOS 3.E.2.b—Demonstrate an understanding of the weighted average cost of capital approach to NPV calculations.

- LOS 3.E.2.c—Calculate the NPV and IRR using time value of money tables.

- LOS 3.E.2.d—Demonstrate an understanding of the decision criteria used in NPV and IRR analyses to determine acceptable projects.

- LOS 3.E.2.e—Compare NPV and IRR focusing on the relative advantages and disadvantages of each method, particularly with respect to independent versus mutually exclusive projects, the "multiple IRR problem" and the cash flow pattern that causes the problem, and why NPV and IRR methods can produce conflicting rankings for capital projects if not applied properly.

- LOS 3.E.2.f—Identify assumptions of the different methods of evaluating capital investment projects.

- LOS 3.E.2.g—Recommend project investments on the basis of DCF analysis.

Part 3 — Section E3. Payback and Discounted Payback

- LOS 3.E.3.a—Demonstrate an understanding of the payback method.

- LOS 3.E.3.b—Identify the advantages and disadvantages/limitations of the payback method.

- LOS 3.E.3.c—Calculate payback periods and discounted paybacks.

- LOS 3.E.3.d—Identify the advantages and disadvantages/limitations of the discounted payback method.

Part 3 — Section E4. Ranking Investment Projects

- LOS 3.E.4.a—Define capital rationing and mutually exclusive projects.

- LOS 3.E.4.b—Rank capital investment projects and recommend optimal investments using the profitability index.

- LOS 3.E.4.c—Determine when the profitability index would be recommended over the NPV rule (for example, independent projects with capital rationing).

- LOS 3.E.4.d—Identify and discuss the problems inherent in comparing projects of unequal scale and/or unequal lives.

- LOS 3.E.4.e—Demonstrate an understanding of the advantages and disadvantages of the different methods of evaluating alternative capital investment projects.

- LOS 3.E.4.f—Identify alternative solutions to the ranking problem, including internal capital markets and linear programming.

Part 3 — Section E5. Risk Analysis in Capital Investments

- LOS 3.E.5.a—Identify alternative approaches to dealing with risk in capital budgeting.

- LOS 3.E.5.b—Demonstrate an understanding of sensitivity analysis and certainty equivalents.

- LOS 3.E.5.c—Identify qualitative considerations in making capital investment decisions.

- LOS 3.E.5.d—Explain why a rate specifically adjusted for risk should be used when project cash flows are more or less risky than is normal for a firm.

- LOS 3.E.5.e—Distinguish among sensitivity analysis, scenario analysis, and Monte Carlo simulation as risk analysis techniques.

- LOS 3.E.5.f—Describe how the CAPM can be used in the capital budgeting process.

Part 3 — Section E6. Real Options in Capital Investments

- LOS 3.E.6.a—Demonstrate an understanding of the concept of real options in the capital budgeting process.

- LOS 3.E.6.b—Identify the four common real options—for example, the option to (a) make follow-on investments if the immediate investment project succeeds, (b) abandon a project, (c) wait and learn before investing, or (d) vary a firm's output or its production methods.

- LOS 3.E.6.c—Identify these real options as either put or call options.

- LOS 3.E.6.d—Demonstrate an understanding of the variables and factors that affect the value of options.

▣ Capital Budgeting Process

Topic overview

Simply stated, capital budgeting is the process of making long-term investment decisions. It is a decision-making process that enables a firm to evaluate the viability of a long-term project and whether it is worth undertaking.

Capital Budgeting

In the course of business operations, firms make two types of investments: current and capital.

Current investments (or **current expenditures**) are short-term in nature; they are investments that can be written off in the same year that the expenses occur. Wages, salaries, many administrative expenses, and expenditures for raw materials in manufacturing are all examples of current investments. An **operating budget** (or **current budget**) is a plan for the operating expenses and revenues associated with activities for the current time period.

Capital investments (or **capital expenditures**) are long-term. A capital investment results in a current cash outlay with the expectation of future benefits. The value of the initial cash outlay is gradually reduced (amortized) over a period of years according to IRS regulations. Examples of capital investments include expenditures for new or replacement equipment as well as investments made in research and design and the development of new products and services. A **capital budget** is a plan of proposed outlays for acquiring long-term assets and includes the means for financing the acquisition.

A firm's stability and future success often depend on its capital investments. Thus firms need a sound capital budgeting process to analyze and control long-term capital investments. Firms often have great difficulty recovering money tied up in bad capital investments.

Capital budgeting applications

Capital budget proposals can come from a variety of sources. For the process of decision analysis, capital expenditures are often grouped in one of the following categories:

- Expansion projects: New machines and equipment bought with the purpose of expanding business operations

- Replacement projects: Replacement of existing machines and equipment

- Mandatory projects: Those that are required by law to maintain safety in the workplace and the safety of consumers and to protect the environment

- Other projects: Some allocations for research and development for new products and/or the expansion of existing products as well as various other long-term investments for buildings, land, patents, and so on

Alternate capital expenditure classifications exist, such as:

- Operating efficiency and/or revenue generation.

- Competitive effectiveness.

- Regulatory, safety, health, and environmental requirements.

Whatever classification scheme a company uses, organizational strategies and objectives will influence the evaluation criteria and decision procedures in making a capital investment.

Project and time dimensions in capital budgeting

Two important aspects of capital budgeting are the project dimension and the time dimension.

Project dimension

Where operational budgeting decisions focus on the income determination, planning, and control of activities for the current time period, capital budgeting decisions look at projects that span multiple accounting periods. A capital budgeting project related to the development of a new product, for example, might span several years from research and design through product fulfillment and customer service.

Life-cycle costing must be used to accumulate capital budgeting costs and revenues on a project-by-project basis and track income over the entire project. For the new product development example just given, costs must be accumulated for all business functions in the value chain over many accounting periods.

Time dimension

Typically, a capital budgeting decision depresses reported income for the current period but has the potential to generate high cash inflows in the future. Therefore, capital budgeting decisions cannot be based solely on the current accounting period's income statement.

Certainly income for any given period is important. For publicly traded companies, income reported in a given period can affect the firm's stock price and can affect bonuses. But excessive focus on short-term accounting can result in investment decisions that forego long-term profitability.

The concept of the time value of money is basic to capital budgeting. The time value of money implies that:

- A dollar (or any other monetary unit) is worth more today than a dollar received tomorrow because that dollar can be invested today to earn a return.

- A dollar tomorrow is worth less than a dollar today because of the interest foregone.

A $10,000 investment made today with the potential for a 15% annual rate of return would be worth $11,500 at the end of the year. But according to the time value of money, had the investment not been made, the opportunity cost is the $1,500 foregone.

Stages of capital budgeting

A capital budgeting project consists of a logical progression of activities. The specific names for the stages or steps vary across firms. In general, firms address all of the stages or steps shown in Figure 3-96 on the next page.

Incremental Cash Flows

An organization and its investors are interested in the firm's cash position. Thus, cash flow and how it is affected by a capital investment project are primary concerns.

Figure 3-96: Stages of Capital Budgeting

Stage 1	**Identification**
	The first stage in capital budgeting is to identify which type of capital budget expenditures are necessary and consistent with organizational goals, objectives and strategies.
Stage 2	**Search**
	The next stage involves thoroughly investigating the initial capital investment proposals and exploring alternative investments.
Stage 3	**Evaluation**
	The third stage is to project revenues, financial and nonfinancial benefits, costs, and cash flows for each alternative and compare them for the project's entire life cycle. Management must assess how the project will affect the organization's resources and whether the firm can absorb the costs.
Stage 4	**Selection**
	The fourth stage is to choose projects chosen for implementation, which typically means selecting those in which the predicted financial benefits exceed costs by the greatest margin. Consideration should also be given to the nonfinancial (qualitative) outcomes.
Stage 5	**Financing**
	The fifth stage is to secure project financing either internally (reinvesting cash) or externally by selling debt and equity in the capital market.
Stage 6	**Implementation and control**
	The final stage is to implement a capital budgeting project and then monitor and evaluate it. Predictions at the time the project was selected need to be compared with actual results. As necessary (and if possible), adjustments may need to be made to obtain optimal results throughout the project life cycle.

Estimating future cash flows is one of the most important tasks in capital budgeting. A firm must be able to evaluate the difference between its cash flows with and without an investment project and where all relevant costs and benefits have an effect during the project.

Key points in evaluating capital investment cash flows are:

- All items affecting cash flows must be examined regardless of whether they are revenues or expenses for the accounting period.

- Sunk costs are ignored because they are historical costs that are not relevant to the investment decision.

- Opportunity costs must be included and are typically treated as a cash outlay at the onset of the project.

- Investments in net working capital are treated as cash outflows at the time they occur.

- The anticipated effects of inflation must be taken into account.

- Depreciation expenses are relevant in capital budgeting only to the extent that they affect the firm's tax obligation on cash flows.

Capital investment projects generally begin with a cash outflow as a payment or commitment of funds. During the life of the investment, different cash flow outcomes are possible. The return on the initial cash outflow may decrease cash expenditures or generate cash inflows. In some circumstances, both outcomes may occur. Based on monitoring and control activities, funds for additional capital investments may be needed.

Relevant incremental cash flows during a capital investment project are categorized based on timing when they occur during the capital investment project—at the start of the project, during the course of the project, or at the end. Figure 3-97 summarizes characteristics of these capital project cash flow categories.

Figure 3-97: Cash Inflows and Outflows during a Capital Budgeting Project

Category	Description	Cash Flow Activities
Initiation	Initial cash investment	■ Outflows to fund the investment and initiate the project ■ Commitments for net working capital ■ Inflows or outflows if there is an asset being replaced
Operation	Interim incremental net cash flows	■ Outflows for operating expenditures ■ Outflows for additional capital investments (if necessary) ■ Commitments for additional net working capital for operations ■ Inflows generated by the investment (e.g., revenues and cash savings) and cash released from net working capital no longer needed for operations
Disposal	Incremental net cash flow for the final year	■ Inflows or outflows related to the investment's disposal ■ Cash inflows from the release of net working capital no longer committed to the investment

Cash inflow increases the cash available to the business; cash outflows or cash commitments decrease available cash. Committing funds to working capital makes those funds unavailable for other uses. Net working capital is the excess of current assets over current liabilities. It is the amount of additional funds available to meet operational requirements.

Understanding the following concepts is important before examining each of these relevant cash flow categories further.

- Direct effect is the immediate effect that a cash inflow, outflow, or commitment has on cash flows.

- Tax effect (or indirect effect) is the change in a firm's tax payments.

- Net effect (or total effect) is the total of the direct effect and the tax effect.

Initiation cash flows

Cash flows during project initiation are generally determined as shown in Figure 3-98. The cost of the asset is subject to various adjustments depending on the net effect of all transactions.

Figure 3-98: Incremental Cash Flows at Initiation

−	Direct effect for the cost of the new asset
−	Additional capitalized expenditures (e.g., for shipping, installation, and modification)
− or +	Increase or decrease in net working capital
+	Net proceeds from the sale of the old asset (if the investment is a replacement project)
− or +	Tax effect due to the sale of the old asset (if the investment is a replacement project)
=	Initiation cash flow

Operation cash flows

Following the initial cash outflows necessary to begin a project, a firm hopes to benefit from cash flows generated during subsequent periods. Future cash flows can generally be determined as shown in Figure 3-99.

Figure 3-99: Incremental Cash Flows during Operations (per Period)

	Net increase or decrease in operating revenue
− or +	Any net increase or decrease in operating expenses (excluding depreciation)
− or +	Net increase or decrease in tax depreciation charges
=	Net change in income before taxes
− or +	Net increase or decrease in taxes
=	Net effect after taxes
+ or −	Net increase or decrease in tax depreciation charges
=	Incremental cash flow for the operating period

Note that the net increase or decrease in tax depreciation charges is first subtracted or added to determine the net change in income before taxes. The net increase or decrease in tax depreciation is later added back in or subtracted out to determine the incremental cash flow for the period. That is because tax depreciation is a noncash expenditure that lowers taxable income. It needs to be considered initially to determine the incremental effect that the project has on the firm's acceptance of the project. It is once again added or subtracted to avoid understating the project's effect on cash flow.

Disposal cash flows

Incremental cash flow at disposal (in the final period, at project termination) is shown in Figure 3-100. Recognition is given to a few activities associated specifically with project termination:

- The salvage value of any sold or disposed assets

- The net tax effect (the taxes or tax savings) related to the asset disposal

- Any change in net working capital (for example, the reinstatement of net working capital to cash flow at project termination)

The shaded lines in Figure 3-100 are cash flows that specifically relate to project termination.

Figure 3-100: Incremental Cash Flows at Disposal

+	Salvage value of any sold or disposed assets
– or +	Net tax effect (taxes or savings) due to the sale or disposal of assets
+ or –	Recaptured increase or decrease in net working capital level
=	Incremental cash flow at disposal

Incremental cash flow example

Consider the following example of incremental cash flow determination involving the purchase of a new machine in a manufacturing operation:

- The cost for the new machine is $80,000.

- Shipping and installation charges for the machine are $20,000.

- The salvage value for the machine after a useful life of four years is $30,000.

No additional working capital is required. The machine will be installed in an area that has no alternative use so there are no opportunity costs. The firm's tax rate is 40%. Projections for net operating revenue (before depreciation and taxes) are shown in Figure 3-101:

Figure 3-101: Projections for Net Operating Revenue

	Year-End			
	1	2	3	4
Net cash flows	$40,000	$42,000	$50,000	$38,000

Incremental cash flows at initiation are shown in Figure 3-102:

Figure 3-102: Incremental Cash Flows at Initiation

Direct effect for the cost of the new asset	($80,000)
Additional capitalized expenditures (shipping or installation)	(20,000)
Initiation cash flow	($100,000)

Incremental (future) cash flows during operations and at disposal are shown in Figure 3-103.

Figure 3-103: Incremental Cash Flows at Operations and Disposal

	Year-End			
	1	2	3	4
Operation cash flows (years 1 to 4)				
Net change in operating revenue, excluding depreciation	$40,000	$42,000	$50,000	$38,000
Net increase in tax depreciation charges*	(33,330)	(44,450)	(14,810)	(7,410)
Net change in income before taxes	$6,670	($2,450)	$35,190	$30,590
Net increase or decrease in taxes at 40% tax rate	(2,668)	980	(14,076)	(12,236)
Net effect after taxes	$4,002	$(1,470)	$21,114	$18,354
Net increase in tax depreciation charges	33,330	44,450	14,810	7,410
Incremental cash flow for years 1 to 4	$37,332	$42,980	$35,924	$25,764
Disposal cash flows (year 4)				
Salvage value of any sold or disposed assets**				$33,000
Net tax effect (taxes due) on the sale or disposal of assets				(13,200)
Disposal cash flow				$19,800

* According to Modified Accelerated Cost Recovery System (MACRS) depreciation schedule for a three-year asset with a depreciable basis of $100,000, the depreciate rates are Year 1 = 33.33%, Year 2 = 44.45%, Year 3 = 14.81%, and Year 4 = 7.41%

** Assumes salvage value is recapture of depreciation and taxed at the ordinary income rate of 40%

The expected incremental cash flows from this capital investment are shown below. (In capital budgeting, the time when initial cash outflows occur is referred to as year 0.)

Figure 3-104: Expected Incremental Cash Flows

	Year-End				
	0	1	2	3	4
Net cash flows	($100,000)	$37,332	$42,980	35,924	$45,564*

* Year 4 operation and disposal cash flows of $25,764 and $19,800.

This incremental cash flow data provides the relevant information necessary to judge the attractiveness of the project. Management would need to assess how the project will affect the organization's resources. Comparisons should be made to other alternatives.

A firm would then need to examine the expected cash inflows and outflows of the capital investment project further using various methods. The following methods are explained in detail in the next two topics of this section:

- Discounted cash flow (DCF) analysis

- Payback method

The DCF methods adjust cash flows by incorporating the time value of money. For this reason, they are widely used in assessing long-run investment decisions.

Income Tax Considerations

Cash flows resulting from capital investments have various tax effects. Under some circumstances, taxes can significantly reduce net cash flows from a project and influence their desirability.

Most tax rules set forth through generally accepted accounting principles (GAAP) for preparing financial statements apply to cash flows from capital investment projects. But there are also special tax rules related to capital investments. In particular, tax rules pertaining to depreciation differ in the:

- Depreciation amount allowable.

- Depreciation time period.

- Depreciation pattern.

An overview of each of these depreciation considerations follows.

Keep in mind that the tax treatment of a depreciable asset can be complex. Whenever a firm invests in an income-producing asset, the productive life of that asset is estimated. The value of any capital asset decreases as its useful life is expended. For accounting purposes, the asset is depreciated over this period.

However, depreciation may not reflect the true value of a capital asset during its useful life as obsolescence may occur at any time. For example, a superior machine is developed that renders an existing one obsolete even though it is not worn out. Furthermore, the depreciation method a firm chooses may be more of a function of the effect on taxes rather than the ability to make a project's book value reflect its true resale value.

In practice, a variety of factors can complicate depreciation. Thorough investigation of the current and applicable tax code and/or consultation with a tax specialist is advisable.

Depreciation amount allowable

Computing the depreciation amount allowable for an asset requires a determination of the asset's depreciable basis. In tax accounting, **depreciable basis** is the amount that can be written off for tax purposes over a period of years.

Typically, the amount allowable is the original cost of the asset. This includes other capitalized expenditures that are necessary to prepare the asset for use (such as shipping and installation charges). Capitalized expenditures are treated as depreciable cash outlays and not as expenses of the period in which they are incurred.

In some situations, the amount allowable can be greater or less than the original investment costs. Tax credits, for example, can reduce the amount allowable below the original cost, and some tax laws permit companies to claim depreciation amounts for specific assets in excess of the investment made.

Depreciation time period

There are three main techniques for determining the depreciation time period for capital investments:

- The taxpayer estimates the useful life.

- Tax authorities estimate the useful life.

- Tax law specifies the allowable life through a series of tax tables (such as the Modified Accelerated Cost Recovery System, or MACRS, pronounced "makers").

Generally, the shorter the allowable life, the fewer periods over which depreciation of the asset can be claimed. This results in a higher depreciable amount per year, higher tax deductions, and greater tax savings.

Depreciation pattern

Tax authorities allow different depreciation patterns (based on the time periods). There are a variety of depreciation methods possible. An overview of a few of the more common methods follows.

Straight-line (SL) depreciation

Straight-line (SL) depreciation allocates expenses equally over the depreciable life of the asset. An equal depreciation amount is taken each year.

The general formula for straight-line depreciation is:

$$\text{Straight-line depreciation} = \frac{\text{Cost - Salvage Value}}{\text{Estimated Useful Life}}$$

An asset costs $10,000 with an estimated useful life of 5 years and a salvage value of $2,000. Using the straight-line depreciation method results in equal depreciation expenses each year over the equipment's 5-year life of:

$$\text{Straight-line depreciation} = \frac{\$10,000 - \$2,000}{5} = \$1,600 \text{ per year}$$

Accelerated depreciation

Accelerated depreciation refers to any method that writes off a capital investment faster than SL depreciation. More of the depreciable amount is written off in the early years of the investment than with the straight-line method. Sum-of-the-years'-digits, declining-balance depreciation, and double-declining-balance depreciation are all examples.

- **Sum-of-the-years'-digits (SYD)**

  Sum-of-the-years'-digits (SYD) is one method to reduce the book value of a capital investment rapidly in the early years and at a lower rate in the later years of the asset's life. The SYD method takes into consideration the estimated salvage value in the same manner as the SL method.

  Let's use the same $10,000 asset with a 5-year life and a $1,000 estimated salvage value to determine the amount of depreciation during the first year using the SYD method. Because this asset has an estimated useful life of 5 years, the sum of the numbers is 15 (as $1 + 2 + 3 + 4 + 5 = 15$).

  The asset is depreciated in the following manner:

  - 33.33% (5/15) in the first year

  - 26.67% (4/15) in the second year

  - 20.00% (3/15) in the third year

  - 13.33% (2/15) in the four year

  - 6.67% (1/15) in the fifth year

  Thus, the depreciation for the first year is $2,667 ($8,000)(0.3333) using the SYD method versus $1,600 using the SL method. During the fifth year, the SYD depreciation is $536 ($8,000)(0.067) versus $1,600 using the SL method. Compared with depreciation using the SL method, depreciation using the SYD method is higher during the early years but lower in the latter years of an asset's life.

- **Declining-balance depreciation**

  Declining-balance (DB) depreciation decreases the asset's value by reducing its book value by a constant percentage each year. Unlike the SL and SYD methods, the DB method does not explicitly use the salvage value in its calculations. However, depreciation expense will be halted when the cost less salvage value has been depreciated. The general formula for the declining-balance method to determine the depreciation charge in any period is:

  $$(1/n)NBV$$

  Where:

  - n = depreciable life of the asset.

  - NBV = asset's net book value at the start of the year (cost – accumulated depreciation).

  For a $10,000 asset with a 5-year life, the depreciation in the first year would be $2,000. The 1/5 determines the fixed percentage or, 20%) that is applied against the declining net book value each year. The net book value for the second year would be $8,000 (the acquisition cost minus accumulated depreciation). Thus the depreciation charge for year 2 would be:

  $$(0.20)\$10,000 = \$2,000$$

The fixed percentage selected is generally the one that reduces book value to salvage value at the end of the asset's estimated life. The asset should never be reduced below the estimated salvage value.

Variations of the declining-balance depreciation method insert multiples.

Depreciation in Year i using the DB method = $m(1/n)NBV$

Where:

- m = multiple.

- n = depreciable life of the asset.

- NBV = asset's net book value at the start of the year.

For example, the double-declining balance (DDB) method doubles the rate in the previous scenario as shown here:

$$2(1/5)\$10,000 = \$4,000$$

The fixed percentage is now $2(1/5)$ or 40 percent. This fixed percentage applied against the declining net book value in year 2 results in:

$$2(1/5)\$6,000 = \$2,400$$

In the third year, the charge would be:

$$2(1/5)\$3,600 = \$1,440$$

In years 1 through 3, the company has a cumulative depreciation expense of $7,840 ($4,000 + $2,400 + $1,440). Because the total depreciation expense is $8,000 ($10,000 - $2,000), the depreciation in year 4 is limited $160 ($8,000 - $7,840) instead of $864 [2(1/5)$2,160]. There would be no depreciation expense in year 5 because the machine has been fully depreciated to its estimated salvage value.

MACRS tables

MACRS tables categorize all business assets into classes (for example, computers and peripheral equipment, office machinery, office furniture, nonresidential real estate, and so on) and then specify the time period over which the assets can be written off in each class (for example, 3-year property, 5-year property, 7-year property, and so on). Depending on the class of an asset, different conventions can be used to adjust the first year depreciation depending on the placed-in-service date.

The IRS provides special tables to determine the percentage of the item's tax basis that can be depreciated each year. The asset's tax basis does not change over the years, only the percentage used as a multiplier changes.

For example, let's assume that the $10,000 asset previous discussed is classified as 5-year asset life category. The following depreciation rates as a percentage apply to the original basis ($10,000), not the depreciable basis ($10,000 - $2,000).

5-Year Asset Life Category

Year	% (rounded)
1	20.00
2	32.00
3	19.20
4	11.52
5	11.52
6	5.76

This table is based on the double declining balance depreciation method, which switches to straight-line depreciation. Year 1 is the year in which the asset is placed in service. This table uses the mid-year convention, which assumes that the asset is placed in service at midyear. Thus, the company can only expense half of the normal amount of depreciation during year 1.

For the $10,000 asset with an estimated salvage value of $2,000, the depreciation expense for year 1 is 0.20($10,000) = $2,000.

Although a full discussion of how income taxes can specifically affect cash inflows and outflows for capital investments is beyond the scope of this text, the following general points can be made about depreciation and tax considerations in profitable companies:

- Depreciation deductions are not cash payments; they are noncash costs that reduce taxable income and taxes.

- A depreciation expense has an effect on the amount of income taxes a firm must pay for a given period.

- Because depreciation reduces taxable income and reduces the tax outflow, depreciation effectively results in a cash inflow.

The decrease in the tax liability due to the depreciation charge is referred to as a **depreciation tax shield**. This tax shield is equal to the depreciation amount multiplied times the tax rate.

Companies tend to favor accelerated depreciation patterns because they result in larger depreciation deductions and cash savings in years when the cash savings have a higher present value. Compared to the SL method, however, accelerated methods result in lower earnings per share (EPS) during the early years but higher EPS during the later years, holding other factors constant.

Progress Check

Directions: Read each question and respond in the space provided. Answers and page references appear on the page following the progress check questions.

1. Capital budgeting is **best** described as

( )   a.   decision making related to current expenditures.

( )   b.   the process of making long-term investment decisions.

( )   c.   the process of planning for short-term investments.

( )   d.   decision making to support operating efficiency.

2. Which of the following items is **not** an example of a capital expenditure?

( )   a.   Heating, ventilation, and air-conditioning system upgrade for EPA compliance

( )   b.   Purchase of a new assembly machine that will cut labor and maintenance costs

( )   c.   Purchase of a new computer server for the research and development group

( )   d.   Project bonuses paid to salaried employees

3. As it relates to relevant cash flow categories, direct effect refers to the

( )   a.   immediate effect that a cash inflow, outflow, or commitment has on cash flows.

( )   b.   change in a firm's tax obligations.

( )   c.   net increase or decrease in tax depreciation charges.

( )   d.   total of the direct effect and the tax effect.

Progress check answers

1. b (p. 3-350)

2. d (p. 3-350)

3. a (p. 3-354)

Discounted Cash Flow Analysis

Topic overview

*Various techniques are available to evaluate capital investment projects. In this topic, one of the more complicated techniques is discussed: **discounted cash flow (DCF) analysis**. DCF analysis adjusts cash flows over time for the time value of money. DCF methods are used to evaluate a capital investment by comparing the equivalent present values of all future net cash flows for the initial investment.*

Two popular DCF methods are covered:

- *Net present value (NPV) uses a specified discount rate to bring all subsequent net cash flows after the initial investment to their present values at the time of the initial investment. NPV emphasizes the dollar amount at the time of the investment.*

- *Internal rate of return (IRR) estimates the discount that makes the present value of all the subsequent net cash inflows after the initial investment equal the initial cash of the outlays of the investment. IRR uses the discount rate as a point of comparison.*

Required Rate of Return

Although each DCF method takes a different approach, they do have some commonalities. NPV and IRR both use the following criteria to evaluate a capital investment:

- Total initial cash flow for the investment

- Expected future cash inflows and outflows from the investment

- Firm's required rate of return for the investment

Topic 1 in this section, "Capital Budgeting Process," covered total cash flow and incremental cash flows. The required rate of return and its use of cost of capital and the weighted average cost of capital (WACC) merit further explanation before the detailed discussions of the NPV and IRR methods.

The required rate of return represents the minimum future receipts the firm will accept in choosing an investment. Stated another way, it is the return that a firm could expect to receive elsewhere for a capital investment of comparable risk. The required rate of return is also referred to as the desired rate of return, the hurdle rate, the threshold, or the (opportunity) cost of capital.

From a practical standpoint, determining the desired rate of return for all potential investments is challenging. At best, it is time-consuming. Identifying and evaluating the gamut of potential investment opportunities available at a given point in time is problematic and costly for a firm. Firms tend to use a couple of methods to expedite the process: a minimum rate of return or the cost of capital.

Minimum rate of return

Firms typically have a minimum rate of return figure that they use to evaluate investments. This rate is usually based on the firm's strategic objectives, industry averages, and common investment opportunities. When a firm uses a minimum rate of return as an investment benchmark, capital investment projects must meet this rate.

Cost of capital

As described in Section C of this part of the CMA Learning System, Topic 3, "Cost of Capital," the weighted average cost of capital (WACC) is a weighted average of the various components a firm uses for financing. WACC is found by determining costs for the individual capital components (for example, issues of preferred or common stock, borrowing through various forms of debt such as loans and bonds, or retained earnings) and then multiplying the cost of each by its proportion in the firm's total capital structure.

Recall the following general formula for the cost of capital:

$$k_a = w_1w_1 + w_2w_2 \ldots + wnkn$$

Where:

- n = different types of financing (each with its own cost and proportion in the capital structure).

- k = cost of a component in the capital structure.

- w = weight that component comprises of the total capital structure.

- k_a = cost of capital (expressed as a percentage).

Section C covers the specific formulas for determining the cost of each component in a firm's capital structure. It also examines how the WACC is used to calculate the relative importance of each source in the total capital structure of the firm (once the individual capital components have been determined).

Recall the formula for the weighted average cost of capital:

$$WACC = k_{dt}w_d + k_e w_e$$

Where:

- WACC = weighted average cost of capital.

- k_{dt} = after-tax cost of debt.

- w_d is the percentage of debt.

- k_e = is the cost of equity.

- w_e = percentage of equity.

Firms often use WACC to evaluate the cost of capital investments that have risk profiles consistent with the firm's overall risk profile, that is, projects of average riskiness for the firm.

Thus, in making capital investment decisions, the cost of capital can be applied as the discount rate to evaluate the present value of project cash flows. It may also provide the basis for the required rate of return and the point of comparison for a capital investment project's internal rate of return.

Net Present Value

Net present value is the present value of a project's future cash flows less the initial investment in the project. It discounts all expected future cash inflows and outflows to the present.

Calculating NPV

In order to calculate NPV, present value (PV) must first be determined.

Present value calculation

Present value (PV) is the equivalent dollar value today of future net cash inflows. It is determined by applying an appropriate discount (based on the required rate of return) to the future cash inflow.

Consider how the present value of $20,000 to be received in one year with a 10% required rate of return is determined.

$$\text{Present Value (PV)} = \text{Amount} \times \text{Discount Rate}$$

Refer to Figure 3-105 to locate the appropriate discount rate.

Figure 3-105: Partial Present Value Interest Factor Table

(n) Periods	10%	11%	12%
1	0.909	0.901	0.893
2	0.826	0.812	0.797
3	0.751	0.731	0.712
4	0.683	0.659	0.636
5	0.621	0.593	0.567
6	0.564	0.535	0.507
7	0.513	0.482	0.452
8	0.467	0.434	0.404
9	0.424	0.391	0.361
10	0.386	0.352	0.322

The discount rate (0.909) taken from the present value interest factor table is the discount factor for 10% in one period.

$$\text{Present Value (PV)} = \text{Amount} \times \text{Discount Rate}$$

$$\$18,180 = \$20,000 \times 0.909$$

Proof of this calculation can be found by determining the cash investment one year from now in the following manner.

Present value of cash now	=	$18,180
Interest for one year ($18,180 × 10%)	=	$1,818
Total cash in one year from now	=	$19,998*

* $2 difference due to rounding of PV interest factor

In other words, $18,180 is the present value equivalent for a $20,000 cash inflow to be received one year from now.

Net present value calculation

Net present value (NPV) is the amount in dollars today that an investment earns after yielding the desired rate of return for each period during the life of the investment.

The steps in determining the NPV for a capital project are:

1. Determine net cash flows for each year.

2. Identify the required rate of return.

3. Determine the discount for each year (using the appropriate present value table) for the required rate of return in step 2.

4. Determine the present values for the net cash flows; multiply the amount for step 1 by the amount for step 3.

5. Total the amounts in step 4 for all years of the investment.

NPV may be used to evaluate investments with uniform net cash flows and with uneven cash flows. Step-by-step examples of both types of calculations are shown here.

Uniform net cash flows example. Uniform cash flow involves an annuity investment. An annuity provides a series of equal cash flows over a specified number of periods. It also requires the use of the present value interest factor annuity table to determine the discount factor. The discount factor varies based on the number of years and the desired rate of return.

Consider the following scenario:

- The desired rate of return for an investment over three years is 10%.

- Net cash flows for each year of the investment are $125,000.

Refer to Figure 3-106 to locate the appropriate discount rate.

Figure 3-106: Partial Present Value Interest Factor Annuity Table

(n) Periods	10%	11%	12%	13%
1	0.909	0.901	0.893	0.885
2	1.736	1.713	1.690	1.668
3	2.487	2.444	2.402	2.361
4	3.170	3.102	3.037	2.974
5	3.791	3.696	3.605	3.517
6	4.355	4.231	4.111	3.998
7	4.868	4.712	4.564	4.423
8	5.335	5.146	4.968	4.799
9	5.759	5.537	5.328	5.132
10	6.145	5.889	5.650	5.426

The discount rate of 2.487 is found using the present value interest factor annuity table for three years at 10%. The present value of the net cash inflows can then be calculated as follows:

PV of Net Cash Inflows = $125,000 × 2.487 = $310,875

An initial cash investment of $300,000 is required. This is the present value of the investment. Subtracting the initial investment from the present value of the net cash inflow yields the net present value for this investment.

NPV = $310,875 − $300,000 = $10,875

The NPV calculation in this example indicates that the initial investment of $300,000 will earn $10,875 in current dollars in addition to a 10% return for each of the three years during the life of the investment.

Uneven cash flows example. A project with uneven cash flow projections over its life starts with the net cash inflows generated each year and then discounts them using the present value interest factor table. The discount factor will vary for each year of the investment.

Consider the following scenario:

- The total initial investment is $90,000.

- The required rate of return over four years is 10%.

- Annual net cash inflows over the life of the investment are $60,000, $40,000, $30,000, and $20,000.

Refer to 3-102 on page 3-383, "Partial Present Value Interest Factor Table," and locate the appropriate values for the four periods.

The following table shows how the cash flows are discounted using the present value interest factor table excerpt to determine the present value for each year.

Figure 3-107: Using NPV to Evaluate a Project

Year	Cash Inflows		Discount Factor at 10%		Present Value
1	$60,000	x	0.909	=	$54,540
2	40,000	x	0.826	=	33,040
3	30,000	x	0.751	=	22,530
4	20,000	x	0.683	=	13,660
Total present value of net cash inflows					$123,770
Less initial investment					90,000
Net present value					$33,770

The NPV calculation indicates that the initial investment of $90,000 will earn $33,770 in current dollars over the life of the project.

Net present value interpretation

NPV values may be interpreted in the following manner:

- An NPV of zero means that the investment earns the same rate of return as the required rate of return.

- A positive NPV indicates that the investment earns a higher rate of return than the required rate; future cash flows are greater than the initial investment cost.

- A negative NPV means that future cash flows will earn a return less than the required rate.

Projects with a positive NPV are acceptable because they add value to the firm. On the other hand, projects with a negative NPV indicate that the firm would lose money in a present value sense. However, a positive NPV does not mean that the project is the best possible investment alternative for a firm. A positive NPV simply means that the investment will earn a higher rate of return than the firm's required rate. Alternate investment opportunities may offer even better returns.

Internal Rate of Return

The **internal rate of return (IRR)** estimates the discount rate that makes the present value of net cash inflows equal to the initial investment. Stated another way, IRR is a discount rate that will make the NPV of an investment zero (if the rate is used as the required rate of return to compute NPV).

Internal rate of return interpretation

The internal rate of return method evaluates a capital investment by comparing the estimated internal rate of return to a predetermined criterion. This criterion is based on whatever rate the firm uses to evaluate investments, such as its minimum rate of return, the rate from another desirable alternate investment, or an industry average. The criterion rate serves as a cutoff point. Projects below this cutoff rate are rejected, unless they are mandatory projects.

Internal rate of return calculation

The internal rate of return method has two fundamental steps:

1. Determine the rate of return that makes the present value of net cash inflows equal the investment's initial amount.

2. Compare the estimated rate of return with the firm's required rate of return (the criterion cutoff) to assess the investment's desirability.

Similar to NPV, IRR may be used to evaluate investments with uniform net cash flows and with uneven cash flows. Examples of both types of calculations follow.

Uniform net cash flows example

The steps in determining IRR for a capital project with uniform net cash flows are:

1. Determine the total initial investment for the project (total cash outflows and commitments).

2. Identify the predetermined criterion cutoff rate of return (the required rate).

3. Determine net cash inflows for each year.

4. Divide the initial investment (step 1) by the annual cash flow (step 3) to obtain the IRR factor (which is basically the present value annuity factor for an annuity, PVIFA).

5. Refer to a present value annuity table to locate a discount rate at the specified number of years that matches the IRR factor (or the one closest to it).

6. Compare the IRR rate (step 5) to the chosen criterion cutoff rate (step 2).

If the calculated IRR exceeds the criterion cutoff rate (which serves as the desired rate of return), the project is a desirable investment.

Consider the following scenario:

- The total initial investment is $35,000.

- The predetermined criterion rate is 10%.

- Net cash inflows for each of the next three years are $15,000.

The IRR factor can then be calculated as follows:

IRR Factor = $35,000 ÷ $15,000 = 2.33

Refer to Figure 3-106, "Partial Present Value Interest Factor Annuity Table," to locate the IRR value.

In this example, IRR equals 13% (using the present value interest factor annuity table for three periods and interpolating to the nearest table value, 2.361).

Because the criterion cutoff rate (serving as the required rate of return) is 10% and the IRR value for the project is very close to 13%, the project is a desirable investment. If the desired rate of return would have been 14%, the project should be rejected.

Uneven cash flows example

For a project with uneven cash flow projections, the IRR calculation becomes trial and error and interpolation. Cash flows must be discounted at various rates until a rate is found that makes the present value equal to the initial investment.

In practice, computer spreadsheet programs and financial calculators make determining the IRRs of changing cash flows fairly easy. The following numerical example helps to illustrate the concepts behind the procedures.

Consider the following scenario:

- The total initial investment is $10,675.

- The criterion cutoff rate is 10%.

- The predicted annual net cash inflows over the life of the investment are $6,000, $4,000, and $3,000.

Refer to Figure 3-105, "Partial Present Value Interest Factor Table," and locate the appropriate values for the three periods.

The following table shows how the cash flows are discounted using the present value interest factor table to determine the present value for each year.

Figure 3-108: Total Present Value of Net Cash Inflows at 10%

Year	Cash Inflows		Discount Factor at 10%		Present Value
1	$6,000	x	0.909	=	$5,454
2	4,000	x	0.826	=	3,304
3	3,000	x	0.751	=	2,253
Total present value of net cash inflows					$11,011

The present value for the net cash flows for the three years ($11,011) is greater than the total initial investment ($10,675). The discount rate needs to be raised to get a present value closer to the project investment. The next table shows a discount rate of 12%. (Refer to Figure 3-105 and locate the appropriate values for the three periods at 12%.)

Figure 3-109: Total Present Value of Net Cash Inflows at 12%

Year	Cash Inflows		Discount Factor at 12%		Present Value
1	$6,000	×	0.893	=	$5,358
2	4,000	×	0.797	=	3,188
3	3,000	×	0.712	=	2,136
Total present value of net cash inflows					$10,682

At a 12% discount rate, the present value for the net cash flows for the three years ($10,682) is close to the total initial investment ($10,675). Because the criterion cutoff rate is 10%, the project should be accepted.

Comparison of NPV and IRR

The same basic assumption underlies both the NPV and IRR methods: risk, or uncertainty, is not a major problem. In addition, both NPV and IRR consider:

- The time value of money.

- The initial cash investment.

- All cash flows after the initial investment.

A major difference is that the end result of NPV is a dollar figure whereas the final computation for IRR is a percentage. Therein is an advantage for NPV, as the NPV values of individual projects can be added to estimate the effect of accepting some possible combination of projects. Because IRR yields a percentage, multiple projects cannot be added or averaged to evaluate any combination of capital investment projects.

Another advantage of the NPV method is its usefulness in evaluating a project in which the required rate of return varies over the life of the project. The total present value of the cash inflows can be determined and compared with the total initial investment to evaluate the attractiveness of a project. Again, it is not possible using the IRR method to infer if the project is unattractive. Different required returns for each year means that there is no single rate of return or a single IRR value.

NPV is also more reliable than IRR when there are several alternating periods of net cash inflows and net cash outflows because it can lead to maximizing shareholder wealth.

Both methods have some reliability cautions:

- NPV is only as reliable as the discount rate that is selected. An unrealistic discount rate can result in an erroneous decision to accept/reject a project.

- A capital investment project should not be accepted solely on the basis of a high IRR value. A high IRR result must be looked at further to assess if an opportunity to invest cash flows at such a high IRR is realistic.

- NPV and IRR have different reinvestment rate assumptions. NPV implicitly assumes that the firm can reinvest all cash inflows at the required rate of return. By contrast, IRR implicitly assumes that the firm can reinvest all cash inflows at the IRR. The reinvestment rate underlying NPV is generally considered to be the more appropriate assumption.

But among all the various methods to analyze capital investments, the DCF methods are theoretically some of the most reliable. The NPV and IRR methods will typically yield similar results as long as there are no differences in:

- The project size (the amount of the initial investment).

- The net cash flow pattern.

- The life of the project.

- The cost of capital over the life of the project.

If any of the cash flows in the analysis other than the initial investment are negative, IRR will yield multiple answers, all correct and all absurd. In such situations, only NPV should be used.

Accounting Rate of Return

As noted previously, there are several techniques that analysts can use to evaluate and select capital investments. NPV and IRR were discussed in detail here as they are two of the more conventional methods. Accounting rate of return (ARR), also called the average rate of return or return on investment, is another method for analyzing capital budgeting projects. The ARR differs from the NPV and IRR in that it focuses on accounting income rather than cash flow.

Although there are several definitions of ARR, one common definition of ARR is the ratio of average accounting income to the initial investment. Some calculations of ARR use average investment (beginning value + ending value)/2 in the denominator.

$$ARR = \frac{EBIT\,(1 - tax\ rate)}{Net\ initial\ investment}$$

Consider the following example for a capital investment in new equipment with an expected useful life of 5 years.

- $40,000 = operating profits a year before taxes

- 40% = company's tax rate

- $100,000 = net initial investment

$$ARR = \frac{\$30,000(1 - 0.40)}{\$100,000} = 0.18\ or\ 18\%$$

In this example, the ARR 18% indicates the rate at which each dollar of investment generates after-tax operating income.

The ARR percentage is influenced by using the net initial investment in the calculation. This makes the denominator larger than it would be if average level of investment is used.

Using the average investment, ARR becomes:

$$ARR = \frac{EBIT\,(1 - tax\ rate)}{(Beginning\ value + Ending\ value)/2}$$

Using the previous example, if the ending value were 0, then the ARR would be:

$$ARR = \frac{\$30,000(1 - 0.40)}{\$100,000/2} = 0.09\ or\ 9\%$$

The annual depreciation that must be deducted to get EBIT also influences ARR. Because of these factors, many companies calculate ARR using an average level of investment, recognizing that the book value declines over time. In doing this, the ratio is sometimes referred to as "average rate of return."

The advantages of using accounting rate of return are:

- The concept is easy to understand; the method provides a simple measure of profitability.

- The calculation uses numbers reported in financial statements.

- The calculation considers income earned throughout a capital investment's useful life.

- The calculation provides an indication of how the accounting numbers reported will change if the investment is accepted.

Similar to IRR, ARR (either the accrual method or the average method) indicates a rate of return percentage.

The disadvantages of using ARR in financial analysis of investments are:

- The method uses book earnings rather than cash flow (unlike NPV and IRR) and ignores depreciation as a source of cash inflow.

- It ignores the time value of money.

- It ignores the time sequence of net earnings.

Progress Check

Directions: Read each question and respond in the space provided. Answers and page references appear on the page following the progress check questions.

Match each term with its application.

1. _____ Present value

2. _____ Net present value

3. _____ Internal rate of return

4. _____ Required rate of return

5. _____ Cost of capital

a. Proportional average of the various components a firm uses for financing

b. Estimates the discount rate that makes the present value of net cash inflows equal to the initial investment

c. The amount in dollars today that an investment earns after yielding the desired rate of return for each period during the life of the investment

d. Minimum future receipts an investor will accept in choosing an investment

e. The equivalent dollar value today of future net cash inflows

6. What is the importance of the criterion rate in internal rate of return calculations?

( )   a.   Projects below this rate are rejected.

( )   b.   Projects above this rate are rejected.

( )   c.   The rate is used to find the discount rate in a present value annuity table.

( )   d.   The rate is used to find the discount rate in a present value interest factor table.

Progress check answers

1. e (p. 3-385)

2. c (p. 3-366)

3. b (p. 3-369)

4. d (p. 3-364)

5. a (p. 3-365)

6. a (p. 3-370)

Payback and Discounted Payback

Topic overview

*The **payback method** in capital budgeting determines the number of years needed to recoup the net initial investment in a capital budgeting project. Payback represents the break-even point for the investment.*

Uses of the Payback Method

Similar to the NPV and IRR techniques, the payback period (PP) does not distinguish between types of cash inflows (whether the cash inflow is the result of operations, the disposal of a piece of equipment, the restoration of working capital, and the like). As a simple measure of cash inflows, the PP can also be used to evaluate capital investments having uniform net cash flows or uneven cash flows.

Uniform net cash flows example

The following calculation determines the payback period of a capital investment if a series of uniform cash flows is expected:

$$\text{Payback Period} = \frac{\text{Total Initial Investment}}{\text{Expected Annual Net Cash Flow}}$$

Consider the following scenario:

- The total initial investment is $600,000.

- The expected annual net cash flow is $175,000.

In this case, the calculation would be:

$$\text{Payback Period} = \frac{\$600,000}{\$175,000} = 3.43 \text{ Years}$$

Uneven cash flows example

In situations in which the annual cash inflows are uneven, determining payback becomes a cumulative calculation. The net cash inflows are accumulated until the initial investment is recovered. Straight-line interpolation is used if the payback amount falls within a year.

The formula for the payback period is as follows:

$$\text{Payback Period} = \text{Years Until Full Recovery} + \frac{\text{Unrecovered Cost at the Beginning of the Last Year}}{\text{Cash Flow During the Last Year}}$$

Consider the following scenario:

- The total initial investment is $30,000.

- The predicted annual net cash inflows over the life of the investment are $10,000, $12,000, $16,000, and $14,000.

The following table shows the figures.

Figure 3-110: Payback and Uneven Cash Flows

Year	Net Cash Flow	Cumulative Net Cash Flow
0	– $30,000	– $30,000
1	10,000	– 20,000
2	12,000	– 8,000
3	16,000	8,000
4	14,000	22,000

After two years, the project requires another $8,000 to pay for itself. In year 3, the project is expected to generate $16,000 in net cash inflows. This means that for this investment, payback will occur sometime between year 2 and year 3. The project needs $8,000 more after year 2 to recover its initial investment. Dividing the unrecovered cost at the beginning of the last year by the cash flow during the last year ($8,000/$16,000) results in 0.5 years. Thus, the payback period for the project is 2.5 years.

$$\text{Payback Period} = 2 + \frac{\$8,000}{\$16,000} = 2.5 \text{ Years}$$

Payback method interpretation

When using the payback method, firms typically choose a target payback period (or maximum cutoff period) for a project. The target payback period represents what the firm considers to be the maximum acceptable length of time for a project. Projects with a payback shorter than the target payback period are accepted; those with a payback longer than the target payback period are rejected. In the previous example, if the firm had set the maximum acceptable target payback for the $30,000 investment as 3 years, the investment should be accepted because the actual payback is achieved in 2.5 years.

Typically, the higher the risk of a project, the shorter the target payback period should be. That is because quickly recovering risky investments is desirable. When comparing two or more investment projects, those with shorter payback periods are generally preferable.

Advantages and Disadvantages of the Payback Method

The payback method has distinct advantages and disadvantages. Primary ones are listed in Figure 3-111.

Figure 3-111: Advantages and Disadvantages of the Payback Method

Advantages	Disadvantages
■ Uses a simple calculation ■ Produces results that are easy to understand ■ Provides a rough measure of liquidity and risk	■ Ignores the time value of money; adds cash flows without regard to timing ■ Ignores cash flows occurring after the payback period ■ Provides no measure of profitability ■ Promotes the acceptance of short-term projects if the target payback period is too short

In some situations, the quick measures of liquidity and risk are beneficial to indicate the risk of losing a capital investment in a high-risk situation. In a rough sense, projects with shorter payback periods are less risky. Projects with shorter paybacks also tend to provide an organization with greater flexibility because funds for other projects are available sooner.

Because of its basic limitations, the payback method can provide only a partial picture of whether an investment is worthwhile. It is, therefore, best used in conjunction with other capital budgeting techniques.

Discounted Payback

The **discounted payback method** attempts to address one of the shortfalls of the payback period calculation—ignoring the time value of money. Discounted payback uses the present values of net cash inflows (rather than the undiscounted dollar amounts of net cash inflows) to determine a payback period.

Similar to the NPV method, the present values of net cash inflows are estimated using the firm's desired rate of return. The time period necessary for the cumulative net present values of net cash flows to equal the initial project investment is the present value payback period.

Figure 3-112: Discounted Payback and Even Net Cash Flows

Year	Net Cash Inflows		Discount Factor at 10%		Present Value of Net Cash Flows	Cumulative Present Value of Net Cash Flows
0	− $16,000		0		− $16,000	− $16,000
1	6,000	x	0.909	=	5,454	− 10,546
2	6,000	x	0.826	=	4,956	− 5,590
3	6,000	x	0.751	=	4,506	− 1,084
4	6,000	x	0.683	=	4,098	3,014

The project will recover its initial investment between year 3 and year 4. The amount needed in year 4 to reach present value (PV) payback is $1,084. The discounted payback period is then determined as follows:

$$\text{Discounted Payback Period} = 3 + \frac{\$1,084}{\$4,098} = 3.26 \text{ Years}$$

This is in contrast to the simple payback method:

$$\text{Payback Period} = \frac{\$16,000}{\$6,000} = 2.66 \text{ Years}$$

The payback method gives a different answer than the discounted payback calculation because it does not discount cash flows.

Progress Check

Directions: Read each question and respond in the space provided. Answers and page references appear on the page following the progress check questions.

1. Which of the following statements about using the payback method in capital budgeting is **false**?

   The payback method:

   ( )   a.   represents the break-even point for an investment.

   ( )   b.   provides a rough measure of project liquidity.

   ( )   c.   takes into account the time value of money.

   ( )   d.   provides a rough measure of project risk.

2. What is the payback period for a capital budgeting project in which the total initial capital investment is $900,000 and the expected annual net cash flow is $150,000?

   ( )   a.   3 years

   ( )   b.   5 years

   ( )   c.   6 years

   ( )   d.   7 years

3. Which of following statements accurately compares the discounted payback and payback methods?

   ( )   a.   Both methods provide simple measures of project profitability.

   ( )   b.   Discounted payback uses the present values of net cash inflows; payback does not.

   ( )   c.   Discounted payback ignores cash flows after the payback period expiration; payback does not.

   ( )   d.   Both methods distinguish between types of cash inflows.

Progress check answers

1. c (p. 3-377)

2. c (p. 3-377)

3. b (p. 3-379)

Ranking Investment Projects

Topic overview

The capital budgeting topics covered thus far have examined analysis methods that result in accept/reject decisions for single, conventional, independent projects. In the real world, there are many scenarios that can (and often do) complicate decision analysis. In this topic, some of those potential difficulties are examined along with methods for ranking investment projects.

Capital Rationing

Capital rationing refers to situations in which there is some constraint on a firm's investment program that limits the total amount of capital expenditures that can be made during a given period (for example, a year). Budget ceilings often result in capital rationing as well as control policies mandating internal financing of capital expenditures.

Consider the following scenario for evaluating three capital investments:

- The capital rationing limit is $10,000.

- The desired rate of return is 10%.

Figure 3-113: Capital Rationing and Net Present Value

Project	Cash Inflow Year 0	Cash Inflow Year 1	Cash Inflow Year 2	Net Present Value at 10%
A	– $10,000	$30,000	$5,000	$21,000
B	– 5,000	5,000	20,000	16,000
C	– 5,000	5,000	15,000	12,000

Based on this data, the firm can invest in either project A or in projects B and C. Because of the capital rationing limit, it cannot invest in all three, even though they are all attractive on an individual basis. Although projects B and C individually have lower NPVs than project A, they collectively have the higher NPV ($28,000 for B and C versus $21,000 for A). On this basis, it would seem logical to select projects B and C.

When capital rationing is present, a firm must attempt to select some combination of capital investment projects that will provide the highest level of returns possible while not exceeding the constraint. Choosing solely on the basis of NPVs is not necessarily the best method. In some situations, a firm needs to use additional analysis to ensure that project(s) with the highest NPV per dollar outlay of the initial investment are selected. One such analysis technique is the profitability index.

Profitability index

The **profitability index (PI)** (or **benefit-cost ratio**) compares the present value of future cash flows with the initial investment on a relative basis. It is a ratio of the present value of future net cash flows to the initial cash outflow:

$$PI = \frac{\text{PV of Future Cash Flows}}{\text{Total Initial Investment}} = \frac{\sum_{t=1}^{n} \frac{CF_t}{(1+r)^t}}{CF_o}$$

The profitability index for the three projects discussed previously is shown in Figure 3-114.

Figure 3-114: Profitability Index

Project	Total Initial Investment (1)	PV of Future Cash Flows (2)	Profitability Index (2)/(1)
A	$10,000	$12,000	1.2
B	5,000	11,000	2.2
C	5,000	7,000	1.4

On this basis, project B has the highest profitability index and project C is the next highest. Given the capital rationing limit of $10,000, projects B and C should be chosen over project A.

In this particular situation (as in most situations), the NPV method and the profitability index result in the same accept/reject decision. But although the two techniques generally lead to the same conclusion, they can rank alternative projects in different orders.

The general interpretation of a profitability index is that projects with a PI greater than 1.0 are acceptable; projects with a PI below 1.0 are rejected.

Given a choice between the two ranking methods, the NPV method has the advantage of expressing the net dollar contribution of a project. The profitability index provides only a measure of probability. Although a major benefit of using the profitability index to rank investments is its simplicity, the primary limitation is that it cannot be used when more than one resource is being rationed over multiple periods.

The profitability index ranking using the cost of capital will not lead to choice of the optimal set of investments, with the possible exception of single-period capital rationing. Thus, the profitability index cannot be used when capital is being rationed over more than one period.

Mutually Exclusive Projects

As the name implies, mutually exclusive projects are those in which the acceptance of one precludes the acceptance of the other. In other words, two mutually exclusive projects cannot both be selected for funding.

When faced with the situation of mutually exclusive projects, determining which projects are acceptable or unacceptable is insufficient. Conceivably, independent analysis of two mutually exclusive projects could indicate that they are both desirable alternatives. Or, in some situations, the capital budgeting analysis methods covered thus far—net present value, internal rate of return, payback, discounted payback, and profitability index—may yield contradictory results. When faced with the decision of choosing between mutually exclusive projects that have contradictory rankings, the reasons for the conflicting rankings should be understood.

Analysis methods often yield conflicting results because of project differences pertaining to:

- The size of the cash flows (that is, scale or size problem).

- The pattern of the net cash flows (that is, timing problem).

- The length of the useful life.

Figure 3-115 provides an overview of these situations and general comments about them.

Figure 3-115: Problems in Comparing Project Investments

	Where ...	Comments
Scale (or size) problem	Sizes of cash flows (including initiation cash flow) differ	Whenever there is a conflict in ranking between NPV and IRR, the NPV method is preferable.
Timing problem	Timing of cash flows differs	Whenever there is a conflict in ranking between NPV and IRR, the NPV method is preferable.
Length of useful life	Projects have unequal useful lives	Special adjustments need to be made to "equalize" the life of the projects before NPV and IRR can be calculated. If there is a conflict in ranking between NPV and IRR, the NPV method is preferable.

The NPV method of ranking alternative project always leads to the correct project selection. Using the NPV method, projects with the best potential to add incremental dollar value to the firm are typically chosen.

Alternate Ranking Methods

Beyond the traditional payback, net present value, and internal rate of return methods for evaluating capital investment projects, analysts can use several alternate methods, linear programming and internal capital markets, can be used.

Linear programming

Linear programming is an optimization technique that can be used to determine the maximum value of some equation subject to stated linear constraints. Applied to ranking of capital investments, a firm desiring to select a group of projects with the highest total net present value can develop a series of programming equations that specify the desired outcome (for example, to maximize NPV) given various cash outflow constraints.

Linear programming models can be useful for evaluating capital budgeting scenarios when resources are limited. The task of selecting different values and performing manual calculations to determine which combination satisfies the constraints and yields the highest NPV is greatly simplified by using a computer for the calculation. Unless whole numbers are specified for results, the computer may even yield fractional projects—recommendations for half of one project, two-thirds of another project, and so on. If capital investments involve warehouse space or tonnage of a raw material, partial square footage (1,000 square feet of 2,000 square feet available) or partial tonnage (200 tons of 300 tons available) could be selected to reach a maximum NPV. But if fractional projects are not feasible (for example, the project being evaluated is whether to buy a piece of equipment or purchase a building), the program can be limited to whole number (integers).

Although linear programming can be helpful in capital budgeting, some cautions exist. Devising and maintaining the sophisticated programming models can be expensive. "Good" data is required; applying poor data to costly sophisticated analysis may lead to erroneous and potentially costly errors. Because capital investments generally present themselves progressively, forecasting all future investment opportunities to be used in a model is sometimes problematic.

Internal capital markets

Often, management imposes capital rationing constraints as provisional limits to aid in financial control. Management, for example, may adopt constraints to prevent managers from overstating investment opportunities. Such internal budget constraints are not driven by any inefficiency in the external capital market, but rather maximization of net present value is driven by internal budget constraints (lack of financial resources for capital projects) or the lack of other resources (such as management time or the availability of skilled labor and capital equipment). By imposing such limits on spending, managers and/or divisions are forced to set realistic priorities and cash flow forecasts.

One of the major drivers in capital rationing is a lack of financial resources for capital projects. Firms that face internal capital constraints are forced to prioritize available capital projects in alignment with company strategy and available funds.

Progress Check

Directions: Read each question and respond in the space provided. Answers and page references appear on the page following the progress check questions.

1. Capital rationing is best described as

( ) a. limits on an investment program that prevent a firm from undertaking all projects with positive net present values.

( ) b. comparisons of the present value of future cash flows with the initial investment on a relative basis.

( ) c. capital budgeting acceptance criteria based on subjectively determined cutoff points.

( ) d. capital budgeting acceptance criteria used when one project is dependent or contingent on another.

Questions 2 through 4 relate to the table below:

Project	Cash Inflow Year 0	Cash Inflow Year 1	Cash Inflow Year 2	Net Present Value (NPV) at 6%	Profitability Index (PI)
A	− $15,000	$10,000	$15,000		
B	− 5,000	5,000	10,000		
C	− 5,000	8,000	7,000		
D	− 10,000	− 10,000	4,000		

2. Calculate the net present value for projects A through D. Net present value of 1 for a single sum at 6% is 0.9434 for one period, 0.89 for two periods, and 0.83962 for three periods.

A: _____   C: _____

B: _____   D: _____

3. Calculate the profitability index (PI) for projects A through D.

A: _____   C: _____

B: _____   D: _____

4. Given a capital rationing limit of $20,000 in year 0, which of the following project combinations should the company accept?

( )   a.   A + B

( )   b.   A + C

( )   c.   B + C + D

Progress check answers

1. a (p. 3-383)

2. See table below. (p. 3-383)

3. See table below. (p. 3-384)

Project	Cash Inflow Year 0	Cash Inflow Year 1	Cash Inflow Year 2	Net Present Value (NPV) at 6%	Profitability Index (PI)
A	− $15,000	$10,000	$15,000	$7,783.91	1.519
B	− 5,000	5,000	10,000	8,616.95	2.723
C	− 5,000	8,000	7,000	8,777.15	2.755
D	− 10,000	− 10,000	4,000	−15,874	−0.59

4. c (p. 3-383)

    NPV of A + B = $7,783.91 + 8,616.95 = $16,400.96

    NPV of A + C = $7,783.91 + $8,777.15 = $16,561.06

    NPV of B = C + D = $8,616,95 + 8,777.15 + $2,993.95 = $20,388.05

    Accepting the projects B, C, and D produces the highest NPV.

Topic 5: Risk Analysis in Capital Investment

Topic overview

By definition, risk implies uncertainty and instability. In several areas of Section C of this part of the CMA Learning System, "Corporate Finance," risk was discussed extensively as it relates to financial instruments. In capital budgeting, risk has different implications.

Fundamentally, there are no risk-free capital investments. Consider just a few reasons why that is an accurate statement:

- *Future cash inflows can vary unexpectedly throughout the life of a project.*

- *The rate of return used in calculations may not be accurate for the life of the project.*

- *The cost of financing may increase during the life of a project.*

- *New mandatory regulatory factors can require additional investments at any given point in time.*

- *The life of the related product or service could be significantly shorter or longer than anticipated.*

- *Inflationary or recessionary economic conditions may impact the value of cash flows.*

- *Domestic or global political events may impact project cash flows or the viability of the project as a whole.*

Because of all these types of risk associated with capital budgeting, it is always a challenge to select capital investment projects. This topic looks at some of the ways to minimize the uncertainty.

Sensitivity Analysis

Sensitivity analysis as it pertains to capital investments is a "what-if" technique evaluating how NPV, IRR, and other indicators of the profitability of a project change if the discount rate, labor or materials costs, sales, or some other factor varies from one case to another. The purpose is to assess how sensitive the NPV, the IRR, or another specified profitability measure is to a change.

Sensitivity analysis can be used to answer questions such as:

- What happens to NPV if cash flows increase or decrease by 10% for each year of the project?

- Will NPV remain positive throughout a project if there is no cash inflow in the second year of a three-year project?

- What will happen to NPV if the discount rate increases from 8% to 10% or decreases from 8% to 7%?

- What would happen to the NPV if a major redesign of the product, requiring additional capital investments, is necessary in year 3 in order to address competitive new products?

- What would be the impact on NPV if the project is extended for three years, with decreasing cash flows and increased maintenance costs in the extended years?

To further understand how sensitivity analysis can be used to answer such "what-ifs," consider the following scenario:

- Annual net cash inflows over the life of investment A are $2,000 and $3,000.

- Annual net cash inflows over the life of investment B are $3,600 and $1,400.

- The total initial investment for each project is $3,200.

Given this information, what happens to each project if the discount rate changes from 10% to 12%? Refer to Figure 3-116 on the following page.

The NPVs of both projects decline when the discount rate increases from 10% to 12%. The percentage change in the NPV for project A is –10.9%, whereas the change for project B is –8.0%. Thus, project A is more sensitive to changes in the discount rate and poses a higher risk than project B if the discount rate changes.

Certainty Equivalents

The certainty equivalent (CE) approach to selecting projects attempts to separate the timing of cash flows from their risk. The expected cash flow is converted into an amount that has a higher probability of actually materializing. These cash flows are then discounted at a risk-free rate (such as the rate for a United States Treasury bill). In practice, only a small percentage of firms report using the certainty equivalent approach.

Figure 3-116: Changes in Discount Rate (continued on next page)

Project A at 10%

Year	Cash Inflows		Discount Factor at 10%		Present Value
1	$2,000.00	×	0.909	=	$1,818.00
2	3,000.00	×	0.826	=	2,478.00
Total present value of net cash inflows					$4,296.00
Less initial investment					3,200.00
Net present value					$1,096.00

Figure 3-116: Changes in Discount Rate (concluded)

Project A at 12%

Year	Cash Inflows		Discount Factor at 12%		Present Value
1	$2,000.00	×	0.893	=	$1,786.00
2	3,000.00	×	0.797	=	2,391.00
Total present value of net cash inflows					$4,177.00
Less initial investment					3,200.00
Net present value					$977.00

Project B at 10%

Year	Cash Inflows		Discount Factor at 10%		Present Value
1	$3,600.00	×	0.909	=	$3,272.40
2	1,400.00	×	0.826	=	1,156.40
Total present value of net cash inflows					$4,428.80
Less initial investment					3,200.00
Net present value					$1,228.80

Project B at 12%

Year	Cash Inflows		Discount Factor at 10%		Present Value
1	$3,600.00	×	0.893	=	$3,214.80
2	1,400.00	×	0.797	=	1,115.80
Total present value of net cash inflows					$4,330.60
Less initial investment					3,200.00
Net present value					$1,130.60

Comparison of Projects A and B

Project	NPV at 10%	NPV at 12%	Dollar Change	NPV % Change
A	$1,096.00	$977.00	−$119.00	−10.86%
B	$1,228.80	$1,130.60	−$98.20	−7.99%

In other words, if a firm has an expected cash flow of $15,000 in year 5 of an investment and the forecaster thinks that an 80% yield (or $12,000) of that expected cash flow is realistic, that amount is then discounted at the risk-free rate.

The following steps are used to determine certainty equivalents:

1. Project the expected cash flows of the investment.

2. Identify the certainty equivalent factors, or the percentages of the expected cash flows that are certain.

3. Multiply the expected cash flows by the certainty equivalent factors to determine the certain cash flows.

4. Calculate the present value of the project by discounting the certain cash flows at a specified risk-free discount rate.

5. Calculate the net present value of the project by subtracting the initial investment from the present value of the certain cash flows.

6. Evaluate the net present value of the project; a zero or positive value is acceptable and a negative value should be rejected.

To better understand how certainty equivalents are applied, consider the following scenario:

- Annual net cash inflows over the life of a five-year investment are $10,000, $8,000, $7,000, $6,000, and $5,000.

- Certainty equivalent factors are estimated over the life of the investment at 90%, 85%, 70%, 60%, and 45%.

- The total initial investment for the project is $18,000.

- The risk-free rate of return is 3%.

Given this information and applying the certainty equivalent approach, here's what an evaluation of the project looks like.

Figure 3-117: Project Evaluation and Certainty Equivalent Factors (continued on next page)

Year	Expected Cash Inflows		Certainty Equivalent Factor		Certain Cash Flow
1	$10,000	×	0.90	=	$9,000
2	8,000	×	0.85	=	6,800
3	7,000	×	0.70	=	4,900
4	6,000	×	0.60	=	3,600
5	5,000	×	0.45	=	2,250

Figure 3-117: Project Evaluation and Certainty Equivalent Factors (concluded)

Year	Certain Cash Inflows		Discount Factor at 3%		Present Value of Certain Cash Flow
1	$9,000	×	0.971	=	$8,739.00
2	6,800	×	0.943	=	6,412.40
3	4,900	×	0.915	=	4,483.50
4	3,600	×	0.888	=	3,196.80
5	2,250	×	0.863	=	1,941.75
Total present value of net cash inflows					$24,773.45
Less initial investment					18,000.00
Net present value					$6,773.45

The positive NPV value indicates that the project is acceptable.

Other Approaches to Dealing with Risk

The capital asset pricing model and simulations are two additional approaches that are useful in dealing with capital budgeting risk.

Capital asset pricing model (CAPM)

The capital asset pricing model was discussed in Section C of this part of the *CMA Learning System*, "Corporate Finance," as it relates to finding the required rate of return on a stock or portfolio. The CAPM also has application in capital budgeting. The formula for the CAPM in capital budgeting is:

$$E(R_a) = R_f + \beta_a \left[E(R_m) - R_r \right]$$

Where:

- $E(R_a)$ = required rate of return on an asset (project) being evaluated.
- R_f = risk-free rate.
- ßp = beta of an asset (project).
- $E(R_m)$ = return on a market portfolio.

The premise behind using the CAPM in capital budgeting is treating a project in the same manner as a share of stock. The rationale is that the return from a project is linked to the return on the firm's total assets or to the return in an industry, just as a stock or market portfolio. With this assumption, the beta of the company is used as the beta for the project. In the event a project is not a typical investment for a company, an average industry beta can be substituted. This is called the "pure play" approach.

Once the project's required rate of return is identified, NPV can be calculated. Expected cash flows are discounted using the rate; the total net present value of cash flows is subtracted from the total initial project investment. A zero or positive NPV means that the project can be accepted as it will preserve the required rate of return.

If multiple projects are being evaluated, the one with the higher beta is considered more risky.

Simulations

Simulations allow testing of a capital investment project before it is accepted. Because the actual future values for cash flows and discount rates for investment projects are not known, hypothetical cash flows and discount rates are assumed and can be studied using a simulation model.

In capital budgeting, simulations can be used to approximate:

- The expected NPV, IRR, and PI.

- The dispersion about an expected value.

When attempting to evaluate more than one risky investment, the NPV or IRR for each project can be simulated several times and average NPVs, IRRs, and standard deviations can be computed and ranked. Repeating the process many times also allows values to be plotted on a frequency distribution graph to show the distribution of the NPVs and IRRs. Looking at the distribution curves provides a reasonable assessment of the risk level of a project.

Many simulation software programs are available. Use of these programs creates many more scenarios than can be done by hand. Some of these programs can also draw graphs of the results. Perhaps the best-known computer simulation model in capital budgeting is the Monte Carlo simulation tool, which in essence simulates a gambling roulette wheel with a model of a project.

Use of Specifically Adjusted Rates

Under most circumstances, risky capital projects are less desirable than safe investments. Firms typically demand a higher rate of return for riskier projects or they use conservative estimates for cash flows.

Many firms use their company cost of capital as the yardstick to discount the cash flows on all new investments. In situations in which new projects are more or less risky than is normal for the firm, using the company rate can create problems.

The firm's cost of capital is an appropriate discount rate when capital projects have the same average risk as the firm's existing business. However, care and discretion must be used in determining what exactly constitutes similar risk.

Using the firm's cost of capital rate arbitrarily for all new projects can lead to erroneously accepting or rejecting a project regardless of its risk only because it offers a higher rate of return than the company's cost of capital. The problem is twofold:

- Good low-risk projects may be rejected.

- Poor high-risk projects may be accepted.

When in doubt, analysts should assess the relative risks of projects on an individual basis and use a rate specifically adjusted for the project risk. By doing this, every project has its own opportunity cost of capital.

Qualitative Considerations in Capital Investments

As previous content has demonstrated, there are a variety of quantitative methods available for evaluating capital budgeting projects. Most of the techniques discussed have distinct strengths and weaknesses. As a result, managers should and often do use multiple criteria for evaluating investment projects. Collectively, multiple methods mitigate the potential for estimation errors and/or incorrect decisions that are not in the best interests of the firm or shareholders.

In addition to quantitative methods, a firm also should recognize qualitative factors that can influence investment decisions. Important qualitative considerations include:

- Management may not have the necessary information to make capital budgeting decisions (for example, type of information or frequency).

- Loan provisions may limit borrowing.

- The firm may have self-imposed capital rationing limits.

- Decision-makers may be risk averse.

- Conflict may exist between decisions to take on a project and performance evaluation of managers. (For example, a manager might be concerned about how a project will affect a bonus plan based on reported annual accrual accounting numbers.)

- A firm may not have sufficient/qualified personnel to successfully implement capital projects.

- Management may assess whether the investment can increase customer loyalty and retention.

Capital investments are often strategic in nature. As such, qualitative factors are important considerations although they may be difficult to estimate.

Progress Check

Directions: Read each question and respond in the space provided. Answers and page references appear on the page following the progress check questions.

Match the different approaches to dealing with risk with the appropriate description.

1. _____ Sensitivity analysis

2. _____ Certainty equivalent approach

3. _____ Capital asset pricing model

4. _____ Simulations

a. The use of a hypothetical situation (similar to the real one) to help make a decision

b. A measure of the extent to which one factor varies when another factor changes

c. The conversion of projected cash flows into an amount that has a higher probability of actually materializing

d. The use of a firm's beta or an industry beta in an assessment of project risk

5. Which method is best suited to comparing the net present values for two capital investment projects when the cash flows vary?

( ) a. Sensitivity analysis

( ) b. Certainty equivalent approach

( ) c. Capital asset pricing model

( ) d. Computer simulation

Progress check answers

1. b (p. 3-390)

2. c (p. 3-391)

3. d (p. 3-394)

4. a (p. 3-395)

5. a (p. 3-390)

Topic 6   Real Options in Capital Investments

Topic overview

Decisions to accept or reject capital budgeting investment proposals depend on risk. Investors and suppliers of capital both require a risk-adjusted return that they deem appropriate. In particular, investors typically go to great lengths to evaluate project risk. However, today's competitive business environment coupled with other influencing factors such as technology and regulatory constraints can raise havoc with capital budgeting investments. Real options provide some flexibility in adjusting projects after they have been accepted.

Definition and Types of Real Options

Once a project is under way, real options (or managerial options) allow management to make changes that will affect subsequent cash flows and/or the life of the investment. They are important considerations in capital budgeting, as they give management the opportunity to alter a previously made decision. Real options allow managers to potentially amplify good decisions or mitigate poor ones that can result in loss to the firm. These allowances add value to the firm.

The discounted cash flow valuation model has its roots in bond and stock investments. Investors in these types of securities can be described as passive, as there is nothing they can do to alter interest rates or returns. Options and securities allow an investor to be an active participant and respond to changing circumstances. In capital investment projects, real options are often embedded so that management can exercise them at its discretion when doing so is in the firm's best interest.

Specifically, real options include the following:

- **Expand**
  The expand option involves making follow-on investments if the immediate investment project succeeds. An expand option is especially valuable when uncertainty is high but a firm's product or service market is growing rapidly. If early project/service results are favorable, a firm may stand to make follow-on investments that are extremely profitable even if taking on negative NPV projects. Such projects are generally dubbed as being of strategic value to the firm. A common adage is that today's investments can generate tomorrow's opportunities.

- **Abandon**
  An option to abandon (or contract) allows the flexibility to abandon a project if early termination is deemed appropriate. The abandon option can be used to evaluate existing projects or to evaluate new investment proposals.

  The abandon option is often used to evaluate ongoing projects, assess their profitability/unprofitability, and decide whether continuing the projects or releasing the funds for use elsewhere is the better choice. For example, a firm may be better off selling a piece of equipment tied to a capital investment that is no longer desirable.

Akin to a put option on a stock, an abandon option is like an insurance policy. For example, if the equipment investment is disappointing, a firm could abandon the project and recover a price equal to the sales value of the equipment.

When abandonment is applied with new projects, the option of abandoning a project at a later date may affect the selection.

- **Postpone**

  Postponing involves waiting and learning more before investing further. When there is no uncertainty, timing of an investment is easy. NPV can be calculated at various future investment dates and the date that offers the highest current value selected. The "wait-and-see" option is the equivalent of owning a call option on an investment project. The call option is exercised when the firm commits to the investment project. Deferral is desirable when uncertainty about the investment is high and the immediate cash inflows lost or postponed are small.

  Exercising the option negates the ability to take advantage of potential gains in future value. But as long as the project has a positive NPV and the cash flows are attractive, the exercise option may be desirable (before the option contract expires).

- **Adapt**

  Adapting—the ability of a firm to vary output or production methods in response to demand—allows the firm to swap or exchange its output mix as demand changes. Given the myriad tumultuous and competitive market situations, companies often build flexibility into their manufacturing operations so they can respond quickly to any changes and produce the most valuable set of outputs.

An investment project's net worth can be viewed as the traditional NPV of the investment in combination with the value of its real options. Evaluating the merits of these real options is important given the outcomes they can have. Options can sometimes:

- Turn an accept decision into a postponement.

- Convert a reject decision into an acceptance.

- Result in early project termination and release cash flows for other projects.

In light of these real options, discounted cash flow analysis and the resulting determination of NPV can be said to provide a sound foundation and starting point. But as possible, the discounted cash flow approach should be adapted to accommodate real options. They can limit the downside of a project by better managing the uncertainty associated with the future.

Valuation of Real Options

A firm essentially acquires an option to cover the risk of one asset with another. But the real options discussed here (expand, abandon, postpone, and adapt) are much more complicated in practice. Each investment opportunity can be affected by a host of variables, including:

- Timing of the real option decision points.

- The cash flows necessary to exercise the option.

- Variable interest and investment rates.

- The unpredictability of current and future commodity, labor, and other variable costs affecting the cash flows.

- The standard deviation, market risk, and other factors that will affect demand for the project's goods or services.

Because assets can take on a nearly infinite number of future values, the general binomial method of option valuation and the Black-Scholes formula can be used to evaluate investment returns for a variety of intervals or subperiods. Programming applications can identify the possible investment outcomes. Numbers can be entered in specific formulas to track the risk of options (which can change week by week, day by day, and sometimes hour by hour.)

The binomial method is typically used when the number of possible outcomes is limited. The Black-Scholes formula recognizes a wider continuum of potential outcomes and is generally thought to be the more accurate of the two methods, as it accounts for a more realistic range of possible outcomes. But it cannot be applied to every situation. For those applications, the binomial method can still provide a reasonable measure of an option's value.

Note: Options are discussed in more detail in Section C of this part of the CMA Learning System, "Corporate Finance." That section also includes information on the general binomial method and the Black-Scholes formula.

Progress Check

Directions: Read each question and respond in the space provided. Answers and page references appear on the page following the progress check questions.

1. Which option would a firm most likely choose if there is a high probability of capturing additional future cash flows beyond the current estimates contained in the cash flow projections?

    ( ) a. Expand

    ( ) b. Abandon

    ( ) c. Postpone

    ( ) d. Adapt

2. If a firm needs to fund a new technology with relatively uncertain demand potential, the **best** type of option is to

    ( ) a. expand.

    ( ) b. abandon.

    ( ) c. postpone.

    ( ) d. adapt.

Progress check answers

1. a (p. 3-399)

2. c (p. 3-400)

Bibliography

Afterman, Allan B. *SEC Regulation of Public Companies.* Englewood Cliffs, New Jersey: Prentice Hall, 1995.

American Society of Association Executives. *ASAE's Essentials of the Profession Learning System:* Module Five, Membership/Using Technology Effectively, and Module Seven, Finance Administration. Washington, D.C.: American Society of Association Executives and Eagan, Minnesota: Holmes Corporation, 2002.

Arens, Alvin A., and James K. Loebbecke. *Auditing: An Integrated Approach,* 8th edition. Upper Saddle River, New Jersey: Prentice Hall, 1999.

Bernstein, Leopold A. *Financial Statement Analysis: Theory, Application, and Interpretation,* 3rd edition. Homewood, Illinois: Irwin, 1983.

Blocher, Edward J., Kung H. Chen, and Thomas W. Lin. *Cost Management: A Strategic Emphasis,* 2nd edition. New York: McGraw-Hill Irwin, 2002.

Bodnar, George H., and William S. Hopwood. *Accounting Information Systems,* 3rd edition. Boston: Allyn and Bacon, 1987.

Brealey, Richard A., and Stewart C. Meyers. *Principles of Corporate Finance,* 4th edition. New York: McGraw-Hill, 1991.

Campanella, Jack, editor. *Principles of Quality Costs,* 2nd edition. Milwaukee, Wisconsin: ASQ Quality Press, 1990.

Cartin, Thomas J. *Principles and Practices of TQM.* Milwaukee, Wisconsin: ASQ Quality Press, 1993.

"Database Management System," Webopedia Web site, www.webopedia.com/TERM/d/database_management_system_DBMS.html.

Delaney, Patrick R., Ralph Nach, Barry J. Epstein, and Susan Weiss Budak. *GAAP 2003.* Hoboken, New Jersey: Wiley, 2002.

Epstein, Barry J., Ralph Nach, and Steven M. Bragg, *Wiley GAAP 2006.* New York: John Wiley & Sons, 2005.

Evans, Matt H. *Course 11: The Balanced Scorecard,* www.exinfm.com/training/pdfiles/course11r.pdf.

Financial Accounting Standards Board, Statements of Financial Accounting Concepts Nos. 1, 2, 4, 5, 6, 7. Financial Accounting Standards Board: Stamford, Connecticut: 1978-2000.

Frederick, William C., James E. Post, and Keith Davis. *Business and Society: Corporate Strategy, Public Policy, Ethics,* 7th edition. New York: McGraw Hill, 1992.

Garrison, Ray H., and Eric W. Noreen. *Managerial Accounting,* 10th edition. Boston: McGraw-Hill/Irwin, 2003.

Gelinas, Ulric J., Jr., Steve G. Sutton, and Allan E. Oram. *Accounting Information Systems,* 4th edition. Cincinnati, Ohio: South-Western College Publishing, 1999.

Gibson, Charles H. *Financial Statement Analysis: Using Financial Accounting Information,* 7th edition. Cincinnati, Ohio: South-Western College Publishing, 1998.

Greenstein, Marilyn, and Todd M. Feinman. *Electronic Commerce: Security, Risk Management, and Control.* Boston: McGraw Hill Higher Education, 2000.

Hargrave, Lee E. *Plan for Profitability: How to Write a Strategic Business Plan.* Titusville, Florida: Four Seasons Publishers, 1999.

Hilton, Ronald W., Michael W. Maher, and Frank H. Selto. *Cost Management: Strategies for Business Decisions,* 2nd edition. Boston: McGraw-Hill Irwin, 2003.

Horngren, Charles T., George Foster, and Srikant M. Datar. *Cost Accounting,* 10th edition. Upper Saddle River, New Jersey: Prentice-Hall, 2000.

Hoyle, Joe B., Thomas F. Schaefer, and Timothy S. Doupnik. *Advanced Accounting,* 6th edition. Boston: McGraw-Hill Irwin, 2001.

Juran, Joseph M., and Blanton Godfrey, coeditors-in-chief. *Juran's Quality Handbook,* 5th edition. New York: McGraw-Hill, 1999.

Kaplan, Robert S., and David P. Norton. *The Balanced Scorecard: Translating Strategy Into Action.* Boston: Harvard Business School Press, 1996.

Kaplan, Robert S., and David P. Norton. *The Strategy-Focused Organization.* Boston: Harvard Business School Press, 2001.

Kaplan, Robert S., and David P. Norton. "Using the Balanced Scorecard as a Strategic Management System." *Harvard Business Review,* January-February 1996.

Kieso, Donald E., and Jerry J. Weygandt. *Intermediate Accounting,* 9th edition. New York: Wiley, 1998.

Kieso, Donald E., Jerry J. Weygandt, and Terry D. Warfield. *Intermediate Accounting,* 10th edition. New York: Wiley, 2001.

Larsen, E. John. *Modern Advanced Accounting,* 10th edition. New York: McGraw-Hill, 2006.

Laudon, Kenneth C., and Jane P. Laudon. *Management Information Systems*, 8th edition. Upper Saddle River, New Jersey: Pearson Prentice Hall, 2003.

Madden, Bartley J. *CFROI Valuation—A Total System Approach to Valuing the Firm.* Boston: Butterworth-Heinemann, 1999.

McMillan, Edward J. *Budgeting and Financial Management Handbook for Not-for-Profit Organizations.* Washington, D.C.: American Society of Association Executives, 2000.

Moscove, Stephen A., Mark G. Simkin, and Nancy A. Bagrandoff. *Core Concepts of Accounting Information Systems,* 5th edition. New York: Wiley, 1997.

Nicolai, Loren A., and John D. Bazley. *Intermediate Accounting,* 5th edition. Boston: PWS-Kent Publishing Company, 1991.

Olve, Nils-Göran, and Anna Sjöstrand. *The Balanced Scorecard.* Oxford, United Kingdom: Capstone Publishing (a Wiley Company), 2002.

Ratliff, Richard L., Wanda A. Wallace, Glenn E. Sumners, William G. McFarland, and James K. Loebbecke. *Internal Auditing: Principles and Techniques.* Altamonte Springs, Florida: Institute of Internal Auditors, 1996.

Roszkowski, Mark E. *Business Law.* New York: Addison Wesley, 1997.

Tague, Nancy R. *The Quality Toolbox.* Milwaukee, Wisconsin: ASQ Quality Press, 1995.

U.S. Securities and Exchange Commission, www.sec.gov.

Van Horne, James C., and John M. Wachowicz, Jr. *Fundamentals of Financial Management,* 9th edition. Englewood Cliffs, New Jersey: Prentice-Hall, Inc., 1995.

Young, S. David, and Stephen R. O'Byrne. *EVA® and Value-Based Management: A Practical Guide to Implementation.* New York: McGraw Hill, 2001.

Index

目　　录

出版说明

关于 CMA 考试教材

本教材的基础是美国管理会计师协会（IMA）所开发的知识体系。虽然本教材的基础是 CMA 考试所测试的知识体系以及已经公布的涵盖该考试四个组成部分的学习要点（LOS），但是 CMA 考试教材方案的开发者并没有参考当前的题库。而且，阅读本教材并不能保证一定能够通过考试。对考生来说至关重要的是，理解美国管理会计师协会认证部（ICMA）公布的所有学习要点、学习与这些要点有关的概念和计算以及牢牢掌握如何解答 CMA 考试中的单项选择题和问答题。

本教材的目的是为了帮助考生进行学习，但应当认识到出版商和作者并不提供法律或者专业方面的服务。

致谢

IMA 非常感谢对本书的最初英文版本做出贡献的各个专家，他们是注册管理会计师金伯利·弗兰克·沙伦博士（Kimberly Frank Charron），注册管理会计师尼尔·J·汉农（Neal J. Hannon），注册管理会计师和注册会计师查尔斯·R·哈特尔（Charles R. Hartle）、丹尼斯·L·奈德（Dennis L. Neider）以及卡尔·V·孟可尼（Carl V. Menconi）。

此外，我们还非常感谢以下几位专家，这些专家对本书的第二版做出了非常大的贡献，他们是注册管理会计师和特许金融分析师吉尔·贝尔博士（Jill Bale），注册管理会计师和特许金融分析师肯特·贝克博士（Kent Baker），注册管理会计师肯尼思·科尔博士（Kenneth Cole），注册管理会计师索雷弗·杜塔博士（Saurav Dutta），注册管理会计师卡伦·L·杰特（Karen L. Jett），注册管理会计师和特许金融分析师乔·兰兹（Joe Lanz），保罗·迈尔森博士（Paul Miesing），注册管理会计师露·佩特博士（Lou Petro），特里·里坦伯格博士（Terri Rittenburg），注册管理会计师肖彭·万博士（Siaw－Peng Wan）。

最后，我们还要感谢以下几位对本书中文部分的翻译校对工作做出了非常大贡献的专家学者。他们是美国管理会计师协会顾问、香港科技大学会计学教授杨继良，注册管理会计师罗鹏，注册管理会计师韩保庆，以及李若女士。

版权所有

册管理会计师）学习系统资料的行为都属非法，并严重地违背了 IMA（管理会计师协会）的《职业道德规范声明》。

任何 CMA 或 CMA 考生，若未事先获得 IMA 和经济科学出版社的授权，以任何形式复制、翻印或发行 CMA 学习系统资料或内容都会面临法律诉讼，同时还会将这一行为报告给 ICMA（注册管理会计师协会），并立即取消其 IMA 会员资格和 CMA 考试资格。

读者有责任确保自己所使用的 CMA 考试资料来自有授权的渠道或个人。如果对资料的可信性或资料提供的途径有任何怀疑，请联系 IMA 客户服务处，致电（800）638 – 4427 或（201）573 – 9000，或者 Email：IMA@ imanet. org。

本书所引用的各种 FASB 文件，其版权归财务会计准则委员会（FASB）所有，地址为 401 Merritt 7，P. O. Box 5116，Norwalk，Connecticut 06856，U. S. A，并经允许复印。这些文件的完整版本可从 FASB 处获得。

CMA 资格

注册管理会计师（CMA）资格为公司管理层和财务专业人员提供了衡量管理会计领域知识和能力方面的客观指标。CMA 资格在全球范围内被各种组织内的专业会计人员作为重要的资质证明，它已成为提升专业技能和扩展专业视野的一种重要途径。

CMA 考试包含四个部分，其目的是开发和考核批判性思考能力和决策制定技能，并且可以满足以下目标：

- 通过确定专业人员的作用、知识体系以及获得这些知识的课程，使得管理会计和财务管理成为一种受人认可的专业。
- 鼓励在管理会计和财务管理领域实施较高的教育标准。
- 确定度量个人在管理会计和财务管理领域的知识和技能的客观指标。
- 鼓励持续的职业发展。

获得 CMA 资格的人员可以从以下几个方面受益：

- 可以与其他人员广泛交流业务知识和战略性财务技能。
- 获得最新的专业知识和技能，这些对企业的成功非常重要。
- 致力于卓越，这种卓越建立在强大的职业道德基础与终身学习基础之上。
- 在职业发展、工资水平及升迁机会上获得优势。

CMA 资格由美国管理会计师协会独家授予。

对考生的整体期望

CMA 考试的内容既包括一定深度的会计专业知识，也包括非常广泛的组织问题，这些问题对于管理会计师发挥专业人员的"商业合伙人"角色非常重要。

获得 CMA 资格需要付出很大的努力，完成四个部分的考试可能需要两年的学习时间。但这笔投资将使考生终身受益，能为他们的职业发展奠定坚实的基础，提升其职业发展水平。

如果考生希望通过这四个部分的考试，就必须制定一个严密的学习计划并切实执行该计划。IMA 为考生提供了很多资源、工具和方案，这些都有助于考生的学习和考试。我们鼓励考生充分利用这些有利条件，以最大化自己的学习效果。

如果希望得到关于 CMA 资格、CMA 考试或者 IMA 所提供的考试资源方面的更多信息，请访问网站 www. imanet. org。

前言

　　欢迎学习美国管理会计师协会 CMA 考试教材的第三部分，即战略管理。

　　第三部分考察的是成本管理的战略方面的知识。这部分以对战略规划概述开篇，主要关注当代成本管理方法和实践是怎样使企业在激烈的竞争中获得成功的。在这一部分，我们将主要阐述一个企业如何制定有别与众多竞争者的与众不同的战略，以及它怎样使其消费者和股东获得价值提升的基本理论。然后，我们将讨论理解产品和服务市场的重要性，以及怎样使卓越的组织能力和富有前景的价值机会最好地结合起来。随后，我们探讨的主要内容是风险管理的原则、如何有效地选择和管理不同的金融工具以帮助企业实现战略和目标、在决策过程中相关资料的重要性以及获取利润过程中分析和定价的战略意义。最后，本书以怎样用战略眼光看待资本预算和关于资本投资项目的不同技巧讨论为结尾。

CMA 考试的第三部分

　　CMA 资格考试由四个部分组成，前三部分的应试顺序可以颠倒，但只有在通过前三个部分的考试之后才能参加第四部分的考试。

　　CMA 考试的第三部分包括 110 个单项选择题，旨在全方位地测试考生的认知能力，考试时间为 3 个小时，计算机答题。这部分内容是在参考 ICMA 所制定的考试大纲和学习要点的基础上编写的，而且内容提要直接反映在各个教材的目录中。考试大纲和学习要点均可以从 IMA 的官方网站上下载。

　　在准备第三部分的考试时，考生应了解教材中涵盖的所有概念和各种计算方法，这一点非常重要。同样非常重要的是，考生应学会如何完成一个全面的选择题考试。为此，考生最好能制定一份详细的学习计划。

制定学习计划

　　CMA 资格考试的第三部分使用单项选择题的形式考察考生对该部分的概念、术语以及计算的理解情况。制定一份详细的学习计划是取得考试成功的重要保证，除此之外，严密地管理该学习计划对于取得成功也非常重要。考生在制定学习计划时可以参考以下建议。

　　1. 由于可以在一年中的任何时间参加第三部分的考试，因此考生的考试准备应该具有结构性。这意味着需要就特定知识点的学习设定目标日期，并将这些目标作为优先完成的事情。

　　• 考生应当确定与 ICMA 联系并注册参加第三部分考试的时间。在注册之后，应在学习计划中清楚标明参加考试的日期。

　　• 根据注册考试日期制定计划，决定第三部分学习的开始和结束日期。考生应全力以赴准备考试，第三部分学习的合理参考时间是 150 个小时。考生所需的实际时间长短取决于考生当前对第三部分知识的掌握程度，以及考生对考试的了解程度和对通过考试的信心。

- 回顾第三部分中的各个章节和问题，并且评估对每个章节的熟悉程度和掌握程度。

2. 跟踪学习进展，完成学习计划中每个部分的学习。考生最好在不超过 6 个月的时间内完成第三部分的学习。

3. 根据学习计划评估学习进展情况。完成与各章相关的练习题。

在线学习资料

为帮助考生顺利通过 CMA 考试，我们在互联网上提供了很多有价值的资源。考生可通过 www. imanet. org/china/examtools 了解所有可用的在线资源。

第1章
战略规划

本章内容简介

如今的商业竞争非常激烈。各个组织天天都面临着种种内在或外在的挑战和变化，这些挑战和变化影响着它们的运行甚至是生存。有些挑战和变化是不可避免的，有些是人为的结果，有些则是不可预知的。

战略规划将帮助一个组织主动地迎接这些不管是人为的还是不可预知的挑战和变化。当然仅仅一份战略规划并不能保证一个组织获得成功。但是假如没有一个深思熟虑的战略规划，一个组织却更可能成为市场竞争的牺牲品，而不是胜利者。

历史上，战略规划作为一种自上而下的活动成为企业精英们的专利。但是在 20 世纪 90 年代，战略规划变成一个更加大众化的活动而广受关注。今天，集体的主动性被普遍采用。

随着战略规划演变，管理会计师开始成为一个更为重要的角色。成本管理不再只是对产品或服务成本及财务报告的被动检查。现在，一个成本管理系统必须有助于企业的战略管理并且能够使它有效地处理影响企业成功的重要问题。本章将用简洁的语言描述在战略和战术规划、生产范式和业务流程绩效等领域中的核心概念，这些概念是不同层次的每一个管理会计师都应该知道的。

学习要点说明

注册管理会计师（CMA）考试包含很多学习要点，这些学习要点由管理会计师协会确定。学习要点描述了注册管理会计师考试要求掌握的所有知识点和技能，并且细分为各个章节。注册管理会计师考试教材解释了学习要点所包含的各个部分，是对学习要点的有力支持。学习要点可以帮助考生以不同的方式或通过不同的问题情景理解这些概念。考生还应该练习学习要点中所提到的全部或者部分计算，或者完成计算过程中的缺失部分。学习要点不能代替对 CMA 考试教材内容的研究和学习，但是可以确保考生达到学习要点所设定的目标。

注册管理会计师教材中所包含的学习要点是一个完整的集合，并且是到目前为止最新的版本。考生可以浏览 IMA 的官方网站 www.imanet.org，点击"认证"部分查看和下载关于学习要点的最新 PDF 文件。

学习要点

1.1 战略和战术规划

- LOS 1.1.1：讨论战略规划如何帮助一个组织确定的路径选择以达到其长远目标和任务。
- LOS 1.1.2：确定一个战略规划的合适时限。
- LOS 1.1.3：确定在战略规划过程中应该对哪些外部要素进行分析，理解怎样通过这些分析认清组织的机遇、局限和挑战。
- LOS 1.1.4：确定在战略规划过程中应该对哪些内部要素进行分析，并解释怎样通过这些分析认清组织的优势、劣势和竞争优势。
- LOS 1.1.5：阐述和理解怎样通过对外部和内部要素的分析确立一个组织的总体任务，并通过完成这个总体任务来实现那些更长远的目标，比如企业的多元化经营、增加或减少生产线或者进入新市场。
- LOS 1.1.6：知道资本预算和能力规划在战略规划中的作用。
- LOS 1.1.7：解释为什么短期目标、实现这些目标的战术以及经营规划（总预算）必须和战略规划一致，并且服务于长期战略目标的实现。
- LOS 1.1.8：解释为什么绩效评价和其他报告体系必须与战略和经营措施进度的度量保持一致，并对这些度量提供支持。
- LOS 1.1.9：知道成功的战略/战术规划的基本特征。
- LOS 1.1.10：定义应急规划并讨论它的重要性，尤其是当外部要素的变化将对战略规划起负面影响的时候。

1.2 生产范式

- LOS 1.2.1：定义什么是适时制（JIT）并阐述其中心目标。
- LOS 1.2.2：知道采用适时制的运营效益。
- LOS 1.2.3：定义术语看板并描述其在适时制中的应用。
- LOS 1.2.4：解释工作单元并阐述它和适时制的关系。
- LOS 1.2.5：定义什么是物料资源规划系统（MRP），并指出它的优点。
- LOS 1.2.6：使用MRP计算完成一个成品订单所需要的子单元。
- LOS 1.2.7：解释外包概念并指出选择外包的优点和局限。
- LOS 1.2.8：阐述对约束理论的理解及其分析步骤。
- LOS 1.2.9：定义并计算产量贡献并解释其与约束理论的关系。
- LOS 1.2.10：怎样理解限制驱导式排程法系统作为管理产品流通的一个工具。
- LOS 1.2.11：讨论为什么约束理论和作业成本法是相互补充的分析工具。
- LOS 1.2.12：知道其他现代生产概念，比如自动化、机器人的使用、计算机辅助设计、计算机集成制造以及弹性生产范式。

1.3 业务流程绩效

- LOS 1.3.1：定义什么是价值链分析。
- LOS 1.3.2：知道价值链分析的步骤。

- LOS 1.3.3：理解怎样通过价值链分析更好地了解一个企业的竞争优势。
- LOS 1.3.4：定义什么是增值作业，并解释增值概念和绩效改善的关系。
- LOS 1.3.5：解释流程分析，并阐述怎样通过业务流程重组改善业务流程绩效。
- LOS 1.3.6：分析一系列任务、活动和流程。
- LOS 1.3.7：定义什么是帕累托原理。
- LOS 1.3.8：怎样理解流程绩效的标准检查。
- LOS 1.3.9：知道标准检查在创造竞争优势中的作用。
- LOS 1.3.10：将作业管理原则运用于流程绩效的改善。
- LOS 1.3.11：理解持续改进技术、作业管理和质量指标之间的关系。
- LOS 1.3.12：理解持续改进（改善）概念及其与执行理想标准和质量改进的关系。
- LOS 1.3.13：定义什么是最佳实务分析，讨论一个组织怎样通过它改善绩效。

第 1 节
战略和战术规划

本节内容简介

一个企业的战略决定了它计划实现其目标的大方向。它代表着一个组织的集体意愿。企业的战略应该是它的核心竞争力与行业机会或威胁的有效结合。

战略规划（有时被称为长远规划）需全面考虑一个企业和它所在的行业、竞争者和环境之间的关系。在这个规划中，一个组织需标明它的目标和在实现这个目标中必须克服的困难，并且确定前进和克服困难的方法。虽然以往这些仅仅是高级管理层的职责，但是现在企业的每个职员都要参与到这个过程之中。深思熟虑的战略规划可以帮助一个组织熟练地度过动荡的时期，不管这个时期是好还是坏。

战略和战略规划

每一个管理有效的企业都会制定不同层次的战略和战略规划。尤其是主管和经理，他们通常会花很多时间来制定一个能够达到企业目标的战略，这些战略通常会形成正式的战略规划。

战略

战略是一个宽泛的概念。企业通常需要制定不同层次的战略。

图表 3 –1 展示的是企业通常制定的三个层次的战略：

- 整体性（或者多种业务）。
- 竞争性（或者一种业务）。
- 职能性（一种业务内）。

图表 3 –1　不同层次的战略

整体性	• 关注全部商业机遇，包括扩展海外市场、兼并和收购 • 分别使用财务和非财务的术语定义企业的价值 • 集中精力确定、建立或者获取重要的资源和能力 • 确定组织将进入什么行业及怎样把各种业务联系起来 • 决定在企业的各个业务中如何分配组织资源 • 设定企业将做和不将做什么的限制
竞争性	• 决定一个企业怎样在一个行业中实现自己，也就是该企业怎样在一个行业中创造价值 • 洞悉企业的服务对象，并知道如何向它们传递价值 • 把专门的活动和过程结合起来，使企业创造独特的价值 • 联合企业的各种活动，全力加强企业在竞争中的潜在优势
职能性	• 加强企业的竞争战略 • 设定市场营销、金融、科研、技术、运营等计划和目标 • 关注各种职能的协调 • 确定各种活动或流程，以帮助企业最大限度地扩大其竞争优势 • 阐明企业各种职能是否及怎样与竞争战略保持一致

整体性战略考虑的是企业大局，决定了恰当的业务组合，指出了企业的竞争环境

（即所处市场）。相反，竞争性战略和职能性战略则更注重具体战术上企业应当怎样在一个行业中竞争。虽然不同层次的战略会产生不同的结果，但是它们必须是一致的。

当然，不同企业的战略很不一样。比如，Dell、IBM 和东芝虽然处在同一个商业电脑的竞技场上，但它们争夺市场配额的战略却各不相同。相应的，不同的战略需要不同的任务、技术、优势和控制系统。

在当今充满竞争的环境里，企业的战略必须是动态的。企业战略的优势并不是由其初始行动决定的，而取决于它能否更好地：

- 预见竞争对手的行动。
- 预见并且/或者影响不断变化的消费者需求。
- 在一个不断变化的竞争环境中利用各种优势（比如：规范、技术、经济、全球机会或者事件）。
- 应对、选择并且执行备选的竞争战略。

对于一个有效的竞争战略来说，预见性和准备是非常关键的。它必须能对竞争对手、客户或者其他重要要素的每一种可能情况做出迅速的反应。

战略规划

图表 3-2 对战略规划进行了概念描述。

图表 3-2　战略规划的要素

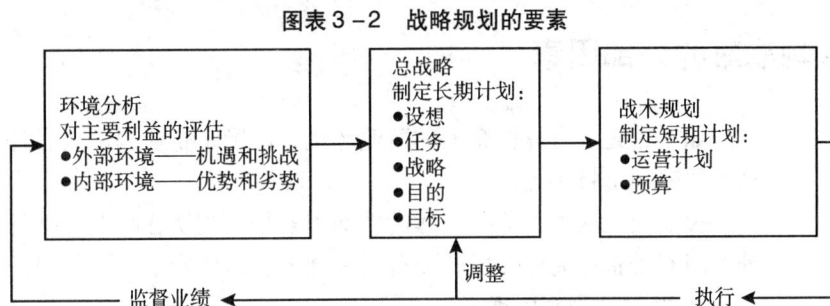

请记住，图表里只是概念化的表述，目的是为战略规划过程提供一个总图。实践中，战略规划的术语和方法在各种企业中不尽相同。企业设计各自的运营模式，并对战略规划过程的细节精益求精。企业本质、市场和利益相关者、规模、资源、组织能力和其他要素如生产过程的参与者及其力量、利益，最终指明了塑造运营模式的额外细节。

战略规划以多长时限为最佳？一年、三年、五年、十年都可以，并没有一定之规。企业根据不同行业、竞争程度（比如新的竞争对手）以及产品或服务的更新换代速度来制定不同时长的战略规划。比如，技术密集型的业务就应当制定时限较短的战略规划，以适应快速的变化及市场竞争压力。

很明显地，战略规划过程高度相关。核心要素相互关联；完成一个要素的同时要回顾以前的要素，并进行一些调整。最后，所形成的战略规划可以使我们洞悉一个企业怎样才能使自己保持持续的竞争优势。

战略与战略规划的关系

实际上，战略制定和战略规划有很多重合的地方。但是这两个过程在概念上有重大区别。

从根本上讲，战略制定产生新的战略，而战略规划则涉及怎样实施这些战略。其他区别包括：

- 战略制定产生组织目标；而管理人员则创造战略以实现这些目标。
- 战略规划形成实施战略并达到目标的战略。
- 战略规划是一个典型的按照时间表和规定程序进行的系统化过程。
- 理想的状态是战略应根据获知的机遇和挑战持续重估。

不考虑概念和进程上的相互重合或不一致，战略制定和战略规划都将不同程度地处理如下一些核心因素：

- 外部因素——认清企业的机遇、限制和挑战。
- 内部因素——认清企业的优势、劣势和竞争优势。
- S. W. O. T.（优势、劣势、机遇和挑战）分析——确定哪些帮助或者阻碍企业发展的因素。
- 长远设想、任务和目标——制定企业总体设想和任务，并制定企业长远目标。
- 实现长远目标的战术——制定短期计划和战术。

这些因素随后将逐一详述。

分析影响战略的外部因素

如果首先没有评估企业的商业环境，即确定企业内部或者外部正在或将要发生什么，战略制定将是无用功。

影响企业战略的那些具体的外部因素是由它所在行业和外部大环境决定的。各种外部因素是企业商业环境的典型组成部分。这些影响企业战略的重要外部因素包括：

- 法律和规范因素。
- 市场力量、行业趋势和竞争。
- 技术更新。
- 利益相关者群体及其社会利益。
- 全球化的趋势、新兴市场和非政府组织（比如联合国和世界银行等）。

在战略规划过程中，必须考虑到所有这些外部因素。

法律和规范因素

针对不同行业，法律和规范可能会相互关联。但是这两个因素也有一些明显的区别。

法律因素

法律要素是由法人实体（比如：联邦、州、郡/省或市的法律）颁布的行为准则；它们通过惩罚威胁强制实施。一系列的法律因素能影响产品/服务的成败，比如：

- 专利权。

- 版权。
- 商标。
- 反托拉斯法。
- 贸易保护主义。
- 产品/服务的责任问题。
- 环境责任。
- 关于就业的法律和诉讼。
- 遵守萨班斯—奥克斯利法案（SOX）。

规范因素

规范因素（或规范）是用来控制或监管各种行为的原则或规则。理论上讲，规范是自愿的。但很多情况下，规范具有法律效力。比如，假如一个企业不遵守规范因素，它很可能进不了目标市场。

法人主体代理机构和非政府组织（比如行业自律组织和专业协会）经常制定规范和处罚。不像法律因素有惩戒威胁强制实施，规范因素最常见的是通过自律、罚款和/或者限制权利等方式来保障实施。

影响企业战略的规范因素通常包括：

- 社会规范（并不限于如下举例）
  - 环境保护局（EPA）——对空气、水和土壤污染的限制标准。
  - 职业安全与卫生管理局（OSHA）——保护美国劳工安全和健康的标准。
  - 联邦贸易委员会（FTC）——保护消费者利益、要求厂家真实宣传和禁止厂家合谋（比如，限定售价和分配市场）的规范。
- 行业规范（并不限于如下举例）
  - 联邦航空局（FAA）——对机场、航运控制、安全问题和路线的要求。
  - 联邦通信委员会（FCC）——对广播和电视频率的规范。
  - 食品和药品管理局（FDA）——对食品和药品行业以及医疗器械制造业的安全要求。

法律和规范因素与战略规划的关系

法律和规范因素对组织战略的影响是非常普遍的。下面举几个简单的例子来说明法律和规范因素是怎样影响一个组织的。

- 影响一个企业选择怎样的方式参与竞争（比如通过反托拉斯法和许可证要求）。
- 限制全球运营（比如，通过贸易保护）。
- 阻碍或者促进技术创新（比如，通过关于税收和专利的政策）。
- 影响人力资源实务（比如，通过平等就业机会/反歧视法、工资和价格控制、《家庭和医疗假期条例》及雇员安全和健康规范）。
- 限制营销活动（比如，通过 FTC 控制）。
- 施加环境义务（比如，通过 EPA 控制）。
- 提高资本要求（比如，通过要求企业采用先进技术以达到政府监管要求）。

由此可知，许多法律和规范因素是针对特定行业的，有一些是跨行业的。有些法律和规范要素甚至是专门针对某个公司的。

上述法律和规范因素，由于会导致潜在的重大成本从而会很大程度上直接影响管理会计。比如，EPA 或者 OSHA 规范的变化可能会要求企业增加巨额资金投入以符合规定。

其他几个对管理会计有特别影响的因素：

- 证券交易委员会（SEC）用于保护投资者利益和维护证券市场诚信的法律和规范。
- 萨班斯—奥克斯利法案关于内部控制的调整。
- 国内税务署（IRS）的法令。
- 国会对最低工资和/或加班补贴的调整。
- 由州政府监管的保险和银行业委员会对业务行为方式及各种金融工具记账方式的规范。

市场力量、行业趋势和竞争

历史已经证明，政府放松管制、全球化、科技创新、苛刻的消费者、变化的人口和社会预期等因素使看似非常稳定的商业竞技场发生戏剧性的变化。因此，战略规划很重要的一部分便是行业分析，也就是对那个充满竞争的竞技场进行彻底的评估，内容包括企业必须面对的竞争者以及竞争的结构和范围。

同战略规划的其他方面一样，没有一个明确的方法用来确定竞争范围或预见竞争对手行动。但是绝大多数行业分析都会考虑如下因素：

- 新竞争对手的进入。
- 替代品的威胁。
- 买方的谈判能力。
- 供应商的谈判能力。
- 现有竞争对手之间的竞争。

迈克尔·波特创立了一个模型以确定这五种因素分别以及共同决定竞争力和盈利性所起的作用。图表 3 – 3 展现了波特的模型。

图表 3 – 3　推动行业盈利的五种力量

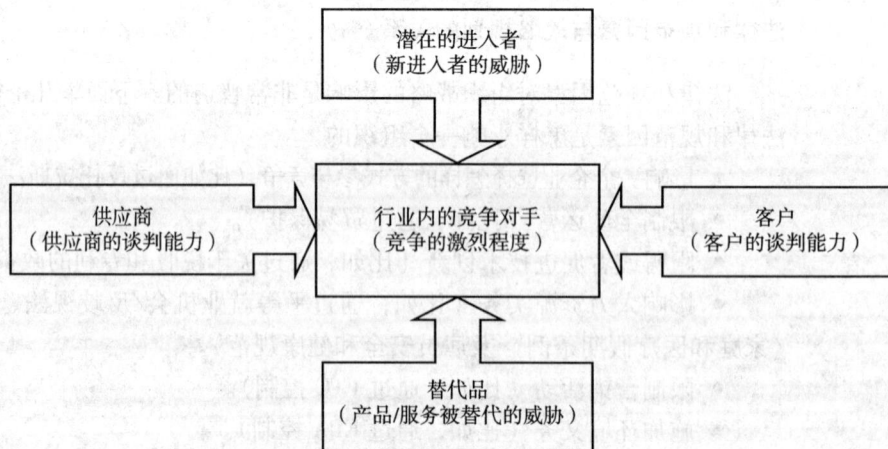

资料来源：改编自迈克尔·波特的《竞争优势——创造与保持优异业绩》。

接下来关于波特五力模式的讨论是对波特两本书《竞争战略：产业与竞争者分析技巧》（1980）和《竞争优势：创造与保持优异业绩》（1985）以及由戴伊和雷布斯坦合著的沃顿商学院的《动态竞争战略》（1997）里面观点的综合。

新竞争对手的进入

一个新进入市场的企业（新成员）通常带有新的能力和资源。为了和新成员竞争，市场中的原有企业会降低销售价格或者提高产品的成本，从而可能导致盈利性下降。

新竞争对手的威胁取决于进入壁垒的大小。进入壁垒对充满希望的新成员非常不利，会降低它们的预期利润。

进入壁垒的例子包括：

- **原有企业的成本优势**

这个优势包括原有企业的廉价劳动力或低资本成本、获取原材料的更好途径、政府补贴、有利的地理位置、领先的技术和产品设计以及不断积累的经验。对于一个刚起步的企业，没有任何经验，它的成本通常要比原有企业高；为了积累经验，高额的起步损失和低于或接近成本的售价通常是正常的。

- **规模经济**

规模经济通常被定义为随着每期产量增加而导致的单位成本下降，它可以阻止一个新成员的进入。为对抗原有企业的强烈反应，新成员需要在更大规模和更高风险水平上进行生产。如果一个新成员决定采用小规模生产，那么它将面临成本劣势。设施、研究、营销、销售队伍范围和分销等规模经济实例都潜在地要求巨额的进入投资。

- **产品/服务差异**

差异是指一个新成员必须克服的品牌认同感及现有消费者对原有产品的忠诚度。新成员必须投入时间和金钱打造自己的品牌。而且假如企业进入失败的话，这种投资并不能保证企业成功或使其获取残值。

- **转换成本**

假如一个买家想放弃一个供应商的产品和服务转而购买另一个新进入供应商的产品和服务，其一次性转换成本是非常巨大的。购买/安装新设备、重新培训员工是两项比较常见的转化成本。新成员必须能节省大笔费用或带来潜在的绩效改善才能确保买家放弃以前的供应商而转向自己。

- **渠道拥挤**

许多分销渠道能力有限，或具有限制制造商生产线数量的排他性权利。说服分销商接受一条新生产线通常需要花费很多时间。一个新成员可能要向分销商支付较高的利润以抵消给其带来的额外成本，否则新成员可能要被迫去寻找一个缝隙市场。

- **原有企业的预期反应**

进入壁垒可能会提高或降低，取决于原有企业保护自己过去地位的强烈程度。那些资产雄厚、持久力强的原有企业，如果愿意在短期内减少利润以维护其市场占有率，这将对新成员产生巨大打击。如果原有企业不太在乎以前的新成员，或不太愿意维护自身的地位，就会鼓励新成员。

替代品的威胁

当一个令人满意的替代产品或服务——既拥有相同功能并能够提供同样好处——出现时，平均价格会降低，其利润空间也会受挤压。产品和服务的价值也就随之减少。所以说，更加便宜但又令人满意的替代品也构成威胁。

电子监视器和警报系统对保安企业的影响仅仅是一个行业受到可用替代品威胁的一个例子。另一个例子是顾客现在可以直接在网上而不用通过传统的分销渠道购物。面对这种情形，关键是在揭示产品或服务相似点的同时，寻找超越这些相似点的差异化机会。例如保安行业的例子，企业可以将保安和电子监控系统作为一个增值包同时提供，并把保安定位为监控系统的熟练操作者。

买方的谈判能力

商品和服务的买方（客户）和卖方（供应商）可以有各种各样的关系。在大规模营销的情况下，他们的关系可以是紧密整合的精益生产系统，也可能是一个领域的两端。买方力量的增强或阻碍特别取决于谈判杠杆和价格灵敏度。

谈判杠杆：一般来讲，杠杆是任何用以形成优势的战略或战术手段。如下因素可增强买方谈判杠杆：

- **几个关键客户的大量购买**

在这种情况下，卖方有些依赖于几个关键客户。一旦关系紧张，卖方就会遇到问题。

- **客户可以轻易转换产品**

假如提供的产品或服务差异性不大、转换成本较低或容易获得低成本替代品，客户可能会转换供应商。

- **向后整合的能力**

当前价格和/或其他条件可以使备选方案比继续外购更有吸引力（比如，购买上游供应商的产品，或把一些以前外包的产品改为家庭作坊式的生产）。

- **客户的"内幕知识"**

假如客户知道供应商的成本和利润，或了解到供应商需要这份业务来补偿其过剩的生产能力或减轻其他方面的压力，客户就会获得谈判杠杆。

价格敏感度：价格敏感度是测量低价格对客户是否重要的指示器。如下因素将提高敏感度：

- **产品或服务影响终端产品的质量**

相对于那些对终端产品质量影响非常小的产品/服务来说，对于那些一旦出现问题将对终端产品质量产生重大影响的产品或服务，买家会更关注其价格。

- **产品或服务价格与客户总成本相关**

高价产品更易受到更加严格的采购审查，而低价杂项产品则通常不在成本备案的分析范围内。

- **买方利润**

当客户利润率非常低时，他们通常要求供应商做出价格让步。在企业的生死关头，这种要求价格让步的压力非常紧迫。

如果买方未觉察到相互竞争的供应商之间的差异，价格敏感度将会进一步加强。

供应商的谈判能力

供应商忍受客户谈判的能力可以反映有助于提升买方谈判力量的情况。供应商的谈判能力由如下因素决定：

- **供应商相对客户的规模大小**

一个较大的供应商对一个小的、分散的小客户来说有明显的优势和杠杆。

- **客户对供应商产品或服务的依赖程度**

依赖程度随着客户买不到等价物、投入不易贮藏（所以买方不能积蓄存货）或转换成本较高的程度不同而不同。

- **向前整合的威胁**

如果供应商可以把产品直接卖给最终使用者，客户谈判杠杆将较低从而不能取得更好的价格。

现有竞争对手之间的竞争

在某些情况下，竞争者可以共存。而在另外一些情况下，直接的竞争对手经常运用各种战术来谋取市场份额，如暂时性降价、特别的促销、广告闪电战、进攻性地推出新产品、提高客服质量、延长保证保修等。随着竞争者的跟进，这些做法的价值会逐渐下降。

电信运营商削减价格以全力赢取新客户、弥补固定成本的做法而出名。但是，这种行为通常会使利润减少，而市场份额却没有任何变化。

如下因素对竞争者关系状况有代表性影响：

- **竞争结构**

当几个势均力敌的竞争者或许多小企业共享一个市场时，竞争最激烈。高层竞争者之间的对抗可能会升级；一旦企业倾向于对抗和报复，不稳定性通常会随之产生。在有众多小企业的情况下，这些公司可能会采取一些其他公司不太注意的行动。但是，假如有一个起主导地位的竞争者，当追随者想在主导者的庇护下共存时，竞争通常会减少。

- **成本结构**

当固定成本较高时，产能利用就会被强调。任何产能过剩都会导致降价和新一轮的价格竞争。

- **产品或服务差异**

如果不存在差异，客户通常关注的是价格、期限等，这样竞争就会很激烈。相反，如果差别太大导致客户有不同的偏好，喜欢不同的品牌，那么竞争就会减少。产品差异会促使买方对个别供应商产生偏好和忠诚。自然地，企业总是寻求可以持续的差异（比如，一个很难模仿的、保持有用性的、客户愿意付费的特色）。

- **客户的转换成本**

把客户和供应商绑定在一起的客户转换成本有效地防止了竞争对手对客户的抢

夺。比如，改变电脑操作系统会给客户带来操作的中断和高昂的成本。

- **竞争对手战略及目标的多样性**

当所有竞争者拥有相似的战略、成本结构、管理哲学的时候，它们很容易就能预见到各自的目标并且能准确地预知面对市场改变所采取的行动。但是，当竞争者拥有不同的背景（比如外资、国有、小型私企和大型企业）时，它们各自的行为和活动就很难预知。

- **高退出壁垒**

甚至当利润非常低时，退出壁垒也会使企业陷入困境。比如，企业宁愿忍受生产能力过剩所带来的利润外流，也不肯把它卖给其他的厂家，因为害怕其以后将会威胁企业的其他市场。同时，管理人员出于对企业或员工忠诚的感情原因，也会抵制经济上合理的退出决策。

五种力量与战略规划的联系

波特认为这五种力量——新竞争者的进入、替代品的威胁、买方的谈判能力、供应商的谈判能力以及现有竞争对手之间的竞争——作为一个整体决定了该行业竞争的激烈程度以及盈利性。换句话说，这五种竞争力量的合力决定了企业获取超过资本成本的投资回报率的能力。

在五种力量均对行业（比如，制药业）有利时，利润非常可观。而在五种力量的一种或几种出现问题（比如在航运业）时，即使管理得再好企业也很少能够有好的回报。波特指出行业的盈利性不是产品外观的函数，也不是服务是包含高科技还是落后技术的函数，它是由产业结构决定的。这就是为什么一个看起来很普通的产品（比如汽车修配用零部件）利润非常之高，而一个迷人的高科技产品（比如一部手机）并不能给所有企业都带来高额利润。

很大程度上，这五种力量并不是固定不变的。从这个方面来讲，它们：

- 在各个行业都有所不同。
- 随着市场的变化而变化。
- 在每个行业中都不是同等重要的。
- 容易受高增长和市场需求影响（假如一个产业吸引了过多的竞争者就会导致过分拥挤）。

自然地，不同企业有自己独特的优点和缺点，从而影响它们处理甚至改变产业结构的能力。

在战略制定过程中，理解产业结构是一个非常重要的开端。不同的力量会呈现重要作用。最强的一个或多个力量在战略规划和战略制定过程中起着越来越重要的作用。

技术创新

所有行业都必须考虑技术创新的战略含义，以下几点便是证明：

- 技术可以创造行业替代品（比如，无线电话替代了有线电话）。
- 技术可以减少大规模分销的需要，从而为新成员开辟市场（比如，以网络为基础的电子商务技术代替传统的分销渠道）。

- 技术可以加速新产品的设计，并促进制造业短期生产的发展，从而导致激烈的竞争或垄断。
- 根据其被采用的领域，技术可以而改变一个企业与其供应商或者买方的力量平衡。
- 技术可以改变产业结构，从而促进或破坏平均盈利性。

那些知道获取和利用技术的企业通常更善于获得或继续保持竞争优势。某种程度上讲，技术创新既是一个外部因素也是一个内部因素。技术影响一个企业提供什么样的产品和服务、怎样生产该产品和服务、怎样服务客户以及必须和谁竞争等。同样地，技术也会影响一个企业的战略意图和竞争策略。

技术评估的特点

技术不仅涉及各个企业，也关系到一个企业的各项活动。考虑到技术涉及面之广以及它对营销成功的重要性，一个企业应当在持续发展的基础上对其技术能力进行评估。

《工商管理硕士便携本》（布鲁纳等人，1998）列出了技术评价的五个步骤：

1. 确认核心技术。
2. 分析现在和将来潜在的技术变化。
3. 分析技术带来的竞争性影响。
4. 分析企业的技术优势和劣势。
5. 建立企业的技术优先权。

第一步：确认核心技术。

在技术评估的第一步，所有对企业有影响的技术都要被确认。这涉及到现在的和将来的以及企业内部及外部的技术。

应该考虑的一般分类如下：

- 生产技术。
- 制造或服务加工技术。
- 具有支持功能的技术（比如营销、客服、金融和会计）。
- 信息管理技术。
- 竞争企业所用的技术。
- 本企业产品和服务的卖方或买方所采用的技术。

应当关注那些当下还没有被采用的技术，特别是那些将来有可能被采用的技术。比如一个尚未发展电子商务的小企业可以去观察其他行业电子商务的发展情况以及它如何影响这些企业当下的产品和加工。

第二步：分析现在和将来潜在的技术变化。

这一步涉及评价所有确认的重要技术的短期及长期变化。复杂技术可能会包含多层次的分支技术。评估必须考虑到所有的分支技术。

分析潜在变化的指南如下：

- 技术评估应当由那些技术专家来指导进行。
- 评估应当由其他人有建设性地检验并质疑，以避免根据毋庸置疑的常识进行预测的可能性。

- 技术开发具有多样性。对竞争企业十分关键的技术可能要比对该企业竞争优势而言必要但不重要的技术发展得更快。

- 成熟技术也不总是更新缓慢，特别是需要技术进步和更新换代时。当一项新技术为新成员提供机会时，成熟技术也会发生迅速变化。

第三步：分析技术带来的竞争性影响。

这一步旨在回答下列关键问题：

- 什么样的技术或技术进步能给一个企业带来最大的竞争优势？

- 什么样的技术或技术进步会成为竞争企业手中最大的威胁？

- 什么样的技术或技术进步能对行业结构的变化产生重大影响？

具有竞争性影响力的技术通常可以划分为如下几类：基础技术、关键技术、决定技术。

- 基础技术被广泛应用于某一行业中。这种技术已经被很好地理解了。它十分必要，但是并不提供竞争优势。

- 关键技术，顾名思义，就是对竞争优势有关键作用的技术。这种技术有助于企业生产出差异性产品或服务。有些情况下，该技术能使企业依靠低成本进行竞争。专利、非专利技术或技术应用的领先经验通常构成了一个企业的关键技术优势。

- 决定技术是指那些具有重塑行业或改变整个竞争基础潜力的技术。它经常会取代关键技术。当开发出决定技术的企业并非是该行业的龙头企业时，改变行业领导权的机会就出现了。由于许多市场龙头企业觉得决定技术太异乎寻常或觉得这类技术会与现存的产品、服务和流程产生冲突，它们往往会忽视决定技术，这种态度是十分危险的。

第四步：分析企业的技术优势和劣势。

管理者必须根据技术分类和开发每项技术的潜在成本评估企业的优势和劣势。评估过程中，管理者应将本企业的优势和劣势与它的竞争者相对比，不但要看眼下，还要顾及将来的变化。

正像在 S. W. O. T. 分析（企业的优势、劣势、机遇和挑战的分析）中，评估往往会因为骄傲、不情愿揭露本企业弱点或看不得别的企业优势而发生歪曲。为了确保客观，最好能够组织一个团队来进行评估，该团队应包括理解技术的科技专家和专攻经营及营销的管理者。

第五步：建立企业的技术优先权。

基于技术评估的结果，企业可以设立出一套尝试性的优先项目，这套项目可以涉及产品、服务、加工技术等多方面的采购、开发和使用。技术评估同样也应考虑建立高度整合技术系统的利弊——企业目前是否具有高度整合的技术系统或者正在考虑建立这样的体系。

- 整合的好处：整合促进数据库的同步更新。决策制定可获得最新的数据。与独立应用相比，整合可以降低数据录入和处理成本。

- 整合的风险：系统整合需要巨额的投资、全面的设计、周到的项目管理和执行以及及时的系统特征培训和过渡过程。整合是一个系统工程。整合往往需要企业牺牲较长时期（比如，两年或更长的时间）的增长和灵活性，这会使企业相对竞争对手而言资源受限、不堪一击。更重要的是，一旦计划失败，消费者会不满意，经济上会遭受损失，并会使整个企业变得更加脆弱。

技术评估与战略规划的关系

通过企业领导和各职能部门管理者之间的互动，技术评估中所获得的对企业的洞察可以衍生出企业的技术战略。

一个健全的技术战略应包括如下特点：

- 提高企业中技术战略的地位。
- 为企业的协作和竞争战略提供支持。
- 短期目标和长期目标计划以及包括总目标和分布目标的重大项目。
- 资源配置。
- 与企业财务计划和预算协调一致。
- 衡量成就的标准。

技术战略也应当是易懂的并且易于交流的。关键人物所作的承诺必须得到保障。

在始终牢记企业战略定位的同时，技术战略应对企业创新和技术发展建立基本的优先权和承诺。只有这样，技术评估才能形成技术战略，并最终成为整个战略规划的一部分。

利益相关者和它们的社会利益

利益相关者一般包括个人、单位、团体、组织和其他群体。它们以投资或者获取利息的方式参与一个企业的成功或行动。它们包括：

- 执行官。
- 经理和员工（包括他们的家人）。
- 公司董事会。
- 股东。
- 公司所处行业。
- 客户。
- 竞争对手。
- 供应商。
- 业务伙伴。
- 咨询顾问。
- 债权人。
- 特殊利益群体——行业、政治、客户等。
- 工会。
- 政府监管机构。
- 公司所处社团。
- 国家。
- 环境——植物、动物、生态系统、自然资源。
- 教育机构。
- 媒体。
- 未来一代。

在战略规划中，确定各个股东理解他们对公司的预期和潜在影响，并确保他们的需求和利益得到保障是非常重要的。即使不在董事会任职，股东也能够停止提供资源和支持，并可以潜在地决定公司的合法性。

在对社会负责任的同时使股东价值最大化

股东价值最大化是针对营利公司而言的，一般是指一家企业的市场价值。利润最大化需要考虑边际成本和一条需求曲线。当然，一家企业应赚取至少等于风险资本成本的利润。尽管利润最大化和股东价值最大化对企业成功很关键，但二者并不是企业的惟一目标。

经营的社会责任是指组织应当成为一个好的公司并担当积极改善民生的社会义务。这种做法的前提是公司必须承担与利润最大化相补充的社会义务，而不只是争夺最大化的利润。这个原理表明公司行为应该平衡所有利益相关者的要求，因此公司领导者对所有利益相关者而不仅仅是公司的执行官和股东具有信托责任。

公司在试图承担社会责任时自然会遇到很多挑战。一些常见的例子如下：

- 会计实务——内部交易。
- 广告——准确的真实的产品/服务说明。
- 公司重组——临时解雇。
- 多样化问题——种族、民族、性别取向。
- 员工隐私问题——药物检测、药品依赖、艾滋病。
- 骚扰问题——性别或年龄歧视。
- 环境问题——污染、动物权利。
- 跨国经营——行贿、任人惟亲及其他在别国被接受的但却挑战企业道德规范的问题。
- 竞争——掠夺性定价，反托拉斯行为。

利益相关者分析

大多数组织会使用一些利益相关者分析模型评估道德挑战及怎样最好地尽到社会责任。利益相关者分析给组织提供了一个框架，使其能够权衡所有要求及利益相关者利益，从而使其作出对社会负责任的决策。

利益相关者分析一般使用矩阵。图表 3-4 给出了该方法的主要步骤。

图表 3-4　股东分析框架的步骤

步骤 1	确认利益相关者；使主要参与者集体献计献策
步骤 2	确定利益相关者需要；通过面谈、集中座谈、调查问卷等收集信息观点
步骤 3	用矩阵将组织目标和利益相关者需要列出来
步骤 4	用符号标示组织目标和利益相关者需要的效用（例如，用 +，-或?）
步骤 5	以所记录的效用为基础制定决策

用以上方式所作的利益相关者分析使决策能够：

- 改变组织目标。
- 满足利益相关者需求。

- 减少潜在的纠纷。
- 如果可以共存或接受就通过。

图表 3-5 列举了利益相关者分析的一个例子。在这个分析中，一个产品分销商计划建造自动化仓库，并安装昂贵的高科技传动装置。这个矩阵分析了利益相关者。此分析指出不存在所谓的"正确"方式；与此表存在差异是可能的。利益相关者分析的意义就是处理这样的利益相关者问题，并且做出深思熟虑、一致合理的决策。

图表 3-5　利益相关者分析例证——使一家产品仓库实现自动化

（＋或－）	公司	员工	消费群体	供应商	政府监管人员
损害和收益	－更高成本 ＋更高利润	＋更多自由时间 －更少的时间和潜在的解雇	＋更低的价格 ＋对市场的快速反应；更少的损坏	－新硬件	＋权力和影响
权利和义务	＋价值 ＋所有者和股东的利润	＋竞争的市场地位	？可能的质量问题 ？公共利益	？满足需求的能力	＋保护公众 ＋规范行业

实施利益相关者分析也可采用其他一些可行方法。一些企业通过回答一系列指导性问题来进行利益相关者分析：

- 谁是主要的利益相关者？
- 每个利益相关者最重要的价值是什么？（例如，每个利益相关者的损害和收益是什么？）
- 争议的权利和责任是什么？
- 什么样的原则和规定是相关的？
- 一些相关的类似案例是什么？
- 应该做些什么？

利益相关者分析与战略规划的关系

有许多方法可以管理一个企业。施乐的管理模式不同于富士通。嘉信理财处理事情的方式不同于德科。但是所有企业都与其利益相关者相互作用影响。

利益相关者分析有助于公司形成其企业社会责任感。它明确了好的公民身份在企业中的作用。通过利益相关者分析，一个企业应该学会：

- 人们对组织及其所处行业的看法。
- 基于何种考虑，公司应该重新思考或重新评价它的地位。
- 公司应该怎样改变以改善自己的地位。

股东价值和利益相关者分析不是相互独立的。与公司目标一致的、权衡费用和收入的明显决策通常是很谨慎的行为。然而，挑战仍然存在。例如，一个组织会面临为了许多人的利益而必须牺牲一个人利益的情况。但是大多数组织也会力求为所有利益相关者做正确的事，同时为股东赚取满意的利润。

全球化

全球化指一个组织将业务转为国际化经营。全球化反映了组织战略，是对世界范围经营进行整合的过程。

虽然全球化很普遍且成为许多组织设定的目标，但是一个组织不可能简单地在一夜之间就变成全球化的经济实体。业务从国内到全球的迁移一般会经历一系列相对可以预知的阶段。

- **出口**

对于多数公司这是初始阶段。开始时，公司通过对客户、进出口公司及独立的代理商或分销商进行直接销售，将产品或服务出口到国外。来自出口的国际销售额一般只占所有收入的一小部分。它们被看作是国内销售的辅助。

- **国际分部和销售子公司**

随着国际销售重要性的不断提高，公司很可能建立独立的国际分部和/或销售子公司。在此阶段，国内和国际业务之间需要有更强的沟通和联系。

销售子公司一般是在销售额相当大的一个或多个国家设立的经营分支。子公司的规模可以是相对较小的办公室，也可以是商店、服务中心或制造厂等，这取决于业务的数量和性质。

- **跨国公司**

随着销售量和国家数量的大幅提高，一家公司进入到跨国公司阶段。跨国公司一般会在一些国家经营业务，并且将每一个国家的业务都看作是相对独立的实体。跨国公司通常会保持诸如融资、招聘、营销等一些职能工作的全球协调。或者这个公司可能变成有多个地域总部、更加协调的地区化结构。

- **全球化公司**

对于全球化公司，整个世界是一个市场。国家间没有地域界限。公司的总部可设在任何地方。

全球化公司的特征如下，但并不仅限于此：

- 全球战略规划。
- 产品和服务的全球化设计和营销。
- 技术和创新的全球化追求。
- 在所有业务中分享全球化的技术和创新；运用到单个市场。
- 只要成本、质量和周期时间有利且需求充足，就开发产品和服务。
- 在发现的最物美价廉地区寻求资源（如资金、原料、零件、保险和人力等）。
- 员工在各国家间自由流动。

- **联盟、合伙、合资等**

本阶段不一定要取代跨国公司或全球化公司。但是它给组织提供了一条渠道，可以将一些以前无法得到的资源（如研发和设计、技术、员工、生产设施等）变为资本。

下面是该阶段的两个例子：

- 一家大型的电信公司将技术资源分包给其他国家，包括主要竞争对手。
- 两家国际电子公司集中资源，联手设计开发精密的计算机芯片，并将其分销到120多个国家。

全球化与战略规划的关系

有时，全球化各阶段的命名和分类会与上面的稍有不同。当然，很明显，并不是每个公司都会按部就班地经历每个阶段。一些可能会由于合并收购等原因加快步伐。另一些则故意演变得非常慢，可能花几年的时间从出口商转变成跨国公司或全球化公司。一些公司的这些阶段会有所重叠。例如，在多个国家有业务的公司可能在一个国家处于出口商的阶段，而在另一个国家已是跨国公司。但是不管怎样命名，阶段的数量及公司全球化的时间构架都有助于认识全球化的进程。

随着一家公司全球化进程的推进，它需要获得另外的技术和才能。随着公司变成羽翼丰满的跨国企业或者全球化公司，它的各种活动和职能也在发展进化。例如，随着全球化进程的深入，国际融资技巧和税务知识也变得越来越重要。

分析影响战略的内部因素

为了对影响战略的外部因素评估进行补充，一个组织必须实施内部能力分析。这两种评估方法——外部（从外部看）和内部（从内部看）——有助于公司确定其当前的能力，并消除其与行业成功所需能力的差距。

内部能力分析的评估内容

内部能力分析尤其有助于确保公司拥有资源、技能和方法去实现自己的战略和战术目标。

- **资源**

资源的内部评估会考虑能够支持或妨碍组织主动权的融资、设施、装备及其他基础设施问题。评估资源需要审查财务报表、其他分析工作及定量信息。支持增长战略需要资本投资分析。支持正在进行的项目需要价值链分析和审查作业成本法的信息（注意：价值链分析的其他信息会在本章第 3 节"业务流程绩效"中提到）。

- **技能**

技能评估须检查员工的当前教育水平，需要的核心知识和技能，以及需要的特定技术及组织技能。当公司面临竞争压力时，员工必须做好充分准备。为了保险起见，应该作出培训的承诺。

- **流程**

当对获得竞争优势所必需的组织流程进行评估时，需要考虑周期时间和各种能力问题（注意：流程分析会在本章第 3 节"业务流程绩效"中进一步探讨）。

怎样评估内部资源，技能和生产

对于内部能力分析没有统一的方法，因为每个公司都是独特的。组织可能从以下例子中选择所需的工具和技术：

- 美国国家质量奖标准（用于自评）。
- ISO9001 质量认证体系和 ISO14000 环境管理体系的要求（用于差距分析）。
- 标杆流程（理解同业最佳）。

- 竞争分析（例如，分析竞争对手业务的五种力量，市场份额等）。
- 员工能力评估（确定当前知识、技能、经验和才智）。
- 培训需求分析（确定能支持组织主动权的培训需求）。
- 内部倾听设置（收集客户数据等）。
- 员工调查（确定员工是否理解企业的重心，评估目前工作环境、补偿方法、管理等方面的状况和/或问题）。
- 审计（确保流程在规定的限度内进行）。

无论一个组织选择怎样的方式评估内部因素，内部事务的优先权都不应该低于公司面临的外部环境挑战。若没有合适的内部能力，一个组织很难被迫去处理外部事务。内部缺口会限制一个组织实现其战略性的外部主动权。

内部能力分析与战略规划的关系

从定义看，内部能力分析有两个阶段。第一个阶段是获得一个关于目前处境的快照，并确定缺口。第二个阶段是做出将关键缺口缩小到想要水平的决策。一些缺口的处理可能相当简单而且直接；另一些可能需要花相当的资本和时间去处理。开发新能力的成本和收益需要仔细权衡。

不同的能力支持不同的竞争优势。一个组织未来的成功通常取决于它发展的能力。需要财务投资的能力是有风险的，因为回报不确定；一些投资可能无法挽回。但是即使没有投资也会有风险，因为：

- 落后于竞争对手。
- 不能持续盈利。
- 损害现有能力，以致失去机遇。

许多企业的战略规划停滞是因为它们不能评估内部能力。不理解完成战略所需要的内部要求和能力，用意良好的战略就会变成经营计划。最后，在评估内部能力并妥当处理它们时，适当的勤奋有助于使公司为将来的机遇做好准备。

S. W. O. T. 分析（优势、劣势、机遇和挑战分析）

S. W. O. T. 是优势、劣势、机遇、挑战四个词语的首字母缩写词。S. W. O. T. 分析为确定各种因素提供了一个框架，这些因素将会帮助或阻碍公司在其经营环境中的发展。S. W. O. T. 分析有时也被称作当前境况分析。

环境分析框定了公认的大背景，并确定了一家组织必须处理的顶尖问题；S. W. O. T. 分析将在另一个层次上聚焦战略规划。公司一般会通过 S. W. O. T. 分析为战略规划收集额外的信息。

从本质上来说，S. W. O. T. 分析提供了对那些来自内部和外部详细分析中的数据进行组织的方法。优势和劣势在组织的内部分析中被确定；机遇和挑战是对公司营运环境进行的外部分析的一部分（外部环境实质上是可能对组织产生影响的所有外部因素）。

优势

确定组织优势应回答这个问题：公司真正擅长的是什么？换句话说，是什么技能、能力和核心竞争力帮助组织实现目标并保持竞争地位？

组织优势可能是以下几种：

- 强大的领导阶层。
- 金融稳定。
- 组织的学识。
- 研究开发。
- 创新产品设计。
- 突破性的技术。
- 产品开发。
- 产品组装。
- 强大的分销渠道。
- 强大的市场地位。

一个或多个优势可以提供竞争优势，帮助组织在市场上独树一帜。例如，如果一家公司有杰出的研发能力，那么它可以把精力集中在机构内部产品的开发上，以建立或加强一项竞争优势。相反的，把资源分散到太多的领域会削弱组织的竞争地位。

劣势

确定组织劣势应回答这个问题，公司需要改善什么？什么是我们需要的但现在尚未具备的？更确切地说，劣势是组织缺少的技能、能力及竞争力，它们会妨碍组织完成自己的目的。劣势也可以被认为有待提高的机会。更进一步说，前面列示的优势的例子可能是或者会变成劣势。换句话说，一项能力可能变成一项缺陷。

面对不足，一个组织一般有三种选择：

- 调整目标使其可以达到。
- 进行必要投资以获取所需的知识和/或技能。
- 找到另外一家有所需的专门技术的组织，然后将该需求外包给或形成联盟。

例如，有一家小的制造公司，它没有资金或者能够安装热处理高炉的工厂。它可以使"劣势"外包，或者若此能力对于公司运作至关重要，则它应该为此投入资本金。

机遇和挑战

机遇一般被描述为能够帮助组织实现目标并增长到更高水平的事件、趋势等。机遇的例子是指有一些机会去：

- 拓展客户基础——机遇因需求、有利的人口转移等造成的客户数量增加。
- 提供新的接触客户的渠道——分销渠道或服务绑定等。
- 提高产品/服务对客户的吸引力——新的广告宣传媒介，或把竞争对手客户吸引过来的新的包装方法。
- 利用竞争对手的弱势——通过投资机遇促进客户接受公司的产品/服务。

挑战是一个组织增长的障碍。它们经常因事件、趋势和竞争对手的行动而产生。挑战的例子是可能是这样一些情况：

- 降低企业客户基础的规模——因为经济下滑、不利的人口移动、客户的自给自足等。
- 开通客户渠道更加困难或花费巨大——因为客户购买习惯发生改变或者与更小的供应商进行买卖等。
- 降低企业产品/服务对客户的吸引力——价格战或其他导致客户选择其他产品的活动。
- 超过企业产品/服务的提供能力——降低价格或新的有重大提高的产品/服务出现（例如，技术的竞相提高）。

与优势和劣势相似，机遇和挑战是二元的——同一事件或趋势既可以是机遇，也可能是挑战。企业处理机遇和挑战的方式不同。总之，一个组织应该注意为机遇提供资本，而对挑战予以还击。

S. W. O. T. 加权平均的例子

在实施 S. W. O. T. 数据分析时，加权平均是很有用的。

例如：

对 S. W. O. T. 数据使用加权平均法进行战略选择，具体做法如下。

ABC 公司已经确定了能够影响其市场吸引力和业务优势的下列因素。每一项都赋予一个不同的比重，这些比重加起来的和为1。级别从1（最高）到5（最低）。

市场吸引力	比重	级别（1 到 5）
市场规模	0.3	4
市场盈利性	0.4	5
分销结构	0.2	4
政府监管	0.1	2

业务优势	比重	级别（1 到 5）
单位成本	0.4	3
客户忠诚度	0.5	2
品牌声誉	0.1	4

经过计算，市场吸引力的加权平均数为4.2，业务优势的加权平均数为2.6，具体计算过程如下。因为较高的市场吸引力可能会吸引其他对手进入市场，所以建立在较低业务优势上（而不是试图开发较高的市场吸引力）的战略规划应该是最有利的。

市场吸引力 = (0.3 × 4 + 0.4 × 5 + 0.2 × 4 + 0.1 × 2 = 4.2)

业务优势 = (0.4 × 3 + 0.5 × 2 + 0.1 × 4 = 2.6)

T. O. W. S. （挑战、机遇、劣势、优势）矩阵的使用

S. W. O. T. 分析为确定帮助或妨碍组织发展的因素提供了一个框架，T. O. W. S. 矩阵则把此过程推进到下一步。使用 S. W. O. T. 的分析数据，T. O. W. S. 矩阵系统性地确定了这些数据的关系，并通过将优势与机遇进行匹配，用机遇降低劣势，用优势

战胜挑战，从而减少劣势、避免挑战等方法帮助制定战略。

T. O. W. S. 矩阵中的变量不是新的；它们直接来自于 S. W. O. T. 分析。T. O. W. S. 矩阵的独特之处在于战略的形成是建立系统的方法上。T. O. W. S. 也被称为境况分析。

图表 3 - 6 展示了基本的 T. O. W. S. 分析。

图表 3 - 6　T. O. W. S. 矩阵

内部因素 外部因素	优势 5~10 个内部优势	劣势 5~10 个内部弱势
机遇 5~10 个外部机遇	优势 - 机遇战略 利用优势把握机遇	劣势 - 机遇战略 克服劣势把握机遇
挑战 5~10 个外部挑战	优势 - 挑战战略 利用优势避免挑战	劣势 - 挑战战略 最小化劣势，并避免挑战

在编制 T. O. W. S. 矩阵和分析形势时有很多不同的方法。例如，组织可以从确定重要问题开始。另一些方法可能从确定组织目标开始，或者将注意力放在机遇上。另外的想法是或者以分析外部环境开始，或者从组织内部资源开始。没有一个方法一定是最好的。

T. O. W. S. 矩阵提供了一个确定关系的良好框架，但是随着多种因素被确定及组合数目的提高，它会变得很复杂。一旦关系组合被确定，一个衡量体系可以用来帮助形成战略选择。" + "可用来表示公司优势和外部机遇的匹配关系；"0"可用来表示一个不存在的关系；或者，" - "表示一个很弱的关系。

但是管理专家提醒我们，不能通过简单地将这些正号、零、负号的数目加总来解释这个矩阵。T. O. W. S. 矩阵中的关系通常都有不同的潜能，应该被进一步评估。可以开发类似的表格用来分析战略组合（优势 - 机遇，劣势 - 机遇，优势 - 挑战，劣势 - 挑战）。

编制此矩阵的时间点是另一个需要考虑的问题。如前所述，因为内部和外部环境是动态的，所以可能需要有多个 T. O. W. S. 矩阵。

尽管存在这些潜在的复杂问题，T. O. W. S. 矩阵可以为组织确定利用优势来把握外部环境机遇的前景远大的战略提供相对直接的方法。

S. W. O. T. 分析与战略规划的关系

S. W. O. T. 分析的结果通常需要组织进行进一步整理。组织面临着以下问题：

- 优势、劣势、机遇和挑战之间存在什么样的关系？
- 公司有必要的资源和能力去抓住机遇消除挑战吗？
- 有多少竞争对手已经有相同的资源和能力了？
- 有市场准入壁垒吗？
- 企业有途径获得竞争优势吗？
- 获得一项特别的资源或能力会给公司带来成本缺陷吗？
- 有替代品吗？
- 组织结构允许充分利用自己的资源、能力支持潜在的增长/改变吗？

在评估所有优势、劣势、机遇和挑战时的难点是区分它们的优先次序，然后确定适当的行动。基本想法是：

- 构建优势。
- 消除弱势。
- 利用机遇。
- 最小化挑战。

在处理优势和劣势时，观念应该能够快速转变。现在正确可行的可能马上就会有所不同。例如，今天的优势，可能马上就会因一项技术革新或政府法规的改变而不复存在。

S. W. O. T. 分析是战略规划很重要的一部分，因为它把组织内部与外部评估结合在一起，使其变得可行可用。它有助于将环境分析的松散结果联系在一起，并且回答许多以前未解决的组织难题。确定的机遇和限制为战略规划中合理的目标和行动计划提供了信息。

注意：在优势创造过程中 S. W. O. T. 分析数据的使用将在第 2 章"战略营销"中讨论。

长期设想、任务、目标和目的

组织的目标和战略不能靠碰运气和直觉。必须将它们明确表述且传达给公司中负责实现它们的人。因此，战略规划的重要一步是正式地写出公司的设想、任务、使命、目标和目的。

设想

组织的设想描述是对组织未来成就的指导性反映，该设想是以组织对社会的贡献情况进行描述的。对于组织为将来一代做什么及组织想要被怎样定位，设想做了简要的概述。图表3－7 给出了设想描述。

图表3－7 设想描述

波音公司
［我们的设想是］大家齐心合力，共同打造在航天业领军的全球化企业。
通用的土星分部
［我们的设想是］将研发和生产的交通工具行销美国，通过员工团结、技术和商业体系做到在质量、成本和客户满意度方面领先世界，并将知识、技术和经验传播给整个通用公司。

不幸的是，太多设想描述没有内在精神的，并且很容易只是通过改变组织名字而在企业间互用（例如，"XYZ 会努力成为世界级企业，并致力于创造超凡的客户期望值"）。一个明确的设想描述是引人注目的，并能团结组织的每个人。它能反映组织的价值观，并鼓舞和挑战管理者和员工去同心协力。

任务

任务描述是组织的指南针。与设想描述相类似，任务描述是由组织价值观塑造而成。任务描述简要说明了一个组织的商业地位。它表达了一个组织应该怎样持续向设想迈进，并明确阐述了组织试图为客户做的事情。任务描述回答了"我们为什么经营"这个问题。在回答这个问题时，任务描述必须是精确的、容易理解的、有激励性的并可转化为行动的。

图表3-8展示了公司任务描述的两个例子。

图表3-8 公司任务描述

西南航空
西南航空的任务是致力于提供最高质量的客户服务，使顾客感受到温馨、友好、自尊和公司精神。
万怡大酒店
［我们的任务是］给讲求实惠、追求质量的旅游者提供干净、舒适、维修良好、有吸引力、服务一流的中等价位的住宿设施。

目标

一般来讲，目标是指被瞄准的对象。目标总结了为完成任务和实现设想一个组织希望达到的结果。目标是总的指导方针；它们不会过于明确或者可以计量。目标阐述了希望得到的最终结果或最终收益；它并不指明实施方案。组织一般会制定战略和战术目标。

战略目标

战略目标由组织最高层制定。顾名思义，战略目标是企业战略规划的一部分；它们本质上是长期的。战略目标的例子是企业多元化经营、生产线的增加或减少、新市场渗透等。战略目标需要在战术水平上实现其他目标。

战术目标

战术目标一般由组织中下层的业务（也被称作责任中心和战略性业务单元）或职能部门制定。战术目标是短期的，通常持续时间在一年之内。"将生产线利润提高10%"就是战术目标的一个例子。

用于战略及战术目标的观念

就像组织战略必须是动态的一样，战略及战术目标也必须是动态的。新事物通常是竞争的范围，如新成员、技术改变、经济剧变等。目标需要进行修正或改变，以反映正在发生的内部和外部改变以及目前的挑战和机遇。目标应该一年至少评估一次。

目的

目的提供了用于支持目标的细节和行动。好的目标明确了用于跟踪进程和绩效——预想的行动、行动的时间、预想的绩效水平、负责行动的职能或个人——的定量措施。

多个目的可以支持一个目标。在这种情况下，必须达到所有目的以获取目标的收益；没有一个目的可以单独保证目标的实现。对上述"将生产线利润提高10%"的例子进行拓展，一些支持性目的可以是：

● 营销团队 A 在 30 天内确定客户对产品 X 质量的认可程度。团队 A 对这些客户认知进行排序不能够并分别赋予权重。

● 生产团队 B 在 30 天内开发产品 X 的包括所有使用设备的生产流程图。

● 会计团队 C 在 30 天内进行产品 X 的盈利性分析，确定了利润率百分比和投资周转率。

还有另一些目的需要制定。总之，所有目的都会支持将生产线利润提高 10% 这个目标。

作为目的所要求的简明性提示，首字母缩略词 SMART 经常被使用。目的应该是明确的、可测量的、可持续的、可实现的和时间确定的。

战术与长期战略目标的合作

如前所述，战略规划是长期的——一般来说，期限在 1～10 年之间，视业务的性质而定。与之相比，营运计划关注的是新的财政年度，因此牵涉到更多的战术问题。战略规划先于营运计划；战略规划为制定更加详细的战术计划提供了基础。从这种意义上来说，战略规划是宏观的，营运计划是微观的。图表 3-9 概括地比较了战略规划和营运计划。

图表 3-9 战略规划和营运计划的比较

	战略规划	营运计划
焦点	揭示了长期和短期计划；为预算提供基础	给每个具有详细收入和费用预算的业务制定具体目标
检查事项	确定并分析如下事项： ● 全球化市场的新成员 ● 经济环境 ● 多元化的计划	确定并分析如下事项： ● 季度收益 ● 存货水平 ● 重要的资本支出 ● 营销计划 ● 生产计划
制定	自上而下；反映内外部因素的综合分析	自下而上；为即将来临的一年建议具体选择
控制	每年进行检查并按需要更新以反映高层次的变化	全年定期检查、更新/修正，以应对不断变化的需求（如滞后的主要产品销售额、竞争对手的新定价，新开辟的分销渠道等）

预算与战略规划的关系

战略规划和营运计划导致了预算的形成。预算是对一段时期内被提议的管理活动的定量表述。预算有很多优点。无论组织是何种类型何种规模，预算都能：

● 通过确定实现组织目标、目的所需的资源和责任，给组织未来一段时间提供蓝图。

● 有助于确定潜在的瓶颈/问题，促进业务更加顺利的进行。

● 充当通讯装置，指出所有部门和员工在确定时期内的预期业绩。

- 提供一个涉及营运方针及监控标准的参考框架。
- 通过将预期和实际结果相比较，促进部门和员工的业绩评估。

预算是对管理人员关于利润、现金流量和财务状况预期的量化。组织编制各种营业预算（生产、研究和设计、营销、分销、管理等）。总预算与这些单个预算相协调构成整个组织的年度综合预算。

组织战略和战略规划为年度总预算提供了基础和起点。很自然的，总预算必须与战略及战略规划一致，并要为公司的长期战略目标、任务及设想的实现服务。

图表 3 - 10 展示了通过预算程序，战略是怎样在战略规划中流动的。战略以广阔的前景为起点。在预算水平上，关注点变得相当明确。

图表 3 - 10　组织战略流程

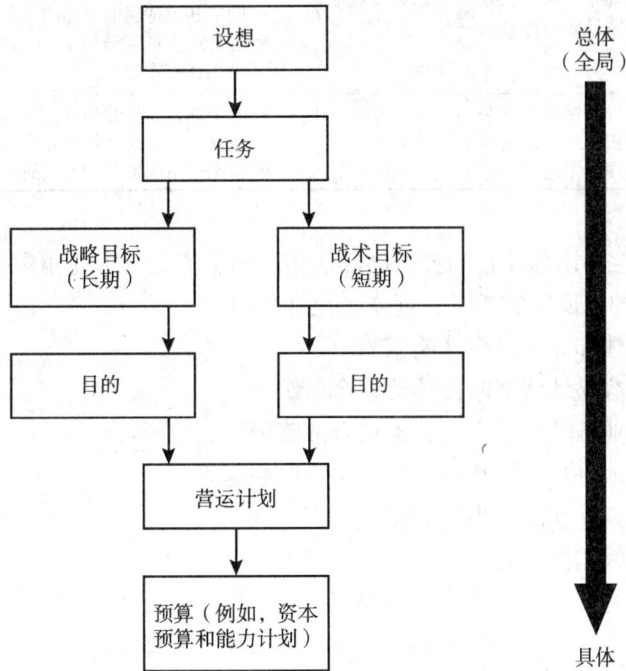

平衡记分卡的战略使用

平衡记分卡是由罗伯特·卡普兰和戴维·诺顿在 20 世纪 90 年代初发展的，最初是为了帮助公司更好地管理同金融工具有关的无形资产。长期以来，公司也已经采用平衡记分卡以建立长期战略规划目标与短期行动的联系。

按照卡普兰和诺顿的观点，企业为记分卡引入了另外的管理程序；当单独或集合使用记分卡时，它能促成一个成功的战略管理体系。图表 3 - 11 总结了记分卡的拓展使用。

图表 3-11 作为战略管理系统的平衡记分卡的使用

额外的平衡记分卡程序	关注点/意图	例子
转化企业设想和战略	高级主管采取行动将组织成功的长期动因转化为整体目的,以及在整个组织营运水平上能实施的措施	• 对组织战略达成共识和承诺,主管团队制定平衡记分卡,将公司的设想描述转化成便于理解的有意义的战略 • 诸如"优质服务"、"以顾客为目标"都是对实施该战略的人员的进一步要求
传达战略并建立其与组织的联系	经理采取行动给整个组织传达战略,并建立其与部门或个人目标的联系	• 中层经理通过制定业务单元记分卡并对下属员工进行相关教育将战略推进下一个水平 • 制定内部业务流程和学习及革新目标,以支持财务和客户目标的实现;制定目标,并将奖励同绩效衡量联系在一起
业务规划	能够使组织整合所有业务主动权和财务规划、排序、分配资源以支持长期战略目标的行为	• 采取措施以建立所有变化项目和资源配置及长期战略优先权的联系 • 为平衡记分卡衡量设立短期目标 • 确定和支持完成目标的必要投资 • 进行适当的检查(一月、一季度、一年)以确保目标是正在被完成
反馈和学习	通过反馈及关于公司、部门和员工是否正在或已经完成了预算目标的复核程序,促进战略学习	• 制定规定,持续检查记分卡衡量、市场状况、客户价值建议、竞争对手行为和内部能力 • 组织战略的生存能力,战略管理体系被评估或重新评估

卡普兰和诺顿注意到公司已经从拓展的平衡记分卡使用中获得了许多收益。这样一个整合的、反复的战略管理体系允许公司:

- 阐述和更新组织战略。
- 更容易地将战略传达给整个组织。
- 使业务单元和个人目标符合战略。
- 将战略目的、长期目标和预算联系起来。
- 确定并实施恰当的战略主动权。
- 持续监督绩效。
- 将持续学习并入营运改善。

成功的战略/战术规划的特征

对于战略家来说,组织及其所处行业是复杂的不断变动的目标。企业为了回应影响竞争平衡的事情而不断变动。战略规划流程——无论组织有多大或多小,或这个方法正式或不正式——有助于公司形成竞争性战略。它也有一些局限。理解优点和不足有助于认识成功战略规划的构成。

战略规划的益处

战略规划提供如下益处:

- 分析挑战和机遇的系统性方法,检查一些组织战略为什么比其他组织的更具有竞争性和盈利性前景。
- 为制定有效的营运预算提供合理框架。
- 是提供经理思考战略和怎样最好地实施它们的组织学习机会。

- 使经理决策和行动符合整体性战略的一次实践（例如，获得经理的认同，并展示他们的决策和行动如何支持公司项目）。
- 是财务和非财务绩效衡量的基础。
- 将战略、目的、营运计划等传达给各个管理层的渠道。
- 为处理新形势提供指导。

战略规划的局限

战略规划不是解决所有组织问题的万能药。战略规划的一些关键不足是：

- 此流程涉及大量努力、时间和费用。
- 事实上，基于预测的规划是不精确的科学；由于一系列原因，规划可能被证明是不正确或者失败的。
- 固定的做事方法可能会妨碍做出改变。
- 规划可能会变成官僚做法，以致完全不能接受新观点和战略想法。

应急规划

好的战略规划是基于极有可能发生的事件。但是战略规划不应该忽视在当今商业环境中的环境不确定性。

应急规划的定义

越来越多的战略规划会包含应急规划这一部分，以帮助对付引起企业严重问题的情况变动。应急规划为可能发生的假设分析情况作准备，用来处理个别的非计划事件。应急规划的目的是提供更快的反应时间，并为面临非预期发展和可能的危机时期的管理者提供必要的指导。

应急规划的对象

许多事件或情况会发生，并会对组织产生严重破坏。应急规划的典型事由是：

- 更低的销售额或利润水平。
- 能夺取市场份额的新成员。
- 政府规定。
- 缺乏重要主管人员或经理/重要雇员更换的持续计划。
- 关键设施的损坏。
- 计算机系统损坏/信息安全问题。
- 灾难恢复。
- 利率的突然变动。
- 资本有效性缩水。
- 工会活动。
- 并购和接管。

实际上，应急规划不能涵盖所有情况。大多数制定应急规划的组织都会选择不超过六个重要事件。重要性和可能性通常会影响应该选择哪些事由进行规划。

应急规划的步骤

在大多数公司中，应急规划是在战略规划完成之后才准备的；战略规划过程为制定应急规划提供了有价值的数据。但是应急规划一般是处理短期战术战略而不是长期战略。

图表 3 – 12 概括了应急规划的基本步骤。

图表 3 – 12　应急规划的步骤

步骤 1	确定需要应急规划的可能情况（事件、假设分析等）
步骤 2	估计上述事件发生的潜在影响（在财务状况、竞争地位等方面）
步骤 3	制定战略与战术规划以处理每个可能发生的情况
步骤 4	确定触发点或警告信号
步骤 5	异地储备计划
步骤 6	定期检查计划并在必要时进行修正（至少跟战略规划同步）

应急规划不存在标准模式。

理想中，应急规划应该是简明的，但是需要包含足够的细节以在必要时指导行动。挑战越严峻，细节越必要。

图表 3 – 13 列示了一些与会计有关的应急规划的例子。

图表 3 – 13　与会计有关的应急规划的例子

事　由	计　划
在总账结账时电脑系统的缺失	• 确定电脑使用的异地（外包）地点/服务 • 确认有公司培训过的人员在远程工作
首席财务官或其他重要财务人员的流失	• 持续计划 　• 确定将被培训的主要人员 　• 确定来自另外部门的后备人员 • 外聘的条件/步骤
主要产品/服务销售量下滑	• 确定分析和/或改变的领域 　• 资源备用计划 　• 员工下岗问题

进度检查

提示：完成以下各题，参考答案随后给出。

1. 整体性战略可以被最佳地表述为（　　）

   a. 一份详细计划，描述为获得超额投资回报公司将会做些什么

   b. 用财务和非财务术语表述的企业价值观的定义

   c. 基于买方权力、供货商权力、竞争、替代品威胁、对手五种力量的行业吸引力的分析

   d. 关于企业价值链中每项活动是怎样影响成本和差异的全局描述

2. 以下描述了影响行业盈利性的五个动因的特点，除了（　　）

   a. 随着行业的不断演进，它们保持不变

   b. 它们因行业而异

　　c. 它们易受到高增长和高市场需求的影响

　　d. 在任何一个行业中，它们的重要性都是不相同的

找出与该术语匹配的描述。

3. _____差异性 　　　a. 随着每期产量的增加，带来的单位成本下降

4. _____规模经济 　　b. 创造市场新成员必须克服的品牌认同和现存客户忠诚度

5. _____渠道拥挤 　　c. 源于有限的能力或限制制造商生产线数量的排他性关系

6. "我们相信公司和员工的主要责任是以合理的价格为公众提供最现代实用的服务。"此描述是公司的（　　）

　　a. 设想

　　b. 任务

　　c. 战略目标

　　d. 目的

进度检查答案

1. b

2. a

3. b

4. a

5. c

6. a

第2节
生产范式

本节内容简介

从定义上，范式是指一个例子或者一种模型。而范式转变就是指人们观察及处事的范式发生巨大转变。

起初，适时制和外包代表了制造业的范式转变。约束理论同样也背离了传统生产方式。这些新生产方式出现以后，用于决策的信息种类以及搜集数据的方式都发生了改变。最终，管理会计师的角色也由此发生了改变，信息报告的效率和效果都得到了改善。

适时制生产（JIT）

此处涉及所有需要生产出最终产品的生产过程，该过程包括从设计到运输以及原材料向前转变的各个步骤。适时制是指一种综合性的生产和存货控制方法，即在每个生产阶段，需要多少材料就购进多少。其目标是通过减少乃至消除资源浪费进行精益生产，即按照需要量而不是持有大量的安全存货生产生产线零件。只在需要的时候才生产产品。

在适时制中，需求来自于对某种产品的需要。理论上，是市场从该系统的最终位置"拉动"了替代产品。需求引发了每一个步骤，并在整个生产过程中拉动产品生产——从一端客户对最终产品的需求全部回归到另一端对原材料的需求。适时制的这种"需求拉动"特征对系统内每一点的质量水平和协调性都要求很高，以确保即使在低库存量的情况下，商品和经营都依然流畅。这常常就要求与更少的供应商保持更密切的合作。

JIT 和 MRP 系统的区别

适时制中的需求拉动策略和传统生产过程中所运用的"推动型"物料需求计划系统完全不同。

MRP 推动系统的基本前提是：

- 需求预测
- 标明用于生产最终产品的材料、零件和部件任务的物料清单
- 明确数量的材料、零件、部件和产品存货，以预测必需的产出

在 MRP 系统里，主生产计划明确了生产各部分的数量和时间。一旦计划的生产开始实行，不管产出是否需要，各部门都在整个系统中推动产出。

例如：

下面展示了一个公司如何使用 MRP 系统来计算生产 P 产品的部件以及抵消前置期。

P 产品的构成	A 部件的构成	B 部件的构成
$2 \times A$	$1 \times C$	$2 \times C$
$3 \times B$	$2 \times D$	$2 \times E$

如果需要 100 件 P 产品：

A 部件	2×P 产品的数量	=2×100	=200
B 部件	3×P 产品的数量	=3×100	=300
C 部件	1×A 部件的数量	=1×200	
	+2×B 部件的数量	+2×300	=800
D 部件	2×A 部件的数量	=2×200	=400
E 部件	2×B 部件的数量	=2×300	=600

所需的前置期为：

P 产品	1 周
A 部件	2 周
B 部件	2 周
C 部件	3 周
D 部件	1 周
E 部件	1 周

P 产品的交付日期一经确定，就可以制定日程计划明确何时订购和收取各部件来满足对 P 产品的需求。

周数

		1	2	3	4	5	6	7	
P	需要下达							100	P 前置期＝1 周
	订单日期						100		
A	需要下达						200		A 前置期＝2 周
	订单日期				200				
B	需要下达						300		B 前置期＝2 周
	订单日期				300				
C	需要下达				800				C 前置期＝3 周
	订单日期	800							
D	需要下达				400				D 前置期＝1 周
	订单日期			400					
E	需要下达				600				E 前置期＝1 周
	订单日期			600					

这个例子中的 MRP 系统是建立在对 P 产品及 P 产品各组成部件的需求上的，兼顾了从内部或外部供应商获得各部件的前置期。

MRP 系统的优点

MRP 系统的优点有：

- 对各功能部门之间的协调性要求不是那么高；每个人只需遵照物料清单。

- 有计划地改善；即使需求不确定或相对不可预测时产量也满负荷。
- 可预测的原材料需求；可以利用大宗购买或者梯度价格。
- 更有效的存货控制；可以规划用完原材料或生产最终产品。
- 一旦产品在向客户运输过程中受损或丢失，手头仍然有多余的存货来满足订单。
- 新的顾客需求做出快速反应；可以直接向新客户供应现有存货，而不必等接到订单后才开始生产产品。
- 更优的生产过程控制；使工具替换和机器准备的时间最小化。

MRP 系统最主要的缺点在于有可能造成存货积压。各工作站可能会收到尚未准备处理的部件。

JIT 系统的要素

JIT 系统主要有以下特征：

- 生产过程被分成各个制造单元——生产最终产品所必需的相关生产过程被分组，然后为了彼此相近、改善沟通、快速反馈等继续将其按逻辑分为更小的组。
- 技能丰富的工人——对工人采取跨职能的训练，这样他们就可以按需执行各种各样的操作与任务，使整个生产过程流畅不间断。
- 减少准备时间——减少获取生产用工具、设备和材料的时间。
- 减少生产前置期——减少从下达订单到最终产品生产完毕所需的时间。
- 可靠的供应商——仔细筛选供应商，以确保按时运送高质量商品以供适时制使用（有时在一天甚至更短时间内）

实行 JIT 时"看板"的使用

在实行 JIT 系统时，可以采用各种方法；最常见的一种方法就是"看板"。看板来源于日语"Kanban"，其书面意思是"可视的记录或卡片"。在 JIT 环境下，工人们使用看板在各工作单元或部门之间有序传达确定数量的材料或部件的需求。工人们只有在收到看板以后才会做出反应。一个生产过程完成后，工人们就将看板贴在已完成的订单上，然后一起传递到下游的工作单元。

看板是一种典型的信息卡片，上面记载了部件、所需数量，交货地点等。然而，看板也可能是标签、盒子、箱子、一系列篮口朝里的篮子或其他可视的指示器。

JIT 系统的优点及局限

JIT 的总的优点主要有：
- 明显的生产优先权。
- 减少了准备和生产的前置期。
- 不会发生生产过剩的情况。
- 改善的质量控制（更快的反馈）和更少的物料浪费。
- 更为简易的存货控制（低存货甚至零存货）。
- 更少的书面工作。
- 与供应商关系密切。

JIT 系统集中力量控制总生产成本（与原材料或直接制造人工等单个成本相对）。通常，生产成本下降而现金流量和营运资本水平提高。一些专门的财务方面的优点在于：

- 更低的存货投入。
- 持有和处理存货的成本降低。
- 存货发生过时、破坏或减损的风险降低。
- 更少的空间投入（生产和存货所需的空间）。
- 可以对顾客要求做出更快的反应，从而带来更大收入。

可以直接追踪一些可能会被归入间接费用的成本项目。人工、装运和其他一些使用别的方法随意分摊的成本可能是可追踪的。

JIT 系统虽然有许多优点，但也存在不少局限。常见的有：

- 没有缓冲存货；如果生产过程需要待料就可能增加停工时间。
- 依赖供应商来维持足够的存货以满足难以预料的需求；对供应链的高度依赖。
- 可能发生供应商某产品缺货情况；重要部件的缺乏可能会使整条生产线瘫痪。
- 收到未预料到订单时的潜在加班费用。

需要注意的是，在某些市场和特定条件下，偶尔的缺货比其他选择更可取。

外包

外包是指公司向外部厂商购买而不是在公司内部自行生产商品/服务的过程。通过这种方式，组织可以集中资源来提升企业核心竞争力，对于企业核心竞争力之外的专业化任务则依靠其他一些在此方面更高效、更有效果、更了解的企业的专业知识。今天，许多公司都将信息技术、数据处理和人力资源模块等的重要部件外包出去。

术语"自制或外购决策"指的就是外包。自制或外购决策分析（本书第4章会详细介绍）分析对比了公司内部自己生产和外包给外部厂商的相关成本。

一些企业还将外包理念延伸为一种"契约式生产"，即其他公司实际上负责生产第一家企业产品的一部分。如果一个企业生产能力过剩或拥有专业知识而另一个企业生产能力不足或缺乏专业知识时，这种契约式生产就是一种双赢的合作关系。

外包的优点及局限

有许多战略方面的原因会促使一个组织选择外包。当然，在组织内部不具备某种能力时，外包为小企业提供了资源和专业知识。对于一些大企业来说，外包能提升许多专门职能。

下面总结了外包的一些主要优点：

- 使得管理层和雇员可以集中精力于核心竞争力和产生战略性收入的活动。
- 通过获取外部的专业知识和生产规模改善效率和效果。
- 能以合理的成本获取新技术，而且没有过时风险。
- 在不发生间接费用（如员工、福利、空间）的情况下获得某项能力从而降低了费用。

- 可能改善产品/服务的质量和/或及时性。

虽然外包有许多优点，但是它并不适用于所有的活动和职能。以下几点是考虑外包时必须注意的：

- 外出寻找特别的专业知识可能花费更多。
- 会使公司内部的专业知识和能力荒废。
- 会降低处理控制。
- 可能会降低对质量的控制。
- 可能导致灵活性下降（依赖于外部供应商）。
- 可能会缺少个性化的服务。
- 产生私人和机密的问题。
- 会导致"知识泄密"，使竞争者获得专业知识、生产规模、客户等。
- 存在员工道德和忠诚度问题。

约束理论

本杰明·富兰克林曾说过这样一句格言"时间就是金钱"。而艾利·高德拉特博士则把这则古老的格言延伸为"目标不是省钱而是挣钱"。

1990 年，高德拉特博士提出了约束理论，这是一门建立在生产环境基础上的总体管理哲学。约束理论的首要目标就是提高生产速度。

约束理论假设每个系统在追求某个目标时都有至少一个制约因素限制产出。系统就是为达到某一目标而连接相互合作的处理过程的网络。制约因素是指限制性的要素——使产品循环时间放缓的瓶颈或障碍。循环时间是某一过程从开始到结束所用的时间。制约因素管理是指识别、分析、理解并排除过程障碍的过程。

高德拉特认为在任何一个给定的时间里在一个系统里只存在一个制约因素，这个瓶颈因素制约了整个系统的产出。系统中的其他组成部分是非制约因素（非瓶颈因素）。总的来说，约束理论强调关注系统制约因素，暂时忽略那些非制约因素。这样，这个理论对循环时间和过程改进有着深远的影响（而不是使有限的时间、能量和资源覆盖整个系统，这样不一定能产生实质结果）。

然而，当一个制约因素加强时，整个系统却不会无限地变强。制约因素只是会转移为系统的另一个要素。（比如，其他的一些因素成了瓶颈或障碍。）这个系统比以前要强但是仍未达到它可能的那么强。

约束理论的基本原理

存货、经营费用、产量贡献和限制驱导式排程法都是约束理论中的一些基本概念。

存货

存货是指系统投资购买用于转售商品的资金。一般的，它是指库存物品，但更广义上它还包括所有的资产。

经营费用

在约束理论里，经营费用是指系统将存货转变为产量所花费的资金。经营费用包括了直接和间接人工、辅料、外部承包人、利息支付和折旧等方面的花销。雇员负责将存货转变为产量。

产量

产量贡献（或产量、产量边际）是约束理论中对产品盈利性的衡量。它是指整个系统通过产品和/或服务销售获得的收益比率。

产量可以由下列公式表示：

产量 = 销售收入 – 直接材料成本

这个式子假设材料成本包括所有购进的零部件和材料处理成本。约束理论还假设人工是固定成本，而不是直接变动成本。另外，所有非组织内产生的现金以及其他成本如分包成本、销售佣金、运输成本等必须从销售收入中扣除。

我们可以举一个简单的例子来看看产量的计算：

- $100 = 产品的销售收入
- $20 = 从外部供应商购进的部件成本
- $10 = 销售佣金（销售额的 10%）
- $5 = 运输成本

则：

产量 = 销售收入 – 直接材料成本

产量 = （$100 – $20 – $10 – $5）= $65

限制驱导式排程法（DBR）

限制驱导式排程法（DBR）是指平衡生产流以使其通过制约因素的约束理论方法。鼓表示制约因素，绳子是先于并且包含制约因素的程序序列，而缓冲是指使鼓运转的在产品投入量的最小值。限制驱导式排程法的目标是通过对程序进行仔细的时间和日程安排为制约因素做好准备，从而使业务流顺畅通过制约因素。

约束理论的步骤

约束理论包括五个主要步骤，这些步骤用来集中精力改进那些最可能对整个系统产生正面影响的制约因素。图表 3 – 14 总结了这五个步骤。

在约束理论中，产量（T）、存货（I）和经营费用（OE）将营运和财务措施联系在一起。

图表 3 – 14　约束理论的五个主要步骤

步骤 1　识别系统中的制约因素
　　第一步，组织识别出系统的哪个部分是最薄弱的环节，即制约因素，然后判定它是物质性制约因素还是政策相关问题。
　　例如：管理会计师和经理、工程师共同绘制生产线生产过程的流程图。他们确定出每一个步骤的顺序以及所需的时间。
　　这样，系统的制约因素就会确定（如，耗时最长的子过程——在产品闲置时间过长的区域）。

步骤2	决定如何充分利用制约因素
	组织使用每一个受到制约的零件，无须受制于潜在的昂贵变化和/或升级，以此来"充分利用"制约因素。
	例如：改变关键机器的时刻表；重新部署雇员。
步骤3	次要的其他东西
	一个恰当的计划用来"开发"制约因素，组织调节系统企业要素以使制约因素发挥最大功效，然后评估结果，看制约因素是否依然阻碍系统运行。如果是，组织进行到第4步。如果不是，制约因素已经被消除了，直接跳到第5步。
	例如：进一步的分析是看那些使得通过限制的流量最大化的行为。会计师会把注意力集中在产量上，建议通过减少设备准备次数和时间及使用限制驱导式排程法等方式来加快（简化）流程。没有带来价值增值的活动被消除。这个想法是要保持制约因素繁忙而不累积存货和增加在产品。
步骤4	提升制约因素
	如果一个组织到达了第4步，那就意味着步骤2和步骤3没有有效地消除制约因素。那么在这一环节，组织就会采取任何必要的措施去消除它以提升制约因素。这可能会使现存系统发生很大的变动，如重组、清算或设备改建。因为这些一般需要大量的预先投资，组织在推行这种做法之前必须确定制约因素不会在步骤1到步骤3过程中被突破。
	例如：管理人员考虑怎么增加系统的能力（如果步骤2和步骤3证明制约因素的减轻不令人满意）。可能需要额外的劳力和更多/新的设备。
步骤5	回到步骤1，但是要小心惯性
	当一个制约性因素被突破以后，组织会再次重复以上的步骤，寻找其他限制系统运行的因素。同时，它监控与随后的制约因素有关的变化将如何影响已经突破的制约因素，由此避免解决方案的惯性。
	例如：组织考虑对制约因素做出战略性反应。目标是提高产量。产品或流程可能会被重新设计，难以用机器制造的产品可能被抛弃，等等。

正如管理会计公告4HH"约束理论管理系统基础"所指出的：

- 当T增加或OE减少时净利润增加。
- 通过增加销售收入或减少生产变动成本可以增加T。
- 只要I不变，增加净利润的措施也可以增加投资报酬率（ROI）。
- 如果I减少，即使净利润没有增加，投资报酬率（ROI）也会增加。
- 当T增加或者创造T的时间减少时，现金流量增加（假定节省的时间被用于得到更多的T）。

约束理论试图在减少存货、经营费用和其他投资的同时最大化生产力。不像传统的运行措施注重直接人工效率、单位成本以及公司如何有效地生产一个产品，约束理论强调组织应如何有效地生产产品来获得最优的市场成功。产品流量由市场需求来支配而不是大宗生产、便宜的原材料来源、机器效率或低廉的直接人工。

换句话说，T、I和OE措施使公司理解它正创造多少收益以及怎样最好地充分利用能力以提高盈利性。

约束理论报告

约束理论注重消除制约因素以及提高/加快周期或交货时间。在执行约束理论过程中所使用的绩效标准也指出了关键的成功要素。组织通常会编制一份约束理论报告以强调精选的运营数据和产量边际。约束理论报告对确认盈利性和关键成功要素很有价值。

图表3-15给出了约束理论报告的一个例子。

图表3－15　约束理论报告示例

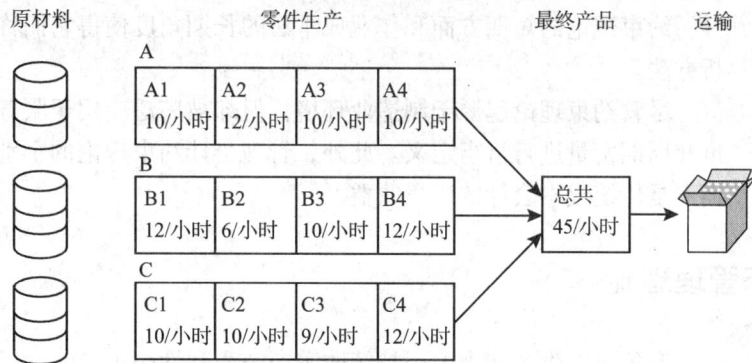

约束理论报告有各种形式。由上述简化的约束理论报告可以得出主要的几点是：

● 最终产品是由三个组成零件构成：A、B 和 C。

● 每一零件是不同的系列线性操作的结果。（例如：A 零件由原材料开始，然后依次通过 A1、A2、A3 和 A4 操作；B 零件的原材料依次通过 B1、B2、B3、B4 操作，依此类推。）

● 最慢的操作是 B2（每小时 6 个）；这个约束性操作的产出是最薄弱的环节，决定了整个系统的产出。

成功地识别了系统约束之后，可以采取步骤减少或者消除它。管理会计公告4HH "约束理论管理系统基础" 对开发和提升制约因素进行了如下区分：

● 开发制约因素改变了组织如何利用制约因素而不花费更多的钱（例如：减少内部准备时间以增加效用或最优化活动）。

● 提升制约因素要求投资更多的钱来增加被制约资源的能力（例如：买另一个设备或对一项活动进行外包来减轻约束）。

自然地，一个组织只有将制约因素发挥到极致后才应花更多的钱来提升制约因素。

约束理论和作业成本法

那些执行约束理论的组织通常使用作业成本法（ABC）。作业成本法是分配产品和服务成本的会计技术，它使企业可以确定生产出来的每一个产品和服务的实际成本。作业成本法的产生是用来处理与传统成本管理系统有关的问题，该方法能精确地算出生产和服务的实际成本，为经营决策提供有用信息。

与约束理论近似，组织采用作业成本法来估计产品盈利性。

但是，在用这两种成本管理方法来估计盈利性时存在以下几点不同：

● 约束理论使用短期方法来进行盈利性分析（强调与材料有关的成本）；而作业成本法检查长期成本（包括所有产品成本）。

● 约束理论考虑如何通过关注生产制约因素和看似合理的短期产品组合调整来提高短期盈利性。

● 作业成本法不考虑资源约束和生产能力，它分析成本动因和精确的单位成本以便进行长期的战略定价和利润计划决策。作业成本法通常被用作计划和控制的工具。

约束理论的短期方面和作业成本法的长期角度使得它们称为互为补充的盈利性分析方法。

尽管约束理论起源于制造业环境，但却被广泛应用于服务业。按照企业本质对速度和周期衡量进行恰当定义。此外，管理会计约束理论的个别推论用来估计企业会计而不是传统成本会计的产量收益。

其他生产管理理论

竞争……生产能力……持续改善……盈利性……

组织不断努力，以求精益求精并利用增长机会。除了上述生产范式以外，为了达到更好、更快、更多盈利的经营要求，组织还可从其他的一系列现代生产管理技术中进行选择。

许多组织已经采用了图表3－16所列示的一些或全部创新性方法来尝试降低成本、增加产量、改善质量和增加他们对消费者的总体反应。

图表3－16 现代生产方法

技 术	描 述
自动化/机器人	• 使用可重新编程的、多功能的机器人（机器）通过可变的程序化动作来操纵材料、零件、工具或专门设备。 • 运用机器人来完成各种重复性工作。
能力管理和分析（能力规划）	• 展示了一个涉及战略、战术和经营方面的重要的决策领域。 • 包括一个循环往复的步骤： 　• 检查长期的需求预测； 　• 把预测转化为能力要求； 　• 配比能力要求与现有设施； 　• 识别能力要求与预计可用性之间的不匹配； 　• 设计规划以克服不匹配并选择最好的备选方案。
计算机辅助设计（CAD）	• 在产品开发、分析、设计调整时使用计算机以提高产品质量和性能。 • 通常用在工程设计的绘图或实际布局步骤中。
计算机辅助制造（CAM）	运用计算机计划、控制和操作一个生产设备。
计算机整合制造（CIM）	• 是指将公司内所有工厂和办公职能通过计算机信息网络完全整合在一起的制造系统。 • 使用计算机来控制设计、工程、制造、逻辑、仓储和分销、客户和供货商、销售和营销活动以及会计等信息的整合和流动。
并行工程	• 将产品或服务设计与贯穿产品或服务生命周期的所有企业单元和职能的投入进行整合。 • 强调上游预防 vs. 下游纠正。 • 试图在保持消费者要求的同时，平衡在产品和服务设计中的各方需求。
弹性制造系统（FMS）	使用自动化设备的计算机网络，该设备能灵活生产一个或更多种零件或一个产品的不同变形。

进度检查

提示：完成以下各题，参考答案随后给出。

1. 适时制（JIT）与传统的物料需要计划（MRP）系统相比，最大的优点是什么？（　　　）

　　a. 增加系统内任何层次上的存货量

　　b. 最大化生产运转以适应整条生产线

　　c. 以需求拉动战略来替代推动制造战略

　　d. 减少过度生产的风险

2. 一个大的半导体制造商计划应用约束理论（TOC）方法来增加生产能力。管理会计师如何最好地支持这个创举？（　　　）

　　a. 确定外包成本以缓解长期关键制约因素

　　b. 设计缓冲管理工作表以便于数量分析

　　c. 提供净利润、投资报酬率和现金流量的数据

　　d. 提供作业成本数据

找出与该术语匹配的描述。

3. _____需求拉动　　a. 一个用来克服供给和需求不匹配的循环往复的决策制定过程

4. _____看板　　　　b. 一个从外部供货商购买产品或服务而不是自己生产的决定

5. _____外包　　　　c. JIT 系统要求密切协调以确保在低存货量的情况下产品和经营顺畅流转

6. _____能力管理　　d. 一个指明特定数量的材料或零件需求按顺序从一项操作或一个部门转移到另一个的可视信号

7. 一个组织会从 TOC 方法中直接得到如下好处，除了哪个以外？（　　　）

　　a. 减少瓶颈

　　b. 增加盈利性

　　c. 改善长期计划和控制

　　d. 提高产品和服务质量

进度检查答案

1. d

2. d

3. c

4. d

5. b

6. a

7. c

■ **第3节**
业务流程绩效

本节内容简介

具有竞争力使组织不仅仅是赶上或超越行业竞争对手。如今客户需求得更多而不是更少。借助因特网，客户通常信息灵通，对价格合理、质量上乘的商品和服务有无限的来源。组织不断地被挑战以应对那些增长的客户预期，而分析业务流程绩效是一个解决办法。许多技术可以用来分析业务流程绩效。

价值链分析

在客户看来，组织是如何做出那些明智选择的，例如集中精力做什么、怎么最好地创造价值等？许多组织通过价值链分析来获得成功。

价值链分析已经成为战略规划过程中必不可少的一部分。同战略规划一样，价值链分析是一个持续不断地收集、评估和交流信息的过程。价值链分析的最基本意图是帮助管理者洞察一个组织的未来并执行商业决策以获得和保持竞争优势。

相关术语

一些基本术语有助于理解价值链分析。

价值

当用于企业时，价值这个术语一般指一个专门资产的价值、希求或效用。但是，价值在某种程度上是相对的。它可能被用于所提供的一个单独产品或一项服务、一组资产或一个完整的企业单元。价值也可用于衡量市场价值、股东权益等。

价值活动

价值活动描述了在一个既定行业里，组织必须实施的从处理原材料（在制造业）到最终产品的生产和服务的集体活动。根据所处行业，一些企业可能会从事好几种活动而其他一些企业可能负责一项活动。在一个组织里，企业单元可能是进一步划分的子集。

例如：一个服装公司可能从最初的布料开始，设计、制造衣服，然后和零售商签订广告和销售合同。另一个服装公司可能把制造过程包给别人，通过组织的企业单元集中精力进行销售和营销，并依靠零售商进行分销。

价值链

价值链是一些相互依存的活动组成的系统，每一项活动都意图为最终产品和服务增加价值。自然地，价值链的发展取决于行业。图表3-17展现了制造业中的一个典型的价值链。在服务业中，没有购置原材料这一环节，其他活动和操作也可能有变化，并/或承担不同程度的重要性。

图表3－17　制造业中典型的价值链

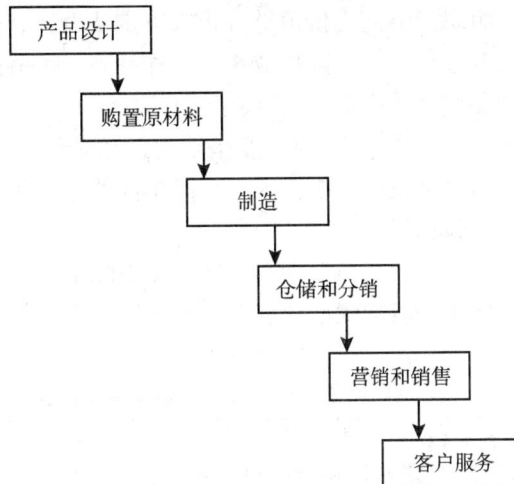

成本动因

成本动因是能引起活动成本变化的任何因素，例如直接人工工时、机器工时、电脑时间、医院床位占用等。为了更有意义地分析（除了每一个创造价值活动的总成本分析外），需要弄清楚引起重要成本的原因。企业检查结构性成本动因和执行性成本动因。结构性成本动因是指决定驱动企业产品或服务成本的经济结构的长期企业决策。执行性成本动因反映了怎样最好地使用资源（包括人力和物力）以达到组织目标和目的的企业经营决策。

供应链

在价值链分析中，组织检查整个供应链。供应链是指参与到生产、设计、销售、运输和使用公司产品或服务过程中的分销商、运输商、储存机构和供货商的延伸网络。

价值链分析定义

有了上述术语，价值链分析就可以下定义了。价值链分析（VCA）是指组织用于评估客户价值感知重要性的一个战略性分析工具。它包括用于确定当前成本和绩效标准，并评估整个供应链中哪些环节可以增加客户价值、减少成本的一整套工具和程序。

价值链分析的独特好处在于它关注整个价值链，而不只是组织参与的那些活动。供应商、分销商及参与到价值链中的其他各方，其成本和毛利都对终端用户的最终价格及产品或服务的营销策略产生影响。

价值链分析中的步骤

价值链分析的目的在于关注产品或服务的总价值链，并确定哪一部分或哪几部分支持企业的竞争优势和战略。理论上讲，竞争优势和竞争战略不能在作为一个整体的组织层面甚或企业单元层面上得到有效的检查。因为价值链将企业分成截然不同的战略活动，组织能够使用价值链分析来决定从设计到分销到客户服务这些操作中哪个环节可以提升客户价值、降低成本。这样一来，价值链分析有助于识别盈利来源并理解有关活动和程序的成本。

管理会计公告 4X "评估竞争优势的价值链分析"，检查了价值链分析的实务和技术。它指出价值链分析要求一个战略性的框架作为起点来组织和分析内、外部信息以及总结经验和建议。

价值链分析没有一个标准程序，在实际中各有不同。管理会计公告 4X 中提到的价值链分析的一般步骤如图表 3 – 18 所示。

图表 3 – 18　评估竞争优势的一种价值链方法

步骤 1　内部成本分析

这一步确定盈利来源以及内部程序或活动的相关成本。内部成本分析：

- 识别企业价值创造过程。
- 确定产品或服务总成本中每一个价值创造过程应分摊的部分。
- 识别每一过程的成本动因。
- 识别过程之间的联系。
- 评估获得相对成本优势的机会。

步骤 2　内部差异分析

在这一步骤，检查创造和维持出众差异的来源。主要关注客户对公司产品和服务的价值感知上。和步骤 1 近似，内部差异分析首先要求识别内部价值创造过程和成本动因。利用这些信息，企业可以进行差异分析以便：

- 识别客户价值创造过程。
- 评估提升客户价值的差异战略。
- 确定最可持续的差异战略。

步骤 3　垂直链接分析

垂直链接分析是对步骤 1 和步骤 2 的更广泛应用，它包括一个行业中所有的上游和下游价值创造过程。垂直链接可以识别哪些是对竞争优势或劣势最关键或最不关键的活动。它包括从原材料来源到产品处置和/或回收的所有环节。垂直链接分析是：

- 识别行业的价值链并对价值创造过程分摊成本、收入及资产。
- 诊断每一个价值创造过程的成本动因。
- 评估获得可持续竞争优势的机会。

管理会计公告指出图表 3 – 18 描述的三种分析——内部成本分析、内部差异分析和垂直链接分析相辅相成。组织首先检查它们的内部运行，然后扩大到评估它们在行业中的竞争地位。

一般，价值链分析会产生大量数据，这些数据需要仔细解释，以辨别出能够最好地创造顾客感知价值的关键信息。

价值增值概念和质量

质量，像战略和战略规划一样，有许多定义、描述和大量方法。质量管理专家们坚持认为是客户最终定义哪些构成产品和服务的质量。但是他们也很快就注意到质量是客户对产品或服务提供的价值的理解，这种理解不是静止的而是不断变化的。当一个产品或一项服务成熟起来（通过创新），当备选方案（行业竞争）可以拿来作为比较基础时，客户对质量的理解就会变化。以任何现有的消费者电子产品为例——电脑、电话、电视——如今客户对质量的理解（源于创新和竞争）甚至已远不同于一两年前。从这点看，有人会说质量是当客户成为回头客而产品没有被退回来。

内部和外部客户

在质量领域，客户是任何一个受组织程序、产品以及服务影响的人。企业有内部和外部客户。

内部客户是指收到来自于另一雇员、部门或企业单元的信息、产品或服务产出的雇员、部门或企业单元。甚至在一项工作流程中的下一个人也是内部客户。在这种理念下，所有与工作有关的活动都可以被认为是雇员之间或内部客户与内部供应商之间的一系列的交易。

外部客户是指一个接收信息、产品或服务的人或组织。一般来说，外部客户被认为是组织之外的最终使用者。

价值链分析和质量绩效

由于组织努力追求质量绩效，从最高执行官到第一线雇员，每个人都有责任向外部客户或最终使用者创造或贡献企业流程、产品、服务的价值。

供应商也起着至关重要的作用。组织从由行业分析和/或战略得出的外部客户要求开始。企业进一步确定内部客户—供应商之间的关系及要求，以及和外部供应商之间的关系及要求。一系列操作产生了最终产品或服务。当每一个内部客户和供应商得到了他们在价值链上的需要时，外部客户也就得到了最好的服务。

图表3-19例举了管理会计公告4R"管理质量改善"中的客户—供应商价值链。

图表3—19　客户—供应商价值链

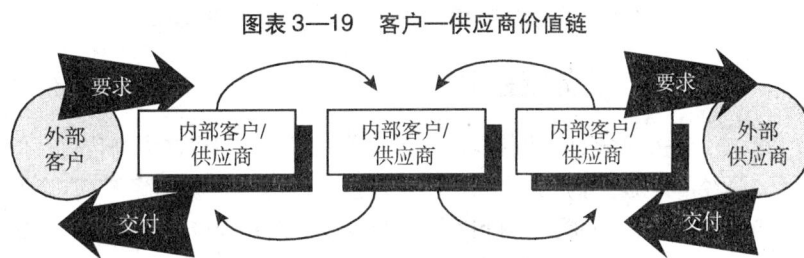

增值的概念是指那些把资源转变为符合外部客户要求的产品和服务的活动。非增值活动可以被消除，同时在最终使用者看来，产品或服务的功能、绩效或质量也没有退化。在产品和服务普遍等价或产出被认为是日用品的行业中，增值活动可能是在卖给客户或随同销售提供更多服务之前的一些额外捏造或定制。那些和材料移动或重做有关的活动最可能是非增值的。

客户—供应商价值链的目标在于把价值整合到工作流程中的每一方面。通过去除非增值活动，工作流程会更有效，并最终产出质量更高的产品或服务。

流程分析

为了理解流程分析，首先理解流程的概念是很重要的。流程是指投入材料和/或资源、增加价值、并为内部或外部客户提供产出的一项或一组相关的活动。一个流程往往横跨几个部门单元，如会计、销售、生产和运输。

企业必须认识并理解那些带来企业利润的业务流程。做到这一点的一种方法就是流程分析。流程分析是指可用以检查和衡量使流程运转的基本因素的一系列分析方法的集合。它也能识别那些最需要改进的流程。

流程特征

IMA 自学课程"高级流程分析和改进"描述了有助于识别一个良好流程的三个特征。

- **效果性**：当一个流程产出预想结果或达到/超过客户要求时，该流程是有效果的。客户认为一个有效果的流程是高质量的。
- **效率性**：当一个流程以最小的浪费、费用和/或周期时间达到结果时，该流程是有效率的。该流程有很高的产出与投入比。
- **适应性**：当一个流程很有弹性并能对变化了的要求和新竞争做出快速反应时，该流程是有适应性的。

一个流程应专注于以上三种特性。例如：一个流程以成本来说可能是行业中最有效果的，但是如果没有人愿意买这个产品，那么它就是一个坏的流程。

"高级流程分析和改进"提示在衡量流程好坏时，以下四个问题很有帮助：

- 从客户角度看，流程是否一直产出高质量的产品或好的服务？
- 流程是否能产出以满足客户随时随地的需要？
- 流程生产的产品是否具有成本方面的竞争力？
- 流程是否能与顾客不断变化的需求保持一致？

流程再造/业务流程重组

有关质量的一个错误假定是改善流程只有以生产力为代价。但是经验告诉我们质量提高经常伴随着生产力提高。质量改进可以减少浪费和降低/消除重做的必要。从而，在生产流程中需要的原材料和资源就会变少。以较少投入获得产出，就是生产力的提高。

但是通过全面质量管理（TQM）获得的流程改进和生产力提高，一般是通过调整系统和减少投入获得的增量收益。流程再造和业务流程重组提供了更深入、更彻底的好处。

流程再造

流程再造详细地图示流程，评估和质疑流程，然后全面地重新设计流程以消除不必要的步骤，减少错误机会并降低成本。所有非增值活动都被消除。

业务流程重组

业务流程重组（BPR）是基础分析，彻底地在企业内部和企业之间重新设计业务流程以获得巨大的业绩改进（例如：成本、质量、速度和服务）。迈克尔·哈默和詹姆士·钱皮在 20 世纪 90 年代早期在他们《再造企业》一书中首次提出了 BPR 这一概念。BPR 提倡这样一个观点：有时候忘记过去，彻底地重新设计和重组一个企业以降低成本和增加产品和服务质量是必要的。

那么，再造怎样才能产生工作流程的彻底变化？哈默和钱皮对 BPR 的主要方面进行了拓展：

- 基础的——BPR 强迫人们去关注那些目前开展业务所采用的司空见惯的规则和假设。企业必须回答两个问题：我们为什么要做这些我们现在做的事情？我们为什么要以这种方式做它？
- 彻底的——BPR 是指重新发明，而不是改进或修正。彻底地重新设计是指抛弃现存流程，创造新的工作方式。
- 戏剧性的——BPR 不是轻描淡写。它是当需要"重磅爆炸"来减轻严重情况时使用的。如果你只是需要对流程进行轻微的改进，那就不需要再造。
- 流程——BPR 事关流程定位，它格外重视那些需要投入并为客户创造有价值产出的一连串活动。

BPR 模型认为多数大企业的工作流程是基于不再有效的技术、人员以及组织目标的假设上的。它还认为信息是达到彻底改变的一个关键能力。

图表 3 - 20 列出了支撑 BPR 成功的普通工具和策略。

图表 3 - 20　业务流程再造的基础

流程定位	组织关注的是横跨组织边界的整个流程，而不是按照事先定义的组织边界所狭义确定的任务。
目标	公司的目标是突破，而不是小的改进。
打破陈规	旧的传统和假设故意被抛弃了。
创造性地使用技术	当前的/艺术性技术可作为使组织以彻底不同方式进行工作的一项能力。

流程再造和业务流程重组是强药剂。许多计划好的再造都因为各种原因失败了。对哈默和钱皮的最初尝试也经历了一点挫折，再造甚至被指责为精简机构和裁员的掩护。然而成功的故事则说明虽然敢闯敢拼会有危险、引起痛苦，但是再造的最后收获也是戏剧性的。

质量、生产力、流程改进之间的联系

质量、生产力、流程改进有如下重要关系：
- 生产力暗示努力改进现存状况。
- 提高生产力要求持续的质量改进。
- 持续改进需要不断的组织学习、流程改进和再造。

只有通过持续的生产力提高，一个组织才能具有长期竞争力。

帕累托原理的应用

为了改进流程和生产力，组织需要建立现实的优先次序。帕累托原理常常被运用。简单说来，帕累托原理是指绝大多数结果是由相对少数原因造成的，即80%的结果源于20%的可能起因（例如：原材料、机器或操作者）。帕累托原理在1950年由质量倡导者约瑟夫·朱兰最先定义，在19世纪按意大利经济学家韦尔菲多·帕累托命名。

百分数（80%和20%）不总是精确的，"至关重要的少数和微不足道的多数"这一表达常与帕累托原理联系起来。朱兰最先提出这一说法。但是他和其他一些质量专家随后逐渐意识到在质量上没有微不足道的问题，所有问题都值得注意。朱兰最终把"微不足道的多数"改为"有用的多数"，但是"至关重要的少数和微不足道的多数"依然是常用的术语。

实践中，帕累托原理被应用为评级体系，即一种按优先次序管理项目的方法，或是一种有秩序地思考问题及其效果的方法。帕累托图用来向组织显示作为结果的发生频率或成本（时间或金钱）。这样一来，图表直观地展示了哪些情况是最重要的。

流程图

每个流程都需要来自供应商的服务和产品。同样，每个流程也为其他一些流程——它的客户生产服务或产品。流程图用符号显示来自供应商的投入、工作活动的次序以及提供给客户的产出。

理解流程的最好方法之一就是画流程图。流程图是指服务或产品所遵循的实际或理想途径的图示。它提供了流程中各步骤的直观顺序，说明了各部分之间的关系，并指出了流程做的或应做的。

在流程改进以前，需要理解它当前运作状况。一个当前流程的流程图有助于提供流程自始至终的全景。在完全理解流程之前试图改变或改进它是不明智的，因为会突然插入很多问题。

图表3-21显示了一个简单的流程图，该图描绘了为会议购置办公用品的流程，该图包括常用的流程图符号。

还有许多其他的符号可以用来画流程图。例如，此处简单的流程图可以更详细和增加一些其他信息。

还有几种流程图。一些更常见类型的流程图在图表3-22中显示。

每一种流程图都可用来突出流程或任务中的不同方面。组织应该选择最适合它们打算确定的流程的流程图。要注意精确记录实际流程并避免不必要的复杂化。使用者要对符号有一些常规了解。

因为流程图能个性化地满足多种需求，因此它们能提供许多有用的信息。流程图有一些特别的好处：

- 通过说明各步骤之间关系提供流程运作的清晰图景。
- 显示组织与内部客户及供应商之间的关系。
- 为探讨一个现存流程或项目提供一个共同参考和标准语言。
- 作为流程改进活动的起点。

图表3-21 会议用品流程图示例

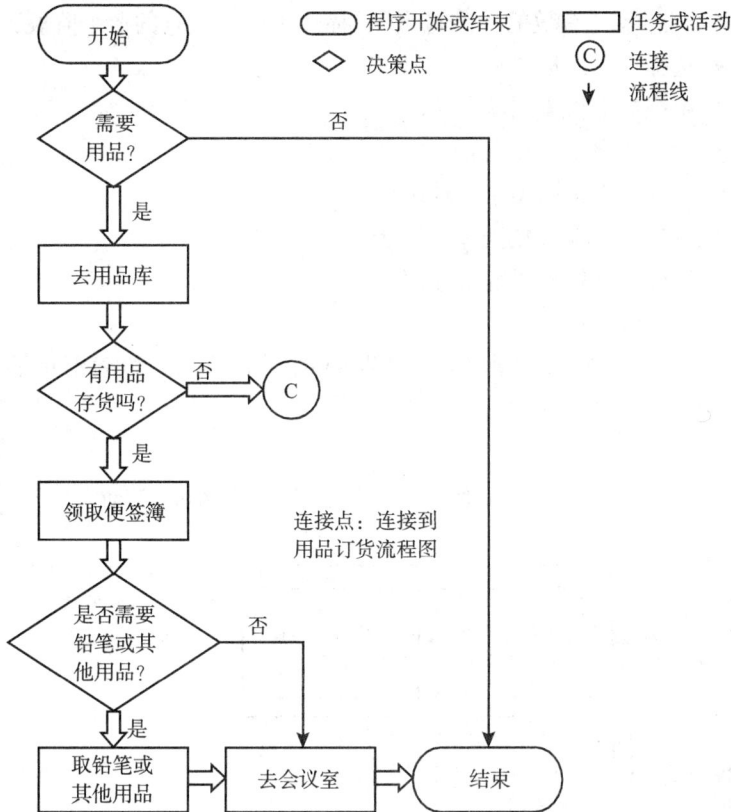

图表3-22 流程图的种类

自上而下的流程图	简单、容易构建的流程图，重点强调一个流程或项目中的主要步骤。这种流程图包含的信息比较有限，但在突出重要流程步骤方面有用。
详细的流程图	包括流程中每一阶段的大量信息。这种流程图显示流程中绝大多数步骤，并详细描述每一阶段。
布局流程图	显示流程的流动及负责各步骤的团队或雇员。这种流程图展示流程概貌及每一步应做的事情。
工作流图形	展示流程中人员、材料、文档或信息的运动。这种运动被标示在代表工作地点的图形上。该图可以使组织识别工作流中任何无效或其他问题。

标准检查

标准检查这个词是用来描述衡量产品、服务和实务与最佳绩效水平相比的水平的持续的、系统的过程。许多人认为标准检查是捕捉同类里最好的信息，但是实务中它还有更广泛的应用。更常见的是，最佳水平近似于行业领先者的外部标准。但是，标准检查也可以基于内部标准信息或其他有类似流程的组织（行业之外）的衡量标准。

流程绩效标准检查

最初，标准检查主要是由制造企业用来改善产品的。现在标准检查也被普遍应用于服务业、客户服务和其他类型的员工部门。最佳水平可以是财务或非财务标准。管理会计公告4V"有效的标准检查",描述了标准检查的七个阶段:

- 选择、排序标准检查项目。
- 组织标准检查团队。
- 记录各自的工作流程。
- 研究、识别同类中最佳绩效。
- 分析标准检查数据并识别能力。
- 执行标准检查研究的建议。
- 重塑检查标准。

图表3-23显示了管理会计公告4V中的流程表,该表汇总了七个阶段中每一阶段的活动。

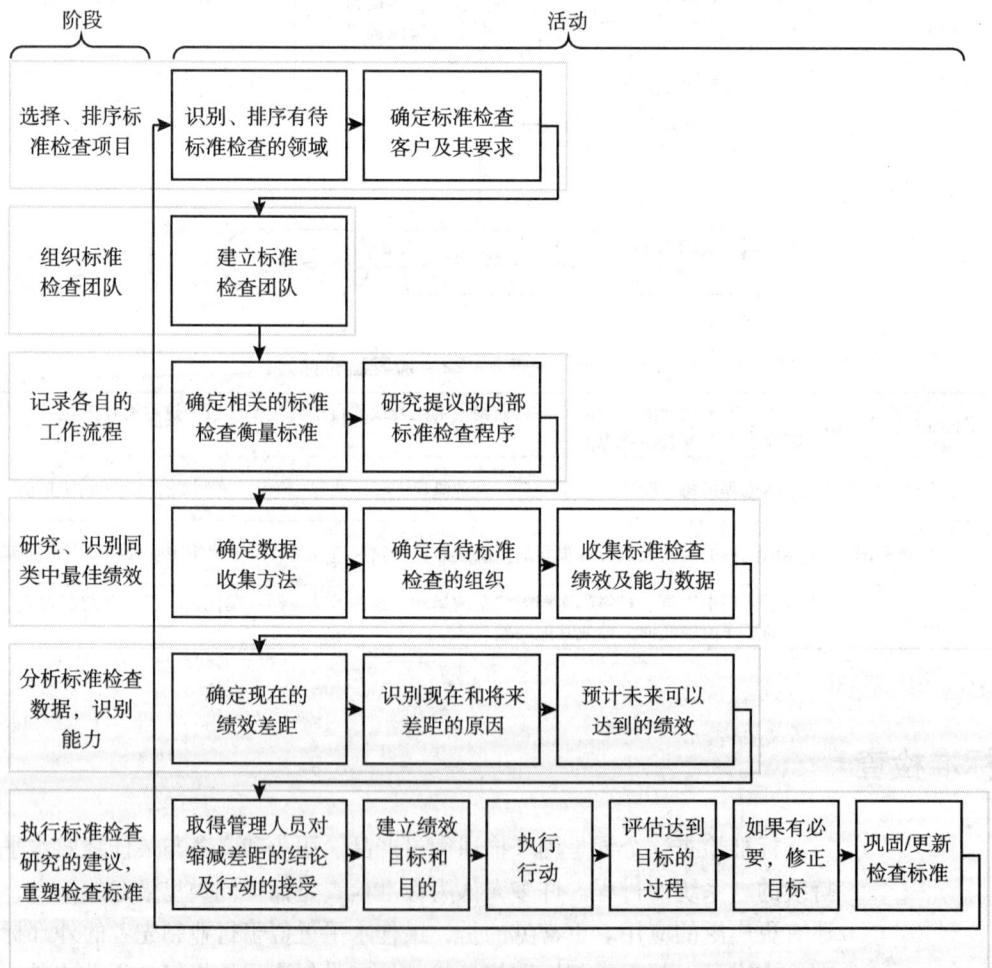

图表3-23 标准检查的阶段及活动

标准检查和创造竞争优势

20世纪90年代标准检查的研究蓬勃出现。不幸的是,许多组织误用标准检查。

各种形式的标准检查研究（最佳实务、功能、流程及竞争）自由地进行着，一般没有联系。经常作无效的比较（例如：比较高负债型公司与完全依靠收益融资的公司的增长，或者比较低成本环境中的公司与硅谷公司的增长）。因为这些误用，绝大多数标准检查研究都不是特别符合成本效益原则。

但事实是：如果设计良好、应用恰当，标准检查是帮助一个组织形成竞争力的有用工具。通过标准检查，企业识别最佳水平，然后进行研究，以帮助确定怎样采用那些水平以提高绩效。管理会计公告 4V 指出，标准检查提供了一种设定绩效目标并获得市场领先地位的理性方法（把个人情绪排除在任何争论之外）。因为标准比较建立在最佳业绩基础上，所以它提供了一种关于需要改变什么的准确评价。

战略性标准检查

应该注意的是，虽然多数标准检查研究关注的是操作（这是这项讨论的意图），但是一项标准检查项目也可以以战略为焦点。战略性标准检查是指通过把标准检查结果融合在战略规划过程中从而在企业战略层次应用流程标准检查。这样做有助于组织增长对于处理战略性业务问题的理解和能力，例如：

- 建立核心竞争力来保持竞争优势。
- 开发一条新的业务线。
- 瞄准专门的战略转移（例如：进入新市场或开发新服务）。
- 进行一项购置。
- 创建能对不确定性进行快速反应的组织。

作业管理法

这节前面提到的作业成本法，与作业管理法是相关概念。但二者的差异性特征常被混淆。管理会计公告 4CC "执行作业管理法：避免隐患" 引证国际高级制造业协会（非营利合作成员组织，支持对制造业具有战略重要性的领域）的词汇表来区分作业成本法与作业管理法。

- 作业成本法（ABC）是衡量活动、资源、成本项目的成本及绩效的一套方法。确切地说，按照消耗，资源分摊给活动，活动分摊给成本项目。ABC 承认成本动因与活动的因果关系。
- 作业管理法是一门学科，它关注活动的管理，该活动被看作提高顾客收到的价值及由提供价值得到的利润的途径。作业管理法包括成本动因分析、活动分析及绩效衡量，这些作为主要数据来源来自 ABC。

对于任何想要努力保持或提高竞争地位的公司来说，要点是 ABC 和 ABM 都是有价值的实践。ABC 回答了消耗了什么这个问题。ABM 则以流程的观点提出了什么导致成本产生这一问题。

ABM 原理和流程改进

ABM 在流程、产品、市场绩效中使用 ABC 数据，并检查怎样重新安排和改善资源的利用以增加客户和其他利益相关者的价值。但是 ABC 更多的是对当前状况的静态分析，重点在控制现存成本，而 ABM 是面向未来、以变化为导向的。ABM 努力避免不必要的成本并使现有资源最大化利用。

基于 ABM 的信息，组织通常能够：

- 做出更好的决策。
- 改善绩效。
- 提高总资源的收益。

总之，ABM 支持流程再造和业务流程重组，因为它帮助组织增加组织流程中消耗资源所创造的价值，并便于对再造影响进行衡量。

组织实行 ABM 有许多原因。图表 3－24 总结了组织在不同发展阶段从 ABM 中的受益情况。

图表 3－24　ABM 的一般应用

如果一个组织的经营是	那么 ABM 有助于
成长	<ul><li>重新配置非增值工作</li><li>改善流程和活动</li></ul>
平稳	<ul><li>识别非增值成本</li><li>优先考虑改进和效果改善</li><li>分离/消除成本动因</li><li>确定产品/服务成本</li></ul>
下降	<ul><li>消减成本</li><li>精简机构</li><li>进行裁员</li></ul>
受能力限制	<ul><li>确定产品/服务的成本</li><li>做出产品/服务的决策</li><li>确定活动的能力</li><li>识别瓶颈</li></ul>

ABM 和质量改进

ABM 有时被错误地认为可以代替质量努力、JIT 系统、流程再造、BPR 和标准检查。相反，ABM 通过提供一个整合的信息系统支持质量管理和其他创新：

- 建立报告责任。
- 便于衡量结果。
- 能够设立优先次序。

特别就质量来说，ABM 系统通过以下途径方便质量执行：

- 确定活动成本。
- 增加质量相关成本的可见性。
- 提供容易包含在质量成本报告里的质量成本标准。

因为传统会计系统关注职能（例如：研究和设计、生产、销售和营销等），收集质量成本数据比较有问题。使用 ABM 法，因质量不好引起的活动成本就比较好确认。

持续改进（改善）概念

改善是日本人用来描述组织内任何层次持续改进的术语。前提是每一流程——从最重要的开始——被检查、执行、改进时，整个企业也在改善。改善承认革新是有价值的，但是也认为革新总的来说没有持续增加的改进贡献大。

改善过程常被喻为"改进的楼梯"。一步一步，组织采用持续的流程：进行改进，保持改进，进行改进，保持改进等。尽管每一步可能很小，但组织却向上持续改进。

持续改进经常是基于一些标准的（组织的绩效预期和目标）。标准使企业得以确认制造和销售产品或服务的成本并确定成本超额的原因。

组织可以在以下几点基础上形成标准：

- 活动分析。
- 历史数据。
- 标准检查。
- 市场预期。
- 战略决策。

例如，公司标准检查可以用来比较企业和其他类似企业的现有成本结构。一旦标准确定，就可以执行一系列持续的改进来提高效率和效果，并减少差异。

最佳实务分析

最佳实务一般指在一种情况下可以产生显著结果的流程或技术，在另一种情况下可被应用或改用以提高效果、效率、质量、安全、创新和/或其他绩效标准。最佳实务分析是指差距分析中的集合性步骤。差距分析一般是指当前状态和理想状态之间的差距，或者"组织现在什么样与希望是什么样之间的差距"。当前状态是指当前实务，理想状态是指最佳实务。

最佳实务分析评价怎样使企业现有绩效水平达到最佳实务，然后确定逻辑上的下一步以转变到理想的绩效水平。

典型活动有：

- 确定差距（通过与内部经营数据比较）。
- 确定引起差距的原因。
- 检查对最佳实务存在有贡献的因素。
- 形成建议和执行最佳实务的途径。

实行最佳实务分析的技巧和工具是多样化的。定性和定量工具都被使用。这些工具中的绝大多数与TQM和改善共通。

有人认为最佳实务分析是业务流程改进创新（价值链分析、流程分析、业务流程再造、评估标准、全面质量管理和渐进改善）之后的补充。通过最佳实务分析，绩效改进变得可以诉求。

进度检查

提示：完成以下各题，参考答案随后给出。

1. 下面哪一个说法最能概括价值链分析的特点？（　　　）

 a. 它强调企业的职能结构

 b. 它检查企业的等级结构

 c. 它检查不同的战略活动

 d. 它提倡产品/服务的差异性

找出与该术语匹配的描述。

2. ＿＿＿＿＿价值链分析　　a. 没有竞争力的企业交换有关类似的制造流程的信息

3. ＿＿＿＿＿标准检查　　　b. 飞机内能移动座位的航班可为长途旅行乘客提供更多空间

4. ＿＿＿＿＿作业管理法　　c. 一个检查过去、现在和未来绩效的内部系统

5. 下面哪种说法准确地指出了作业成本法（ABC）与作业管理法（ABM）的不同？（　　　）

 a. ABC 提供关于流程、产品和市场绩效的信息，而 ABM 寻找改进它们的方法

 b. ABC 提供可诉求的信息，而 ABM 是解释性数据的来源

 c. ABC 寻求改变成本和成本动因，而 ABM 注重对它们的理解

 d. ABC 主要是面向未来的，而 ABM 基本上是历史性的

进度检查答案

1. c

2. b

3. a

4. c

5. a

战略营销

本章内容简介

营销向来被认为是一门融合了科学和艺术的学科。从科学的角度看，营销整合了企业的所有职能。它力求使企业做到最好，并通过广告、销售和其他技巧性策略来影响顾客。存在很多正式的营销工具，都能提供建立营销策略的框架。从艺术角度看，经验、直觉和创造性在制作一份成功的营销策略过程中都扮演着重要的角色。所有这些营销活动就是采用不同方式但能成功销售的原因，如戴姆勒克莱斯勒、宝马、福特、通用和本田等公司。

在很大程度上，营销具有无限的可能性。但是鉴于工业壁垒变化、新的竞争对手以及前所未有的消费者需求等这些普遍存在的生存压力，市场导向型战略成为区别成功企业和一般企业的重要特征。无论何种企业或者行业，市场导向型战略可助其达到成功；市场导向型战略提供了一种清晰的系统化的方法来确认、了解并且使其符合顾客的价值观。在组织设想、任务和战略规划中经常可以看到类似战略营销、市场导向、以顾客为中心的营销战略等字眼。当与企业整体性、竞争性、职能性战略联系起来时，这种以顾客为中心的营销方式有利于实现大股东价值。

市场导向型战略讲求团队合作。管理会计师需要了解一个企业建立和维持其市场导向型战略的基础，这样，他们才可以提供及时的信息并且为企业的生存发展做出贡献。本章关注战略营销的以下几个方面：企业内的战略角色，营销信息管理，市场细分、目标及定位，产品和服务管理，定价战略，促销组合与分销策略。

学习要点说明

注册管理会计师（CMA）考试包含很多学习要点，这些学习要点由管理会计师协会确定。学习要点描述了注册管理会计师考试要求掌握的所有知识点和技能，并且细分为各个章节。注册管理会计师考试教材解释了学习要点所包含的各个部分，是对学习要点的有力支持。学习要点可以帮助考生以不同的方式或通过不同的问题情景理解这些概念。考生还应该练习学习要点中所提到的全部或者部分计算，或者完成计算过程中的缺失部分。学习要点不能代替对 CMA 考试教材内容的研究和学习，但是可以确保考生达到学习要点所设定的目标。

注册管理会计师教材中所包含的学习要点是一个完整的集合，并且是到目前为止最新的版本。考生可以浏览 IMA 的官方网站 www. imanet. org，点击"认证"部分查看和下载关于学习要点的最新 PDF 文件。

学习要点

2.1 企业内的战略角色

LOS 2.1.1：确定企业总体战略和营销程序的相互关系。

LOS 2.1.2：说明对企业营销战略设定程序的理解，以及达到这些战略营销目的的目标和方法。

LOS 2.1.3：说明对优势、劣势、机遇和挑战分析（SWOT）的理解。

LOS 2.1.4：解释识别客户需要以及提供价值来满足这些客户需要的重要性。

LOS 2.1.5：定义并说明对业务组合概念的理解。

LOS 2.1.6：说明对营销过程的理解，包括分析营销机遇、选择目标市场、开发营销组合及管理营销活动。

LOS 2.1.7：说明对营销分析、计划、执行和控制之间相互关系的理解。

LOS 2.1.8：定义行业中的战略组，讨论为什么它们要求不同的营销战略。

LOS 2.1.9：定义波特的三种一般战略。

LOS 2.1.10：说明对行业演变期竞争变化的理解。

LOS 2.1.11：辨别萌芽、成长、震荡、成熟、衰退行业的不同。

LOS 2.1.12：说明对全球化对产业结构的影响的理解。

LOS 2.1.13：确定内部竞争优势及其组成部分，包括效率、质量、创新和客户满意度。

LOS 2.1.14：说明对价值创造链的理解。

LOS 2.1.15：确定独特的竞争力、资源和能力。

LOS 2.1.16：确定营销战略失败的原因及保持竞争优势的途径，包括持续改进和标准检查。

2.2 营销信息管理

LOS 2.2.1：确定营销信息需求。

LOS 2.2.2：说明对营销信息开发过程的理解，包括内部数据收集、营销情报和营销调查。

LOS 2.2.3：定义客户关系管理（CRM）。

LOS 2.2.4：确定收集、分配和利用营销信息的有效方法。

2.3 市场细分、目标及定位

LOS 2.3.1：确定目标营销步骤，包括市场细分、目标及定位。

LOS 2.3.2：确定并定义大众营销、细分营销、补缺营销以及微观营销。

LOS 2.3.3：说明对细分消费者市场、企业市场和国际市场的理解。

LOS 2.3.4：确定有效细分的要求。

LOS 2.3.5：说明对市场目标的理解，包括评估和选择细分市场。

LOS 2.3.6：定义定位战略。

2.4 产品和服务管理

LOS 2.4.1：区分产品和服务。

LOS 2.4.2：对产品和服务进行分类，包括消费品、工业品和其他交易实体。

LOS 2.4.3：说明对产品属性、品牌、包装、标签和产品支持服务的理解。

LOS 2.4.4：说明对生产线决策和产品组合决策的理解。

LOS 2.4.5：说明对服务营销的理解，包括服务营销战略的本质和特征。

LOS 2.4.6：说明对新产品开发战略和产品生命周期战略的理解。

2.5 定价战略

LOS 2.5.1：说明影响定价决策的内部和外部影响因素。

LOS 2.5.2：说明对一般定价方法的理解，包括成本法、价值法及竞争法。

LOS 2.5.3：讨论管理会计师在定价决策中的作用。

LOS 2.5.4：说明对新产品定价战略的理解，包括市场撇脂法和市场渗透法。

LOS 2.5.5：说明对产品组合定价战略的理解，包括生产线定价、备选产品定价、后续产品定价、副产品定价及成组产品定价。

LOS 2.5.6：说明对价格调整战略的理解，包括折扣和折让定价、差别定价、心理定价、促销定价、地理定价、国际定价。

LOS 2.5.7：说明对买方或卖方弹性和讨价还价能力是怎样影响价格的理解。

2.6 促销组合与分销战略

LOS 2.6.1：定义营销传播组合。

LOS 2.6.2：说明对整合营销传播程序的理解，包括对整合营销传播的需求。

LOS 2.6.3：确定并定义整合传播组合的组成部分，包括广告、促销、公共关系以及人员推销。

LOS 2.6.4：说明对广告程序的理解，包括设定广告目标、决定广告预算、制定广告战略和进行广告评估。

LOS 2.6.5：说明对促销程序的理解，包括促销目标、工具、战略和评估。

LOS 2.6.6：说明对公共关系的理解，并确定相关工具。

LOS 2.6.7：说明对作为促销组合要素之一的人员推销程序的理解。

LOS 2.6.8：确定在特定情况下营销组合的最有效组成（广告、促销、公共关系及人员推销）。

LOS 2.6.9：定义关系营销。

LOS 2.6.10：说明对直销模式及其优点、直销形式、整合促销程序和道德问题的理解。

LOS 2.6.11：定义分销渠道的本质和功能。

LOS 2.6.12：说明对分销渠道行为和组织的理解，包括垂直、水平和混合营销系统以及渠道分散趋势。

LOS 2.6.13：说明对分销渠道设计决策的理解，包括分析客户服务需求、定义渠道目标和限制、确定和评估主要的备选方案以及全球执行。

第 1 节
企业内的战略角色

本节内容简介

市场导向型战略试图面对当今全球化商业环境中无处不在的竞争。通过市场导向型战略，公司可以评估市场以及组成市场的客户，并把这些信息作为一个重要组成部分纳入到商业战略中。

战略与营销的联系

公司的战略确定了其经营范围和目的，并且概括了其长期目标和能力，以及要达到这些目标所必需的行动和资源。营销战略把客户观点加到了这个组合中来。除了倾听客户的声音，营销战略必须要符合整体的企业战略规划优先次序，并且要支持企业整体性、竞争性和业务单元或职能性战略。

制定营销战略与整体性战略有一些相似之处：

- 分析——要针对组织的目标市场确定设想。
- 制定战略——筛选并制定合适的目标市场战略和目标。
- 执行活动——执行并管理营销程序战略，达到每个目标市场客户的价值要求。

战略营销把营销创新提升到一个新的高度。它将企业及其面临的竞争环境连接到一起，并且试图处理不断变化的情况并提供较多的客户价值。它使市场导向法成为营销战略制定的必然选择，而营销战略制定又为下列各项提供了一个基础：

- 环境监测。
- 决定目标客户和服务客户。
- 指导产品/服务的规格。
- 确定竞争对手。

在战略营销中，营销是整个企业的活动而不仅仅是一个专门的职能。组织业绩比销售收入的增加更重要。

战略营销程序

绕过最好、最著名的商学院和大量的商业课本，关键是战略营销程序必须符合、联合并支持整体性战略。战略营销程序为组织设想、任务、战略、目标和目的提供蓝图。战略营销程序支持目标市场层面上的详细计划。

图表 3－25 对战略规划和战略营销的关系进行了简单的陈述。

图表 3-25　战略规划与战略营销程序

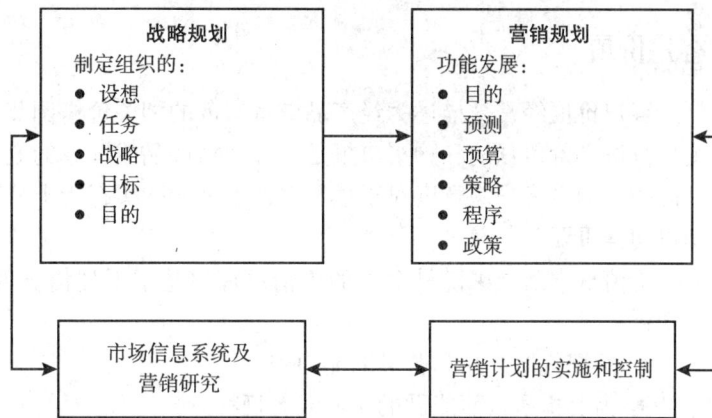

就大部分模型而言，组织会根据情况调整营销程序中的步骤和术语。尽管结果比手段重要，但是所有的营销模式都可以说明图表 3-26 中总结的各个阶段。本章接下来的内容充分阐述了各种战略营销的不同阶段和活动。

图表 3-26　战略营销程序

阶　段	采取的行动	结　果
分析营销机遇	• 系统分析环境因素（比如：合作的、竞争的、经济的、社会的、政治的和法律的因素） • 确定优势、劣势、挑战、机遇和反挑战 • 定义产品/服务的客户及其偏好	确认营销活动中的盈利机会和潜在限制
	• 确认兴趣市场的子集（细分） • 判断各子集需求的不同	市场细分，并针对相应的价值要求阐明企业的价值主张
	• 使用各种营销传感法来理解现在发生的和很可能发生的事情	不断地研究市场
设立目标	• 通过销售、市场占有率、客户保持率、利润贡献率和客户满意度来阐明管理人员预期 • 确定业绩标准	指明营销目标（从组织目标中衍生出来或者与其一致）
选择目标市场	• 确认客户需求和满足这些需求要做的事情 • 预测总的市场规模和潜在增长率	在给定市场及竞争的情况下竞争（如果客户需求变化，可能是一个或多个细分市场），决定怎样、何时、何地进行竞争
开发营销组合	• 制定针对目标市场的战略并达到组织目标 • 决定产品、价格、促销和地点（分销渠道）	产品战略、定价战略、促销战略以及分销战略
管理营销结果	• 实施营销计划 • 根据预定进度执行营销任务	协调执行营销计划
	• 测量营销计划结果 • 比较实际结果和计划目标 • 决定必要的调整措施	控制营销计划

客户价值和客户满意度

在目前的商业环境中，昨天还被认为是优秀的组织绩效，在今天也许就只能合乎要求，到明天也许就不合格了。一个企业想要在竞争中获得胜利，它的营销策略必须支持客户价值和客户满意度。

客户价值

客户价值经常被描述为经产品或者服务的相关价格调节过的市场认知品质的一种测量方法；价值预期和购买决策是以客户对产品或服务的效益扣除总成本后的感知为基础的。测量客户满意度对于预测客户未来的购买行为十分重要，但测量用户价值感知也同样重要。

价值从本质上来说是个人的事情；客户基于下列情况的不同而拥有不同的价值感知：

- 负担优质产品和服务的能力。
- 为负担质量而能做的交换或者牺牲。
- 对产品和服务是否与其价格相符的感知。

一些客户也许愿意支付较高的价格来选择快递方式送货。而另一些也许愿意等待比较长的时间，这样可以支付较低的价格。

在分析用户价值感知时，组织努力了解导致客户做出购买决策的原因——为什么客户认为一种产品或服务比其他的更有价值。企业一般进行用户价值分析，来进一步检查价值的两个组成部分（产品和成本）并帮助进行直销以提高客户对产品价值的感知。

战略营销的一个关键目标是拉近与客户的距离，并且培养与他们的关系，以便了解他们的真实需要和预期。这种了解必将像组织影响客户满意度的每一部分一样，最终渗透到整个企业中去。

客户满意度

客户满意度反映了客户使用产品或服务的感觉比其原有的价值预期好的程度。当（与竞争对手提供的预期和价值相比）客户有一次好的使用经历并且感觉非常满意时，也就产生了较高的客户价值。

组织一般通过各种措施收集定量和定性数据来评估客户满意度。当两种数据整合在一起时，公司得到了综合的反馈，这使企业未来战略营销计划和决策程序更容易也更有效，并且增加了企业做出更好的企业决策的机会。

为了获得并保持客户满意度，组织需要：

- 通过适当的程序、衡量方法和数据来确定客户满意度和不满意度。
- 及时从客户那里收集关于产品/服务和近期交易的反馈信息。
- 如果可行，收集并综合关于竞争对手和/或检查标准的客户满意度的信息。
- 保持与当前企业战略一致的客户满意度措施。

业务组合概念

一个组织要想满足所有客户而且不陷入试图无所不能的陷阱，那已经不只是挑战了。不管你信不信，满意度的高低和一些客户无关。但是，有一些其他的核心客户——战略群组——他们对组织的成功和存活非常重要，所以他们的需求必须被满足。

上一章的帕累托原则中提到了"战略规划"。总有一群核心客户对组织盈利性至关重要。理论上，总销售收入的80%来自于20%的客户。和那些数量少但关键的客户联系是非常重要的。在某种程度上，组织必须关注这些核心客户。

那么一个组织怎样区分客户并如何决定涉足何种业务呢？业务组合分析、迈克尔·波特的一般竞争战略、商业周期以及客户盈利性分析等概念是非常重要的，它们都很重视组织想把资本投资到最可行方面的需求。

业务组合分析

组合分析不是营销学特有的。例如，金融机构用组合模型在组合单元之间（例如，股票、产品、企业等）平衡风险和收益，继而选择出最优组合。

由于组合分析适用于营销，因此可以帮助组织制定出合适的产品和业务组合，以提供不相关的多样化从而不受经济下滑的影响。大部分组织倾向于经营多种有不同增长率和回报率的产品和业务。管理层也希望制定一个有多种收益、提供充足现金流并保持长期利润的组合。以百事公司（PepsiCo）为例，该公司是百事（Pepsi）、菲多利（Frito-lay）和纯品康纳（Tropicana）的母公司，拥有多种产品、生产线和业务。

标准化组合模型

在营销中，咨询公司开发了多种组合战略。最著名的三种标准化组合模型是：
- 波士顿咨询集团的增长/占有率矩阵。
- 麦肯锡公司的多因素分析。
- 理特管理顾问公司的战略业务单元系统。

在这些标准化模型中有一些基本的相似点和差异。这三种模型都提供了产品或业务分类系统，并且包括矩阵分析。

从概念上说，波士顿咨询集团（BCG）模型和麦肯锡多因素分析具有相似的做法，包括：
- 建立——意味着采取行动来增加市场占有率（甚至以短期收益和现金流量的减少为代价）。
- 保持——保护市场占有率和竞争地位。
- 收获——最大化短期收益和现金流量（即使以减少市场占有率为代价）。
- 撤出——要求消除这项业务（通过清算或者卖断）。

除了这些相似之处，每个模型都采用了有细微差别的方法。下面是对这些模型的概述。

波士顿咨询集团（BCG）的增长/占有率矩阵

BCG业务组合模型把企业机遇分成了四个类别——明星、钱牛、问号和狗——每一种需要有不同的整体性战略和营销方法。
- **明星（保持）**

属于明星组的业务在高增长环境中保持着较高的市场占有率。组织需要集中精力（专业知识、技术应用、人员等）来增加运营的客户价值。明星产品需要被小心地培养并且注意保持在增长市场中的竞争优势。

- 钱牛（收获）

钱牛类业务在较低的或者是下降的环境中占有较高的市场占有率。它们一般被称作"珍宝"，而且被描述为今日仍能提供现金以支持其他创新的昨日明星。按净额算，它们仍能提供巨大的正现金流。

- 问号（建立）

问号类业务有较低的市场占有率，但是有较高的增长潜力。这组业务经常引起注意（因为它们也许会成为成功的明星，并且最后成为钱牛），但是它们不应该分散企业对核心业务的注意力。问号类业务可能数量很大，但货币销售收入很小。组织从该组不会得到很多利润。

- 狗（撤出）

尽管一些人也许会认为把企业称为"狗"是很恶俗的，但事实上有很多企业确实经营着那些没有价值的买卖。狗类业务指的是市场占有率和增长率都很低的产品。简单说，它们没有盈利能力。

图表3-27对BCG模型的四种情况进行了说明。

图表3-27 波士顿咨询集团（BCG）图

BCG的研究表明，根据经验，高市场占有率与高投资报酬率（ROI）及较低成本之间高度相关。换句话说，单位成本会随一段时间生产的产品数量（以及积累的经验）而降低。BCG模型用一些业务支持稳定的、高的市场占有率以便为其他业务提供现金流。

麦肯锡公司的多因素分析

麦肯锡模型认为存在有两个决定企业评价的一般变量：行业吸引力和业务定位（优势）。每个变量都被多个行业因素影响。对于不同的行业，因素的重要性也不同。总之，在麦肯锡模型中有9部分，参见图表3-28。

图表 3 - 28　麦肯锡公司的业务定位/行业吸引力分析

业务定位			
强	S	I	I
平均	H	S	I
弱	H	H	S
	低	平均	高

行业吸引力

I=投资和保持/增长/建立或重建
S=选择性投资收益
H=收获/撤出

根据图表 3 - 28，一般来说有 6 种行动路线：

* 投资并持有。
* 投资等待增长。
* 投资建立或者重新建立。
* 选择性投资（在有希望的领域）。
* 收获（榨取）钱牛。
* 出售（卖出）狗。

理特管理顾问公司的战略业务单元系统

理特管理顾问公司（ADL）组合概念围绕战略业务单元（SBUs）展开。一切企业运作都被划分为 SBUs，SBUs 被放在一个有 24 格的矩阵中。决定企业评价的两个一般变量为：行业成熟度（从萌芽到衰退）和竞争地位（从主导地位到衰弱和无法存活）。

ADL 模型用"交通灯"分类表示：

* 绿色——意味着高市场占有率/或一个有吸引力的市场。
* 黄色——表示中等市场的特点。
* 红色——代表低市场占有率/或一个没有前途的成熟市场。

图表 3 - 29 列示了 ADL 模型。

图表 3 - 29　ADL 战略业务单元表

竞争地位				
领先	G	G	G	G
壮大	G	G	G	Y
顺利	G	G	Y	R
维持	G	Y	R	R
衰弱	Y	R	R	R
无法存活	R	R	R	R
	萌芽期	成长期	成熟期	衰退期

行业成熟度

G=绿色	Y=黄色	R=红色
（建立）	（保持）	（清算）

3 - 481

基于上述矩阵分类，ADL 模型为每个 SBU 设计了一般战略（建立、保持或清算），并且构建了合适的战术计划（关注、进入或多样化）。

三种模型的变异有很多；其他咨询师也设计了不同的方法，许多公司也根据自己的实际应用进一步改进了这些模型。例如通用电气设计了一个延伸了上述三个标准模型特点的模型。

通用电气模型

BCG 模型认为市场占有率是盈利能力的惟一决定因素，而通用电气（GE）则发展了一种综合了更多信息并考虑更多影响市场长期吸引力的其他因素的模型。

在 GE 模型中，企业按行业吸引力和业务优势（与麦肯锡模型类似）分类。每一方面都以图表 3 – 30 中列示的影响因素的复合指数为基础。

图表 3 – 30　通用电气模型中行业吸引力和业务优势的组成部分

行业吸引力		业务优势	
·市场规模 ·市场增长率 ·市场盈利性 ·定价趋势 ·竞争（密度和竞争） ·市场进入壁垒 ·差异化的机会	·需求的可变性 ·市场细分 ·分销结构 ·技术进步 ·世界范围	**市场定位** ·国内市场占有率 ·全球市场占有率 ·市场占有率增长 ·与处于领先地位的竞争对手相比的市场占有率	**竞争优势** ·领先质量创新 ·客户忠诚度 ·技术 ·营销 ·与处于领先地位的竞争对手相比的相对利润 ·与处于领先地位的竞争对手相比的相对成本 ·财务或投资资源途径

一旦企业按照其行业吸引力和业务优势被分类，它们就被放入图表 3 – 31 的 3 × 3 矩阵（与麦肯锡模型类似）中。

图表 3 – 31　通用电气的行业吸引力和业务优势模型

		业务优势		
		强	平均	弱
	高	A	A	B
行业吸引力	中	A	B	C
	低	B	C	C

解释指南根据企业在 GE 矩阵中的位置对它们进行了排序。

● **A 级优先（绿色区域）**

行业吸引力和业务优势都很高，这类企业应当"建立"。

● **B 级优先（黄色区域）**

行业吸引力和业务优势都是中等，这类企业应当"持有"。

● **C 级优先（红色区域）**

行业吸引力和业务优势都很低，这类企业一般"收获或出售"。

其他组合模型

除了以上讨论的四种模型，还有其他很多模型。比如修正的风险报酬和随机（随机变量）模型、结合模拟的定制组合模型等。这些更为复杂的模型超出了产品或业务分类，并且给资源配置提供了操作指南。随着时间推移，组织会采纳并应用业务组合概念来做客户组合分析。

组合管理模型的优点和局限

总之，业务组合管理模型试图提供对创造可行的战略性备选方案、估计每个备选方案价值并识别其固有风险必要的概念和战略。各种模型为选择备选方案、权衡风险和机遇、理解组合中各组成要素如何互相影响提供了一个框架。

组合模型提供了一个相关快照。然而，在应用组合管理模型时，我们必须警惕网格测量是相当主观而且很难进行明确评估的。业务组合模型不能被用作"食谱"式计划工具。

一般竞争战略

一个企业要想在行业中生存和繁荣发展必须达到两个基本要求。组织必须：
- 提供客户想买的东西。
- 可以持久面对竞争。

迈克尔·波特提出了三种一般竞争战略，很多企业单独或者综合利用这些战略来开发可持续战略来超过行业竞争对手。
- 成本领先（同等质量、更低成本）。
- 差异化（价值高于溢价）。
- 关注（瞄准特定部门）。

图表3-32总结了每种战略的关键特征。具体情况决定了企业最好的战略选择。

图表3-32 一般竞争战略

战 略	描 述
成本领先	• 促成相对一般竞争对手来说的更低成本（但是不是以牺牲质量、服务或其他为代价） • 要求积极开展内部规模经济、严格控制成本及间接费用、警觉地追求成本降低，避开边际客户账户等 • 尽管竞争压力较大，但回报率仍在行业平均水平以上 • 提供较高的利润，使其可以再投资来维持成本领先 **例子**：折扣零售业的沃尔玛、折扣经纪业的嘉信理财、折扣汽车业的现代公司
差异化	• 把重点放在创造一种客户认为独特或者优良的并且愿意为其支付溢价（与其对手的价格相比）的商品或服务 • 采取多种形式，比如产品或服务的设计和特色（如耐用或者方便）、品牌忠诚度、优质客户服务等 • 倾向于降低价格敏感度和产生较高的利润 • 不忽略成本；在不影响差异化的领域推行降低成本 **例子**：钟表业的劳力士，软饮料业的可口可乐和百事，零售业的诺德史顿

续表

战 略	描 述
关注	• 关注范围狭小的战略目标（比如：特定买方群体、生产线部门、地域性市场） • 试图比竞争对手（这些对手的竞争范围更广泛）更有效率或更有效果地为目标市场提供优异服务 • 在目标市场（但不必在行业内）中获得成本领先或差异化 **例子：**针对高端跑车爱好者的保时捷，针对能买得起得、无须排场的、航空旅行的西南航空

行业演变

行业演变还是战略制定和业务组合开发得另一个重要因素。

产品生命周期（PLC）是一个用来分析行业演变可能过程的概念——用来预测行业结构的转变。它基于行业要经历多个可以预知的时期或阶段的假设。不同时期反映了行业销售收入增长率状况。竞争性战略和战略营销创新必须适应不同时期买方多样性和偏好的变化。

PLC 分类

基本的 PLC 可分为：萌芽期、成长期、震荡期、成熟期和衰退期。

• **萌芽期**

萌芽期（也被称作导入期、出现期）描述的是一个新行业或是由于新技术、买方需求变化或确认未满足需求而改革了的行业。因为最初的买方惯性和产品试验，进入期以几乎水平的增长率为特征。例如，多年以来一直处于萌芽期的数码照相。

• **成长期**

就像这个名字一样，产品被证明是成功的，随后买方掀起购买热，快速增长开始出现。比如，无线技术进步后，手机行业随之繁荣起来。

• **震荡期**

在客户接触和使用新产品以后会变得更精明，这样震荡也随之发生。供应商和客户聚集在市场领先者周围，这样一来迫使边缘玩家退出市场。手机制造商一度充斥着市场，但是当主要制造商出现后，很多都会退出舞台。

• **成熟期**

当产品在市场上畅销时，市场就成熟了，增长率会稳定在较高水平。例如，微波炉现在就是日用厨具。

• **衰退期**

顾名思义，在衰退期，增长最终逐渐停止，新的产品替代品出现。除非努力更新产品，否则将面临结束。比如，当品牌药品失去专利权，而一般替代品进入市场时，品牌就开始衰落。

图表3-33展示了典型的 PLC 阶段及其与销售收入和利润的相互关系。起初，利润落后于销售收入，这是因为在导入阶段费用一般很高。当产品成熟后，销售收入和利润都开始下降（但利润一般先于销售收入开始下降）。

图表3-33　产品生命周期曲线

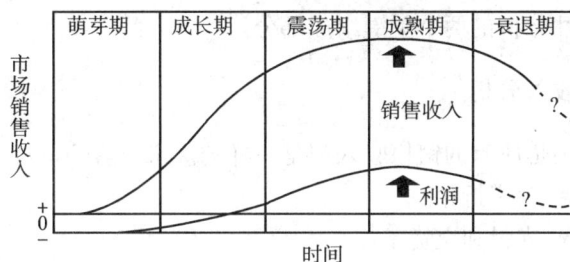

有时我们也采用其他的PLC分类。例如，"过渡"描述了一个行业从快速增长到成熟的转变过程。产品快速增长直到在市场上畅销（比如，微波炉）。"分割"描绘了在一个行业中有数量众多的小企业但是缺乏主导力量（比如，草坪护理）。"重建"有时被用来描述一个现存的行业从衰退中重新振作（一般是因为新一代技术或者幸存的竞争对手集中精力来降低成本和改善生产力来维持市场占有率）。当制造商把手机定位为多功能手机从而可以传送和接收音乐、游戏、文本、图片及其他类型数据时，手机进入了一个新阶段。

PLC 经验总结

多年以来，对PLC阶段可以得出如下观测结论：

- 不同的行业，每个阶段的持续时间不一样。
- 两个阶段之间的分界点并不总是清晰的。
- "S"型曲线可能发生变化，有时行业会跳过一个阶段（比如，跳过成熟期，直接从增长期到衰退期）。
- 对不同行业而言，每个阶段的竞争实质可能很不一样。

全球化的影响

全球化为PLC阶段带来了新的空间。有广泛的全球竞争的行业存在着很多不同的机遇和挑战（例如，电信、汽车以及消费类电子产品）。

国际竞争会影响传统分类。比如，生命周期的阶段会因国家的不同而不同。一个行业也许在一个国家正在快速增长，而在另一个国家正在衰退。

在不同的国家，企业的竞争和营销战略也各不相同。必须将全球标准化的优点和局限与本土化的潜在优势进行评估。一个经典的案例是：韩国汽车制造商在美国市场为了与日本及美国汽车竞争，而对现代汽车采用的定位战略（低价并且延长产品保质期限）。

客户盈利性分析

企业是从购买产品和服务的客户那里获得利润，而非来自制造产品或提供服务。这个简单的前提就是支撑客户盈利性分析的关键概念。

客户盈利性分析追踪并报告客户的收入和成本；这使企业可以确定特定客户的盈

利性（或者不盈利性），并提供提高利润所必需的信息。收入分析和成本分析是客户盈利性分析的两个关键组成部分。

客户收入分析

不是所有的销售收入都是一样的。来自客户的净收入因如下因素的不同而不同：
- 销售折扣。
- 支付和交货条款。
- 销货退回与折让。

不同的客户也许会带来大致相同的总销售收入。但是收入分析可以为这些销售产生的净收入描绘出另一幅完全不同的画面。

在图表 3 – 34 中展示了来自两个不同客户的基本收入分析。

图表 3 – 34　客户收入分析

	客户 A	客户 B
总销售收入	$600 000	$580 000
减：销售折扣	(30 000)	—
净发票额	$570 000	$580 000
减：销货退回与折让	10 000	5 000
净销售收入	$560 000	$575 000
减：现金折扣	—	8 000
加：财务（利息）费用	$4 000	—
净客户收入	$564 000	$567 000

尽管来自客户 B 的初始总销售收入比来自客户 A 的少 $20 000，但是客户 B 的净客户收入却比客户 A 多 $3 000（$567 000 – $564 000）。

客户成本分析

为了补充客户收入信息，客户成本分析确定了与服务各种客户相匹配的成本活动及成本动因。和收入数据相似，可以点对点地对个别客户或细分市场进行比较。图表 3 – 35 显示了对成本类别可以进行的比较。

图表 3 – 35　客户成本分析分类

分类	描述	例子
单位成本	卖给客户的每一单位产品所消耗/使用的内部资源	销售佣金，运输成本，每单位补货成本
批次成本	每次销售所消耗/使用的内部资源	订单处理成本和发票成本
服务支持成本	与销售数量或批次无关的，为服务客户而消耗/使用的内部资源	销售费用、月报成本、逾期支付收款成本
分销渠道成本	用于服务客户的每一分销渠道所消耗/使用的资源	区域仓库、分销中心、零售网点的运营成本
销售支持成本	不能被追溯到单位、批次、客户或分销渠道的，用于维系销售和服务活动所消耗/使用的内部资源	用以支持销售、支付工资、附加福利或奖金的公司一般性支出

一段时间内各种活动的成本动因及其每项成本分类的分配率都可以追踪和分析：

- 接受订单。
- 处理订单。
- 交货。
- 加快接受订单、处理订单、交货的速度。
- 客户访问数量。
- 开出账单。
- 销售退回与折让。
- 补货。
- 销售服务。

我们可以区分服务不同客户的成本差异，然后，比较净利润。

总之，通过追踪和分析收入和成本数据，公司可以：

- 识别那些对于一些或者全部客户不盈利的活动或过程。
- 衡量客户盈利性。
- 识别并且发展最有盈利性的客户。
- 改变业务以增加平均水平客户的利润贡献，并且提高表现最差部门的利润。

关于不同客户的信息越精确，企业就可以越好地重组客户关系，并且把不盈利的客户变成盈利的。

S. W. O. T. 分析

理解行业竞争对于制定现实的战略规划和营销战略是至关重要的。企业评估其内部竞争优势和核心竞争力也同等重要。内部和外部评估的一个重要目标是确定怎样使企业区别于竞争对手的能力的价值最大化。

CMA 学习体系本册第一章"战略规划"，详细描述了进行 S. W. O. T. 分析——评估组织优势、劣势、机遇、挑战的要素。下面介绍在优势创造过程中 S. W. O. T. 分析数据的应用。

内部竞争优势

在评价其内部竞争优势时，企业要确定：

- 企业的优势和竞争力。
- 在市场中的合适地位。
- 与竞争对手相比其资源如何。

企业的优势和竞争力

S. W. O. T. 数据可以清楚地描述公司优势。比如，3M 公司以其研发和推广新产品而著名。客户因为 L. L. Bean 享有盛名的客户服务而认可它。索尼以其产品质量、可信度和耐用性而享誉消费类电子产品界。其他能带来竞争优势的独特能力是广告、分销等，或者是内部处理能力，如效率、质量、创新等。当然，不同公司有不同的优势——哪怕是在同一行业内。

分析竞争对手可以确定什么是竞争优势。企业一般只分析关键竞争对手——那些瞄准相同市场或细分市场的企业。Tylenol 制造商分析的非处方止痛药竞争对手可能包括 Excedrin、Anacin、Advil、Bayer、Bufferin、Aleve 等。

竞争对手分析（对每一位关键竞争对手）的基本信息包括：

- 业务目标、目的、战略。
- 目标市场和客户基础。
- 现有市场占有率和趋势。
- 能力（财务、技术、经营等）。
- 优势、劣势、缺陷。
- 关键的竞争优势。
- 领导和管理能力。

竞争分析也可以识别可能的新竞争对手。

竞争信息可以从很多渠道获得，比如，年报、行业研究、贸易刊物、普通的企业杂志、报纸、金融分析师报告、政府报告以及来自客户、供应商和推销员的信息。根据环境和详细程度，竞争对手分析可以做得相当复杂。

有了竞争分析数据，企业就有了对每个竞争对手可能的行动和它们对行业变化的反应能力作出预测的依据。

在市场中的合适地位

企业市场规模的关键衡量指标包括：

- 市场占有率——等于某一产品市场中公司销售收入除以所有企业总销售收入。
- 市场潜力——在某一特定时期内产品的最大销售量（满足所有有购买欲望和能力的客户的需求）。
- 销售预测——在某一特定时期内的预期产品销售收入。

市场数据使得企业能够分析市场机遇。管理人员能预测现存市场和新市场的财务吸引力。

与竞争对手相比其资源如何

比较本企业与其竞争对手的资源，一般需要逐项对比如下几项（但不限于此）：

- 人员（领导、管理人员、职员）。
- 研究和设计。
- 技术。
- 制造能力。
- 销售能力。
- 分销渠道。
- 现金状况。
- 贸易关系。

仔细与竞争对手比较内部资源有助于识别核心竞争力。

核心竞争力

客户忠诚度是随情况变化的、脆弱的、稍纵即逝的。这也是为什么组织必须力求获得其产品服务组合之外的认可。一个企业需要被认为拥有核心竞争力组合。

核心竞争力（也叫独特竞争力）一般被定义为在特定主题领域或技能范围内的基础知识、能力或专长。市场里有特定优势的公司可以被认为是在这一领域有核心竞争力。

管理会计公告 4X "评估竞争优势的价值链分析"中，指出组织核心竞争力的如下额外要点：

- 它们由技术的、实物的和人力的资源经过出众的整合创造而成。
- 它们代表着独特技术、无形资产、文化能力等（比如，企业在管理变化、充实团队、推动持续学习方面的能力）。
- 它们是"结缔组织"，将一个企业看似不同的方面连接在一起，并使管理者和雇员可以交流不同业务环境下的见解。

什么使真正的核心竞争力与"同大家一样"的能力相区别呢？有如下 3 方面普遍接受的特征：

- 被提升的客户价值——核心竞争力对客户感知产品或服务的益处有重大贡献。
- 惟一性——核心竞争力可以减少竞争对手模仿带来的威胁。
- 市场杠杆——核心竞争力提供进入各种市场的潜在可能。

核心竞争力中的"核心"表明企业有开发其他产品和服务的坚实基础。核心竞争力的多样化很值得拥有，因为可以减少风险和投资，并且可以促进业务单元之间交流学习和实践。

价值创造

如前所述，价值是由买方感知的，并以购买和使用产品或服务的收益和成本为基础。客户满意度反映了使用体验与客户价值预期的契合程度。与竞争对手提供的产品相比，良好的使用经历会带来出众的客户满意度。价值创造是决定在哪以及怎样才能使企业产品或服务提供较高价值并且随后管理营销能力的过程，该过程使良好的竞争力/价值与结果相匹配。

企业战略和市场是相互联系的，并且二者对竞争优势十分重要。一个企业必须理解当前市场、市场可能怎样变化以及处于竞争劣势的危险。客户如果转向购买新的或者其他的产品，就意味着价值转移发生了。从传统的相机和胶卷转移到数码相机就是价值转移的一个例子。应该对潜在市场转移进行预测，并且制定出反击战略。

注意：价值链分析在本书第 1 章第 3 节 "业务流程绩效"中阐述。

营销战略失败的原因

营销会形成重大战略，但是因为各种原因，计划可能会失效，有时甚至失败。导致失败的主要原因有：

- 缺少组织配合

高层管理人员必须对营销计划全力以赴。对提供的产品和服务怎样支持组织目标必须有清楚的理解和接受。跨功能的支持也要到位。

- 情况分析不正确

较差的预测分析会导致可能高估营销机会、低估竞争、曲解趋势、失去目标受众等错误的产品开发。一些错误构思的努力确实会导致开发出没有市场的产品和服务。

- 营销计划的频率

如果战略被重估得太频繁，就会造成组织对市场的反应不够稳定。反之，如果规划长期不被修正，那么组织就可能无法恰当地应对环境挑战并且可能失去竞争地位。

- 营销与销售脱节

营销与销售具有内在联系。销售人员的职责就是执行营销战略。如果营销不能分享正确的信息（比如，错误或者不合格的间接支持材料），销售就会受到影响。而且，如果营销没能认识到或没能从销售人员那里得到关于客户数据和需求的数据，那么就会导致产品或服务的失败。

- 缺乏或不好的战术规划

对于环境的变化，绝大多数战略营销规划顶多需要一些微调。比如：产品存在一些质量问题，或者竞争对手可能引入了一种新产品。很多产品和服务的失败可以归咎于战术执行以及控制存在问题。营销主管需要不断监督计划执行情况，做出必要的调整，如果实际结果严重背离计划结果，则要考虑更改计划。

即使产品和服务是成功的，组织也应该通过以下实践对目前产品状况进行主动评价：

- 产品或服务审计——以确定目前产品是否应继续、改进、修正或者删除。
- 标准检查——把目前的产品和服务与领先组织的可比较产品和服务进行衡量和比较以获得改进信息。
- 持续改进——为了满足或超过客户需求及愿望并保持竞争优势，执行严格的方法来了解、分析和持续改进产品和服务。

注意：标准检查和持续改进在本书第 1 章第 3 节"业务流程绩效"中详细阐述。

进度检查

提示：完成以下各题，参考答案随后给出。

1. 细分市场并确认重要特点、规模预测及增长预测的战略营销阶段是：（　　）
   a. 情况分析
   b. 战略设计
   c. 程序开发
   d. 战略执行

2. 一个公司面临抉择——投资一个战略业务单元以增加市场占有率，或处置并使用组合中其他业务的投资。这种情形最能反映组合矩阵概念中的哪一个业务种类？（　　）
   a. 明星

b. 问号

c. 钱牛

d. 狗

连线——产品生命周期阶段与适当的行业表现。

3. _____萌芽期   a. 竞争对手全力提高生产力来维持市场占有率

4. _____震荡期   b. 客户接受度和市场最终规模的不确定性比较普遍

5. _____衰退期   c. 买方在选择产品时,更加有识别力

6. 一个公司计划将一种新的消费类电子产品以低于其主要竞争对手产品成本的价格推入市场,目的是用以后年度的较大利润来弥补第一年的预计损失。这体现了哪种竞争战略?(   )

   a. 成本领先

   b. 差异化

   c. 关注

   d. 合并

7. 下列组织能力中,哪一种最可能被认为是核心竞争力?(   )

   a. 生产经营中应用全面质量管理

   b. 完成客户订单时电子商务能力

   c. 外勤销售队伍使用笔记本电脑

   d. 咨询企业的行业经验及其雇员的任职时间

进度检查答案

1. a

2. b

3. b

4. c

5. a

6. a

7. d

■ 第 2 节
营销信息管理

本节内容简介

直到 20 世纪 60 年代，营销领域才提出要提供产品和服务来满足客户需求的概念。这是是对简单地卖给客户企业所生产产品的以工厂为中心的导向的不可思议的飞跃。今天，战略营销支持客户的观点。在一个以客户为中心的组织中，所有单元都为支持客户价值而工作。在以客户价值为重的文化中，雇员的感觉是普遍的——你为客户服务，或者你为服务客户的人服务。

客户关系管理（CRM）是一种帮助组织变成客户驱动型企业的行为准则。客户关系管理准则以客户为出发点——了解他们的需求和偏好——也鼓励与之发展长期合作关系。信息对了解市场和服务这些市场中的客户非常关键。那些客户关系管理最成功的企业都善于收集、解释并运用信息来指导营销和业务战略。

承诺是客户关系管理中的一个重要组成部分。承诺体现了雇员对从产品或服务设计到售后保修和支持的每笔交易客户关注价值的消化程度。（与承诺相反，当一个公司或者一个雇员仅仅是做个样子时，灵活性就很明显了）。雇员应该感到帮助客户就是帮助组织实现战略目标。从客户的需求和期望中得到的信息应该被推广，而且实务和政策应该恰当以使所有雇员觉得对客户满意度负有责任。

建立营销信息

市场驱动型的企业不认为它们可以凭直觉知道客户的需要。这些组织：
- 不懈地研究客户需求和期望。
- 力求理解买方的不同偏好。
- 扩展并越过传统的市场边界。
- 纳入知识和想法的所有相关来源。

在大多数行业中，可获得的信息并不短缺。组织需要分辨出什么信息是它们需要的，然后把这些信息的潜在收益与获取和分析这些信息所付出的成本进行比较。

营销信息系统

满足客户需求的能力以组织首先了解客户和市场需求的努力为基础；开发未来业务机遇的能力以组织预测客户和市场需求的能力为基础。这需要关于长期要求、期望及组织目标和/或潜在客户和市场偏好的信息。

建立一个客户现在购买或要求的产品和服务特色的信息充足的数据库，是一个更好了解客户需求的办法。对现在和未来需求的进一步了解可以通过以下手段获得，比如标准检查、顾问团、客户访谈、焦点小组、调查、环境扫描、雇员的观点、观察等。

因为信息越来越丰富，挑战日渐成为知识管理——解释信息并使其在公司范围内得到理解。组织需要有一个系统化的方法来：

- 主动倾听客户。
- 记录他们听到的。
- 分析他们听到的。
- 在整个组织内传播这些信息。
- 依照这些信息行动。

如果没有这样的系统，公司就将承受不能满足客户的危险，并且会给竞争对手以可乘之机。

有许多种营销信息系统。电子系统是一种标准模式。组织可以根据其特定需求——影响因素包括从企业规模、业务本质到产品/服务组合、收集信息的类型等——设计特定类型的信息系统。例如，一个提供汽车售后配件的批发制造企业的营销信息要求与一个零售服装连锁店的就完全不一样。

图表 3-36 列示了几种常见的营销信息系统。

图表 3-36　营销信息系统的种类

类　　型	关　键　特　征
市场调查研究	针对专门的研究问题收集并分析客户信息
标准化信息服务	信息来自外部卖主；一般是订购或者单独购买（尽管一些服务是免费的）；同样的信息也许会被卖给或者提供给一些客户
管理信息系统（MIS）	内部计算机系统提供各种目的的信息（如订单处理、发票、客户分析等）；包括内部和外部数据来源
数据库系统	特定的管理信息系统（MIS）格式便于进行各种营销应用（比如：客户和产品/服务分析、邮件列表等）
决策支持系统（DSS）	帮助经理和职员进行决策制定的计算机系统；比 MIS 先进
客户关系管理（CRM）系统	系统整合所有有助于与客户进行无缝链接的必要信息，能提供关于客户的详细交易数据
市场（竞争对手）情报系统	用来帮助监管现存的和潜在的竞争对手；包括数据库搜索、客户调查、供应方和其他渠道成员访谈、评估竞争对手的产品或服务、与竞争对手结成战略同盟等

一般来说，营销信息可以被划分为以下两大类：

- 从内部或者外部来源定期取得的信息（比如：环境扫描、SWOT 分析、销售人员、供应方、销售成本分析、保修卡、客户满意度调查和市场占有率）。
- 针对特定情况或问题，根据需求收集的信息（比如：新产品概念研究、品牌偏好研究、广告效果研究）。

营销调研过程

营销调研是为获得营销相关决策所需信息的系统过程。尽管特定的行动和术语会有所不同，但是严格意义上，营销调研过程包括图表 3-37 中列示的步骤。

图表3－37　营销调研过程

步　骤	描　述
定义需求	● 定义有待研究的问题 ● 确定有待完成的特定目标 ● 决定解决该问题的必要信息
确定信息来源	● 确定从内部系统和来源中获取的现存数据 ● 确定支持决策制定需求的外部信息来源（比如，政府机构、行业和贸易组织、学院和大学、私人研究企业和咨询公司） ● 决定是通过定性（比如，观察客户行为）还是定量（比如，调查）的方法收集信息
收集数据	系统收集定性和定量数据（来自访谈、焦点小组等的软数据；来自报告、研究、调查等的硬数据）
分析数据/得出结论	● 对硬数据进行统计解释，通过软数据来确定客户偏好和认知；用来自标准检查的比较 ● 总结发现和结论
传播信息	● 根据数据和优先顺序制定合适的行动计划 ● 通过组织开展客户反馈 ● 计划持续监控；确定提高效率和效果、降低成本、提高利润和市场占有率的途径

进度检查

提示：完成以下各题，参考答案随后给出。

1. 下列组织活动中不属于客户关系管理（CRM）的活动是：（　　　）

　　a. 雇员与呼叫中心目标一致

　　b. 增加网络和公司网站的杠杆作用

　　c. 紧密协调销售、营销、服务和领域支持

　　d. 程序技术改进以最大化与分销渠道成员的联系

连线——营销信息系统与对应描述。

2. _____市场调研　　　　　a. 监督现存的和潜在的竞争对手

3. _____数据库　　　　　　b. 为特定需求收集并分析客户信息

4. _____市场情报　　　　　c. 促进各种营销运用的特定的 MIS 格式

5. _____标准化信息服务　　d. 数据一般从外部卖方购买

进度检查答案

1. a

2. b

3. c

4. a

5. d

第3节
市场细分、目标及定位

本节内容简介

营销有两种基本方法：大众市场法和目标市场法。亨利·福特对其 T 型车的经典论断"客户可以拥有任何他们想要的黑颜色车"代表了大众营销法，在该方法下，公司就提供的产品而言对所有客户一视同仁。目标营销认为所有客户是不同的——他们有不同的需求而且这些需求在不断变化。越来越多的企业认识到它们满足那些独特需求的程度会带来比毕其功于一役的大众营销法更高的回报（尽管成本也高）。

目标营销战略的基本流程如图表 3 – 38 所示。下文对其中列示的主要构成进行了详细阐述。

图表 3 –38　目标营销战略步骤

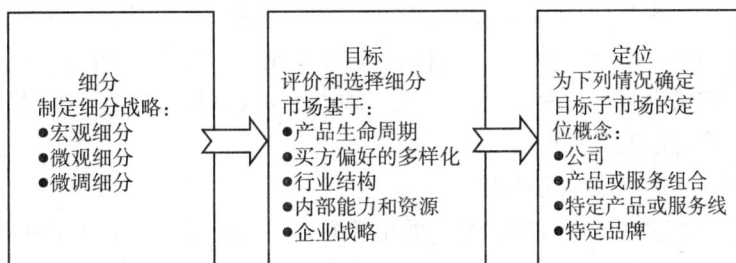

市场细分

市场细分是在特定产品或服务市场里，公司确认和分析有类似特征的买方子集的过程。由此确定的客户子集与现存客户或潜在客户相对同质。

一旦企业选择了将被细分的总体市场的一部分，那么就有无数的方法来细分子集。企业通过一系列相关行动来开始市场细分程序。总的目标是根据它们的共同需要和特征来细分客户和潜在买方。宏观和微观的细分方法常被用到。在一些情况下，甚至可能会有一些细微的细分战略。国际市场会有一些独特的要求。

宏观细分战略

宏观细分一般是对客户或买方数据的第一次细分。以连锁酒店为例，度假旅行者和商务旅行者一般是两组重要的宏观客户群。

进一步宏观标准可以把商务旅行者细分为常住和短住，或者分为想要负担得起的食宿和希望豪华舒适两种。额外的细分标准可能包括商务旅行者的收入。运用帕累托的利润率和收入分析，酒店应该识别出那些贡献酒店80%收入的20%客户。

另一种被称为客户保持战略的宏观细分，是指根据客户的购买行为（比如：增长、保持、衰减或者失去）来划分客户。其他宏观方法包括细分竞争对手的客户和潜在客户或细分消费者市场（终端客户）和分销市场（企业客户）。

微观细分战略

微观细分法基于客户变量的更细微部分。迈克尔·波特在他的著作《竞争优势：创造和保持出众的表现》中讨论了对买方进行分类的多种方法，并认为应针对重要差异对公司所有不同类型的终端用户进行研究。消费类商品和服务的买方与商业/工业商品和服务的买方，其细分客户的变量不同。比如：如果销售消费类商品，公司应研究年龄、收入、住房面积及决策制定者特点。而如果是销售工业、商业或机构产品，公司应根据规模、技术精进程度以及客户怎样使用产品或服务来区分买方。

细分消费者市场

根据波特的理论，在消费者市场中，研究客户之间重要差异的变量包括以下几种：

- **人口资料**

这些变量包括地理位置、年龄、性别、婚姻状况、家庭规模、社会阶层、教育、国籍、职业以及收入。例如，单身商业人士与有孩子的家庭对衣服拥有不同的需要和购买方式。在银行业，年收入、财富和教育程度决定了客户购买何种银行服务以及客户对这些服务价格的敏感程度。

- **客户心理特征**

这些变量说明了客户的生活方式，包括客户的活动、兴趣和观点。这些影响因素很难衡量。尽管如此，生活方式或自我形象可能是重要的购买行为鉴别因素。人口资料也许可以和这个特征结合起来用。例如，家庭健身器材制造商会把18~40岁的、有活力的、对运动感兴趣且关注健康的、付得起运动器材费用的男人和女人进行细分。

- **语言**

在有些行业，如出版商和唱片业，语言决定客户细分，并且决定所有产品和服务的终端用户的细分。比如，许多产品有以多种语言写就的说明书。

- **决策单元或购买程序**

就期望的质量特征和价格敏感度而言，家庭决策过程很重要。例如，一对夫妻可能对一辆车的价格和舒适程度更感兴趣，而其他人也许更关心性能特征。

- **购买诱因**

购买诱因指的是被购买的产品/服务是作为礼物还是买方自用，或者产品/服务是日常使用还是另有他用。买方的用途和信号标准常常因场合不同而不同。例如，给自己买钢笔的客户常常购买实用不贵的钢笔，但如果是作为礼物，那么客户会选择更贵的名牌笔。

- **潜在的买方**

现在不买产品或服务的人可能也代表客户细分。

细分企业市场

研究商业/工业市场中买方之间重要差异的变量可能包括地理位置、标准行业分类（SIC）代码、北美行业分类系统（NAICS）代码或雇员人数。波特给这些变量作了解释：

- **买方行业**

这个变量指出产品怎样被使用及其代表的总购买的百分比。例如，一个小用具制造商购买和使用塑料树脂与一个汽车制造商在汽车内饰使用同样树脂不同。

- **技术精进程度**

买方技术精进程度是对差异性及其带来的价格敏感度的敏感性的一个重要指示器。

- **OEM 与终端用户**

在自己的产品中使用一种产品并且把自己的产品卖给其他厂家的原始设备制造商（OEMs）与自己使用产品的终端用户有不同的价格敏感程度和复杂程度。

- **决策单元或购买程序**

对于消费类产品，在购买决策中的特定个人对购买决策的精明、期望的产品品质和价格敏感度会产生重要影响。

- **规模**

公司一般用这些变量细分买方，例如，它们是一个小企业还是财富 100 强甚至500 强公司。根据波特的理论，规模可以用三个变量衡量：订单规模、年总购买量或公司规模。

- **所有权**

所有权结构可以影响买方动机。例如，私人公司与公共公司可能重视不同的产品特征，或者分支机构可能会受其母公司的购买决策指导。

- **收入/财务优势**

通过这个变量，公司按收入细分客户，例如，收入少于 1 百万美元的，或者在 5百万美元到 1 千万美元之间的。根据波特的理论，买方的盈利性和财务资源可以决定其对价格的敏感程度、购买频率和信贷需求。

精细的细分战略

很多影响因素一起来帮助企业识别微小细分——在一些情况下，甚至是细分成只有一个。

考虑下边的例子：

- 对于一个公司业主来说，CRM 系统能力使企业可以以无缝链接方式回应独特的客户偏好；企业可以基于独特的客户需求和预期在产品和服务中提供更有吸引力的价值。
- 在企业和家庭电脑领域，戴尔使个人和企业客户可以设计自己的电脑系统，以此来满足特定需求，而价格则可与大量生产的电脑相比。
- 卡西欧卖出超过 5 000 种不同的手表，因为有效的系统设计使得以低成本生产这些不同种类成为可能。

当考虑精细的细分时，组织必须评估：

- 提供符合成本效益的定制产品（比如数据库知识、计算机辅助设计技术以及适时制存货系统）的内部能力。
- 客户对特别定制产品的要求/期望。
- 亲密客户关系的优势（比如：价值机会和潜在的市场进入壁垒）。

国际市场细分

在任何国际营销战略中与客户保持紧密关系都是很关键的。但是，就像按照逻辑可预期的，超出国内市场定位的范围带来许多变量和挑战，这些变量和挑战必须被消化并进行处理。

在很大程度上，国际细分都是独特的；尽管一些细分会有相似之处，但是没有两个完全相同。在国内或地区内可以应用的，在国际上完全不可以用的说法太保守。

国际市场细分必须考虑企业的全球性。但是它必须把当地/区域喜好作为影响因素考虑，而且要考虑怎样来适应以下变量：
- 区域文化和价值观。
- 当地营销需求。
- 可用技术水平。
- 分销结构。
- 竞争对手。
- 经济环境。
- 政治环境。
- 贸易影响，比如，关税和配额。

很多企业通过与当地细分市场相关联的大规模定制获得了国际成功。很多国内细分市场调查得出的消费者和工业的特征依然适用，这取决于地理位置。当然，也有一些是不相关的（源于当地情况）。

总之，任何国际化营销中的基本推动力与国内的相同，即支持了该区域不断变化的需求和喜好的企业反应和增值活动。尽管活动应全球一致，但是它们也必须保持关于优势和竞争的本土化意识。

有效细分的要求

细分一般带来较高收入的事实并不是细分市场的惟一动力。组织可以获得以下大量的额外好处（当然不仅限于此）：
- 对建立和执行战略营销程序的重要洞察力。
- 弄清企业自己的竞争地位。
- 营销目标和战略的清楚定义。
- 营销组合变化的坚实基础。
- 产品开发和资源分配指南。
- 将营销和其他业务活动有力地整合以支持企业满足客户需求。

这些潜在的收益要求组织考虑怎样有效地细分市场。图表3-39提供了有效市场细分特征的一览表。

图表3-39 有效市场细分的特征

√	杠杠作用	细分计划是否可以归纳/应用到不止一个产品或服务？
√	逻辑的	细分是否反映了具有比较容易分辨的相同点和/或不同点的逻辑子集？
√	基于研究的	细分是否被准确和全面地分析了？
√	一致的	细分战略是否与整体性、竞争性、职能性战略一致？
√	盈利的	细分战略怎样支持价值创造？细分市场的预计收入—支出比是否是盈利的？
√	普遍的	雇员、供应商、合作伙伴和盟友是否支持细分？有没有什么必须清除的壁垒？
√	双赢	雇员、供应商、合作伙伴、盟友和细分市场怎样做到互利互惠？

市场目标

在目标市场战略中的细分部分，企业确定、研究并分析市场细分。换句话说，机会已经被确定。通过市场目标确定，企业选择最好的细分市场来经营。根据营销大师菲利普·科特勒的说法，目标确定包括制定衡量细分市场吸引力的方法并选择将要进入的市场。目标确定回答了哪些细分市场为公司提供最盈利的机会的问题。目标确定决策的最后结果是企业要为多少客户群服务。

如果你检查市场驱动型公司的目标确定战略，在不考虑行业、规模或其他特征的不同之处的情况下，就会发现一些共同点。在评估细分市场盈利潜力和选择目标市场时，所有的企业都考虑以下方面：

- **产品生命周期**

产品的成熟期、竞争的行业环境和面对的全球竞争对手都会影响目标确定决策。一个新的或正在产生的细分市场与那些处在成熟期或是衰退期边缘的市场提供的潜在机会很不相同。国际竞争的威胁或存在要求我们考虑全球的挑战和机遇。

- **买方偏好的多样性**

目标确定应该考虑细分市场中的买方价值需求。企业可以通过产品和服务专门化实现的显著偏好是否存在？或者产品多样化对买方是否重要？

- **行业结构**

目标确定应该也包括在迈克尔·波特的五种市场力量中。如果一些细分市场表现得过于好以至于不像真的，那么它也许是一个真正的目标。另一方面，也许有一些隐藏的缺点。如果一个细分市场真的很有吸引力，那么其他竞争对手就有可能准备进入同样的市场。

- **内部能力和资源**

组织在目标确定时要现实可行。换句话说，内部和外部资源能否支持目标市场？确定一个不可能达到的目标市场没有什么意义。一个竞争对手可能有出众的差异。除非有一些潜在的缺陷，不然这样的市场虽然很有吸引力但是却不值得进入，因为竞争对手已经占据了主导地位。

- **企业战略**

整体性、竞争性、职能性战略应该有恰当的关系。例如，如果一个组织设定了多样化和重大增长的战略目标，那么目标市场逻辑上必须支持这些战略。

这些因素共同影响如何更好地选择目标市场。

通过目标确定，企业最终必须决定是否：

- **以单一细分市场为目标（单一市场集中化）**

当企业专注于某一特定细分市场的营销时，它的产品或服务就会迎合该市场的需求。比如：雷克萨斯目标确定为那些追求高端汽车的客户。

- **选择性地以几个细分市场为目标（市场专业化或产品专业化）**

通过选择性的目标确定，企业决定将目标确定为用以满足不同客户群的产品和服务独特的不同的细分市场。商业航空公司提供头等舱、商务舱、经济舱以吸引不同的乘客。

- **以所有（或者大部分）细分市场为目标（全面或大众营销）**

有时考虑到大众营销，这种方法将提供同样产品的整个市场（或市场的绝大部分）定为目标。

市场定位

一旦组织选定目标市场，形成市场驱动战略的下一步就是决定它想怎样在选定的细分市场中给自己定位。定位是一个组织希望与其他竞争对手相比客户怎样认知它。定位有不同的层次。定位可能关注：

- 整个公司（比如，以低价闻名）。
- 产品或服务的组合（比如，福特汽车公司意图以其各种核心车型和精品中的极品而出名）。
- 一条专门的产品或服务线（比如，惠普希望客户从其完整的激光或者喷墨打印机系列中选择）。
- 一个专门的品牌（比如，爱慕思希望宠物主人认为该商标代表了较高价值的狗粮或猫粮）。

定位是组织获得和保持市场占有率计划的关键部分。定位的首要任务是把企业的能力与每一个目标细分市场中的客户价值要求进行匹配。期望的结果是在目标细分市场客户的心目中获得持久地位。

从根本上说，定位是关于组织希望消费者怎样认知它的产品和服务，以及什么战略是达到这个感性目标所必需的。企业必须决定它们是否想把自己定位在接近竞争对手的位置，这样客户可以进行直接的比较，或者通过差异性战略定位在一个远离竞争对手的位置（比如低成本或独特的特征和好处）。

细分、目标、定位、选择正确的市场战略可以合并或分解一个企业。

- 细分市场提供了用于集中营销的有效方法。
- 目标确定评估了细分市场并使企业能够进入最盈利的市场。
- 定位确定了管理人员希望买方怎么认知企业的产品或服务。

综合起来，这三项可以显著地影响企业的业绩。

进度检查

提示：完成以下各题，参考答案随后给出。

1. 以下变量都与新设立的公司细分消费者市场有关，除了：（　　）

   a. 语言

   b. 决策单元或购买程序

   c. 收入/财务优势

   d. 购买诱因

2. 一家美国公司的塑料部门计划在全球范围推广一种新的塑料树脂。下面哪一种细分变量比较重要需要调查？（　　）

   a. 人口资料

   b. 决策单元

   c. 客户心理特征

   d. 购买诱因

连线——市场战略与对应行为。

3. ＿＿＿＿细分　　　　a. 提供了一个集中营销的有效方法

4. ＿＿＿＿目标确定　　b. 确定了管理人员希望买方怎么认知企业的产品和服务

5. ＿＿＿＿定位　　　　c. 评估了细分市场并使企业能构进入最盈利的市场

进度检查答案

1. c

2. b

3. a

4. c

5. b

第4节
产品和服务管理

本节内容简介

当被问到描述一种产品和一项服务的区别的时候，很多人一般会说一个产品是一个"实体商品"，而把服务定义为一个"过程"。本节就产品和服务管理的一些方面进行讨论。

产品和服务的区别

图表3-40中列示的基本属性一般用来说明产品和服务的差异。

图表3-40　产品和服务的属性

产　品	服　务
有形商品	无形商品
持久商品	不持久
可以被储存	交付时消费/使用
很容易标准化	交付变异使得很难标准化
交易导向	高度个性化
质量更容易被内部控制	质量受客户认知影响很大
低感情投资	高感情联系和高客户敏感度

组织和客户间的无形交换也许是区别产品制造和服务环境的关键。因为服务是无形的，它们在交付前不可测量、测试或查实。像对一件被制造的产品那样检查服务的质量或召回有缺陷的服务是不可能的。

除了这些基本特征，区分一个企业是产品制造还是服务提供企业还是有些困难的。所有组织都可以说成为客户提供服务——甚至那些传统的实体商品制造商。近似的，服务业组织也有有形的组成部分。请看下面的例子：

● 通用汽车公司制造汽车，但是在它们的业务组合中也有并不是交付有形的终端产品给客户的纯服务程序。通用汽车金融服务公司（GMAC），是通用的全资控股子公司，提供各种各样的融资服务（比如，汽车、房子、保险）。

● 诺德史顿提供有形的服装但是在业内却以提供优异的客户服务而知名。

● 联邦快递是一家运输公司，但是它们的名字一般使人联想起隔夜快递服务和可以使客户更方便地得到关于装载货物信息的技术服务创新。

● 银行和金融业被认为是服务行业，但是仍可举出很多它们也提供有形产品的例子。

让产品和服务本来清楚的界限变得模糊的另一个事实是所有组织都有服务部门，这些部门不直接从事生产或其他经营活动，但是却提供一些形式的对整个组织成功很重要的支持或服务。比如人力资源、内部审计、成本会计、采购、法律、日托和雇员自助餐厅。

产品属性

只有当有购买产品或服务能力的买方有需求，并且耐用产品和服务可以满足这种需求时，市场才会存在。有需求的人们购买产品和服务来满足组织或家庭需要。因此，导致了"消费品"和"工业品"的分类。但是和产品与服务分类相似的是，工业和消费范畴也有重叠。工业企业也许提供最终构成消费品的组件，或者它们在生产过程中使用消费品。

除消费和工业分类外，还有其他的可交易实体。政府是其中最值得注意的一个。美国联邦和州政府都对各种产品和服务提供招标的机会和合同。迅速发展的全球市场也给无数的供应商提供了全球政府采购机会。

企业还试图确定为什么人们购买特定的产品和品牌。消费品和工业品买方依照可预测的决策顺序进行决策：

- 确认——确认一种需求或一个问题。
- 研究——收集产品/供应商的信息来满足需求或解决问题；确定备选的产品和供应商。
- 评估——评估所有备选产品的重要属性。
- 购买决策——选择一种产品来购买或一个供应商来签订合同。

尽管两类买方的主要决策步骤都是相同的，但是问题和活动却会大不相同。一般来说，消费者购买比供应商评估和工业采购的购买标准要少得多。

消费品和工业品买方进行购买决策的购买标准和品牌是否关键这类问题总是引起人们的兴趣。

品牌化

品牌化一般被用来描述一种通过创造一个独特的名字和/或符号（比如，标志、商标或包装设计）来识别一种产品或一个制造商的营销战略。品牌化的目标是将一种产品或服务与其竞争对手的产品或服务相区别。

下面的术语和概念是关于品牌化的：

- 品牌是一个实际的术语、标志、设计或它们的组合。对于国际商业机器公司来说，IBM 就是一个品牌。
- 品牌名称是品牌可以称谓的那部分。IBM® 是被用作产品和服务广告的品牌名称。
- 服务标志或者商标（®或™）也是品牌的一部分，并且通过第一次使用制度被法律保护，意味着第一个公开使用服务标志或者商标的企业对其有所有权。
- 品牌权益指的是品牌的价值或优势，反映了与品牌相关的所有资产和负债（比如，客户忠诚度和支付溢价的意愿、被认知的质量和流行程度、被认知的价值、知晓、市场占有率、价格以及分销指数）。

在战略营销中，品牌化创新的目的是反映组织目标和设想并且与企业价值观相联系。一个战略品牌意识应创造客户价值和股东价值。

图表 3-41 中列示了一个强有力的品牌提供给买方和卖方的重要好处。

图表 3 - 41　品牌的作用

对买方的好处	对卖方的好处
• 帮助快速准确地识别/再识别产品 • 减少购买危险；提供质量担保和连贯性 • 提供因购买了象征质量、地位和威望的品牌的心理奖励	• 促进增强财务业绩的重复购买 • 促进新产品介绍，因为客户熟悉该品牌 • 提供促销的关注点 • 创造与竞争对手不同的基本差异 • 帮助建立品牌忠诚度

与定位类似，品牌化也有不同的等级。组织可以选择以下品牌化战略：

• 一种特定的产品（比如，宝洁的象牙牌香皂，海飞丝洗发水或包替纸巾）。
• 整条生产线（比如，奔迈公司的掌上电脑系列）。
• 一个公司的名字（比如，快餐业的麦当劳）。
• 一个组合战略（比如，通用电气的名字和 GE 标志与惠而浦厨具组合使用）。
• 私人品牌（比如，西夫韦商店与供应商签订合同来把西夫韦商标贴在西夫韦杂货店出售的超市产品上）。

利用合适的杠杆作用，品牌化为企业可见度、市场占有率和较高的销售收入提供重大机会。投资者也关注一个公司品牌的估计价值。

标签和包装

有点儿滑稽的是，据说你不能根据一本书的封皮来判断这本书的好坏。但是在产品标签和包装中通常并不是这样。组织经常会竭尽全力来评价它们的目标客户、客户看到产品时的状态、意图是否是诱惑购买、产品将怎样被使用等。近似的，买方希望通过产品的标签和包装了解一些事情。

一般来说，标签和包装是推广/支持品牌意识的整合营销传播计划的一个部分，并达到任何监管要求。对大多数产品（特别是消费品）来说，企业应充分考虑有竞争力的标签和包装，以及怎么得到客户的注意并促使其放弃其他产品而挑选特定产品。

关于加标签的一般考虑因素

加标签有很多目的，列示在图表 3 - 42 中。

图表 3 - 42　关于加标签的一般考虑因素

目　的	例　子
监管规定	• 符合现存的指南或要求（比如食品保鲜期、营养配方信息或基本资格） • 产品使用的安全声明
推荐用途	• 一般的使用说明和预期产品用途 • 玩具、游戏等的适宜年龄
警告	• 危险用法/危险警告（比如不能接触皮肤或吸入有害气体的警告） • 健康损害（比如香烟警告） • 提示（比如非处方和处方药的过敏和相互反应警告）
一般信息	• 生产者想要推广的一般信息，该信息与产品或品牌识别有关 • 关于环保的信息（比如，可回收标志或无动物试验） • 关于产品问题/支持以及保证退款的联系信息

关于包装的一般考虑因素

包装承担着三项一般功能：展示、便利和保护。

- **展示**

精明的经销商都知道展示与产品同样重要。包装显示了主要在外观上的关注点，这些外观为产品提供了真正的个体特性并提高了其知名度和价值。从库存展示到有创意和难忘的定制展示，选择无穷无尽。

- **便利**

产品供应商需要不断创新并以客户为中心来进行包装以满足客户需要。便利的考虑因素包括从使用更轻的包装材料到产品的容易打开和合上的特性或者是其他更复杂的应用。

- **保护**

保护性包装一般包括产品包装的所有方面，比如防止在运输中的损伤，在储藏或使用过程中保持产品的完整/货架期，确保客户安全等。保护性产品包装的范围包括纸箱、泡沫包装、泡沫聚苯乙烯、缓冲材料、塑料覆膜、收缩薄膜包装、安全印章等。

产品支持服务

无数研究表明客户会因为产品的后续服务而不再买该产品。缓慢的交付、差劲的售后服务、不正确的发票、不予答复的修复以及对保修或服务电话令人愤怒的不答复或迟缓答复都是造成客户服务抱怨的常见原因，如果忽视这些事情，会进一步造成客户的失望。但是如果没有恰当处理关于产品特性或怎样操作等这类日常咨询，甚至都会造成客户不满。

要想让客户开心并防止客户流失，那么要求用与新产品/服务的说明、产品的生产和配送同等程度的事先筹划和严密要求来支持服务。这些程序必须恰当，以便为每一个客户联系提供及时、满意的解决方案，而不管这些联系是亲自来访、通过电话中心或者互动语音系统（IVR），或者是通过公司网站及其他媒介。

公司必须展示一种建立和维持客户认为合适的售后支持系统的承诺。一个以 25～50 岁年轻专业人士为目标的软件公司，应该通过网络提供基本的客户服务，并且给客户可以直接存取数据库文件的权限。但是一个小商品制造商只能通过和善的代理人员来提供售后支持，甚至没有考虑过其他方法。

现在，大家普遍认为客户忠诚度十分重要。必须把提供售后客户支持看作是购买产品或服务不可分割的一部分。有效的支持服务必须要在提供个性化支持和节省成本的技术之间找到平衡。不管选择何种支持程序，它们都必须是对客户需求的自然反应。

生产线和产品组合决策

一个企业也许只有一种产品、一条生产线或者各种生产线的组合。生产线和产品组合决策处理的是一个企业怎么管理新开发产品和现存产品之间的关系。在战略营销中，公司在生产线和产品组合决策中正逐渐采用团队方法。

该方法一般有几种组织层次。特定个人会因组织的不同而不同。但十分常见的是如下参与交叉职能团队的个人组合在一起：

- 单个产品或品牌经理——与研发、经营、财务、销售、广告、其他部门和SBUs一起、作为产品发起人或宣传者的人。

- 产品组经理——管理一组产品或品牌并在一个拥有几种产品或品牌的企业中承担产品组责任的人。

- SBU 主管/经理——对产品组合业绩、产品购置决策、研发次序、新产品决策、资源分配等负有首要责任的人。

现在，小企业和大公司都认识到仅仅有好的或有前途的商品是不足以获得成功的。在竞争压力极大、买方需求不断变化的情况下，产品要想获得成功就必须执行市场驱动导向并注重提供优良客户价值的产品战略。不断的组织学习是作出新的和现存产品组合决策的关键。最后，营销组合要素必须以符合成本效益的方式实现目标市场的目标。

产品开发

在今天复杂而且迅速变化的商业环境中，创新是竞争成功的关键。但是选择最好的战略来获取创新机会并不是一个简单的任务。

那些成功创新的组织具有：

- 支持创新的文化。
- 识别机会的有效程序。
- 把想法转变成成功的新产品的便捷程序。

换句话说，新产品要有细致的计划。市场驱动型公司必须拥有恰当的程序以完成图表 3-43 所列示的活动。企业的规模和类型、内部资源和能力、对新产品增长率的要求和外部客户需求形成了特定的组织战略。

图表 3-43 新产品计划

活 动	描 述
形成想法	• 从对现存产品的额外改进到新产品创造 • 一般包括一系列资源：公司人力、客户、竞争对手、发明者、购买者和渠道成员 • 一般在现存产品和市场介入范围内确定目标（比如，与整体性和 SBU 战略一致）；支持更开放式的研发
筛选和概念评估	• 尽快排除那些没有前途的想法来节省时间和金钱投入 • 把拒绝好点子的危险控制在可接受的水平
业务分析	• 评估新产品概念的商业绩效 • 评价预计收入、开发成本和利润规划 • 形成一个执行/拒绝决策
产品开发和测试	• 把概念转换成一个或多个原型（研发部门而不是已有的制造程序产生的） • 如果可行，通过试用测试取得客户反馈 • 建立用以评估商业生产的平台（比如，产品是否可以在期望的质量和成本水平上被更大量地生产）

续表

活　　动	描　　述
市场进入和测试	• 包括目标和定位战略（以概念评估开始，并经过产品开发） • 包括类似选择名字、包装、环保考虑、产品信息、安全和服务考虑等活动 • 测量买方对新产品的反应 • 评估对一种或多种定位战略的反应
商业化	• 确定营销计划 • 把推广活动与企业职能结合起来 • 执行营销战略 • 监管和控制产品投放

新产品计划可以被用于有形产品和服务。应该说产品和服务不应该先被开发，然后再寻找市场，而应该一步步地执行计划程序。

产品生命周期

正如前述的产品生命周期（PLC）所指出的，一个行业会经历很多可预测的阶段和时期。营销战略必须调整到与不断变化的情况一致，并且要反映购买方多样性以及每个阶段的偏好。

图表 3 - 44 总结了在基本的产品生命周期阶段的一般营销方法。

图表 3 - 44　在不同产品生命周期阶段的营销方法

PLC 阶段	营销战略
萌芽期	• 把产品消息通知给目标客户——建立一般性了解 • 通过类似广告等品牌开发活动来创建品牌 • 收回开发成本
增长期	• 通过营销活动强化品牌 • 通过下列活动建立市场进入的竞争性壁垒： 　• 获得市场占有率 　• 降低成本 　• 继续开发产品
震荡期	• 保护和改进品牌名称 • 使企业特有的能力与市场价值机会匹配
成熟期	• 维持忠诚的客户 • 通过产品的重新定位来重新开发产品以吸引不同的细分市场
衰退期	• 修改/重新包装产品 • 降低管理、产品开发和营销的成本

服务企业的营销策略

如前所述，产品和服务有一些固有的不同。服务的独特之处在于它是无形的，不可被储存，而且必须在被生产出来的同时或稍后立即被消费。服务往往充满变数；它不像产品那样可以将一致性和质量制造到货物中。

另一个有区别的特征是，服务一般离不开提供服务的人。在服务组织，一线雇员不仅仅是交付商品，他们自己就是商品。比如，人们在接收银行柜员、商务航线的空乘人员、医院职员的服务的时候记住的是他们的礼貌、高效和专业性。

服务行业建立品牌识别一般要求与业务的有形方面建立联系——提供服务或与服务有某种联系的人员。这就是为什么航空公司经常展示它们的雇员，或者医院以医师和护理人员做广告。一些公司雇用知名人士来推销它们的服务。多年来，美国运通用名人做广告来为其信用卡建立品牌识别。

服务营销传递给人们的除了品牌化和定位以外还有另外一个重要的组成部分。服务企业必须是竞争对手导向的。通过邮件、电话和亲身调查从客户收集到的竞争信息，对竞争对手的观察，公开发布的客户和竞争数据，以及标准检查都应该被整合到营销战略中。

对于产品和服务之间的所有这些差别，我们也必须注意到服务营销和产品营销的成功有一个共同的基本特征：以客户为焦点。服务营销的成功者经常与客户交谈来了解他们的真实需要，并且预测出在未来他们需求变化后需要何种服务。客户成为战略营销程序的一部分。

国际营销

从概念上说，国际营销战略和国内战略是相似的。一个组织需要执行一种系统方法，来确保所形成的战略一致、联合并支持整体性、竞争性、职能性战略。但是全球环境远比国内市场复杂和不确定；为制定成功的营销战略，还需要做一些基础性修改。

全球市场机会分析

在决定追求哪个目标时，企业需要客观地估计公司的竞争力和能力将如何支持其扩张到国际市场。评估国外市场必须评价总部所在国的制约（比如，政治、法律、经济）和目标市场所在国的制约（比如，经济、政治、竞争性、文化、分销结构、货币、地理）。该政府是否有会影响到全球经营扩张的贸易限制、反托拉斯法案或其他法律因素？东道国的政治和经济气候是否支持国外新成员进入市场？

当然，及时沟通、全球供给网络和国际金融市场都可以支持全球市场扩张。但是市场分析必须全面地评估全部的假定事件和潜在的威胁。

适应目标市场

营销组合一般必须根据国际目标市场进行调整。产品本身需要调整，从品牌名称、功能/型号、包装到服务和保修条款。定价、促销和分销也都需要调整。

公司必须决定产品和战略在国际市场中的标准化程度（比如：在多个国家标准化）或者在不同的国家和地区间根据客户的不同进行调整。同样的产品或服务是否能在几个不同的全球市场吸引客户？或者在何种程度上国家或地区的偏好要求产品和服务进行调整？

试图在所有的市场推广同一个全球品牌一般是有问题的。一个品牌的形象在全世界范围内很少相同。例如，在美国本田汽车是质量和信赖的同义词；但是在日本，所有的汽车质量是确定的，没有差别。本田汽车在日本象征着速度、年轻和活力。

通过筛选收集到的信息和考虑到的目标调整，企业可以制定国际营销战略，并且通过执行和控制计划进一步推行。

全球合作

一些参与全球市场竞争的企业选择与其他组织结成合作关系。合资企业和战略联盟可以在获得市场准入和扩大单个企业能力方面提供极大的优势。但是，必须再次考虑收益和局限。国际合伙关系可以为双方提供好处。但是，很多合伙关系因为合作伙伴间的利益不对称或力量失衡而破裂。当国际合伙关系失败时，新出现的跨国公司通常也处在一个明显不利的地位。

总之，全球竞争是知识密集型和信息密集型的。成功进入国际市场需要的不仅仅是简单调整国内营销战略。在全球市场中增加销售收入及低成本劳动力和/或原材料的诱惑并不意味着可以不预先考虑和计划。

进度检查

提示：完成以下各题，参考答案随后给出。

1. 在产品生命周期的哪个阶段广告费用最高：（　　　）
   a. 萌芽期
   b. 震荡期
   c. 成熟期
   d. 衰退期

2. 一个医药器材公司的营销、销售和区域支持人员最终确定了营销计划并在新产品推广中协调行动。这个产品计划程序可以被描述为：（　　　）
   a. 进入市场
   b. 业务分析
   c. 商业化
   d. 筛选

连线——产品和服务营销术语与对应行为。

3. _____品牌化　　　　　　a. 推广/支持品牌意识和满足所有监管要求的整合营销传播活动
4. _____生产线和组合决策　　b. 关于企业怎么管理新的和现存产品之间关系的活动
5. _____标签和包装　　　　　c. 创造一个独特的名字或/和符号来识别一种产品或一个制造商的活动

进度检查答案

1. a
2. c
3. c
4. b
5. a

■ **第5节**
定价战略

本节内容简介

随着企业和消费者需求越来越苛刻、全球竞争加剧、大多数市场增长缓慢以及无数其他行业因素带来竞争压力，进行合适的产品定价对大部分企业来说已成为一项重要的活动。如为了获得市场占有率或产生快速的投资报酬率而定价过高，那么这种产品或服务有可能卖不出去；如果定价太低，则可能会得到收入很多，但是却损失了盈利。

价格还对买方的产品价值认知也有重大影响。一旦实施，价格战略就很难改变，特别是情况变化需要大幅提价的时候。

可以说，定价决策有重大影响。所以公司怎样给产品合适的定价呢？基本做法是考虑内部和外部因素并且分析多种定价方法和战略。

内部和外部影响因素

影响企业为其产品定价的因素有很多。图表3－45展示了这些内部和外部因素。

图表3－45　影响定价的内部和外部因素

内 部 因 素	外 部 因 素
• 材料成本	• 行业
• 开发/制造成本	• 产品成熟和产品生命周期各阶段
• 管理费用	• 买方价值认知
• 人工成本	• 买方价格敏感度
• 周期	• 分销渠道
• 上市时间	• 直接竞争
• 预计产品或服务寿命	• 来自替代品的威胁
• 服务成本	• 政府法律和其他规章
• 产品组合	• 经济状况
• 捆绑机会/交叉销售	• 市场可承受的价格
• 目标成本	
• 公司目标和战略配合	
• 大宗购买的客户折扣	

定价方法

价格一般以成本、需求、竞争或是综合考虑三者为基础。定价有很多种方法。企业一般有下列几种基本方法：

- 成本法。
- 价值法。
- 竞争法。

成本法

作为企业定价方法之一的成本法被描述为"设定底线"。这种定价方式揭示了产品的最低可能价格。成本法有两种计算方法：

- **盈亏平衡法**

盈亏平衡法用来建立参考的框架；它不是独立的定价方法。本质上，它决定了以一个固定价格要卖出多少单位才可以收回所有固定和变动成本。公式如下：

盈亏平衡（单位）＝总固定成本/（单位价格 − 单位变动成本）

一旦知道了盈亏平衡值，企业就可以评估超过这个价格定价以获得利润的可行性。选定的价格一般比盈亏平衡价高，包括了需求和竞争的影响。

- **成本加成法**

在成本加成法下，企业通过准确分析单位成本来计算产品或服务的售价。代表最低可接受投资报酬率（比如，10% ~ 30%）的利润率被加到成本中以设定价格。

公式如下：

价格＝平均单位成本/（1 − 加价百分比*）

*加价百分比以小数表示

成本加成法揭示了产品的最低合理价格。如果市场状况不支持该价格，那么企业必须重新考虑其战略。

成本法定价面临的挑战在于准确计算应分摊给产品或服务的所有成本。企业有忽略应包括在成本中的合法项目（比如，研究成本、客户商誉以及管理费用）的倾向。

价值法

价值法（或增值法、需求法）估计产品或服务对买方的价值。价值法定价的目标是确定买方对满足其需求的产品或服务愿意支付多少价格。

用价值法定价时，企业根据它认为客户看重并愿为其支付较高价格的独特特征为其产品或服务设定一个价格。各种影响因素，比如产品性能、服务和质量，都会造成差异化。

价值法被广泛应用于消费品和工业品的定价。网络拍卖是价值法的最新运用。

竞争法

顾名思义，竞争法（市场法）考虑了竞争对手的价格。企业考虑市场中其他类似产品或服务的价格，并试图把自己的价格设在这些价格界限内。设定的价格要么等于竞争价格、要么高于或低于一定的百分比。

航空业是竞争法定价的一个典型例子。市场领先者通常宣扬费用上升或下降，行业中的其他企业随之调整自己的价格。

新产品定价战略

公司投入大量的时间、精力和金钱来开发或获得新产品。不幸的是，没有水晶球可以用来预测新产品推出后市场的可能反应。

在设定新产品价格时，企业必须考虑：

- 产品成本。
- 预计产品寿命。
- 预测买方对备选价格的反应。
- 可能的竞争反应。

下面是两种基本的新产品定价战略：市场撇脂法和市场渗透法。

市场撇脂法

市场撇脂定价法为新产品设定一个较高的价格，目的是从那些愿意支付较高价格的细分市场中获得最大收入。基本的逻辑是向买方传输了这样的思想——价格高的产品提供了更高的价值。

当以下情况存在时，就可以为新产品设定一个较高的价格：

- 产品性能或优点支持较高的价格。
- 质量和外观支持较高的价格。
- 有足够的买方愿意以此价格购买该产品。
- 少量生产的成本不高。
- 竞争者不容易进入市场。

用市场撇脂法定价的挑战是较高的定价也许证明是不现实的。买方也许不认同该价值主张，而且可能没有足够的需求。一个较高的价格也会给竞争对手留下太多的操作空间。

市场渗透法

市场渗透法是一种新的产品定价战略，即用一种相对较低的市场进入价格来建立销量和市场地位。设定较低价格的目的是吸引大量的买方以赢得较大的市场占有率。

在如下情形下，可以设定一个较低的初始渗透价：

- 在客户对价格敏感的新的或者不发达的市场中。
- 当产品优点非常多而且由此很想要时。
- 因销售量增大而带来较低的生产和分销成本时。
- 较低的价格能获得足够的差异以阻止竞争对手时。

市场渗透法的主要优势是供应商可以迅速强势占领市场，并且理想上会很快成为市场领先者。用低价来削弱竞争的缺点是可能会牺牲盈利性。而且可能会发生意外并引发价格战。

推出新产品以及设定合适的价格要求仔细的分析和机敏的宣传。错误的定价会损害产品的价值主张。

麦肯锡最近的一份研究报告表明 80%～90% 的不好的定价决策都是企业对产品定价过低。试图将低价调高和提升产品价值主张的困扰不只是一种痛苦；对许多企业来说，那是不可能的任务。

产品组合定价战略

　　如果一个企业有不止一种产品（或服务），管理人员就必须评估这些产品之间的相互关系。必须仔细考虑产品组合中的相同和不同之处，并且做出基于成本、需求和/或竞争的定价决定。

　　一般来说，不是所有的产品都具有同样的盈利性。价格结构处理的就是考虑相互关系的情况下怎样给产品组合中的单个产品定价。

　　单个产品也许是针对同样的目标市场或者不同的终端用户。很多事例证明了这一点：

- 化学产品制造商，类似孟山都公司和陶氏化学，出售同样的用于农作物、草皮和观赏植物及建筑物保护的除草剂和杀虫剂；销售给商业或家庭用的同样产品。
- 大的连锁企业，像家得宝、山姆会员商店和好市多出售许多相同的产品给企业和消费者。
- 汽车制造商用本质上相同的车体和外加豪华性能来针对不同的目标市场。
- 百货公司和超市提供商店品牌和高级品牌。

　　有很多种不同的方法用来给多种产品定价。图表 3 – 46 总结了常见产品组合战略的关键特征。

图表 3 – 46　产品组合定价战略

战略	描述
生产线定价	• 在生产线项目之间设定价格梯级 • 基于这个等级的零件的性能、优点或其他方面定价 比如：洗车，按不同价格提供基础、中等和奢华的不同服务；不同规模的快餐菜单项目卖不同价格
备选产品定价	• 一旦客户开始购买，就试图增加他们的消费金额 • 包括选择性附件来增加产品或服务的总价 比如：一个轮胎经销商提供终身保换保证，以便在新轮胎购买价格上附加额外的收费；家电在被购买时附加延期保修协议
后续产品定价	对必须和主产品一起使用或补充主产品的产品收取较高的价格 比如：剃须刀制造商对剃须刀收取较低的价格，但通过销售该种剃须刀的替换刀片来弥补（或收取更多的）利润；某些软件的升级
副产品定价	• 对副产品定格来使主产品的价格更有竞争力 • 对低价值的副产品定价以便处理掉它们 比如：将不可食用的肉类加工产品售出以制作宠物食品、肥皂、化学用品和化肥；废木材/木屑销售给定向结构板制造商来用作再生建材
成组产品定价	在同一包装中组合几种产品，以优惠价格一并销售 比如：旅行套装中包括旅店和飞机票；配套的唇膏和指甲油一起搭卖；电影录像片和 DVD 与 CD 唱片一起搭卖

价格调整战略

　　定价战略需要持续监控。不断变化的外部市场环境、竞争对手行为、产品生命周期的变化和其他因素都可能会带来下列价格调整战略：

- 折扣和折让定价——降低价格来回馈提前或立即支付的买方。
- 差别（歧视）定价——根据客户、产品、地点的差异调整价格，但要考虑罗宾森－帕特曼法和克莱顿法第一部分的要求。
- 心理定价——为心理效果调整价格；试图让买方在一个感性认知而不是理性的基础上做出回应（比如，定价在 \$799 而不是 \$800，或者用 99 美分来代替 \$1）。
- 促销定价——临时降价来获得短期销售或者通过优惠券、回扣、买一赠一等方式来促销某一商品。
- 地理定价——考虑客户的地理位置来调整价格（比如，以区域为基础的运输成本）。
- 国际定价——基于国际市场环境来调整价格。

改变产品或服务的价格是很常见的。但是不管提价还是降价，价格调整可能会是一件危险的主张。

价格弹性和其他定价影响因素

需求的价格弹性衡量当所有其他因素不变时，价格变动对需求数量的影响。它常被用来感知买方对备选价格的敏感度。

需求的价格弹性计算公式如下：

需求的价格弹性＝需求数量变化百分比/价格变化百分比

这个比率一般情况下是负数，因为价格上涨时，需求数量会减少。但是，常常用绝对值，所以价格弹性以正数的形式出现。进一步说，因为计算用的是比例变化，所以计算结果是无单位的数字，与用来表示价格和数量的单位无关。

如果价格越低人们购买的越多，那么需求数量就相对有弹性；价格变化会引起需求数量的更大变化。然而，在某些情况下，会出现相反的现象，即价格越高人们购买的越多；当买方不能评估产品或服务或者认为高价产品有较大名气时，他们将价格和质量等同起来。不管人们过多购买是因为高价还是低价，只要需求数量百分比变化比价格百分比变化大，价格都被认为是相对有弹性的。

如果价格变化导致需求数量较小的变化，那么需求数量被认为是相对没有弹性的。如果一种产品的需求数量没有弹性，价格的上涨就会引起收入的提高，因为因数量相对少量的减少而导致的收入损失比因价格上涨导致的收入增加小。

用价格弹性来估计价格/数量关系是非常理论化的。企业可以用除了价格弹性以外的（或与价格弹性一起）其他方法来估计客户对备选价格的敏感程度。试销、对价格和数量数据的历史分析、价格点消费者调查都是可用的。这些方法和管理人员的经验和判断相结合，有助于估计销售对价格的敏感度。

买方或卖方的讨价还价能力

买方或卖方的讨价还价能力都会影响价格。思考以下例子：

- 一个大买方对卖方施压要求折扣价格。
- 一个处于主导地位的卖方，如果处于垄断地位，就可以要求并收到一个较高的价格。

● 一个处于主导地位的卖方可以承受低价销售以驱逐其他竞争对手。

注释：本书第 1 章第 1 节 "战略和战术规划" 中详细分析了买方或卖方的讨价还价能力。

公共政策影响

公共政策是影响产品或服务定价的另一个因素。各种法律法规、道德考虑和产品税负都会影响产品或服务的定价。

法律限制

很多定价实践要经过政府检查。比如在美国，政府法规禁止下列行为：

● 价格限定——在分销渠道中竞争对手之间串谋。
● 价格歧视——不以成本为基础，对不同的客户收取不同的价格。
● 价格欺骗——用一个初始高价误导买方，然后降到正常水平。
● 信息披露不完全/欺诈——违反价格信息、利率、信贷条件和其他财务费用的形式上的或可获得性的要求。

道德考虑

在本质上，道德考虑比法律要素要主观一些，但在定价中却仍很重要。很多企业在定价决策和实践上，自愿制定和应用道德指南。但是什么是道德的或什么是不道德的一般很难清楚界定。

美国处方药行业的高价经常被政府、企业和消费者关注。尽管供应商辩解说高价药费是因为研发成本，但是还是有很多批评家质疑该行业的定价，并寻求对其价格进行控制。

税负考虑

公共政策和压力常常通过税负来对定价施加压力。比如，销售税也许会影响到特定商品的价格。烟草税和燃气税就是两个常见的例子。

进度检查

提示：完成以下各题，参考答案随后给出。

1. 一个公司的市场研究表明工业客户愿意为突出的技术优势支付高价，基于该研究公司对新产品收取明显高于现存产品的定价。这种定价战略是：（　　　）

a. 成本法

b. 成本加成法

c. 竞争法

d. 增值法

2. 下列特征中不属于市场撇脂法的是：（　　　）

a. 质量和外观支持较高的价格

b. 较低的价格提供竞争性差异

c. 市场新进入者的威胁很低

d. 认为价格与优良价值等同的战略

连线——定价战略与对应描述。

3. _____ 捆绑定价	a. 定价在 $99 而不是 $100 来吸引买方
4. _____ 折扣或折让定价	b. 同一包装中组合几种产品，以优惠价格一并销售
5. _____ 渗透定价	c. 降低价格来回馈提前或立即支付的买方
6. _____ 心理定价	d. 用一种相对较低的市场进入价格来建立销量和市场地位

进度检查答案

1. d
2. b
3. b
4. c
5. d
6. a

第6节
促销组合与分销战略

本节内容简介

在电影《梦幻之地》中有一句很流行的台词："你盖好了，他就会来。"但是离开促销和分销战略来开发产品或服务无疑是很危险的。组织必须让人们了解它们的产品和服务，并且说服买方、分销渠道成员以及公众全去购买它们的品牌。

营销传播组合

传统观点是，营销依靠关注产品的要素的组合。传统的营销4"P"是：

• 产品——提供给客户的商品和服务；包括类似于包装和保修等所有与产品相关的性能。

• 价格——客户以美元或美分支付的产品或服务成本。

• 地点（或分销）——产品或服务被交付给客户的物理地点。

• 促销——所有的广告、个人销售和其他销售产品和服务相关的活动。

客户需求驱动战略营销，今天很多销售商考虑用4"C"进行营销：

• 消费者或客户，代替了产品。组织认识到它必须关注客户并且必须研究客户需求，然后设计产品和服务以满足这些需求。

• 成本，代替了价格。在计算价格前应进行成本分析。成本分析着眼于产品和服务的总价值主张，并考虑客户在决定购买前关心的每一件事情。

• 便利，代替了地点。因为消费者认为看重时间，所以便利和成本/价值经常相互联系。比如，网上订购可以使潜在客户购买更容易，也因此增加销售收入。

• 沟通，代替了促销。企业用广告、公共关系和其他技术手段来和客户交流。组织应该听取客户的需求（通过他们的言谈举止）而不是告诉客户他们需要什么。

每周，全球的公司花费数十亿美元来促销它们的产品。所有企业，不管是大的还是小的，不管是预算充足还是资源有限，都需要有效管理它们的促销支出来确保该项花费支持企业向市场推销产品的整体性、竞争性、职能性战略。

一般来说，促销战略描述的是一系列相关的传播活动——促销组合——企业用来和客户、目标市场和其他相关受众交流。广告、促销、公共关系、人员推销和直销都是构成促销战略的工具。促销战略的目的是达到经理人员对其每一个目标受众的期望传播目的。

图表3-47给出了每一种促销工具的基本定义。

图表3-47　促销组合

广告	特定赞助商资助的用来描述组织、产品或观念等的任何形式的非个人传播；试图通过提供关于产品和/或服务的说服性的销售信息来影响买方行为
促销	各种各样的促销活动，包括利用互联网、样品、优惠券、购买点广告、贸易展示、竞赛和贸易奖励；针对目标买方，与公众交流，回应特殊需要，和/或新创一种奖励措施来推动购买产品和/或服务

续表

公共关系	通过商业媒体来传播公司及其产品，但是赞助商不直接付费；鼓励相关媒体（比如，贸易杂志）在媒体传播过程中报道公司发布的信息
人员推销	销售人员（或销售团队）与一个或多个潜在买方之间的语言交流，目的是告知客户相关信息并说服他们购买产品或服务
直销	多种传播渠道，包括直接发送邮件、目录、电话营销、电视直销节目、电视销售、广播销售、印刷品销售（杂志和报纸）、网上商店和售货亭；使公司可以直接与买方接触

　　每一种方式都有其特定的目的、优势和局限性，每一次促销的范围也大不相同。通过一系列的计划、执行和评估活动，促销战略把所有这些要素组合成为一个整合营销传播（IMC）战略，从而运用每种形式优点并形成符合成本效益的促销组合。

　　整合营销传播越来越多地取代了传统的分散的营销方案。IMC的基本特征是：

- 综合方案——在计划过程中考虑广告、促销、公共关系、人员推销和直销。
- 统一信息——所有信息都支持一个统一的营销主题。
- 目标方案——所有方案都关注相同或者相关的目标市场。
- 协调执行——所有的传播组成部分互相协调。

　　关系营销是IMC的重要组成部分。关系营销的目的是发展并保持客户和销售商之间的互相满意程度。

广告、促销和公共关系

广告

　　组织通过一种或多种媒体（比如，电视、广播、印刷品、互联网、直接邮件和户外广告）以付费广告的方式来进行传播。

　　一旦确定并描述了目标受众，就要经过四个基本步骤进行广告宣传：

- 设立特定的广告目标。
- 预算广告费用。
- 开发有创意的战略。
- 评估该战略的效果。

设立特定的广告目标

　　广告的目的很多，从一般层面的知名度与曝光率到具体层面的利润贡献率。

　　在一般水平上设定广告目标首先考虑的是，没有办法确定对购买行为的影响。这使得对多大的广告曝光率才会增加人们购买产品的可能性的评价存在问题。

　　广告目标与公司盈利目标联系的越近，就越需要加强与客户购买决策的联系，并影响其购买决策。但是因为受影响销售和利润的其他因素的影响，其具体影响很难测量。

　　除了这些问题，广告也有如下这些优点：

- 曝光成本低。
- 多种媒体。

- 曝光率控制。
- 一致的文书内容。
- 有机会进行创意设计。

预算广告费用

决定广告的最佳预算很有挑战性，因为有很多其他因素能够影响销售。预算通常试图提高促销效果（与过去结果相比）。

图表3-48列示了企业常用的预算方法。

图表3-48　广告预算方法

方　法	描　述
目标和任务	● 设定传播目标；确定为达到目标必须要完成的任务；加总成本 ● 普遍做法，但是其准确度取决于营销团队的经验
销售百分比	● 按销售百分比计算 ● 一般以过去的支出为基础
竞争均势	● 基于竞争对手的花费 ● 很难考虑到不同竞争对手的促销战略（比如，特定目标、促销目的和促销组成部分）
能支付的全部	● 管理人员设定有多少钱可以花费在促销上 ● 受大多数公司普遍存在的预算限制的现实驱动

开发有创意的战略

有创意的战略以目标市场和定位战略为指导。有创意的主题试图与买方有效交流预期形势。

促销活动一般用来完成以下活动之一：

- 保持现状，支持已建立的品牌。
- 改变市场状况（比如，重新定位一个品牌、扩展一个品牌市场、推出新产品）

广告文书被用来提供特定信息（比如，产品的优点），或者它们被用来传播更微妙的意象与象征。

评估该战略的效果

评估标准应该在执行广告战略前被设定好。

对广告活动有效性的衡量给企业提供了关于未来决策用信息的反馈。

如前所述，广告对销售的影响很难确定，因为有其他影响销售和利润的因素存在。有时可以利用历史数据来进行回归分析。

一些例子如下：

- 如针对主要媒体的尼尔逊收视率，统计研究公司（SRI）对广播听众的测量，黄页的使用或其他媒体等服务。
- 通过回忆测试来测量客户对特定广告的了解程度。
- 试销。
- 消费者特定小组。

促销

如图表3-47（促销组合）所示，一个促销计划包括了很多活动。组织可能对各种客户进行直接的促销活动：

- 工业买方——用互联网、贸易展示、样品、应用指南和产品信息报告以及一些钢笔、日历和便签本等特制的广告用品来使其记住品牌和公司名字。
- 消费者——采用优惠券、折扣、竞赛和其他奖励；对消费者关心的活动提供赞助（比如，维萨赞助良种赛马中的三重冠），或个人运动会（比如，美国邮政赞助自行车比赛的兰斯·阿姆斯特朗）。
- 价值链成员（批发和零售）——用互联网、目录和产品信息以及特制的广告用品。
- 销售人员——用奖励性（比如，竞赛、奖励和认可程序）和信息性（比如，销售终端成套赠品）活动来激励和支持公司销售队伍。

如果不考虑可能的促销活动和目标受众的多种多样，那么促销活动的计划、执行、评估中使用的战术与广告活动的非常相似。必须定义要完成的传播任务，必须确定特定目标，必须编制预算，而且必须用成本效益法来进行评估。

促销目标

总之，促销的目的是为了建立销量。促销可以将价值链上的不同群组确定为目标，并且提供额外价值或激励以促进立即销售。

促销预算

用确定广告预算的同样方法（目标和任务，销售百分比，竞争均势，能支付的全部）来确定促销预算。

促销评价

评价促销效果的方法可以帮助企业识别那些可以提供最好结果/成本组合的促销活动。评估评价促销目标的完成情况。例如，可以用制定并转化为采购的合同数量来评估一场贸易展示。或者企业可以追踪其发出的优惠券和回扣。

促销的最大好处是，它提供了各种各样的传播、奖励和定价能力。奖励和价格促销一般会成功地增加销售。很多种类的促销都很容易被追踪和评估。

促销需要注意的是它不能被用作广告或人员推销的替代品；它可以用作增加其他促销创新。控制对防止滥用奖励、优惠券和免费券也很重要。

公共关系

公共关系主要是通过在商业媒体上发布公司信息来获得公众的理解和接受。因为公司不对媒体报道付费，所以公开宣传是一种符合成本效益的促销方法。

公共关系通常和出版物而不是产品或服务打交道，并被用来建立和保持在大众或雇员中的良好名声。比如，公开宣传一些正面的社区参与、故意透露给财务分析师的消息或者参与和支持慈善活动的声明。

一般来说，人们喜欢从他们知道和喜欢的人那里买东西。越来越多的企业客户和消费者希望了解产品背后的公司。随着人们道德、社会、环境意识的提高，他们希望那些和他们打交道的公司也有同样的价值观。很多组织聘请公共关系企业或者顾问来主动获取公共宣传机会。

但是公共关系也有不利的方面。尽管，媒体报道是免费的而且符合成本效益，但是公司不能总是控制广告文本尽可能和其他促销战略一致。因此，如果媒体认为某个话题涉及公众利益，那么可能对企业的公开宣传是负面的。

人员推销和直销

通过人员推销，销售人员可以和买方进行面对面交流。直销用邮件、电话、电视和电脑接触同样的客户。

公司经常组合运用这两种方法。尽管促销战略在执行中各有不同，但是这两种方法都允许组织与目标受众进行一对一交流。

人员推销

人员推销名副其实是个人交流的一种，目的是告知客户并说服他们购买产品或服务。其特定销售责任从简单接受订单到执行咨询性销售。

目标市场、特定产品特性、分销渠道、分销政策和定价战略都是形成营销人员角色的关键影响因素。销售角色必须同组织销售战略一致。

关系营销是一种高度咨询性的人员推销方法。它通常指的是一个团队（比如，一个销售人员，一个技术支持代表和一个营销经理）评价客户需要并且用产品或服务来满足这种需要。价格与此有关，但并不是销售的首要驱动力。

通过关系营销，团队成员（单独行动或者合作）可以：
- 直接与潜在的或当前的客户交流。
- 听取他们关心的事项。
- 回答特定问题。
- 提供额外信息。
- 告知、说服、推荐产品或服务。

与人员推销角色作用相同的是，关系营销使企业可以得到最大的自由来调整广告文书来满足客户信息需求。这种咨询关系使公司可以建立客户满意并且增加长期客户忠诚度。

直销

直销的首要目标是获得单个买方的购买反应。

直销方法

组织可以选择各种直销方法，如图表3–49所示。

图表3-49　直销方法

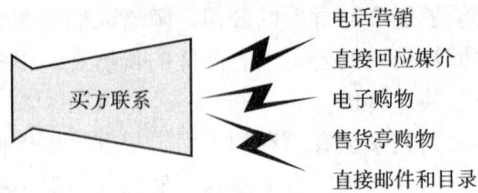

买方联系

电话营销
直接回应媒介
电子购物
售货亭购物
直接邮件和目录

电话营销。电话营销用电话在买方和卖方之间建立直接联系。目标是完成所有或部分销售功能。这种方法的优点是沟通成本低且迅速。

直接回应媒介。直接回应媒介的目标是说服听取或者阅读广告的客户定购产品或服务。广播、杂志和报纸提供了广泛的直销广告渠道。电视途径（比如，家庭购物网）宣传了低于标签价格的折价产品。客户使用免费电话下订单。特定产品（类似音乐唱片、家居用品和杂志）可以通过带有免费电话或者邮件订购地址的电视广告进行销售。

直接回应媒介的优点是成本很低。在低成本下，对买方的投资报酬率也可能很大。

电子购物。通过电子购物，公司可以通过电脑从它们的供应商那里订货，而且消费者和企业也可以通过互联网下订单。

电子购物的优点有：

- 促进标准产品的日常再次买。
- 支持处理标准订单任务的外勤销售人员。
- 减少订单循环和存货。
- 削减成本。
- 监控客户偏好。

一些买方仍然拒绝使用电子系统与供应商联系，但是电子联络处于增长趋势。随着互联网虚拟购物的增长，越来越多的企业会对电脑用户开展直销。

售货亭购物。售货亭在概念上和自动售货机类似，但是它们使买方可以从一家小便利店或者从一个零售中心（比如，大型超市）柜台或者其他公共场所（比如，机场）购买。一些售货亭有网络连接（比如，发布航班信息甚至提供飞机票或者飞行险）。买方以前购买过的熟悉的产品非常适合售货亭销售。卖方可以招徕很多顾客，而买方获得了便利。

直接邮件和目录。用邮件联系潜在买方一般会带来通过回复邮件或电话而下的订单。在有些情况下，该方法鼓励买方访问零售商店或网站来查看产品并进行购买。

直销战略

直销的范围变化很大，但所有直销都要如下一些基本的战略制定步骤：

- 确定目标市场。
- 设定目标。
- 定位战略。
- 制定一个传播计划。

- 执行和管理该计划。
- 评估与预期业绩相比的实际效果。

直销可能是与客户联系（比如，户外服装市场的宾恩）的首要方式，或者也许是企业在一些组合（比如，女士内衣零售商"维多利亚的秘密"对目录、直接回应媒介、电视广告和电子购物的运用）中采用的几种方法之一。

直销的道德问题

直销协会（DMA）是直销行业的首要专业协会。该协会倡导的一般哲学是：自律的道德措施比政府强制更好。

该协会鼓励广泛使用与各种直销关注问题有关的合理的企业实务，比如（但不限于）：

- 使用术语（比如，诚实；对提供的产品及其代表含义有清晰的表述；披露；邮资、运费和处理）。
- 事先同意的营销（消费者同意在未来连续或定期收到并支付产品或服务，除非和直到消费者取消该计划）。
- 对儿童营销（比如，父母对孩子的责任和来自/关于孩子的信息）。
- 特定提供和要求（比如，"免费"这个词的使用、价格比较、证明书、保证）。
- 彩票（比如，获胜的机会、规定、奖品和奖金）。
- 履行情况（比如，产品可获得性及运输）。
- 营销信息的收集、使用和保持（比如，私人信息的收集、使用和转移，销售名单的运用和信息安全）。
- 在线营销（比如，在线的商业引导）。
- 电话营销（比如，合理的时间、谈话录音、自动拨号设备的使用）。
- 集资（比如，提供关于资金利用的财务信息）。
- 法律、法规和规章（比如，美国邮政总局、联邦商务部、联邦通信委员会和联邦储备委员会的法律规章，其他的联邦、州、地方法律对广告、营销活动和企业交易的规定）。

有关直销道德问题的特定信息和涉及其他措施的额外信息，请登陆 DMA 网站，www. thedma. org/guidelines/ethicalguidlines。

分销渠道

分销渠道是指一组相互关联、相互依靠的机构和代理商组成的网络。分销渠道中的各方相互协作并共同努力把产品分销给终端用户。一个有效的分销渠道是创造并保持组织竞争优势的重要影响因素。

图表 3－50 展示了关于消费品和工业品分销渠道的简单例子。

图表 3–50　普通的分销渠道

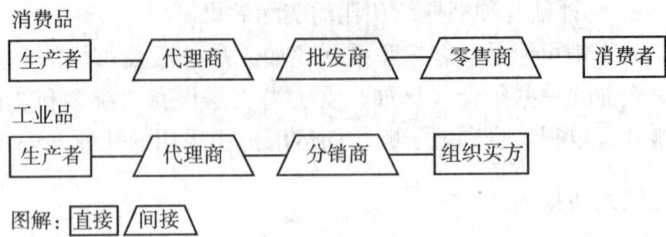

分销渠道的增值功能

强有力的分销渠道在把产品从生产者传递给终端用户的过程中要完成几个必要的增值活动，如图表 3–51 所示。

图表 3–51　分销渠道的功能

活　动	描　述
营销中介	为生产者和终端用户减少交易的次数
产品存货	帮助达到客户对产品购买时间和种类偏好的要求
运输	消除买方和卖方之间的地理/区域差距
融资	促进货币兑换功能
处理和储存	把大的数量分割成许多单个订单；维持存货和汇集装运单
广告和促销	传播产品的可获得性、地点、性能和优点
定价	设定买方和卖方的交换基础
减少风险	提供保险、退货政策和期货交易机制
人员推销	提供销售、产品信息及支持性服务
服务和维修	提供基本的客户支持和服务

行业的本质、企业的目标市场和定位战略、产品组合和许多其他营销因素共同决定了为了支持分销需要什么样的特定职能和组织需要为其承担什么责任。

分销渠道组织

企业从不同类型的分销渠道中进行选择。

传统渠道

在传统分销渠道中，独立组织之间是垂直的联系。每一个组织自力更生，很少协调和关注分销的总体表现。渠道成员之间的交流是非正式的。大家关注交易（买方—卖方交易），而不是整个渠道的协调。

垂直营销系统

垂直营销系统法（VMS）把渠道作为一个协调的或者程序化的系统进行管理。一个企业被指派为渠道管理者。渠道管理者指导渠道活动，设定经营规则和指南，提供管理协助，并为参与渠道的其他组织提供各种支持性服务。VMS 渠道主要应用在零售业，在商业、工业和服务行业正越来越流行。

垂直营销系统网络有4种类型。图表3-52列示了这4种类型和主要特征。

图表3-52 垂直营销系统的分销渠道

类型	主要特征
所有者型 VMS	• 渠道协调者拥有这个从供应源头到终端用户的分销渠道 • 包括渠道协调者的大量资本投资 比如：拥有自己经销商的汽车制造商；控制着"从地面到油罐车"的经营的石油公司
契约型 VMS	• 也许包括渠道参与者之间的各种正式协议，包括独立零售商的特许和自愿连锁 • 契约方案可能由制造商、批发商和零售商发起 比如：连锁快餐店；连锁旅店；其他小连锁零售店
支配型 VMS	其中某一渠道成员因具有财务状况、品牌优势或其他专门能力从而能够影响其他渠道成员 比如：计算机操作系统制造商；主要软件公司；电脑芯片制造商
关系型 VMS	• 与支配型 VMS 有同样的特征，但不是一个渠道成员可以控制其他成员 • 有亲密的交流和分享关系 比如：提供无线电话硬件和服务合同或者销售卫星电视硬件和合同的消费电子连锁店

一般来说，只要恰当设计和管理，VMS渠道的业绩才可能比传统渠道的好。尽管没有严格的规则来监管经营，但是有很多控制方式。参与的企业有义务做出让步，并为VMS的整体业绩共同努力。

水平营销系统

在水平营销系统中，两个或更多的不相关也不互相竞争的企业一起合作来利用某一特定机会。组织合作是因为每一个独立的企业都缺少适当的资源（比如，资金、技术或人力）来单独完成工作或者因为它们害怕风险。这种关系也许是暂时的合作或者变成长期关系。在有些情况下，这些公司会组成合资公司或其他战略联盟。

水平合作的一个例子是一家独立的汽车保险公司和一家私人信用管理企业可以提供对方的信息给各自的客户。

混合营销系统

随着客户细分市场和分销渠道潜力的增加，一些公司采用了一种混合的（多渠道）方法。当一家公司采用两种或者更多的分销渠道来达到一个或多个客户细分市场时，混合或多渠道营销就产生了。

混合或多渠道营销的一个例子是：一个生产商直接配送给零售商，零售商再卖给特定的客户细分市场，同时这个生产商也利用代理商配送给其他客户细分市场。这个生产商可能也直接销售给特定的客户细分市场。这是一种典型的方法，即企业既通过互联网又通过实体店铺进行营销。

渠道分散趋势

要保持竞争优势或者提高客户满意度和组织的效果，就要经常检查分销渠道经营。时常地，组织战略问题或成本效率问题要求重组或者重建渠道系统。

考虑下面的例子：

• 采用直销方法的企业发现间接渠道（比如，批发商、分销商、代理商或零售商）可以更好地服务部分客户。

- 当市场成熟时，组织可能追随低成本的大规模的商家而不是专用产品连锁店。
- 可能在现存客户范围内实施直销方案以利用方便购买的机会（通过邮寄目录或免费电话购物）。
- 互联网也许被用来绕开传统分销商（比如戴尔电脑的供应商和客户之间的虚拟整合）。

很多因素导致渠道分散，脱媒也许是最主要的因素。脱媒指的是企业从价值链中离开。这个术语通常是指买方通过互联网直接从制造商网页（像上文提到的戴尔电脑的例子）上购买。互联网给卖方提供了脱离以前所必需的伙伴或与分销渠道联系的潜力。中间人（分销商和/或零售商）经常从销售中被排除掉。

可以从以下事件中看出脱媒的例子：

- 航空公司在网上售票，绕开旅行社和经销商网站，比如 Travelocity 和 Expedia。
- 娱乐公司在它们发行的 CD 和 DVD 中嵌入超链接和促销广告来把客户直接带到公司所拥有的在线零售商处，并把客户从零售渠道拉走。
- 汽车制造商提供按单定制系统，使在线卖方可以直接从工厂订购，或者给客户提供新产品价格、新车和二手车的在线存货及与二手车折价价值和代理商网站的链接，迫使代理商向客户披露汽车和卡车的价格。
- 消费者通过熟悉的品牌制造商网站在线购买服装，绕过传统服装零售商。

这样的好处是客户更方便了，周转时间更短了，一般来讲价格更低了。但是，因为传统中间人被排斥和关键渠道功能被重新分配，以致出现了渠道冲突。

随着买方上网购买产品和服务，很多传统零售商和供应商被疏远了。但是，会产生一种重新居间的行为，被驱逐的分销商或新的加入者会以一种新的身份回来。认识到公司和其客户直接关系中存在关键差距和未被满足需求的企业可能作为增值的中间人重新加入这个系统。

渠道设计

渠道的类型（传统型、VMS、水平型或混合型）和密度水平（紧密的、选择性的、排他的）对渠道包括多少组织层级以及中间人的特定类型产生影响。比如，一种工业品的生产商也许会在独立的（受托的）制造代理商和分销链中做出选择。

影响渠道设计的一些因素是：
- 消费者需求和偏好——目标终端客户希望在哪购买产品。
- 产品特征——产品的复杂程度、特殊应用要求以及必要的服务。
- 制造商能力和资源——集合资源以及大生产商与中间人的谈判能力（或者相反，对小生产商的限制）。
- 必要功能——把产品从生产者移动到终端用户的必要职能（比如，储存、运输以及服务）。
- 中间人的有效性和技能——中间人的经验、能力和动机。

选择渠道战略

采用何种渠道是一个关键的营销决策；它影响其他每个营销决策（比如，定价、传播决策、销售人员）。选择渠道要考虑的因素有：

- 组织总体战略。
- 渠道目标。
- 终端用户所在地和期望得到的服务水平。
- 不同渠道的市场进入潜力。
- 产品或服务成本。
- 经济考虑（收入—成本对渠道战略的影响）。
- 关于弹性和控制的考虑。
- 法律和道德考虑（比如，特许代理和区域协定）。

关于主要备选方案的优点和缺点都应该被考虑。比如，所有直接对消费者或终端用户进行的销售也许会导致不可承受的成本损失。另外，引入中间人可能明显降低生产者对终端用户关系的控制程度。中间人也许会帮助达到财务目标，但是同时也降低了对产品如何售出以及出售给谁的控制。中间人经常会要求一些支持（比如，培训、市场调查和其他能力构建计划）。

如果多种选择可以带来利润，组织需要平衡成本和其他考虑。

关于国际化的考虑

虽然其他国家也有代理商、批发商和零售商，但分销模式和网络会有很多其他的重大差异。归纳跨越国界的分销实践是不可能的。进行全球扩张的企业必须：

- 学习其有利益关系的国家的分销模式。
- 研究技术趋势（比如，卫星通信）、区域合作（比如，欧盟）以及运输服务。
- 评估全球市场动荡的潜力。
- 调查货币问题和银行机构。
- 确定资本和资金要求。
- 评估战略的产品配合。

不管是国内还是全球，市场驱动战略的首要目标是使公司的价值链与不断变化的客户和竞争要求一致。分销渠道是价值链的核心。简而言之，强有力的分销渠道可以带来竞争优势。

进度检查

提示：完成以下各题，参考答案随后给出。

1. 营销的 4C 指的是：（　　）
   a. 消费者/客户、创造力、成本、沟通
   b. 客户、竞争、公司、成本
   c. 消费者/客户、成本、便利、沟通
   d. 客户、竞争、成本、渠道组织
2. 一个以正常交易的买方—卖方关系为特征的分销渠道，采购部门选择供应方并且决定什么时候需要商品，这种分销渠道是：（　　）
   a. 所有者型垂直营销系统

    b. 契约型垂直营销系统

    c. 传统型分销渠道

    d. 排他型分销渠道

3. 关系营销的关键特征是：（   ）

    a. 高度咨询性的人员推销

    b. 说服接听广告的潜在买方购买该产品

    c. 通过商业媒体获得公共理解和接受

    d. 客户和企业都可以通过互联网来下订单

4. "能支付的全部"的广告预算方法主要受什么影响：（   ）

    a. 过去的支出

    b. 竞争对手的花费

    c. 有创意的广告文书设计

    d. 普遍存在的预算限制

进度检查答案

1. c

2. c

3. a

4. d

公司理财

本章内容简介

公司理财是提升核心业务目标和完成战略目标的基础。营利企业、非营利机构和公共实体都必须支付各种各样的成本。所有投资，不论是短期还是长期，都必须支持组织的核心能力。简单来说：公司理财必须支持组织战略，确保任何短期障碍都不会扰乱长期战略。

组织可以从几种金融工具中做出选择。

管理会计师经常被要求去评价一种工具对于组织的适当性。为了达到这个目的，会计师需要理解不同工具的一般用途、拥有或发行它们的经济风险和收益。他们也必须确保组织能够从所选择的投资中获得足够的投资报酬率以补偿融资成本。

谨慎的投资决策有助于确保任何企业的财务稳健性。尤其是对于上市公司，财务稳健和价值创造可促使投资者购买公司的股票、债券和证券。

本章分析了公司理财的主要概念、范围、从基本的风险管理原则到短期、长期金融工具的有效选择和管理。

学习要点说明

注册管理会计师（CMA）考试包含很多学习要点，这些学习要点由管理会计师协会确定。学习要点描述了注册管理会计师考试要求掌握的所有知识点和技能，并且细分为各个章节。注册管理会计师考试教材解释了学习要点所包含的各个部分，是对学习要点的有力支持。学习要点可以帮助考生以不同的方式或通过不同的问题情景理解这些概念。考生还应该练习学习要点中所提到的全部或者部分计算，或者完成计算过程中的缺失部分。学习要点不能代替对 CMA 考试教材内容的研究和学习，但是可以确保考生达到学习要点所设定的目标。

注册管理会计师教材中所包含的学习要点是一个完整的集合，并且是到目前为止最新的版本。考生可以浏览 IMA 的官方网站 www. imanet. org，点击"认证"部分查看和下载关于学习要点的最新 PDF 文件。

学习要点

3.1　风险和报酬

- LOS. 3.1.1：计算报酬率。
- LOS. 3.1.2：确定并阐述不同种类的风险（系统性［市场］、非系统性［公司］、行业、国家等）。
- LOS. 3.1.3：阐述风险和收益之间的关系。
- LOS. 3.1.4：计算预期报酬，报酬的标准差和变异系数。
- LOS. 3.1.5：辨别对于风险的不同态度，以及它们可能对风险管理的影响。
- LOS. 3.1.6：定义组合并区分单一证券风险和组合风险。
- LOS. 3.1.7：定义风险价值（VAR）。
- LOS. 3.1.8：阐述分散投资。
- LOS. 3.1.9：区分系统性和非系统性风险。
- LOS. 3.1.10：阐述个别证券怎样影响组合风险。
- LOS. 3.1.11：定义 β 系数并阐述对证券 β 系数的理解。
- LOS. 3.1.12：使用资本资产定价模型（CAPM）和套利定价理论（APT）计算预期风险调整报酬率。
- LOS. 3.1.13：定义套期保值并阐述怎样运用套期保值管理金融风险。

3.2　金融工具

- LOS. 3.2.1：定义并确定债券、普通股和优先股的特点。
- LOS. 3.2.2：确定并描述债券的特征，诸如期限、面值、票面利率、赎回条款、保证条款、赠与发行方和投资方的期权、契约、限制条款。
- LOS. 3.2.3：定义不同种类的股利，包括现金股利、股票股利和股票分割。
- LOS. 3.2.4：确定和讨论影响企业股利政策的因素。
- LOS. 3.2.5：说明普通股和优先股的股利发放程序。
- LOS. 3.2.6：使用折现现金流量法对债券、普通股和优先股进行估值。
- LOS. 3.2.7：阐述股利折现模型。
- LOS. 3.2.8：阐述相对或比较估值法，如市盈率、市账率和市销率。
- LOS. 3.2.9：阐述衡量债券利息率敏感度的久期。
- LOS. 3.2.10：阐述所得税怎样影响筹资决策。
- LOS. 3.2.11：定义并阐述衍生金融工具及其支付结构和应用。
- LOS. 3.2.12：区分期货和远期交易。
- LOS. 3.2.13：阐述期权。
- LOS. 3.2.14：基本理解布莱克—舒尔茨期权估价模型和二项式期权估价模型，以及一个变量的变化将怎样影响期权价值（不要求计算）。
- LOS. 3.2.15：定义并确定其他来源的长期筹资如租赁、可转换证券、权证和留存收益的特点。

3.3　资本成本

- LOS. 3.3.1：定义资本成本并阐述它在资本结构决策中的应用。
- LOS. 3.3.2：确定加权平均（历史的）资本成本及其各组成部分的成本。
- LOS. 3.3.3：计算边际资本成本并阐述运用边际成本而不是历史成本的意义。
- LOS. 3.3.4：阐述资本成本在资本投资决策中的应用。
- LOS. 3.3.5：阐述所得税对资本结构和资本投资决策的影响。

3.4　流动资产管理

- LOS. 3.4.1：定义营运资本并确定其组成部分。
- LOS. 3.4.2：解释短期财务预测在营运资本管理中的益处。
- LOS. 3.4.3：确定影响现金水平的因素。
- LOS. 3.4.4：确定持有现金的三种动机。
- LOS. 3.4.5：阐述企业公司怎样监管现金流入和流出并进行未来现金流预测。
- LOS. 3.4.6：确定加快现金回收的方法。
- LOS. 3.4.7：计算锁箱法的净收益。
- LOS. 3.4.8：定义集资银行并讨论企业怎样利用它。
- LOS. 3.4.9：阐述补偿性余额的用途。
- LOS. 3.4.10：确定减缓支付的方法。
- LOS. 3.4.11：通过汇票和零余额账户定义应付款项。
- LOS. 3.4.12：阐述支出的浮账和透支系统。
- LOS. 3.4.13：定义电子商务并讨论它在企业中的应用。
- LOS. 3.4.14：定义不同种类的有价证券，包括货币市场工具、短期国库券、中期国库券、长期国库券、回购协议、联邦机构证券、银行承兑汇票、商业票据、可转让存单、欧洲美元以及其他有价证券。
- LOS. 3.4.15：阐释有价证券选择时的变量，包括安全性、适销性、收益、期限和可税性。
- LOS. 3.4.16：阐述在选择有价证券时对风险和收益的权衡。
- LOS. 3.4.17：列举持有有价证券的原因。
- LOS. 3.4.18：确定持有应收账款的原因和影响其水平的因素。
- LOS. 3.4.19：阐述信贷条件变化的影响。
- LOS. 3.4.20：定义违约风险。
- LOS. 3.4.21：阐述决定最优信用政策的影响因素。
- LOS. 3.4.22：计算平均回收期。
- LOS. 3.4.23：确定持有存货的原因及影响其水平的因素。
- LOS. 3.4.24：确定并计算存货的相关成本。
- LOS. 3.4.25：定义前置时间和安全库存。
- LOS. 3.4.26：阐述经济订货量（EOQ）及一个变量的变化会怎样影响 EOQ 的（不需要计算）。
- LOS. 3.4.27：定义适时制和看板存货管理系统。

3.5 流动资产筹资

- LOS.3.5.1：阐述风险是怎样影响一个企业流动资产筹资政策的（积极的，保守的等）。
- LOS.3.5.2：描述不同种类的短期信贷，包括贸易信贷、短期银行贷款、商业票据、信用额度、银行承兑汇票，并确定它们的优劣。
- LOS.3.5.3：估计年度成本和没接受现金折扣的实际年利率。
- LOS.3.5.4：计算有补偿性余额要求和/或承诺费的银行贷款的实际年利率。
- LOS.3.5.5：描述不同种类的担保短期贷款，包括应收账款融资和存货融资。
- LOS.3.5.6：阐述应收账款转售并计算转售成本。
- LOS.3.5.7：阐述筹资的期限匹配或套期保值。

第1节
风险和报酬

本节内容简介

在当今的经济环境下要想成功，组织必须成功地管理各种各样的经营风险和财务风险。较差的风险管理可以导致效率低下、业务流失或者企业终结。

本节首先介绍了经营风险和财务风险的不同，然后分析了财务风险和报酬的一些内容。

风险的种类

按照传统的说法，风险是指不能从投资中获得预期报酬的可能性。风险暗示了一种不确定程度。报酬的潜在变动性越大，投资的风险越大。提供了"担保"投资报酬率的一年期美国短期国库券（T－bill）被认为没有风险。股票或者一些其他可变的投资工具的年报酬率都是内在高风险的；报酬可能比预期少得多，或者最坏的情况甚至是少于最初的投资。

公司风险主要分为两类：经营风险和财务风险。

经营风险

经营风险是指企业在筹资决策前其经营中的固有风险。与产品和服务的生产及营销有关的一系列经营决策都是经营风险的常见例子。经营风险的其他原因包括需求、销售价格和投入成本的变动性；随投入成本的变化而调整产出价格及及时地、符合成本效益地开发新产品的能力；外汇风险；成本固定的程度。企业筹资方式不影响经营风险。

经营风险中包括的是可保风险。正如管理会计公告2A"术语：管理会计词汇表"所述，可保风险包括财产及其他有形资产的损坏和损失；因侵权负债而带来的收入、利润或净值减少；员工意外伤害或疾病而产生的成本。大多数组织都有正式的风险管理程序以减轻可保风险。

但是经营风险和可保风险一般都不是管理会计师的直接领域。本质上说，财务风险才是其管辖范围。

经营杠杆系数

经营风险经常用经营杠杆系数（DOL）来衡量。DOL是指营业利润百分率变化与销售收入百分率变化之比。公式是：

DOL＝边际贡献/营业利润

边际贡献等于销售收入减去变动成本。营业利润等于边际贡献减去固定成本。

财务风险

财务风险是与债务融资相联系的风险。债务融资提高了税前（但息后）收益的变动性。因此，和经营风险一起，财务风险会引起净利润和每股收益的不确定性。

注意：不同的金融工具会在本章第 2 节"金融工具"中详细讨论。

金融工具选择数量的增多以及日益提高的复杂程度都会影响投资风险，影响程度不容小觑。影响投资报酬变动的其他主要因素是：

- 利率、汇率及商品价格的不确定性。
- 金融交易的时间敏感性。

财务杠杆系数

财务风险经常用财务杠杆系数来衡量。DFL 是指 EPS 百分率变化与营业利润百分率变化之比。公式是：

DFL = 营业利润\\{营业利润 − 利息费用 −［优先股股利\\(1 − 税率)］}

总杠杆系数

经营风险和财务风险合起来被称作总杠杆系数（DTL），它是经营杠杆和财务杠杆的产物。

DTL = DOL × DFL

或

DTL = 边际贡献\\{营业利润 − 利息费用 −［优先股股利\\(1 − 税率)］}

风险管理

因为错误管理财务风险存在潜在后果，大多数公司会通过实施风险管理程序以尽力控制它们的影响。尽管这种程序的形式和细节因公司而异，但是风险管理程序的基本步骤仍可概括为图表 3 − 53 列示的内容。

图表 3 −53　风险管理程序的步骤

第一步：确定公司的风险容忍程度
这一步确定组织对风险的态度。公司会接受重大的财务风险吗？公司是只想承担选择性风险吗？企业必须消除所有风险吗？

第二步：评估风险
在这一步，风险的特定本质必须被确定。（例如：风险是同利率或汇率的潜在变化有关吗？如果不是，主要的风险因素是什么？）风险必须被量化以便做出风险水平是否是组织可接受的决策。

第三步：实施恰当的风险管理战略
风险管理战略确定必须采取什么样行动去管理风险。各种战略都是可能的。

第四步：监管风险及管理战略
定期监管评定现状或风险中任何意想不到的变化（由于市场的多变性等）。本步骤也要考虑选择的风险管理战略是否有效。战略调整也是必要的。

除了对风险管理制定明确的目标和战略外，组织一般确定主要人员的角色和责任，并建立决策制定的等级。同时，也要考虑怎样衡量和报告业绩结果。

风险管理有助于降低公司未来现金流的变动性。由此，拥有稳定的现金流也会增加公司价值。具有稳定现金流的公司一般被认为更稳定（低风险），从而能在信贷市场上获得有利的借款地位。

注意：本章第 2 节"金融工具"关注能被用作风险管理工具的投资工具。

套期保值、投机、套利和期限匹配

一般来说，四个过程体现了公司使用金融工具管理风险的方式：套期保值、投机、套利和期限匹配。

套期保值

套期保值是降低价格、利率或汇率不利波动所带来的风险的方法。公司通过使用另一个反向投资工具来对原来的投资进行套期保值。

套期保值的一般形式包括期货合同，把价格波动风险转移给其他方的卖出和卖方期权，或者同时卖出和买入交割期不同的商品和服务的权利。套期保值协议或交易的目标是降低或消除一个公司的风险。

注意：本章第 2 节"金融工具"对于衍生金融工具的讨论更详细地介绍了期货和期权。

投机

投机涉及打赌市场变动方向导致的风险。不像套期保值试图降低风险，投机因为对特定投资价格的上涨或下跌下赌注，所以承担了很大的风险。

投机的目标是尽力预测未来以期获得快速巨大的收益。就因为这样，投机协议或交易提高了一个公司的风险。

套利

套利是指在一个市场买入一个投资工具而同时在另一个市场卖出，目的是利用不同市场的价格差获得收益。

套利协议或交易的目标是从市场无效中获利。真正的套利不应该影响一个公司的总体风险。

期限匹配

期限是指发行方偿还证券前剩余的时间长度。到期日是指本金偿还日，即最后一次付款的到期日。

期限匹配是指通过匹配公司负债与资产的期限来对冲风险的管理方法。在实践中，期限匹配尽力用短期融资为短期项目提供资金，用长期资产为长期项目提供资金。期限匹配的一个例子是一个公司为一个历时五年的项目购买设备，同时用相似久期的资金为项目融资。

注意：本章第 5 节"流动资产筹资"也将讨论期限匹配。

计算报酬率

公司和投资者一般不会为了好玩而承担风险；他们一直在寻求与风险相当的投资报酬率。报酬（或报酬率）是指持有一项投资一段时间而获得的金额与初始投资金额之比。当然，不是所有报酬率都以利得结束。金融投资或资产的所有者在一段给定时期内也可能遭受损失。报酬率反映了投资市场价格的任何变化，一般用投资的初始市场价格的百分比来表示。

最简单地说，报酬率的计算是用收到的现金支付（如股利或利息）加上市场价格变化（折旧或价格损失），然后除以证券的初始价格。

例如，报酬率，也被称为一段时期内普通股的持有期回报（HPR）可表示为：

$$R = \frac{(P_t - P_{t-1}) + D}{P_{t-1}}$$

式中：

- R 表示报酬率（持有期回报）。
- P_t 表示期末股票价格。
- P_{t-1} 表示期初股票价格。
- D_t 表示期末现金股利。
- t 指持有期。

例如：

假设一名投资者一年前花 \$20 买了一只普通股，现在这只股票价格上升到 \$22。在这期间，公司给每股发放了 \$2 现金股利。这只股票的一年持有期回报是多少？

- P_t（以前的股票价格）= \$2
- P_t =（当前的股票价格）= \$22
- D_t =（现金股利）= \$2

$R = [(\$22 - \$20) + \$2] / \$20 = \$4 / \$2 = 0.20$ 或 20%

持有期（t）可以是任何时长。在本例中，R 代表了该普通股一年的持有期回报。因此，该普通股的报酬率是 20%。

风险和报酬之间的关系

风险是财务决策中重要的考虑因素。在理性市场条件下，有更大预期风险的那些投资应该比低风险投资提供更大的预期报酬率。

对资本市场历史的大量研究认为给投资者的报酬一般都是对他们所承担风险的反映。比如，下面是对美国投资工具的归纳（基于很长一段时间的历史数据——一般是几十年——所以平均报酬率不会因异常高或低的报酬率的波动而扭曲）。

- **短期国库券的风险和报酬**

美国短期国库券（期限短于一年的美国政府证券）是非常安全的证券。它没有违约风险。违约风险是指借款到期时借款方不能偿还利息和/或本金的风险。因为期限短，所以价格（容易受通货膨胀影响）相对稳定。短期国库券有最稳定的报酬率。

- **债券的风险和报酬**

美国政府债券和公司债券的期限比短期国库券长。它们也有另外一面：价格随利率变化波动。从历史上看，当利率下降时债券价格会上升，而利率上升时债券价格会下降。因此，债券价格和利率之间存在反向关系。

类似于美国短期国库券，政府债券没有违约风险。而公司债券一定有违约风险。在一段时间内，债券报酬率要高于短期国库券报酬率。平均来说，公司债券的报酬率略高于政府债券。

- **股票的风险和报酬**

股票是表明在一个公司拥有所有权（权益）的投资。股票投资者也直接分担企业风险。

平均来说，股票报酬大大高于长短期国库券的稳定报酬。从历史上来看，美国小企业股票的投资报酬超过了美国大企业股票的投资报酬。

注意：本章第 2 节"金融工具"给出了债券、普通股和优先股的其他信息。

风险价值

管理风险时，组织不能仅仅依靠历史数据。管理风险的人在承担风险前应该了解风险。如前所述，长期的历史业绩对报酬率进行了平均化，从而包含了异常高或低的报酬率的波动。但是正如名字所暗示的，"历史的"表明是对风险的回顾总结。当回顾一个组合时，历史波动性表明在过去某段时期内该组合的风险有多大。它对组合的当前市场风险没有指示作用。风险价值使公司具备评估当前风险的能力。

风险价值是在给定时期内、给定的特定可能性水平（置信水平）下的最大损失。不像回顾风险度量标准衡量的是历史波动性，VAR 是前瞻的。它量化了将要承担的市场风险。

表 3-54 概括了 VAR 的关键概念。

表 3-54　风险价值（VAR）的特点

应　用	VAR 可用于任何能够定期按市场表现合理估价的组合。VAR 不能用于不动产或其他非流动资产。
时间跨度/范围	VAR 评估特定时期内的组合表现，如一个交易日、一周或一月。
基准货币	VAR 以货币度量风险。任何货币都可以使用。
VAR 度量结果	得出的 VAR 度量结果用一个数字概括了组合的市场风险。

VAR 可以用以下方法计算：

- **历史法**

该方法重新组织了一段时期内的实际历史报酬，把它们按从坏到好的顺序排列。历史法认为从风险角度来看，历史不会重演。柱状图将报酬频率同损失联系在一起。最终得出的置信水平提供了一个最差情况下日损失也不会超过的百分比。（例如，如果我们投资 \$1 000，那么我们有 95% 的信心认为我们最差的日损失也不会超过 \$40（\$1 000 × 4%））。

- **方差—协方差法**

方差—协方差法认为股票报酬率服从正态分布。估计了预期（或平均）报酬率和标准差，正态分布曲线就可以画出来。通过观察正态曲线，一个人能准确地看到最坏百分比在曲线上的位置。被关注的这个百分比是期望置信水平和标准差的函数。

- **蒙特·卡洛模拟**

蒙特·卡洛模拟是指随机进行试验的任何方法。该方法开发了一个未来报酬率模型，并通过该模型运行大量的假设试验。

风险和报酬的态度

评价风险和报酬之间的权衡是股东财富最大化的一个主要组成部分。

股东财富是一个公司普通股的市场价值。股东财富是流通在外普通股股数与每股市价（普通股在交易所，诸如纽交所，交易的价格）的乘积。

股东财富最大化（SWM）是指股东购买力最大化。在有效市场里，股东财富最大化就是当前股票价格最大化。它给评价各种投资和融资战略的时机和风险提供了便利的框架，它用现金流衡量报酬。从财务角度看，SWM 一般被认为是企业的主要目标。

确定性等值（CE）是指投资者在偿付和给定投机之间无所谓时不得不接受的现金金额。它回答了下面这个问题，为替代有风险的现金流，一个投资者能够接受的最低确定性偿付是多少？图表 3－55 总结了关于投资者确定性等值和预期货币价值之间关系的一般原则。

表 3－55　确定性等值和对风险的态度

当确定性等值	则
小于预期价值	风险厌恶（风险厌恶态度）
等于预期价值	风险无差异（风险无差异或中立态度）
大于预期价值	风险喜好（风险渴求态度）

风险厌恶指投资者不喜欢风险，对于风险更大的投资需要更大的报酬率来激励。因此，比起低风险投资，高风险投资应该给投资者更高的预期报酬。换句话说，一个投资的风险越大，需要更高的预期报酬去补偿购买并持有该项投资的投资者。相反地，投资者对低风险投资预期获得较低的预期报酬。一般来说，大多数投资者是风险厌恶者，对不断提高的风险寻求较高的报酬。

在讨论投资报酬时，对于确定性没有真正或者单一的衡量方法。确定性等值处理的是预期报酬；投资的实际报酬可能会不同。例如，低风险投资的实际报酬可能会远高于风险投资的报酬。

风险一般随时间增长，就好像越远的预测不确定性和/或变动性就越大一样。

概率分布、风险和报酬

除了无风险国库券，实际报酬率经常被认为是服从概率分布的随机变量。概率分布显示随机变量（例如，投资）可能的所有数值以及每个值发生的几率。

概率分布中有三个主要的描述性统计指标：

- 预期报酬。

- 标准差。
- 协方差。

预期报酬

预期报酬率是可能报酬的加权平均，这个平均数代表了发生的可能性。它是对概率分布集中趋势的衡量。预期报酬的公式是：

$$\overline{R} = \sum_{i=1}^{n} (R_i)(P_i)$$

式中：

- $\overline{R}$ 表示预期报酬。
- R_i 表示第 i 种可能的报酬。
- P_i 表示该报酬发生的概率。
- n 表示可能性的总数。

标准差

标准差是一个统计指标，显示了围绕投资预期（最可能发生）报酬的变异或离散程度。它展现了围绕均值（平均数）的分布，计算方法是：方差的平方根。计算公式为：

$$\sigma = \sqrt{\sum_{i=1}^{n} (R_i - \overline{R})^2 (P_i)}$$

在上面等式中，对中值的离差（$R_i - \overline{R}$）进行平方，以消除负号的问题。一般来说，标准差越高，报酬的变动性和总风险就越大。

例如：

在给定的概率分布下，预期报酬和报酬的标准差的计算过程。

可能的报酬，R_i	发生的可能性，P_i	预期报酬 $\overline{R}$ 的计算 $(R_i)(P_i)$	方差 σ^2 的计算 $(R_i -)^2$ (i)
-0.02	0.10	-0.002	$(-0.02 - 0.10)^2(0.10) = 0.00144$
0.05	0.20	0.010	$(0.05 - 0.10)^2(0.20) = 0.00050$
0.10	0.40	0.040	$(0.10 - 0.10)^2(0.40) = 0.00000$
0.15	0.20	0.030	$(0.15 - 0.10)^2(0.20) = 0.00050$
0.22	0.10	0.022	$(0.22 - 0.10)^2(0.10) = 0.00144$
	$\sum = 1.00$	$\sum = 0.10 = \overline{R}$	$\sum = 0.01288 = \sigma^2$
			标准差 $= (0.01288)^5 = 0.11349$ 或 11.349%

在本例中：

- 该分布的方差 $= 0.01288$。
- 该分布的标准差 $= 11.349\%$。

变异系数

当比较不同投资的风险或不确定性时，若它们的投资规模不同，则标准差可能存在误导。计算变异系数有助于对规模的不同进行调整。

变异系数（CV）为相对风险提供了度量方法。变异系数用标准差除以分布的均值。

$$CV = \frac{\sigma}{R}$$

例如：

符合正态分布的投资 A 和投资 B 有以下特点。

	投资 A	投资 B
预期报酬，$\overline{R}$	0.06	0.18
标准差，σ	0.04	0.06

基于对这两项投资的标准差的比较，较大的是投资 B(0.06)，看起来它好像比投资 A 风险大。然而，相对于预期，投资 A 的方差更大。为了调整这些差异，变异系数提供了度量单位预期报酬的风险的方法。

	投资 A	投资 B
变异系数	0.04/0.06 = 0.67	0.06/0.18 = 0.33

使用相对风险作为度量指标，变异系数为 0.67 的投资 A 比变异系数为 0.33 的投资 B 风险更大。更高的变异系数表明更高的相对风险。

投资组合的风险和报酬

常言道，不要把所有鸡蛋都放在一个篮子里，投资者也很少会只持有单一种类的投资。相反，他们会对多种投资进行组合。

简单地说，投资组合指两种或两种以上资产的混合。一个投资组合可以包括现金、债券、股票、基金或其他投资的任意组合。

投资组合的风险

投资组合的风险和报酬不同于单一投资的风险和报酬。用于评价投资组合风险的计算比单一投资的标准差和方差更复杂。

协方差和相关系数是很有用的组合度量指标。它们都是两组随机变量（如投资组合中的两项投资报酬）趋同程度的统计度量指标。

协方差

方差衡量的是单一随机变量自身，协方差拓展了这个概念，衡量一个随机变量怎样随另一随机变量变动。协方差展示了投资组合中两个不同资产预期一起而不是相互独立的变动的方式——报酬相互变动的方式。

例如：

• 股票的预期报酬和股票的卖出期权按相反方向变动，所以它们的协方差为负。

（注意：在本章第2节"金融工具"中讨论了期权。）

- 同一行业两只股票的预期报酬最有可能同向变动，所以协方差为正。
- 股票和无风险短期国库券组合的预期报酬的协方差为零，因为不论股票报酬如何变动，无风险资产的报酬都不会变动。

随着投资组合中资产数目的增多，各种证券两两之间的协方差变得更加重要。资产之间的变动越不同，组合的风险就越小。

随机变量 X、Y 之间协方差的基本符号是：

$Cov_{x,y}$

使用预期数据计算两个资产报酬的协方差：

$$Cov_{1,2} = \sum_{i=1}^{n} \{ P_i [R_{i,1} - E(R_1)] [R_{i,2} - E(R_2)] \}$$

式中，

- $R_{i,1}$ 表示资产1在状态i的报酬。
- $R_{i,2}$ 表示资产2在状态i的报酬。
- P_i 表示状态i发生的概率。
- $E(R_1)$ 表示资产1的预期报酬。
- $E(R_2)$ 表示资产2的预期报酬。

例如，使用以下两种资产的报酬数据和相关的概率计算协方差。

首先，我们必须计算每项资产的预期报酬：

$$E(R_1) = \sum_{i=1}^{n} P_i R_{i,1} = 0.25(0.06) + 0.50(0.16) + 0.25(0.26) = 0.015 + 0.080 + 0.065 = 0.160$$

$$E(R_2) = \sum_{i=1}^{n} P_i R_{i,2} = 0.25(0.25) + 0.50(0.10) + 0.25(0.05) = 0.0625 + 0.0500 + 0.0125 = 0.125$$

P_i	$R_{i,1}$	$R_{i,2}$	$(R_{i,1}) - E(R_1)$	$(R_{i,2}) - E(R_2)$	$P_i [(R_{i,1}) - E(R_1)] [(R_{i,2}) - E^*(R_2)]$
0.25	0.06	0.25	-0.100	0.125	-0.00313
0.50	0.16	0.10	0.00	-0.025	0.00000
0.25	0.26	0.05	$+0.100$	-0.075	-0.00188
$Cov_{1,2} = \sum_{i=1}^{n} \{ P_i [R_{i,1} - E(R_1)] [R_{i,2} - E(R_2)] \} = -0.00501$					

协方差为负，所以这两种资产的报酬反向变动。

投资组合协方差的计算取决于单一证券的方差和所有证券两两之间的相关系数。还需要将每一对证券的加权相关系数做成矩阵。可能有非常多的两两组合，这取决于组合中的投资数量。而且，协方差的值可能从无穷大到无穷大，故以平方单位表示。

相关系数

为了简化对协方差的解释，用协方差除以随机变量标准差。得出的结果称为相关系数。计算两种证券（1和2）预期报酬相关系数的公式是：

$$\text{Corr}_{1,2} = \frac{\text{Cov}_{1,2}}{\sigma_1 \sigma_2} \text{可推出 Cov}_{1,2} = \text{Corr}_{1,2} \sigma_1 \sigma_2$$

其中：

- σ_1 和 σ_2 分别是组合中证券1和证券2可能报酬的概率分布的标准差。

理解两个随机变量（本例中的资产1和资产2）相关系数的关键特征是：

- 相关系数衡量的是两个随机变量的线性相关程度。
- 相关系数没有单位。
- 相关系数总是介于 -1.0 到 $+1.0$ 之间。即 $-1 \leqslant \text{Corr}_{1,2} \leqslant +1$
- 相关系数为正数代表证券的同向变动。相关系数为 $+1.0$ 代表随机变量之间完全正相关。这意味着一个证券的变动导致另一个证券的精确的可度量的正向变动。即 $\text{Corr}_{1,2} = +1.0$。
- 相关系数为负数代表证券的反向变动。
- 相关系数为 -1.0 代表随机变量之间完全负相关。这意味着一个证券的变动导致另一个证券的精确的可度量的反向变动。即 $\text{Corr}_{1,2} = -1$。
- 相关系数为0代表变量之间没有线性相关关系，意味着不能使用线性方法基于 R_2 预测 R_1。即 $\text{Corr}_{1,2} = 0$。

风险厌恶型投资者一般愿意分散持有，目的是包含不那么完全正相关的证券。

例如：

$$\sigma_P = \sqrt{w_1^2 \sigma_1^2 + w_2^2 \sigma_2^2 + 2w_1 w_2 \text{Corr}_{1,2} \sigma_1 \sigma_2}$$

如果 $w_1 = 0.40$，$w_2 = 0.60$，$\sigma_1 = 0.05$，$\sigma_2 = 0.09$。

现在假设相关系数分别为 $+1$，0，和 -1。请使用上述数据计算组合的标准差 σ_p。结果显示，组合的标准差在相关系数为 $+1$ 时最大，为0时下降，为 -1 时继续下降。

当 $\text{Corr}_{1,2} = +1$ 时，$\sigma_p = [(0.40)2(0.05)2 + (0.60)2(0.09)2 + 2(0.40)(0.60)(1)(0.05)(0.09)]1/2$

$= [0.00040 + 0.00292 + 0.00216]1/2 = 0.074$

当 $\text{Corr}_{1,2} = 0$ 时，$\sigma_p = [(0.40)2(0.05)2 + (0.60)2(0.09)2 + 2(0.40)(0.60)(0)(0.05)(0.09)]1/2$

$= [0.00040 + 0.00292 + 0.0]1/2 = 0.058$

当 $\text{Corr}_{1,2} = -1$ 时，$\sigma_p = [(0.40)2(0.05)2 + (0.60)2(0.09)2 + 2(0.40)(0.60)(-1)(0.05)(0.09)]1/2$

$= [0.000400 + 0.00292 - 0.00216]1/2 = 0.034$

如上例所示，组合的标准差随着相关系数从 $+1$ 到0再到 -1 而逐渐下降。

投资组合的报酬

组合的报酬率是构成组合的所有投资的预期报酬率的加权平均数。权重代表每一投资在组合中所占的比例，权重之和一定等于100%。

组合预期报酬率的一般公式是：

$$\overline{R}_P = \sum_{i=1}^{n} W_i \overline{R}_i$$

式中：

- $\overline{R}_p$ 表示组合的预期报酬。
- W_i 表示该项证券投资占全部资金的比例或比重。
- $\overline{R}_i$ 表示证券 i 的预期报酬。
- n 表示组合中不同证券的数目。

典型的组合投资战略是组建一个有效组合（或最佳组合），从而在给定风险下报酬率最大，或给定报酬率下风险最小。

假设投资组合中资产 A 占 40%，预期报酬率为 12%；资产 B 占 60%，预期报酬率为 18%。则该投资组合的报酬率是：

$$\overline{R}_p = 0.40(12\%) + 0.60(18\%) = 4.8\% + 10.8\% = 15.6\%$$

分散化

分散化是指在组合中持有各种不同的投资。其目的是降低组合的变动性（或风险）。

只要不同投资不都朝同一方向完美地一前一后变动（它们不是完全正相关的），那么分散化就可以降低组合风险。例如，若投资组合中的十只股票全部来自同一行业，则它们倾向于产生高度相关的报酬。因此，这些公司的业绩值一般会按相似的方式上下波动。组合中来自不同行业的股票越少，则组合就越可能有较低的相关系数和较低的组合报酬变动性。也就是说，不同行业的各个股票在同一时间或以同一速率价值上下波动的概率很低。

图表 3-56 列示了组合分散化所带来的变动性抵销。

图表 3-56 分散化和组合风险

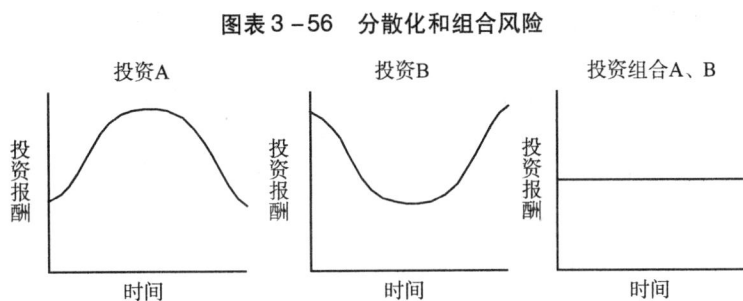

设计良好的投资分散化会降低组合上下波动的潜力，并会在各种经济环境下创造更稳定的业绩。

系统性和非系统性组合风险

大量的市场研究审视当随机选择的投资被合并到加权组合中时分散化对组合风险的影响。如图表 3-57 所示，最初组合风险（标准差）的降低程度很大，然后随着更多投资加入到组合中来，其逐渐变小直至停止。

图表 3 - 57　组合风险的降低

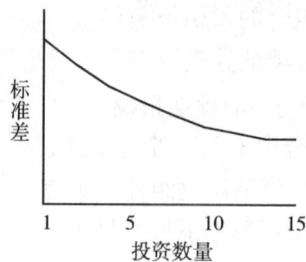

标准差

投资数量

在较小的组合中，分散化能显著地降低变动性，但是随着持有大量投资（一般 15 ~ 20 种不同的投资）的组合规模增大，这种改善就越来越不显著了。

如果用标准差衡量组合的总风险，它由两种风险组成：

- 系统性风险。
- 非系统性风险。

系统性风险

系统性风险（也叫做市场风险、不可分散风险或不可避免风险）与基于市场整体的报酬波动有关。因为威胁大多数（或所有）企业并影响大部分市场的不可避免的国内外经济变化或其他事件，系统性风险对所有投资都是一样的。投资者遭遇系统性市场不确定性时，投资价值通常会全面下滑。例如，这也是为什么经济体系风险或全球风险会使股票一同波动。

非系统性风险

非系统性风险（也叫做个别风险、可分散风险或可避免风险）不受政治、经济等因素或一般市场波动影响。它只同特定公司或者行业有关。

大多数人估计一只股票的总风险（标准差）中 60% ~ 75% 来自非系统性风险。例如，行业中新产品的出现会使一个公司的产品过时。人力资源管理出现问题或一次罢工会对一个公司或整个行业产生负面影响。

大多数来自于非系统性风险的变动性是可以通过分散化避免的。因此，非系统性风险有时也被称作可分散风险。持有分散化组合降低了非系统性风险，这是因为市场的不同部分在不同时间表现不同。

图表 3 - 58 展示了分散化怎样使非系统性风险达到最小，但是却不能消除系统性风险。

图表 3 - 58　组合中的系统性和非系统性风险

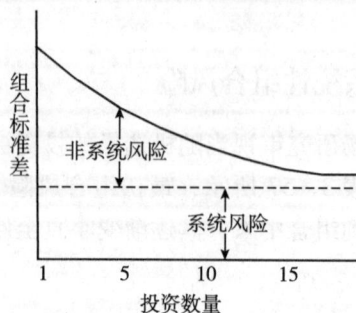

组合标准差　非系统风险　系统风险　投资数量

当组合含有有限数量投资时，非系统性风险极其重要。对于一个合理的、充分分散的组合来说，系统性风险更加重要的。例如，这是为什么市场波动（上升或下降）带动组合一起变动。

市场风险和 β 系数

因为大多数投资者都进行投资分散化，所以最好在组合的背景下判断风险。一项投资对于整个组合风险的贡献要看整个市场下滑时该投资最可能受到怎样的影响。

β 系数描述了一项投资对于市场变动的敏感度。它定量地衡量一项给定投资相对于总体市场的变动性。

特别地，β 系数用来表示市场每变动 1%，投资者期望一项投资的价格变动的数量。

- 美国短期国库券的 β 系数为 0；报酬固定，不会受市场变动影响。
- 所有股票的平均 β 系数为 1。
- β 系数大于 1 的股票对市场变动显著敏感；该股票放大了总体市场的变动。
- β 系数小于 1 的股票比市场变动显著不敏感；该股票和市场同向运动但程度小于总体市场。

另一种描述 β 系数的方法是 β 系数大于 1，则变动性高于总体市场；β 系数小于 1，则变动性低于总体市场。

一个充分分散的组合中的系统性（市场）风险是风险的主要决定因素，单个投资的 β 系数反映了其对市场波动的敏感度。换句话说，充分分散的组合其标准差同 β 系数成比例。β 系数为 1 的分散化组合的系统性风险是 β 系数为 2 的分散化组合的系统性风险的一半。

资本资产定价模型

资本资产定价模型是通过建立风险和报酬率之间的关系来评价组合的经济模型。CAPM 模型的思想是投资者在接受无风险资产（例如，短期国库券）之外的风险时，要求额外的预期报酬。换句话说，要求报酬率和无风险报酬率之差就是风险溢价。

CAPM 模型的基本前提是在完全竞争市场里，风险溢价同 β 系数成正比例变动。组合中每项投资的预期风险溢价应该随 β 系数成比例提高。这意味着组合中所有投资应该在一条斜线上，这条线被称作证券市场线。

证券市场线（SML）是 CAPM 模型的图示。SML 为评价不同组合项目的相对价值提供了一个检查标准。SML 开始于无风险的短期国库券（它的 β 系数为 0），其向右上方倾斜。把不同的 β 系数代入 CAPM 公式中可得出 SML 线上不同的点。

图表 3-59 展示了 CAPM 模型的风险溢价、β 系数和 SML。

其中：

- R_f 表示无风险报酬率（短期或长期国库券）。
- K_m 表示市场组合报酬。
- SML 表示证券市场线。

图表3-59 风险溢价、β系数和 SML

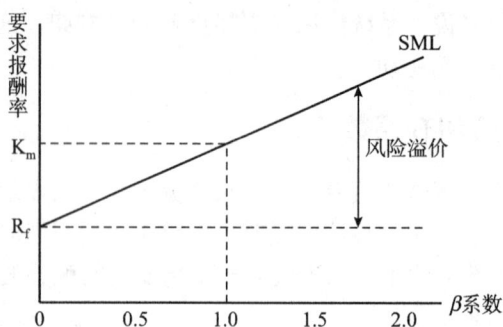

如果目的是要保持组合风险较低，则应该选择 β 系数较低的投资。相反，如果想要较高报酬，则应将 β 系数较高的投资加入组合中。

当无风险资产的报酬率、股票或组合的 β 系数及市场组合的报酬率已知时，CAPM 模型可用来计算股票或组合的要求报酬率。

CAPM 的公式是：

$$K_e = R_f + \beta(K_m - R_f)$$

式中：

- K_e 表示要求报酬率。
- R_f 表示无风险利率（例如，美国短期或长期国库券报酬率）。
- β 表示公司的 β 系数。
- K_m 表示市场组合报酬率。

对于使用短期国库券还是长期国库券作为 CAPM 的无风险利率存在很多争议。证据表明，在作资本预算决策时，管理人员更经常使用长期国库券而非短期国库券作为无风险利率的替代。

例如：

利用 CAPM 计算股票的要求报酬率。假设：

- $R_f = 8\%$（美国国库券的无风险利率）。
- $\beta = 1.50$（公司的 β 系数）。
- $K_m = 12\%$（市场组合报酬率）。

$$K_e = R_f + \beta(K_m - R_f)$$

$$K_e = 0.08 + 1.50(0.12 - 0.08) = 14.0\%$$

CAPM 被认为是单因素模型。它建立了风险（β）和预期报酬率之间的正向关系，将市场组合作为其中普通的一个点。虽然此模型有时因过于简单而被指责，但是它确实提出了关于风险及为补偿投资者风险而需要必要的风险溢价的观点。

套利定价理论（APT）

代替 CAMP 解释风险和报酬率的另一种方法是套利定价理论（APT）。APT 宣称为风险和报酬率之间的正向关系提供了更广泛的解释。在 APT 中，预期报酬率是两个或两个以上影响因素的函数，通过套利保持均衡。

APT 认为证券报酬率对若干因素的变动（如利率、通货膨胀、行业改变、盈利公告等的未预期变化）敏感而且套利效力普遍存在。回顾一下本章前面的讨论，套利是指利用本质上相同的资产或产品的多种价格，在便宜的市场买进，再到价格更高的市场卖出。APT 考虑到了多种因素，被认为增加了风险和确定性的范围。

二因素模型

二因素模型可用以下计算表示。

证券的实际报酬率为：

$$R_j = a + b_{1j}F_1 + b_{2j}F_2 + e_j$$

式中：

- R_j 表示证券的实际报酬率。
- a 表示当两因素价值为 0 时的报酬率。
- F_1 和 F_2 表示因素 1、2 的（不确定的）价值。
- b_{1j} 和 b_{2j} 表示反应系数，代表了一个因素一单位的变化引起的证券报酬率的变化。
- e_j 表示误差项，代表了与本关系式无关的特定风险或影响。

证券的预期报酬率为：

$$\overline{R}_j = \lambda_0 + b_{1j}(\lambda_1) + b_{2j}(\lambda_2)$$

式中：

- $\overline{R}_j$ 表示证券的预期报酬率。
- λ_0 表示无风险证券的报酬率。
- λ_1 和 λ_2 表示与特定因素有关的各种风险的风险溢价。
- b_{1j} 和 b_{2j} 表示反应系数，代表了一个因素一单位的变化引起的证券报酬率的变化。

例如：

利用二因素模型计算股票的预期报酬。假设：

- $\lambda_0 = 8\%$（美国国库券的无风险报酬率）。
- λ_1 和 λ_2 分别为 6% 和 -2%。
- b_{1j} 和 b_{2j} 分别为 1.2 和 0.8。

$$\overline{R}j = \lambda_0 + b_{1j}(\lambda_1) + b_{2j}(\lambda_2)$$
$$\overline{R}j = 0.08 + 1.2(0.06) + 0.8(-0.02)$$
$$\overline{R}j = 0.08 + 0.072 - 0.016 = 13.6\%$$

在本例中，第一个因素是风险厌恶型的，要求更高的报酬率；第二个因素提供价值，因此降低了预期报酬率。λ_s 代表因素风险的市场价格。

多因素模型

当考虑两种以上的因素时，APT 计算原则同样适用。通过加入更多因素和反应系数将公式进行拓展。随着抽样规模（从中选择因素）的增大，APT 的结果也在改变。

在使用 APT 模型时，需要特别注意的是：

- 抽样失真的可能性。
- 选取不适当因素的可能性。

- 两个因素支配此关系的趋势。
- 复杂的计算。

尽管有这些挑战，APT 仍然为资产定价和保持均衡的方法提供了额外的视角。在公司理财中，APT 有助于为资本预算决策建立要求的报酬率（或折现率）。

注：股利折现模型将会在下节"金融工具"中讨论。

进度检查

提示：完成以下各题，参考答案随后给出。

1. 下面哪项举例说明了财务风险：（　　）

    a. 与企业普通股相关的风险

    b. 以较低的利率让新顾客赊账

    c. 企业用负债为实际投资筹资的程度

    d. 遭到因工负伤员工的起诉

2. 股票投资的标准差可描述为（　　）

    a. 预期报酬率的变动性

    b. 对市场变动的敏感度

    c. 风险和报酬率之间的权衡

    d. 围绕平均报酬率的变异程度

找出与下列术语匹配的描述。

3. _____相关系数　　　a. 使投资者对某一时点风险无所谓的现金额

4. _____证券市场线　　b. 评价不同组合项目相对价值的一个检查标准

5. _____确定性等值　　c. 投资组合中两只股票一起变动的程度

6. 投资分散化的主要优点是（　　）

    a. 降低汇率风险

    b. 使非系统性风险最小化

    c. 降低系统性风险

    d. 处于更有利的借款地位

进度检查答案

1. c

2. d

3. c

4. b

5. a

6. b

第2节
金融工具

本节内容简介

金融工具证实了双方之间的交易。它有货币价值或记录了一笔货币交易。对于交易中的一方，金融工具代表了一项投资；对于另一方，该工具是一种责任或义务。

投资和筹资决策的风险及报酬

企业对金融资产（例如，股票和债券）和实物资产（例如，厂房和设备）都会作出投资决策。下面介绍的是与金融资产有关的投资决策。与实物资产有关的投资决策会在本书第5章："投资决策"中讨论。

组织投资金融资产的原因包括：

- 确保流动性——以便及时支付日常现金债务。

- 使得收到但不需立即使用的现金产生利息收入。

筹资允许组织通过债务或权益资本追求长期目标。债务筹资是指组织在特定日期之前偿还债权人所借资金的一种法律义务或责任。权益筹资代表出售一个公司的所有权。债务和权益涉及风险和报酬率之间的权衡：

- 债务成本由利率表示；利率是可以免税的费用。

- 权益的价值可用股票价格或者公司资产的净价值表示；权益资产的股利不可免税。

- 公司进行债务筹资的方式（例如，贷款合同的种类）可能影响经营；权益股东可以通过实施特定的表决权进行控制。

每个公司都应有适当的投资和筹资战略。图表3－60总结了投资和筹资战略应关注的基本方面。

图表3－60　投资和筹资的基本考虑要素

投　　　资	筹　　　资
● 公司目标	● 债务筹资与权益筹资
● 政策方针	● 短期筹资与长期筹资
● 投资工具的选择和投资组合的结构	● 固定利率支付与浮动利率支付
● 投资活动的角色、责任及职权	● 担保债务与非担保债务
● 财务控制	● 表内融资与表外融资
● 业绩评价	● 税负考虑

一项投资政策反映了组织的风险承受能力；借款过程中债务和权益的混合决定了一个公司的杠杆，并同企业的资本结构密切相连。

在筹资过程中，筹资组合应该使以股票价格衡量的公司价值最大化，并且使企业的加权平均资本成本（WACC）最小化。通过将被融资资产的现金流入与现金流出相匹配来降低潜在风险。

所得税对筹资决策的影响

许多筹资决策很大程度上取决于税收影响。一般来说，在公司水平上，债务有税收优势，因为利息支付可以减少企业的应纳税所得额（可以避开联邦税和州税），而股利和股票回购不行。如果公司权衡了债务税收收益与财务困境成本，则与该筹资相关的利息税屏蔽倾向于支持更高的杠杆。

根据权衡理论，最优的资本结构涉及对利息税屏蔽引起的债务收益与财务困境和代理成本引起的债务成本之间的权衡。代理成本是指委托人授权给代理人所引起的直接或间接费用。代理人是被委托人授权代表其实施某些任务或服务的人。财务困境是指太多债务导致公司财务状况的全面削弱。破产是财务困境的极端情况。有各种经济理论挑战权衡理论。税收屏蔽命题的争论在于借款引起的利息支付的税收减免能否影响公司价值。

估价

估价是指为判定一项资产或公司的价值而将风险和报酬联系到一起的过程。理解估价概念要求对价值和相关的价值概念有基本的了解。

对于资产或公司，价值有不同的含义。资产一般指金融资产——对发行者的货币索取权，一般是票据资产，如债券、普通股或优先股。

相关的价值概念包括以下内容。

* **持续经营价值**

持续经营价值是指作为持续经营主体的公司的价值。此价值取决于产生未来现金流而非资产负债表资产的能力。

* **清算价值**

清算价值指偿付所有债务后变卖实体所能实现的货币额。

* **每股清算价值**

如果实体变卖所有资产，偿还所有债务（包括优先股），并在股东中分配剩余金额，那么股东将会收到的每普通股的实际金额。

* **账面价值**

账面价值指资产负债表上的资产持有价值。它是资产的会计价值——资产成本减累计折旧。

* **普通股每股账面价值**

普通股每股账面价值是指股东权益与普通股平均股数的比率。每股账面价值与每股清算价值或每股市场价值几乎没有关系。

* **市场价值**

市场价值指在给定时间内投资者买卖资产的市场价格。市场价值的关键性决定因素是供给与需求。

* **内在价值**

内在价值是对资产理论价值的度量。虽然不能代表实际价值，但内在价值为决定是否买卖一项金融资产提供了基础。内在价值也被称作基础价值。

一般来说，一项资产的价值受以下因素影响：

- 一段时期内资产的现金流。
- 现金流的增长率。
- 现金流的风险。

现金流的度量指标是

- 普通股和优先股的年度股利和每股价格变动。
- 债券持有人收到的年利息加上价格变动。

增加的现金流会提高资产价格。如果价格下降，现金流会变得更不确定。在财务管理中，基本目标是保持/提高现金流且控制/降低风险。继而支持股东财富最大化。

风险很难估计。未来现金流必须以适当利率折现到现值以反映风险。因此，估价中的一个关键概念是：资产的价值（资产的价格）是所有与资产相关的现金流的现值。

本节接下来的内容介绍了各种债务和权益工具的特点。其中包括估价，估价是财务管理的基础活动，它估计了债券、普通股及优先股的内在价值。投资在第四节"流动资产管理"及第五节"流动资产筹资"中介绍。为了便于讨论，短期国库券（期限短于一年）被归类为短期债券，在随后对资产的讨论中进行介绍。

债券

债券指发行的期限长于一年的债务工具（贷款）。购买债券的投资者通过借钱赚取利息，而借钱人（发行人）获得所需资本（现金）。

债券可以是短期、中期和长期的。虽然这些划分会有些不同，但一般的范围是：

- 短期债券：2~5 年。
- 中期债券：5~10 年。
- 长期债券：10~30 年。

期限较长的债券一般比期限较短的债券支付更高报酬（收益）。因此，正常的收益曲线的形状是向上倾斜。

发行人和债券类型

有许多由不同来源发行的债券。图表 3-61 列示了一般的类型。

图表 3-61 债券的一般类型

类 型	描 述
公司债券	• 由美国的大型和小型公司发行 • 用于给增长、扩张及其他活动筹资
政府公债	• 由美国政府的声誉担保 • 用于维持政府工作和为国家债务支付利息 • 如美国中期债券、长期债券、储蓄债券
市政公债	• 由城市和州发行 • 用于支持建设项目和其他活动
代理债券	• 由联邦、州和地方机构发行 • 包括抵押出借人（如，Ginnie Mae、Fannie Mae 和 Freddie Mac）发行的债券及用于支持经营并为特殊项目筹款的其他代理债券
国际债券	同时在多个国家上市，通常由国际银行的伦敦支行和证券经销商发行

债券合同

债券发行各方之间的书面法律协议被称做契约（或信托契据）。

契约定义债券发行的细节，包括：

- 债券发行的条款和条件。
- 利率。
- 债券到期日。
- 保护性保证条款（对发行人的限制）。
- 违约事项。
- 次级条款。
- 偿债基金条款（由借款方支付到一个单独的保管账户；用来在到期日偿还债务并使债权人确信有充足的基金可用来还债）。
- 将被抵押的担保财产（如果有）。
- 受托人的任命和职责。

保证条款

保护性保证条款对合同期内公司可能实施的某些行为设定了约束（限制）。它们是债券合同中特别重要的特征。

有两种保证条款：

（1）负保证条款。

负保证条款限制或禁止借款方的某些行为。支付过多股利，将资产抵押给为他出借人，出售主要资产，与其他企业合并，获取更多的长期债务，这些都是负保证条款可能处理的行为。

（2）正保证条款。

正保证条款明确了借款方许诺实施的行为。正保证条款的例子包括维持某些比率，保持担保品状态良好，及时偿付利息和本金。不能遵守正保证条款可能导致债券发行人违约。

债券管理

债券由有资格的受托人管理。受托人是被债券发行人选择作为债券持有人官方代表的第三方。个人或机构都可以作为托管人；银行经常管理债券。

受托人的责任包括：

- 鉴别债券发行的合法性。
- 保证所有合同义务都被履行；偿债基金和利息被适当地支付和应用。
- 若借款方不能履行义务则发起恰当的行动。
- 在法律诉讼中代表债券持有人。
- 管理赎回。

债券发行人给受托人付报酬；受托人报酬被包括在借款成本中。

债券的术语

一般来说，债券是在到期日偿还本金和利息的承诺。

债券本金

本金（也称账面价值或面值）代表了债券发行时的货币金额。账面价值是债券到期时借出方被偿付的金额。大多数债券是按 $1 000 的倍数出售。

债券利息

债券上标明的利率被称为票面利率（或票面收益率）。债券的票面利率是有竞争性的；利率要与同期发行的其他债券的利率相比较。

有三种债券利率：

- 固定利率——支付一贯相同的利率。
- 浮动利率——利率随经济变化而变化。
- 零利率——不支付利息（债券大幅折价出售，全价赎回，相当于复利增长到票面价值）。

如果票面利率和债券支付额在出售时是固定的，则债券被归为固定收益证券。传统上，大多数债券以固定利率出售。这是债券一般被认为是保守投资、风险低于股票和其他有更大变动报酬率的投资的主要原因。

在首次发行（债券出售）后，债券通过经纪人在二级市场（发行后证券交易的二手市场）上以类似于股票交易的方式买卖。在二级市场，债券的价格随利率浮动。如果市场利率下降，价格会高于账面价值；市场利率高于债券票面利率意味着债券将被以低于面值的价格出售（折价）。

债券票面利率以面值的百分比表示。利率通常按半年或一年支付。例如，如果半年付息债券的票面利率是 7%，则对于每 $1 000 面值的债券，发行人需每 6 个月支付债券持有人 $35。

零息债券是一个特例。顾名思义，零息债券在到期前不支付利息。利息累积（增长）在到期时一次性支付。

"息票"这个词最初产生是因为债券持有人传统上会收到标明债券条款的凭证，该凭证附带息票，在收取债券利息时应撕下该息票以换取现金。绝大部分新债券以电子形式发行（类似于股票购买）。然而，许多息票凭证仍然存在，因为它们还没到期。

债券期限

债券一般都有确定的期限。这是债券债务到期支付、义务了结的最后日期。账面价值是债券到期日价值。

债券通常在寿命期内被买卖。一些债券可以提前偿还（赎回）。在到期日，债券持有人收到债券的面值。面值 $1 000 的债券在到期日值 $1 000（只要发行人不违约）。

债券评级

债券评级使投资者能在实际购买债券前评价买入债券的一般风险。

通常，信用机构基于若干因素对债券发行进行评级，包括：

- 发行者目前的财务状况。
- 未来财务前景。
- 担保债券的担保品（如果有的话）。

穆迪投资服务和标准普尔是两家知名的信用评级服务公司。图表 3-62 提供了它们的评级及一般特征。

图表 3-62　穆迪投资服务和标准普尔评级

穆迪	标准普尔	
Aaa	AAA	
Aa	AA	一般被认为是高质量债券
A	A	
Baa	BBB	
Ba	BB	有点问题；缺少一些高质量的特征
B	B	
Caa	CCC	质量差；有违约风险
Ca	CC	
C	C	垃圾债券（高投机性的债券，违约风险高于平均几率）
–	D	

下面是理解债券评级的一些关键点：

- 债券评级适用于债券发行，而不是公司。
- 美国短期国库券不用评级，因为它们有联邦政府作担保。
- 级别可以在债券寿命期内上下调整；级别降低意味着未来发行债券需要提供更高的利率以吸引购买者。
- Aaa 和 AAA 级债券的利率最低。
- 因为垃圾债券存在违约风险，它们是高收益债券。
- 垃圾债券有更高的违约几率，但是在某些环境下，它们也可能是新兴实体，并提供很高的利润报酬。

债券收益

债券的票面利率从来不变，但是通货膨胀和其他利率的变化影响债券的价值。

收益率和回报率

当期收益率是以年利息与债券当前价格的百分比表示的年报酬率。10 年期、面值 $1 000、年利率 5% 的债券连续十年每年可获利 $50。如果债券的当前价格是 $1 250，则当前收益率是 4%（$50 ÷ $1 250）。如果债券当前价格等于面值，则当期收益率等于利率。

到期收益率指从购买到到期日债券的实际报酬率，假设所有收到的支付都以原始债券票面利率再投资。到期收益率考虑：

- 债券寿命期内利率与价格的关系。
- 购买价格与面值的关系（基于债券是以高于还是低于面值价格购买的任何利得与损失）。
- 任何再投资的票面利息或利息支付。

通货膨胀和债券净报酬

通货膨胀会吞噬一个债券的报酬。如果债券报酬率高于通货膨胀率，则债券产生一个正的报酬率。如果债券报酬率低于通货膨胀率，则债券产生一个负的报酬率。考虑下面的例子：

- 如果债券报酬率是6%，通货膨胀率是4%，则债券产生2%的净报酬率。
- 如果债券报酬率是6%，通货膨胀率是8%，则债券产生 –2% 的净报酬率。

债券久期

到期收益率的计算假设所有收到的支付都以原始债券的票面利率再投资。然而，债券受通货膨胀影响。如果利率下降，投资者收到的利息支付和本金将不得不以更低的利率再投资。因此，当利率下降时，债券投资者面临再投资风险。

久期给出了债券/组合价值对到期收益率变动的大致敏感度。因此，债券久期考虑了对于收益率变化债券价格怎样变化。久期最好的解释是对于到期收益率的1%变化，价格变化的大致百分比。久期是价格收益率关系的近似，因为此关系是一条曲线，而非直线。

凸性度量了随着利率变化债券价格变化的曲率。利率上升引起的价格变化小于利率下降引起的价格变化。

图表3-63列示了价格—收益率曲线。债券价格上涨快于下跌。

图表3-63 债券价格—收益率曲线

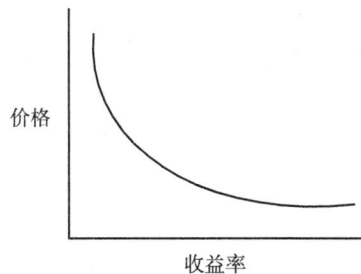

债券久期由价格变化对收益率变化的百分比决定。

有效久期 =（收益率下降时的债券价格 – 收益率上升时的债券价格）/ [2 ×（初始价格）×（以小数形式表示的收益率变化）]

通常被表示为：

$$有效久期 = \frac{V_- - V_+}{2V_0(\Delta y)}$$

式中：

- V_- 表示收益率下降 Δy 时的债券价值。
- V_+ 表示收益率上升 Δy 时的债券价值。
- V_0 表示当前债券价格。
- Δy 表示为得到 V_- 和 V_+ 的收益率变化，以小数形式表示。

有效久期展示了对于收益率 1% 的变动，价格变动的平均百分比。例如，10 年期、半年付息、票面利率 9% 的债券，为获得 8% 的收益率，当前定价是 \$1 067.95。如果收益率降低 50 个基准点变为 7.5%，则债券价格会上升到 \$1 104.22。如果收益率上升 50 个基准点变为 8.5%，则债券价格会下降到 \$1 033.24。使用前面的公式，债券的有效久期将会是：

$$有效久期 = \frac{\$1\ 104.22 - \$1\ 033.24}{2(\$1\ 067.95)(0.005)} = \frac{\$70.98}{10.6795} = 6.65$$

因此，有效久期 6.65 意味着 1% 的收益率变化会造成大约 6.65% 的价格变动。

债券久期为什么重要？理解债券价格将怎样随着利率变动而变动，可以使投资者根据自己对债券怎样表现的看法而买卖或持有债券。投资者可以使用久期去比较发行日、到期日、票面利率和到期收益率不同的债券。

下面是一些涉及债券久期的关系。在其他特征不变的情况下：

- 越高（低）的票面利率意味着越低（高）的久期。
- 越长（短）的期限意味着越高（低）的久期。
- 越高（低）的市场收益率意味着越低（高）的久期。

债券担保

债券可以有担保（资产担保），也可以无担保。

担保债券

担保债券是以特定资产（例如，存货、不动产或固定资产）或特定项目产生的收入作为担保品的债券。担保债券为投资者提供了违约时对一项资产的留置权。

无担保债券

无担保债券（信用债券）只有以借款人良好的声誉、正直和信用作保证，而没有任何特定的担保品。当持有无担保债券时，投资者只有一般索取权，而不是对某项特定资产的索取权。因为无担保债券的风险高于担保债券，所以它们通常支付更高的收益率。

债券清偿顺序和清算

债券通常被分为同级、优先、次级，以同其他债务责任相联系。这些清偿顺序影响了清算的先后顺序。如果违约的债券发行人同时拥有担保和无担保债券：

- 担保债券持有人首先被偿付；然后才是无担保债券持有人。

- 高级无担保债券持有人先于次级信用债券持有人被偿还。

对于同一资产或财产次级（非优先）债务意味着其优先权低于其他索取权。换句话说，次级债务是在发行人偿还其他债务之后才偿付。债务级别越低，投资者的风险越大。

债券估价

债券的价值是折现现金流量之和。确定债券价值的步骤是：

- 计算利息支付的现值。
- 计算面值的现值。
- 将两个现值加总。

债券估价的传统方法是以相同的折现率将所有现金流折现。利息和面值必须以市场利率（类似债券折现的利率）折现。

当面值和票面利率已知时，下面的公式用于确定债券的价值。

$$V_b = I(\text{PVIFA}_{k,n}) + F(\text{PVIF}_{k,n})$$

式中：

- V_b 表示债券价值。
- I 表示每期利息。
- PVIFA 表示年金现值利息系数。
- F 表示债券的本金或面值。
- PVIF 表示现值利息系数。
- k 表示折现率。
- n 表示期数。

例如：

一家公司发行的 15 年期、每年支付利息的债券还有 5 年到期。在发行时，债券票面利率为 10%，面值为 \$1 000。现在，投资者对风险相似债券的要求报酬率为 8%。债券价值的计算如下：

- 确定年利息（10% × \$1 000 = \$100）。
- 使用年金现值表以折现率 8% 折现 \$100 的年利息 5 年。
- 使用现值表以折现率 8% 折现 \$1 000 的面值 5 年。
- 加总这两个现值。

$$V_b = I(\text{PVIFA}_{k,n}) + F(\text{PVIF}_{k,n})$$
$$V_b = \$100(3.9927) + \$1\,000(0.6806)$$
$$V_b = \$399.27 + \$680.60 = \$1\,079.87$$

债券的价值是 \$1 079.87。这是投资者愿意为债券支付的价格。在本例中，债券价值高于面值。因为折现率低于票面利率，所以债券溢价出售。（如果折现率高于票面利率，则债券折价出售。）

利率、票面利率及期限的改变都会影响债券价格。这些经济因素和时间跨度会影响债券价值。

理解债券估价的其他要点包括：

- 当市场利率下降时，更低的票面利率意味着老债券支付的利息高于新债券支付的利息。从债券持有人角度来看，这导致了再投资利率风险。息票债券的再投资利率随着市场利率上升和下降，从而导致了再投资利率风险。

- 债券价格与市场利率反向变动——如果利率上升，票面利率较低的债券价格下降。
- 利率变动的大小影响债券价格——利率变动越大，债券价格波动越大。
- 随着到期日的临近，债券价格将逐渐接近票面价值。债券价格逐渐接近本金（票值）的运动叫做趋同。

股票

股票是权益投资工具；它表示在公司中的所有权地位（权益）。股东购买公司的股票，基于拥有的股份比例对公司的资产和利润拥有索取权。

权益所有权的水平取决于拥有的股数及流通在外的股数。流通在外的股数是指一家公司由股东持有的股数。

所有权的计算是用投资者的股数除以所有流通在外的股数。例如，如果一家公司有流通在外的股票 10 000 股，一个投资者有 200 股，则此投资者拥有公司 2% 的所有权。

一级和二级市场

一家公司经常为了获取额外的资金而由私有变为上市公司。一级市场是产生证券的地方，二级市场是投资者之间交易证券的地方。股票初始发行给投资者是在一级市场。之后的交易是在二级市场。

一级市场

随着扩张资金需求的增长超过了通过个人投资、贸易信贷、信用额度、贷款和风险资本可以产生的资金，管理人员会去找同意承销股票发行的投资银行。在投资中，承销指投资银行承担了从发行公司购买新发行的证券然后再卖给公众的风险。按照定义，一级市场是投资者有机会购买新发行股票的市场。

承销商帮助企业编制招股说明书。招股说明书是正式的书面说明，目的是为了向公众销售证券。它在证券交易管理委员会备案，并向所有投资者公开。招股说明书包括很多细节，如证券怎样定价、每只股票的发行价格、发行公司的规模和目标。

一级市场基本上与首次公开发行（IPO）是同义的。通过承销，投资银行以约定价格购买所有公开发行份额。公司用收到的钱为经营提供资金。在 IPO 之后，股票在二级市场上交易，但是公司不再收到额外收入。之后的股票价格由投资者购买时愿意支付的金额决定。

在一家公司上市后，它可以在一级市场继续发行新股。惟一的不同是股票不再是初始（IPO）发行，而是增资发行。

二级市场

按照定义，二级市场是投资者从另一个投资者而非发行公司那里购买资产的市场。这是二级市场的定义性特征——投资者之间相互交易。他们从其他投资者那里买卖已经发行的证券，而不牵涉发行公司。

二级市场一般是股票市场的同义词，包括纽约股票交易所（NYSE）、纳斯达克和所有世界上主要交易所。

股票的市值

股票的市值（流通在外股票的最新报价）决定了企业的市场资本总额。市场资本总额（或资本）由目前每股市场价格与流通在外股数的乘积决定。拥有 3 000 万每股价格 \$30 流通股的公司，它的市场资本总额为 \$9 亿。

市场资本总额是用来对股票进行分类的方法之一。图表 3-64 展示了基于市场资本总额的股票分类。根据市场资本总额，公司通常分为大型、中型、小型和微型。

图表 3-64　基于资本化的股票分类

大型	大于等于 \$150 亿
中型	大于等于 \$20 亿，小于 \$150 亿
小型	大于等于 \$3 亿，小于 20 亿
微型	小于 \$3 亿

资本总额的一些指定是任意的。例如，取决于数据来源，微型的分隔点可能是 \$2.5 亿而非 \$3 亿。

大型股票是指市场资本总额高于其他公司的公司股票。它们通常定期发放股利，公司规模通常会减轻公司失败的风险。

中型股票是指市场资本总额在大型和小型股票之间的股票。类似于大型股票，中型股票也有大量的股数进行交易，只是与大型股票相比，公司规模更小一些。不如大型公司那么成熟。一般来说，这些公司比更大公司的增长潜力更大，但同时风险也大。

小型股票是指市场资本总额相对小于平均公司的股票。它们有巨幅增长的潜力。但是它们也有更不稳定的可能性。

不同种类股票的投资报酬通常按不同轨道运动。微型股票被认为是这些股票中风险最大的。

下面是普通股的其他分类：

- 蓝筹股——最大的和最持续盈利的上市公司的股票。
- 成长型股票——有很强增长潜力，销售收入、收益、市场份额增长超过整个经济的公司的股票。
- 周期型股票——收入高度依赖于经济周期（例如，经济增长和下滑）的公司的股票。
- 防御型股票——相对于大多数经济状况保持稳定和不受影响的保守型股票。
- 价值型股票——当比较收益和其他绩效度量值时此股票看起来不贵。
- 收益型股票——资金雄厚、具有通常产生稳定收益的良好纪录的公司的股票。
- 投机型股票——该股票是对真实价值有待证明的公司的风险型投资。

要注意因为公司不断变化，上述资本总额及其他分类都不是一成不变的。

其他的两种股票分类是普通股和优先股。普通股和优先股有一些明显的差异（也有相似点）。它们各自的特征给公司和投资者提供各种各样的风险和报酬。

普通股和优先股的分类是股票余下内容的重点。

普通股

普通股代表对一个公司的权益所有权。也就是说，普通股的所有人对公司的资产拥有所有权，对收益有分享权。总起来说，普通股持有人拥有公司。普通股没有到期日，但是股东可以通过在二级市场上出售股票来清算投资。

权益特点

普通股不能保证投资者能赚到钱。普通股的权益所有权意味着所有者分享公司的财富和损失。

普通股的每股市值是股票的当前交易价格。如果股票价值提高，股东会从他们投资的资本增值上获益，也可能获得股利。

股利（或支付）代表利润分享。除非董事会已经宣布，否则不要求公司支付股利。支付随收益和董事会决定发放的额度变化。公司通常每季度支付现金股利，但是他们也以股票的形式支付股利。

- **现金股利**

现金股利以现金的形式支付，通常是用支票。现金股利一般是应税的。

- **股票股利**

股票股利以额外的股票（而非现金）支付。股票股利允许公司为投资同时又能回馈投资者的方式保留资金。公司发行股票股利时，一般没有税收结果，直到股东将股票卖掉才会产生税收问题。

- **股票分割**

股票分割类似于股票股利，因为它们是非现金股利支付。但是与股票股利相比，股票分割通常引起更多股票的发行。

公司一般分割股票以降低股票价格，使价格更具吸引力并促进交易。基本原理是当股票价格很高时，个人投资者不愿买股票或者因为股票成本太大，或者因为认为股票价格已经到了顶峰。

股票能以各种增量分割：2:1，3:1，3:2 等。在2:1 分割中，持有100 股的股东将会收到另外100 股。如果股票现在以每股 $100 的价格交易，则股价会降到大约 $50。如果股价恰好降到了 $50，总市值保持不变（200 股每股 $50 同最初 100 股每股 $100，都为 $1 000）。虽然总市值一开始不变，但如果股价最终上涨，股东可以从中受益。

虽然不是股利，但股票也可以经历反向分割。在反向分割时，股票数量下降，股价由此上升。例如，1:2 的反向分割中，100 股每股 $1 的股票变为50 股每股 $2 的股票。反向分割经常用于保持该股票在股票市场上的最低牌价，或者用于增强该股票对回避低价股票的投资者的普遍吸引力。

股票分割和反向分割都不会引起任何应税利得或损失。

总之，股利被认为是拥有普通股的一种激励。定期发放股利的公司一般经历过了增长期，不能从再投资利润中获取很多好处，因此，选择以股利形式分享这些利润。由此可见，公司所处的生命周期阶段会影响其股利政策。

如果公司收益下滑，公司可能决定降低或终止现金股利，这可能标志着对公司未来期望的下滑并导致股价下降。

投票权

普通股的所有权让股东有权对公司的重要事件进行投票，诸如：

- 选举公司董事会成员。
- 公司规章制度的政策和变更。
- 股票期权计划的批准。
- 并购。
- 审计师的指定。

一般来说一股对应一个投票权。公司以两种方式管理投票权：传统或累积。

- **传统投票权**

传统投票权（也称多数投票权、多数原则投票权或法定投票权）是指选举董事会的股东被限定为对每位被提名者一股一权的公司投票制度。每个股东的投票权总数等于其拥有股数与空缺职位的乘积。例如，有 5 位提名人竞争空缺的董事席位，则一个有 500 股股票的股东对每个提名人都能投 500 票，总计可投 2 500 票。

传统的多数投票权法阻止少数股东选举自己（少数）的候选人。

- **累积投票权**

累积投票系统允许股东给不同候选人投不同数量的票。继续上面的例子，持有 500 股的股东能把这些投票权平均分给 5 位候选人，在一些候选人组合中分配这些投票权，或把 2 500 票全部投给一个候选人。

累积投票权试图通过提高少数股东选举某些数量董事的几率来给少数股东在公司治理中更多的权力。

一些公司发行有不同投票权的不同级别的股票。如果允许某类股东拥有额外投票权，一小群人能在拥有不到多数股权的情况下控制公司的方向。

股东一般通过邮寄股东签署的委托书的方式进行投票。另外，他们可以在公司年度会议上亲自投票。一些公司允许电话投票或网上投票。

股东签署的委托书是一项法律文书，在年度会议前不久必须寄给每一位股东。股东签署的委托书列示公司年度会议上要谈到的问题，并包括对公司提案和董事会成员进行投票的选票。提交代理选票就是授权其他某些人（通常是管理层）在开会时代表投资者进行投票。如果管理层收到超过 50% 的有投票权的股票代理，他们就能够选举整个董事会。然而，如果投资者不返回股东签署的委托书，他们的选票将不算在内。在年会上投出的选票越少，随之构成多数选民需要的股数就越少。

优先购股权

一些普通股有优先购股权。按照定义，如果公司另外发行股票，优先购股权允许当前的股东保持他们在公司的所有权比例。有优先购股权的股东有权利（但不是义务）在其他任何人之前购买新股，以便保持自己当前的权益所有权水平。

清算价值

在违约或清算时，普通股股东拥有对公司资产的最后索取权。特别地，只有在债券持有人、其他债务持有人和优先股股东的索取权被满足后，普通股股东才有公司资产的剩余索取权。但是普通股股东承担有限责任，并不对公司债务负责；其损失不超过原始投资额。

普通股估价

普通股的报酬率会发生变化。如前所述，在某些年，可能不发放股利。在另一些年，股利可能比前几年高或低，这取决于公司的股利政策、盈利性及资金可得性。

普通股估价需要仔细预测未来增长率和未来股利。这种预测多取决于：

- 年股利。
- 股利增长率。
- 折现率。

有三种可能的估价情况。随着时间的推移，股利可以保持不变（零增长）、以固定速率增长或以变动速率增长。投资者使用估价模型将他们的结果与现存价格进行比较，以确定股票是高估、低估或恰当定价。

零增长普通股估价（无股利增长率）

下面的公式用于零增长股票的估价。

$$V_o = \frac{D_1}{(1+k_s)^1} + \frac{D_2}{(1+k_s)^2} + \frac{D_3}{(1+k_s)^3} + \cdots + \frac{D_\infty}{(1+k_s)^\infty}$$

式中：

- V_o 表示估计的普通股价格。
- D 表示普通股每股固定年股利。
- k_s 表示投资者对普通股的要求报酬率（权益成本）。

要求报酬率取决于普通股的风险。如果有风险，投资者就期望高的报酬率。换句话说，必须有更高的回报去激励投资者投资。

此公式可进一步简化为：

$$V_o = \frac{D}{k_s}$$

例如：

一家公司在每年末支付每股现金股利 $5。分析师预测政策不会改变。若预期报酬率为 12%，普通股价值计算如下：

$$V_o = \frac{D}{k_s} = \frac{\$5}{0.12} = \$60.00$$

固定股利增长率普通股估价

投资者预期股利每年按照固定增长率增长。例如，如果公司最近支付的股利是

$5，按股利年增长率5%计算，下一年的股利将会是：

$5(1 + 0.05) = $5(1.05)^1 = $5.25

随后第二年的股利是：

$5(1 + 0.05)(1 + 0.05) = $5(1.05)^2 = $5.51 未来几年可依此类推。

固定增长率普通股的价值也可用要求报酬率对未来股利进行折现来确定。这种估价方法会在阐述股利折现模型的应用的随后内容中讲述。

变动股利增长率普通股估价

当股票以不同速率在两个或多个期间内增长时，用此方法估计股票价格。当普通股有变化的股利增长率时：

- 分别预测将来的股利。
- 利用现值表将预测的股利折成现值。
- 计算增长期末终值的现值。
- 加总所有现值。

例如：

一家公司去年支付每股现金股利 $5。分析师预测股利在未来三年将会以年增长率20%的速度增长，然后趋于正常，以后均以 5% 的增长率增长。当要求报酬率为 12% 时，计算普通股今天的股价：

$$P_3 = \frac{D_3(1 + g)}{k_s - g}$$

$$P_3 = \frac{$8.64(1.05)}{0.12 - 0.05} = \frac{$9.07}{0.07} = $129.57$$

式中：

- D_1、D_2、D_3 表示第 1、2、3 年分别的股利。
- PVIF 表示现值利息系数。
- P_3 表示第 3 年的普通股股价。
- k_s 表示普通股的要求报酬率。
- g 表示固定（年）股利增长率。

年份	收益		按12%计算的 PVIF		收益的现值
1	$D_1 = $5(1.20) = 6.00	×	0.8929	=	$5.36
2	$D_2 = $6.00(1.20) = 7.20$	×	0.7972	=	5.74
3	$D_3 = $7.20(1.20) = 8.64$	×	0.7118	=	6.15
	$P_3 = 129.57$		0.7118		92.23
				总现值	$109.48

在本例中，在第 3 年末普通股的价格是 $129.57。加总折现价值，估计的股票价格是 $109.48。

优先股

与普通股类似，优先股也代表对公司的部分所有权。然而，二者存在一些重要差异。在某种程度上，优先股更像债券而不是普通股。因为这个原因，优先股经常被描述为有着债务和权益特征的混合体。

权益特点

优先股一般发放固定股利；股利金额不会随收益波动。"优先"也意味着优先股股东有权在普通股股东获得股利之前得到确定的股利。

固定的股利降低了投资者风险，但是它也限制了财务报酬。当市场下滑时，优先股的变动较小。但是市场上扬时，股东也不能指望巨大的价格利得。事实上，股利是不能被保证的。董事会（他们表决股利事宜）可以选择不发放固定股利。

投票权

优先股股东一般没有普通股股东那样的选举权。如果公司不能发放固定股利或在贷款协议或债券契约上违约，则可以授予优先股股东特别投票权。

清算价值

在违约和破产时，对于公司资产，优先股股东比普通股股东有更大的索取权。因为优先股优于普通股，所以当公司经营失败时，优先股股东有比普通股股东更大的可能性收回投资。如果发生资产清算，优先股只有在偿付短期和长期债务持有人之后才可以得到清偿。

特性

在纳税申报表中，公司支付给股东的股利不能免税。这是公司使用优先股筹资的最主要缺点。

下面是优先股其他的重要特性：

- **累积股利**

不像普通股股利不要求公司必须支付，优先股股利是一种义务，不管公司收益如何。当发行优先股时，公司经常承诺发放固定年股利。然而，如果公司没有足够的收益进行支付，则股利支付是可以自由决定的。在某些情况下，未支付的优先股股利可以累积。

许多优先股有累积股利的特征，这要求所有未支付的累积股利将来应先于普通股股利被公司用收益偿付。应该注意，如果公司无意发放普通股股利，则也没有偿付拖欠的累积优先股股利的要求。

- **参与特征**

当普通股股利达到一定金额，此特征允许优先股参与提高的股利。参与的确切金额各不相同，它由一些预先确定的公式决定，这些公式将额外的优先股股东支付额与普通股股东支付额的增加联系到一起。

参与优先股给予优先股优先的收益索取权和额外报酬的机会。不幸的是，对于投资者来讲，参与特征不像累积特征那么常见；绝大多数优先股报酬率限制为固定股利率。

● **提前兑回条款**

优先股有明确的兑回价格（或赎回价格）。它在股票发行时就已确定；它高于原始发行价格并会随着时间降低。

提前兑回条款赋予优先股发行人以兑回价格买回（或兑回）全部或部分发行的股票，而不必用更贵的价格买回股票，诸如在公开市场购买股票，或提供给优先股股东一个高于市场价值或其他同类证券的价格。

● **可转换特征**

优先股发行有时有可转换特征（或转换特征）。持有人有权选择将可转换优先股转换成特定数量的普通股。公司会设定可转换优先股转换为普通股一个固定的转换率。一旦转换，优先股就退市了。

当优先股同时有提前兑回条款和转换特征时，如果当前优先股市值价格远远高于兑回价格（由于转换特征）时，公司能够通过兑回股票来迫使转换。

如前所述，普通股没有到期日。除非优先股被强制赎回，否则优先股不会到期。提前兑回条款和可转换特征使公司自由退役优先股（那些不能强制赎回的）而不会潜在地让它们永远流通在外。

优先股估价

如果公司在每年末支付固定股利，则可以用下面方式估价：

$$V_P = \frac{D}{(1+K)^1} + \frac{D}{(1+K)^2} + \frac{D}{(1+K)^3} + \cdots + \frac{D}{(1+K)^\infty}$$

式中：

● V_p 表示优先股的市值。
● D 表示普通股每股固定年股利。
● k 表示折现率。
● ∞ 表示无穷大。

此等式可被简化为：

$$V_P = \frac{D}{K}$$

一旦股利和折现率的信息可获得，优先股的价值就可以直接计算出来。

例如：

一家公司发行了优先股。优先股的面值是 \$100，每股年现金股利是 \$7。市场上同类优先股的折现率是 8%。下面确定该公司发行的优先股的价值。

$$V_P = \frac{D}{K}$$

$$V_P = \frac{\$7}{0.08} = \$87.50$$

虽然年股利率是固定的，但是折现率的改变会随着时间的推移影响股票价格。

- 如果市场折现率下降，优先股的价值将会上升。
- 如果市场折现率上升，优先股的价值将会下降。

股利折现模型的应用

股利折现模型（DDM）是估计普通股价值的一种方法，该方法中普通股内在价值是以预期未来股利折现值（现值）为基础的。

股利折现模型是一种折现现金流量分析法。有几种不同的 DCF 模型以及随之不同的 DDMs 可供组织使用。不存在最好的方法。所用方法应该考虑如下几点：

- 现金流的度量——相对权益的股利和自由现金流。
- 预计持有期——预计持有期是有限的还是无限的。
- 预期股利模式——零增长（不增长）、增长、稳定（固定）增长和超常增长。

基本的股利折现模型

基本的股利折现模型可用如下公式表示：

$$V_s = \sum_{t=1}^{\infty} \frac{D_t}{(1+k_s)}$$

式中：

- V_s 表示普通股每股内在价值。
- D_t 表示第 t 期普通股每股预期股利。
- k_s 表示投资者对普通股的要求报酬率（权益成本）。

基本的股利折现模型假设投资者购买普通股后计划无限期持有。因此，有时它也被称作无限期估价模型。

固定增长股利折现模型

固定增长股利折现模型是假设每股股利每期按固定的、预计不会改变的速率增长的一种估价方法。此模型代表了单阶段增长模式。用 $D_0(1+g)^t$ 代替基本模型中的 D_t 可得到以下公式。

$$V_s = \sum_{t=1}^{\infty} \frac{D_0(1+g)^t}{(1+k_s)^t}$$

式中：

- D_0 表示当期普通股每股股利。
- g 表示固定股利增长率。

如果 k_s 大于 g，公式能被进一步简化为著名的戈登固定增长模型（或称戈登模型）：

$$V_0 = \frac{D_1}{k_s - g}$$

式中：

- V_0 表示预计普通股价值。
- D_1 表示第 1 年预期普通股每股股利。
- k_s 表示普通股要求报酬率。

- g 表示固定（年）股利增长率。

例如：

一家公司只是在去年支付过每股 \$3 股利。分析师预期股利每年以 6% 的固定速率增长。如果投资者期望收到 12% 的报酬率，则 ABC 股票的内在价值是多少？

在本例中：

- $D_1 = \$3.00(1.06) = \$3.18$。
- $k_s = 0.12$。
- $g = 0.06$。

$$V_o = \frac{D_1}{k_s - g} = \frac{\$3.18}{0.12 - 0.06} = \frac{\$3.18}{0.06} = \$53.00$$

要求报酬率与增长率之间关系的要点在图表 3 - 65 中给出。

图表 3 - 65　戈登模型的要点

若……	则……
k_s 与 g 之间的差别加大	→ 股票价值下降
k_s 与 g 之间的差别缩小	→ 股票价值上升
k_s 与 g 之间的差别有细微的变化	→ 股票价值会有很大的变化

相对（或可比）估价模型的应用

相对估价是另一种估价方法，该方法定义"可比的"并选择一个标准价值度量同公司进行比较。价值一般是某些形式的多重收益、权益账面价值或销售收入。基于内在价值的资产可能是便宜的，但是基于相对定价和目前市场定价的资产可能是昂贵的。

本质上，在 DCF 估价模型中用到的相同变量（例如，要求报酬率、预期增长率等）也在相对估价估算中被使用。两种估价方法的主要差别是 DCF 估价的假设是清楚的（明确定义或表述），而用于相对估价模型的那些假设则不太清晰（这些假设提供模型要满足的条件）。

选择可比企业是相对估价的基础。可比企业是指与被估价的单个企业有相似业务和行业特征的企业。

在相对估价中，分析师：

- 试图控制/最小化企业间差异（如规模）。
- 计算每个可比企业的倍数，然后求它们的平均值。
- 计算被估价的单个企业的倍数。
- 将单个企业的倍数与平均值比较。
- 基于单个企业的特点（如增长率或风险），评估两个倍数之间的任何差异。

例如，如下市盈率，其中：

可比企业的市盈率 = 18

单个企业的市盈率 = 10

一个分析师可能认为单个企业的股票便宜（或者低估了），因为它的倍数低于平均值。相反，如果此倍数高于平均值，则股票会被认为很贵（或者高估了）。

三种常见的相对估价模型是市盈率（P/E）、市账率（P/B）及市销率（P/S）。

市盈率

市盈率（P/E）是用来估计普通股价值的最常见倍数。用每股收益（EPS）衡量的收益能力是投资价值的主要决定因素。有两种市盈率；二者之间的区别在于怎样计算分母中的收益。

- 当前 P/E

当前 P/E 使用最近 12 个月的收益。该 P/E 在最流行的财务出版物上很常见。

当前 P/E = 每股市价/前 12 个月的 EPS

- 预测 P/E

预测 P/E 使用下一年的预期收益（或是下一个财政年度或下一季度的预期收益）。

预测 P/E = 每股市价/未来 12 个月的预测 EPS

预测 P/E 依靠 DDM 为稳定企业创建固定倍数模型，然后解释影响股票 P/E 的DDM 中的因素。

例如：

一家公司公布上一个财政年度的收益为 \$1 000 万。分析师预测未来 12 个月 EPS为 \$1.00。这家公司有 1 500 万股票流通在外，每股市价 \$15。基于这些信息，计算当前 P/E 和预测 P/E。

上一年的 EPS = \$10 000 000/15 000 000 = \$0.67

当前 P/E = \$15.00/ \$0.67 =22.39

预测 P/E = \$15.00/ \$1.00 =15.0

使用 P/E 的优势包括：

- 它们通常被用于投资界。
- 研究表明 P/E 差异和长期平均股票报酬之间存在重要关系。

使用 P/E 的一些劣势有：

- 如果收益是负的，得出的 P/E 是没有用的。
- 收益的变动使解释 P/E 变得困难。
- 管理人员的判断（在会计实务允许范围内）可能会扭曲收益。

市账率

市账率（P/B）（或市价对账面价值的比率）表明市场愿意为权益付出的金额。账面价值是一个累积数额，它一般是正值，即使公司报告为亏损或 EPS 为负值。市账率可表述为：

市账率 = 权益的市值/权益的账面价值 = 每股市价/每股账面价值

其中：

权益的账面价值 = 普通股股东的权益 = （总资产 – 总负债） – 优先股

例如：

使用下面表格中的信息，计算这家公司的 P/B。

200X 年权益的 账面价值（百万）	200X 年的销售 收入（百万）	200X 年流通在外 股数（百万）	200X 年 5 月 15 日的价格
$14 015	$9 450	3 400	$9.50

每股账面价值 = 权益的账面价值/流通在外股数

每股账面价值 = $14 015/3 400 = $4.12

P/B = 每股市价/ 每股账面价值 = $9.50/ $4.12 = $2.31

使用 P/B 的优势包括：

- 即使当 EPS 为负时，账面价值作为累积数额也通常为正值。
- 账面价值度量指标比 EPS 更稳定，所以当 EPS 高、低、变动不定时它可能比 P/E 更有用。
- 账面价值为持有大量流动资产（例如，金融、投资、保险和银行业）的企业提供了度量企业净资产的恰当指标。
- P/B 可用于评价一个预计将要歇业的公司。
- 研究表明 P/B 有助于解释长期平均报酬的差异。

使用 P/B 的劣势包括：

- P/B 忽略了非实物资产的价值（例如，商誉和人力资本）。
- 当被比较企业间的资产规模有重大差别时，P/B 可能会产生误导。
- 股东的真实投资可能因不同的会计惯例而被隐藏起来。
- 技术改变和通货膨胀会导致资产的账面价值和市场价值有重大差异。

市销率

市销率（P/S）显示了市场愿意为一美元销售收入付出的金额。P/S 是边际净利润、股利支付率和增长率的正函数；是风险的反函数。

市销率可表示为：

市销率 = 权益的市值/总销售收入 = 每股市价/每股销售收入

例如：

使用下面表格中的信息，计算这家公司的 P/S。

200×年权益的 账面价值（百万）	200×年的销售 收入（百万）	200×年在外流通 股数（百万）	200×年 5 月 15 日的价格
$14 015	$9 450	3 400	$9.50

每股销售收入 = 销售收入/流通在外股数

每股销售收入 = $9 450/3 400 = $2.78

P/S = 每股市价/每股销售收入 = $9.50/ $2.78 = $3.42

P/S 有以下优势：

- 即使对处于困境的企业，该比率也可以提供有意义的度量指标。
- 销售收入数额比 EPS 和账面价值更可信，因为前者不会像后者那样容易操纵或扭曲。
- 因为不像 P/E 倍数那么容易变动，P/S 倍数更趋向于稳定。

- 从成熟的或循环的行业到新建的尚没有收益记录的企业等一系列股票的估价，P/S 都有用。
- 研究表明 P/S 差异和长期平均股票报酬差异之间存在重要关系。

P/S 有以下劣势：

- 高销售收入并不必然代表由收益和现金流度量的营业利润。
- P/S 不能捕捉公司间成本结构的不同。
- 虽然 P/S 不像 EPS 和账面价值那样容易被扭曲，但是收入确认实务会扭曲销售收入预测。

衍生金融工具

衍生金融工具是指特征和价值衍生自另外更基本的金融工具的基础价格或价值的金融工具。原生资产（也被称作基本品）可以是债券、权益投资、商品或货币。

衍生金融工具涉及两方之间的合同。支付在双方间进行。支付额可以是：

- 特定事件（例如，超过某个最小值的原生资产的价格）引发的事先确定的金额。
- 特定数量原生资产价值的改变引起的金额；特定数量原生资产被称为合同的名义数量。

财务会计准则委员会（FASB）公告 133 号"衍生金融工具和套期保值活动"及 138、140、141、145 号公告对其的修订都涉及了衍生金融工具的会计准则。在定义衍生金融工具时，133 号注意了以下几点：

- 它包括一个或多个原生资产。
- 它有一个或多个名义数量或支付条款或二者兼有。
- 它不要求初始净投资，或与预期对市场变化有相似反应的其他合同相比金额更小。
- 净结算（合同支付额）一定是现金付款、易于转换成现金资产的交付或其他衍生金融工具。

不可避免地，新的衍生金融工具将会出现。在说明这些特点时（并非用被认为是衍生金融工具的金融工具定义衍生金融工具），FASB 的意图是确保 133 号公告能够被应用于新的衍生金融工具——只要它们的特征与该公告中列出的特征类似。

公司不使用衍生金融工具筹集资金，但是对它们进行买卖以预防市场因素的不利变动。例如，一家公司可以用一种衍生金融工具管理其原生投资的风险，并防护价值的浮动。

从概念上说，有两类基本类型的衍生金融工具：期权和远期合同。随后内容会集中在这些衍生金融工具上。另外一些衍生金融工具（例如，期货和互换）是期权和远期合同的结合或者变种。它们的特征会被简要介绍。

衍生金融工具是有风险的复杂工具。本书关于它的信息只是为了提供一个概览。这些内容概括的信息多数来自于：

- 马克·A·特朗布利的《衍生与套期会计》。
- 金融理财师协会（AFP）的学习体系：财产。

- 管理会计公告 No. 4 "理解金融工具"。

许多其他来源也致力于衍生金融工具这一主题。关于买卖衍生金融工具的其他指导，强烈推荐参考这些资料。

期权

期权（或期权合同）双方之间的一个合同，其中合同买方有权（但不是义务）买卖约定数量的原生资产。

主要特征和术语

下面是与期权合同有关的显著特征和术语。

- 拥有期权进行买卖的一方是期权的所有者（也称为期权的买方或持有人）。另一方是期权的卖方。
- 原生资产可以是有形的（如股票、商品或货币），也可以是无形的（如指数价值或利率）。
- 买方期权给予期权所有人在特定时期内以固定价格从卖方那里购买原生资产（也称作基本品）的权利（而不是义务）。
- 卖方期权给予期权所有人在特定时期内以固定价格出售给卖方原生资产的权利（而不是义务）。
- 预购价格（或行权价格）指合同的固定价格。
- 行权日期（也称到期日、截止日）是买方可以对原生资产行权（买或卖）的最后一天。
- 期权定金是期权的初始购买价格；它通常以每单位为基础。期权合同卖方提前从买方（持有人）那里收到期权定金。如果买方选择行使期权，则卖方有义务履行合同（买或卖原生资产）。
- 欧式期权是允许持有人只能在到期时才能行使期权的一种合同。
- 美式期权是允许持有人在到期之前的任何时间都可行使期权的一种合同。

偿付结构

期权有不同的偿付结构：

- 如果原生资产的价格等于预购价格，则该期权被称为平价期权。
- 如果合同立即行权，则一般被称作溢价期权的期权要求对持有者进行支付。
- 如果持有者没有动力行使合同，则该期权被称为折价期权。
- 如果买方期权的预购价格超过原生资产价格，则该期权被称为折价期权；如果原生资产价格高于买方期权的预购价格，则该期权被称为溢价期权。
- 如果卖方期权的预购价格超过原生资产期权，则该期权被称为溢价期权；如果原生资产价格高于卖方期权的预购价格，则该期权被称为折价期权。

以下是一些买方期权和卖方期权偿付结构的简化例子。

买方期权例子。买方和卖方之间签订了一个 30 天的商品期权合同；预购价格为每单位 $50。期权定金是每单位 $2。在到期日有两种情况：

- 如果市场价格小于等于 $50 的预购价格，持有人（买方）不会行使期权，因为以当前市价购买商品比行使期权便宜。买方损失 $2 的期权费。

● 如果市场价格大于预购价格与期权定金之和（$50 + $2 = $52），持有人（买方）会行使期权并从中获利。

卖方期权例子。买方和卖方之间签订了一个 60 天的商品期权合同；预购价格为每单位 $30。期权定金是每单位 $1。在到期日有两种情况：

● 如果市场价格大于等于 $30 的预购价格，持有人不会行使期权。持有人可能会售出商品而不是行使期权以赚取更多利润。

● 如果市场价格低于预购价格与期权定金之差（$30 − $1 = $29），持有人可通过行使期权赚取利润。

在制定期权合同时，双方都不被要求必须拥有原生资产。例如，在涉及股票的期权中，期权卖方不必当前就拥有股票。卖方可以在不实际拥有股票的情况下提供给买方买股票的期权。然而，如果持有人行使了买方期权，卖方必须交付股票。如果卖方还没有股票，他必须到公开市场购买合同规定的股票，并将其交付给期权买方。如果当前市价超过预购价格，期权卖方只能收到预购价格作为支付。预购价格和市场价值之差是必须承担的损失。

期权有非对称偿付结构。买方期权持有人有获得无限收益和有限损失的可能。如果不行使期权，它会到期终止。如果一单位也不成交，则持有人的仅限于期权定金——为购买期权而支付的价格。买方期权的卖方可能经历无限的潜在损失（除非合同被"补进"，这意味着卖方已经拥有了基本品）。另一方面，卖方期权持有人面临着无限收益和有限损失，卖方期权的卖方面临的只是有限损失（但收益也是有限的）。

期权一般用于杠杆作用或保护作用。用期权做杠杆为持有人提供了用以获得期权定金（是实际市价的一部分）的原生资产的权益。因为期权提供了在有限时间内以固定价格购买原生资产的权利，所以在到期前它们通过预防价格波动提供保护作用。这将风险限制在损失期权定金之内（除非还没有原生资产）。

买方期权的偿付图如图表 3−66 所示。

图表 3−66 买方期权的偿付

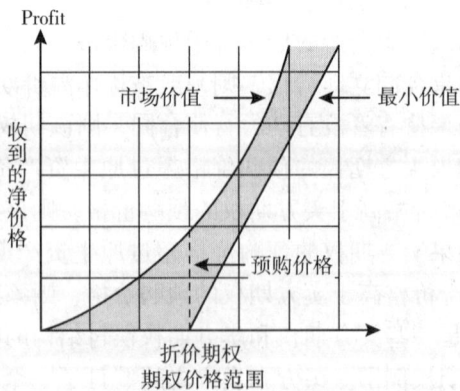

如买方期权的偿付图所示：

● 市场价值（市场价格）与最小价值（最低价格）不同。

● 曲线和直线间的阴影部分代表市场价值超过最小价值。

只要期权价格继续提高，投资者愿意支付超过最小价格的期权定金。然而，随着市场价值曲线接近最小价值线，投资者就不愿意为期权支付期权定金了，因为期权价格的进一步提高将会产生最小的期权价值增长。

期权的价格和价值

在某种程度上，期权价格或价值取决于原生资产的预期未来价值（如一些简单例子所示）。

在讨论期权时，管理会计公告 No. 4M 指出了影响期权理论价值的如下因素：

● 原生资产的当前价格。

● 期权到期前的时间。

● 原生资产的价格波动性。

● 期权的预购价格。

● 与期权合同同时到期的无风险收益证券（通常为短期国库券）的利率。

● 普通股和附息证券的任何预期股利和利息的现值。

实际上，要用数学公式计算理论期权价值。而且，资产负债表会计要求衍生金融工具必须作为资产或者负债以公允价值列示在资产负债表上（取决于具体合同）。会计师必须能够确定衍生金融工具的价值。

关于期权估价，公告 133 号参考了公告 107 号"关于金融工具公允价值的披露"，公告 107 号描述了估计衍生金融工具公允价值的如下三种途径：

● 定制调整——用于市场价格可得且公允价值的估算是建立在市场报价基础上的衍生金融工具。

● 定价模型——主要用于以期权为基础的衍生金融工具，其中各种参数是估计的（布莱克—舒尔茨期权估价模型和二项式期权估价模型将会在下文讨论。）

● 折现现金流量法——适用于以远期为基础的衍生金融工具，其中未来现金流量需要被估算，当前折现率用于计算估计现金流量的净现值。

注：折现现金流量法将在本书第 5 章"投资决策"中详细介绍。

布莱克—舒尔茨期权估价模型（以创立者费雪·布莱克和梅隆·舒尔茨的名字命名）认为大量交易资产的价格以持续的变动形式遵循几何布朗运动。当用于股票期权时，此模型包含了股票的持续价格波动、货币时间价值、期权的预购价格和期权到期的时间。

布莱克—舒尔茨期权估价模型的主要假设包括：

● 股票在期权寿命期内不支付任何股利

● 使用欧式行权条款；卖空原生资产是可能的。

● 市场是有效的；股票交易是连续的。

● 没有交易成本或税收；没有手续费。

● 无风险利率存在、保持不变且对所有到期日都一样。

● 原生股票的报酬率服从正态分布。

二项式期权估价模型通过迭代数学计算对期权估价。它运用二项式网格（树）

追踪期权主要原生资产的演变。网格中的每个节点或时间点均代表原生资产在估价日和到期日之间某个特定时点的一个可能价格。价格演变形成了期权估价的基础。

二项式期权估价模型的主要特征是：

- 采用风险中立法估价。
- 假设到期前原生资产价格随着时间只能提高或降低。
- 消除套利的可能性。
- 假设市场充分有效。
- 缩短期权久期。

布莱克—舒尔茨期权估价模型和二项式期权估价模型比用于远期和期货定价的折现现金流量法复杂得多。但实际上，通过使用计算机电子制表软件和科学计算器，它们也不会非常难用。事实上，布莱克—舒尔茨期权估价模型和二项式期权估价模型的数学计算通常很接近实际的期权价格。

远期合同

远期合同是双方在未来某日以约定价格买卖特定数量资产的定制合同。远期合同与期权有本质相同，因为双方都有义务履行合同条款。

主要特征和术语

与远期合同相关的一些主要特征和术语如下：

- 在远期合同中，一方购买合同；另一方通常被称作订约方。
- 原生资产可以是有形的（如商品或货币）也可以是无形的（如股票指数或债务工具）。
- 同意在未来特定日期购买原生资产的一方为多头（或被称为做多远期合同）。
- 同意在未来特定日期出售原生资产的一方为空头（或被称为做空远期合同）。
- 交付价格（或合同价格）指合同中规定的购买/出售价格。
- 交付日期（或到期日）指合同规定的未来日期；合同交付在到期日发生。
- 原生资产数量和交付日期在合同签订时设定；无须支付初始费用（期权定金）。

远期合同的订约方经常是一家银行、证券商或外汇市场（FX）的交易商（远期合同最常见应用是用外汇支付）。在很多情况下，这些主体作为"做市商"进行服务，促成两方间的私人合同。

远期合同不在有组织的交易所交易。这是与在标准交易所交易的期货合同的主要区别。

偿付结构

在不必交付期权定金的情况下，合同的初始价值对于双方来说是零。合同在签署时没有价值。远期价格决定合同的价值。多头在原生资产价格上升时获得价值，在原生资产价格下降时损失价值。相反，空头在原生资产价格下降时获得价值，在原生资产价格上升时损失价值。

远期有对称偿付结构；有利和不利头寸的利得和损失是相等的。随着原生资产价值的改变，远期合同多头和空头的价值会成比例增加或减少，这取决于所持头寸。

远期合同例子。显示远期合同应用的一个简单情景可以是一个美国进口商60天到期的欧元发票。不管60天内货币汇率发生什么波动，购买60天交割的欧元远期合同都会锁定汇率。

期货合同

期货合同（或期货）是以远期为基础的合同，它在概念上类似于远期，但在行使上不同。基本差异是不像远期（经常通过中间人私下磋商），期货是在有组织的交易所交易的标准化合同。

例如，在美国，交易期货在：

- 纽约商业交易所（如金属、石油和光纤）。
- 芝加哥期货交易所（如牲畜、木材和肉）。
- 芝加哥交易所的国际货币市场部（如外汇期货）。

交易所规定名义数量和到期日。它们也要求在合同期间基于原生资产的变化进行日常结算。利得和损失计入利润账户。

期货通常在到期前抛售。它们很少用实际交割进行清算。最后的清算通常以现金支付完成。期货合同多头和空头的偿付结构与远期合同的偿付结构完全相同。

互换

互换是双方（订约方）交换（或互换）未来现金支付的私人约定。类似于远期合同，互换合同通常由中间人促成。互换以一系列远期合同和特定日期的支付互换为特征。

最常见的互换是利率互换——双方（通常在中间人的帮助下）互换约定金额的未来利率支付。本金是名义的，因为它不会永远不转手，而只是被用于计算支付金额。

在被称作普通型利率互换的最简单的利率交换中，涉及以固定利率支付交换浮动利率支付：

- A方同意给B方一系列远期支付，数额等于事先约定的固定利率乘以名义本金。
- B方同意给A方一系列远期支付，数额等于浮动利率乘以相同的名义本金。

相同货币互换之初，A方和B方一般不会互换本金。当支付到期时，净利息由欠钱的订约方支付。也就是说，适当的订约方支付固定利率和浮动利率支付额的差额。互换结束时，因为双方开始时不交换名义本金，所以没有资金的交换。

使用利率互换的主要动机是降低利率不利变动的风险。为了将自己的资产和负债的固定或浮动特性配比起来，订约方会将固定利率义务转化为浮动利率义务（反之亦然）。

例如，假设A、B双方都想要借$1 000万5年。A比B有更好的信用等级。给双方提供的条款如下：

	固定利率	浮动利率
A	10.00%	6 月期的 LIBOR * +0.50%
B	11.00%	6 月期的 LIBOR +1.00%

- 伦敦同业拆放利率

假设:
- A 方想要以浮动利率借款。
- B 方想要以固定利率借款。
- A 方比 B 方有更高的信用等级,可以支付比固定或浮动市场更低的利率。
- 在两种市场上,B 方比 A 方支付得都多,但是在浮动利率市场以浮动利率(LIBOR)加上 1% 进行支付花费相对较少。

因为 A 方在固定利率市场有比较借款优势,而 B 方在浮动利率市场有比较借款优势,双方签订能产生净优势的利率互换合同,该净优势通常在双方之间分割。

使用互换的可能风险是任一订约方可能在约定利息支付流上违约,从而潜在地让另一方为原始支付流负责。使用第三方中间人有助于减轻这种风险。

有许多其他类型的互换,也有许多其他类型的利率互换。其中一些更常见的是,以一种货币表示的义务转换成另一种货币的货币汇率互换;将一种商品的浮动价格转换成固定价格的商品互换。

其他长期金融工具

除了以上介绍的投资工具,还有其他公司可以用于长期筹资的工具。图表3-67 总结了关于租赁、可转换证券、购股权证及留存收益的主要特点。

图表3-67 其他长期金融工具

投 资	描 述	主要特征
租赁	资产所有者(出租方)授予另一方(承租方)在某一时期内使用该资产的权利,并因此获得一定报酬的法律合同	• 约束承租人支付租赁合同约定的支付 • 可采用各种形式: • 经营性租赁:短期、可撤销租赁,出租人承担所有权风险 • 融资性租赁(也称全部收回租赁或资本租赁):通常不可撤销、租期内全部支付(摊销)、承租人担负风险。也就是,承租人担负维修、保险和纳税的责任。
可转换证券	包含用该证券交换一定数量另一种证券期权的固定收益证券或优先股	• 通常用于将该证券转换成一定数量的另一种权益证券 • 允许一家公司以低于直接发行债券或普通股的资本成本筹集资金;当可转换证券被转换时,债务从资产负债表上移走
购股权证	直接从公司购买普通股的长期买方期权	• 给予债券持有人或优先股股东按给定价格购买普通股的权利 • 价值源自投资者认为股价会超过预购价格的预期
留存收益	一家公司寿命期内的净收益减去现金股利或股票股利	• 代表一家公司留存在企业的全部收益(没有以现金形式分配给所有者或未因股票股利而转成实收资本) • 基本上代表权益资本的最便宜成本,因为它允许一家公司自己进行再投资

进度检查

提示：完成以下各题，参考答案随后给出。

1. 下面哪项准确描述了债券收益（　　　）

    a. 质量高债券通常比等级低债券收益低

    b. 短期债券通常比长期债券收益高

    c. 固定利率债券比零息债券收益高

    d. 担保债券比无担保债券收益高

2. 当利率较低时，下面哪种债券在二级市场上最有吸引力？（　　　）

    a. Aaa 或 AAA 级债券

    b. 零息债券

    c. 浮动利率债券

    d. 美国短期国库券

连线——融资工具与恰当描述。

3. 普通股	a. 双方在未来某日按约定价格买卖特定数量资产的约定
4. 优先股	b. 双方交换未来现金支付的私人约定
5. 期权	c. 直接从公司购买普通股的长期买方期权
6. 远期合同	d. 提供公司部分所有权和固定股利的工具
7. 购股权证	e. 允许买方有权在特定日期或之前以规定价格买卖原生资产的合同
8. 互换	f. 提供公司资产的权益利益并分享公司收益的工具

9. 股票分割与现金股利间之间的主要区别是（　　　）

    a. 现金股利不会导致任何应税利得或损失；股票分割是应税的。

    b. 股票分割不会导致任何应税利得或损失；现金股利是应税的。

    c. 现金股利按季支付；股票分割按年授予。

    d. 股票分割按季支付；现金股利按年授予。

进度检查答案

1. a

2. c

3. f

4. d

5. e

6. a

7. c

8. b

9. b

第 3 节
资本成本

本节内容简介

正如管理会计公告 4A "资本成本" 中所给出的定义，资本成本是组成企业资本结构的各种资金来源的成本的组合。它反映新投资所必须赚取的从而使股东权益不会被稀释的最低报酬率。

资本成本的定义

一家公司的管理团队承担着保障资产的效率性和盈利性，同时最大程度地减少公司投资所引起的资本成本的任务。为履行这一委托责任，管理人员作出各种影响企业资本结构的筹资决策。

公司基本上通过两种来源获取资本：贷款人和股东。一家企业的总资本代表了债务资本和权益资本的结合。管理会计公告（SMA）4H "资本成本的运用" 将这些资本组成部分描述如下：

- **债务资本**是指总资本中从附息工具如票据、债券或贷款的发行中取得的那部分资本。
- **权益资本**是指总资本中从股东的永久投资如实收资本或留存收益中取得的那部分资本。一家企业可以发行新的普通股或优先股，或者可以选择将收益留存而不作为股利发放。

企业为形成资本所做的每一个行为——无论明确的还是含蓄的——都有一个相关成本。总资本成本反映一家企业筹资的各种组成部分的比例平均数。

决策资本结构时应考虑资本成本。公司用资本成本作为标准衡量投资决策和更有效地管理营运资本（例如，应收账款、存款和应付账款）会从中受益。资本成本在衡量和评估业绩上也很有价值。比如，资本或净资产的实际和预期报酬可以与它们各自相关的资本成本相比较。

计算资本成本

资本成本是通过确定各类资本成本，然后将每一组成部分的成本与该部分在企业总资本结构中的比例相乘而得到的。SMA 4A 提供的资本成本一般计算公式如下：

$$k_a = p_1 k_1 + p_2 k_2 \cdots + p_n k_n$$

式中：
- n 表示不同种类的筹资（每一种筹资在资本结构中都有自己的成本和比例）。
- k 表示资本结构中各要素的成本。
- p 表示要素在所组成的总资本结构中的比例。
- k_a 表示资本成本（用百分比表示）。

资本成本举例

图表3-68列示了一家公司所使用的各类筹资：

图表3-68 资本成本举例

类型（n）	税后成本（k）	资本结构的百分比（p）
债务	4%	30%
优先股	8%	20%
普通股	18%	50%

$$k_a = p_1 k_1 + p_2 k_2 + \cdots + p_n k_n$$
$$= 0.30(4\%) + 0.20(8\%) + 0.50(18\%) = 1.2 + 1.6 + 9 = 11.8\%$$

在计算资本成本时，使用各种资本组成部分的当前或预期成本通常比依靠历史成本更合适。资本成本的一个主要用途是将新资本投资于新产品、设备或设施等项目上。因此，相关成本是与企业计划筹集的增量资金相关的边际成本，不是企业已经筹集的历史资本成本。

确定资本成本的主要考虑因素是：

- 怎样确定每个单一资本组成部分的成本（k）。
- 怎样确定公司总资本结构中各自的权重（p）。

单个资本组成部分的成本

确定一家企业资本结构中每一个组成部分的成本是计算资本成本的第一步。公司通常使用三种筹资方式：

- 债务。
- 优先股。
- 普通股。

债务成本

债务成本反映债务资本（例如，贷款和债券）的供给者所要求的要求报酬率。税后债务成本的基本公式是：

税后债务成本 $= k_d(1-t)$

式中：

- k_d 表示税前债务成本。
- t 表示企业的边际税率。

确立税后债务成本的考虑因素有：

- 应该使用什么利率（k_d）？
- 应该如何处理不同类型的债务？
- 所得税对利率有何影响？

这个公式不反映任何发行成本因为大多数债务是私下安排的。

税前债务成本大于税后债务成本，原因是一家企业可以在确定应税收益时扣除利息支出。税率越高，税后债务成本越低。

例如：

Blane 公司的债务由 6% 以面值发售的附息债券组成。预计税率为 35% 。债务成本为：

$$税后债务成本 = k_d(1 - t)$$
$$= 6\%(1 - 35\%)$$
$$= 3.9\%$$

债务的现行重置成本（市值）被用于计算资本成本。但是，当涉及一种或更多种债务时，应使用到期收益率的加权平均值来计算债务成本。

债务的加权平均成本计算如图表 3-69 所示：

图表 3-69　使用到期收益率计算的加权平均债务成本

1 债务	2 市值（百万）	3 占总资本的百分比	4 到期收益率*	5 = (3×4)加权成本
发行 A	$45	10.0%	11.2%	1.12%
发行 B	125	27.8	12.4%	3.45
发行 C	280	62.2	13.1%	8.15
总计	$450	100.0%		12.72%

税前加权平均的债务成本：12.7%

按所得税调整（1-0.45）：0.55

所得税后加权平均的债务成本：6.99%

*债券的到期收益率是使所有利息和本金支出的现值等于债券当前价格的折现率。

优先股成本

优先股成本是向股东支付的股利（如果有）和发行成本的函数。因为发行成本可能很高，优先股成本要能反映发行成本。发行成本包括直接成本（如承销费用、申报费用、法律费用和税款）和间接成本（如用在新发行上的管理人员时间）。应将发行成本从优先股售价中扣除以计算净收入。

优先股成本的一般计算公式是：

$$k_p = \frac{D_p}{P_p - F}$$

式中：

- k_p 表示优先股的组成部分成本。
- D_p 表示优先股股利。
- P_p 表示每股现价（当前或预期成本）。
- F 表示以货币表示的发行成本。

例如：

Blane 公司的优先股发放每股 $8 的股利，并以每股 $100 发售。如果公司发行新的优先股，它将支付每股 $2 的承销和其他费用（发行成本）。该公司优先股成本计算如下：

$$k_p = \frac{D_p}{P_p - F} = \frac{\$8}{\$100 - \$2} = \frac{\$8}{\$98} = 8.16\%$$

本例中，优先股成本是以年度股利支付为基础的。如果股利按季支付，上述公式同样适用，这时季度股利率乘以 4 得到名义年度股利率。

发行成本有时按发行的百分比给出。在上例中，发行成本为 2%。因此，优先股成本的分母为 $P_p(1 - F\%)$，其中 F 是一个百分数，而不是货币金额。

因为优先股股利不可以免税，它们代表了税后资金流出。一个支付 11% 股利的优先股（面值为 $100）花费企业税后收益的 $11。如果企业税率为 35%，它每发放一美元股利，必须在税前赚到 $1.54。

当一家公司有多于一种优先股流通在外时，应该使用所有优先股的加权平均股利率。

普通股权益成本

普通股权益成本（或权益成本）是最难计算的资本组成部分。如前所述，权益主要由普通股发行、实收资本和留存收益组成。SMA 4A 将权益成本描述为企业普通股的预期、要求或实际报酬率，如果能赚回，该报酬率将使股票市值不变。这个比率难以估计是因为普通股没有固定的合同支付。

存在着从简单到复杂的各种方法来估计权益成本。三种估计内部权益成本的方法如下：

- 历史报酬率。
- 股利增长模型。
- 资本资产定价模型。

每种方法都有独特的优势和局限。企业可以使用不只一种方法确定一个合理的估计。恰当方法的选择通常是给定情景下可获得信息的函数。

如前所述，公司通过两种途径之一筹集权益：

- 通过将收益留存下来从内部筹资。
- 通过发售新的普通股从外部筹资。

成熟的公司倾向于从内部产生大部分权益。发行成本使在市场中筹集新权益的成本更贵。此外，如果股票被低估，以低于正常价值发售股票将导致损失。换句话说，因为发行成本和低估带来的潜在损失，企业在发行新的普通股（外部权益）之前，通常会使用成本较低的留存收益（内部权益）。

使用历史报酬率估计内部权益成本

顾名思义，确定权益成本的历史报酬率法涉及股东已赚得的历史报酬率。该方法考虑到一位投资者过去购买股票、持有至今并以当前市价卖出所得的报酬率。

比如，一个五年前购买的以每股 $100 发行的普通股，今天以 $110 出售。每年发放 $8 的股利。使用历史报酬率法，投资者的平均报酬率为每年 10%（$8 股利加上 $2 平均年度利得/ $100）。然后用 10% 估计股票的当前报酬率和企业权益资本成本。

如 SMA 4A 所述，使用历史报酬率法意味着：

- 企业业绩在未来不会有重大变化。

- 利率不会发生重大变化。
- 投资者对待风险的态度不变。

虽然历史法相对容易计算，但是它的局限是将来很少与过去一样。

使用股利增长模型估计内部权益成本

股利增长模型反映的是一种市值法。如 SMA 4A 所述，该模型的基本逻辑是股票市价等于预期未来收益的现金流（包括股利和市价增值）折现的现值。这表示当未来收益的现值等于市价时，贴现率等于权益资本成本。它的一个潜在假设是收益将以固定复利增长。

股利增长的计算公式是：

$$k_s = \frac{D_1}{P_0} + g$$

式中：

- k_s 表示内部权益资本成本。
- D_1 表示第 1 期的每股股利。
- P_0 表示第 0 期的每股市价。
- g 表示预期的股利增长率。

例如：

如果 Blane 公司的股票最近以每股 $50 出售，第一年结束的时候，预期股利为每股 $3.50，而且未来股利预期以每年 5% 的速率增长，权益资本成本为：

$$k_s = \frac{\$3.50}{\$50} + 5\% = 12.00\%$$

与其他计算权益资本成本的方法类似，股利增长率也是一种估计。既然这样，这个估计就是 g 的价值。只有当市场期望是股利以此速率增长时，此模型才有用。投资者必须相信过去每股收益的过去趋势将会继续。如果真是这样，可以使用这个趋势（用百分比表示）。

使用资本资产定价模型估计内部权益成本

资本资产定价模型（CAPM）在此之前讨论过，它与组合管理（第 1 节"风险和报酬"）相关。它也用于衡量一家企业的权益资本成本。

CAPM 认为任何证券的报酬率等于无风险利率加风险溢价。无风险利率通常根据美国长期国库券或短期国库券的当前或预计利率决定。风险溢价来自证券的 β 值。

用 CAPM 模型估计权益资本成本的计算公式是：

$$k_s = R_f + \beta(k_m - R_f)$$

式中：

- k_s 表示内部权益资本成本。
- R_f 表示无风险利率（比如，长期国库券或 30 天到期的短期国库券的利率）。
- β 表示股票的估计 β 值（来自经纪商、投资咨询服务公司或企业计算）。
- k_m 表示对整个市场或平均股票的报酬率的估计。

（$k_m - R_f$）被称为市场风险溢价，在 5% ~7%，这取决于估计的日期和分析师使用的数据来源。企业通常加6%到长期国库券利率以得到整个市场报酬率。

例如：

如果国库券收益率为8%，一家企业股票的β值为0.9，市场的预期报酬率为14%，使用 CAPM 模型，那么 Blane 公司的权益资本成本为：

$$k_s = 8\% + 0.9 \times (14\% - 8\%)$$
$$= 8\% + 5.40\%$$
$$= 13.40\%$$

使用 CAPM 模型需要估计等式中的每一项。决定如下事项具有挑战性：

- 使用长期还是短期国库券利率作为无风险利率。
- 估计投资者期望的未来β值。
- 估计整个市场的期望报酬率。

使用股利增长模型估计新权益成本

确定新普通股成本（k_e）必须考虑发行成本和可能的折价损失。用于计算现存权益成本（k_s）的固定增长 DDM 的公式能调整用来计算这两个因素。

新权益成本的计算公式是：

$$k_e = \frac{D_1}{P_0 - (F + U)} + g$$

式中：

- k_e 表示外部权益资本的成本。
- D_1 表示第 1 期的每股股利。
- P_0 表示第 0 期每股市价。
- g 表示预期股利增长率。
- F 表示发行成本。
- U 表示折价损失。

例如：

假设 Blane 公司以每股 \$50 的价格发行股票，其发行成本和折价损失为 \$5。第一年年末的股利预期为每股 \$3.50，并且未来的股利预期将以每年5%的速率增长。新权益资本成本估计为：

$$k_e = \frac{D_1}{P_0 - (F + U)} + g$$

$$= \frac{\$3.50}{\$50 - \$5} + 0.05 = 13.00\%$$

将新权益成本（13.00%）与内部权益成本（12%）相比，两者之差是发行成本和折价损失。这些因素使得新权益成本高出内部权益成本1%。

估计资本成本，尤其是当涉及权益成本时，是不准确的。关于输入的决策和不同模型自身会带来估计的重大差异。

加权平均资本成本

一旦决定了不同资本组成部分，最终目标是计算企业总资本结构中每个来源的相对重要性。换句话说，单个组成部分必须进行加权，以表示每一组成部分对企业资本结构总值的贡献程度。

加权平均资本成本（WACC）是企业总资本成本，反映与典型或平均项目相关的风险。

许多公司使用下面的加权平均资本成本的计算公式：

$$WACC = \sum_{i=1}^{n} w_i k_i$$

式中：

- WACC 表示加权平均资本成本。
- w_i 表示每个资本组成部分所代表的总永久资本的百分比。
- k_i 表示每个资本组成部分的税后成本。
- n 表示资本组成部分的总数。

因为 WACC 包括企业资本结构的全部来源的永久筹资，加权组成部分的总和必须等于 1.0。

通常使用三种加权方案来计算 WACC。

- **账面价值加权**

账面价值加权根据企业资产负债表上显示的会计（账面）价值来衡量每种资本的比例。

- **市场价值加权**

市场价值加权代表在当前市场价格下，企业资本结构中每种资本的当前比例。

- **目标价值加权**

目标价值加权代表基于企业最理想（目标）的资本结构的权重。

账面价值保持稳定是因为它们并不依靠不断变动的市场价值计算负债和权益。它们反映历史成本。但是，使用账面价值会歪曲 WACC，因为账面价值可能与市场有极大的差异。

许多人认为市场价值加权是计算 WACC 最准确的方法，因为市场加权考虑到不断变动的市场条件的影响和每种证券的当前价格。但是，在使用基于实际市场还是目标市场的资本结构加权的优点之间，存在一些争议。因为目标加权代表企业在未来将如何筹资的最佳估计，如果企业向目标结构发展，目标加权是有意义的。

例如：

管理人员认为组合是最理想的，并且希望在筹集未来资本时维持这个目标结构。如果 Blane 公司以目标比例筹集新资本，企业 WACC 的计算如下。

资本组成部分	权　　重	税后成本	WACC
长期债务	0.40	3.90%	1.500%
优先股	0.10	8.16	0.816
普通（内部）权益	0.50	11.80	5.900
			8.276%

*使用历史报酬率（10.0%）、股利增长模型（12.0%）和 CAPM 模型（13.4%）

的平均成本，普通（内部）权益（留存收益）的成本是（10.0% + 12.0% + 13.4%）/3 = 11.8% 。如果管理人员认为某种估计留存收益成本的方法好于其他方法，它可以使用那个成本来代替好几种方法的平均。

因此，在使用外部权益之前，Blane 公司的加权平均资本成本为8.276%。

$$\text{WACC} = (0.30 \times 4.58\%) + (0.15 \times 8.22\%) + (0.55 \times 11.25\%)$$
$$= 0.0865 \text{ 或 } 8.65\%$$

边际资本成本

公司没有无限的资金资源用于投资。简单地说，他们不能超越他们的财务能力去满足财务债务。

市场投资者评价不同公司的财务优点，比较它们，并对单个公司确定合理的限制，如果超过这个限制，投资者将不会愿意提供资金。如果一家企业试图超过其市场确定限度地扩大筹资，资金将只能以高成本获得。（筹集外部资本有发行成本，使得新权益的成本高于留存收益的成本。）

边际资本（MC）是公司筹集的最后一元新资本。边际资本成本（MCC）是超过之前 MC 水平筹资的增量成本。边际资本成本表设定一系列的范围，并详细说明企业筹资超过每个范围最大限度时的增量成本。

MCC 表

编制 MCC 表需要五个步骤：

1. 确定新筹资的恰当权重。
2. 计算与每笔所筹资本相关的组成部分资本成本。
3. 计算新组成部分成本增长的总新筹资的范围。
4. 计算每个总新筹资每个范围的 MCC。
5. 绘制 MCC 表。

设定 MCC 表的断点

建立新组成部分成本增长的总新筹资范围需要设定临界点。临界点（BP）是指一家企业在资本成本增加前所能筹集的总筹资。

MCC 断点的计算公式是：

$$\text{BP}_{RE} = \frac{\text{TF}_i}{w_i}$$

式中：

- BP_{RE} 表示资本组成部分 i 的临界点。
- TF_i 表示从资本组成部分 i 可获得的资金总量。
- w_i 表示资本组成部分 i 所代表的总永久资本的百分比。

使用该公式，临界点可以通过将按一定成本可获得的某一特定资本组成部分资金总量除以其在资本结构中的权重得到。

一个 MCC 表可以包括几个临界点。

例如：

　　Blane 公司期望下一年有 $50 百万的收益来支付普通股股东现金股利或者再投资。企业预期 40% 的股利支付率。因此，公司将会有 $30 百万 [（$50）(1 − 0.40)] 的新留存收益。假设公司的资本结构是 40% 的债务，10% 的优先股和 50% 的权益。那么留存收益的临界点是多少？

$$BP_{RE} = \frac{TF_i}{w_i}$$

$$BP_{RE} = \frac{\$30\ 百万}{0.50} = \$60\ 百万$$

　　因此，Blane 公司在不得不发行外部权益前可以筹集 $60 百万。$60 百万包括 $24 百万（0.40 × $60 百万）的负债，$6 百万（0.10 × $60 百万）的优先股和 $30 百万的内部权益（留存收益——0.50 × $60 百万）。如果公司有一个大于 $60 百万的资本预算，那么它的边际资本成本将增加，因为普通股比留存收益成本更高。

计算 MCC

　　Blane 公司想计算留存收益断点后的边际资本成本。根据股利折现模型，企业留存权益成本为 12%，但当考虑到发行成本和折价时，其新权益成本为 13%。因此，1% 的差异代表了对发行成本和折价成本的估计。管理人员决定给之前计算的普通（内部）权益增加 1 个百分点。因此，新普通股的估计成本为 12.8%，即，11.8% + 1.0%。

　　例如：

　　Blane 公司在留存收益断点 $60 百万后的边际资本成本计算如下：

资本组成部分	权　　重	税后成本	WACC
长期债务	0.40	3.90%	1.500%
优先股	0.10	8.16	0.816
普通（内部）权益	0.50	12.80	6.400
			8.776%

　　因此，留存收益断点 $60 百万后的边际资本成本增长到 8.776%。MCC 表如下：

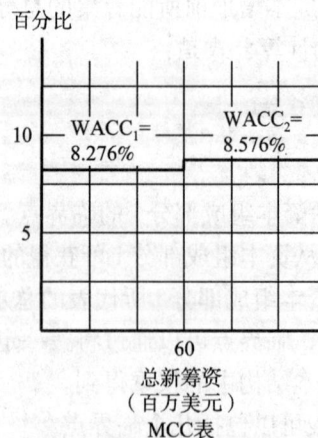

MCC表

MCC 确认了投资者对增加的筹资要求的反应。市场对不同水平实行限制。过量水平会导致随后更高的资本成本。

所得税对资本结构和资本投资决策的影响

税收通过以下方式影响企业的资本结构：

- **大额应税收益的企业**

有大额应税收益（无税收屏蔽）的企业可以通过更多的债务筹资来减免税款——这会增加分配给债务和权益持有者的总现金流。

- **不稳定营业利润的企业**

有不稳定营业利润的企业具有更高的经营风险和更低的企业在低收入年份借款而减免税款的可能性。这些企业可能不想像其他低经营风险的企业那样借那么多款。

在投资决策中使用资本成本

公司必须决定该把收益投向哪儿以获得企业风险范围内最可能的回报率。SMA 4A 指出，企业可将资本成本用作折现率以估计预测现金流现值的现值或估计内含报酬率的门槛比率。

资本成本提供了评价一家企业证券的风险和报酬是高还是低的检查标准。这些评级很重要，原因如下：

- 高风险代表高资本成本；低风险预示着低资本成本。
- 高资本成本（折现率）一般代表企业证券价值被低估；低资本成本代表证券价值被高估。

证券的销售为公司提供了必要的投资资金。如果证券价值低，筹资成本增加。反过来，证券价值高则筹资成本低。

最后，企业的偿债能力取决于其总风险。管理人员必须考虑到各种投资对企业总风险的影响。

进度检查

提示：完成以下各题，参考答案随后给出。

1. 根据下列信息，该企业的资本成本为多少？（　　　　）

类　　型	税后成本	占资本结构的百分比
债务	8%	34%
优先股	9%	26%
普通权益	10%	40%

a. 8%

b. 9%

c. 10%

　　　　d.　27%

2. 下列哪个因素使确定债务成本具有挑战性?(　　　)

　　a. 利息成本有多种计算方式。

　　b. 留存收益易受股利支付影响。

　　c. 普通股没有固定的合同支付。

　　d. 公司未来的业绩水平难以估计。

3. 应用资本资产定价模型去估计企业权益资本成本的一个潜在前提是:(　　　)

　　a. 投资者对风险的态度不变。

　　b. 收益预期以稳定的复利率增长。

　　c. 单个资本组成部分必须按其对企业资本结构的贡献加权。

　　d. 报酬率等于无风险报酬率加上风险溢价。

找出与下列术语匹配的描述。

4. _____资本成本　　a. 公司支付给所有负债资本（如，贷款和债券）的利率

5. _____债务成本　　b. 给股东支付股利（如果有）的函数

6. _____优先股成本　　c. 企业用作筹资的各种组成成分的比例平均

7. _____普通股成本　　d. 企业股票的预期、要求和实际报酬率，如果赚回，股票市值将不变

进度检查答案

1. b

2. a

3. d

4. c

5. a

6. b

7. d

第4节
流动资产管理

本节内容简介

组织营运资本的基本组成部分是现金、有价证券、应收账款和存货。这节着眼于营运资本和每个组成部分的管理。

营运资本术语

营运资本（或流动资本）通常是指公司在流动（短期）资产账户持有的资金。净营运资本是特指企业流动资产和流动负债的差额。净营运资本衡量企业的当前流动性，显示企业有多少现金可用于维护和发展。取决于企业流动负债的水平，营运资本可能为正或为负。

营运资本管理是指关于企业短期资产和负债的决策。营运资本管理政策通常分为：激进的、保守的或温和的。

- **激进的营运资本管理**

激进的营运资本管理政策专注于高的盈利性潜力，尽管存在高风险和低流动性成本。激进的资产管理导致相对于长期投资，流动资产资本被最小化。激进的筹资政策包括更高水平的低成本短期债务和较多的长期资本投资。虽然这降低了资本成本，但它增加了短期流动性问题的风险。

- **保守的营运资本管理**

保守的营运资本管理政策着重于低风险、低报酬的营运资本投资和筹资。保守的政策在流动资产中放置更高比例的资本，但却以牺牲一些盈利性为代价。

保守政策利用高成本资本但延迟债务本金的偿还，或通过使用权益而完全避开债务。

- **温和的营运资本管理**

温和的营运资本管理政策使用能使资产期限与筹资期限相匹配的风险、报酬和筹资战略。筹资的套期保值法涉及使债务与特定筹资需要的期限相匹配。

管理会计公告4N"营运资本管理：现金资源"中简要指出，有效的营运资本管理对所有企业都是重要的。企业需要审视营运资本管理项目的完整运作来确保下列事项的效率：

- 现金管理——管理现金流入和流出。
- 有价证券管理——管理短期投资和借款组合。
- 应收账款管理——管理现金应收款及其支付。
- 存货管理——将各项库存维持在希望水平上（如原材料、在产品、产成品）。

营运资本管理包括现金和证券管理、应收账款管理、存货管理和短期信贷管理。其目标是使经营周期和现金周期两者最小化。

经营周期是存货库存天数加上应收账款收款期。

现金周期是经营周期减去应付款支付周期。

减少存货库存天数和应收账款收款期，同时使应付款支付周期最大化，可以使两个周期最小化，

随后内容将详细研究这些营运资本的每个组成部分。

现金管理

现金管理描述公司管理和投资现金的各种活动。现金管理的主要目标是尽可能高效地、与企业战略目标和风险管理特点相一致地使用现金。

金融和财务部门涉及现金管理。一起运作时，二者必须确保可以及时获得必要的现金资源以维持企业经营，从原材料和其他资源的购买到这些材料和资源的支付、商品和服务的销售及销售收据的搜集。

影响现金水平的因素

流动性要求和企业盈利性及风险政策是现金水平的主要决定因素。

- **流动性要求**

流动性是指将资产迅速且不遭受损失地转换成现金的能力。企业的现金流入（现金进入）和现金流出（现金支出）很少是同步的——这表示它们的金额和发生的时间不同。企业需要控制净营运资本以避免现金流入和流出的不平衡，并确保足够的流动性。

最终，有效的现金管理系统可以增加公司的整体流动性。随之，增加流动性可以增加盈利性并减少还不起债的风险。

- **盈利性及风险政策**

盈利性一般与流动性反向变化。企业必须确定流动资产投资的最佳水平和支持流动性要求的必要的长短期筹资的恰当组合。这些投资必须考虑盈利性和风险的相互关系及利弊权衡。例如，向卖主提供更宽松的信用条件可能会增加应收账款。因此，公司可能必须出售短期证券，减少现金余额和/或增加从银行借来的短期资金以产生现金流。从另一方面来说，尝试去减少银行账户的闲置现金可能导致交易成本的增加。明显地，债务或权益筹资的最优组合在公司或行业之间可能很不相同。

流动性、盈利性、风险及现金的有效管理需要一个现金管理系统，负责管理日常的：

- 收款——如何从客户或其他付款人手中为企业收回资金。
- 集资——如何集中资金，通过将企业收款系统的存款银行（外地银行）和其他银行的现金移到一个主要的集资银行，使得资金得到最有效的利用。
- 支付——如何将资金从集资银行移到企业的支付银行，以对雇员、卖方、投资者和其他收款人进行支付。
- 银行关系——如何管理与银行和其他金融服务机构的关系。
- 现金预测——如何预测未来现金流并预计潜在的短缺或盈余。
- 信息管理——如何发展和维持用于搜集和分析金融数据的适当的信息系统。
- 投资和借款——如何投资过剩的现金余额和满足短期借款要求。
- 补偿——如何偿付劳动者赚得的工资和其他金融福利。

再一次，根据企业规模和性质的不同，这些经营的情况会有所不同。大型国际公司当然会比只有一台设备的小型国内企业拥有更加复杂的现金管理系统。

持有现金的动机

公司需要充足的财务资源（如，银行里的现金余额和证券，还有额外的信用额度和其他短期借款协议）来维持足够的流动性。企业需要管理流动性的原因一般归纳为受交易性、预防性或投机性动机的驱使。

● 交易性动机

持有现金的交易性动机涉及现金流的非同步性。企业必须有充足的现金储备或近现金储备以满足日常业务运作带来的财务支付（比如，小量购买、雇员赔偿、税收和股利）。

● 预防性动机

持有现金的预防性动机是为非预期的现金需求提供一个缓冲。现金流入和流出的不可预知性意味着企业必须维持现金或近现金余额的充足水平以支付费用。

● 投机性动机

投机性动机涉及盈余流动储备的使用，以利用短期投资或其他可能发生的暂时情形。比如，原材料的价格突然下降，如果利用储备资金购买将能节约一大笔钱。

确保适当水平的流动性使持续的衡量、监督和预测活动成为必要。过剩的和不充足的流动性都有缺点：

● 过剩的流动性可转化为潜在的盈利损失，因为资金的使用没有盈利性。

● 如果必须出售证券，则不充足的流动性会导致多种负面成本，如延迟付款、非预期借款的额外利息，或经纪人和管理成本。最糟糕的情况是，过剩的流动性赤字会导致倒闭破产。

现金流管理

预测数据和包含在现金预算里的财务控制为现金管理提供了一个起点。但是有效的现金管理还涉及与收款、支付和临时性投资的日常活动。

必须管理如下种类的现金流：

● **现金流入**——从客户收来的资金；从银行、出借人和其他财务来源获得的资金；从投资者和其他支付者取得的资金。

● **集中流动**——企业业务单元之间的内部转账和企业为创建流动储备而拥有的各种银行账户间的内部转账。

● **现金流出**——从企业流动储备中支付给公司雇员、卖方、股东和其他收款人的资金。

这些现金流的适时性对维持足够流动性、优化现金资源并管理风险很重要。现金流适时性的挑战在于能够及时满足当前和未来的财务债务，并使无收益的（闲置）现金余额最小化，以可接受的成本借入必要的资金，并控制企业面临的财务风险。

企业通常从缩短现金流入时间和延长现金流出时间来获益。加速应收账款可以使企业更快地获得资金；减慢应付账款为企业提供一个更长的时间框架来利用手头上的钱。自然而然地，两者必须谨慎地管理以保障不会危害卖方和客户关系及企业对供应商和出借人的信用声誉。

企业可以使用各种技术来加速收款并控制支付。

加速现金收款的方法

收款系统是用来处理客户支付和聚集流入现金的系列银行安排和处理程序。

企业的收款系统影响现金流入的适时性。企业一般尝试通过减少收款浮差来加速现金收款。收款浮差是付款人邮寄支票和接受企业可以使用这笔资金之间的时间间隔。

收款浮差有三个组成部分：

- **邮寄浮差**——支票寄出与收款人或处理地点收到支票的时间间隔。
- **处理浮差**——收款人或处理地点收到支票与将支票存入金融机构的时间间隔。
- **取款浮差**——支票存入金融机构与收款资金记入企业账户贷方的时间间隔。

图表 3 - 70 提供了收款浮差的简单示意图。

图表 3 - 70　收款浮差的组成部分

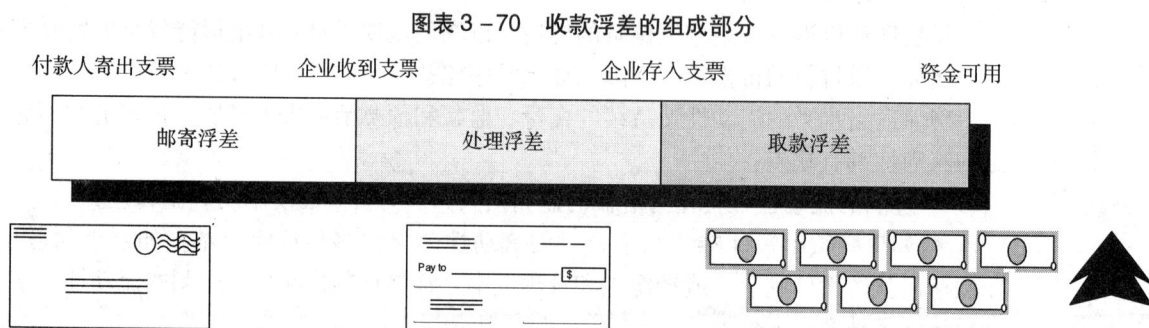

在试图减少收款浮差时，重要的考虑因素包括收款点最理想的数量和地点、是否使用锁箱制度或电子支付系统和如何管理中央集资银行系统。

收款点。根据业务性质，企业通过柜台、邮件和电子方式（通过家庭银行、电讯、个人电脑和互联网）向客户收取付款。总的来说，收款点越多，收款浮差越短，特别是如果收款点和客户很近或靠近联邦储备银行（为了更快地清算支票）。但是，额外的收款点可能会带来更高的经营成本。

锁箱系统。锁箱系统是企业和银行机构之间的一种安排，所有存款都直接由银行接收，并立即存入企业账户。

这种安排为所有汇款设立银行邮政信箱号码，而不是企业地址。锁箱程序对客户是透明的，因为汇款的信封和报表显示了企业名称而不是银行名称。一些企业以锁箱网的形式拥有多个收款地点。

在设置锁箱系统时，企业可以要求银行：

- 影印所有收到的支票。
- 给汇款附上一张支票的影印件。
- 包括随付款一同寄出的信封（通常注明地址变迁）或其他东西。

锁箱系统确保存款在它们被接收的当天处理，这大大减小了处理浮差。邮寄时间浮差和取款时间浮差也可以缩短，这取决于锁箱地点。一旦当天的收据被存入，银行将转寄一张确认存款的小票，而且如果要求，还可以将支票影印件和汇款文件转寄到公司。

锁箱系统的主要缺点是额外的银行服务成本。锁箱系统有固定和变动成本两种。

● **固定锁箱成本**

固定成本包括租借邮政信箱、准备存款、传输汇款数据、余额报告和其他账户维护活动等经常性费用（如，按年或月）。所有固定成本一般都应打包计入每个锁箱维护费。

● **变动锁箱成本**

变动成本的例子包括每一项目的存款和处理费、传输汇款数据费用和影印及缩微拍摄费。

在决定是否使用锁箱系统时，企业需要比较系统的额外成本与从加速资金可用性可能赚得的潜在收益。

锁箱系统的净收益 = 浮差机会成本的减小 + 内部处理成本的减小 - 锁箱处理成本

浮差机会成本是如下项目的函数：

● 所收款项的金额。
● 该项总的收款时间。
● 企业的流动投资或借款利率。

如果收益大于成本，那么锁箱系统是盈利的。

例如：

一家公司正考虑锁箱系统的建议。公司年销售收入 $96 百万（每个月 $8 百万）。年度支票量为 12 000，这批支票的平均金额为 $8 000。支票内部处理成本（假设没有锁箱）为每件 $0.20。公司的年度机会成本为 8%。

一个锁箱的处理器计划每年收取 $8 500 加上每件 $0.45 的处理成本。

没有锁箱

批次	金额	收款浮差天数	总金额
1	$1 400 000	×4 =	$5 600 000
2	4 400 000	×2 =	8 800 000
3	2 200 000	×6 =	13 200 000
总存款	$8 000 000	总浮差成本	$27 600 000
		除以 30 天（日历天数）	$920 000
		年浮差成本（$920 000×0.08）	$73 600

有锁箱

批次	美元金额	收款浮差天数	总金额
1	$1 400 000	×3 =	$4 200 000
2	4 400 000	×1 =	4 400 000
3	2 200 000	×4 =	8 800 000
总存款	$8 000 000	Total Float Cost	$17 400 000
		除以 30 天（日历天数）	$580 000

年浮差成本（$580 000 × 0.08）	$46 400
没有锁箱系统的年浮差成本	$73 600
有锁箱系统的年浮差成本	（$46 400）
锁箱浮差节余	$27 200
固定锁箱成本	（$8 500）
变动锁箱成本（12 000 × $0.45）	（$5 400）
内部处理成本节余（12 000 × $0.20）	$2 400
锁箱的美元净收益	$15 700

　　根据成本/效益分析，考察浮差减少的节余与锁箱成本的权衡，公司的经济效益为 $15 700。

　　电子支付系统。电子支付系统使支付或电子格式的传输更加便利。因为电子系统回避了邮件和人工处理，它们能保证在支付日的资金可得性。在美国，两种主要的电子支付方式是票据自动清算所（ACH）和联邦储备系统电子转账系统。

　　● **票据自动清算所（ACH）**系统提供支票的一种电子备选方案。支付信息以电子方式处理和结算。在美国，联邦储备是 ACH 的主要操作者。增加的可靠性、效率性和成本效益性是主要的优点。ACH 也能传输关于支付的、比支票可能更多的信息。

　　● **联邦储备系统电子转账系统**是联邦储备资金的转账系统。它提供在两个金融机构之间通过他们各自的联邦储备银行账户，进行立即转账资金的实时方式。尽管可靠和安全，使用该系统的费用相对比较昂贵。

　　集资银行系统。集资银行系统系统地将从外地银行和/或锁箱银行收到的存款转账到企业的支付银行，以创造一个以现金方式或为短期信贷、投资交易而持有的流动储备的集中存储。

　　一些银行要求补偿性余额，即保留在该银行的公司存款账户的非无息存款，用于账户服务费用、信用额度或投资。该余额要求可以详细规定为总承诺贷款、承诺贷款中的未使用部分或未清偿借款的百分比。

　　总的来说，集中现金可以减少外地银行的闲置余额，改善对企业现金流入和流出的控制，并促进更有效的投资。自然而然地，会有一些与现金集资系统相关的管理和控制成本。成本应该与其收益的期望值相比较。

减慢付款的方法

　　支付系统是用于向雇员、卖方、供应商、税收机构和其他收款人（如股东和/或债券持有人）支付资金的一系列的银行安排、付款机制和处理程序。

　　企业的支付系统影响现金流出和付款浮差的适时性。付款浮差是付款人寄出支票与资金从付款人账户中扣除之间的时间间隔。

　　付款浮差有三个组成部分。前两个是邮寄浮差和处理浮差，和收款浮差中的两个组成部分一样。在付款浮差中不同的第三个组成部分叫作结算浮差，即收款人存入支票与记入企业账户借方之间的时间间隔。

　　图表 3－71 是付款浮差的一个简单示意图。

图表 3-71　付款浮差的组成部分

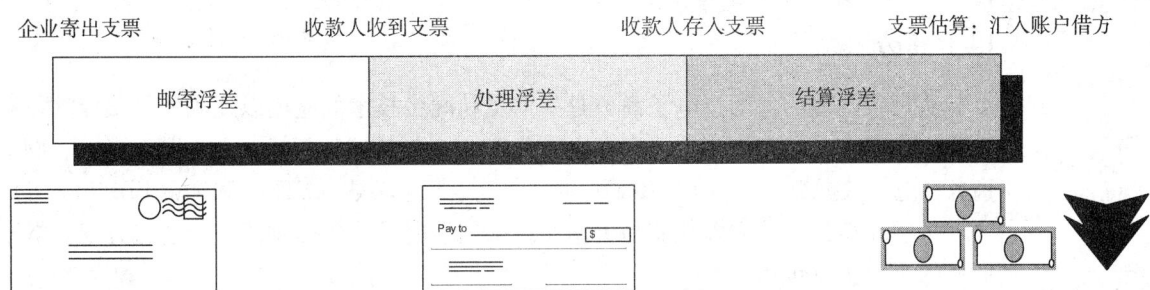

| 企业寄出支票 | 收款人收到支票 | 收款人存入支票 | 支票估算：汇入账户借方 |

邮寄浮差　　处理浮差　　结算浮差

和支付系统相关的一般成本有时间价值成本、过剩余额、交易成本、收款人关系和信息及控制成本。银行和其他机构向公司提供各种服务以帮助控制支付系统成本。特别地，零余额账户系统是企业改善支付程序管理的一个途径。

零余额账户（ZBA）是一个虽然余额保持为零，但企业仍可签发支票的支付账户。从同一银行的一个主账户转账，以补偿任何记入 ZBA 借方的支票。

企业通常在一个主支付账户下，有好几个附属的 ZBAs（比如，用于工资、股利和其他应付款项的单独的 ZBA）。此外，一些 ZBAs 除用于支付外还可以用于收款。拨款偿付是自动的。贷款和借款每天都会进行过账，银行在主账户和 ZBA 之间转账足够资金，以保持 ZBA 的余额为零。

ZBA 系统的优点包括控制账户余额和消除在附属账户中闲置的过剩余额。企业可以更准确地将主账户余额投资到证券上。ZBA 还可以通过提供当地支票签发权同时保持总部资金控制权的方式帮助有若干地址的企业分散应付款项。但是，那些在公司有最终现金管理权的个人必须准确预测支票清算时间并确保主账户有足够储备以补偿相关的 ZBAs。

尽管支付系统的总体目标是及时地、精确地、有成本效益地进行支付，但企业有时会故意尝试减慢支付的清算。集中应付款项和通过汇票的应付款项是减慢支付的两种方法。

集中应付款项。拥有集中应付款项意味着通过一个单一账户（通常是总部或集中处理中心）进行支付。集中支付功能为支票和资金在需要的时候能及时支付提供更有力的保障，而不像分散应付款项系统，有更大过剩余额的可能（同样有增长的转账、协调和管理成本）。

集中过剩现金可以用作贷款偿还或投资。有些情况下，可能通过一个集中账户获得改善了的资金头寸信息，从而使企业因能更久地持有现金而赚得更大的投资报酬。但是，集中应付款项系统要求仔细的监控，以确保延迟付款不会导致现金折扣损失或损害与收款人的关系。

通过汇票的应付款项。通过汇票的应付款项（PTD）是一个付款工具，对付款人而不是付款人的银行签发。不同于普通支票，当 PTD 呈交给银行时不是见票即付的。因此，支付汇票的责任在于签发支票的企业。

当签发人的银行收到支票，银行必须把支票拿给签发人以便最终承兑。那时，企业才存入资金以偿付汇票。使用 PTD 延迟了企业必须有可用资金的时间和允许企业维持较小的银行余额。PTD 的潜在缺点是银行一般征收较高的服务费用和供应商可能更喜欢支票。

电子商务

从现金管理的角度，电子商务是指信息和网络技术的应用以便利贸易伙伴的业务关系。许多格式和交流协议包含在电子商务内，包括因特网、企业内部互联网、网上商务、电子数据交换（EDI）及 EDI 的子集电子资金转账（ETF）和金融 EDI（FEDI）。

虽然北美公司绝大多数交易仍基于纸张，但电子商务提供了一个备选方案。电子商务的主要优点包括：

- 提高生产力，因为它基本上消除了人工处理。
- 减少周期时间。
- 降低错误率。
- 改善现金流预测。
- 改善交流能力。

硬件和软件要求及其相关成本、安全问题、内部人员及贸易伙伴的教育和培训，这些都是实施电子商务的基本考虑因素。如果能恰当地实施和支持，电子商务有利于加强公司与其卖方和客户的关系。

无论复杂还是简单，现金管理系统应该实现下列目标（如 SMA 4N 所列）：

- 加速现金流入。
- 减慢现金流出。
- 最小化闲置现金。
- 最小化与现金流相关的管理成本。
- 与客户和供应商维护良好关系。
- 最小化提供后备流动性的成本。
- 最大化提供给管理人员的财务信息价值。

有价证券管理

公司需要现金以满足持续的财务债务。虽然一些现金储备是谨慎的，但是持有过剩水平的现金涉及几种成本。在银行账户中持有太多闲置的现金不仅带来维护成本，还导致潜在的利息收益损失。这就是为什么公司持有有息有价证券的短期投资组合。

有价证券是在一年或少于一年内到期的投资。通常归类为短期投资（虽然资产负债表会计将初始期限为三个月或三个月以内的证券视为现金等价物、将那些将在一年或少于一年内到期的证券视为短期投资）。

公司为何持有有价证券

具体来说，公司投资有价证券有以下三个主要原因：

- 保持流动性——提供一种准现金（或即时现金）来源，以补偿任何因现金流入不足或不可预见的现金需求而导致的营运资本的不平衡。
- 可控制流出——赚回为可预见的下游现金流出（如利息支付、税收、股利或保险单）而持有的资金的利息。

- 收益的产生——赚回公司没有立即使用的多余现金的利息。

选择有价证券的变量

在投资于有价证券之前，应该仔细考虑如何选择。安全性、适销性、收益、期限和纳税能力都是企业一般评估的特征。

安全性

安全性（本金的保存）是在选择一个证券时的指导性原则和最基本的检验。虽然任何投资都有某种程度的内在风险，但是企业必须评价与证券有关的特定风险，并权衡风险与潜在的财务报酬（或损失）。企业倾向于寻求既安全又有一定水平的收入产生的短期金融工具。

适销性

证券的适销性是指持有人将大量证券在相对快速卖出而不遭受严重价格损失的能力。高适销性是大型二级市场的一个功能。在一个相对不活跃的二级市场的证券被认为流动性较差。

收益

证券的收益（报酬）同利率相关。一些证券提供变动利息，另一些支付固定利率，还有一些（如美国短期国库券）不支付利率但是以折价出售、面值赎回。对于变动利率证券，离到期日时间越长，由于利率变动引起的潜在的价格变动就越大。收益同流动性存在反向关系——证券越流动，收益越低。因此，收益同风险存在正向关系。总之，风险越大，预期报酬越高。

期限

期限是指证券的寿命，它代表了债务清算的日期。到期日各种各样。选择短期证券经常基于企业预测在到期日需要现金。一些证券可能被指定为快速流动，另一些可能被标为不立即使用。

纳税能力

公司应该评价证券的税收含义。企业的有效税率将会决定免税方案的优点和应税投资的税后利率。

有价证券的类型

存在两种主要的债务和权益工具市场：资本市场和货币市场。股票和长期债券（在第 2 节"融资工具"中讨论）在资本市场上买卖。货币市场上交易在一年或一年内到期的短期债务证券。

不像有专门交易所（例如，纽约股票交易所）的资本市场，货币市场是一组市场。货币市场证券的主要发行人是美国政府、外国政府证券经销商、商业票据经销商、银行承兑汇票经销商及其他货币市场专做短期工具的经纪人。

图表3-72提供了各种类型的货币市场证券（大部分来自管理会计公告4M"理解金融工具"和4N"营运资本管理：现金资源"）。

图表3-72 有价证券的种类

工　具	描　述
美国国库券	• 美国财政部的直接债务；以美国政府的信誉作为担保。 • 利率为其他证券提供参考和市场指标。 • 被认为是安全投资，因为它们没有违约风险，在大型二级市场上交易活跃，有较强的适销性。 • 常见类型包括： 　• 短期国库券（T-bills）：没有利息；折价出售、一年内到期、以面值赎回。 　• 中期国库券（T-notes）：按半年计息；有效期为1~10年。 　• 长期国库券（T-bonds）：类似于中期国库券，但是有效期长于10年；一般不会被短期组合购买，除非债券接近到期日。
联邦机构证券（机构证券）	• 有息证券，通常以面值发放和赎回。 • 一般不被美国政府的信用担保，但仍被认为是相当安全的投资和无违约风险。 • 一般比国库券的发行量小；虽不如国库券那么适销但流动性也很强。 • 有限税收；许多可免缴州/地方所得税，但是需缴州特许经销税。
回购协议（再购回协议）	• 从另一方购买证券，通常是银行或同意在特定日期以固定价格买回证券的证券经销商。 • 一般将美国国库券作为原生证券，回购利率会稍低于美国国库券利率。 • 期限有很多种，最短为一夜回购协议。 • 一般被认为是相对安全的投资（因为政府的原生资产）。 • 经常被转移给第三方，以确保如果发行人违约，证券可用于销售。
银行承兑汇票（BAs）	• 本质上是源于商业交易筹资的远期汇票；通常涉及国际贸易。 • 涉及银行承兑的信用证；一般有银行做担保。 • 各种期限和面值。 • 由经销商的活跃的二级市场提供流动性。
商业票据（CP）	• 公司无担保短期贷款。 • 可转让票据但一般持有到期，因为二级市场较弱；一般比类似证券收益高，因为适销性低。 • 期限为1~270天。 • 可以是有息的，也可以是折价发行的；通常折价发行。 • 通常被信用机构评级（例如，穆迪或标准普尔）以帮助投资者评估风险。
拍卖优先股	• 通常是被投资于短期债务工具的其他公司购买的权益。 • 股利率被定期重新制定（通常每7周），以防止价格浮动。 • 如果投资者不想要调整后的利率，他们通常有机会出售股票（除非拍卖过程失败）。 • 有吸引力，因为股利收益的70%免税。
可转让大额存单（CDs）	• 银行或能在货币市场交易的储蓄贷款机构发行的附息存单；一般面值为\$1 000 000。 • 多数期限在1~3个月；有一些可能是几年。 • 有固定和变动利率。 • 如果超过100 000就不能被联邦存款保险公司（FDIC）担保；因此，发行银行应该认真调查。 • 如果由大型现成银行发行，则适销性较高。 • 一般种类有： 　• 欧洲美元CDs，由美国银行和外国银行一般设在伦敦的国外分行发行的面值为美元的CDs。 　• 杨基CDs，外国银行在美国的分行发行的CDs。 　• 储蓄CDs，由储蓄贷款协会、存款银行和信用互助会发行的CDs。

续表

工　具	描　述
欧洲美元存款	<ul><li>一般由美国境外（虽然不必在欧洲）银行持有的不可转换的面值为美元的定期存单；不受美国银行法规约束。</li><li>可以通过多数大型美国银行购买。</li><li>期限从一夜到几年；多数在6个月之内。</li></ul>
短期市政公债	<ul><li>州或地方政府发行。</li><li>两种常见类型：<ul><li>浮动利率的CP工具，利率每周重新设定。</li><li>1~2年到期的长期票据。</li></ul></li><li>短期市政公债有很大的价格稳定性和更好的适销性。</li></ul>

应收账款管理

应收账款是指客户由于公司赊销给自己商品和服务而欠公司的钱。在货物售出、发票寄走后，该项目就被归为应收账款。应收账款被认为是资产负债表上的一项资产。

公司为什么持有应收账款

信用经常被表述销售工具。在决定拓展信用并持有应收账款时，公司会考虑以下因素：

- 总的经济状况
- 目标市场（例如，吸引新客户的必要条件和当前客户的需要）
- 行业惯例（例如，竞争对手提供的信用条件）
- 信用条件下来自利息收入的潜在利润

正如其他流动资产，应收账款要权衡盈利性和风险。拓展信用可以刺激销售和利润。但是一家公司因持有应收账款会产生成本并遭遇潜在的坏账损失。公司必须为应收账款管理实行有效而恰当的政策和程序。

影响公司应收账款管理的一般因素包括：

- 详细的信用政策和销售条款
- 客户信用度评估和客户信用额度确定的条款
- 及时开账单和收回应收账款
- 应收账款准确及时的记录
- 追查过期账户和启动收款程序的条款（如果有必要）

公司信用和应收账款管理活动涉及销售、会计和财务职能部门。

信用条款

信用条款规定了客户收到商品和服务的付款形式和拖延的付款时间以及折扣条款（如果有）。信用期限是指确切到期日（例如，20天、30天）。折扣条款被表述为信用期限和因提前付款而给予的现金折扣。现金折扣是指因提前付款而允许在销售价格上扣减的百分比。例如，25/10 net 30的意思是全部金额在发票日后的30天内到期，但是如果买方在 10 天内付款，就可以得到 25% 的折扣。

常见的公司给予的信用条款如图表 3－73 所示。

图表 3－73　信用展延的类型

形　式	描　述
赊账	• 卖方发票代表买卖双方之间的正式义务，并以应收账款记录该销售。 • 客户收到每笔交易的发票或当期发票的月度报表。 • 按照确定的信用条件和任何折扣，全额付款到期；延迟支付一般要收取费用。 • 包括信用度的定期审查。 • 信用的最常见类型。
分期付款信贷	• 要求客户每月等额偿付，其中包括本金和利息。 • 可能涉及书面合同，详细说明责任条款、信用条款和利率等。 • 经常用于高价值消费品（例如，汽车）。
循环信贷	• 提供持续信贷，而不需要对个人交易进行批准，只要账户状况良好（例如，未清偿的信用低于设定的界线并且支付是短期的）。 • 如果账户过期了，则以该期未清偿的平均金额为基础估计利息费用。
信用证	• 涉及一家银行保证卖方（不是买方）为已达成协议的购买进行支付的信用证工具。 • 买方一般支付开设信用证的费用。 • 通常用于进出口贸易。

延展信用期限和改变折扣条款能影响与应收账款相关的盈利性和风险。明确的公式可用于计算信用期限和现金折扣的改变所产生的影响。以下内容总结了一般概念。

● **延展信用期限**

企业如果预期提高销售收入会带来盈利性的提高，则它会延展信用期限。考虑下面的情景：一家企业将信用条款从 net 30 改为 net 60；信用期限从一个月提高到两个月。更加宽松的信用条款激励了额外的销售。但是延展的信用期限随着客户减慢了支付速度而给企业带来额外的持有成本。

在拓展信用期限时，企业必须比较额外销售带来的盈利与额外应收账款导致的机会成本。如果提高的销售利润超过用额外应收账款进行投资的要求报酬，则改变信用期限是值得的。

● **改变折扣条款**

企业提供现金折扣或改变现有折扣以试图加速应收账款的支付。考虑下面的情景：一家企业现在的收款期平均为 60 天，不提供现金折扣。企业决定提供 2/10、net 45 的折扣条款。一个月后，企业 70% 的客户（美元金额）利用了该现金折扣。

在改变折扣条款时，企业必须确定提高的收款速度是否抵消了提供折扣的成本。如果加速收款的机会成本大于折扣成本，折扣是值得的；如果节余不能抵消现金折扣，折扣就不是一个好办法。

违约风险

曾有个说法认为应收账款顶多像其被偿付的可能性那样好。坏账一般是指应收账款回收缓慢和应收账款的违约部分。当客户不能履行责任条款时，违约就发生了。违约风险是一家公司（一个人）不能偿付债务的利息或本金的风险。

为使违约风险最小化，企业需要设定并维持信用展延、开账单和收款的信用标准。申请人信用信息可以从内外部来源获取。

一般内部信用信息的来源是：

- 申请人完成的信用申请。
- 申请人完成的协议表格。
- 企业与申请人打交道的以往记录（例如，支付历史）。

信用信息的外部来源包括：

- 财务报表——检查审计过的（或未审计的）财务报表和能与行业平均值作比较的相关比率。
- 贸易参考——就其他公司与申请人的实际支付经历联系其他公司。
- 银行和其他领先者——搜寻关于申请人财务状况和可用信用的标准化信用信息。
- 机构——地方或国家机构对于大多数公司的信用史的报告。

有助于最佳信用/收款政策的因素

信用和收款政策涉及对买方信用度的评估、延展的信用期限和要求的收款程序水平。最起码，信用和收款政策获得的收益应该等于它们花费的成本。

为使信用和收款政策的盈利性最大化，一家公司需要变化这些政策。基于信用标准、信用条款和收款支出的最好的可能组合，可以得到最佳方案。通常，存在如下关系：

- 在没有信用标准时，销售收入最大化，但经常被巨额坏账、收款成本和巨额应收账款持有成本所抵消。
- 随着信用标准越发严格，销售收入下降，但平均收款期和坏账损失也下降。
- 随着信用标准越发严格，利润提高到最高点后下降。

平均收款期

平均收款期是指企业用于收回应收账款的平均时间。

下面的比率用于确定平均收款期：

平均收款期 = 365 天/应收账款周转率

算出的比率表明应收账款收回前未清偿的平均天数。

考虑一家企业应收账款周转率为 6.25 的例子：

平均收款期 = 365 天/6.25 = 58 天

为了进一步理解平均收款期，将此度量值与行业均值和提供的信用条款相比较。

与行业均值比较提供了一个相对度量值。例如，如果行业周转率中值是 8.1，平均行业收款期是 45 天（365 天/8.1），则二者存在 13 天的差距。

比起行业均值，58 天平均收款期的好坏更多取决于信用条款。如果信用条款是 30 天，则 58 天的平均收款期将会成为关注的原因。它可能表明对客户的信用调查不充分、较差的信用管理和过期账户的收回过慢。然而，如果信用条款是 60 天，则 58 天表明情况良好，因为只要信用条款允许大多数客户倾向于保留付款。

由此，销售收入和信用条款的改变将会改变平均收款期。例如，销售收入的提高和应收账款投资的降低会提高应收账款周转率（赊销收入/应收账款）。因此，平均收款期降低。

应收账款回收天数

应收账款回收天数（DSO）是度量应收账款的另一种方法。DSO 用特定时期期末的未清偿应收账款除以该期的平均日赊销额计算。

例如：

一家公司汇编了如下应收账款和信用信息：

- 第 3 月月末的未清偿应收账款 = \$155 000
- 信用条款 = net 60
- DSO 平均期限 = 3 个月（90 天）
- 赊销收入历史

1 月 = \$40 000

2 月 = \$50 000

3 月 = \$65 000

平均日赊销额 = (\$40 000 + \$50 000 + \$65 000)/90 = \$1 722.22

DSO = 未清偿应收账款/平均日赊销额

DSO = \$155 000/ \$1 722.22 = 90 天

平均过期 = DSO – 平均的信用条款天数

平均过期 = 90 天 – 60 天 = 30 天

DSO 为企业整体收款效率提供了度量方法。它算出的数字可以与信用政策或历史趋势相比较。在使用 DSO 时要注意它可能被销售量不断改变的趋势或强烈的季节销售波动歪曲。

存货管理

理解存货管理要求对基本存货控制术语有一个了解：

- 存货是指公司储存的所有商品，代表了以备将来使用的供应量。
- 存货清单是指存货中所有项目的列表。
- 项目是指保持在存货中的一种产品；项目是存货中的一个分录。
- 单位指存货项目的标准大小或数量。

按照这些定义，存货控制和存货管理的概念可以解释为：

- 存货控制是指确保存货中每一项数目正确的一系列活动和程序。
- 存货管理是指确定和维持存货要求水平的程序，该水平可确保客户订货能按时地恰当满足。

公司为什么持有存货

存货控制涉及平衡冲突的成本——平衡为提供特定水平客户服务而持有充足存货的成本与用完存货及损失销售的成本。这些成本的交叉点为许多存货控制问题提供了答案，如存什么货、应何时下订单、应订购多少等。

从某种程度上说，每一家公司都持有存货。但是持有存货花费很大，因为有储存处理成本、存货过时风险及与占用资本有关的成本。当资本被占用时，企业必须为了投资而放弃其他盈利机会。这些持有存货的劣势和成本引出了公司为什么要持有存货的问题。

简单地说，存货为供求之间提供了缓冲。但持有存货还有另外很多原因，包括：

- 覆盖供求率的错配。
- 为超过预期和意料之外的客户需求提供充分服务。
- 覆盖延迟的或不充足的供应商送货。
- 购买中的经济实惠（如大宗订单的价格折扣或当价格较低并预期会上升时购买的节省）。
- 生产中的经济实惠。
- 保持持续水平的经营。
- 覆盖紧急事件。

总之，只有当收益超过持有额外存货的成本时，存货水平才应该提高。

经济订货量

经济订货量（EOQ）是存货控制中的经典分析，它定义了订单规模、项目需求量及相关成本之间的关系。

确定 EOQ，需回答以下两个问题：

- 应该订购多少？
- 每年应该下多少次订单？

EOQ 代表了最佳订货规模——在某时点购入定期订购项目的数量，该数量导致总成本最小，即订货和储存成本最小。

- **订货成本**

订货成本包括支付给采购部门雇员的补偿、准备订单的计算机时间的成本、用于产生采购订单的供应成本。

签发订单越频繁，订购过程的成本越大。订货成本（每单）和订货数量（每单数量）间的一般关系如图表 3－74 中的图（a）所示。由此可见，一次订购更多数量以使订货成本最小是有道理的。

- **储存成本**

储存成本（也称持有成本）包括储存处理成本、过时和变坏成本、保险、税收、存货占用资金成本。储存成本随着订单规模的增长而增长，随着订货数量的减少而减少。

图表 3－74 中的图（b）描述了储存成本（每单）和订购量（每单数量）之间的关系。

当把订货成本和储存成本同需求量联系起来时，就可以确定经济订货量了。图表 3－74 中的图（c）阐明了 EOQ。

图表3-74　EOQ与订货成本、储存成本、订货数量间的关系

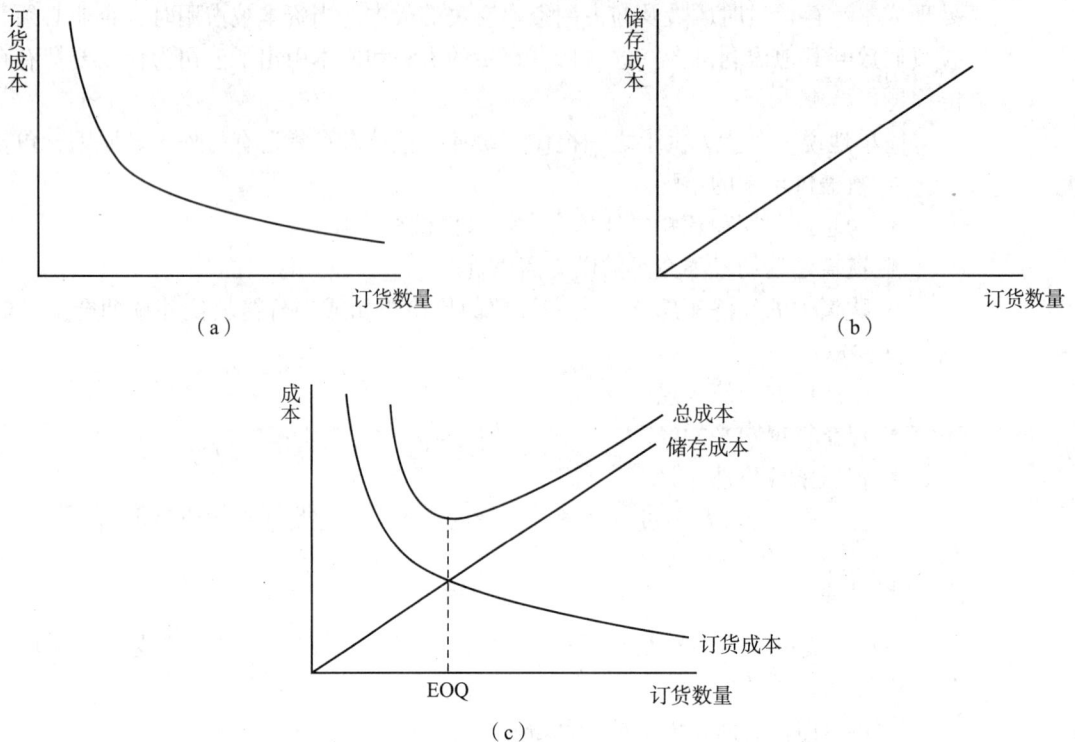

EOQ 公式是：

$$EOQ = \sqrt{\frac{2FD}{C}}$$

式中：

- F 表示每单的固定订货成本。
- D 表示需要的总存货量。
- C 表示每存货单位的储存（持有）成本。

如果持有成本降低，则 EOQ 提高。如果需要的总存货量或每单固定订货成本降低，则 EOQ 也降低。

EOQ 基于以下假设：

- 前置时间固定且已知。
- 需求以相对稳定且已知的速率发生。
- 经营和储存成本已知。
- 补充及时；没有脱销。

EOQ 原则还可用于待生产项目的数量。

例如，假设财务计算器的制造者每年使用某项目 10 000 单位。它的订货成本是每单 $75，储存成本是每年每单位 $1.50。则 EOQ 为：

$$EOQ = \sqrt{\frac{2(10\,000)(\$75)}{\$1.50}} = \sqrt{1\,000\,000} = 1\,000 \text{ units}$$

如果公司每年使用 10 000 单位，则它的 EOQ 是 1 000，公司将会每年订货 10 次

（10 000/1 000）。

虽然被广泛使用，EOQ 也有以下弱点：

- 假设有时是不现实的、不准确的；所有相关因素（需求、前置时间、成本）都完全已知的条件是很少见的。
- 计算是基于估计的成本和预计的需求。
- 在生产准备成本很高的制造环境中，巨量会导致过剩的能力和存货。
- 过大的能力会使过多资本占用在存货上

前置时间和安全存货的影响

实际上，补充不会瞬间完成，当脱销发生时，它们一般会产生许多相关成本。在零售或服务环境中，短缺能导致因销售损失、商誉损失、未来销售损失、声誉损失引起的利润下降。在制造过程中，生产中断可能意义重大、成本高昂，范围从重定计划到员工临时解雇、高价紧急订货再到供货商专门发货。

这些短缺问题可以通过缩短前置时间和持有安全存货被最小化或者被避免。

前置时间

前置时间是指下达订单与存货入库待用之间的时间。前置时间因一些原因而不同。有效的存货管理试图通过缩短以下时间，来缩短前置时间：

- 订单准备（收集订单信息和准备订单的时间）。
- 将订单交给供应商（通过电报、电讯或邮件将订单送抵供应商的时间）。
- 供应商对订单的处理和完成。
- 供应商送出订货。
- 处理发货（将项目入库）。

安全存货

安全存货（或缓冲存货）一般是指计划并以存货形式持有的、用以抵御供求波动或防止生产预测错误和/或短期订货改变的存货量。

EOQ 分析是基于需求和前置时间已知的理论假设，安全存货使用的是涉及概率的模型。安全存货分析试图处理存货系统中的不确定性，特别是需求和前置时间在现实世界中的不确定性。

确定需要保持的安全存货量涉及对脱销的概率和成本同避免这种可能性而持有充足存货的成本进行平衡。可以使用专门的计算（超出本书范围）。但是下面是一些普遍应用的概念：

- 预测的需求量越不确定，企业可能越愿意考虑持有更多的安全存货。
- 补给脱销的前置时间越不确定，企业可能越想保持更多的安全存货。

安全存货分析考虑了与脱销有关的所有成本。但是最后的因素是持有额外存货的成本和占用营运资本的利息收益损失。如果不考虑这些成本和盈利投资损失，企业理论上会持有充足的安全存货以防止脱销发生。

适时制系统和看板

本书第 1 章第 2 节 "生产范式" 中介绍了适时制系统和看板的基本原则。这些概念在存货控制中也适合。

JIT 系统的根本目标是通过用最少的原料、设备、操作人员等满足生产目标，以使生产营运过程中的浪费最少。通过只是在需要时才完成所有操作的方式可以达到这一目标。看板是简单的手工控制方法，可同 JIT 一起确保所有原料确实能够在需要时及时到位。

EOQ 和 JIT/看板之间存在一些相似之处。例如，二者都会监督存货水平和为补货下固定数量订单。然而，主要不同是，在 JIT 和看板中，活动将存货降低到再订货水平，补货只在每次退货后才发生。选择 EOQ 还是 JIT 要取决于公司的具体因素。

JIT 和看板系统只是看似简单。它们的有效执行要求仔细的评估和规划。但是当 JIT 和看板被很好地设计和恰当地应用时，它们能大大降低原材料和在产品存货。随之，这些降低可通过以下方面转换成额外的成本节约：

- 减少必需的生产和仓储空间。
- 降低财产和管理费用。
- 降低存货投资。

最后，JIT 和看板能导致营运资本的更有效使用。

进度检查

提示：完成以下各题，参考答案随后给出。

1. 持有现金的交易动机可最好地描述为：（　　）

   a. 使用过剩流动储备以利用短期投资或其他暂时情况

   b. 使现金流入和流出同步，由此将多余的现金余额投资到短期工具上

   c. 为因现金流入和流出的不可预测性而产生的不可预期的现金需求提供缓冲

   d. 保持充足现金或类现金储备以满足正常业务经营所产生的财务支付

2. 下面哪种技术不会加速收款？（　　）

   a. 锁箱制度

   b. ACH 和联邦储备系统电子转账系统处理

   c. 通过汇票的应付款项

   d. 现金集资银行系统

连线——有价证券与特点。

3. 联邦机构证券　　　　　　a. 银行或能在货币市场交易的储蓄贷款机构发行的附息存款

4. 商业票据　　　　　　　　b. 源自商业贸易筹资的定期汇票

5. 银行承兑汇票　　　　　　c. 相对安全的投资，没有违约风险

6. 可转让大额存单　　　　　d. 通常由投资短期债务工具的其他公司购买的权益

7. 拍卖优先股　　　　　　　e. 公司发行的非担保短期贷款

8. 企业想从延长信用期限中获得的主要收益是：

   a. 提高的盈利性源自增加的销售收入

b. 提高的收入来自过期账户的利息费用

c. 过期账户必要的收款程序减少

d. 相对稳定的需求带来的改善的存货控制

9. 下面哪项准确地表达了经济订货量（EOQ）和安全存货原则的特点？（　　　）

a. 二者都主张将存货降低到预定的再订货水平

b. EOQ 分析假设需求和前置时间完全已知；安全存货使用涉及概率的模型

c. EOQ 分析和安全存货都假设需求可变但前置时间完全已知

d. 二者的前提都是没有存货控制确定性的正确度量

进度检查答案

1. d
2. c
3. c
4. e
5. b
6. a
7. d
8. a
9. b

第5节
流动资产筹资

本节内容简介

短期筹资是指期限在一年或一年以内的债务工具的使用。组织从事短期筹资有一些原因：

- 确保充足流动性以满足立即的现金需求。
- 为流动资产（如应收账款和存货）筹资。
- 使借款利息成本最小化。
- 使不能偿付的风险最小化。
- 通过评估各种短期借款方案使财务弹性最大化。

当为流动资产筹资时，公司理解短期信用选择权的财务影响是很重要的。企业可以从几个不同的短期借款选择权中选择。市场状况和涉及的风险会影响决策。产生最低成本的方法是最受欢迎的。尤其地，流动负债是许多小型企业筹资的一个重要来源。

短期信用的类型

企业通常用如下两种方式之一满足短期借款需求：

- 通过金融中介筹集外部资金（例如，通过银行和金融机构或通过在货币市场投资）。
- 发行商业票据。

大多数企业依靠金融中介完成贷款职能。

有几种短期信用安排是可能的，包括：

- 应计费用。
- 商业信用。
- 无担保短期银行贷款（信用额度和循环信贷）。
- 担保短期贷款（担保应收账款和担保存货）。
- 商业票据。
- 银行承兑汇票。

每项的简要介绍附后。

应计费用

应计费用代表企业尚未支付工资、税收、利息、股利而欠的金额。最常见的应计费用是工资和税收。

应计费用被认为是无息筹资的自发来源。企业可以使用流动资金满足立即的现金需求，一直到应计费用到期支付为止。在这方面，应计费用必须谨慎使用。

商业信用

商业信用是当供应商赋予客户购买时的信用条款时产生的短期筹资的来源。商业信用经常是小型企业短期信用的最大来源。

商业信用代表附有以下条款的间接贷款：

- 卖方根据事先约定条款提供商品。
- 信用出现在卖方账簿的应收账款以及客户账簿的应付账款。
- 信用代表了客户可以一直保持到最后支付期的现金。

赊账（卖方给予买方特定的期间去偿还商品和服务）是最常见的商业信用形式。

注意：赊账条款在本章第 4 节"流动资产管理"的应收账款信用条款中已介绍。

无担保短期银行贷款

无担保短期银行贷款是银行信用的一种形式，它没有特定担保品或资产进行担保。这种贷款的达成是以借方的财务健全性和信用度为基础的。

无担保短期银行贷款是在银行和企业之间磋商而成的。贷款协议规定了贷款条款（例如，应付利息、支付条款、到期日等）。借款人签订期票作为正式的义务，并依据规定条款偿还贷款。

无担保短期银行贷款通常被认为自行清算，即公司用贷款购买的资产或持有的流动资产将产生充足的现金流来偿还贷款。例如，无担保短期银行贷款是对应收账款或存货进行季节性筹资的流行工具。

信用额度和循环信贷是为企业提供快速稳定的短期融资来源的两种无担保贷款。

信用额度

信用额度是指允许企业在特定时期、确定额度范围内借款的协议。借款人可以在信用额（一般是大额的）内借款，但是只需为实际借款额支付利息。

在信用额度内借款是通过专门的短期票据进行的。在同一信用额度内可以发行一系列短期票据。短期票据的期限多种多样；一般来讲，票据期限从一夜到 90 天不等（尽管有一些可能更长）。

信用额度技术上被设定为一定期限（通常是一年），但是大多数可以在到期时持续续借。许多信用额度可以维持几年有效。

循环信贷

循环信贷（也被称为循环贷款或循环信贷协议）允许企业在一定额度内借钱、还钱、再借钱。循环信贷的信用条款类似于信用额度。虽然循环信贷经常被用于短期借款，但是期限经常更长（2 ~ 5 年）。

担保短期贷款

担保短期贷款（或以资产为基础的借款）是以抵押资产做担保品为基础的一种信用形式。应收账款和存货是用于这种担保贷款的最常见的资产；设备、不动产或其他有形资产有时也会被用作担保品。

担保应收账款

在这种协议中，出借人会花时间评估借款人企业；客户购买量、客户付款的及时性、拖欠债务比率以及坏账冲销数量都要被考虑。

基于该评估，可以确定贷款率，被表示为未清偿应收账款的百分数。然后，此百分数可用到抵押应收账款金额上，从而确定借款的最大额度。当贷款生效时，借款人的客户一般直接向出借人付款，出借人再将它们用到未清偿的贷款余额。

担保存货

类似于应收账款筹资，信贷金额受贷款率限制，并表示为存货的百分数。贷款率也考虑了借款人可能卖不掉存货的风险（因为市场状况改变、商品价格浮动、存货过时或损坏）。

一般来说，出借人更愿意以原材料和制成品作抵押，而不是在产品。有时，一些出借人可能为不同的存货计算不同的贷款率。一般而言，存货的贷款率大大小于应收账款的贷款率。

商业票据

商业票据（CP）是由公司发行的无担保期票。CP 低于面值折价出售，并且公司承诺在到期日按面值买回。

主要的信用评级机构通常为特定发行人的商业票据评级。商业票据一般面值为 $100 000。对于公开发行，期限从一夜到 270 天不等。一些私下发行的期限可能长于 270 天。

CP 利率多种多样。该利率是以市场为基础的，是发行公司的信用等级、发行规模和总体市场短期利率的函数。

大多数 CP 通过经销商出售（投资银行机构或商业银行）。一些公司可能直接将 CP 出售给投资人。

一般来说，短期筹资中 CP 的应用：

- 为以低于其他方法的利率借到更多的资金提供广阔的范围。
- 允许借款人避开维持商业银行补偿性余额的费用。
- 推广借款人的名字，因为广泛的市场，借款人的名字变得更加广为人知。

银行承兑汇票

银行承兑汇票（BA）是可转让短期工具，主要为进出口商品筹资。一些银行承兑汇票的发行可以用于易销商品的国内发货和储存。

BA 是指由借款人开据且经银行承兑的定期汇票。承兑汇票意味着银行承担了到期支付汇票的责任。

BA 易于销售，并经常在货币市场上折价。借款人作为预收款收到折价收入，有义务在到期时偿还全部汇票金额给承兑银行。承兑银行向购买 BA 的投资者付款。

短期信用成本最小化

对借款人来说，不同的短期信用选择权有不同的成本。本章特别关注短期筹资的三种成本：

- 没有利用以商业信用提供的现金折扣而导致的成本。
- 与无担保短期银行贷款有关的实际年利率。
- 与担保短期银行贷款有关的应收账款代理成本。

以商业信用提供的现金折扣

商业信用代表企业可以一直投资到特定偿还日期的现金（例如，30、60、90 天）。付款期越长，企业能够使用资金的时间越长。

企业节约下来的短期筹资成本金额取决于信用天数。例如，如果要使用价值 $100\ 000 的信用 30 天，而不是以 2% 的成本借 $100\ 000，企业将节省 $2\ 000（$100\ 000 \times 0.02）。

企业提供商业信用以促进销售。提供折扣以激励客户提前还款，并降低持有应收账款的成本。客户必须权衡折扣和使用商业信用选择权的利弊，然后决定接受折扣、提前还款是否有利。一般而言，企业会接受折扣以节约成本，而并非将信用延续到原定的支付日期。

确定放弃折扣的机会成本的公式是基于如下年利率（365 天）计算的：

$$EID = \frac{DR}{1-DR} \times \frac{365}{N-DP}$$

其中：

- EID = 放弃商业信用折扣的实际年利率。
- DR = 折扣率。
- N = 净付款期。
- DP = 折扣期。

考虑以下情景：

信用条款是 2/10 net 30。接受现金折扣的实际年利率是：

$$EID = \frac{0.02}{1-0.02} \times \frac{365}{30-10}$$

$$= 37.24\%$$

如果企业能够在其他地方以低于 37.24% 的利率借到资金，它应该这样做并且接受商业信用提前付款的折扣。然而，如果超过 37.24%，企业可能想要延迟付款直至明确的到期日。

实际年利率

银行对无担保短期银行贷款收取利息。它们一般征收承诺费，也可能收取补偿性余额。

- **利息率**

收取的利率是由加到诸如优惠利率、英国银行家协会（BBA）伦敦同业拆放利率（LIBOR）、美国短期国库券联邦利率等基准利率上的差额构成的。在确定利率时，银行评估客户偿还贷款的能力。收取的利率反映了银行对贷款风险的评价。利率通常是变动的，并根据基准利率的变化进行调整。

- **承诺费**

除了利息，银行经常对持有信用额度和循环信贷的借款人收取承诺费。承诺费是额度或额度未使用部分的百分数。

- **补偿性余额**

一些银行也可能要求补偿性余额。补偿性余额规定银行要求借款人将贷款的百分数保留在不赚取利息或抵消其他服务费用的存款上。补偿性余额可以具体表示为总承诺、承诺未使用的部分或未清偿借款的百分数。

承诺费和补偿性余额有效地降低了借款人能够使用的资金数量。同时，它们也提高了贷款的实际年利率。换句话说，实际年利率高于银行报价的初始利率。

实际年利率的公式是：

$$EI = \left(\frac{PR + CF}{1 - CB}\right)\left(\frac{365}{M}\right)$$

其中：

- EI = 实际利率。
- PR = 本金利息费（％）。
- CB = 补偿性余额（％）。
- CF = 承诺费（％）。
- M = 贷款天数。

考虑以下情景：

企业协商了一年期利率为 12％ 的 $1 000 000 贷款。承诺费是总额的 0.25％，补偿性余额是额度的 10％。

$$EI = \left(\frac{0.12 + 0.0025}{1 - 0.10}\right)\left(\frac{365}{365}\right) = \left(\frac{0.1225}{0.9}\right) = 13.6\%$$

报价利率是 12％，但是企业实际支付的实际年利率是 13.6％。

应收账款代理成本

应收账款代理业务是指将担保短期贷款的应收账款出售或转让给第三方（应收账款代理商）。应收账款代理商是负责应收账款筹资和管理的公司。

应收账款代理商代理的应收账款由代理商和客户间的合同监管。应收账款代理商检查账户信用并收取应收账款的百分之几作为佣金，具体数额取决于应收账款的金额和质量以及客户整体的财务稳健情况。应收账款代理商也收取利息，利息经常是变动的。

应收账款代理商在客户不能偿还贷款时可以对抵押资产进行清算。为了保护自己免受违约风险，应收账款代理商通常对应收账款的当前价值进行"削价"。使用削价为应收账款代理商提供了缓冲。如果应收账款代理商不得不以令人痛惜的价格出售资产，应收账款代理商仍然还有收回违约贷款金额的机会。

考虑以下情景：

应收账款的面值是 $200 000。削价 15％，总费用（利息费和佣金）是 $30 000。

对于借款企业，该贷款的收入是 $140 000。

　$170 000　应收账款面值 × 削价 t

　　　　　　[$200 000 × (1 - 15％)]

　$30 000　总费用

$140 000　贷款收入

在一些情况下，应收账款代理商协议对于客户是透明的，客户会继续支付给企业，然后，企业再签单付款给应收账款代理商。在另外一些情况下，客户被通知转让，不得不直接对应收账款代理商进行支付。大多数协议没有追索权，即出售公司对于应收账款代理商不能收到的任何应收账款不负责任。

应收账款代理协议也可用于存货。但因为存货是流动性最差的流动资产，削价更高，要求有信托收据。信托收据允许借款人出售存货中的商品并将收入汇给应收账款代理商。

筹资的期限匹配或套期保值法

正如第1节所提到的："风险和报酬、期限匹配是通过将公司资产和负债的期限匹配以对冲风险的营运资本管理方法。"因此，公司试图用短期筹资为短期项目提供资金，用长期资产为长期项目提供资金。

套期保值是降低价格、利率或汇率的不利波动带来的风险的一种方法。公司通过利用另一种投资工具的冲销头寸来对一项投资进行套期保值。

将资本投资到国外业务中的根本原因一般是渴望获得超过要求的报酬。另外的影响因素包括：

- **投资于国际市场缺口**

国内市场可能提供的只是正常的报酬率，跨越不同市场的国际投资可以提供赚取超额报酬的独特机会。

- **降低经营成本**

通过进入外国市场可能得到更低的劳动力成本和其他成本效率。

- **保证必需的原材料**

公司缺少充足的原材料，故在国外投资以获取它们。考虑一下，矿产公司和石油公司怎样到国外经营以确保必需的经营资源。

在国际市场、生产设备和原材料的投资都能帮助企业获得比仅靠国内活动更高的报酬率。

国际机会的一些主要风险包括：

- **税收**

由于不同的税法和对国外投资的不同待遇，税收变得复杂。美国政府对国际经营企业征税不同于国内企业。个别国家对外国公司在本国经营业务的所得征税。

- **政治风险**

应该仔细考虑许多国家从轻度干预经营到征用的政治不稳定的可能性。

- **汇率风险**

根本风险来自汇率的变化。三种专门的汇率风险是外币折算风险、交易风险和经济风险。

折算风险同汇率变化的会计处理有关。当资产和负债从国外经营转换为母公司货币时，可能产生会计利得或损失。

当结算一项专门的国外交易，如买卖外国产品或结算无条件信用证条款时产生的利得或损失就是交易风险。

经济风险是因汇率的不可预测变化导致的公司价值的变化。经济风险是预期未来现金流的函数。

期限匹配和套期保值是企业用来管理外汇风险的两种方法。虽然超出本书的范围，但是许多期限匹配战略和套期保值活动大量存在，企业能用它们来抵消汇率变动带来的损失风险。

进度检查

提示：完成以下各题，参考答案随后给出。

连线——短期信用安排与特点。

1. 应计费用　　　　　　　　a. 以信用额度和循环信贷为例的磋商成交的协议

2. 商业信用　　　　　　　　b. 主要用于为进出口商品筹资的可转让短期工具

3. 无担保短期银行贷款　　　c. 基于贷款率的贷款；一般表示为应收账款或存货的百分数

4. 担保短期贷款　　　　　　d. 供应商和客户之间针对购买的间接贷款

5. 商业票据　　　　　　　　e. 用于满足现金需求的自发无息筹资，当到一定额度时它们就到期需要支付

6. 银行承兑汇票　　　　　　f. 公司发行并以折价出售的无担保期票

7. 利率8%，承诺费25%，补偿性余额10%的$5 000 000贷款的实际年利率为多少？（　　　）

    a. 8%

    b. 8.64%

    c. 9.17%

    d. 11.11%

进度检查答案

1. e

2. d

3. a

4. c

5. f

6. b

7. c

第4章
决策分析

本章内容简介

决策制定对于每个组织来说都是一项关键活动。在任何企业中，每天都要作出各种各样的决策。决策在规模上有大小之分，也可分为单个决策或集体决策。更进一步的，从决策涉及的资源以及财务影响来分，给定的决策可以产生短期或是长期的结果。

管理会计师经常被要求提供用于决策制定的关键数据。本章概述了管理会计师需要知道的关于决策制定过程、相关的成本和收入数据的重要性、本—量—利及边际分析的运用以及成本基础定价法的应用的基本信息。

学习要点说明

注册管理会计师（CMA）考试包含很多学习要点，这些学习要点由管理会计师协会确定。学习要点描述了注册管理会计师考试要求掌握的所有知识点和技能，并且细分为各个章节。注册管理会计师考试教材解释了学习要点所包含的各个部分，是对学习要点的有力支持。学习要点可以帮助考生以不同的方式或通过不同的问题情景理解这些概念。考生还应该练习学习要点中所提到的全部或者部分计算，或者完成计算过程中的缺失部分。学习要点不能代替对 CMA 考试教材内容的研究和学习，但是可以确保考生达到学习要点所设定的目标。

注册管理会计师教材中所包含的学习要点是一个完整的集合，并且是到目前为止最新的版本。考生可以浏览 IMA 的官方网站 www. imanet. org，点击"认证"部分查看和下载关于学习要点的最新 PDF 文件。

学习要点

4.1 决策过程

- LOS 4.1.1：确认并说明对于达成决策所需步骤的理解，即：（i）获取并分析信息；（ii）确定备选的行动过程；（iii）对未来场景作出预测；（iv）选择并验证一项备选方案；（v）实施决策；（vi）评价业绩以提供反馈。
- LOS 4.1.2：说明对于经理应如何评价决策结果的理解。

4.2 相关数据概念

- LOS 4.2.1：区分收入与成本的经济学概念和会计学概念。
- LOS 4.2.2：定义相关收入（预期未来收入）和相关成本（预期未来成本）。
- LOS 4.2.3：识别和确认成本性态类型、成本可溯性和成本相关性，其中成本相关性与有待决策的各种成本对象有关。
- LOS 4.2.4：说明对价值链中出现的各种成本以及这些用来决策（如定价、备选的经营选择权、合约谈判和外包决策）的成本的组成部分的理解。
- LOS 4.2.5：区分在决策制定过程中出现的可避免和不可避免的成本。
- LOS 4.2.6：将相关成本确认为备选行动过程中的增量成本、边际成本和差异成本等，并在给定数据的条件下计算相关成本。
- LOS 4.2.7：定义沉没成本，解释为什么该成本是不相关的。
- LOS 4.2.8：区分用数字衡量的定量因素，包括：（a）财务的（例如，直接人工成本）；（b）非财务的（例如，新产品研发时间的缩短）；
- LOS 4.2.9：将定性因素定义为不能用数字来衡量的结果（例如，雇员的道德水平）。
- LOS 4.2.10：说明机会成本的理解，即因为没有最好地利用一种有限资源而放弃的对收益的贡献。
- LOS 4.2.11：说明所得税对于决策制定过程中相关收入和成本数据的影响。

4.3 本—量—利分析

- LOS 4.3.1：说明对以下项目的理解：当产出水平、销售价格、单位变动成本或固定成本发生变化时，本—量—利（CVP）分析（也称盈亏平衡分析）是如何用来审查总收入、总成本和营业利润行为的。
- LOS 4.3.2：区分关于产出水平的固定成本和变动成本。
- LOS 4.3.3：说明对与相关范围产出有关的总收入和总成本的理解。
- LOS 4.3.4：解释为什么固定成本与变动成本的分类受所考虑的期限影响。
- LOS 4.3.5：说明对如何将单位边际贡献用于 CVP 分析的理解。
- LOS 4.3.6：计算单位边际贡献和总边际贡献。
- LOS 4.3.7：计算达到目标营业利润和目标净利润时盈亏均衡点的销售数量和销售金额。
- LOS 4.3.8：说明对单位销售组合变化如何影响多种产品情况下的营业利润的理解。
- LOS 4.3.9：说明对多种产品情况下没有惟一盈亏平衡点的原因的理解。
- LOS 4.3.10：分析并推荐一个使用 CVP 分析的行动过程。
- LOS 4.3.11：说明对所得税对 CVP 分析的影响的理解。

4.4 边际分析

- LOS 4.4.1：展示熟练运用边际分析进行如下决策：（a）引入一个新产品还是改变现存产品的产出水平；（b）接收还是拒绝特别订单；（c）制造还是购置产品或服务；（d）销售产品还是实施额外程序以出售更增值的产品；（e）增加还是削减一个部门。
- LOS 4.4.2：将相关信息确认为未来收入和未来成本，而这些收入或成本在任何一种边际分析中都会因决策不同而不同。
- LOS 4.4.3：解释为什么在边际决策分析中任何不因方案不同而不同的成本（包括已分摊的成本）都应该被忽略。
- LOS 4.4.4：说明对边际分析中机会成本的理解。
- LOS 4.4.5：计算边际分析决策中机会成本的影响。
- LOS 4.4.6：推荐一个运用边际分析的行动过程。
- LOS 4.4.7：计算产出水平变化对营业利润的影响。
- LOS 4.4.8：计算在存在闲置能力且订单没有长期影响的情况下，接受或拒绝一个专门订单对营业利润的影响。
- LOS 4.4.9：确认在制造还是购买决策中的定性因素，例如产品质量和对供应商的依赖程度。
- LOS 4.4.10：计算制造还是购买产品或服务的决策对营业利润的影响。
- LOS 4.4.11：区分分部增减决策中的可避免成本和不可避免成本。
- LOS 4.4.12：说明对所得税对边际分析决策的影响的理解。

4.5 成本法定价

- LOS 4.5.1：说明衡量产品成本时对成本性态类型、成本可溯性、成本动因和成本相关性的理解。
- LOS 4.5.2：说明对产品或服务需求以及供给能力如何影响产品或服务定价的理解。
- LOS 4.5.3：讨论短期定价决策怎样不同于长期定价决策。
- LOS 4.5.4：计算短期专门产品购货订单的相关成本。
- LOS 4.5.5：讨论长期定价决策中长期稳定并可预见的成本的重要性。
- LOS 4.5.6：说明对市场基础法定价决策的理解。
- LOS 4.5.7：区分成本基础法和市场基础法在定价时的不同。
- LOS 4.5.8：解释为什么在竞争商品市场中经营时通常使用市场基础定价战略。
- LOS 4.5.9：定义并说明对目标定价法和目标成本法的理解。
- LOS 4.5.10：确认在理解客户价值认知、竞争对手技术、产品、成本和财务状况的基础上定价使用的工具。
- LOS 4.5.11：确认制定目标价格和目标成本时的主要步骤。
- LOS 4.5.12：定义价值工程。
- LOS 4.5.13：计算单位目标营业利润和单位目标成本。
- LOS 4.5.14：定义并区分增值成本和非增值成本。
- LOS 4.5.15：定义成本加目标报酬率这一定价技术。
- LOS 4.5.16：定义产品的生命周期和生命周期成本法。
- LOS 4.5.17：定义高峰负荷定价法。
- LOS 4.5.18：在特定的市场环境或机遇中评价并推荐定价策略。

第1节
决策过程

本节内容简介

简单来说，决策制定就是在两个或更多个选项中作出选择。而实际上，这个过程复杂得多。对大部分企业应用来说，决策的制定意味着进行大量的数据筛选，这其中也许只有少数信息是相关的。在决定哪个选项最优的时候，决策制定者最终必须选出可以为企业带来最大收益（一般以美元来衡量）的那个选项。

相关成本和收入

在给定企业环境中作出选择，只需要考虑相关成本和收入。含不相关成本和收入的数据会混淆手头的数据，浪费时间，并有可能导致错误的决策。

将相关成本收入从不相关数据中区分出来的标准有二：（1）它们面向未来；（2）它们因选项而异。

决策制定的步骤

要制定出一个决策，必须将不同选项中的成本和收益进行系统权衡。

大部分组织决策都是基于某类决策模型或过程作出的——不管该决策是由个人负责还是集体参与制定。决策模型为甄别相关和不相关信息并选择选项提供了一个逻辑框架，从而为做出有效决策提供了便利。

由于可能的决策制定方法太多，每一种类型都加以讨论是不可行的。

大多数模型都包括一个定量分析和定性分析的框架，如图表3-75所示。

图表3-75 组织决策制定步骤

步骤一	**收集信息**
	一开始就获得全面的信息有助于确保作为解决办法的短期而快速的定位不是错误地被替代了的下游。
	例如： 一家公司必须决定是否接受一个产品定制要求。考察当前成本指出正常产品销售价格是$400，正常产品单位成本是$200（材料费$50，人工成本$100，管理费$50）
步骤二	**确定备选的行动过程**
	相关数据必须从不相关信息中分离出来。行动过程可以按短期和长期目标来表述。
	例如： 该案例中的选择是接受或者放弃机会。分析认为，该定制要求在单位产品基础上增加额外材料。在完成订单前，将要实施雇员工资的年度增长。该订单对于常规销售将不会产生什么影响，并能在现有能力内完成。
步骤三	**预计未来成本和收入**
	基于相关数据，能够预测不同选项的相关成本和收入。
	例如： 专门订单的估计单位产品成本比当前单位产品成本高10%。额外材料是一次性成本。与客户协商的价格比正常售价高5%。
步骤四	**选择并验证一个选项**
	基于现有信息评价各种潜在选项，以选出最优方案。
	例如： 比较定制产品预测成本和销售价格的上涨，并考虑接受（或拒绝）定制要求给客户商誉带来的可能的影响。经理选择接受订单。

步骤五	实施决策
	实施最优选项。
	例如：实施步骤 4 中制定的决策。
步骤六	评估结果以提供反馈
	评价所选决策的结果为未来做出相同类型决策提供恰当的反馈。同时，指明改进的机会。
	例如：人工成本比预测的要高，因为为完成定制产品而延长生产时间。管理人员认为是预测而不是决策出了问题。应当考虑如何更好地处理未来的定制要求。

评估决策效果

组织业绩在很大程度上取决于有效的决策制定。一个有效的决策制定过程包括了图表 3 - 75 中列出的六个步骤：（1）系统收集信息；（2）确定备选的行动过程；（3）估计未来的成本和收入；（4）选择并验证一个备选方案；（5）实施所选择的最优方案；（6）评估结果并反馈信息。

最后一步——评估决策结果——是很关键的。业绩评价和反馈有助于确保采取的行动过程按预期执行。

取决于决策的性质，可以就如下项目做出决定：

- 预测和实际结果之间的差距。
- 相关成本和收入的恰当分类或不恰当分类。
- 如何通过对过去不满意业绩的根源发挥作用来增强效率、效果和盈利性。

用这种方式来评价决策结果为改善以后的决策制定指出了改进的机会。

进度检查

提示：完成以下各题，参考答案随后给出。

1. 下面哪项是区分相关成本、收入和不相关数据的两个标准？（　　　）

　　a. 流线型活动和增量利得

　　b. 定性和定量的决策结果

　　c. 历史基础和给定的决策环境

　　d. 面向未来和不同的备选项

2. 来自一个新增产品的预期财务利得低于第一季度的预测。下面哪项最有可能是评估决策结果的好处？（　　　）

　　a. 任何业绩不满意的领域都可被确认并纠正

　　b. 可以确认交流共享的企业设想的额外机会

　　c. 可以实施短期快速的定位以提高生产力和收入

　　d. 修正短期和长期目标以使其更现实

进度检查答案

1. d

2. a

第2节
相关数据概念

本节内容简介

在进一步研究决策分析之前，必须理解几个术语和概念。本节关注的就是这些重要术语和概念。

面向未来的成本和收入

相关成本和相关收入

根据定义，相关成本是将要发生的成本或未来的成本。相关收入是预期的未来收入。相关成本和相关收入是指对决策制定者可得的每个选项而言都不同的成本。已发生的成本和收入在决策制定过程中是不相关的，因为不再需要与这些成本和收入有关的任何判断。

可避免成本和不可避免成本

可避免成本（或可逃避成本）是指在决策制定过程中通过采用一种备选方案替代另一种备选方案就可以全部或部分免除的成本。可避免成本可以通过终止一个活动的实施或者提高某项活动的效率来消除。不可避免成本是指无论做出什么企业决策或行动，这项成本都会一直存在。可避免成本是相关成本，而不可避免成本是不相关成本。

增量的及差异的成本和收入

增量成本（即支出或现付成本）是指为在成本对象现有或计划产量基础上获得额外产量而发生的额外成本。差异成本（或净相关成本）是指在决策制定中任两个备选方案的总成本之差。

增量成本和差异成本这两个概念经常交替使用。技术上来讲，增量成本是指不同备选方案之间的成本增加，而减量成本是指成本减少。差异成本既包括不同备选方案之间的成本增加（增量成本），又包括成本减少（减量成本）。这三种成本——增量成本、减量成本和差异成本都属于决策制定中的相关成本。

增量收入是指执行一项备选行动过程中产生的额外收入。差异收入是指任两项备选方案之间的收入差异。收入的变化可能是数量上的也可能是时间上的。

会计人员一般从增量和差异两个方面来审视成本和收入的变化。从经济学角度来看，是使用边际成本和边际收入的概念。边际成本是指多生产一单位产品所产生的成本，边际收入是指多售出一单位产品所获得的收入。会计学和经济学角度之间的根本差异就在于用于单位产出的"边际"。

决策过程中相关数据的重要性

既然相关成本是随决策方案的不同而不同的未来成本，逻辑上在决策制定过程中只应该考虑相关成本。换句话说，如果一项成本不管选择何项都是固定的，那么它就属于不相关成本，不应考虑在决策制定过程中。

如下情境显示了在决策制定过程中只包括相关成本的重要性。一家企业计划购买一台新的复印机，正对不同机型进行评价。同时也考虑将复印机放置在哪里。不同复印机的价格都是相关的应包含在决策制定过程中，因为这些成本会随着复印机性能和优点的不同而不同。不相关成本的例子是办公空间的月租。因为无论企业是否购买新复印机，买哪种机型或放在什么地方，房租都保持不变。

成本性态类型

成本性态类型是指固定成本和变动成本如何对企业活动变化做出反应。

• 对固定成本来说，总成本在活动的相关范围内保持稳定，而单位成本则会随活动的变化而增加或减少。

• 对变动成本来说，单位成本保持稳定，而总成本则会随活动的增减而变动。

注意：本章第3节"本—量—利分析"将详细介绍成本性态类型。

沉没成本

沉没成本（或称过去成本）是指已经发生的且不会因现在或将来的决策而改变的成本。无论选择什么方案，沉没成本都是不变的。除了所得税的潜在影响外，沉没成本不应该包括在为增加或减少现有利润水平的任何当前决策中。历史成本均为沉没成本。

先前购买的用来生产产品（该产品目前已过时）的机器，其购买成本就是一项沉没成本，即使原先设备投资没完全收回。如果所要做出的决定是继续生产这种过时产品，已支付的机器款就是一项过去成本，不能对未来的任何利润水平产生影响。决策制定者应该忽略沉没成本。

机会成本

机会成本是指在决策过程中当选择一个方案而放弃另一个时所放弃的收益。举例来说，一家企业选择升级计算机系统，而不投资于证券。那么从证券中放弃的投资收益代表了一项机会成本。

机会成本一般不记录在会计账中。然而，在制定企业决策时，它们很重要，需要考虑在内。每一个决策方案都会有与之相关的机会成本。如果一家公司选择购买证券而不是新的计算机硬件和软件，那么所放弃的来自提高雇员生产力的可能收益就是机会成本。

在一些情况下，机会成本可以通过确定一个备选方案的财务收益来量化。例如，如果一家公司因为在完成现有订单过程中可能产生的耽搁而放弃了一个专门订单，那么放弃订单可能产生的收益就代表了该项决策的机会成本。但是，在这种情况下现有客户的忠诚度（很难量化），有重要的长期价值，可能超过了这个专门订单潜在收益。现有客户如果因现存订单延期而取消以后订单，那么就会潜在地减少未来的利润。

定性和定量因素

决策方案的结果有时可分为定性和定量两类。

定性因素

定性因素是指不能由数字来衡量的决策结果。例如，客户商誉和雇员的道德素质。

定量因素

定量因素是指可以由数字来衡量的决策结果。定量因素可进一步分为财务量度和非财务量度。

- **财务量度**

就是很容易用财务术语——例如直接人工或直接材料成本来表示的量度。

- **非财务量度**

就是可以用数字但不能用财务术语来表示的量度。例如，以百分数表示的新产品研发时间的减少、已有产品循环周期的缩短或生产力的提高等。

决策分析一般因为定量因素的财务结果而强调它们。但这并不是说定性因素应被忽略。决策制定者最后总是要对两种因素的权衡进行评价。

成本可溯性

成本可溯性是指以经济上的可行方式，利用因果关系将一项成本归因于成本对象的能力。直接成本易于追溯，但间接成本比较难以精确追溯。

在可行的情况下，公司在决策制定过程中需要将成本直接追溯到成本对象和/或企业分部上。例如，地区仓库的房租应当直接由地区分支机构缴纳，而不应包括在公司整体的管理费用中。

未合理分摊的成本会导致成本歪曲。具体来说，分摊普通的固定成本可以使生产线或职能业务单元盈利看起来不如实际那么盈利。

价值链成本

管理会计公告 4X 条"为评估竞争优势进行价值链分析"，将价值链分析描述成团队工作。管理会计师需要与组成价值链的组织的其他职能部门——研发、工程（设计）、生产（制造）、营销、分销和服务——以成功地将公司的产品和服务推广给客户并产生收入。

大多数大型公司按职能的成本、收入、利润和投资中心来组织。在考虑价值链法时，企业应采用流程视角和横向观点，从产品投入开始，到产出和消费者结束。成本和资产应该被追溯和分摊到确认的每一个价值创造过程。如果成本会计信息难以与该过程平行，公司有时就会估计可分摊给价值创造过程的这些成本。

传统的管理会计注重内部数据。通常特别强调制造成本。而与供应商和客户之间的重要联系一般被忽视。在决策制定过程中，评估盈利性可能会遗漏一些重要成本。结果，管理人员就会在不知情的情况下制定导致组织亏损而非公司盈利的决策。

价值链法与传统会计的不同之处在于：

- 既有内部数据也有外部数据。
- 在所有主要的价值创造过程中使用恰当的成本动因。
- 承认贯穿价值链的链接。
- 解释价值链中的上游和下游成本。

在决定产品盈利性时，"上游"成本和"下游"成本与制造成本同等重要。

- 在价值链中，上游成本是指研发和设计成本。
- 在价值链中，下游成本是指营销、分销及服务成本。

在利润图表中，上游和下游成本通常被称为"销售、总务和管理"（SG&A）。在一些企业，这些组合成本包括了企业总成本的一大半。以医药公司为例，研发和营销费用占企业总支出的很大部分。

在为制定决策而尽力确定产品或服务盈利性时，必须检验价值链中各个部分之间的链接。上下游成本之间的各项活动和权衡的影响需要考虑。例如，研究的额外投资可以提高产品质量，降低下游的服务成本。产品打包的创新性设计决策可以提高下游的分销效率。

管理会计师负责追查整个价值链中发生的不同成本。当成本被合理分配时，就可以做出如何降低每一种类成本和改善经营效果及效率的合理决定。对降低成本结构、提高产品认知价值起作用的价值链活动包括：转包、外包活动或自制决策、定价战略和构建最佳分销渠道的决策。

注意：本书第 1 章第 3 节"业务流程业绩"详细讨论了价值链分析。

所得税在决策过程中的影响

在评估投资建议时，所得税是一个重要的考虑因素。在某些情况下，税率、纳税方法以及税负对于相关收入和成本数据的影响将会成为在不同建议之间的决定因素。

折旧费用直接影响应税收入从而影响利润。能在寿命期初冲销折旧可以为其他投资带来更多资金。

税法与时俱进。在评估今天的投资建议时，决策制定者应对现行税法有彻底的理解，并对可能影响当前投资和会计程序的潜在的未来税法变化有所洞察。

进度检查

提示：完成以下各题，参考答案随后给出。

1. 两个投资备选方案在金额和时间上存在不同，例举的是下面哪一项？（　　）

　a. 增量收入

　b. 差异收入

　c. 花费

　d. 净相关成本

2. 下面哪一项没有准确描述沉没成本？（　　　）
   a. 通过取消一项活动，该成本可以被全部或部分消除
   b. 无论正在考虑哪个方案，该成本都相同
   c. 该成本不会影响未来盈利水平
   d. 在决策制定过程中应忽略该成本

进度检查答案

1. b
2. a

第3节
本一量一利分析

本节内容简介

本/量/利分析（CVP）是分析一个组织内总成本、数量和利润之间相互关系的方法。CVP分析法检验了下面几项的相互作用：

- 产品和服务的销售价格。
- 销售量（活动水平）。
- 单位变动成本。
- 总固定成本。
- 销售的产品和服务的组合。

经理可以在各种决策制定情况下使用CVP分析法，例如：

- 提高或降低现存商品和服务的价格。
- 引进一项新产品或服务。
- 为新产品和服务设定价格。
- 拓展产品和服务市场。
- 决定是否重置现存设备。
- 决定制造还是购买产品或服务。

CVP 术语及假设

CVP分析法试图简化收入和成本形态类型的假设。要进一步解释CVP分析法，需要明确一些术语

- 成本一般是指为达成一个特定目标而花费的资源。
- 成本动因是指影响成本的任何因素。成本动因的变动会导致相关成本对象中总成本的变动。成本动因的例子包括制造的产品数量或者装运的打包数量。
- 成本对象是指累计成本数据的项目。例如产品、生产线、客户、工作和组织业务单元。
- 固定成本是指相关范围内无论活动水平如何变化，总量都保持不变的成本。固定成本因管理人员活动而不得不改变。
- 变动成本是指相关范围内总量随活动水平变化而成正比例变动的成本。
- 相关范围是指使变动成本和固定成本假设成立的活动范围。
- 收入是指因交换产品或服务而收到的资产流入。
- 收入动因是指影响收入的因素（例如营销成本、产品销售价格或者销售量）。
- 总成本（或总费用）是由变动成本（与产量有关）和固定成本构成的。总成本由下式表示：

总成本 = 变动成本 + 固定成本

- 营业利润是指总营业收入减去总营业成本（不包含所得税）。营业利润通常由下式表示：

营业利润 = 总营业收入 - 总营业成本

公司有时为了分析的目的而将筹资成本从营业利润中扣除。

- 净利润是指在一段期间内从所有来源中减去费用后的当期收益。净利润由下式表示：

净利润 = 税前收益 - 所得税

净利润可能包括非营业收入和费用。

- 活动水平（也称产出水平、产出量度或产出）是指生产的产品数量或销售的产品数量。活动水平这一术语随行业不同而有所不同。例如，航空空司用乘客英里数、医院可能使用病人天数或占用床位数、旅馆使用占用客房数、高校使用学生学时数来代替产品数量。

下面解释的 CVP 分析专门检验在产出水平、销售价格、单位变动成本或固定成本发生变化时，总收入、总成本和营业利润的行为。CVP 模型假设：

- 总成本可以就与产出水平的关系分为固定成本和变动成本。
- 总收入和总成本在相关范围内与产出数量有线性（直线）关系。

固定成本和变动成本性态

成本性态一般是指企业活动水平变化时成本如何反应。随着企业产出的变化，给定的成本可能会增加、减少或保持不变。

CVP 分析中的一个关键假设是成本按照与活动水平的关系可以分为固定成本或变动成本。图表 3 - 76 总结了在相关范围内固定成本和变动成本在总成本和单位成本基础上的行为表现。注意：从总成本或单位成本角度看，固定成本和变动成本的行为表现各不相同。

图表 3 - 76　相关范围内固定成本和变动成本性态

成本类型	总成本性态	单位成本性态
固定成本	一般不受活动水平变化的影响	反向增减（例如，活动水平降低时该成本增加，反之亦然）
变动成本	与活动水平变化成比例的常规性增减	保持不变

无论什么发生环境（例如制造、零售或服务）成本均固定的例子包括保险费、租金费、财产税、工资和广告费等。

在制造业，变动成本的例子包括直接材料和一部分管理费用如销售佣金和运输成本。在零售业，变动成本的例子包括销货成本、销售佣金和开单成本。在服务业，例如医院，变动成本包括处方药费、医院供给费和病人伙食费。

一段时间的固定成本和变动成本分类：

固定成本和变动成本分类会受所考虑的时间范围的影响。换句话说，一些变动成本可能被重新归类为固定成本。如果期限延伸，固定成本最终可能也会变化。

一般来说，以下原则适用于一段时间的固定和变动成本分类：

- 时间段越短，总成本中可视为固定成本的比例就越高。
- 时间段越长，变动成本的比例就越高。

总的来说，成本是固定还是变动通常是如下项目的函数：
- 相关范围。
- 时间范围。
- 给定的决策环境。

图表3-77的例子进一步阐释了固定成本和变动成本性态。

图表3-77　固定成本和变动成本性态

	总成本10 000件	单位成本	总成本25 000件	单位成本	总成本50 000件	单位成本
直接材料	$16 000	$1.60	$40 000	$1.60	$80 000	$1.60
直接人工	25 000	2.50	62 500	2.50	125 000	2.50
分销	13 000	1.30	32 500	1.30	65 000	1.30
折旧	50 000	5.00	50 000	2.00	80 000	1.60
租金	25 000	2.50	25 000	1.00	40 000	0.80

材料和人工的单位成本在相关能力范围内是固定的。不管公司是生产一件产品还是25 000件产品，折旧和租金的总成本是固定的。然而，当销售增长超出了固定资产25 000件的生产能力，公司就需要增加生产线。单位成本也会随额外的设备而上升，同时也需要更大的空间。

总收入和总成本

CVP模型假设总收入和总成本在相关活动范围内是线性的。换句话说，在一定的产出水平下，总成本预期是以近似的线性比率上升的。图表3-78简单地展示了这种线性关系。

图表3-78　总收入、总成本和产出水平的CVP图

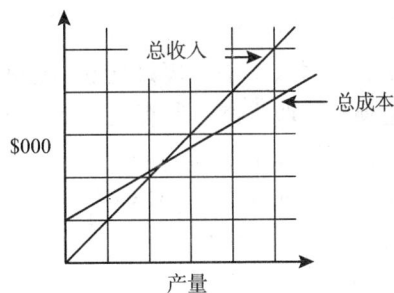

盈亏平衡分析

CVP分析有时也被称作盈亏平衡分析。技术上，盈亏平衡分析只是CVP分析的一部分。

盈亏平衡点，也称作经营性盈亏平衡点，是指总收入等于总成本时的产出水平。该点的营业利润为零。高于该点，营业利润水平为盈利；低于该点，则为亏损。

确定盈亏平衡点是CVP分析和评估各种"如果……怎样"决策的备选方案将如何影响营业利润的关键部分。盈亏平衡点可能由三种不同方法来决定：公式法、边际

贡献法和图表法。以下内容描述了在给定场景下的每种方法：

一家公司的销售代表到客户所在地推销一种新产品。产品的单位售价是 $200。产品固定成本是 $4 000。产品的变动销售成本是 $100，销售数量为 75。

公式法

计算盈亏平衡点的一般公式是：

收入 – 变动成本 – 固定成本 = 营业利润

或者

$(USP \times Q) - (UVC \times Q) - FC = OI$

其中：

- USP = 单位售价。
- Q = 销售数量。
- UVC = 单位变动成本。
- FC = 固定成本。
- OI = 营业利润。

在盈亏平衡点处，营业利润为零。设定及营业利润为零并在公式中代入数字，例子中的盈亏平衡点（以单位表示）计算如下：

$(USP \times Q) - (UVC \times Q) - FC = OI$

$(\$200 \times Q) - (\$100 \times Q) - \$4 000 = \$0$

$\$100 \times Q = \$4 000$

$Q = \$4 000 / \$100 = 40$ 单位

在本例中，销售量少于 40 单位就会造成亏损；销售 40 单位达到盈亏平衡；多于 40 则产生利润。

边际贡献法

边际贡献法是对公式法的代数改编。边际贡献代表了销售收入减去变动费用后剩余的金额。它通过将收入减去所有随产量变化的产出成本计算得出。

边际贡献法基于以下公式：

$(USP \times Q) - (UVC \times Q) - FC = OI$

$(USP - UVC) \times Q = FC + OI$

$UCM \times Q = FC + OI$

$Q = (FC + OI) / UCM$

其中：

- USP = 单位售价。
- Q = 销售数量。
- UVC = 单位变动成本。
- FC = 固定成本。
- OI = 营业利润。
- UCM = 单位边际贡献（USP – UVC）。

设营业利润为零，在边际贡献法中代入数字，本例中盈亏平衡点（以单位表示）

的计算如下：

盈亏平衡点（单位）＝固定成本（FC）/单位边际贡献（UCM）

＝ \$4 000/ \$100 ＝40 单位

贡献利润表通过按成本性态类型将费用项目分组来强调边际贡献。边际贡献利润表确认了边际贡献盈亏平衡的计算。

图表3 –79 贡献利润表

销售收入（\$200 ×40）	\$8 000
变动成本（\$100 ×40）	4 000
边际贡献	4 000
固定成本	4 000
营业利润	\$0

边际贡献百分比/边际贡献率

边际贡献可以通过百分比而不是单位的美元数量来表示。边际贡献百分比（也称为边际贡献率或 CMR）可以通过两种方式来计算。通常边际贡献百分比由单位边际贡献除以售价来表示。

边际贡献百分比 ＝单位边际贡献（UCM）/销售价格

＝ \$100/ \$200 ＝0. 50 或50%

边际贡献百分比也可以用边际贡献除以总收入计算得出。如果售出 40 件，则：

边际贡献百分比 ＝边际贡献/总收入

＝ \$4 000/ \$8 000 ＝0. 50 或50%

边际贡献百分比或 CMR 提供了每美元收入的边际贡献。在该例中，它表明每一美元的50%（相当于 \$0. 50）为边际贡献。

变动成本百分比

变动成本百分比是边际贡献百分比的补数，换句话说：

边际贡献百分比 ＋变动成本百分比 ＝1

在给定的例子中，边际贡献百分比 ＝50%，所以变动成本百分比 ＝50%。给定变动成本为每单位 \$100、变动成本百分比为50%，则售价为：

\$100 ÷0. 50 ＝ \$200

图表法

CVP 图（或称盈亏平衡图）图示了成本、数量和利润之间的相互关系。

- 活动水平（单位量）通过横轴（X）图表示。
- 金额通过纵轴（Y）图表示。
- 总成本和总收入都在图中线性表示，且它们的交点即为盈亏平衡点。

图表3 –80 表示了盈亏平衡分析的 CVP 图标。

图表3-80　盈亏平衡分析的 CVP 图

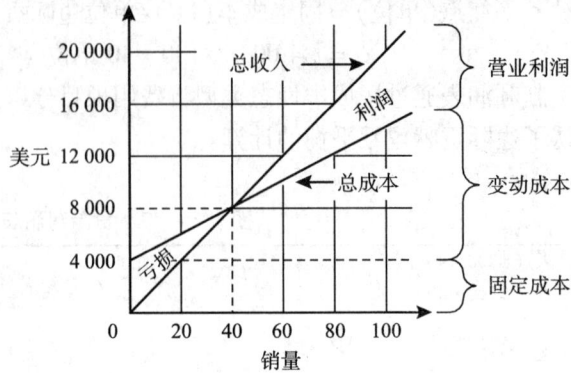

利润表现和备选的经营水平

盈亏平衡分析也可以用来决定要达到目标利润水平——目标营业利润或目标净利润，必须售出多少单位产品。继续前例，设目标营业利润为 \$8 000，计算销售数量及销售金额。

等式法

在这种情况下用到的等式为：

收入 – 变动成本 – 固定成本 = 目标营业利润

或

$$(USP \times QT) - (UVC \times QT) - FC = TOI$$

其中：

- USP = 单位售价。
- QT = 实现目标营业利润的销售数量。
- UVC = 单位变动成本。
- FC = 固定成本。
- TOI = 目标营业利润。

设目标营业利润为 \$8 000 并代入数字，必须销售的单位数量计算如下：

$$(USP \times QT) - (UVC \times QT) - FC = TOI$$
$$(\$200 \times QT) - (\$100 \times QT) - \$4\,000 = \$8\,000$$
$$\$100 \times QT = \$4\,000 + \$8\,000$$
$$\$100QT = \$12\,000$$
$$QT = \$12\,000 / \$100 = 120 \text{ 单位}$$

边际贡献法

设营业利润为 \$8 000 并代入边际贡献法，分子由固定成本加目标营业利润组成：

$$
\begin{aligned}
QT &= (FC + TOI)/UCM \\
&= (\$4\,000 + \$8\,000)/\$100 \\
&= \$12\,000/\$100 = 120 \text{ 单位}
\end{aligned}
$$

贡献利润表如图表 3 – 81 所示：

图表 3 – 81　贡献利润表

销售收入（$200 × 120）	$24 000
变动成本（$100 × 120）	12 000
边际贡献	12 000
固定成本	4 000
营业利润	$8 000

也可以计算盈亏平衡点的收入。回顾前面关于边际贡献百分比或 CMR 的计算：

边际贡献百分比 = 边际贡献/总收入

= $4 000/$8 000 = 0.50 或 50%

在该例中，每一美元的 50%（或 $0.50）就是边际贡献。为了达到盈亏平衡，边际贡献必须等于 $4 000 固定成本。为获得 $4 000 边际贡献，收入必须等于 $8 000。

盈亏平衡收入 = 固定成本/边际贡献百分比（%）

= $4 000/0.50 = $8 000

图表法

图表 3 – 82 显示了利润—数量（PV）图以及产出的变化如何影响营业利润。产出为零时，固定成本水平为 $4 000。盈亏平衡点后的每一单位产品都对营业利润有贡献。

图表 3 – 82　PV 图

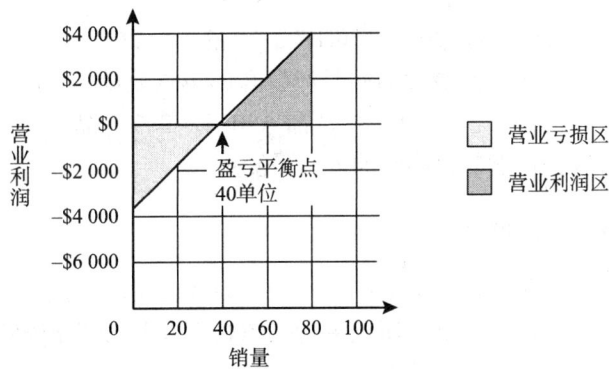

例如，销量为 60 单位，营业利润为：

（$200 × 60） – （$100 × 60） – $4 000 = $2 000

多产品分析

销售组合（或收入组合）是指出售的产品或服务的相对比例。大部分公司有多种产品和/或服务。一般来说，不同的产品和服务盈利性也不同。企业通常努力追求能产生最大盈利的销售组合。如果产品或服务组合中较高边际的项目比例越大，则利润趋向于越大。

考虑下面一家拥有两种产品（A 和 B）的公司的预算方案。

图表 3 – 83　预算方案

	产品 A	产品 B	合计
销量	100	50	150
单位收入（\$200 和 \$125）	\$20 000	\$6 250	\$26 250
单位变动成本（\$125 和 \$75）	12 500	3 750	16 250
单位边际贡献（\$75 和 \$50）	7 500	2 500	10 000
固定成本			4 000
营业利润			\$6 000

因为存在多种产品，在盈亏平衡点上就没有一个惟一的数字。该数取决于销售组合。当销售组合（每售出一单位产品 B 同时售出两单位产品 A）不变时可以用下面的等式：

收入 – 变动成本 – 固定成本 = 营业利润

代入数字，每种产品必须销售的数量计算如下：

收入 – 变动成本 – 固定成本 = 营业利润

$[\ \$200(2S) + \$125S\ ] - [\ \$125(2S) + \$75S\ ] - \$4\ 000 = 0$

$\$525S - \$325S = 0$

$\$200S = \$4\ 000$

$S = 20$

$2S = 40$

其中：

- $2S$ = 达到盈亏均衡时产品 A 的单位数量。
- S_i = 达到盈亏均衡时产品 B 的单位数量。

当销售组合为 40 单位产品 A 和 20 单位产品 B 时，盈亏平衡点为 60。其他销售组合选择可能导致不同的盈亏平衡点。

加权平均贡献法

加权平均贡献法是在公司生产多种产品时应用 CVP 分析的另一种算法。为了确定盈亏平衡点，单位加权平均贡献边际是按预算销售组合中每种产品来计算的。例如，前述产品 A 和产品 B 的销售组合中：

$$\text{加权平均 UCM} = \frac{[\ (\text{产品 A 的 UCM} \times \text{销量}) + (\text{产品 B 的 UCM} \times \text{销量})\ ]}{(\text{产品 A 销量} + \text{产品 B 销量})}$$

$$= \frac{[\ (\text{每单位 } \$75 \times 100 \text{ 单位}) + (\text{每单位 } \$50 \times 50 \text{ 单位})\ ]}{(100 \text{ 单位} + 50 \text{ 单位})}$$

$$= (\$7\ 500 + \$2\ 500)/150 = \$10\ 000/150 = \text{每单位 } \$66.66$$

盈亏平衡点计算如下：

盈亏平衡点 = 固定成本/加权平均 UCM

$= \$4\ 000/\text{每单位 } \$66.66 = 60 \text{ 单位}$

销售产品 A 与 B 的比率为 100∶50（或 2∶1），盈亏平衡点为：

- 60/3 = 20 × 2 = 40 单位（产品 A）
- 60/3 = 20 单位（产品 B）

在该组合中，边际贡献是 $4 000（每单位产品 A $75 × 40 单位 + 每单位产品 B $50 × 20 单位），正好等于公司固定成本 $4 000。因为 60 单位时边际贡献等于固定成本，所以公司刚好在盈亏平衡点。

计算多产品盈亏平衡点的收入也可以用加权平均边际贡献百分比。

加权平均边际贡献百分比% = 总边际贡献/总收入

= $10 000/ $26 250 = 0. 381 或 38.1%

盈亏平衡点的总收入 = 固定成本/加权平均边际贡献%

= $4 000/0. 3809523 = $10 500.00

图表 3 – 84 显示了在盈亏平衡点处总收入、总变动成本和总边际贡献细目分类。

图表 3 – 84 盈亏平衡点的预算方案

	产品 A	产品 B	合计
销量	40	20	60
单位收入（$200 和 $125）	$8 000	$2 500	$10 500
单位变动成本（$125 和 $75）	5 000	1 500	6 500
单位边际贡献（$75 和 $50）	3 000	1 000	4 000
固定成本			4 000
营业利润			$0

使用图表 3 – 83 中的数据，总收入 $26 250 在产品 A 和产品 B 之间的细目分类是：76.2% 的 A 产品（$20 000/ $26 250）和 23.8% 的 B 产品（$6 250/ $26 250）。$10 500 的盈亏平衡收入应该按同样的比率分解。结果如下：

- 产品 A 的盈亏平衡收入为 $8 000（76.2% × $10 500）
- 产品 B 的盈亏平衡收入为 $2 500（23.8% × $10 500）

产品 A 售价 $200、产品 B 售价 $125 时：

- 产品 A 的盈亏平衡点 = 40 单位（$8 000/ $200）
- 产品 B 的盈亏平衡点 = 20 单位（$2 500/ $125）

销售组合变化对于营业利润产生多大影响取决于高边际项目和低边际项目在组合中的原始比例如何变化。通常应用下面的一般原则：

- 由高边际项目向低边际项目变动会使营业利润降低，即使总销售收入可能是增加的。
- 由低边际项目向高边际项目变动会使营业利润增加，即使总销售收入可能是减少的。

企业努力通过销售组合来使收入最大化。许多因素都会影响到诸如生产什么、生产多少以及以哪种产品为重点等决策的制定。有时候，最好的决策可能不总是生产具有最高单位边际贡献的项目。例如，一种产品可能有很高的边际贡献，但是公司未必有能力卖出能够达到盈亏平衡的数量。在多数情况下（特别是当固定资产满负荷运行时），管理人员应该关注每种产品的边际贡献并选择那些在约束性资源下具有最高单位边际贡献的产品。

约束性资源是一种严格制约或限制产品或服务的产量或销量的资源。在制造业，约束性资源的例子包括每机器工时的贡献或者直接材料、零件或熟练工人的可得性。在零售业，展示空间大小也是约束性资源。财务和销售因素在任何环境下都可以成为约束性资源。

当各种产品中每种产品都有多种约束性资源时，要使该组产品总营业利润最大化就存在很大挑战。一家公司可能需要存储最少的商品，即使这些商品不是非常具有盈利性。例如，一家五金商店可能必须持有盈利性稍差的物品，以确保他们能提供给顾客所需的各种商品。

所得税和 CVP 分析

如前所述，净利润通常用营业利润减所得税的差表示。为确定净利润，CVP 分析等式法中惟一需要改变的就是从目标营业利润中扣掉所得税。

设税率为40%，贡献利润表如图表 3－79（目标营业利润为 $8 000）所示。以下为税收的作用：

目标净利润 ＝ 营业利润 －（营业利润×税率）

$\qquad$ ＝ 营业利润×（1－税率）

营业利润 ＝ 目标净利润/（1－税率）

考虑所得税的等式法如下：

收入 － 变动成本 － 固定成本 ＝ 目标净利润/（1－税率）

将本例数字代入上式，得：

$200Q － $120Q － $4 000 ＝ $8 000/（1－0.40）

$200Q － $120Q － $4 000 ＝ $13 333

80Q ＝ $17 333

Q ＝ 216.66 单位

图表 3－85 的贡献利润表包含了所得税的影响，证明了上式。

图表 3－85　所得税和目标营业利润

收入（$200×216.66）	$43 332
变动成本（$120×216.66）	25 999
边际贡献	17 333
固定成本	4 000
营业利润	13 333
所得税（$13 333×0.40）	5 333
净利润	$8 000

进度检查

提示：完成以下各题，参考答案随后给出。

1. 在 CVP 模型中，总收入和总成本（　　　）
   a. 在有限产出范围内保持不变
   b. 与活动水平的变化呈反向增减
   c. 与活动水平的变化成比例增减
   d. 在相关活动范围内以近似的线性比率增长

2. 下面哪个选项不能正确描述盈亏平衡点（　　　）
   a. 营业利润为零
   b. 总收入等于总成本
   c. 盈亏平衡点以上表示盈利；以下表示亏损
   d. 盈亏平衡点以下表示盈利；以上表示亏损

找出与以下项目相匹配的描述。

3. _____相关范围　　　　　a. 企业活动水平变动时成本如何反应
4. _____活动水平　　　　　b. 使变动成本和固定成本假设成立的活动范围
5. _____成本性态　　　　　c. 销售的产品或服务的相对比例
6. _____边际贡献　　　　　d. 产量或销量
7. _____销售组合　　　　　e. 从销售收入中减去变动费用后的剩余部分

8. 如果固定成本 $8 000，变动成本 $100，单位边际贡献 $200，要达到目标营业利润 $34 000 必须卖出多少单位产品？（　　　）
   a. 130
   b. 140
   c. 210
   d. 260

进度检查答案

1. d
2. d
3. b
4. d
5. a
6. e
7. c
8. c

第4节
边际分析

本节内容简介

决策制定涉及在至少两个方案当中做出选择。在某些情况下，有很多种方案可以考虑。但是其他决策可能要求只在两个方案中进行选择，其中一个可能是现状。无论有多少种选择，在决策过程中都需要对这些方案的成本和收益做出评价。

边际分析（也称为增量分析或差异分析）是一种分析决策问题的方法，该方法着重于分析增量成本的增减情况，而不是与活动（或一系列备选活动）相关的总成本和总收益。它通常用于如下几种情况：

- 专门订单及其定价。
- 制造还是购买。
- 销售还是再加工。
- 增加还是减少一个分部。
- 将限制性因素的单位贡献最大化。

应用边际分析的关键因素是决定哪些信息是与决策相关的。正如本章第2节"相关数据概念"中提到的，相关成本相关收入随方案不同而变化并且面向未来。已经发生的成本和收入在决策制定过程中是不相关的。换句话说，在边际分析中，任何在选项之间没有区别的成本，包括已分摊成本，都应当被忽略。

本节详细探讨了组织决策制定中边际分析的应用。

专门订单及其定价

专门订单的定价决策涉及这样的情况：企业有一次性的机会来选择接受还是拒绝一个特定数量产品或服务的专门订单。决定是否接受订单需要评估盈利性（基于相关成本和收入及机会成本）并考虑能力利用情况。

如果存在过剩的能力——比完成订单所需的还多——企业就需要确认与该专门订单相关的非正常发生的变动成本。这些变动成本是相关成本，决定了最低可接受（盈亏平衡点）价格。如果专门订单提供的价格比单位成本高，订单就是盈利的，应该接受。

如果企业以接近或达到全部生产能力进行经营，最低可接受价格就是正常销售价格。当没有过剩能力时，只要给出的价格超过正常价格，就可以接受订单。在充分使用生产能力时，企业也必须考虑接受订单是否会导致失去其他更有利可图的销售。还应评价因损失具有更高边际贡献的销售项目而导致的机会成本。

专门订单成本分析

思考如下情景：
- 产品单位售价是 $4。
- 单位平均变动成本是 $2.75。

- 单位平均固定成本是 $1。
- 单位总成本是 $3.75。
- 正常生产能力是 500 000 单位。
- 固定成本是 $500 000。

一个专门订单要求提供 50 000 单位，单位售价 $3.50。

过剩生产能力

在生产能力过剩的情况下，正确的决策分析是将相关成本与专门订单价格进行比较。相关成本包括生产单位产品的成本（$2.75），专门订单的单位价格（$3.50）。无论订单是否被接受，单位固定成本（$1）是不变的，因此它是不相关的。每销售一单位产品的利润贡献是 $0.75（$3.50 - $2.75），总贡献为 $37 500（50 000 单位 × $0.75）。该订单可盈利，应该接受。

在评估专门订单决策时，一个普遍的错误概念是关注每单位的总成本。如果将每单位的总成本作为参照数，该订单可能会被拒绝，因为单位成本（$3.75）超过了订单价格（$3.50）。

接近或达到全部生产能力

假设企业以接近或达到完全生产能力经营，恰当的决策分析应该考虑任何损失的销售所产生的机会成本。例如，如果专门订单会导致失去一些具有更高边际收益（$1）的销售，那么损失的销售的机会成本就是 $50 000（50 000 × $1）。该订单的净损失的贡献就是 $12 500（$50 000 - $37 500）。接受该订单将会使总利润减少 $12 500，所以应该拒绝该订单。

在大部分相关成本分析情景中，固定制造成本被认为是不相关的。然而，如果企业以接近或达到完全生产能力经营，这种分类就应该改变。例如，当固定资产接近完全生产能力并有一个看上去可以吸收专门订单的相关范围时，如果要达到完全生产能力并完成订单必须有额外的手段，那么制造成本就会增加，增加的固定制造成本对这个决策而言就是相关成本。

正如"专门订单"这个术语所显示的，此类订单一般来说是非预期的且并不频繁。它们一般被认为是短期的，而且只有在它们可以增加总收入的时候才会在那些少见的情况下被接受。定期（长期）接受专门订单定价会破坏标准订价政策。

制造 vs 购买

"制造 vs 购买"这一术语是指外包。正如本书第 1 章"战略规划"中指出的，外包描述了公司决定从外部供应商处购买产品或服务而不是自己生产。要做出是购买还是制造的决定，一般要将内部制造的相关成本与外部购买的相关成本进行比较。在某些情况下，机会成本和定性因素也应该被考虑。

相关成本代表了自己生产的短期成本。这些成本是增量/差异成本并且通常是变动成本。相关成本是可以通过外部购买来避免或消除的成本。

不相关成本是那些无论企业决定内部制造还是外部购买都不会改变的不可避免成

本。它们是沉没成本或未来成本，即使外部购买，也不会改变。一般来说，它们是固定的管理成本和折旧成本。

如果相关成本比买价低，应该决定内部生产。如果外部买价比可避免成本低，理性的决策是外包。

制造 vs 购买成本分析

思考如下情形：一家公司每年制造 5 000 单位产品。在这种产量内，每制造一单位产品的成本如图表 3 - 86 所示。

图表 3 - 86　制造成本

直接材料	$2.50
直接人工	3.50
变动管理费用	1.50
固定管理费用	1.00
单位产品总成本	$8.50

公司可以从外部供应商处以单价 $7.75 购买无限量的该产品。因为相关成本是 $7.50（$8.50 - 保持不变的固定管理费用 $1），故该产品不应外包。如果一直采用内部生产方式生产 5 000 单位，则会增加 $1 250 （5 000 × $0.25）。

考虑机会成本

在制定制造和购买决策时，机会成本也应该考虑在内。常见的制造和购买机会成本是固定管理费用的一部分能否通过外包而减少。另外的常见机会成本是内部生产过程中使用的部分空间能否挪作他用。

如果正在用于内部生产的空间没有其他用途并且闲置，那么机会成本是零。但是如果这些空间能用于其他用途，那么机会成本应该在评估外包时被考虑。

回到这个例子，如果公司能剔除 50% 的固定成本并通过向其他公司出租此空间而获得一年 $6 000 的收入，外包的经济效益将改变该决策。在这种情况下，$6 000 是可避免的固定成本，则来自出租空间的每单位机会成本是 $1.20（$6 000/5 000 单位）。现在的相关成本是 $9.20（$7.50 的初始相关成本加上如果外包企业所能避免的 $0.50 固定成本［即机会成本 1］及 $1.20 的租金损失［即机会成本 2］）。购买的相关成本是 $7.75。比较这两项，外包的潜在节省是每单位 $1.45，或者说是总计 $7 250（$1.45 × 5 000 单位）。

考虑定性因素

针对相关成本的制造 vs 购买边际分析在外包决策中有重要作用。但是除了潜在的边际利润外，成功的外包还要考虑很多因素。除了制造 vs 购买决策的利润抉择外，企业也需要评估同外部供应商打交道的定性因素。这些定性因素的例子包括需要利用外部供应商的独特知识、不寻常的技术人员、获取稀有材料的途径。

传统上，想要控制质量一直是决定制造而不购买的驱动因素。越来越多的买卖组织正在形成准合作伙伴关系或联盟，从而联合起来改善产品和服务。买方公司经常调整制造 vs 购买决策，以与供应商达到互利关系。如果买方组织能被确保现有的质量和服务水平均达到要求并且供应商的工作将不断改善，那么就会带来更低的价格。不好的一面是给予供应商（宽松时生产、繁荣时购买）的不稳定订货会产生反效果，当销售需求很高但缺少材料和工人时可能带来找货问题。

最终决定向外部供应商外包时不应该忽视供应商在可靠和质量方面的信誉，如：

- 保证按时交货以及零部件和材料顺畅流通。
- 保持可接受的质量控制。

保持控制核心竞争力的战略方面也很重要。对于保持竞争地位关键的任何内部能力的外包都需要仔细考虑。

注意：在本书第 1 章第 2 节"生产范式"中有关于外包的目的以及制造 vs 购买决策的优点和局限的其他信息。

销售还是再加工

销售还是再加工涉及在中间处理步骤之前将产品或服务销售出去或者增加进一步的处理程序再以更高的价格卖出产品或服务。销售还是再加工的一个普遍的例子包括对如下事项的决策：

- 在一个产品上加入新特性以提高其功能。
- 提高一项服务的灵活性或质量。
- 修复有缺陷的产品以便按通常方式销售（而不是按残次品折价销售）。

销售还是再加工决策要求分析相关成本。在很多情况下，该决策也涉及对联产品或服务的考虑。该类型的销售或再加工决策的关键是联合成本是不相关的。

联产品或联服务是一项共同投入生产出来的两种或更多种产品或服务。例如，石油提炼产生原油、汽油和天然气。分离点是指在生产过程中联产品能被辨别为单独产品的点。联合成本是指分离点前所发生的全部成本。

联合成本是不相关的，这是因为这些成本是产品或服务为了达到分离点所必须发生的共同成本。因为联合成本无法直接归属到任何中间产品/服务或最终产品/服务上，因此它们与分离点之后的行动决策制定不相关。

对于销售还是再加工决策，只要得到的增量收入（可归属到增加的处理过程的收入）超过发生的增量处理成本，继续加工产品或服务就是有利可图的。这项规则同样适用于联产品和联服务在分离点之后的处理过程。图表 3－87 概括了销售还是再加工决策的步骤。

图表 3－87　销售还是再加工决策的制定步骤

第一步：确定一项产品或服务的售价，或确定在联合生产过程中分离点处每件产品或服务的售价
第二步：若对产品或服务进行再加工，确定每件产品或服务的售价
第三步：计算再加工所产生的增量收入，即第二步减去第一步
第四步：计算增量成本；从增量收入（第三步）中减去再加工成本（或者分离点后每项产品或服务的单独处理成本）
第五步：比较增量收入和增量成本。净值为正支持再加工，为负则表明应在再加工前（或在分离点上）出售

销售还是再加工成本分析

例1：

考虑如下情景，将增量成本和增量收入进行简单的比较：

- 产品单位生产成本为 $4 200。
- 产品单位售价为 $5 000。
- 单位增量处理成本为 $1 500。
- 单位新售价 $5 800。

根据以上信息，产品应该照现在的样子销售而无须再加工。增量收入是 $800（$5 800 – $5 000）。再加工的增量成本（$1 500）超过了增量收入，再加工将导致 $700 的亏损（– $700 = $800 – $1 500）。

例2：

考虑如下关于联产品的情形：

- 一家公司将原材料 A 加工成联产品 B 和 C。
- 每 100 单位原材料 A 可以生产出 60 单位 B 和 40 单位 C。
- 原材料 A 的单位成本为 $5。
- 要将 100 单位原材料 A 加工成联产品 B 和 C 需花费 $100 成本。
- C 产品可以马上以 $5 的单价售出，或者也可以经过再加工后以 $15 的单价卖出。额外的加工成本为每单位 $4。

根据以上给定信息，再加工产品 C 会产生每单位 $6 的净收益。

- 再加工的增量收入是 $10（$15 – $5，即再加工后产品 C 的单价减去分离点处产品 C 的单价）。
- 再加工的增量成本是 $4。
- $6 的净收益是增量收入减去增量成本（$10 – $4）。
- 原材料 A 的成本（$5）和将原材料 A 加工成产品 B 和 C 的成本 $100 就是分离点之前发生的全部联合成本，这些成本是不相关成本。

增加还是减少分部

保留还是淘汰一种产品或服务以及是否增加一种新品的决策很大程度上取决于相关成本分析和该决策会给净营业利润带来的影响。可避免成本必须从不可避免成本当中区别出来。在这个决策分析过程中只有可避免成本才是需要考虑的相关成本。

例如，给定一个由 5 种不同产品组成的生产线，仅仅因为现在的净经营亏损而减掉销售组合当中的一件产品，一般来说是不明智的。相反，应该努力将产品的可溯固定费用和共同固定费用区别开来。如果淘汰掉一种产品，可溯固定费用就是潜在的可避免成本。共同固定费用是不可避免成本，无论产品淘汰还是保留该成本都不会变化。

一旦可避免成本被识别出来，就可以更肯定地确定相关边际贡献并决定增加、淘汰还是保留一个分部：

- 如果节省的可避免固定成本小于将要损失的边际收益，应该保留该分部。
- 如果节省的可避免固定成本大于损失的边际收益，应该剔除该分部因为会提高总的净营业利润。

增加还是减少分部成本分析

例1：

考虑下面一个产品分部报告亏损的利润表：

图表 3－88　利润表

销售		$500 000
变动费用		200 000
边际收益		300 000
固定费用：		
工厂总间接费用*	$60 000	
产品经理工资	90 000	
设备折旧**	50 000	
产品广告费	100 000	
厂房租金***	70 000	
总管理费用*	30 000	400 000
净亏损		$（100 000）

* 代表如果该产品被放弃应重新分配给其他生产线的已分配共同成本。
** 没有转售价值而且没有通过使用报废的设备。
*** 公司所拥有的厂房。

基于对该利润表的评价，公司应当保留该产品。

- 已分配共同成本（*）是不可避免的并且仍会发生。
- 设备折旧（**）是不可避免的费用。
- 厂房（***）是公司自有的，所以不可剔除。

图表 3－89　成本分析

损失的边际贡献	（$300 000）
来自已避免的固定成本的节省：	
产品经理的工资	90 000
产品广告费	100 000
放弃该生产线的净亏损	（$110 000）

放弃该产品所节省的固定成本低于边际贡献，因而公司在短期内保留该产品线是更加明智的选择。

例2：

考虑下面一个展示产品分部边际的利润表

图表 3－90　利润表

	部门 A	公司	没有部门 A 的公司
销售	$500 000	$4 000 000	$3 500 000
变动费用	200 000	2 000 000	1 800 000
边际收益	300 000	2 000 000	1 700 000
固定费用：			

续表

	部门 A	公司	没有部门 A 的公司
工厂总间接费用*	$60 000	$600 000	600 000
产品经理工资	90 000	400 000	310 000
设备折旧**	50 000	300 000	300 000
产品广告费	100 000	300 000	200 000
厂房租金***	70 000	200 000	200 000
总管理费用*	30 000	100 000	100 000
净亏损	$(100 000)	$100 000	$(10 000)

* 代表如果该产品被放弃应重新分配给其他生产线的已分配共同成本。

** 没有转售价值而且没有通过使用报废的设备。

*** 公司所拥有的厂房。

正如以上经营数据表所显示的，在本例中，公司应该保留分部 A。因为含 A 分部，总的净利润会更大。从中止分部 A 中节省的可避免固定成本不如损失的边际贡献多。

最大化限制性因素的单位贡献

当企业满足客户需求的能力受某项决定能力的因素限制时，企业目标就成为使每单位生产能力（限制性因素）的边际贡献最大化。例如：

Barlow 公司制造三种产品：A、B 和 C。每种产品的单位售价、变动成本以及边际贡献如下：

	产品		
	A	B	C
售价	$180	$270	$240
减：变动费用：			
直接材料	24	72	32
其他变动费用	102	90	148
总变动费用	126	162	180
边际贡献	$54	$108	$60
边际贡献率	30%	40%	25%

三种产品使用同样的原材料。Barlow 公司手头只有 5 000 磅原材料，并且由于其供应商工厂的罢工问题，未来几个星期都无法再获得任何材料。管理人员正尽力决定，下周应该集中生产哪种产品以便完成积压的订单。材料成本是每磅 $8。你建议公司下周应该选择哪个订单进行生产？

首先，确定每磅材料每种产品的贡献。然后，生产每磅材料贡献最大的产品。如下所示：

	A	B	C
（1）单位边际贡献	$54	$108	$60
（2）单位直接材料成本	$24	$72	$32
（3）每磅直接材料成本	$8	$8	$8
（4）单位产品需要的材料磅数（2）÷（3）	3	9	4
（5）每磅边际贡献（1）÷（4）	$18	$12	$15

公司应该将其可用材料集中生产产品 A：

	A	B	C
每磅边际贡献（同上）	$18	$12	$15
可用材料磅数	×5 000	×5 000	×5 000
总边际贡献	$90 000	$60 000	$75 000

尽管产品 A 单位边际贡献最低，且边际贡献率第二低，但与其他两种产品相比，它仍是更好的选择，因为产品 A 的每磅材料边际贡献最大，而材料是这家公司的被约束资源。

所得税和边际分析

决策制定过程要求确认各种相关成本。一种相关成本可能是变动的也可能是固定的。一般来说，大部分变动成本都是相关的，因为它们会因选择不同而不同而且又尚未发生；固定成本中大多数是不相关的，因为通常它们对所有选项都是一样的。

一个错误的假设是将折旧费用归类为相关成本。事实上，设施或设备的折旧费是已发生成本中的一部分。购置成本在资产寿命期被分摊。为此，折旧费是沉没成本，通常在决策分析过程中是不相关的。

将折旧费归类为不相关成本也有例外的情况，即考虑税收因素的影响时。在考虑所得税时，折旧费发挥了正效应，因其降低了应税收入从而减少了税费。在这种情况下，折旧降低了公司的税负。

进度检查

提示：完成以下各题，参考答案随后给出。

1. 对于有过剩生产能力的企业来说，一个专门订单的订价决策应该（　　　）
   a. 考虑潜在损失的销售的机会成本
   b. 比较相关成本和专门订单价格
   c. 比较单位总成本和专门订单价格
   d. 评价分离点前的全部联合成本

2. 制造或购买成本分析包括所有如下因素，除了（　　　）
   a. 相关内部成本和外购成本的比较
   b. 考虑机会成本
   c. 评价外部供应商
   d. 增量收入和增量成本的比较

3. 给定如下信息，对销售或再加工一件产品进行决策的利润或亏损？（　　　）
   - 该产品单位生产成本为 $10 000
   - 该产品单位售价是 $6 000
   - 单位增量处理成本是 $1 000

- 新的单位售价是 $6 650
  a. − $350
  b. − $650
  c. + $350
  d. + $650

进度检查答案

1. b
2. d
3. a

第5节
成本法定价

本节内容简介

要在当今的竞争环境中生存，公司必须仔细管理成本和价格。长期的财务成功取决于商品和服务收取的价格是否超过成本以及是否为资金增长、再投资筹资和给投资者满意的回报提供了充足的储备。管理会计师在收集、分析、计量和报告对成本定价决策有重要影响的信息方面扮演着关键的角色。

定价

"定价决策"这个术语一般是指公司就为其产品和服务收取多少价钱而做出的集体决策。没有被普遍接受的定价方法。然而，定价决策在决定企业的成败方面仍然是非常关键的。定价太高，可能会降低销量；定价太低，可能收不回成本。

相关产品和服务成本是定价决策中的一个重要部分。前面的章节中介绍了成本—性态类型、成本可溯性、成本动因和成本相关性等概念，这些当代的成本系统要素：

- 将活动和经营用作中间成本对象以将成本追溯到最终成本对象。
- 按照成本动因将成本分配给最终成本对象。
- 提供有关成本的多种观点（例如，按所消耗的资源、所消耗的活动和所消耗的动因）。
- 通过将各种容易忽略的关系提醒给经理从而促进对产品或服务的成本管理。

设计良好的成本管理系统增加了做出合理定价决策的可能性，同时帮助组织达到其战略目标。其他因素，例如产品或服务的供需以及时间范围，也会影响决策。

供需考虑事项

在几乎没有竞争对手和供不应求的情况下，传统的定价实务就是将产品或服务成本标上高价以产生足够的利润。只要需求保持旺盛、竞争受限，任何成本的上升都可以通过价格提升得到抵消。

以供需为基础的定价方式主要缺陷是它基本无法促进成本管理。许多公司——包括各行各业——曾经为覆盖成本而一直提高价格从而使产品和服务的定价脱离了市场。进一步说，除非有严格的市场准入限制（例如技术领先或大额资本投资要求），否则就会为竞争者进入市场提供机会。随着竞争增加、供大于求，通过将成本标上高价获利来幸存于市场变得困难起来。

时间范围

定价决策通常被分为短期和长期两种。

短期定价决策是一年或一年以内。许多则是六个月或六个月以内。短期决策用于一次性短期专门产品购买订单或对要求更及时生产线和产出量调整的竞争性市场环境的反应。

长期定价决策时间范围超过一年。长期决策一般关注主要市场上的某一产品或服务。

时间范围——短期或长期——最终都是描述哪些产品或服务成本与定价相关。一些定价决策可能既包括短期又包括长期。

短期成本法和定价法

如下情境例举了一次性专门订单的成本法和定价法。一家公司决定投标一项一次性快速周转的机会。其存在过剩的制造能力，所以该订单对于现存销售没有影响。在 100 000 单位正常生产运行水平下，单位变动和固定成本如图表 3 –91 所示。

图表 3 –91　固定成本和变动成本

	单位 变动成本	单位 固定成本	单位 变动及固定成本
制造			
直接材料	$10	—	$10
包装	5	—	5
直接人工	6	—	6
间接制造费用	8	$10	18
总制造成本	29	10	39
广告	4	12	16
分销	7	5	12
总成本	$40	$27	$67

变动间接制造费用（$8）代表了公用事业成本。在正常的 100 000 单位生产运行水平下，固定间接制造费用总成本和单位成本的细节如图表 3 –92 所示。

图表 3 –92　固定间接制造费用单位成本

	固定间接制造费用 总成本	固定间接制造费用 单位成本
折旧	$300 000	$3
原材料获得	100 000	1
工资	200 000	2
工程	400 000	4
固定间接制造费用总成本	$1 000 000	$10

一次性专门订单要求生产 10 000 单位产品。如果公司决定投标该订单，当前固定制造成本（$1 000 000）就会继续发生。公司将要发生的惟一额外支出是材料获得（$10 000）及工程准备（$25 000）。

要求投标的企业指出超过每单位 $35 的任何产品都不具备竞争力。公司为了竞标这个专门订单必须确定短期价格。

必须分析相关成本。只有额外的材料获得和工程准备成本是相关的。广告和分销成本在定价决策中是不相关的。现存的固定制造成本也是不相关的，因为公司是否接受该订单它们都保持不变。相关成本归纳如下：

图表 3 –93 相关成本数据

直接材料（10 000 单位 × $10）		$100 000
包装（10 000 单位 × $5）		550 000
直接人工（10 000 单位 × $6）		60 000
变动间接制造费用（10 000 单位 × $8）		80 000
材料获得	$10 000	
工程	25 000	
固定间接制造费用总成本		$35 000
总相关成本		$325 000

基于这些相关成本数据，单位相关成本为 $32.50（$325 000 ÷ 10 000 单位）。这低于被认为有竞争性的 $35 价格。任何高于该单位成本（$32.50）且低于 $35 的投标价都会为公司营业利润创造贡献。例如，短期价格 $34 可能带来 $15 000 的利润 [10 000 × （$34.00 – $32.50）]。

正如第 4 节 "边际分析" 中关于专门订单定价的讨论，基于单位总成本的定价决策会产生误导并且可能导致该业务无法中标。在本例中，如果用单位总成本来比较，该订单就将要被拒绝，因为公司的单位成本（$67）超出了投标的最高限价（$35）。即使分析时只用单位变动成本，该订单也可能被拒绝（$40 与投标的最高限价 $35 比较）。

长期成本法和定价法

精确的成本信息对公司做出关于产品或服务收费多少及怎样在市场上最好地竞争的决策至关重要。分析方法会做出与成本和价格有关的假设。如果这些限制条件稳定，分析精确就会有更大的可能性。

在给定长期时间范围的情况下，稳定且可预测的成本对定价决策而言更受欢迎。稳定的长期成本会带来价格的更大稳定性并降低持续监督供应商价格和其他相关成本数据的必要。稳定的长期成本也会改善其他规划决策，鼓励更牢固的长期买卖关系。预测变得更容易，顾客关系也更紧密。

市场基础定价法

公司经常必须在几乎没有差异的产品和服务市场上竞争。市场基础定价法一般在这种产品或服务基本相同的情况下流行。

在市场基础定价法环境下：

- 市场力量对产品或服务定价影响较大。
- 顾客不愿付比市场普遍价格更高的价钱。
- 公司一般收取普遍的市场利率。

市场基础定价法基本不允许公司有高于或低于市场利率的定价空间；一家只有判断自由的公司应该这样做。尽管采取市场基础定价法，一家企业：

- 考虑客户期望和想要什么。
- 确定竞争激烈程度。
- 估计客户和竞争对手会对其定价如何反应。

在市场基础定价法中，公司根据预计的客户和竞争对手反应做出关于产品和服务特性以及定价的决策。总目标是避免能导致昂贵的市场混乱或竞争性价格战的定价。同样，市场基础法是合理的定价方法，用于高度竞争和商品型市场，例如航空、石油、天然气、矿石和许多农产品。

成本基础定价法

成本基础定价法（或称成本加成定价法）通过研究成本来开发一项产品或服务并设定价格来覆盖成本，赚取想要的利润。当一定水平的产品或服务差异存在时，成本基础定价法是恰当的，在定价时公司能做出谨慎判断。市场基础定价法被市场条件严格限制，所以成本基础定价法将市场反应作为定价的一个因素：

在成本基础定价法下，企业应该：

- 确定生产和销售产品的成本。
- 确认合理的报酬（加价）。
- 对成本进行加价。
- 必要时调整加价以对市场力量做出反应。

使用成本基础定价法，加价一般被表示为成本的百分数。预定的加价被用于成本基础以确定目标销售价格。

销售价格 = 成本 + (加价% × 成本)

例如，一个产品单位成本 \$50，加价 50%，销售价格 \$75。

成本基础定价法的挑战是确定用什么成本以及最终加价多少。最后，想要的加价被评估，并基于竞争对手收取类似产品的价格和消费者对备选价格的预期反应进行修订。

目标定价法

目前为止讨论的传统定价方法都基于以下理念：

价格 = 成本 + 边际利润

这个等式假设一种产品或服务已经被开发出来，成本已经或可以被确认，并且一旦价格确定该产品或服务很容易营销。

目标成本法提供了一种根本不同的方法来看待价格和成本的关系。目标成本法的基本概念是：

成本 = 竞争性价格 – 边际利润

产品或服务成本通过预计售价减去想要的利润计算。

关键的概念和术语

要理解目标定价法，有几个概念和术语很重要。

目标成本法

目标成本法有很多种定义。管理会计公告 4FF "执行目标成本法"，列举的大部分定义所共有的特征如下：

- 竞争性的市场环境。
- 市场价格驱动成本（和投资）决策的环境。
- 早在产品设计和开发阶段实施成本计划、成本管理和成本降低。
- 交叉职能团队的参与，包括管理会计。

本质上说，目标成本法是一个综合的成本管理过程，它确定了产品或服务的目标成本，然后开发出在确定数量下生产能够获利的产品或服务的原型。它是一种主动型方法，产品和服务成本的管理早在设计开发过程而不是后期的开发生产阶段进行。

目标成本法的根本目标是使企业在竞争的市场环境中获利经营。同样，目标成本法的基础是确定市场基础和价格基础成本。研究设计、工程、生产、营销和会计等交叉职能的参与对于确保提案的产品或服务在销售时产生想要的边际利润是很有必要的。换句话说，交叉职能团队负责设计开发产品或服务以使其按目标成本制造。

目标价格

在目标成本法中，目标价格代表可收取产品或服务的最高价格。它是对潜在客户基于价值认知——对产品服务、质量、及时性和价格等的需要和预期——所愿意支付的价格的估计。目标价格也反映了企业对市场竞争——它们的能力和可能的反应——的了解。最终，目标价格应该带来客户可接受的价格和组织可接受的报酬。

目标成本

在定义目标成本时，SMA 4FF 指出该术语对于不同的公司意味着不同的事情。对某些公司来说，目标成本是目标价格（由市场决定）和目标利润（由管理人员决定）之差。其他定义将目标成本描述为可接受成本和当前成本之差——即为达到可接受成本而必须从成本中减掉的金额。

可接受成本

可接受成本是目标价格和目标利润之差。实际上，可接受成本代表一个企业为达成其利润目标可以赋予其产品的最大成本。

单位目标营业利润和单位目标成本

目标成本法和目标定价法中其他重要的概念是单位目标营业利润和单位目标成本。

- 单位目标营业利润是公司为售出的每单位产品或服务而努力赢得的营业利润。
- 单位目标成本是预计的长期的单位产品或服务成本。

单位目标成本通过从目标价格中减去单位目标营业利润来确定。如果一单位产品以目标成本生产并以目标价格销售，公司就可以获得目标营业利润。

如下情境显示了单位目标营业利润和单位目标成本。因日益激烈的市场竞争，一家企业需要将其单位售价从 \$100 降到 \$75。在这个较低的价格水平上，企业预期年销售量从 10 000 单位增加到 12 000 单位。管理人员希望在销售收入中赚取 15% 的目标营业利润。当前的单位总成本为 \$80。

总目标销售收入 = 12 000 单位 × $75 = $900 000

总目标营业利润 = 15% × $900 000 = $135 000

单位目标营业利润 = $135 000 ÷ 12 000 = $11.25

单位目标成本 = 目标价格 – 单位目标营业利润

= $75.00 – $11.25 = $63.75

目标定价法中，产品的市场价被看作是给定的。单位目标成本通常低于单位产品或服务的全部成本。正如上例所示，单位目标成本为 $63.75，当前的（全部）单位成本为 $80。但是为了盈利，公司必须收回其全部成本。因此，所有的成本——固定的和变动的——都与目标成本计算相关。在此情况下，为改善产品或服务及整个生命周期的生产过程，企业将不断地面临目标成本法的挑战。

图表 3-94 概括了企业用来设计提议的新产品或服务以及建立目标价格和目标边际的基本技术（SMA 4FF）。

行业和竞争性分析与市场评估及逆向工程数据相结合，有助于促进目标价格的设定。财务计划和分析可以推动目标边际利润的确定。内部成本分析和成本图表促进了允许成本和当前成本的比较及目标成本的确定。

图表 3-94 目标成本过程工具

工具	描述
市场评估工具	用来评估市场和客户对计划产品或服务的需求的几种方法，包括调查、焦点小组、访谈和对现在、未来或以前客户的顾客评论卡片。
逆向工程（拆卸分析）	获取并拆卸竞争对手产品以调查他们的设计、材料、可能的制造过程、属性、质量和成本。
行业和竞争性分析	用来理解竞争对手以及如何最好将企业及其产品和服务定位在竞争优势上的分析工具。可能包括各种各样进行综合的行业和竞争性分析的战略（如麦克尔·E·波特战略）。
财务计划和分析	具体的财务计划和报表分析，以检验过程、数量和收入之间的关系。该方法同时也从整体、专门分部线及单个产品（或服务）上关注成本和投资；允许对计划的产品或服务进行比较。
内部成本分析	确定产品和服务成本及对当前供给的投资，以估计在现存和计划的产品/服务特征及处理特征下计划的新产品或服务的成本。该工具通常用作业成本法（ABC）来确认与专门的成本发生活动有关的成本。
成本图表	对基于各种制造变量的详细的成本信息数据库进行维护和使用；促进对计划的新产品或服务的不同设计、材料、制造过程和终端用户功能的成本规划。该技术帮助经理事先确定其他选择的效果。·

目标成本法过程

正如目标成本法没有统一的定义，其实施步骤也无明确规定。目标成本法在任何一家公司都倾向于基于特定的企业环境进行演化。然而，SMA 4FF 给出了普遍适用于大多数目标成本法应用的步骤，如图表 3-95 所示。

图表 3 - 95　目标成本法步骤

- 在考虑市场需求和竞争情况下建立目标价格。
- 建立目标边际利润。
- 确定必须达到的成本。
- 计算当前产品和过程的可能成本。
- 建立目标成本——即必须被减掉的成本额。
- 建立一个交叉职能团队，使他们从最初的设计阶段就参与实施过程。
- 在设计过程中使用一些工具，如并行工程法、价值工程法和质量功能配置法。
- 一旦生产开始进行，就实行成本缩减（例如，通过持续改进法和生命周期成本法）。

一旦确定目标成本，随之而来的就是实现该成本的挑战。对于交叉职能团队的强调促进了企业各职能部门之间的高度相互依赖。公司会努力改变不同方法以达到可以实现目标成本的产品/服务和流程设计。大多数企业使用了并行工程法、价值工程法、质量功能配置法和持续改进法以及生命周期成本法中的一些方法。

并行工程法

并行工程法是组织在过程之初就通过使用来自所有业务单元和职能的投入及评价设计产品或服务，预计问题并平衡各方需求。该方法强调保持客户需求和上游预防而非下游修正。

价值工程法

价值工程法是一项消除当前成本和允许成本之间差距的重要技术。它是针对客户需求而对产品或服务设计、材料、规格和生产过程的系统分析。

需要区分增值成本和非增值成本。增值成本是指将资源转化为与客户需求一致的产品或服务的成本。它们是客户认为增加产品或服务价值或效用的成本。相反，非增值成本对客户偏好来说并不重要。在制造业，增值成本的例子可能是与设计、装配、工具和机器相关的成本。非增值成本的例子可能是邮件快递费、返工成本或陈旧存货成本。

实际上，要分清增值成本和非增值成本很难。在特定情况下，一些成本可能两类成本都可以归入。在制造过程中，测试成本或订货成本通常很难区分是增值成本还是非增值成本。

价值工程法的目标是权衡总的成本和收益以及增加产品最终价值。使用交叉职能团队可以最好地实现该过程，因为设计、开发、生产和成本之间的权衡都包括在其中了。管理会计师通常被要求评估因消除非增值活动和相关成本而产生的潜在节省。

在很大程度上，"价值工程"和"价值分析"这两个术语是可以互换使用的。一些企业在设计开发阶段使用"分析"而在开发后阶段使用"工程"。

质量功能配置法

质量功能配置法（QFD）是一种将客户对产品或服务的要求转化成开发和生产每一阶段的适当技术的结构化方法。QFD 过程通常被称为"倾听顾客心声"。

产品生命周期成本法和生命周期成本法

目标成本法假设由于市场情况——因价格、质量和性能的竞争，产品或服务价格是稳定的或随时间减少的。公司必须在产品或服务的生命周期中对这些竞争性压力做出反应。

正如本书第2章"战略营销"中所讨论的，产品生命周期（PLC）是基于一个行业（及其产品和服务）要经历很多可预见的步骤或阶段这一前提的概念。

目标成本法被用来减少产品或服务整个生命周期当中的总成本。在应用目标成本法原则时，企业必须定期重新设计产品和服务以便在降低价格的同时提高价值。

生命周期成本法追踪并积累整个生命周期中与产品或服务相关的所有真实成本。捕捉所有成本为各种使成本最小化的规划决策提供了重要信息。

持续改进成本法

第1章"战略规划"中提到，"改善"是日本人用来描述企业在所有层次上持续改进（CI）的一个术语。一旦产品或服务进入生产阶段，改善成本法就成为一个全面而持续的降低成本的方法。改善成本法（与其他CI实务，如全面质量管理和约束理论相结合）被用在为降低产品或服务成本而进行的各次重新设计之间，这种成本降低是通过提高供应链效率和整个生产过程中生产力实现的。

成本加目标报酬率定价法

此前讨论的成本基础定价法，描述了设定价格的一个一般公式，即在成本基础上加一个加价百分比。成本加目标报酬率法是以目标投资报酬率为基础确定加价的一种方法。

目标投资报酬率是一家企业必须挣到的目标营业利润除以它的投入资本。企业通常设定一个目标投资报酬率。

如下例举了成本加目标报酬率定价法：

- 一种产品的单位全部成本为 $1 000。
- 预期销售数量为 10 000。
- 税前目标报酬率为 20%。
- 投入资本（长期或者固定资产加流动资产）为 $10 000 000。
- 总目标营业利润为 20% × $10 000 000。
- 单位目标营业利润为 $2 000 000 ÷ 10 000 单位，或者 $200。

基于以上信息，想要的单位目标营业利润是 $200。给定单位全部产品成本为 $1 000，加价百分比是：$200 ÷ $1 000 = 20%。

20%的加价代表以单位全部产品成本百分比表示的单位营业利润。

最大负荷定价法考虑事项

迄今为止，所有讨论过的定价法都是以某种方式基于成本的。在一些情况下，定价中也必须考虑非成本因素。最大负荷定价法就是这样一种情况。

最大负荷定价法是基于需求和物质能力限制而对产品或服务多收费或少收费的一种实务。在该方法下，即使实质成本没有显著不同，价格也在细分市场之间不同。

当如下情境出现时，采用最大负荷定价，价格可能上升或下降：

- 当需求接近能力限制时，价格上升。
- 当宽松或剩余能力存在时，价格下降。

最大负荷定价法被用于很多行业，如航空、旅店、汽车租赁、电力设施和通讯等。

进度检查

提示：完成以下各题，参考答案随后给出。

1. 哪些特点将传统定价法与目标定价法区别开来？（　　）
    a. 传统定价法基于价格等于成本加边际利润的假设，而目标成本法暗示了成本等于竞争价格减去边际利润。
    b. 传统定价法基于成本等于竞争价格减去边际利润的假设，而目标成本法暗示了价格等于成本加边际利润。
    c. 传统定价法以成本的百分比标注价格，而目标成本针对竞争对手法标注价格。
    d. 传统定价法针对竞争对手标注价格，而目标成本法以成本的百分比来标注价格。

找出与以下项目相匹配的描述。

2. _____市场基础价格　　a. 一般在存在一定水平的产品或服务差异而且公司在定价时能行使适度自由时使用。

3. _____成本基础价格　　b. 一般在竞争性环境中使用，以使企业能够盈利经营。

4. _____目标价格　　c. 一般在产品或服务等价的情况下以及当公司基本没有定价自由时使用。

5. 哪种方法对企业在设计过程中努力消除当前成本和允许成本之间差距最有用？（　　）
    a. 逆向工程法
    b. 产品生命周期成本法
    c. 价值工程法
    d. 质量功能配置法

6. 在目标成本法过程中使用交叉职能团队有什么主要好处？（　　）
    a. 改善对如何获得和保持竞争优势的分析。
    b. 对成本图表数据库更准确的输入和维护。
    c. 对客户需求的更现实的市场评估。
    d. 对计划的产品或服务产生想要的边际利润提供更好的保证。

进度检查答案

1. a
2. c
3. a
4. b
5. c
6. d

投资决策

本章内容简介

无论是以债务还是以权益形式存在，资本都是一种有限的组织资源。银行对于其可提供的借贷规模是有限制的。甚至绝大多数稳定的公司也只能借债到一定水平或者发行有限数量的普通股来筹集资本。

基于组织资本资源有限性这一现实，每个企业都必须仔细评估其投资项目。通常，管理会计师在决定一个投资是否稳健或值得实行方面发挥着举足轻重的作用。本章内容以资本预算过程概述为起点，然后回顾了一些便于在两个或多个投资方案中做出明智选择的基本原则。

学习要点说明

注册管理会计师（CMA）考试包含很多学习要点，这些学习要点由管理会计师协会确定。学习要点描述了注册管理会计师考试要求掌握的所有知识点和技能，并且细分为各个章节。注册管理会计师考试教材解释了学习要点所包含的各个部分，是对学习要点的有力支持。学习要点可以帮助考生以不同的方式或通过不同的问题情景理解这些概念。考生还应该练习学习要点中所提到的全部或者部分计算，或者完成计算过程中的缺失部分。学习要点不能代替对 CMA 考试教材内容的研究和学习，但是可以确保考生达到学习要点所设定的目标。

注册管理会计师教材中所包含的学习要点是一个完整的集合，并且是到目前为止最新的版本。考生可以浏览 IMA 的官方网站 www. imanet. org，点击"认证"部分查看和下载关于学习要点的最新 PDF 文件。

学习要点

5.1 资本预算过程

- LOS 5.1.1：定义资本预算。
- LOS 5.1.2：说明对项目投资决策制定过程中应用资本预算的理解。
- LOS 5.1.3：确定项目资本预算开发和实施的步骤或阶段。
- LOS 5.1.4：确定并计算一个资本投资项目中税前和税后的相关现金流。
- LOS 5.1.5：说明对所得税如何影响现金流的理解。
- LOS 5.1.6：区分现金流量和会计利润，并讨论增量现金流、沉没成本和机会成本与资本预算的相关性。
- LOS 5.1.7：解释资本预算过程中净营运资本变动的重要性。
- LOS 5.1.8：讨论资本预算分析中通货膨胀的影响如何被反映出来。
- LOS 5.1.9：描述事后审计在资本预算过程中的作用。

5.2 折现现金流量分析

- LOS 5.2.1：说明对两种主要的 DCF 法、净现值（NPV）和内含报酬率（IRR）的理解。
- LOS 5.2.2：说明对使用加权平均资本成本法计算 NPV 的理解。
- LOS 5.2.3：用货币时间价值表计算 NPV 和 IRR。
- LOS 5.2.4：说明对为确定可行项目而进行 NPV 和 IRR 分析时所用的决策标准的理解。
- LOS 5.2.5：重点比较 NPV 和 IRR 的相对优点和缺点，特别是关于独立与互斥项目、"复合内含报酬率问题（multiple IRR problem）"及导致该问题产生的现金流类型以及为什么 NPV 和 IRR 使用不当会产生矛盾的资本项目排序。
- LOS 5.2.6：确定评估资本投资项目的不同方法的假设。
- LOS 5.2.7：在 DCF 分析的基础上推荐项目投资。

5.3 回收期与折现回收期

- LOS 5.3.1：说明对回收期法的理解。
- LOS 5.3.2：确定回收期法的优点和缺点/局限。
- LOS 5.3.3：计算回收期和折现回收期。
- LOS 5.3.4：确定折现回收期法的优点和缺点/局限。

5.4 评级投资项目

- LOS 5.4.1：定义资本分配和互斥项目。
- LOS 5.4.2：利用获利能力指数为资本项目评级并推荐最优投资。
- LOS 5.4.3：确定什么时候推荐获利能力指数而不是 NPV 规则（例如，资本分配中的独立项目）。
- LOS 5.4.4：确认并讨论当比较规模不等和/或时间长度不等项目时的内在问题。
- LOS 5.4.5：说明对评估备选资本投资项目时不同方法的优缺点的理解。
- LOS 5.4.6：确认评级问题的备选解决方案，包括内部资本市场和线性规划。

5.5 资本投资的风险分析

- LOS 5.5.1：确认资本预算中应对风险的备选方法。
- LOS 5.5.2：说明对敏感性分析和确定性等值的理解。
- LOS 5.5.3：确认制定资本投资决策时的定性考虑。
- LOS 5.5.4：解释为什么当企业项目现金流比正常情况风险高或低时应该使用一个专门的风险调整利率。
- LOS 5.5.5：区分敏感性分析、情景分析和蒙特卡洛模拟等风险分析技术。
- LOS 5.5.6：描述资本预算过程中如何使用 CAPM 模型。

5.6 资本投资的实物期权

- LOS 5.6.1：说明对资本预算过程中实物期权这一概念的理解。
- LOS 5.6.2：确认四种普通的实物期权——例如，如下事项的期权：（a）如果当前投资项目成功则追加投资；（b）放弃一个项目；（c）投资前等待和了解；或者（d）使公司产出或生产方法多样化。
- LOS 5.6.3：确认实物期权是买入期权还是卖出期权。
- LOS 5.6.4：说明对影响期权价值的变量和因素的理解。

第 1 节
资本预算过程

本节内容简介

简单来说，资本预算是制定长期投资决策的过程。它是一个企业评估长期投资项目生存能力及其是否值得投资的决策制定过程。

资本预算

在企业经营过程中，企业会进行两种类型的投资：流动投资和资本投资。

流动投资（或流动支出）本质上是短期的；它们是在费用发生同一年即可注销的投资。工资、薪金、许多管理费用和制造业原材料支出都是流动投资的例子。经营预算（或流动预算）是对与短期活动有关的经营费用和收入的计划。

资本投资（或资本支出）是长期的。一项资本投资可以导致伴随未来收益预期的当前现金支出。按照 IRS（译者注：即 Internal Revenue Service，美国国内税务局）的规定，初始现金支出的价值会随时间而逐渐下降（摊销）。资本投资的例子包括新添或重置机器设备的支出以及新产品和服务的研究、设计和开发投资。资本预算是获得长期资产的建议支出的计划，包括为购置筹集资金的方法。

企业的稳定和未来的成功常常取决于它的资本投资。因此企业需要稳健的资本预算过程来分析控制长期资本投资。企业要收回不良成本投资通常有很大的困难。

资本预算应用

资本预算计划可以有很多来源。对于决策分析过程，资本支出常被归入下面几类中的一类：

- 扩张性项目：为扩张业务经营而购置新机器设备。
- 重置性项目：替换现存的机器设备。
- 强制性项目：法律要求的项目，目的是为确保工作场所安全、消费者安全和保护环境。
- 其他项目：用于新产品研发和/或现有产品扩张以及各种其他长期投资如厂房、土地、专利等的一些拨款。

还有一些备选的资本支出分类，例如：

- 经营效率和/或收入的产生。
- 竞争效果。
- 法规、安全、健康和环境要求。

无论公司使用哪一种分类表，组织战略和目标都会影响资本投资中的评价标准和决策过程。

资本预算项目和时间范围

资本预算的两个重要方面是项目范围和时间范围。

项目范围

经营预算决策关注于当期活动的利润确定、计划和活动，而资本预算决策则关注跨越几个会计期间的项目。例如，一项与新产品开发有关的资本预算项目，可能从研发设计到产品完成和顾客服务需要好几年的时间。

生命周期成本法必须被用来按项目累计资本预算成本和收入并追踪整个项目的利润。对于上述新产品开发的例子，必须累计几个会计期间价值链中全部业务职能的成本。

时间范围

一般，资本预算决策降低当期的报告利润，但是却有在未来产生高现金流入的潜力。因此，资本预算决策不能仅仅基于当前会计期间的利润表。

当然，任何给定期间的利润是重要的。对于上市公司来说，给定期间报告的利润可以影响到企业股价以及红利。但是过分关注短期会计会导致放弃长期盈利性的投资决策。

货币时间价值这一概念对资本预算而言是基本的。货币时间价值是指：

- 今天的一美元（或任何其他货币单位）比明天收到的一美元更值钱，因为可以将今天这一美元投资以赚取报酬。
- 明天的一美元没有今天的一美元值钱因为它放弃的利息。

今天投资 $10 000 美元，预计年报酬率 15%，那么其在年末的价值就是 $11 500。但是，根据货币时间价值，如果没有进行这项投资，机会成本就是放弃的 $1 500。

资本预算阶段

一项资本预算项目包括活动的逻辑进程。各阶段或步骤的具体名称因企业而异。总的来说，企业会涉及图表 3-96 中显示的所有阶段或步骤。

增量现金流量

一个组织及其投资者都会对企业现金状况感兴趣。因此，主要关心的就是现金流以及它如何受资本投资项目的影响。

图表 3-96　资本预算的阶段

阶段 1　**确认**	资本预算的第一阶段就是确认哪种类型的资本预算支出是必要的并与组织目标、目的和战略一致。
阶段 2　**调查**	接下来的阶段包括全面调查初始资本投资计划，发掘备选投资。
阶段 3　**评价**	第三阶段是预计并比较每一个备选方案整个生命周期的收入、财务和非财务收益、成本和现金流。管理人员必须评价该项目将怎样影响组织的资源以及企业能否承受这些成本。

续表

阶段4	**选择** 第四阶段是选择将要实施的方案，一般是选择那些预计财务收益超过成本并产生最大边际的项目。此外，非财务（定性）结果也应予以考虑。
阶段5	**筹资** 第五阶段是取得项目筹资，可以是内部筹资（再投资现金）也可以是通过在资本市场出售债务和权益进行外部筹资。
阶段6	**实施和控制** 最后阶段是实施资本预算方案，然后对它进行监督和评价。选择该项目时的预测需要与实际结果进行比较。必要的话（并且可能的话），可能需要做出调整以在项目生命周期中获得最优结果。

预计未来现金流是资本预算中最重要的任务之一。企业必须能够评价存在和不存在投资项目两种情况下现金流的差异以及项目中所有相关成本和收益会产生影响的地方。

评价资本投资现金流的关键点是：

- 所有影响现金流的项目，不管是该会计期间的收入还是费用，都必须检验。
- 应忽略沉没成本，因为它们是与投资决策不相关的历史成本。
- 必须包括机会成本，一般在项目开始时作为现金支出处理。
- 净营运资本投资作为该投资发生时的现金流出处理。
- 必须考虑通货膨胀的预计影响。
- 在资本预算中，只有影响企业税负现金流的折旧费用才是相关的。

资本投资项目一般开始于作为资金支付或承付的现金流出。在投资期间，不同的现金流结果是可能的。初始现金流出的报酬可能会降低现金支出或产生现金流入。在某些情况下，两种结果都可能出现。在监督控制活动的基础上，可能需要追加资本投资的资金。

资本投资项目中的相关增量现金流根据它们在该项目的发生时间——项目初始、整个项目过程及项目结束——进行分类。图表3－97概括了这几类资本项目现金流的特点。

图表3－97　在资本预算项目期间的现金流入和流出

类别	描述	现金流活动
初始期	初始现金投资	• 为投资提供资金并启动项目的流出 • 净营运资本的承付款 • 替换资产时的流入或流出
经营期	期间增量净现金流	• 经营性支出的流出 • 额外资本投资（如果必要）的流出 • 用于经营的额外净营运资本的承付款 • 投资产生的流入（例如，收入和现金节省）以及经营中不再需要的净营运资本释放的现金
处置期	最后一年的增量净现金流	• 与投资处置相关的流入或流出 • 不再用于投资的净营运资本释放的现金流入

现金流入增加了企业的可用现金；现金流出或现金承付减少了可用现金。用作营运资本的资金无法转作他用。净营运资本是流动资产超过流动负债的部分。它是可用

来满足经营要求的额外资金。

在进一步检验相关现金流类型以前，理解以下概念是非常重要的。

- 直接效应是现金流入、流出或承诺对现金流产生的直接影响。
- 纳税效应（或间接效应）是企业纳税支付的变化。
- 净效应（或总效应）是直接效应和纳税效应的加总。

初始期现金流

项目初始阶段现金流的确定通常如图表 3–98 所示。资产成本经常根据所有交易产生的净效应进行各种调整。

图表 3–98　初始期增量现金流

–	新资产成本的直接效应
–	额外的资本性支出（例如，为运输、安装和调试）
–或+	净营运资本的增加或减少
+	旧资产出售的净收入（如果该投资是重置性项目）
–或+	旧资产出售的纳税效应（如果该投资是重置性项目）
=	初始期现金流

经营期现金流

为了启动项目而付出了必要的初始期现金流后，企业希望从随后期间中产生的现金流中获益。未来现金流的确定一般如图表 3–99 所示。

图表 3–99　经营期（每个期间）增量现金流

	经营收入的净增加或减少
–或+	经营费用（除了折旧）的任何净增加或净减少
–或+	税法折旧费用的净增加或净减少
=	税前利润的净变化
–或+	税负的净增加或净减少
=	税后的净效应
+或–	税法折旧费用的净增加或净减少
=	经营期增量现金流

需要注意的是，应先减掉或加上税法折旧费用的净增或减少来确定税前利润的净变化。随后，为确定该期间的增量现金流，再把该税法折旧的净增加或减少加回或减去。这是因为税法折旧是可以降低应税收入的非现金支出。为了确定项目对接受该项目的企业的增量影响需要开始时将它考虑在内。之后再次将它加上或减去是为了避免低估项目对现金流的影响。

处置期现金流

处置期（在最后阶段，项目终止时）的增量现金流如图表 3–100 所示。需要确认一些专门与项目终止相关的活动：

- 任何出售或处置资产的残值。

- 与资产处置有关的净纳税效应（税负或纳税节省）。
- 净营运资本的任何变化（例如，在项目终止时净营运资本重新回到现金流中）。

图表 3－100 的阴影部分是与项目终止有关的现金流。

图表 3－100　处置期增量现金流

+	任何出售或处置资产的残值
－ 或 ＋	由于出售或处置资产而产生的净纳税效应（税负或纳税节省）
＋ 或 －	净营运资本水平重新收回的增加或减少
＝	处置期增量现金流

增量现金流的例子

例如，在制造经营过程中购买一个新机器，请确定其增量现金流：

- 新机器的成本为 $80 000。
- 机器的运输费和安装费为 $20 000。
- 机器四年使用寿命后的残值为 $30 000。

不需要额外的营运资本。该机器被安装在没有其他备选用途的领域，因而不存在机会成本。公司税率为 40%。净经营收入（折旧和纳税前）的预测如图表 3－101 所示。

图表 3－101　净经营收入预测

	年末			
	1	2	3	4
净现金流	$40 000	$42 000	$50 000	$38 000

初始期增量现金流如图表 3－102 所示。

图表 3－102　初始期增量现金流

新资产成本的直接效应	($80 000)
额外资本性支出（运输或安装）	(20 000)
初始期现金流	($100 000)

经营期和处置期的增量（未来）现金流如图表 3－103 所示。

图表 3－103　经营期和处置期的增量现金流

	年末			
	1	2	3	4
经营期现金流（第一到四年）				
经营收入的净变化（不包括折旧）	$40 000	$42 000	$50 000	$38 000
税法折旧费用的净增加 *	(33 330)	(44 450)	(14 810)	(7 410)
税前利润的净变化	$6 670	($2 450)	$35 190	$30 590
税率为 40% 时税负的净增加或净减少	(2 668)	980	(14 076)	(12 236)
税后净效应	$4 002	$(1 470)	$21 114	$18 354

续表

	年末			
	1	2	3	4
税法折旧费用的净增加	33 330	44 450	14 810	7 410
第一年到第四年的增量现金流	$37 332	$42 980	$35 924	$25 764
处置期现金流（第四年）				
任何出售或处置资产的残值**				$33 000
出售或处置资产的净纳税效应（应交税金）				(13 200)
处置期现金流				19 800

　　*根据修订的加速成本回收制度（MACRS）的折旧图表，一个三年期资产，其折旧基数为$100 000，折旧率为第一年：33.33%，第二年：44.45%，第三年：14.81%，第四年：7.41%。

　　**假设残值是折旧的回收，按普通收益40%的税率纳税。

　　这项资本投资的预期增量现金流如图表3-104所示。（在资本预算过程中，将初始期现金流出的时间作为第0年。）

图表3-104　预期增量现金流

	年末				
	0	1	2	3	4
净现金流	（$100 000）	$37 332	$42 980	$35 924	$45 564*

　　*第四年经营期和处置期现金流为$25 764和$19 800。

　　增量现金流数据提供了判断项目吸引力的必要的相关信息。管理人员有必要评价项目将怎样影响组织资源。应将该项目与其他备选方案进行比较。

　　然后，企业需要进一步利用各种方法审视资本投资项目的预期现金流入和流出。在本章下两节中将详细解释如下方法：

- 折现现金流量（DCF）分析。
- 回收期法。

　　DCF法通过考虑货币时间价值来对现金流量进行调整。为此，该方法被广泛用于评价长期投资决策。

所得税考虑事项

　　来自资本投资的现金流量会产生各种纳税效应。在某些情况下，税负能明显减少项目净现金流并影响其合意性。

　　通过编制财务报表的通用会计原则（GAAP）阐明的绝大多数纳税规则适用于资本投资项目的现金流量。但也有与资本投资相关的专门的税务规则。特别是，与折旧有关的税务规则在如下方面存在差异：

- 可允许的折旧金额。
- 折旧期。
- 折旧模式。

如下是对这些折旧考虑事项的概述。

记住，对可折旧资产进行的税务处理可能很复杂。只要企业投资于可营利资产，就要估计该资产的生产寿命。任何资本资产的价值都会随其使用寿命的消耗而减少。为了会计目的，该资产应在使用期内折旧。

然而，折旧可能没有反映资本资产使用寿命中的真实价值，因为过时随时都可能发生。例如，当开发出一个更高级的机器时，现存的可能就要过时了，尽管它还没有坏掉。进一步说，企业选择的折旧方法可能更多的是纳税效应的函数，而不是使项目账面价值反映其真实转售价值的能力的函数。

实际上，许多因素会使折旧变得复杂化。建议对当前的或适用的税法进行彻底调研并/或咨询税务专家。

可允许的折旧金额

计算一项资产可允许的折旧金额要求确定资产的折旧基数。在税务会计中，折旧基数是在一段年限内为纳税目的而冲销的金额。

一般来说，可允许金额是资产的原始成本。这包括为准备资产投入使用（例如运输和安装费）所必须的其他资本性支出。资本性支出被作为可折旧现金支出而不是其发生期间的费用进行处理。

在某些情况下，可允许金额可能比原始投资成本高或低。例如，税额减免可使可允许金额降至原始成本以下，同时一些税法还允许公司有权要求特定资产折旧金额超过投资。

折旧期

确定资本投资折旧期三种主要技术：

- 纳税人估计使用寿命。
- 税务机构估计使用寿命。
- 税法通过一系列纳税表（例如修订的加速成本回收制度，或 MACRS，发音如"makers"）详细规定可允许的寿命。

一般来说，可允许的寿命越短，该资产折旧可要求的期间就越短。这导致了每年有更高的可折旧金额，更高的应税收益减免额以及更大的纳税节省。

折旧模式

税务机构允许不同的折旧模式（基于时期）。有各种各样可能的折旧方法。下面概述几种比较普遍的方法。

直线折旧法（SL）

直线折旧法（SL）将费用平均分配到资产的折旧寿命中。每年提取相等的折旧金额。

直线折旧法的一般公式为：

直线折旧 =（成本 - 残值）/预计的使用寿命

一项资产成本为 \$10 000，预计使用寿命 5 年，残值 \$2 000。使用直线折旧法，在这 5 年间每年形成相等的折旧费用：

直线折旧 =（\$10 000 - \$2 000）/5 = \$1 600 每年

加速折旧法

加速折旧法是指比 SL 法更快冲销资本投资的任何方法。与直线法相比，在投资的初始几年该方法冲销较多的折旧金额。年数总和法、余额递减法及双倍余额递减法都是加速折旧法的例子。

- **年数总和法（SYD）**

年数总和法（SYD）是在资产寿命的初始几年快速减少资本投资账面价值、在最后几年又采用较低折旧率的一种方法。SYD 法与 SL 法以同样的方式考虑了预计残值。

与上例相同，$10 000 的资产，5 年的使用寿命，$1 000 的预计残值，使用 SYD 法确定第一年的折旧金额。因为该资产预计使用寿命为 5 年，年数总和为 15（即 1 + 2 + 3 + 4 + 5 = 15）。

该资产通过下列方式折旧：

- 第一年：33.33%（5/15）
- 第二年：26.67%（4/15）
- 第三年：20.00%（3/15）
- 第四年：13.33%（2/15）
- 第五年：6.67%（1/15）

因此，在 SYD 法下，第一年的折旧为 $2 667（$8 000）(0.3333)，而在 SL 法下为 $1 600。第五年，SYD 法下的折旧为 $536（$8 000）(0.067)，而 SL 法下为 $1 600。与 SL 法的折旧相比，SYD 法在资产寿命的前几年折旧高，后几年折旧低。

- **余额递减法**

余额递减法（DB）通过每年以固定比率降低资产账面价值来减少资产价值。与 SL 法和 SYD 法不同，DB 法在计算中没有直接使用残值。然而，当按成本减残值提取折旧时，折旧费用将被中止。余额递减法的一般公式确定了任何期间的折旧费用都等于：

(1/n) NBV

其中：

- n 为资产的折旧寿命
- NBV 为资产在年初的净账面价值（成本 - 累计折旧）。

一项有 5 年寿命的 $10 000 资产，第一年的折旧应该是 $2 000。1/5（或 20%）确定了用于每年减少净账面价值的固定百分比。第二年的净账面价值为 $8 000（购置成本减累计折旧）。因此，第二年折旧费用为：

(0.20) $8 000 = $1 600

选定的固定百分比一般是在资产预计寿命结束时将账面价值减少到残值。资产永远不应该减少到低于预计残值。

余额递减法的变形是加入乘数。

使用 DB 法计算第 i 年的折旧 = m(1/n)NBV

其中：

- m = 乘数。

- n = 资产的折旧年限。
- NBV = 资产在年初的净账面价值。

例如，双余额递减法（DDB）的比率是前面例子中的二倍：

2(1/5) $10 000 = $4 000

固定百分比现在变为 2(1/5) 即 40%。该固定百分比用于第二年净账面价值会产生如下结果：

2(1/5) $6 000 = $2 400

第三年，该费用为：

2(1/5) $3 600 = $1 440

从第一年到第三年，公司累计折旧费用为 $7 840（$4 000 + $2 400 + $1 440）。因为总折旧费用为 $8 000（$10 000 - $2 000），第四年的折旧就限制在 $160（$8 000 - $7 840）而非 $864[2(1/5) $2 160]。第五年将没有折旧费用，因为该机器已经全部折旧完，只剩预计残值了。

● MACRS 图表

MACRS 图表将所有的企业资产进行分类（例如，计算机和外围设备、办公器械、办公家具、非住宅房产等）并详细规定每类资产被冲销的期限（例如，三年期财产、五年期财产、七年期财产等）。根据资产类别以及投入使用的日期，可以使用不同的惯例来调整第一年的折旧。

IRS 提供了专门图表来确定每年能被折旧的项目纳税基数百分比。资产的纳税基数在各年间不变，只作为乘数的百分比会变。

例如，假设前面提到过的 $10 000 资产被归入五年期资产类别。下面的折旧率作为百分比被用于原始基数（$10 000），而非折旧基数（$10 000 - $2 000）。

五年期资产类别	
年	% （四舍五入）
1	20.00
2	32.00
3	19.20
4	11.52
5	11.52
6	5.76

该表基于双余额递减法，并转换到直线法。第一年是资产开始投入使用的一年。该表使用了半年惯例，即假设资产在年中被投入使用。因此，公司只能将第一年正常折旧金额的一半费用化。

对于价值 $10 000、估计残值 $2 000 的资产，第一年的折旧费用为 0.20（$10 000）= $2 000。

尽管全面讨论所得税如何专门影响资本投资的现金流入和流出超出了本节的范围，但下面一些关于营利公司折旧和纳税考虑事项的一般观点还是可以得出：

- 折旧减免不是现金支付；它们是非现金成本，可减少应税收入和税负。
- 折旧费用对公司给定期间必须支付的所得税金额有影响。

- 因为折旧抵减了应税收入并减少了纳税流出，折旧实际上带来现金流入。

因折旧费用引起的纳税义务的减少被称为折旧税盾。该税盾等于折旧金额乘以税率。

公司倾向于采用加速折旧模式，因为在现金储蓄有更高现值的年份，它们可以产生更大的折旧减免和现金储蓄。然而，与 SL 法相比，在其他因素不变的条件下，加速法导致了初始几年每股收益（EPS）较低，最后几年较高。

进度检查

提示：完成以下各题，参考答案随后给出。

1. 下面哪项最好地描述了资本预算？（   ）

    a. 与当前支出相关的决策制定

    b. 制定长期投资决策的过程

    c. 制定短期投资计划的过程

    d. 制定决策以支持经营效率

2. 下面哪项不是资本支出的例子？（   ）

    a. 为遵循 EPA 而升级加热、通风和空调系统

    b. 购买一项新的可以减少人工和维护费用的装配机器

    c. 为研发小组购买新的计算机服务器

    d. 支付给付薪员工的项目津贴

3. 因直接效应与相关现金流类别有关，直接效应是指（   ）。

    a. 现金流入、流出或承付对现金流的直接影响

    b. 公司纳税义务的变化

    c. 税收折旧费用的净增加或减少

    d. 直接效应和纳税效应之和

进度检查答案

1. b

2. d

3. a

第 2 节
折现现金流量分析

本节内容简介

　　评估资本投资项目有各种可用的技术。本节将讨论较复杂的工具之一：折现现金流量（DCF）分析。DCF 分析随时间推移按货币时间价值调整现金流量。DCF 法通过比较初始投资的所有未来净现金流量的等值现值来评价资本投资。

　　本节讨论了两种常见的 DCF 法：

　　● 净现值（NPV）使用专门的折现率将所有初始投资后净现金流量折为初始投资时的现值。NPV 强调投资时的美元金额。

　　● 内含报酬率（IRR）估计使所有初始投资后净现金流量的现值等于投资支出的初始现金的折现率。IRR 将该折现率用作比较点。

要求报酬率

　　尽管每个 DCF 方法都有不同的方式，它们还是有一些共同点的。NPV 和 IRR 都使用以下标准来评价资本投资：

　　● 该投资总的初始现金流。

　　● 投资所产生的预期未来现金流入和流出。

　　● 企业对该投资的要求报酬率。

　　本章第 1 节"资本预算过程"讨论了总现金流和增量现金流。要求报酬率及其对资本成本和加权平均资本成本（WACC）的使用应在详细讨论 NPV 和 IRR 两种方法前作进一步解释。

　　要求报酬率代表了企业在选择一项投资时可以接受的最低未来收入。换句话说，它是企业在其他风险相似的资本投资中预期收到的报酬。要求报酬率也指想要报酬率、最低可接受报酬率、门槛或（机会）资本成本。

　　在实用立场上，为所有潜在投资确定想要报酬率是很有挑战性的。即使在最佳情况下，该法也是费时的。确认并评估给定时点所有可行的潜在投资机会对企业来说既困难又费钱。企业趋向于使用两种方法来加速该过程：最低报酬率或资本成本。

最低报酬率

　　企业一般有一个最低报酬率来评估投资。该报酬率通常基于企业的战略目标、行业平均值和普通的投资机会。当企业将最低报酬率作为检查标准时，资本投资项目必须满足该报酬率。

资本成本

　　正如本书第 3 章第 3 节"资本成本"所述，加权平均资本成本（WACC）是企业用于筹资的各组成部分的加权平均。WACC 通过确定单个资本组成部分（例如优先股或普通股的发行，各种债务如贷款和债券的借款，或留存收益）成本，然后将每一项成本乘以各自在企业总资本结构中的比例来确定。

回顾下面关于资本成本的一般公式：

$$k_a = k_1 w_1 + k_2 w_2 \cdots\cdots + k_n w_n$$

- n = 不同类型的筹资（每种类型都有自己的成本和在资本结构中的比例）。
- k = 资本结构中每一组成部分的成本。
- w = 每一组成部分在总资本结构中的权重。
- k_a = 资本成本（以百分比表示）。

第 3 章讨论了确定企业资本结构中每一组成部分成本的具体公式。同时，也审视了如何利用 WACC 计算企业总资本结构中每一来源的相对重要性（一旦确定单个资本组成部分后）。

回顾加权平均资本成本的公式：

$$WACC = k_{dt} w_d + k_e w_e$$

- WACC = 加权平均资本成本。
- k_{dt} = 税后债务成本。
- w_d = 债务百分比。
- k_e = 权益成本。
- w_e = 权益百分比。

企业经常使用 WACC 来评价与企业总风险情形一致的资本投资成本，也就是具有企业平均风险的项目。

因此，在制定资本投资决策时，资本成本可以用作估算项目现金流现值的折现率。它也可以为要求报酬率和资本投资项目内含报酬率的比较点提供基础。

净现值

净现值是项目未来现金流现值减去初始投资。它将所有预期的未来现金流入和流出折现。

计算净现值（NPV）

计算 NPV，必须首先确定现值（PV）。

现值计算

现值（PV）是未来净现金流入在今天的等价货币价值。通过对未来现金流入使用适合的折现率（基于要求报酬率）来确定该值。

确定一年以后收到的以 10% 为要求报酬率的 $20 000 的现值。

现值(PV) = 金额 × 折现率

参见图表 3 - 105 来确定适合的折现率。

图表 3 - 105　部分现值利息系数表

(n) 期间	10%	11%	12%
1	0.909	0.901	0.893
2	0.826	0.812	0.797
3	0.751	0.731	0.712
4	0.683	0.659	0.636
5	0.621	0.593	0.567
6	0.564	0.535	0.507
7	0.513	0.482	0.452
8	0.467	0.434	0.404
9	0.424	0.391	0.361
10	0.386	0.352	0.322

摘自现值利息系数表的折现率（0.909）是按 10% 计算的一个期间的折现系数。

现值（PV）= 金额 × 折现率

$18 180 = $20 000 × 0.909

要证明该式，可以用下面的方式确定从现在开始一年后的现金投资。

现在的现金现值 = $18 180

一年的利息（$18 180 × 10%）= $1 818

从现在开始一年后的总现金 = $19 998 *

* $2 的差异源自 PV 利息系数的四舍五入。

换句话说，$18 180 是从现在开始一年后收到的 $20 000 现金流入的等价现值。

净现值计算

净现值（NPV）是一项投资在投资寿命期内每期获得想要报酬率后所赚得的今天的美元金额。

确定资本项目 NPV 的步骤如下：

1. 确定每年的净现金流。

2. 确认要求报酬率。

3. 按步骤 2 中的要求报酬率确定每年折现率（使用恰当的现值表）。

4. 确定净现金流的现值；将第 1 步与第 3 步中的数相乘。

5. 将第 4 步中该投资的各年数加总。

NPV 可以用来评估有均匀净现金流和不均匀现金流的投资。这两类计算的例子将在此一步一步介绍。

均匀净现金流的例子。均匀现金流涉及年金投资。年金在特定期间内提供一系列等额现金流。该方法也需要年金现值利息系数表来确定折现系数。该折现系数随年数和想要报酬率的不同而不同。

思考以下情境：

● 一项三年期投资的想要报酬率为 10%。

● 该投资每年的净现金流为 $125 000。

参见图表 3 - 106 来选择恰当的折现率。

图表 3 - 106　部分年金现值利息系数表

(n) 年份	10%	11%	12%	13%
1	0.909	0.901	0.893	0.885
2	1.736	1.713	1.690	1.668
3	2.487	2.444	2.402	2.361
4	3.170	3.102	3.037	2.974
5	3.791	3.696	3.605	3.517
6	4.355	4.231	4.111	3.998
7	4.868	4.712	4.564	4.423
8	5.335	5.146	4.968	4.799
9	5.759	5.537	5.328	5.132
10	6.145	5.889	5.650	5.426

在年金现值利息系数表中三年期 10% 的利率水平下可以找到 2.487 的折现率。然后计算该净现金流入的现值：

净现金流入的 PV = \$125 000 × 2.487 = \$310 875

初始现金投资需要 \$300 000。这是该投资的现值。从净现金流入的现值减去初始投资就得到了该投资的净现值。

NPV = \$310 875 - \$300 000 = \$10 875

本例中净现值的计算表明，初始投资 \$3 000 000，除在投资寿命期内每年获得 10% 的报酬率外，还会获得 \$10 875 当前美元报酬。

不均匀现金流的例子。在投资寿命期内有不均匀现金流预测的项目，先计算每年产生的净现金流入，然后再使用现值利息系数表对其进行折现。该投资每年的折现系数都不同。

思考以下情境：

- 总的初始投资为 \$90 000。
- 四年的要求报酬率为 10%。
- 投资寿命期内年净现金流入为 \$60 000、\$40 000、\$30 000 和 \$20 000。

参见表 3 - 102 "部分现值利息系数表"，选择这四个期间的恰当值。

图表 3 - 107 显示了如何使用摘录的现值利息系数表来折现现金流以确定每年的现值。

图表 3 - 107　使用 NPV 法评估项目

年份	现金流入		10% 的折现系数		现值
1	\$60 000	×	0.909	=	\$54 540
2	40 000	×	0.826	=	33 040
3	30 000	×	0.751	=	22 530
4	20 000	×	0.683	=	13 660
净现金流入的总现值					\$123 770
减去初始投资					90 000
净现值					\$33 770

NPV 法计算表明 \$90 000 初始投资在投资寿命期内会赚取 \$33 770 的当前美元报酬。

净现值解释

净现值可以按如下方式解释：
- NPV 为零表示该投资报酬率与要求报酬率相等。
- NPV 为正表示该投资报酬率高于要求报酬率；未来现金流大于初始投资成本。
- NPV 为负表示未来现金流赚取的报酬率低于要求报酬率。

NPV 为正的项目可以接受，因其增加了企业价值。另一方面，NPV 为负的项目表示企业从现值的意义上看可能会赔钱。然而，NPV 为正并非意味着该项目是企业最好的可能投资方案。NPV 为正只意味着该投资会赚得比企业要求报酬率更高的报酬率。备选的投资机会可能会提供更好的报酬。

内含报酬率

内含报酬率（IRR）估计了使净现金流入的现值等于初始投资的折现率。换言之，IRR 是使一项投资 NPV 为零的折现率（如果该报酬率被用作要求报酬率来计算 NPV 的话）。

内含报酬率解释

内含报酬率法通过比较估计的内含报酬率和预先确定的标准来评价资本投资。该标准以企业用来评价投资的任何一种报酬率，如最低报酬率、另一个想要的备选投资报酬率或行业平均值为基础。该标准报酬率被用作取舍分界点。低于该点的项目应被拒绝，除非它们是强制性项目。

内含报酬率的计算

内含报酬率法有两个基本步骤：

1. 确定使净现金流入现值等于投资初始金额的报酬率。

2. 比较企业估计报酬率和企业要求报酬率（取舍分界标准）以评价投资的合意性。

与 NPV 类似，IRR 可能被用于评价有均匀净现金流和非均匀现金流的投资。两类计算的例子如下。

均匀净现金流的例子

确定均匀净现金流资本项目 IRR 的步骤如下：

1. 确定项目的总初始投资（总现金流出和承付）。

2. 确认预先确定的标准取舍分界报酬率（要求报酬率）。

3. 确定每年的净现金流入。

4. 用年现金流（第 3 步）除以初始投资（第 1 步）以获得 IRR 系数（基本上，就是一项年金的年金现值系数，PVIFA）。

5. 参考年金现值表找出特定年数下与 IRR 系数相匹配（或与它最贴近的）的折现率。

6. 比较 IRR（第 5 步）和选定的标准取舍分界率（第 2 步）。

如果计算出来的 IRR 大于标准取舍分界率（用作想要报酬率），该项目就是想要的投资。

思考以下情境：

- 总初始投资为 $35 000。
- 预先确定的标准率为 10%。
- 随后三年每年净现金流入为 $15 000。

IRR 系数计算如下：

IRR 系数 = $35 000 ÷ $15 000 = 2.33

参见图表 3 – 106 "部分年金现值利息系数表"，查找 IRR 值。

本例中，IRR 等于 13%（用年金现值利息系数表，查找三年期系数，内插至最贴近的表值 2.361）。

因为标准取舍分界率（用作要求报酬率）是 10%，而该项目的 IRR 值非常接近 13%，这个项目是想要的投资。如果想要的报酬率是 14%，该项目就该被拒绝。

不均匀现金流的例子

对于不均匀现金流项目来说，IRR 计算变成了试验、错误和内插。现金流必须用各种折现率折现，直至找到可以使现值等于初始投资的折现率。

实际上，计算机制表程序和财务计算器可以使变化现金流的 IRR 确定变得很容易。下面的数学例子有助于理解该过程背后的概念。

思考以下情境：

- 总初始投资为 $10 675。
- 标准取舍分界率为 10%。
- 投资寿命期内预计的年净现金流入为 $6 000、$4 000 和 $3 000。

参见图表 3 – 105 "部分现值利息系数表"，查找这三个期间的恰当值。

图表 3 – 108 显示了如何利用现值利息系数表折现现金流以确定每年的现值。

图表 3 – 108　10% 折现率下的净现金流入总现值

年份	现金流入		10% 的折现系数		现值
1	$6 000	×	0.909	=	$5 454
2	4 000	×	0.826	=	3 304
3	3 000	×	0.751	=	2 253
净现金流入总现值					$11 011

三年净现金流现值（$11 011）大于总初始投资（$10 675）。需要提高折现率以使现值更接近于该项目投资。12% 折现率的图表如图表 3 – 109 所示（参见图表 3 – 105 并查找折现率为 12% 的三个时期的恰当值）。

图表 3 - 109   12% 折现率的净现金流入总现值

年份	现金流入		12% 的折现系数		现值
1	$6 000	×	0.893	=	$5 358
2	4 000	×	0.797	=	3 188
3	3 000	×	0.712	=	2 136
净现金流入总现值					$10 682

折现率为 12% 时，三年净现金流现值（$10 682）接近于总初始投资（$10 675）。因为标准取舍分界率为 10%，所以该项目可以接受。

NPV 和 IRR 的比较

两种方法的共同基本假设是：风险，或者说不确定性，不是主要问题。此外，两种方法都考虑：

- 货币时间价值。
- 初始现金投资。
- 初始投资后的所有现金流。

一个主要区别是 NPV 的最终结果是美元数量，而 IRR 的最终结果是百分比。就这一点而言，净现值法占优势，因为单个项目的 NPV 值可以相加，从而能评价接受项目某种可能组合所产生的效果。因为 IRR 产生的是百分比，多个项目不能相加或平均来评价任何资本投资项目组合。

NPV 法的另一个优点是，在评价项目寿命期内要求报酬率不断变化的项目时，该方法很有用。为评价项目吸引力，可以确定现金流入总现值并与初始投资比较。同样，无法用 IRR 法来推断项目是否具有吸引力。每年不同的要求报酬意味着没有单一报酬率或单一 IRR 值。

当净现金流入和净现金流出有几个备选期间时，NPV 比 IRR 更可靠，因为它能使股东财富最大化。

两种方法都有一些可靠性方面的警告：

- NPV 仅像所选的折现率那么可靠。不现实的折现率会导致接受/拒绝项目的错误决策。
- 资本投资项目不应仅仅因为有高 IRR 值而被接受。高 IRR 结果应进一步关注以评价以如此高 IRR 投资现金流的机会是否现实。
- NPV 和 IRR 有不同的再投资报酬率假设。NPV 法暗含着企业可以以要求报酬率对所有现金流入进行再投资的假设。相反，IRR 法暗含着企业可以以 IRR 对所有现金流入进行再投资的假设。NPV 法的再投资报酬率一般被认为是更恰当的假设。

但是在所有分析资本投资的各种方法中，DCF 法在理论上是最可靠的。只要以下方面没有不同，NPV 法和 IRR 法一般会产生相似的结果：

- 项目规模（初始投资金额）。
- 净现金流模式。
- 项目寿命期。
- 项目寿命期内的资本成本。

如果分析中除了初始投资外的任何一笔现金流为负，那么 IRR 法会产生多种结果，所有结果都对但所有结果都不合理。在这种情况下，只能使用 NPV 法。

会计报酬率

如前所述，分析师们能使用多种技术来评价和选择资本投资。NPV 和 IRR 在此已作了详细讨论，因为它们是更传统方法中的两种。会计报酬率（ARR），也被称为平均报酬率或投资报酬，是分析资本预算项目的另一种方法。与 NPV 和 IRR 不同的是，ARR 关注会计利润而非现金流。

尽管会计报酬率有很多种定义，一个通行的定义是平均会计利润与初始投资的比率。一些 ARR 计算使用平均投资（起点值 + 终点值）/2 作为分母。

ARR = EBIT × (1 − 税率)/净初始投资

如下是对预期使用寿命 5 年的新设备进行资本投资的例子。

- $40 000 = 一年的税前营业利润
- 40% = 公司税率
- $100 000 = 净初始投资

ARR = $30 000(1 − 0.40)/ $100 000 = 0.18 或 18%

本例中，18% 的 ARR 表示每一美元投资产生税后营业利润的比率。

ARR 百分比受计算中使用净初始投资的影响。这使得该分母大于使用投资平均水平的分母。

使用平均投资，ARR 变成：

ARR = EBIT × (1 − 税率)/[(起点值 + 终点值)/2]

使用先前的例子，如果终点值为零，那么 ARR 为：

ARR = $30 000(1 − 0.40)/($100 000/2) = 0.36 或 36%

为得到 EBIT 而必须减掉的年度折旧也会影响 ARR。因为这些因素，许多公司用投资平均水平计算 ARR，发现账面价值会随时间推移而减少。这样做时，该比率有时被称为"平均报酬率"。

使用 ARR 的优点是：

- 该概念易于理解；该方法提供了一种衡量盈利性的简单方法。
- 计算使用的是财务报表的报告数据。
- 计算考虑了整个资本投资使用寿命内赚得的利润。
- 计算提示了如果投资被接受，那么会计报告数据将如何变化。

类似于 IRR，ARR（无论是权责发生制方法还是平均法）给出了一个报酬率百分比。

在投资财务分析中使用 ARR 的缺点是：

- 该法使用账面收益而非现金流（不像 NPV 和 IRR），同时忽视了折旧也是一种现金流入的来源。
- 忽视了货币时间价值。
- 忽视了净收益的时间顺序。

进度检查

提示：完成以下各题，参考答案随后给出。

找出与该术语匹配的描述。

1. _____现值　　　　　　a. 公司用于筹资的各种组成部分的比例平均。

2. _____净现值　　　　　b. 预计使净现金流入现值等于初始投资的折现率。

3. _____内含报酬率　　　c. 一项投资在投资寿命期内每期获得想要报酬率后所赚得的今
　　　　　　　　　　　　　　　天的美元金额。

4. _____要求报酬率　　　d. 在选择投资时投资者将收到的最低未来收入。

5. _____资本成本　　　　e. 未来净现金流入的今天的等价美元价值。

6. 在内部报酬率计算中标准比率的重要性是什么？（　　　）

　　a. 低于该比率的项目应被拒绝。

　　b. 高于该比率的项目应被拒绝。

　　c. 该比率用来在年金现值表中查找折现率。

　　d. 该比率用来在现值利息系数表中查找折现率。

进度检查答案

1. e

2. c

3. b

4. d

5. a

6. a

第3节
回收期和折现回收期

本节内容简介

资本预算中的回收期法确定了一项资本预算项目收回净初始投资需要的年数。回收期代表了投资的盈亏均衡点。

回收期法的使用

与 NPV 和 IRR 技术类似，回收期（PP）不区分现金流入的类型（不管现金流入是经营的结果还是设备的处置、营运资本的收回及其他类似种种）。作为现金流入的一种简单衡量方法，PP 也可用来评价均匀或不均匀净现金流的资本投资。

均匀净现金流的例子

如果预期是一系列均匀现金流，则确定一项资本投资回收期的计算如下：

回收期 = 总初始投资/预期年净现金流

思考以下情境：

- 总初始投资为 $600\ 000$。
- 预期年净现金流为 $175\ 000$。

本例中，计算应为：

回收期 = $600\ 000$/ $175\ 000$ = 3.43 年

不均匀现金流的例子

在年现金流入不均匀的情况下，确定回收期是一项累计计算。累计净现金流入直至初始投资被收回。如果回收期不是完整的年数，可以使用直线内插法。

回收期公式如下：

回收期 = 在全部收回前的年数 + 最后一年年初时的未收回成本/最后一年的现金流

思考以下情境：

- 总初始投资为 $30\ 000$。
- 投资寿命期内预计年净现金流入为 $10\ 000$、$12\ 000$、$16\ 000$ 和 $14\ 000$。

图表 3 – 110 列出了数据。

图表 3 – 110　回收期和不均匀现金流

年份	净现金流	累计净现金流
0	– $30\ 000$	– $30\ 000$
1	10 000	– 20 000
2	12 000	– 8 000
3	16 000	8 000
4	14 000	22 000

两年后，该项目还需要 $8\ 000$ 才能收回本。第三年，该项目预期产生 $16\ 000$

净现金流入。这意味着对该投资而言，回收将发生在第二至第三年间的某个时间。第二年后，该项目还需要 \$8 000 来收回初始投资。最后一年年初的未收回成本除以最后一年的现金流（\$8 000/ \$16 000）等于 0.5 年。因此，项目的回收期为 2.5 年。

回收期 = 2 + \$8 000/ \$16 000 = 2.5 年

回收期法的解释

在使用回收期法时，企业一般为项目选择一个目标回收期（或最大取舍分界期）。目标回收期代表了企业考虑项目可接受的最大时长有多长。回收期比目标回收期短的项目可以接受；回收期比目标回收期长的项目应被拒绝。在前例中，如果企业将 \$300 000 投资的最大可接受目标回收期定为 3 年，该项投资因实际只需 2.5 年即可回收而应被接受。

一般来说，一个项目风险越高，其目标回收期应该越短。这是因为人们想要快速收回风险投资。在比较两个或更多投资项目时，有更短回收期的项目一般更受欢迎。

回收期法的优点和缺点

回收期法有很明显的优点和缺点。主要内容如图表 3 – 111 所示。

图表 3 – 111　回收期法的优点和缺点

优点	缺点
• 计算简单 • 结果容易理解 • 大致衡量了流动性和风险	• 忽视了货币时间价值；不考虑时间的情况下加总现金流量 • 忽视了回收期后发生的现金流 • 未衡量盈利性 • 如果目标回收期太短的话，促使接受短期项目

在某些情况下，对流动性和风险的快速衡量对于显示错过一项高风险环境下资本投资的风险是有好处的。大致说来，回收期越短的项目风险越低。同时，回收期越短的项目越倾向于为组织提供越大的灵活性，因为提供给其他项目的资金很快就可用了。

因为回收期法的根本局限，它提供的只是一项投资是否值得的部分方面。因此，最好与其他资本预算技术一起结合使用。

折现回收期

折现回收期法试图解决回收期计算的一个缺点——忽视货币时间价值。折现回收期利用净现金流入的现值（而非未折现的净现金流入的美元金额）来确定回收期。

与 NPV 法类似，净现金流入现值用企业想要的报酬率来预计。使净现金流的累计净现值等于初始项目投资的必要期间就是现值回收期。

图表3－112 折现回收期和均匀净现金流

年份	净现金流入		10%的折现系数		净现金流现值	累计净现金流现值
0	－ $16 000		0		－ $16 000	－ $16 000
1	6 000	×	0.909	=	5 454	－ 10 546
2	6 000	×	0.826	=	4 956	－ 5 590
3	6 000	×	0.751	=	4 506	－ 1 084
4	6 000	×	0.683	=	4 098	3 014

该项目在第三至第四年间可以收回初始投资。为实现现值（PV）回收第四年所需的金额为 $1 084。折现回收期计算如下：

折现回收期 = 3 + $1 084/ $4 098 = 3.26 年

相比之下，简单回收期为：

回收期 = $16 000/ $6 000 = 2.66 年

回收期法与折现回收期法计算结果不同，是因为它没对现金流折现。

进度检查

提示：完成以下各题，参考答案随后给出。

1. 下列哪项关于资本预算中使用回收期法的陈述是错误的？（　　）

回收期法：

a. 代表了一项投资的盈亏平衡点。

b. 粗略衡量了项目流动性。

c. 考虑了货币时间价值。

d. 粗略衡量了项目风险。

2. 一个资本预算项目总初始资本投资为 $900 000，预期年净现金流为 $150 000，该项目的回收期是多少？（　　）

a. 3 年

b. 5 年

c. 6 年

d. 7 年

3. 下面哪项陈述准确比较了折现回收期法和回收期法？（　　）

a. 两种方法都简单衡量了项目盈利性。

b. 折现回收期法使用了净现金流入的现值，而回收期法没有。

c. 折现回收期法忽视了回收期结束后的现金流，而回收期法没有。

d. 两种方法都区分了现金流入的类型。

进度检查答案

1. c

2. c

3. b

第 4 节
评级投资项目

本节内容简介

迄今为止讨论过的资本预算章节已经审查了形成对单一、传统或独立项目采取接受/放弃决策的分析方法。在真实世界里，有许多能（并经常）使决策分析复杂化的情况。本节将连同投资项目评级方法一起，审查那样一些潜在困难。

资本分配

资本分配是指对企业投资项目有某种约束的情形，该约束限制了企业给定期限（如一年）内所能做出的资本支出总金额。预算上限通常导致资本分配以及要求进行资本支出内部筹资的控制政策。

思考以下评价三项资本投资的情形：

- 资本分配限额为 $10 000。
- 想要报酬率为 10%。

图表 3 – 113　资本分配及净现值

项目	现金流入 第 0 年	现金流入 第 1 年	现金流入 第 2 年	净现值 10% 折现率
A	– $10 000	$30 000	$5 000	$21 000
B	– 5 000	5 000	20 000	16 000
C	– 5 000	5 000	15 000	12 000

基于上述数据，该企业可以投资项目 A 或项目 B 和 C。因为资本分配限额，企业不能三个都投资，尽管每个项目单独看都很有吸引力。尽管项目 B 和 C 的 NPV 都比 A 低，但它们合起来的 NPV（B、C 合起来为 $28 000，A 为 $21 000）更高一些。基于此，选项目 B 和 C 看上去更合逻辑。

当进行资本分配时，企业必须尽力选出一些可以产生最高可能报酬水平同时又不超过约束的资本投资项目组合。仅仅基于 NPVs 进行选择并不一定是最好的方法。在某些情况下，企业需要使用额外一些分析，以确保所选项目能够带来每一美元初始投资支出净现值最高。这种分析技术之一是获利指数。

获利指数

获利指数（PI）（或效益 – 成本比率）将未来现金流现值与初始投资在相对基础上进行比较。它是未来净现金流现值与初始现金流出的比率：

$$PI = \frac{\text{未来现金流现值}}{\text{总初始投资}} = \frac{\sum_{t=1}^{n} \frac{CF_t}{(1+r)^t}}{CF_0}$$

上面讨论的三个项目的获利指数如图表 3 – 114 所示。

图表 3 - 114　获利指数

项目	总初始投资（1）	未来现金流现值（2）	获利指数（2）／（1）
A	$10 000	$12 000	1. 2
B	5 000	11 000	2. 2
C	5 000	7 000	1. 4

在此基础上，项目 B 有最高的获利指数，C 其次。假定资本分配限额为 $10 000，则应该选项目 B 和 C 而不选 A。

在这个具体情况下（大多数情况也一样），NPV 法和获利指数会导致相同的接受／拒绝决定。但是尽管两种技术一般形成同样的结论，它们对于备选方案的评级顺序却不同。

获利指数的一般解释是 PI 大于 1.0 的项目可以接受；PI 低于 1.0 的应该拒绝。

如果两种评级方法之间进行选择，NPV 法在表示一个项目的净美元贡献方面占优势。而获利指数仅仅提供了对于盈利性的衡量。尽管使用获利指数进行投资评级的一个主要好处是简洁，但主要局限在于当在多个期间分配一种以上资源时它就无法使用了。

使用资本成本进行获利指数评级不会选出最优的投资集合，除非可能的单一期间资本分配。因此，获利指数不能在多于一个期间分配资本时使用。

互斥项目

顾名思义，互斥项目是指接受了一个就不能接受另一个的项目。换句话说，两个互斥项目不能被同时选中进行筹资。

在面对互斥项目情况时，决定接受或不接受哪个项目是不够的。可以相信的是，对两个互斥项目的独立分析可能显示两个项目都是想要的备选方案。或者，在某些情况下，目前为止讨论过的资本预算分析方法——净现值法、内含报酬率法、回收期法、折现回收期法和获利指数法——可能会产生矛盾的结果。在对具有评级矛盾的互斥项目之间进行选择决策时，应当理解其评级冲突的原因。

分析方法常常导致互相冲突的结果，这是因为项目存在如下差异：

- 现金流规模（即规模或大小问题）。
- 净现金流模式（即时间问题）。
- 使用寿命长度。

图表 3 - 115 概括了这几种情况及对其的一般评述。

图表 3 - 115　比较项目投资时的问题

	情况	评述
规模（或大小）问题	现金流规模（包括初始现金流）不同	在 NPV 和 IRR 评级之间无论何时存在评级冲突，NPV 法都优先。
时间问题	现金流时间不同	在 NPV 和 IRR 评级之间无论何时存在评级冲突，NPV 法都优先。
使用寿命长度	项目有不同的使用寿命	在计算 NPV 和 IRR 之前，需要做一些专门的调整以使项目寿命相等。如果 NPV 和 IRR 之间存在评级冲突，NPV 法优先。

用 NPV 法给备选项目进行评级总是可以带来正确的项目选择。使用 NPV 法，一般可以选出最有潜力给企业带来增量美元价值的项目。

备选评级方法

除了使用传统的回收期法、净现值法和内含报酬率法来评价资本投资项目外，分析师们还可以使用一些替代方法，如线性规划和内部资本市场法。

线性规划

线性规划是用来确定一定线性约束下某些公式最大值的一种最优化技术。在用于资本投资评级时，企业如果想要选出具有最高总净现值的一组项目可以设计一系列规划等式，这些等式应在给定各种现金流出的约束下明确规定想要的结果（例如，使 NPV 最大化）。

线性规划模型对评价资源有限时的资本预算情境很有用。选择不同价值并进行手工计算以确定哪种结合可以满足约束并产生最高的 NPV 这项任务，因使用计算机而大大简化了。除非明确规定结果是整数，否则计算机甚至可能得出分数的项目——推荐半个这个项目，三分之二个另一个项目等。如果资本投资涉及原材料的仓储空间或吨位，可以选择部分平方英尺（可用的 2 000 平方英尺中的 1 000）或部分吨位（300 吨中的 200 可用）以达到最大 NPV。但是如果分数个项目不可行（例如，要评价的项目是购买一项设备还是一栋建筑），该项目就应该限定为整数。

尽管线性规划有助于资本预算，但仍需谨慎。设计并维护复杂的规划模型较为昂贵。要求有"优良"的数据；将不好的数据用于高成本的复杂分析可能导致错误的和潜在高成本的差错。因为资本投资一般表现得很激进，预测要在模型中用到的所有未来投资机会有时很困难。

内部资本市场法

通常，管理人员将资本分配约束作为临时限制来辅助财务控制。例如，管理人员可能利用约束来防止经理夸大投资机遇。这种内部预算约束并非受外部资本市场的任何无效率驱使，而是净现值最大化受内部预算约束（资本项目缺少资金来源）或其他资源缺乏驱使（例如管理时间或可用的技工和资本设备）。通过在花费上设置这种限制，经理和/或部门会被迫设置现实的优先权和现金流预测。

资本分配的主要动因之一是资本项目缺乏资金来源。面对内部资本约束的企业被迫将可行的资本项目设为优先以与公司战略和可用资金一致。

进度检查

提示：完成以下各题，参考答案随后给出。

1. 资本分配可被最好地描述为（　　　）

　　a. 投资项目限额以防止公司接受所有具有正净现值的项目

　　b. 在相对基础上比较未来现金流现值和初始投资

c. 基于主观确定的取舍分界点的资本预算接受标准

d. 在一个项目独立或依附于另一个项目时使用资本预算接受标准

2～4 题参见下图：

项目	现金流入 第 0 年	现金流入 第 1 年	现金流入 第 2 年	净现值 6%	获利指数
A	− $15 000	$10 000	$15 000		
B	− 5 000	5 000	10 000		
C	− 5 000	8 000	7 000		
D	− 10 000	− 10 000	4 000		

2. 计算项目 A 到 D 的净现值。折现率为 6%，1 的净现值为：1 期 0.9434，两期 0.89，三期 0.83962。

A _____　　　　C _____

B _____　　　　D _____

3. 计算项目 A 到 D 的获利指数（PI）？

A _____　　　　C _____

B _____　　　　D _____

4. 给定资本分配限额为第 0 年 $20 000，公司应接受下面哪个项目组合？（　　　）

a. A + B

b. A + C

c. B + C + D

进度检查答案

1. a

2. 见下表

3. 见下表

项目	现金流入 第 0 年	现金流入 第 1 年	现金流入 第 2 年	净现值 6%	获利指数
A	− $15 000	$10 000	$15 000	$7 783.91	1.519
B	− 5 000	5 000	10 000	8 616.95	2.723
C	− 5 000	8 000	7 000	8 777.15	2.755
D	− 10 000	− 10 000	4 000	− 15 874	− 0.59

4. c

A + B 的净现值 = $7 783.91 + 8 616.95 = $16 400.96

A + C 的净现值 = $7 783.91 + $8 777.15 = $16 561.06

B 的净现值 = C + D = $8 616.95 + 8 777.15 + $2 993.95 = $20 388.05

接受项目 B、C 和 D 可以产生最高的 NPV。

第5节
资本投资的风险分析

本节内容简介

按照定义，风险暗示了不确定性和不稳定性。在本书第3章"公司理财"的很多部分，风险因与金融工具有关而被广泛讨论。在资本预算中，风险有着不同的含义。

基本上，没有无风险的资本投资。这是一个正确的陈述，原因在于：

- 在整个项目寿命期内，未来现金流入会发生不可预期的变化。
- 计算所用的报酬率可能对项目寿命期来说并不准确。
- 在项目寿命期内筹资成本可能会上升。
- 新的强制性规定因素可能在任何给定的时点上要求额外的投资。
- 相关产品或服务的寿命可能大大短于或长于预测。
- 通货膨胀的或衰退的经济环境可能影响现金流的价值。
- 国内或全球政治事件可能影响项目现金流或项目整体生存能力。

因为所有这些与资本预算相关的各类风险，选择资本投资项目一直就是一个挑战。本节研究一些使不确定性最小化的方法。

敏感性分析

因与资本投资有关，敏感性分析是一种"如果，则……"技术，用来评价 NPV、IRR 和其他项目盈利性指标在折现率、人工或材料成本、销售收入或其他一些因素从一种情况变为另一种情况时如何变动。目的是评估 NPV、IRR 或其他专门的盈利性衡量指标对于变动有多敏感。

敏感性分析可用来回答如下问题：

- 如果项目每年现金流上升或下降 10%，NPV 会如何变化？
- 如果一个期限为三年的项目在第二年没有现金流入，整个项目的 NPV 还会是正的吗？
- 如果折现率从 8% 上升到 10% 或者从 8% 下降到 7%，NPV 会发生什么变化？
- 如果为了面对竞争性新产品而必须在第三年追加资本投资以对产品进行重大的重新设计，NPV 会有什么变化？
- 如果项目延长了三年，而这三年内现金流减少、维护成本上升，对 NPV 会产生什么影响？

为进一步理解敏感性分析如何用来解答这些"如果，则……"式问题，思考以下情境：

- 投资 A 寿命期内年净现金流入为 \$2 000 和 \$3 000。
- 投资 B 寿命期内年净现金流入为 \$3 600 和 \$1 400。
- 每个项目的总初始投资为 \$3 200。

给定以上信息，如果折现率从 10% 上升到 12%，每个项目会发生何种变化？参考图表 3 – 116。

当折现率从 10% 上升到 12% 时，两个项目的 NPVs 都下降了。项目 A 的 NPV 变动百分比为 – 10.9% ，项目 B 的 NPV 变动百分比为 – 8.0% 。因此，项目 A 对折现率的变化更敏感从而在折现率变化时形成比项目 B 更高的风险。

图表 3 – 116　折现率的变化

年份	现金流入		10% 的折现系数		现值
项目 A，折现率为 10%					
1	$200 000	×	0.909	=	$1 818.00
2	300 000	×	0.826	=	2 478.00
净现金流入的总现值					$4 296.00
减去初始投资					3 200.00
净现值					$1 096.00
项目 A，折现率为 12%					
1	$2 000.00	×	0.893	=	$1 786.00
2	3 000.00	×	0.797	=	2 391.00
净现金流入的总现值					$4 177.00
减去初始投资					3 200.00
净现值					$977.00
项目 B，折现率为 10%					
1	$3 600.00	×	0.909	=	$3 272.40
2	1 400.00	×	0.826	=	1 156.40
净现金流入的总现值					$4 428.80
减去初始投资					3 200.00
净现值					$1 228.80
项目 B，折现率为 12%					
1	$3 600.00	×	0.893	=	$3 214.80
2	1 400.00	×	0.797	=	1 115.80
净现金流入的总现值					$4 330.60
减去初始投资					3 200.00
净现值					$1 130.60

比较项目 A 和 B				
项目	净现值（10%）	净现值（12%）	美元变化	NPV 变动百分比
A	$1 096.00	$977.00	– $119.00	– 10.86%
B	$1 228.80	$1 130.60	– $98.20	– 7.99%

确定性等值

对于选择项目而言，确定性等值（CE）法试图将现金流的时间与它们的风险分离开。预期现金流被转换成实际上更可能的确定金额。然后这些现金流以无风险利率（例如美国国库券利率）进行折现。实际上，只有一小部分企业使用确定性等值法进行报告。

换句话说，如果企业在一项投资的第五年有预期现金流 $15 000，预测者认为该预期现金流获得 80% 的收益（或 $12 000）是现实的，该数额就会以无风险利率来折现。

要确定确定性等值，须采取以下步骤：

1. 预测投资的预期现金流。
2. 确认确定性等值系数，或者确定的预期现金流的百分比。
3. 用确定性等值系数乘以预期现金流以决定确定的现金流。
4. 通过用特定的无风险折现率折现确定现金流量来计算项目现值。
5. 从确定现金流量的现值中减去初始投资来计算项目净现值。
6. 评价项目的净现值；如果净现值为零或正，则接受，为负则拒绝。

为了更好地理解如何应用确定性等值，思考以下情境：

* 一个五年期投资的年净现金流入为 $10 000、$8 000、$7 000、$6 000 和 $5 000。
* 在投资寿命期内估计的确定性等值系数为 90%、85%、70%、60% 和 45%。
* 项目的总初始投资为 $18 000。
* 无风险报酬率为 3%。

给定以上信息并应用确定性等值法，下面显示的是如何评价该项目。

图表 3 -117　项目评估和确定性等值系数

年份	预期现金流入		确定性等值系数		确定现金流
1	$10 000	×	0.90	=	$9 000
2	8 000	×	0.85	=	6 800
3	7 000	×	0.70	=	4 900
4	6 000	×	0.60	=	3 600
5	5 000	×	0.45	=	2 250

年份	确定现金流入		3% 的折现系数		确定现金流现值
1	$9 000	×	0.971	=	$8 739.00
2	6 800	×	0.943	=	6 412.40
3	4 900	×	0.915	=	4 483.50
4	3 600	×	0.888	=	3 196.80
5	2 250	×	0.863	=	1 941.75
净现金流入的总现值					$24 773.45
减去初始投资					18 000.00
净现值					$6 773.45

正 NPV 值表明该项目可接受。

其他处理风险的方法

资本资产定价模型和模拟法是处理资本预算风险的另两种有用的方法。

资本资产定价模型（CAPM）

资本资产定价模型在 CMA 学习体系本书第 3 章 "公司理财" 中，因其与找出股票或组合的要求报酬率有关而讨论过。CAPM 模型在资本预算当中也有应用。资本预算中的 CAPM 公式为

$$E(R_a) = R_f + \beta_a [E(R_m) - R_r]$$

其中：

- E(R_a) 表示要评估的资产（项目）的要求报酬率。
- R_f 表示无风险利率。
- β_a 表示资产（项目）的 β 值。
- E(R_m) 表示市场组合报酬。

在资本预算中使用 CAPM 背后的前提是用对待一支股票的方式对待一个项目。基本原理是一个项目的报酬与该企业总资产的报酬或行业的报酬相联系，正如股票或市场组合。在该假设下，公司的 β 值用作项目的 β 值。在项目不是公司典型投资的情况下，行业平均 β 值可以被替代。这就是"单一业务"法。

一旦确定了项目的要求报酬率，就可以计算 NPV 了。预期现金流利用该报酬率进行折现；从总初始项目投资中减去现金流的总净现值。NPV 为零或正意味着该项目可接受，因其可获得要求报酬率。

如果要评价多个项目，则 β 值越高的项目可以认为其风险越大。

模拟法

模拟法允许在接受资本投资项目之前对其进行测试。因为投资项目现金流和折现率的真实未来价值是未知的，而假设的现金流和折现率是假定的，可以用模拟模型来研究。

在资本预算中，模拟法可用来估计：

- 预期 NPV、IRR 和 PI。
- 预期值的离散度。

当试图评价不止一项风险投资时，每个项目的 NPV 或 IRR 都可以被模拟多次，并且可以计算并评级平均的 NPVs、IRRs 和标准差。多次重复这一过程也使各值分布于频率分布图中以显示 NPVs 和 IRRs 的分布。观察分布曲线可以合理评估项目风险水平。

有许多模拟软件程序可用。使用这些程序可以比手工操作创造出更多情境。其中一些程序还可以画出结果的图表。也许最有名的资本预算计算机模拟模型是蒙特·卡洛模拟工具，它实际上用一个项目模型模拟了轮盘赌。

专门调整利率的使用

在大多数情况下，风险资本项目没有安全投资有吸引力。一般地，项目风险越高，企业就会要求越高的报酬率，或者对现金流进行保守的估计。

许多企业也使用它们公司的资本成本作为折现所有新投资现金流的准绳。当新项目的风险高于或低于企业的正常水平时，使用公司比率就会产生问题。

当资本项目与企业现存业务平均风险一样时，企业资本成本就是合适的折现率。然而，在确定什么项目恰好等同于类似风险时，还是要审慎判断。

武断地对所有新项目使用企业资本成本率容易导致在不管其风险的情况下，仅仅因为该项目提供了比公司资本成本更高的报酬率而错误地接受或拒绝一个项目。会造成双重问题：

- 好的低风险项目可能被拒绝。
- 不好的高风险项目可能被接受。

在产生疑问时，分析师们应当在单个项目基础上评估它们的相对风险，并使用专门调整的利率来衡量项目风险。通过这样做，每个项目都有自己的机会资本成本。

资本投资的定性考虑事项

如前面内容所展示的，评价资本预算项目有很多定量方法。大多数讨论过的技术都有独特的优点和缺点。因此，经理们应该并且通常也确实使用了多重标准来评价投资项目。总的来说，多重方法减轻了估计错误和/或不符合企业或股东最大利益的不正确决策的可能性。

除定量方法外，企业也应确认影响投资决策的定性因素。重要的定性考虑事项包括：

- 管理人员可能没有必要信息以做出资本预算决策（例如，信息或频率的类型）。
- 贷款条款可能限制了借款。
- 企业可能有自我强加的资本分配限额。
- 决策制定者可能是风险厌恶者。
- 在接受项目的决策和经理业绩评价之间可能存在冲突（例如，一个经理可能关注于项目将会如何影响以报告的年度会计数据为基础的奖金计划）。
- 企业可能没有足够的/有资格的人员来成功实施资本项目。
- 管理人员可能评价投资是否会增加顾客忠诚度和持续力。

本质上，资本投资常常是战略性的。正因如此，尽管定性因素很难估计，它们仍是很重要的考虑事项。

进度检查

提示：完成以下各题，参考答案随后给出。

连线——处理风险的不同方法和恰当描述。

1. _____敏感性分析　　　　a. 使用假设的情景（近似于真实情况）以帮助制定决策。
2. _____确定性等值方法　　b. 衡量另一种因素变化时一种因素变动程度的方法。
3. _____资本资产定价模型　c. 将预测现金流转换成实际上更可能的确定金额。
4. _____模拟法　　　　　　d. 评价项目风险时使用企业的或行业的 β 值
5. 当现金流变化时，下面哪种方法最适合比较两个资本投资项目的净现值？（　　　　）
   a. 敏感性分析
   b. 确定性等值法
   c. 资本资产定价法
   d. 计算机模拟法

进度检查答案

1. b
2. c
3. d
4. a
5. a

第6节
资本投资的实物期权

本节内容简介

接受或拒绝资本预算投资建议的决策取决于风险。投资者和资本提供者都要求他们认为恰当的风险调整报酬。特别地，投资者一般竭尽全力评价项目风险。然而，今天竞争性的企业环境伴随着其他一些影响因素，如科技和规定的限制，会严重损害资本预算投资。实物期权为接受项目后做出调整提供了一定的弹性。

实物期权的定义及类型

一旦项目开始实施，实物期权（或管理期权）允许管理人员做出一些会影响随后现金流和/或投资寿命周期的变动。它们是资本预算中的重要考虑事项，因为它们为管理人员更改以前决策提供了机会。实物期权允许经理们潜在地强化好的决策或减轻不好的可能导致企业损失的决策。这些准许增加了企业的价值。

折现现金流估价模型在债券和股票投资上是有渊源的。这类证券的投资者可以被描述成被动型的，因为他们没有办法改变利率或报酬。期权和证券允许投资者成为主动的参与者并对变化的环境做出反应。在资本投资项目中，经常包含实物期权，这样管理人员就可以在这样做对企业最有利的时候按照自己的意愿实施该权利。

具体来说，实物期权包括以下内容：

- 扩张

扩张期权涉及在直接投资项目成功的情况下的后续投资。在不确定性很高但企业产品或服务市场快速增长的情况下，扩张期权尤其有价值。如果早先的项目/服务结果是可喜的，企业可能会坚持继续进行获利极高的投资，哪怕项目 NPV 为负。这样的项目通常号称对企业有战略价值。有一句格言是这样说的：今天的投资孕育了明天的机遇。

- 放弃

如果尽早中止项目被认为是合适的时候，放弃期权（或合约）给予了放弃项目的弹性。放弃期权可以用来评价现存项目或新的投资建议。

放弃期权经常用来评价正在进行的项目，评估它们的盈利性/不盈利性，并决定继续该项目和抽回资金另作他用哪个选择更好。例如，企业可能因出售不再有吸引力的资本投资中的一件设备而情况好转。

类似于股票的卖方期权，放弃期权就像一个保险单。例如，如果设备投资令人失望，企业就可能放弃该项目并收回等于设备出售价值的价格。

放弃期权被用于新项目时，过些时日放弃项目的权利可能会影响选择。

- 延迟

延迟涉及并在进一步投资前等待并了解更多。不存在不确定性时，投资的时间选择就比较简单。NPV 可以在各种未来的投资日期进行计算，而且可以选择能提供最高当前价值的日期。"等待并观望"期权相当于在投资项目上面拥有卖方期权。当企业实施投资项目时，就行使了卖方期权。当投资的不确定性很高并且损失或延迟的直接现金流入很小时，延迟是想要的。

行权就排除了利用潜在的未来价值利得的能力。但是只要项目 NPV 为正且现金流很吸引人，那么企业就会想行权（在期权合约到期前）。

- **适应**

适应——企业有能力变换产出或生产方法以对需求做出反应——允许企业在需求变化时转换或调换其产出组合。在无序和竞争的市场环境下，企业通常在生产经营中融入一定的弹性，这样他们就可以对各种变化作出快速反应并生产出价值最大的产出组合。

投资项目净值可以被看作是投资与其实物期权价值相结合的传统 NPV。在给定可能结果的情况下，评价这些实物期权的优点是非常重要的。期权有时可以：

- 将接受决策转为延迟。
- 将拒绝决策转为接受。
- 导致尽早中止项目并抽回资金用于其他项目。

根据这些实物期权，折现现金流分析及其得出的 NPV 可以说提供了坚实的基础和起点。但是，尽可能的，折现现金流法应当随时调整以适应实物期权。通过更好的管理与未来有关的不确定性，可以限制项目的不利方面。

实物期权的估价

本质上，公司获得期权是为了用一项资产补偿另一项资产的风险。但此处讨论的实物期权（扩展、放弃、延迟和适应）实际上更复杂。每个投资机会都会受很多变量影响，包括：

- 实物期权决策点的时间选择。
- 行使选择权所必需的现金流。
- 变动的利率和投资率。
- 当前及未来的商品、劳动力和其他影响现金流的变动成本的不可预测性。
- 标准差、市场风险和其他影响该项目产品或服务需求的因素。

因为资产可能具有无限大的未来价值，期权估价的一般二项式法和布莱克—舒尔茨公式可用来评价各种时间间隔或不完整期间的投资报酬。规划应用能识别可能的投资结果。也可以将数字代入专门的公式来得出期权风险（每周、每天、有时每小时都会发生变化）。

二项式法一般在可能结果数量有限时使用。布莱克—舒尔茨公式确认更广泛统一的潜在结果，并且通常认为这两种方法中它更准确，因为它考虑了更现实范围的可能结果。但它不能用于所有情况。对于那些情况，二项式法可能会提供期权价值的合理度量。

注意：本书第 3 章 "公司理财" 中详细讨论了期权。该章也包含了一般二项式法和布莱克—舒尔茨公式的信息。

进度检查

提示：完成以下各题，参考答案随后给出。

1. 如果很有可能捕捉到现金流预测中所包含的当前估计以外的额外未来现金流，企业最可能选择什么期权？（　　　）

 a. 扩展

 b. 放弃

 c. 延迟

 d. 适应

2. 如果企业要为潜在需求相对不确定的一项新技术筹集资金，最好的期权类型是？（　　　）

 a. 扩展

 b. 放弃

 c. 延迟

 d. 适应

进度检查答案

1. a

2. c

参考文献

Afterman, Allan B. *SEC Regulation of Public Companies*. Englewood Cliffs, New Jersey: Prentice Hall, 1995.

American Society of Association Executives. *ASAE's Essentials of the Profession Learning System*: Module Five, Membership/Using Technology Effectively, and Module Seven, Finance Administration. Washington, D. C.: American Society of Association Executives and Eagan, Minnesota: Holmes Corporation, 2002.

Arens, Alvin A., and James K. Loebbecke. *Auditing*: *An Integrated Approach*, 8th edition. Upper Saddle River, New Jersey: Prentice Hall, 1999.

Bernstein, Leopold A. *Financial Statement Analysis*: *Theory, Application, and Interpretation*, 3rd edition. Homewood, Illinois: Irwin, 1983.

Blocher, Edward J., Kung H. Chen, and Thomas W. Lin. *Cost Management*: *A Strategic Emphasis*, 2nd edition. New York: McGraw-Hill Irwin, 2002.

Bodnar, George H., and William S. Hopwood. *Accounting Information Systems*, 3rd edition. Boston: Allyn and Bacon, 1987.

Brealey, Richard A., and Stewart C. Meyers. *Principles of Corporate Finance*, 4th edition. New York: McGraw-Hill, 1991.

Campanella, Jack, editor. *Principles of Quality Costs*, 2nd edition. Milwaukee, Wisconsin: ASQ Quality Press, 1990.

Cartin, Thomas J. *Principles and Practices of TQM*. Milwaukee, Wisconsin: ASQ Quality Press, 1993.

"Database Management System," Webopedia Web site, www. webopedia. com/TERM/ d/database_ management_ system_ DBMS. html.

Delaney, Patrick R., Ralph Nach, Barry J. Epstein, and Susan Weiss Budak. *GAAP* 2003. Hoboken, New Jersey: Wiley, 2002.

Epstein, Barry J., Ralph Nach, and Steven M. Bragg, *Wiley GAAP* 2006. New York: John Wiley & Sons, 2005.

Evans, Matt H. *Course 11*: *The Balanced Scorecard*, www. exinfm. com/training/pdfiles/ course11r. pdf.

Financial Accounting Standards Board, Statements of Financial Accounting Concepts Nos. 1, 2, 4, 5, 6, 7. Financial Accounting Standards Board: Stamford, Connecticut: 1978 – 2000.

Frederick, William C., James E. Post, and Keith Davis. *Business and Society*: *Corporate Strategy, Public Policy, Ethics*, 7th edition. New York: McGraw Hill, 1992.

Garrison, Ray H., and Eric W. Noreen. *Managerial Accounting*, 10th edition. Boston: McGraw-Hill/Irwin, 2003.

Gelinas, Ulric J., Jr., Steve G. Sutton, and Allan E. Oram. *Accounting Information Systems*, 4th edition. Cincinnati, Ohio: South-Western College Publishing, 1999.

Gibson, Charles H. *Financial Statement Analysis*: *Using Financial Accounting Information*, 7th edition. Cincinnati, Ohio: South-Western College Publishing, 1998.

Greenstein, Marilyn, and Todd M. Feinman. *Electronic Commerce*: *Security, Risk Management, and Control*.

战略管理（第二版）

Boston: McGraw Hill Higher Education, 2000.

Hargrave, Lee E. *Plan for Profitability: How to Write a Strategic Business Plan*. Titusville, Florida: Four Seasons Publishers, 1999.

Hilton, Ronald W., Michael W. Maher, and Frank H. Selto. *Cost Management: Strategies for Business Decisions*, 2nd edition. Boston: McGraw-Hill Irwin, 2003.

Horngren, Charles T., George Foster, and Srikant M. Datar. *Cost Accounting*, 10th edition. Upper Saddle River, New Jersey: Prentice-Hall, 2000.

Hoyle, Joe B., Thomas F. Schaefer, and Timothy S. Doupnik. *Advanced Accounting*, 6th edition. Boston: McGraw-Hill Irwin, 2001.

Juran, Joseph M., and Blanton Godfrey, coeditors-in-chief. *Juran's Quality Handbook*, 5th edition. New York: McGraw-Hill, 1999.

Kaplan, Robert S., and David P. Norton. *The Balanced Scorecard: Translating Strategy Into Action*. Boston: Harvard Business School Press, 1996.

Kaplan, Robert S., and David P. Norton. *The Strategy-Focused Organization*. Boston: Harvard Business School Press, 2001.

Kaplan, Robert S., and David P. Norton. "Using the Balanced Scorecard as a Strategic Management System." *Harvard Business Review*, January-February 1996.

Kieso, Donald E., and Jerry J. Weygandt. *Intermediate Accounting*, 9th edition. New York: Wiley, 1998.

Kieso, Donald E., Jerry J. Weygandt, and Terry D. Warfield. *Intermediate Accounting*, 10th edition. New York: Wiley, 2001.

Larsen, E. John. *Modern Advanced Accounting*, 10th edition. New York: McGraw-Hill, 2006.

Laudon, Kenneth C., and Jane P. Laudon. *Management Information Systems*, 8th edition. Upper Saddle River, New Jersey: Pearson Prentice Hall, 2003.

Madden, Bartley J. *CFROI Valuation—A Total System Approach to Valuing the Firm*. Boston: Butterworth-Heinemann, 1999.

McMillan, Edward J. *Budgeting and Financial Management Handbook for Not-for-Profit Organizations*. Washington, D. C.: American Society of Association Executives, 2000.

Moscove, Stephen A., Mark G. Simkin, and Nancy A. Bagrandoff. *Core Concepts of Accounting Information Systems*, 5th edition. New York: Wiley, 1997.

Nicolai, Loren A., and John D. Bazley. *Intermediate Accounting*, 5th edition. Boston: PWS-Kent Publishing Company, 1991.

Olve, Nils-Göran, and Anna Sjöstrand. *The Balanced Scorecard*. Oxford, United Kingdom: Capstone Publishing (a Wiley Company), 2002.

Ratliff, Richard L., Wanda A. Wallace, Glenn E. Sumners, William G. McFarland, and James K. Loebbecke. *Internal Auditing: Principles and Techniques*. Altamonte Springs, Florida: Institute of Internal Auditors, 1996.

Roszkowski, Mark E. *Business Law*. New York: Addison Wesley, 1997.

Tague, Nancy R. *The Quality Toolbox*. Milwaukee, Wisconsin: ASQ Quality Press, 1995.

U. S. Securities and Exchange Commission, www. sec. gov.

Van Horne, James C., and John M. Wachowicz, Jr. *Fundamentals of Financial Management*, 9th edition. Englewood Cliffs, New Jersey: Prentice-Hall, Inc. , 1995.

Young, S. David, and Stephen R. O'Byrne. *EVA*® *and Value-Based Management*: *A Practical Guide to Implementation*. New York: McGraw Hill, 2001.

索引

A

B

C

D

E

I

J

K

L

M

Q

R

S

T

U

V

W

Z

ZBA. *See* zero balance account ZBA   参见零余额账户

zero balance account（ZBA），267   零余额账户

zero coupon bond，207   零息债券

zero growth valuation formula，219   零增长估价公式

图字 2007 - 78

CMA Learning System part 3：Strategic Management

© 2007 Institute of Management Accountants，All rights reserved

© 2007 中英文双语版专有出版权属经济科学出版社

责任编辑：周国强
责任校对：杨晓莹
版式设计：代小卫
技术编辑：邱　天

战略管理（第二版）（英汉双语）
美国管理会计师协会（IMA）　主编
杜美杰　译
经济科学出版社出版、发行　新华书店经销
社址：北京市海淀区阜成路甲 28 号　邮编：100142
编辑部电话：88191350　发行部电话：88191540
网址：www.esp.com.cn
电子邮件：zgq@esp.com.cn
汉德鼎印刷厂印刷
德利装订厂装订
880×1230　16 开　44.75 印张　1350000 字
2007 年 11 月第 1 版　2011 年 7 月第 4 次印刷
印数：5501—8000 册
ISBN 978 - 7 - 5058 - 6607 - 2/F · 5868　定价：130.00 元